Latin American Politics
and Development

About the Book and Editors

The third edition of this highly regarded text has been completely updated and revised to reflect the complex political and economic developments that have occurred in Latin America over the last five years. The extensive revision includes new introductory and concluding chapters, several chapters by authors new to the volume, and thoroughly updated chapters on each country in the region.

Wiarda and Kline emphasize the trend toward democratization as the organizing theme of the book, covering such pressing issues as the continuing debt crisis, political unrest, and the international drug trade. Organizing their analysis around Latin America's unique background and its position in the world economy, Professors Wiarda and Kline describe the patterns of political development to the present, the dynamics of political behavior, and the constant tension between those who favor a political regime in keeping with the authoritarian past and those who prefer a Latin American version of democracy.

Within this framework, experts on the twenty Latin American countries give updated analyses of South America, Central America, and the Caribbean. Finally, the coeditors offer a conclusion about Latin America and its alternative futures.

Howard J. Wiarda is professor of political science at the University of Massachusetts–Amherst. **Harvey F. Kline** is professor and chairman of the Department of Political Science at the University of Alabama–Tuscaloosa.

Third Edition, Fully Revised and Updated

Latin American Politics and Development

EDITED BY

HOWARD J. WIARDA
University of Massachusetts–Amherst

HARVEY F. KLINE
University of Alabama–Tuscaloosa

Westview Press
Boulder, San Francisco, & Oxford

Copyright © 1985, 1990 by Westview Press, Inc.

Published in 1990 in the United States of America by Westview Press, Inc., 5500 Central Avenue, Boulder, Colorado 80301, and in the United Kingdom by Westview Press, Inc., 36 Lonsdale Road, Summertown, Oxford OX2 7EW

First published in 1979 by Houghton Mifflin Company

Library of Congress Cataloging-in-Publication Data
Latin American politics and development / edited by Howard J. Wiarda
  and Harvey F. Kline.—3rd ed., fully rev. and updated.
    p. cm.
  Includes bibliographical references.
  ISBN 0-8133-0820-8. ISBN 0-8133-0821-6 (pbk.)
  1. Latin America—Politics and government. I. Wiarda, Howard J.,
1939- . II. Kline, Harvey F.
F1410.L39 1990
320.98—dc20
                                                                                          89-27203
                                                                                          CIP

Printed and bound in the United States of America

The paper used in this publication meets the requirements of the American National Standard for Permanence of Paper for Printed Library Materials Z39.48-1984.

10   9   8   7   6   5   4   3   2

Contents

Illustrations

Tables

Figures

Maps

Preface
to the Third Edition

The first edition of this book was published in 1979, the second in 1985, and the third in 1990, and a great deal transpired in Latin America in these intervening years. The 1970s was a period of authoritarianism and corporatism throughout the region: Fourteen of the twenty countries discussed in this book were under military-authoritarian rule, and in three others the military was so close to the surface of power as to make the distinction between civilian and military almost meaningless. That left only Colombia, Costa Rica, and Venezuela as democracies, and even those countries should be described as still-incomplete democracies. Despite the prevalence of authoritarianism, however, the countries of Latin America continued, generally throughout the 1970s, to prosper with growth rates of 5, 6, or even 7 percent per year and to experience accelerated social change.

Since that time, twelve countries in Latin America have undertaken major transitions to elective government. Along with the changes in the Soviet Union, Eastern Europe, and China, these transitions to democracy in Latin America must count as among the major epochal events of the late twentieth century. Of course, democracy has not yet been consolidated in some countries (and could be reversed), there are many partial and incomplete democracies, and some countries (a handful) have not democratized at all. To students of Latin America, these openings toward democracy have been very heartening, and they are well analyzed in this book. These changes are not only important for the individual countries, but they have also altered the way scholars view the area: away from "corporatism" and "bureaucratic authoritarianism" as explanatory models and toward "transition to democracy."

During the 1980s, however, the Latin American economies fared badly. The worldwide recession of the early years of the decade, which continues to plague Latin America today, the drying up of traditional markets, lack of competitiveness (as compared with East Asia), and the crisis of unpaid (and unpayable) international debts had a devastating effect on the Latin American economies. Some countries slipped backward economically while many others experienced little or no growth. The 1980s has thus been referred to as the "lost decade" in Latin America. Meantime, the conflicts in Central America (Guatemala, El Salvador, Nicaragua,

Panama) persist. And, with the region's continued economic troubles, investment has dried up, giving rise to the fear that Latin America may be even worse off in the future.

So, while many political developments of the 1980s look hopeful for Latin America, the economic situation looks bleak. One of the most critical questions, in fact, is whether the dismal economic situation might not undermine the region's democratic institutions and give rise to a new period of authoritarianism.

As in the earlier editions, the book's authors, who represent the leading and most distinguished scholars in the field, wrestle vigorously with these difficult questions. And once again, Latin America provides a fertile, "living laboratory" for the study of the complex themes of economic growth (or the lack thereof), social change, and political modernization.

It is heartening for us as authors and editors to see this new edition published by Westview Press. This book has become one of the main texts in the field of Latin American politics, used in scores of college and university courses, and it has helped educate an entire generation of students, young scholars, and foreign policy makers about Latin American affairs. They all know this book and the sterling collection of scholars who have contributed to it. Numerous times, at professional meetings or policy forums, strangers have come up to us to introduce themselves and say that they enjoy using our book in their courses. On other occasions, in trains and planes, we have had people sitting next to us who, unexpectedly, pulled the book out of their bags and proceeded to read. These kinds of experiences make research and teaching worthwhile. So hats off to Westview, our collaborators, and our students.

We should add that in this edition, a chapter on the country of Haiti has been added while the chapter included earlier on the Commonwealth of Puerto Rico, unfortunately, for space considerations, has had to be dropped.

Howard J. Wiarda
Harvey F. Kline

Latin American Politics and Development

Part 1

The Latin American tradition and process of development

HOWARD J. WIARDA
HARVEY F. KLINE

1
The Context of
Latin American Politics

Latin America is one of the most interesting and exciting research areas in the world. In Cuba, Mexico, Peru, Venezuela, Argentina, Nicaragua, Colombia, Brazil, and elsewhere throughout the continent, some of the globe's most innovative social and political experiments are being carried out. Latin America is undergoing profound revolutionary change—socially, economically, politically, psychologically—and it is seeking to devise new institutional arrangements to manage the complex transformations that are currently under way. Industrialization, urbanization, accelerated social change, and the "revolution of rising expectations" are having momentous effects, altering old political relationships and forging new ones. Latin America is vibrant, dynamic, and changing. At the same time, the area has achieved a new status in terms of its rising strategic importance and wealth of natural resources in an age when the world community has become acutely aware of its dependence on such resources. People in the United States, because of a common New World heritage and because they have always considered that Latin America lies within the U.S. sphere of influence—a situation that is now changing—have long thought of Latin America as having a special relationship with the United States.

The nature of the transformations going on in Latin America is different than is commonly imagined. Most North Americans have a picture, based on news headlines and *New Yorker* cartoons, of a Latin America governed by comical, mustachioed men on horseback who gallop in and out of the presidential palaces with monotonous regularity. Another image is of poor but happy peasants with big sombreros either taking siestas under the palm trees or dancing gaily in the streets. Neither of these images conforms to the realities of the area. The revolutionary transformations now taking place are not just palace revolts that substitute one man on horseback for another but profound social revolutions that affect all areas of national life. Latin America is not comic opera or the stuff of cartoons. Instead, the area's politics and the clash of social forces have become deadly serious; the stakes are high, and the outcome is still uncertain.

3

Often people speak of Latin America in writings and policy pronouncements as if it were a single entity. It is and it isn't. In fact, the area is characterized by immense diversity. Argentina is as different from Paraguay as France is from Portugal. There is a world of difference between the cosmopolitan societies of Rio de Janeiro, São Paulo, Buenos Aires, and Mexico City and the provincialism of Asunción or Santo Domingo. Yet within this context of diversity, which makes it imperative that one knows each country of the area individually, there are also important common characteristics of language, culture, institutions, and social and historical backgrounds. This factor of unity amid diversity makes Latin America an exciting living laboratory for the study of comparative social and political change.

Not only is Latin America diverse, but it faces—and has always faced—a profound identity crisis. We must therefore ask not only whether Latin America exists as a unit but what is it, what is its essence. Is it Western, non-Western, developing, Third World, or what? The answer is complex. With strong roots in Roman law, Catholicism, and the Iberian sociopolitical tradition, Latin America is Western; yet it represents a particular Luso-Hispanic variant of the Western tradition, and its social and cultural underpinnings are quite different from the variant established by the British in North America. Moreover, because of its strong Indian and (in the circum-Caribbean and Brazil) African subcultures, Latin America is sometimes classified as a non-Western area. Although these countries were integrated into the emerging Western, capitalist world economy as colonies and exporters of precious metals (it is seldom mentioned that the gold and silver from Latin America helped initiate the Industrial Revolution), Latin America as a whole received few of the benefits. It long remained on the margin of the world economic system and was considered to be a supplier of raw materials but destined to lag behind in terms of economic growth.

After about 170 years of independent life, the Latin American countries cannot be included in the category of "new nations." Latin America is seldom considered a part of the First World of developed capitalist countries (the United States, Western Europe, Japan) or the Second World of socialist countries (Soviet Union, China, Eastern Europe—Cuba and Nicaragua are the only socialist states in the Western Hemisphere), but it does not comfortably fit into the Third World category either. By virtually any criterion, almost all the Latin American nations are more developed than the Third World nations of Africa or South Asia; they tend to be transitional countries, neither fully developed nor wholly underdeveloped. Moreover, when the Latin American countries follow a Third World foreign policy, they usually see themselves as leaders of the Third World, not merely members of it. Many scholars, emphasizing the ill fit of any of the existing categories and pointing to the distinctive features of the Latin American tradition, have begun referring to the area as a Fourth World of development. In doing so they mean, not just what economists sometimes have in mind when they talk about the more advanced developing nations, but an entire political-cultural tradition and a developmental model that are fundamentally different from those of the rest of the world.

But if Latin America has evolved as a unique fragment of the Greco-Roman-Hispanic tradition, integrated into a world pattern of change and interaction but with a style and institutions all its own and with strong institutions and political dynamics, then we must try to comprehend what that tradition is and how its institutions function. We must deal with the issue of how and why Latin American development has taken the path it has as well as with how the Latin American tradition reflects and interacts with broader, global patterns of change and modernization. Moreover, in coming to grips with the main themes of Latin American development, we must seek to understand that tradition on its own terms, shedding commonly held prejudices about the area and our frequently ethnocentric biases. We must put away our stereotypes and misconceptions and come to know Latin America through an understanding of its own institutions and processes. A greater modesty regarding the supposed superiority of North American civilization and an appreciation of another culture area with which we are less familiar are indispensable if we are to comprehend Latin America.

Latin America today is an area of immense vibrancy and sometimes dizzying change, of clash and conflict, of complex efforts to deal with developmental issues of great importance, of attempts to retain what is valuable in its own traditions and past (strong family ties and interpersonal relations, a strong sense of community, intense individualism, an ethical view of people and society) while also accommodating itself to the modern world. Although the traditional institutions and holders of power (such as the oligarchy) remain strong, the winds of revolution are sweeping through the area. The conflicts between these forces are fierce and deep-rooted and lie at the heart of Latin American politics and the process of change.

James Reston of the *New York Times* once remarked that people in the United States seem willing to do anything for Latin America except read about it or seek to comprehend it. It is our hope that in this book you will not only read about Latin America but also try to understand it. Given the United States' political and strategic interests in the area, the massive Hispanic immigration into the United States, and the country's vulnerability to commodity and raw-material shortages, Latin America is now more important to the United States than ever before. And given the crises that U.S. social and political institutions are experiencing, it may even be that one can learn something from the way Latin Americans have dealt with contemporary change—instead of thinking they must always "learn" from the United States.

LATIN AMERICA

Latin America—broadly defined as Middle, Central, and South America and the Caribbean—is a vast area. It encompasses 8 million square miles (21 million square kilometers) of land (19 percent of the world's total) and contains roughly 350 million people. It comprises eighteen Spanish American countries; Brazil, Haiti, and seven other new states (six former British colonies and one Dutch one); and a number of dependencies of France, Britain, the Netherlands, and the United States. This book concentrates on the Luso-Hispanic countries of Latin America— the vast area colonized by Spain and Portugal—and Haiti. References to Latin America thus can be understood to exclude the other present or former British, Dutch, and French colonies or territories: Guyana, Suriname, Belize, Jamaica, Trinidad and Tobago, and other smaller islands.

The countries of Latin America are diverse. Some are, or think of themselves as, predominantly white and European (Argentina, Chile, Costa Rica, Uruguay); some are heavily Indian and mestizo, mixtures of Indian and European (the Andean countries of Ecuador, Peru, and Bolivia; Mexico; and the countries of Central America). In some the racial mix is black and mulatto or black, mulatto, and white (northeast Brazil, the Caribbean islands, and the circum-Caribbean countries); in others the social and racial configurations involve complex interrelations of Indian, European, and black. Some of the countries are based largely on subsistence agriculture, some have heavy industry, but the majority are a mixture of backward areas and modern urban centers. Per capita income, literacy rates, and other social indicators show remarkable variation.

Although the diversity of the area and the special features of each country must be recognized, the common features are equally significant. And though we may lament the simplistic notions of journalists and government officials—when they talk of a single "Latin American policy" for all the nations of the area—we must acknowledge that there are cogent reasons for treating the countries comparatively and as part of a single culture area. In their common Iberian colonial past, their institutional foundations, their struggles for independence, their cultural commonalities and continuities, and their often parallel development processes, the nations of Latin America have had some remarkably analogous experiences. This book seeks to understand both the distinctiveness of the Latin American nations and, especially in Parts 1 and 4, their common patterns and experiences.

Latin America is diverse not only in terms of its peoples and societies but also in terms of its geography and resources. It contains one of the world's highest and most majestic mountain ranges, the Andes, and its peaks serve as the backdrop for the Pacific countries of South America (Colombia, Ecuador, Peru, and Chile). Northward, the Andes level out into lower ranges and plateaus in Central America and Mexico. The vast fertile plains in Argentina, Uruguay, Brazil, and Venezuela support large-scale agri-industry, but the meagerness of the soil in the highland areas makes it impossible to eke out even subsistence agriculture. Natural resources are abundant in some areas (Venezuela, Brazil, Mexico, Chile, Peru) and almost nonexistent in others. For the resource-poor nations, the absence of natural resources means that no national development plan or formula can effect more than modest changes in the basic pattern of poverty. Even Fidel Castro has cautioned that revolution in countries with slim resources could cause more despair than benefits.

The tropical coastal regions of Brazil and the circum-Caribbean are suitable for sugarcane production (and also in earlier times for slave-plantation agriculture—hence the large importation of Africans to these regions), and the highlands of Central America, Brazil, and Colombia are suitable for coffee trees. There are also vast areas (the llanos of Colombia, much of the Amazon Basin, denuded mountainsides) that currently are not able to support any form of profitable agriculture. And even though Latin America has some of the world's greatest river systems (the Orinoco, Amazon, and Río de la Plata), they are often unsuitable for internal transportation.

Some geographical features of Latin America have retarded efforts toward development and national integration. The Andes on the Pacific and the coastal escarpments on the Atlantic slowed internal colonization in the early years and helped account for the fact that almost all the major cities lie on or close to the coast. The steep mountains and the secluded valleys partly explain the historical lack of contact among the towns of the area and the localism of the small community or the *patria chica* ("little country"). One's "whole world" could be encompassed by an isolated valley, and the *patria chica* or the local hacienda, often self-sufficient and virtually self-governing, could be the setting for all of one's life experiences. Before the onset of modern communications and transportation, geographic provincialism impeded the development and growth of a sense of national loyalty. It also helped—and still helps—prevent the development of integrated national economies, political communities, and nation-states.

Latin America's main population centers lie on the coast, and the interior of the continent remains largely empty. With such vast empty spaces and with a population density about one-sixth that of the United States or Western Europe and one-ninth that of Asia, it would appear that Latin America does not have a severe population problem. But many of the interior areas are not particularly hospitable for reasons of either health or climate, and much of the land is infertile and unsuitable for agriculture. To date, the Latin American interior has been a static frontier, not a dynamic one.

Latin America has an abundance of natural resources, but often they are not juxtaposed in a way that is conducive to the development of modern industry, or they are the wrong kind of resources. The abundant gold and silver found during the colonial era were used largely to benefit the colonizing countries rather than for internal development, and those minerals also contributed to a get-rich-quick mentality, repeated cycles of boom and bust, and a system of exploitation that still marks the area. There is some coal and iron ore in Latin America, but they are generally of inferior quality, and because the two are seldom in proximity, the coal cannot readily be used in iron smelting. It is sometimes said that steel is the key to the development of a modern industrial base, but few of the Latin American nations possess the resources to produce a substantial amount of it. Venezuela and perhaps Brazil are the major exceptions.

Oil is another story. Venezuela, part of which seems to float on oil, was for a long time the richest Latin American nation in known reserves; today Mexico claims to have the largest reserves. It is no accident that Venezuela has the highest per capita income in the area, and the wealth generated by oil helps explain why Venezuela is one of the few Latin American nations to enjoy continuous democratic government since 1958. Ecuador, Colombia, Argentina, Brazil, and Peru are also oil producers, and new finds in the Caribbean may transform that area. Latin America contains other mineral resources: copper and nitrate in Chile; tin in Bolivia; emeralds and coal in Colombia; and small deposits of nickel, gold, manganese, and bauxite in several other countries. Brazil's Amazon Basin has huge and largely untapped quantities of numerous precious and industrial metals, and this fact partly explains why Brazilians think of their country as the future of Latin America.

Nature, however, has in general been relatively stingy with Latin America, and there is nowhere near the amount of resources possessed by the United States during its historical development period. In Latin America, the obstacles to development have been all but insuperable: steep mountains coming right to the water's edge, dense tropical jungles, an incredibly chopped-up landscape, rivers and farmland whose location has hindered development, scarce and inaccessible minerals. Geography and nature have played critical and not necessarily friendly roles in Latin American history.

THE ECONOMIES

Latin America was settled as a colonial area and exploited chiefly for the benefit of the colonizing countries. Under the economic conception then prevalent (mercantilism), the colonies existed to enrich the home countries, Spain and Portugal. Much of Latin America's wealth was drained away to Europe, through Spain and Portugal and on to the Netherlands and Great Britain, where it helped stimulate the rise of capitalism. From the beginning Latin America has been on the margin of the emerging world system of capitalist economies, an area to be milked dry by the exploiting powers with little of its wealth used for internal improvements.

One need not be an economist to recognize poverty, and the impoverishment of this area is what will first strike most visitors. The poverty, the result of a rigid socioeconomic structure that benefits chiefly the wealthy and centuries of exploitation and deprivation, is most visibly present in the bloated bellies of the children, the widespread malnutrition-related diseases, the shacks that pass for houses, and the malformed bodies of both old and young. Poverty is the way of life of perhaps 70 percent of the Latin American population, and it ranges from a depressingly severe level in most countries to the relative prosperity of Argentina and Venezuela. The aim of the contemporary revolution in Latin America is to relieve this poverty.

Historical economic patterns throughout Latin America have varied considerably, and these different patterns still help account for the differing socioeconomic configurations of the area. In Brazil, the Caribbean islands, and the low-lying mainland rim of the Caribbean, slave-plantation systems were established, necessitating the large-scale importation of Africans as laborers. In other areas, large cattle ranches were established and gradually concentrated; many of today's immense estates have their origins in the vast tracts the Spanish Crown granted to the conquistadores. Some areas, such as Costa Rica, had neither precious metals nor vast numbers of Indians to enslave, so they remained largely empty during the colonial era and thus escaped the full weight of the Spanish colonial heritage. When these areas were finally settled, less of the get-rich-quick attitude prevailed, and a society of mostly self-sufficient, medium-sized family farms emerged instead of the usual pattern of large estates dominated by a European elite, along with a large servile class, either black or Indian.

The hacienda was probably the classic institution of the nineteenth century. During this period the system of great estates begun in the colonial period was expanded and consolidated: The Argentine pampa was enclosed and divided into private estates, communal Indian lands were brought under private ownership, and areas of cultivation and grazing were expanded. The hacienda was a self-contained unit socially, economically, politically, religiously. The hacendado had absolute sway, and his tenants and peasants were largely caught up in a system of peonage that differed little from earlier slavery. Not only did the hacienda generate wealth for its owner, but the numbers of acres, cattle, and peasants were also symbols of social status or prestige. The large estate was thus both a capitalist enterprise and a feudal one. It helped perpetuate the two-class, exploitative, authoritarian structure established during the colonial period.

The hacienda economy was agriculturally centered. The peasants eked out a subsistence existence on their own small plots, and the hacienda produced chiefly commodities (tobacco, coffee, sugar) for the world market. Even today, although many of the Latin American economies are still predominantly agricultural, they are oriented toward producing for the world market, and hence the countries must import basic foodstuffs to feed their own populations.

Toward the end of the nineteenth century commerce was increasingly stimulated, and the process of industrialization began. Industry remained incipient and small-scale until after World War I and the market crash of 1929, however, when the markets for Latin America's exports dried up and it was impossible to import manufactured goods. Industrialization thus took the form of "import substitution"—that is, the production locally of goods that had previously been imported. Although industrialization proceeded rapidly, with the pace obviously varying from country to country, agriculture remained predominant, and subsistence continued to be the way of life of most Latin Americans. Today the amount of gross national product (GNP) generated through agriculture and the amount generated through industry are approximately the same in the majority of the countries.

Industrialization quickened the pace of life and led to accelerated social change. It served to break down the traditional isolation of the *patria chica* and helped further the integration of the Latin American economies into the world marketplace. It also stimulated foreign investment in the area and paved the way for the modern multinational corporation. These changes brought some economic betterment, but they also cast Latin America into a position of subservience and dependency with regard to the advanced industrial nations, principally the United States.

Although some of the bigger and richer countries—like Mexico, Argentina, Brazil, and Venezuela—have at times made progress in becoming more self-sufficient in terms of both food production and industrial output, the majority of the Latin American countries remain locked in the historical pattern of exporting raw materials for the world market and importing manufactured goods. That pattern was often beneficial to Latin America up to the 1920s, as the money Latin America received for its exports remained roughly equivalent to what it had to pay to import manufactured goods, but since that time the costs of the imported manufactured goods have risen far faster than the prices Latin America is able to charge for its exports. The result has been that the countries of the northern tier (North America, Western Europe, Japan) have forged ahead and Latin America has lagged increasingly behind, with mounting trade deficits, balance-of-payments problems, woefully low wages, and underdeveloped economies. The gap between the industrialized nations of the North and the raw-material-producing ones of the South has widened.

The situation is made worse by the fact that the essentially one-crop or one-resource economies of Latin America (tin for Bolivia, nitrate and then copper for Chile, sugar for Cuba and the Dominican Republic, coffee for Brazil, Colombia, and the countries of Central America, bananas for Ecuador) are subject to fluctuating world market prices, changing demands and consumption habits, and the import quotas set by the major powers, chiefly the United States. If, as occurred during World War I, nitrate could be produced chemically instead of being mined, the bottom would drop out of the Chilean economy. If the price of sugar were to fluctuate downward by a few cents per pound, the Cuban and Dominican economies could be ruined and their political systems toppled. If North Americans were to decide to drink beer instead of coffee, Colombia and Brazil could similarly slide into chaos. Or, if the United States wants to punish Cuba or the Dominican Republic, all it would have to do is reduce the quota of sugar imported from them. The Latin American economies are vulnerable to impersonal, outside forces over which they have no control.

The instability of both world market prices and consumption habits subjects the Latin American countries to political pressures and to boom-and-bust cycles whose effects are devastating and, for those countries, intolerable. They are now bargaining for stable markets and prices, and the rising demand for commodities and raw materials has given them a stronger negotiating position. Many are banding together to form blocs of commodity and raw-material producers similar to the Organization of Petroleum Exporting Countries (OPEC) oil cartel (of which Venezuela is a leading member). There are now cartels of bauxite-producing countries, copper-producing countries, coffee-producing countries, and banana-producing countries. Other countries are renewing efforts to diversify their economies and to industrialize. But the very effort to industrialize is producing new social forces (the rise of sizable middle-class and trade-union organizations) that are challenging the internal structure of social and political power. The dynamics of these changes, the processes of social, economic, and political modernization, lie at the heart of the analyses in this book.

Most of the Latin American economies are no longer ranked as "underdeveloped" or "low income," but they have not reached the stage of being "industrialized market economies" either. Rather, they are classified by the World Bank as "middle-income countries," with Haiti, Bolivia, Honduras, El Salvador, and Nicaragua at the lower end of that scale; Brazil, Mexico, Argentina, Chile, Uruguay, and Venezuela at the upper end; and the other countries occupying intermediary positions. According to various measures of social and political modernization, the Latin American countries are also intermediate, neither so backward and uninstitutionalized as other Third World areas nor so developed as the industrial nations (Table 1.1).

Although the Latin American economies have modernized rapidly since World War II, important continuities with the past still remain. Increasingly drawn into a world capitalist system, the Latin American systems have nonetheless retained a number of distinct historical features.

Table 1.1   Indices of Modernization in Latin America

	GDP[a] per capita (US$) (1986)	Manufacturing as % of GDP (1986)	% of Urbanization (1986— preliminary est.)	Life Expectancy (years) (1985)	Literacy Rate (%) (1981–1986)[b]
Argentina	2,361	21.5	84.9	70	94.2
Bolivia	926	10.0	47.7	53	63.2
Brazil	2,525	25.9	74.5	65	68.7
Chile	2,306	20.9	84.0	70	91.7
Colombia	1,330	21.7	66.6	65	81.0
Costa Rica	1,971	22.0	49.5	74	89.8
Cuba	—	—	—	77	—
Dominican Republic	1,319	17.1	53.3	64	69.4
Ecuador	1,326	17.1	52.7	66	85.2
El Salvador	892	17.4	41.8	64	66.9
Guatemala	1,282	16.0	32.7	60	56.6
Haiti	342	15.1	26.9	54	36.9
Honduras	780	12.9	40.4	62	59.7
Mexico	2,407	24.1	69.7	67	87.9
Nicaragua	862	26.4	56.9	59	72.3
Panama	2,513	8.9	51.5	72	85.8
Paraguay	1,829	16.3	43.9	66	92.0
Peru	1,250	23.4	67.7	59	86.0
Uruguay	2,738	18.4	85.0	72	96.3
Venezuela	2,762	20.5	81.3	70	86.0

[a]Gross domestic product
[b]Year of rate varies within this range.

Sources: Inter-American Development Bank, *Economic and Social Change in Latin America: 1987* (Inter-American Development Bank, Washington, D.C., 1987); World Bank, *World Development Report 1987* (Oxford University Press, New York, 1987).

One is apt to go astray if one thinks of the Latin American economies in terms of the U.S. capitalist model. Latin America is indeed a part of the capitalist world, but it often practices its own special form of capitalism. In keeping with Latin America's historical traditions of central control, the capitalism of Latin America has generally been not one of laissez-faire and individual initiative but a system of state capitalism, with a comparatively large public sector and a great deal of central direction. Although many Latin American countries experienced significant "privatization" movements in the 1980s (that is, government enterprises were sold to the private sector), one should still keep in mind the concept of state capitalism and its implications. In many respects, the modern Latin American economies represent an updated, modernized extension of the semifeudal, exploitative "milk-cow," mercantilist system of the colonial period.

Latin America was in severe economic straits throughout the 1980s, and most of the countries were deeply in debt. They were unable to repay those debts, but they could not repudiate them without severe consequences; nor could they grow as long as the debt burden hung over their heads. There was little foreign aid available to them, and private investment declined as well. U.S. and other multinational corporations shied away from investing in the area, and local Latin American capital fled abroad. Without capital, either foreign or domestic, there could be no growth, and at the beginning of the 1990s, it was not certain that the economic situation would improve.

CLASSES AND SOCIAL FORCES

Latin America has long essentially had a two-class society of lords and peasants, elites and masses, even though there has always been a small middle sector composed of artisans, craftspeople, soldiers, and petty bureaucrats. During the colonial era the two-class system consisted basically of a small group of Spanish (or Portuguese) elites and a large mass of peasants, workers, Indians, and slaves. Within these major sectors, there was ample room for rivalries and further gradations. The small European elite never numbered more than a few percent of the population, and the huge mass was Indian, African, or racially mixed. The system was sharply pyramidal and rigidly hierarchical; there was almost no possibility of social mobility or movement from one class to another. The society had caste overtones as well as class criteria: The elite was not only wealthy but white; the lower classes were not only poor but Indian, African, or of mixed racial background.

It should not be surprising that this two-class pattern was established in the sixteenth century. What is remarkable is that it persisted throughout the seventeenth and eighteenth centuries. The institution of the hacienda perpetuated the same two-class system throughout the nineteenth century, despite the achievement of independence and the writing of a host of democratic constitutions. As late as the 1960s social anthropologists stated that the same two-class pattern, albeit modified in various particulars, still existed, yet several decades of fairly rapid economic growth had led to complex changes.

The onset of modernization and industrialization in the nineteenth century—and the acceleration of this process in the twentieth—gave rise to some new social forces that made the historical system more complex. The growth of commerce helped stimulate the emergence of a new class of businesspeople, and in some instances they challenged the power of the traditional hacendados. In most cases, however, this newer wealth was gradually joined with the older wealth, through marriage and other means, so that the historical oligarchic pattern was continued and even strengthened. The immigrant communities—Italians, Germans, Syrians, Jews, Japanese, English, North Americans—that began coming to Latin America in the late nineteenth century were often co-opted and assimilated in much the same fashion. Although in some ways they maintained separate identity, many of the new immigrants prospered, married into the elite Latin American community, and became leading members of society.

At least until recently the growing middle class or middle sectors in Latin America represented a distinctive but parallel phenomenon. As economic growth accelerated, a sizable (20–40 percent of the population, depending on the country) middle sector began to emerge, consisting of small-business people, merchants, clerks, government workers, and the like. But the members of these middle sectors were deeply divided on political issues and showed little consciousness as a class. They often aped aristocratic ways, despised the lower classes (from which they had recently risen), and frequently were more politically conservative than the real aristocrats. Hence, although in terms of income there appeared to be a growing "middle class" in Latin America, in terms of social and political attitudes the old two-class system was perpetuated.

The basic dividing line lay between people who worked with their hands and those who did not. Neither the upper nor the middle classes worked with their hands; manual labor was done only by peasants and workers. The continuing two-part division of society seemed to mean that no middle-class society, with all its presumed middle-class virtues— moderation, pragmatism in politics, democratic social and political ideas— had yet emerged in Latin America. The Southern Cone countries of South America—Chile, Argentina, and Uruguay—were perhaps the first exceptions to this generalization, and by the mid-1980s all of the other more developed Latin American countries, and even some of the moderately developed ones, seemed to be developing "classes" in the strict sense.

Even within the basically two-class system, the lower classes were further differentiated. Varying forms of tenancy and of wage labor existed in the countryside, and some peasants migrated en masse to the cities where they formed a large but unorganized subproletariat. Trade unions formed by skilled workers, the "elite" of the lower classes, became major power contenders in many of the countries.

Thus, while Latin America continues to have an essentially two-class society, within that structure there are various gradations, and even though Latin American society is still rigidly hierarchical and pyramidal, and social mobility is limited, new avenues for advancement have opened up. Business, the army, government service, and university or technical training all provide ways for the upwardly mobile to rise in the social scale. Nevertheless, many of the old class barriers persist, and the basic two-part division of society implies a situation of on-again, off-again class warfare. No apathetic, "safe," middle-of-the-road bourgeois society has emerged anywhere in Latin America. All of these factors most likely signal the continuation of what Kalman Silvert has called a conflict society.

THE POLITICAL CULTURE

Political culture is a term used to describe the basic values, ideas, and behavioral patterns that govern a society. It covers a large spectrum and is fraught with dangers of misuse. One must avoid stereotyping cultures, as the old "national character" studies did in the past, and one must also recognize that any society may have several cultural currents existing simultaneously. Additionally, one must realize that political culture presents a general and composite picture and that individual persons and behavior within a society may sometimes fit the ideal type at best imperfectly and sometimes not at all. Nevertheless, when employed carefully, the concept of political culture is useful and helps one understand the differing assumptions on which distinct political societies are based.

It is probably safe to say that although North American political culture is strongly Lockean and liberal, that of Latin America, historically at least, is strongly elitist, hierarchical, authoritarian, corporatist, and patrimonialist. The elitism of Latin American society stems from the Iberian tradition of nobility, a medieval tradition that had reached its fruition in Spain and Portugal precisely at the time the discovery of the Americas provided new lands and slaves so that any aspiring Spanish conquistador could live like an aristocrat. Elitism stemmed also from the long history of Spanish political theory, which argued that society should be governed by its "natural elites" and which was skeptical of the capacity of the masses to govern wisely and well.

Elitism, hierarchy, and authoritarianism all had a powerful base in traditional Spanish Catholicism, particularly as articulated in the writings of Saint Thomas Aquinas and his disciples. This was not the only tradition in Spanish thought, but for a long time it remained the dominant one. Political authority emanated directly from God or from the "natural order" of the universe. Both power and society were organized hier- archically from the top down: God, archangels, angels, cherubim, ser- aphim, and so on down to humans—but only certain types of humans. First came kings, who received their power directly from God, and then nobles, whose authority over land and people was similarly assumed to be God given. Occupying positions progressively further down the hierarchy were the lesser nobility; then soldiers, artisans, craftspeople; then workers, day laborers, and peasants. In the New World, Indians and African slaves were still lower in the hierarchy.

Although Latin society was thus structured hierarchically by rank, it was also structured vertically in terms of society's major corporate groups: army, church, nobility and landowners, bureaucracy, university, and so on. In the twentieth century, corporatism as a manifest ideology has earned a bad reputation because of its association with fascism, but in Latin America, corporatism is not necessarily fascistic but has to do with the historical Latin tendency to divide society vertically and functionally into its component groups. Latin American society is hence a society of place, of position, and external appearance and manners are essential in signaling to others what rank or status one holds and therefore how one should be treated. It is a system organized along both class and corporate lines.

All of these features, grounded in medieval Catholic political philosophy and natural law, served to reinforce each other. Corporatism, elitism, hierarchy, and authoritarianism helped foster a rigidly stratified system in which mobility was difficult at best. If one was born into a certain position in society, one generally stayed in that position. At each level in the hierarchy one was expected to accept one's station in life as God given and conforming to the natural ordering of the universe. There could be no questioning of the system. Society was thought of as fixed and immutable; for over 300 years it remained locked in this pattern.

But even though Latin American society was authoritarian and hierarchical, it was also patrimonialist and paternal. Thus, although elitism and authoritarianism were considered to be natural and God given, the elites had a Christian obligation to take care of those less fortunate than themselves. The people who owned land and labor might run their estates in an absolute fashion, but in theory, they also had to be just and fair. Although the peasant or worker owed an obligation of labor to the *patrón*, he in turn was obligated to look after the welfare of his workers. And even though the political authorities could rule autocratically and expect loyalty from their subjects, they had an obligation not to overstep the bounds of "right" behavior. Patron-client relations were thus a two-way process, whether at the level of the local hacienda or in the national political system. Patrimonialism as it applied to the state system emphasized the features of centralization, authoritarianism, and modernization under elite hegemony but within some quite carefully defined bounds. In many ways, these traditions of hierarchy, authoritarianism, elitism, corporatism, and patrimonialism are still strongly present in Latin American political society.

In the nineteenth century, however, a new framework of ideas and values—liberal, republican, and egalitarian, sometimes secular and rationalist—was superimposed upon the earlier tradition. Scholars continue to argue about the degree to which these values took hold and the variations among the countries of Latin America. Liberal and democratic ideas were often incorporated in laws and constitutions, but the underlying structures of landownership and authority often remained elitist. By now, however, in most Latin American societies two basic conceptions, two political cultures, exist side by side: one elitist, hierarchical, and authoritarian; the other liberal and democratic. Although frequently these two traditions are so far apart that they do not touch and provide little basis for social and political compromise, most Latin American nations now represent complex fusions of both (as in the growth of Christian democracy or authoritarian socialism). These two fundamentally opposed conceptions of society and the role and functions of the people in it lie at the heart of much nineteenth- and twentieth-century political conflict. They help account for the concepts of "the two Brazils" or "the two Venezuelas" that are frequently found in the literature, and they also help explain the deep divisions found in Latin American political society. In addition, they explain why at times (as through the mid-1950s and in the late 1960s and 1970s) most Latin American countries have had authoritarian, dictatorial governments and at others (the late 1950s and since the mid-1980s) the majority of the governments have been elected.

Although a liberal-democratic tradition was superimposed on the authoritarian tradition in the nineteenth century, in the twentieth century a third, socialist, tradition has appeared. In most of Latin America, socialism is still a minority strain. But socialism has come to power in Cuba and Nicaragua; in Chile, political opinion is about equally divided electorally among conservative, liberal, and socialist conceptions; social-democratic governments have come to power in several countries; and clearly, among young people generally, socialist sentiment is sometimes popular. Hence, the real question may be, not whether socialism is coming to Latin America, for it has, but rather whether it will be fused with the older traditions or whether, as in Cuba, it will seize power by itself and eventually eliminate the other, older traditions.

What was once a fairly unified, stable, monolithic Latin American political culture (conservative, traditional, authoritarian) has now become a deeply divided and unstable one. The old values are no longer universally held, yet the newer ones are sometimes only incompletely established. Moreover, the distances between such wholly different societal concep-tions—feudalism, liberalism, socialism—are so vast as to be virtually uncompromisable. The overlaps among and fusions of quite distinct and often wholly opposed ideas and views of society tend to make Latin America even more of a conflict society than was the case earlier.

Of course, not all of the Latin American countries exhibit all of these traits and patterns, at least not to the same degree. The pattern of elitism, authoritarianism, hierarchy, corporatism, and patrimonialism here ascribed to traditional Latin American culture is an "ideal type" that does not always mirror existing reality. It fits only some countries, or if all, then to varying degrees. In some countries (such as Peru and Mexico), traditional Spanish institutions were strong; in others, weak. Some countries that lacked strong Hispanic institutions endeavored later to create them; in others (such as Chile), the liberal and republican tradition was strong right from the beginning; in still others (Paraguay, several of the Central American countries), both the traditional Hispanic and the liberal institutions were historically so weak that chaos, clan politics, and caudilloism became endemic. These variations stand out clearly in the country chapters.

CONCLUSIONS AND IMPLICATIONS

Latin American society has long been riven by geographic, economic, social, and political-cultural divisions that have retarded both national integration and development. But the great forces of twentieth-century change are now overcoming those barriers and altering the foundations on which Latin American society has rested. These are no longer the sleepy "banana republics" they once were; rather, Latin American society has become vibrantly alive, and far-reaching social changes are sweeping the area.

Although the changes have been immense, the problems remain at least equally large. Poverty, malnutrition, and malnutrition-related diseases are endemic; illiteracy rates remain high; the majority of the population is ill housed, ill clothed, and ill fed; health care is poor; wages are low; inflation is rampant; and the standards of living of peasants and slum dwellers are woefully inadequate. In addition, the existing social and political institutions are often unable to cope with the immense changes. The fabric of Latin American society is deeply divided; and, although changes are occurring, the institutional structure to manage these changes has not developed at the same pace.

And yet Latin America is not failing altogether in dealing with its developmental dilemmas. New formulas are being tried, and new institutions are being experimented with. A single-party system in the context of an institutionalized, now somewhat tired, revolution proved for a long time to be more or less functional in Mexico. Colombia, Costa Rica, and Venezuela have developed into more or less institutionalized and consolidated democratic systems. Peru, Panama, Bolivia, Ecuador, and Honduras have had military regimes come to power that, with varying degrees of enthusiasm and success, have stressed nationalist and developmentalist themes; more recently, a form of democracy has again been tried in all these countries. In Paraguay, an old-time caudillo regime remained in control for a long time, but it too instituted changes. Conservative, authoritarian, state-capitalist military regimes were established in Brazil, Argentina, Chile, and Uruguay in the 1970s; but in all of these countries, the military was eventually replaced with elected presidents. Cuba continues to be ruled by a socialist regime that has not been as successful in encouraging economic growth as other Latin American regimes, but for a time it carried out some of the most successful social programs—in housing, health care, education, and social services—in all of Latin America. Nicaragua also embarked on a socialist course, but the March 1990 election seemed to indicate a change in direction.

Hence the variety of alternatives being weighed and experimented with in the effort to deal with the new pressures and social forces of modernization makes Latin America exciting to study, and an exploration and assessment of these various alternatives and their degrees of success or failure form the basis of the analyses presented in this book.

2
The Pattern of
Historical Development

Latin America is a product of its past in ways that North America is not. In many respects, Latin America remains dominated by institutions and practices first established during the colonial era; in many ways, it is still a semifeudal area. Because the weight of history is so strong, one must come to grips with Latin America's past in order to understand its present.

THE CONQUEST

The conquest of the Americas by Spain and Portugal fully a century before the English colonies were established was one of the most incredible epic adventures of all time, and its significance reached beyond the Americas. Columbus's first steps in the New World and the subsequent conquest in the next several decades of almost all of Latin America constituted the initial phase of a European expansionism and colonialism that would eventually encompass the entire world. Latin America was the first non-European continental area to be Westernized.

The contact of Europeans with the native Indian populations gave rise to a clash of cultures that persists today. It gave rise also to some of the earliest comparative anthropological and sociological studies of non-European cultures and societies, and it resulted in the Christianization, to a greater or lesser degree, of Latin America. The gold and silver brought back by the Spanish helped make the Industrial Revolution possible, and the conquest immensely expanded human knowledge and frontiers. It stimulated worldwide exploration and trade and helped turn the focus of commerce and power from the Mediterranean to the Atlantic. The conquest also led to new patterns of social, political, and race relations and to innovative experiments in the effort to colonize and govern distant lands. In a very short period of time the known world had doubled in size; so had human vistas.

Although it is conventional to begin a history of Latin America in 1492, this is yet another reflection of Western biases, as the area had already been settled by large Indian civilizations long before the Europeans arrived. It has been estimated that whereas the Indian population of North America numbered only 3 million at the time of European colonization and generally consisted of dispersed and small-sized tribes, the number of Indians in Latin America was about 30 million and many of them were grouped into settled, large civilizations. These differences in number and complexity shaped the subsequent histories of the two areas to a major extent and help explain the differences in society and race relations that persist in the two parts of the Americas.

North Americans largely "solved" their Indian problem by either killing the Indians or, later, confining them to reservations. In Latin America there were, in many areas, too many Indians to be killed; although the Spanish conquest involved barbarism toward the Indians at least equal to that of the English colonists, the sheer number of Indians in Latin America dictated a policy of assimilation rather than one of annihilation. The Indians were generally subdued rather than slaughtered, Indian leaders were often co-opted into working with or for the Spaniards, and the Spanish usually replaced the Indian aristocracy at the top of the social pyramid without destroying the pyramid per se.

North America was settled mainly by families, but Latin America was conquered by conquistadores who did not bring their families along because they viewed the conquest as a military campaign. The immense differences in the number of Indians and the level of their civilizations between the two parts of the Americas also implied a greater racial intermingling and less manifest racial prejudice in Latin America than in North America. This situation applied to blacks as well as to Indians. Miscegenation and more relaxed racial attitudes led to predominantly mestizo or mulatto societies in many countries of Latin America, which helps to explain the sense of national inferiority (on racial and cultural grounds) that many Latin Americans still feel and the sense of superiority toward the area—bolstered by old-time racial prejudices—that North Americans still harbor.

The Indian culture was so strong and so well established that it pervaded the Spanish and Portuguese colonies to a degree as yet perhaps unrecognized. The larger-scale Indian civilizations practiced a form of elitism and theocracy on which the Spaniards simply imposed a new layer. The Latin American tradition of political absolutism and arbitrary rule by local caciques (chiefs) has its roots as much in Indian traditions as in the Spanish. Moreover, the Aztec, Inca, and Mayan civilizations of Latin America were proud cultures with major accomplishments, and they affected the Spaniards almost as much as the Spanish culture did the Indians. Hence, the clash of cultures in Latin America was far more of a two-way process of interaction between Indian and European than in North America. In some realms of life, Indian ways prevailed; in other realms, complex mixtures of the two cultures resulted; for instance, in religion there is a mixture of Catholicism and Indian beliefs. Some nations like Mexico and Peru are immensely proud of and preoccupied with their Indian pasts and have sought to elevate the mestizo to a new racial and national type.

Although assimilation and the fusion of Indian and European cultures were the rule in some areas, separation was the rule in others. In the highlands of Latin America, the Indians remained all but untouched by the conquest, and the conquest was such a shock to the Indians in some regions that they withdrew into a shell of isolation. In Guatemala, Peru, Bolivia, and elsewhere, the distance between the Indian and European cultures is still almost unbridgeable, and there are essentially two nations within the same borders. In Guatemala, for example, some 50 percent of the population does not speak the national language, lives completely outside the money economy, is wholly uninvolved in the national social or political life, and may not even be cognizant of being part of an entity called Guatemala.

The conquest proceeded in stages and took different forms in different areas. It is useful to review this process and the distinct patterns of colonization, race relations, landholding systems, and colonial structures to which the conquest gave rise, since these early patterns strongly shaped the internal structures of the independent nations that eventually came into being.

The first area to feel the impact of Spanish conquest and colonization was the island of Hispaniola, which flourished for some thirty years until the supplies of gold and Indian labor began to decline. Hispaniola also served as the launching pad for the conquests of Cuba and Puerto Rico. But these islands, like Hispaniola, had little gold or silver, and after their Indian population was decimated, as much by European diseases as by force of arms, African slaves were brought in. The islands were eventually dominated by grazing, agriculture, and later, large plantations (not by mining), and their socioracial patterns were henceforth shaped by the relations between Africans and Europeans rather than Indians and Europeans.

Hernando Cortés undertook the conquest of Mexico from Cuba. In Mexico, Yucatán, and present-day Guatemala, the Spanish found, not small Indian tribes as on the islands, but large-scale civilizations with populations numbering in the millions. The incredible impact the discovery and presence of these civilizations had on the Spanish and the story of how Cortés captured the Aztec chief Montezuma and conquered his empire are now the stuff of legend. The Spanish were awed and impressed but hardly immobilized by the riches and cities of the Indians. The conquest of the extensive Aztec civilization was aided by several factors: the use of the horse, which the Indians had never seen before and which was probably more effective than firearms; the resentment of the Aztecs on the part of other tribes, whom Cortés cleverly employed as allies; the fortuitous circumstance that Cortés arrived the same year Indian prophecies had said that a "great god" would sail across the waters from the east; and the disintegration of Indian resistance once Montezuma was captured.

But in Mexico, unlike the islands, the Indian civilization was stronger and therefore never entirely subdued or eliminated; there were simply too many Indians. The result was a sometimes thin Spanish veneer of "civilization" with a huge Indian subculture, incompletely Hispanicized and Westernized, underneath. The Spanish became the overlords and absolute rulers, the Indians the laborers and peasants. The Spanish Crown granted the conquistadores the right to Indian labor (*encomienda*), a right that carried the obligation to Christianize the Indians and treat them justly. But Spain was far away and unable to enforce its edicts completely and regularly, so there were many abuses of the system and grants of labor soon became de facto grants of land also, with the Christianizing duties often forgotten. The later hacienda system, so important in shaping Latin American history and society, was formed on this same two-class lord and peasant relationship, a relationship that was based as much on race and caste as it was on class. Few African slaves were brought to the mainland (except along the Caribbean coast) since the supply of Indian labor seemed inexhaustible; hence, race, class, and social relations in Mexico and most of the mainland would be written in terms of the interactions between Europeans and Indians, not Europeans and blacks.

From Mexico the conquest proceeded south to Guatemala and down the isthmus through Central America. In the meantime, Brazil was being settled by the Portuguese, and other Spanish galleons had explored the Venezuelan coast and sailed up the Río de la Plata to claim Argentina, Paraguay, and Uruguay. Vasco Núñez de Balboa had crossed Central America at Darien (present-day Panama) to gaze upon the Pacific. And in an epochal feat, the Pizarro brothers and a handful of men conquered the Inca empire, which stretched across what is now Ecuador, Peru, and Bolivia. In the process the area of Colombia came under the hegemony of the Spanish Crown, and Chile followed shortly thereafter. From Bolivia the conquest spilled across the Andes into Argentina, which, despite its fronting on the Atlantic, was initially settled more from the western than the eastern side. The conquest of the entire continent was completed within eighty years, as compared with the three centuries that it took for North America to be settled.

Where the Spaniards found large numbers of Indians to enslave or to force to work in the mines or on the land, as in Peru, Ecuador, and Bolivia, the same kind of rigid two-class landholding and hacienda system emerged as in Mexico and Guatemala. What is now Paraguay is a fascinating special case because, for a time, the Spanish Crown granted the overlordship of the Guaraní Indians to the Jesuit order. In Central America, Venezuela, and Chile, precious metals were not readily available and there were smaller numbers of Indians to enslave, so the Spanish presence was generally weaker, the church less important as an institution, and the system of the hacienda less pervasive. In Uruguay and Argentina, there were no precious metals and far fewer Indians. These areas were only lightly colonized, and generally later, so they never felt the full weight of the authoritarian Spanish colonial system as Mexico and Peru did.

Thus, the Spanish presence and institutions affected different Latin American areas in varying degrees. Characterized by colonial neglect, the less-affected areas often developed a stronger sense of self-reliance. In areas where there were fewer Indians to enslave, the Spanish settlers often had less aversion to manual labor, and class and caste lines were not so rigidly drawn. Because the yoke of the colonial past was often lighter, these areas frequently had fewer obstacles to overcome in their later drive to develop and modernize. The possibilities for national development and democratization in Latin America have been generally inversely proportional to the degree of Spanish colonial heritage experienced. In countries where Indians and gold were prevalent and Spanish institutions strong, as in Mexico, Guatemala, Peru, Ecuador, and Bolivia, the difficulties of development and democratization have proved almost insuperable (except perhaps in Mexico—and there only by violent revolution). In countries where Indians and precious metals were scarce and Spanish institutions therefore weak, as in Venezuela, Chile, Costa Rica, Argentina, and Uruguay, the possibilities for development and democratization have been better.

The conquest of Brazil by the Portuguese represents a parallel but distinctive case. Brazil was established on an authoritarian, elitist, hierarchical, corporatist, patrimonialist, and semifeudal basis just as the Spanish colonies were. But Portugal had neither the will nor the power to colonize such an immense area effectively, and Portugal's colonization efforts were always more relaxed and easygoing than those of the Spanish. Further, the Portuguese enclaves were largely limited to the coast and only later spilled over the mountainous escarpment into the interior. Since there were few Indians to enslave, the Portuguese imported African slaves, but the plantation system and race relations in Brazil were never so rigid and unyielding as in the Spanish colonies. Brazil represents a variant on the main themes of Latin American conquest and colonization, although in the Portuguese colony, too, elitist, oligarchic, and two-class patterns prevailed.

By 1570, several decades before the first British colonies were established in North America, the Spanish and Portuguese conquest of Latin America had been all but completed. It was a remarkable feat accomplished in a short span of time, and Spain became, briefly, the major power in the world.

COLONIAL SOCIETY: PRINCIPLES AND INSTITUTIONS

The institutions colonial Spain and Portugal carried with them to the New World were a direct reflection of the Spanish and Portuguese themselves in 1492. An understanding of these institutions serves as the beginning point for comprehending modern-day Latin America and also for contrasting the foundations of Latin American society with those of North America.

In 1492 Spain had just completed the reconquest of its own peninsula from the Moors, North Africans of the Muslim faith who had dominated Iberia since the eighth century. The effort to drive out the Moors had been both the culmination of a long effort at national unification and a religious crusade. No mercy was asked for—or given to—the infidels. The conquest of the Americas was similar in the sense that the Indians were also heathens who had to be Christianized and Hispanicized—or else! The conquest of the Americas was an extension of Spain's reconquest and "purification" of its own peninsula.

Because of Spain's and Portugal's long struggles against the Moors, the development of feudalism and a stable lord-vassal system was slower and distinctly different from that in the rest of Europe. Feudalism in Iberia was tied to conquest: As the fighting Spanish knights and nobles drove the Moors farther south, they received the right to the lands they had conquered and the labor of the people who lived on those lands. Spain had just begun to develop a pattern of feudal landownership when the conquest of the Americas occurred.

Feudalism was brought to the New World, where it received a new lease on life, at a time when it had already begun to fade away elsewhere in Europe. The Spanish Crown used the New World lands and grants of Indian labor to reward middle-class elements and the lower nobility— who would not have been able to gain such extensive wealth and the titles that went with it on the peninsula itself—and thus to buy their loyalty and keep them from rebelling against royal authority. The Crown employed the time-honored patronage practice of doling out lands, labor, and titles in return for loyalty and the further centralization of authority in the Crown itself. When the Spaniards arrived in the New World, they found conditions particularly propitious for a new form of feudalism: abundant lands, a ready-made (Indian) peasantry, and a virgin society ripe for conquest in which they would constitute the new elite. Whereas on the peninsula all available land and labor had already been partitioned, in the New World every would-be Spanish grandee could become the overlord of vast estates.

The late fifteenth century was important also because it was during that period that the principal Spanish kingdoms of Aragon and Castile were unified through the marriage of Ferdinand and Isabella. Further, Spain unified under authoritarian, absolutist, centralized, and patrimonialist auspices, and these features were carried to the New World through the Spanish colonial system. The early-sixteenth-century model of a pyramidal, centralized, authoritarian, corporate, contractual state system, the ideal of Spain's golden century of national accomplishment, would continue to serve as an ideal for many years. In several countries

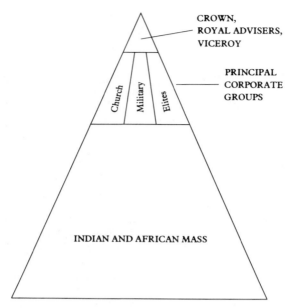

Figure 2.1 The Corporate-Authoritarian Structure of Latin American Political Society, Sixteenth Century

of Latin America whose subsequent history has been as chaotic, this sixteenth-century authoritarian model is still regarded as the ideal toward which a nation should strive (see Figure 2.1).

The institutions that Spain brought to the New World from 1492 on were reflections of Spain itself and of its historical developmental drives. The political tradition that Spain enshrined was one of authoritarian and patrimonialist rule. Power emanated from the top down, from king to viceroy (literally vice king) to local cacique, hacendado, or landowner. It was absolutist and centralized to the core.

Beneath the king came the major corporate and vested interests: church, army, nobility. Each of these interests had its own powerful traditions and prerogatives, its own courts and codes of conduct, its own jurisdictions and responsibilities. Each owed loyalty to the king and constituted his strong right arm in religious, military, and economic affairs, respectively. The king could not always enforce his decrees in colonies several thousand miles away, but centralized absolutism nonetheless remained the ideal. So did the idea of a harmonious, vertically organized structure of corporate orders, all similarly authoritarian and hierarchical in their respective spheres but ultimately revolving around and subservient to the Crown or the central state.

The religious institutions of Catholicism and the church bolstered and reinforced the state concepts. The church was an instrument of the state and of the conquest. Because of the long crusade against the Moorish infidels and the preoccupation with maintaining the purity of the Catholic faith, the Spanish church was more intolerant and absolutist than its European counterparts. Catholic beliefs at the time, inspired by Saint Thomas and a remarkable group of sixteenth-century Spanish, Jesuit political theorists, emphasized authority, absolutism, and the natural inequalities—hence, the hierarchy of humankind. These concepts not only helped undergird and bolster the idea of a strong central state and monarchy, but they provided a convenient rationalization for subjugating the Indians. In Spain, the church was more than just another interest group, and Catholicism was more than merely just another religion: They were the backbone of the regime, a part of the state system, at the base of the political culture, and the moral and theoretical foundations of society and the political order.

The economic system was organized on an exploitative basis. Under the prevailing theories of neomercantilism, the colonies were considered to exist solely for the benefit of the colonizing country, and hence their ample resources were drained away. To fight European wars and to provide glitter to Crown and church, Spain and Portugal milked the colonies dry. This marked the beginning of Latin America's dependency position in relation to the major colonial powers. The Latin American "periphery" was exploited for the benefit of the European "core."

Society was organized along similarly hierarchical and two-class lines. Except in a few localized cases, Latin America never developed a class of medium-sized family farmers, as in North America, nor did a sizable commercial middle class arise. Rather, Latin America consisted of a small elite at the top controlling a huge mass of Indian or African slaves, serfs, tenant farmers, peasants, and day laborers at the bottom. These social classes had been rigidly stratified in the Old World; in the New World, class considerations were further reinforced by racial ones. Each class and caste in the hierarchy enjoyed its own special rights and obligations. This was the "feudal ideal," although it was seldom mentioned that the upper classes monopolized most of the rights and the lower classes most of the obligations. Since this structure was thought to be natural and in conformity with God's just ordering of the universe, little change was possible. In many areas of Latin America, the structure of an essentially two-class, patron-client system persists today, and it is almost as rigid and unyielding as in colonial times.

Intellectual life and the educational system were grounded upon many of the same principles. Education was private and reserved only for the elites; it followed from the hierarchical and nonegalitarian premise that there was no need for mass public education. Education and intellectual life were infused with Catholic, Thomistic premises. The method of learning was scholastic and deductive, based upon the rote memorization of absolute truths from which principles of correct conduct could be deduced. There was no sense of science, empiricism, or observation to arrive inductively at agreed-upon knowledge. Learning, education, and intellectual life were closed and absolutist.

It should not be surprising that the Spanish and Portuguese colonies were established on the basis of semifeudal institutions. Spanish Catholicism was probably more intolerant than that of other areas of Europe, and the special nature of Iberian feudalism, the way the Spanish kingdom had been unified, and a distinct political tradition helped make Spain and Portugal different from the other European powers. Of at least equal importance was the time period in which the colonies were settled, a factor that makes the colonies the product more of historical accident than of some supposed evils residual in the Hispanic tradition.

The Spanish and Portuguese colonies were founded on a set of fifteenth- and sixteenth-century institutions that were absolutist, authoritarian, hierarchical, Catholic, feudal or semifeudal, two-class, corporatist, patrimonialist, orthodox, and scholastic to their core. By contrast, the British colonies to the north, established fully a century and more later, were founded on a set of institutions and practices that were fundamentally different from those prevailing when the Iberians came to America. In the seventeenth century, when colonial North America was effectively settled, the first steps toward limited, representative government were already under way, and the protestant Reformation had broken the monopoly of Catholic absolutism and led to greater religious (and political) pluralism. Economically, capitalism had begun to supersede the feudal and patrimonialist conceptions. Socially, a more pluralistic and predominantly middle-class society had come into existence. And intellectually, the scientific revolution ushered in by Galileo and Newton had taken place, and there was an emphasis on empiricism and experimentation. The differences between the sixteenth century, when the Latin American colonies received their indelible imprint, and the seventeenth, when North American society took firm shape, and the major distinguishing characteristics of the two cultures that developed in the Americas are summarized in Table 2.1.

The differences are stark. They imply entirely different life-styles and world views and wholly distinctive social, economic, and political institutions and behavior. They provide clues as to why one part of the Americas was condemned to lag behind while the other forged ahead. If there is validity in dividing a course on the basic history of Western civilization into pre-1500 and post-1500 components, then it is easy to see that Latin American institutions were grounded on essentially feudal and medieval conceptions, dating from the period before that historical breaking point, while those of the United States were based upon the more modern world emerging from the seventeenth century on. This difference has nothing to do with any alleged inherent superiority of liberal, Protestant, northern, Anglo-Saxon civilization. Rather, it has to do with the contrasting time periods in which the societies in Latin America and North America took definitive shape and the distinct,

Table 2.1   Contrasting Foundations of Latin and North American Society

	Latin America, 1492–1570	North America Seventeenth Century
Political	Authoritarian, absolutist, centralized, corporatist	More liberal, early steps toward representative and democratic rule
Religious	Catholic orthodoxy and absolutism	Protestantism and religious pluralism
Economic	Feudal, mercantilist, patrimonialist	Emerging capitalist, entrepreneurial
Social	Hierarchical, two-class, rigid	More mobile, multiclass
Educational and Intellectual	Scholastic and deductive	Empirical

alternative sets of institutions that the earlier and later colonizers transplanted to the New World.

Given the times and circumstances, therefore, it is not surprising that the Latin American colonies were founded on a semifeudal basis. What is remarkable is the perseverance of those institutions. The absolutist, authoritarian, two-class, patrimonialist, Catholic, scholastic, mercantilist, and corporatist institutions of Latin America lasted from the period of conquest and settlement in the sixteenth century through the era of institutionalization in the seventeenth century and the reforms of the eighteenth century. Indeed, efforts to reform these colonial institutions in the Americas in order to bring them abreast of the rest of Europe generated so much antipathy that they helped precipitate the separation of the colonies from Spain. Moreover, many of these same semifeudal institutions, although necessarily remodeled, were carried over after independence in the nineteenth century and continued to survive into the twentieth.

THE WARS OF INDEPENDENCE—AND AFTER

The wars of independence in Latin America did not bring about such a sharp break with the past as is often imagined. They meant more a separation from Spain and Portugal than a profound transformation in the social structure. Although the apex of the pyramid, the Crown, was removed, the basic hierarchical and elitist order of society remained intact. When social revolt did accompany the independence struggle (as in Mexico, where a major Indian uprising occurred), it was quickly snuffed out, and conservative rule was reestablished.

The causes of the independence struggles in Latin America were complex. The example of the United States, as well as the ideals of liberty, equality, and fraternity stemming from the French Revolution of 1789, had an effect, particularly on Latin American intellectuals who used these concepts to frame a rationalization for independence. The liberal, Enlightenment reforms of the Spanish Bourbons (such as the expulsion of the Jesuits from the Spanish colonies in 1767) had also stimulated resentment in the colonies, and the ineptness of the Spanish and Portuguese kings in the late eighteenth and early nineteenth centuries led to a belief on the part of the colonists that they could manage their own affairs better than the colonizing countries could. A rising merchant class in the colonies had grown impatient with the monopoly systems of Spain and Portugal and wished to be free to trade with whomever it wished.

A critical factor was the growing impatience of the Spanish criollos (people of Spanish descent born in the New World) with the fact that major colonial positions were filled by *peninsulares* (colonial officials sent from the Iberian peninsula). The criollos wished to have political power, and doubtless the attendant salaries and perquisites, commensurate with their growing economic wealth, yet they were blocked in this desire by the Crown's policy of appointing peninsula-born officials to the major posts. Frustrated, the criollos became increasingly impatient, and independence sentiment grew. When Napoleon Bonaparte of France captured Spain in 1808 and placed his brother on the throne, the Latin American criollos refused to accept his authority and moved to take power until the legitimate king could be restored. Later, when the legitimate king did return to the throne but refused to accept the liberalizing reforms proposed by the colonists, the final break came.

The wars of independence lasted some fifteen years and involved epic struggles. But since the Spanish garrisons stationed in the Americas were small (it is a measure of the success of the Spanish colonial enterprise that such a modest armed force was used to maintain it for 300 years) and located only in the major centers, the actual fighting was limited. The first revolts, in Argentina and Mexico, were quashed. Simón Bolívar carried out a long struggle against the Spanish in Venezuela and then helped to liberate the present countries of Colombia and Ecuador. José de San Martín finally defeated the Spanish forces in Buenos Aires and then marched his army over the Andes to drive the Spanish from Chile.

But the key to the liberation of South America was the defeat of the large Spanish force attached to the viceroyalty of Peru, centered in Lima. San Martín proceeded north from Chile by ship while Bolívar went south from Colombia over land, and in the decisive Battle of Ayacucho in 1824, the royalists were routed. Ayacucho marked the virtual end of the wars for independence in South America. Meanwhile, the revolt in the other main center, Mexico, had foundered for several years until the victory over the Spanish forces was won in 1821. Once Mexico had been freed, the colonies in Central America became independent, although there was little fighting there. Because the Spanish colonial system was so highly centralized, the liberation of the main centers at Caracas, Buenos Aires, Santiago, Bogotá, Quito, and Lima and in Mexico was followed by the freeing of the rest of the colonies, chiefly by administrative fiat.

In Brazil, the situation was different. When Napoleon's forces occupied Portugal, the royal family set sail for Rio de Janeiro—the first time European royalty had ever set foot in the New World. Later, when the French were driven out of Portugal and the king was called back in 1821, he left his son Pedro in Brazil as regent. Although summoned subsequently to succeed his father in Lisbon, Pedro determined to stay in Brazil. Hence, when Brazil became independent in 1822, it did so as an independent monarchy, not as an independent republic. The republic would come later. The transition to independence in Brazil was thus peaceful, and the continuity provided by the monarchy enabled Brazil to escape the chaos that was characteristic of the Spanish colonies during their early years of independence.

The disintegrative tendencies set loose in Spanish America during the wars of separation continued for a time after independence. The confederation of Gran Colombia split up in 1830 into the separate nations of Venezuela, Colombia, and Ecuador, and the United Provinces of Central America fragmented in 1838 into five small city-states. Bolivia's independence also came late and was, in the words of historian Hubert Herring, a "vague afterthought of the wars of independence," while Paraguay gained independence more as a result of its struggles with the Argentines than of those with the Spanish. What is now the Dominican Republic was forcibly reunited with Haiti (which had become independent from France in 1804 through a slave revolt) from 1822 to 1844 before the island of Hispaniola was permanently divided into these two nations, and Uruguay was established with British assistance as a buffer state between the two giants of South America, Argentina and Brazil. Panama was a distant province of Colombia until the United States helped guarantee its independence in 1903 in order to secure the rights to build the Panama Canal. Cuba remained a Spanish colony until the war of 1898, a fact that shaped the island's history of frustrated nationalism.

Within each of the new republics the situation was similarly chaotic, disorderly, and fragmented. The removal of the Spanish Crown had eliminated the one unifying element in the colonies, setting loose a variety of centrifugal forces and creating a legitimacy vacuum. The criollo conservatives attempted to fill that vacuum along with the caudillos and the armies left over from the independence struggles, but neither could effectively stem the disintegrative forces at work, and power continued to drain away from the center. In the absence of an effective central authority, power came to be lodged in local or regionally based caudillos, rival elite factions, and the self-contained haciendas. Power was diffuse, decentralized; little real authority was exercised by the people who occupied the presidential palaces. The semifeudal system was perpetuated.

Almost universally the new nations of Latin America adopted constitutions providing for democratic, representative rule. At the time this seemed the only acceptable alternative to colonialism and monarchy. But often enshrined in these constitutions were numerous articles that helped preserve corporate privilege and autocratic rule. The constitutions were thus more a reflection of the area's historical forms of government and traditions than a sharp break with the past, including as they did extensive powers for the executive, various measures to limit suffrage and preserve oligarchic rule, and a special place and privileges for such groups as the church and the army. Much of Latin America's history after independence would be written in terms of the conflict between these divergent republican and autocratic tendencies.

The political instability of the time was often accompanied by economic disorder and, in some countries, reversion to a more primitive form of existence. With the disruption of old trade patterns, commerce came virtually to a standstill, and many mines and plantations ceased to function. The comings and goings of various caudillos led to so much disruption that markets and prices were unstable, crops and cattle were destroyed, fields were abandoned, and agriculture and production declined. In many areas, peasants and Indians went back to a pre-Columbian type of subsistence agriculture.

The politics of the first decades after independence, roughly 1820–1850, are more easily understood if we remember that the wars of independence had been conservative movements, not liberal ones. They were aimed at preserving oligarchic privilege and the status quo, not sweeping them away. Many royalist commercial and landed elites had only reluctantly come around to the independence cause when they grew convinced it could result in an increase in their wealth and trade. The wars of separation from Spain were aimed at reasserting the power and institutions of traditional society, not destroying them. The wealth and power of the church remained largely intact after independence, and the importance of the hacienda and of the semifeudal two-class system was enhanced. It was not flaming radicals or liberals who inherited power after Spain was driven out but generally conservative oligarchs and their agents. The independence armies frequently stepped in to fill the vacuum left by the withdrawal of the Crown.

But the criollo oligarchy was often a bedraggled element that was unable to rule effectively or maintain order. In some countries, rival regionally based oligarchic families competed for the national palace and all the spoils and opportunities for land and social advancement that holding presidential power implied. Juan Manuel de Rosas in Argentina and Antonio López de Santa Anna in Mexico were caudillos in this early classic mold, dominating their countries by force and bravura during the first thirty years of independence. The prevailing pattern, however, involved the frequent coming and going of rival caudillos and elite or would-be elite families, whose constant alternation in power helped retard the development of most of the nations of the area. Only Brazil, under its emperor, and Chile, whose conservative elite quickly reasserted itself after independence, escaped this era of chaotic, disruptive, caudillo politics.

Hence, the first thirty years of independence were marked by a general lack of progress throughout Latin America and by efforts to devise new institutional formulas necessitated by the withdrawal of royal authority. Precisely because this era was so chaotic and governments so prone to breakdown, this period gave rise to a number of what would become the historic drives of Latin American development policy. These may be identified as the quest, given the prevailing instability, to secure and maintain order at all costs; to populate and thus to fill the area's vast empty spaces; to control and civilize the Indian and African elements so as to prevent future social upheavals; to strengthen the oligarchy through immigration and a general Hispanicizing of the population; to maintain and strengthen existing structures such as the army and, in many areas, the church; to fill the organizational void and correct the historic *falta de organización* (absence of organization); and to develop a political model that would reflect the area's earlier glory and its hopes for the future. That model was frequently the authoritarian-autocratic model of sixteenth-century Spain and Latin America.

THE EARLY STAGES OF MODERNIZATION

By the 1850s some order had been brought out of the earlier chaos in most countries. The first generation of postindependence caudillos and criollos had died or faded from the scene, and newer Liberal parties had emerged to vie with the traditional Conservatives. The Liberals were not usually very liberal, however, and usually consisted of one group of rival first families organized to contest the power and privileges held by another elite group. Many times these families were in commercial agriculture instead of owners of self-contained haciendas. The Liberals stood for some of the classic nineteenth-century freedoms, including separation of church and state and free trade. By stimulating a greater competition for power, the rise of the Liberals resulted in an expansion of suffrage and an increase in the voting population to perhaps 3–5 percent.

The 1850s was a period of gradual, incipient socioeconomic changes. Cattle ranches and plantations began to recover from the earlier devastations, and new lands were opened for cultivation. In the Argentine pampa and elsewhere, the practice of common landholdings gave way to private ownership, and the system of large estates started to expand.

There was a commercial quickening, new banks opened, and in the cities a merchant and artisan class, often stimulated by European immigrants, emerged. Foreign capital, chiefly British, provided a catalyst for investment and production. New national industries began to grow: guano in Peru, sugar in Cuba, mining in Chile, agriculture (meat, hides, wool) in Argentina and Uruguay, rubber and coffee in Brazil. The first railroads and highways were built, docks and port facilities were constructed, and national economic infrastructures began to develop. In economic terms, the 1850s and 1860s saw the first stages of modernization.

Yet conditions were different in Latin America than in the United States or Europe, simply because the northern countries went through the process first. In many Latin American countries there were debates between policymakers who favored high tariff barriers, in order to encourage nascent industry, and those who favored low tariffs, in order to base economic growth on foreign trade. The key economic fact was that, at least in the short run, British (and later U.S.) manufactured goods were less expensive than those produced locally, because of economies of scale and higher levels of technological development.

Increasingly, the policymakers favoring low tariffs, often but not always calling themselves Liberals, won the debate. The most beneficial policy seemed clear, as indicated in this statement by the Colombian treasury minister Florentino González in 1847:

> In a country rich in mines and agricultural products, which can sustain a considerable and beneficial export trade, the law should not attempt to encourage industries that distract the inhabitants from the agricultural and mining occupations. . . . Europe with an intelligent population, and with the possession of steam power and its applications, educated in the art of manufacturing, fulfills its mission in the industrial world by giving various forms to raw materials. We too should fulfill our mission, and there is no doubt as to what it is, if we consider the profusion of natural resources with which Providence has endowed this land. We should offer Europe raw materials and open our doors to her manufactures, to facilitate trade and the profit it brings, and to provide the consumer, at a reasonable price, with the products of the manufacturing industry.[1]

Following what later was to be called "comparative advantage," the decisions made reinforced the dependency position of Latin America that had begun during colonial times. Latin America was cast as an exporter of primary products, and its industry lagged. The ramifications of these decisions were evident from then on in Latin America, even during the energy crisis of the 1970s and the debt crisis of the 1980s.

Although there was considerable economic resurgence during the 1850s and 1860s, the political situation had not stabilized. Rival caudillos, frequently heading competing Liberal and Conservative factions, continued to vie for control of the national palaces. Instability remained the rule. In some countries, the Conservatives and the Liberals alternated in the presidency; in others, a Conservative or a Liberal caudillo might manage to hold on to power indefinitely. Despite the frequent instability, however, the economic structure continued inexorably to change, giving rise to new social forces as yet only dimly foreseen. In many countries, Liberal policies led to the consolidation of large commercial farms, with the concurrent loss of holdings by small farmers. In some, the first wars over land—which continue today—began.

In the 1870s and 1880s the political situation began to stabilize. There were two basic patterns—a third one was to emerge somewhat later. The first, exemplified by Argentina, Brazil, and Chile, involved the gradual consolidation and joining of older (landed) and newer (commercial) wealth into a system of strong oligarchic rule. With few interruptions, oligarchic rule in these countries continued until 1930, through a period of unprecedented stability and economic growth. Indeed, the entire span from the 1880s to 1930 may be considered the heyday of oligarchic power throughout Latin America.

The second pattern, similarly stabilizing and consolidating, involved the coming to power of a new type of order-and-progress caudillo. Porfirio Díaz in Mexico is the prime example, although in Guatemala, Venezuela, and the Dominican Republic the situation was parallel. No longer so unrefined as their man-on-horseback predecessors and no longer interested solely in power for its own sake, the new order-and-progress caudillos sought to promote national economic growth and to bring Latin America abreast of the rest of the world. They surrounded themselves with advisers who brought a positivistic, scientific, and progressive approach to national development. Under both the consolidating oligarchies and the order-and-progress caudillos (frequently intertwined, since the new breed of caudillos often ruled at the behest of powerful national oligarchies), the Latin American nations began to enjoy significant economic growth for the first time.

Law and order were now established, often brutally. New national armies and police forces were set up, replacing the unprofessional and caudillo-led armed bands of the past. The police and army enforced order in the countryside and served as agencies for increased national and central direction. As oligarchic power was consolidated, the great estates expanded, and peasants and Indians were impressed into the labor force and obliged to sacrifice their communal lands and small holdings.

Along with political consolidation came greater economic growth. New roads and railroads were built, the first telegraphs and telephones were introduced, and import and export facilities—docks, storage facilities, shops—were constructed and improved. Large amounts of capital began to flow in, initially chiefly from Europe, but by the 1890s, in at least some of the countries, the United States had replaced Great Britain as the major source of foreign investment and trade. Manufacturing and industry burgeoned, and immigration from Europe was encouraged.

Previously empty areas began to be filled, and new lands were opened for rubber, coffee, sugarcane, cacao, and tobacco production. The number of commercial establishments multiplied, and previously sleepy towns and port cities began to grow and come alive with activity. There was a general economic quickening as more money became available and business and trade picked up. New government agencies were established to administer these new activities, and the national infrastructure—bureaucracies, communications structures, armies, and so on—started to take definitive shape. The drive to modernity had commenced, and some of the historical goals and aspirations of Latin American development policy began to be fulfilled.

It must be remembered, however, that in the majority of the countries, development and modernization occurred under elite, authoritarian, and oligarchic auspices, not democratic ones. Still, the general economic stimulus gave rise to new sociopolitical forces whose growth helped undermine the oligarchic order. A new middle class appeared in the urban areas, and its members began pushing for political influence commensurate with their increased economic wealth. By the first decades of the twentieth century some strong trade unions, often rural as well as urban—cane cutters and tobacco workers, for example—had emerged, and they similarly demanded a bigger piece of the omelet and threatened to scramble it if their demands were not met. These pressures mounted. In 1910 dissatisfaction with the Díaz regime and Mexican middle-class impatience with the barriers to advancement and spoils, coupled with deep-seated and long-smoldering resentment on the part of peasants and Indians because of the encroachment of the big estates onto lands they had previously farmed, led to a revolt against the old dictator that triggered the twentieth century's first great social revolution. In 1916 Argentina's newly enfranchised middle-sector voters wrested control from the oligarchy for the first time, and in 1920 Chile's middle sectors united with the workers to unseat the oligarchy. This pattern would be repeated in numerous countries of the area in 1930, when the big upheaval came.

In addition to the consolidating-oligarchy and order-and-progress caudillo patterns of the period, a third pattern involved direct U.S. intervention in the Caribbean part of Latin America, both to ensure political stability and to secure and expand U.S. economic and strategic interests. In the aftermath of the Spanish American War of 1898 the United States emerged as a major industrial and economic center and an aspiring world power. As a result of that war, the United States acquired Puerto Rico and other areas as territories and established a protectorate over Cuba. Panama also took on independence as a protectorate of the United States, with its national territory divided by the U.S.-controlled Canal Zone. Under the now-infamous Roosevelt corollary to the Monroe Doctrine, the United States intervened in the Dominican Republic in 1904 to prevent European creditors from using force to collect unpaid debts and to take over the administration of all customs receipts. During the first two decades of the twentieth century U.S. Marines intermittently occupied and intervened in the Dominican Republic, Haiti, Nicaragua, Panama, and Cuba.

The role of the United States in these countries was in many ways similar to that of the order-and-progress caudillos and produced many of the same results. The marines pacified the countryside and built roads and port facilities. Through the establishment of marine-created national guards, power and administration were centralized just as in the caudillo regimes. Moreover, by bringing order to the nations' finances, conducting land surveys, and reorganizing the national systems of land titles, the United States helped facilitate further U.S. investment and production. Naturally, the people who were in a position to benefit most from these changes (again similar to the order-and-progress caudillos) were the large foreign investors and those Latin Americans who already possessed land, capital, and good connections. The third major developmental pattern of the period thus involved the wedding of foreign and domestic capital with the use of North American military power to join the emerging Latin American bourgeoisie with U.S. strategic and private economic interests. This pattern also served generally in Latin America to reinforce conservative, oligarchic rule.

By the 1920s a change in the situation was due. Pressure for the United States to withdraw its military forces from the Caribbean increased, and the Latin American middle sectors and trade unions were insisting on the need for a national restructuring—or else! The military officer corps, no longer drawn solely from the aristocratic ranks, was becoming restless. The final triggering cause was the world market crash of 1929, which ruined the market for Latin America's exports. Oligarchic rule was undermined, and the need for basic change became obvious to all. In 1930 a rash of revolutions brought on by the economic crash swept Latin America and signaled, not just another dreary round of military coups, but a profound reordering of the sociopolitical structure. The heyday of the oligarchy was over, and a new era of middle-sector-dominated politics had begun.

CONCLUSIONS AND IMPLICATIONS

The weight of the feudal and semifeudal past, of the colonial era and its institutions, hung heavier over Latin America than over North America. Indeed, in many ways the heavy hand of the past still continues to weigh upon and shape Latin American countries in a fashion that is not true for the United States. In many countries, authoritarianism, elitism, a two-class system, hierarchy, patrimonialism, and corporatism have proved to be remarkably persistent, durable features.

But within this context considerable change is nevertheless possible. Latin American history is hardly the total failure that some detractors of the area would have us believe it to be. Indeed, given Latin America's background and the historic geographic, social, and economic barriers to development, the accomplishments have been notable. It must be remembered, however, that the changes ushered in to this point have most often come under oligarchic auspices, not democratic ones. However, these changes have given rise to new social forces, principally labor and the new middle sectors, and these have challenged and helped undermine oligarchic rule.

NOTES

1. Quoted in Miguel Urrutia, *The Development of the Colombian Labor Movement* (New Haven, Conn.: Yale University Press, 1969), pp. 6–7.

3
The Acceleration
of Modernization,
1930 to the Present

The year 1930 was a turning point in Latin American history. Not only did the older oligarchic order break down—at least temporarily—but the modernization process greatly accelerated. The middle sectors became a dominant force in politics but were deeply divided. The trade unions had become a power group to be reckoned with. The new rulers of Latin America, cognizant of the weaknesses of economies based solely on raw-materials and commodities exports, turned increasingly to industrialization as a means of stimulating growth and lessening reliance on expensive imports. But accelerated industrialization led to even more accelerated social transformations. A new set of pressures began to be felt, and cumulatively they added up to profound social revolution. Let us trace the chronology of these changes and analyze the major areas of Latin American society that are presently undergoing restructuring.

THE POST-1930 PERIOD OF
LATIN AMERICAN DEVELOPMENT

The political responses to the wave of revolts that swept Latin America in 1930 were far from uniform, and a variety of alternative development strategies were tried. The host of new parties and movements that emerged, ranging from moderate to social democratic to Communist, challenged and sometimes defeated the older elitist Conservative and Liberal factions. Socialist, anarchist, Communist, and anarcho-syndicalist influences were strong within the trade unions. A number of Christian-Democratic parties and Catholic trade unions, business groups, and student associations were formed. Fascist and manifestly corporatist movements and regimes also attracted support.

Despite the wide variety of new movements and ideologies that sprang up in the 1920s and 1930s, there were some common political responses as well. In general, the Latin American systems in the 1930s and on into the 1940s sought to adapt to change, but that did not imply the destruction of the system per se. They attempted to accommodate themselves to the new currents and forces that modernization had spawned without sacrificing entirely the institutions of the past. Their formula was, not to destroy the older established order, but to mold and reorder it to fit the new realities.

The general Latin American way of responding to the social pressures of the times was to add on and assimilate the new corporate groups and power contenders that had begun to challenge the system (the middle sectors and the trade unions) without necessarily repudiating or destroying the older centers of influence (see especially Anderson, *Politics and Economic Change in Latin America*).* Latin Americans sought to expand and remodel the prevailing hierarchical and elitist order, but they did not necessarily shake off the tradition of elite-dominated rule. The new groups were to be accommodated and brought into the system, but they would have to play by the rules of the game and not seek to topple the prevailing structure. They had to go along with and accept the benefits that accrued, or they would be suppressed.

The management of this process of change involved some clever politics on the part of those elite groups that had historically governed Latin America and those newer middle-sector elements that now were moving into positions of power. Both groups saw that for things to remain the same, they would have to change, which implied a granting of recognition and certain benefits to the middle and labor sectors, but at a price. In return for legal standing and certain social programs, for example, the labor movement was often organized under strict government control and regulation. The status quo was hence changed, but it was also preserved. The nature of this evolution, as well as the continuity with the older tradition, is presented in Figure 3.1.

Three major arenas of change are apparent between these two images and time frames of the Latin American sociopolitical structure. First, in the post-1930s period the number of vertical corporate groups or power contenders expanded to include both the older elements (army, church, oligarchy) and the newer ones (business, middle-sector, labor). Second, the size of the middle sectors expanded horizontally, and third, skilled and organized workers became differentiated from the peasants and/or Indian masses and were given a special place in the hierarchy. In these ways, the Latin American systems sought to respond to change and modernization and proved adaptable in the process.

But four other points are of at least equal importance. One, the hierarchical, pyramidal societal structure was retained; two, the top-down system of rule by elites remained intact (although the relative power of the several elites may have shifted); three, the line separating

---

*All references are to the suggested readings found at the end of Chapter 7.

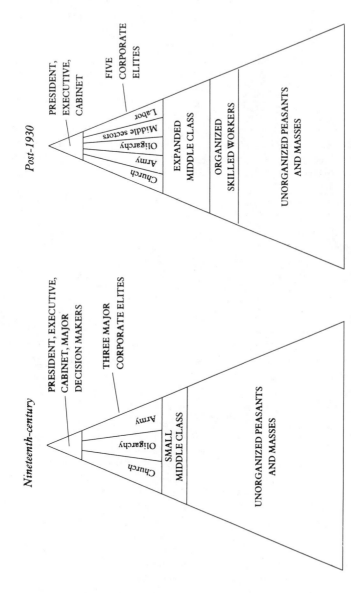

Figure 3.1 Continuity and Change in the Latin American Sociopolitical Structure

the "effective nation" (elites and middle class, a few from the organized working class) from the rest was still sharply drawn; and four, the essentially two-class nature of Latin American society, in which the middle sectors come frequently to share the values of the historical elites (such as disdain for the common people and for manual labor), persisted. Note also the remarkable continuity of the post-1930s structure with the sixteenth-century model depicted in Figure 2.1. Thus, although much had changed in Latin America since the nineteenth century, much also remained the same. Whether such an essentially elitist, hierarchical, and pyramidal system could continue to cope with and manage the forces that modernization set loose, or whether that system would be overthrown by revolution, has been a question at the heart of the political struggles in virtually all the national political systems treated in this book.

Although the effort to adapt to change while also preserving the traditional structure was probably the dominant Latin American pattern from the 1930s on, a great number of variations within that basic pattern could and did occur, and in some nations the basic model itself was attacked and overthrown. The middle sectors emerged predominant in some countries; instead of oligarchic rule, the prevailing pattern in Chile, Uruguay, and Venezuela was one of general dominance by the new (albeit frequently internally divided) middle-class groups and parties. Mexico developed a single-party system, although power within the official party came to be lodged not so much with the labor and peasant sectors as with an emergent bourgeoisie.

In Brazil and Argentina, a new kind of populist leader rose up in the persons of Getúlio Vargas and Juan Domingo Perón, respectively, and they both gave benefits to and expected support from the new middle and labor sectors. Social-Democratic parties vied for and sometimes won power in Costa Rica, Peru, and Venezuela. In contrast, strong-arm dictators emerged in Cuba, the Dominican Republic, El Salvador, Haiti, Honduras, Nicaragua, Paraguay, and Guatemala, and despite all their authoritarian practices, they also signaled a partial break with the past. These dictators were from middle-class and often racially mixed social origins, rather than from the old oligarchy, and they undertook a considerable number of nation-building development projects. In many countries, democratic rule was established for a time; in others, the elites recaptured power after having been temporarily deprived of it.

But the prevailing situation in all the countries was a new legitimacy crisis, a deepening fragmentation, and hence, often a pattern of oscillation between any or all of these phenomena. Latin America had become increasingly a conflict society in which the old norms and institutions were being questioned while the various new groups were badly divided as to what future directions their countries should take. A democratic government might come to power briefly, only to be followed by a new military regime, or else populist politicians would instigate a needed reform program, only to be replaced by a conservative oligarchic government that rescinded it. There were strong challenges from the left in Brazil, El Salvador, and other nations, defensive actions from the right, increased fragmentation in the center—and repeated clashes among all these groups.

A few of the countries of the area—Mexico, Chile, and Uruguay for a time, Costa Rica, Venezuela, and perhaps Colombia—seemed able to deal fairly well with these competing, divisive crosscurrents. But in the rest (and eventually even in some of the countries mentioned), the divisions helped produce an increased fragmentation. The conflicts were often so deep, the gaps among the contending groups and classes so vast, the bitterness so intense that no government—left, right, or center—could come to power, govern effectively, and hope to survive for long. As the divisions became more intense, governments and the political systems were increasingly unable to function effectively. Breakdown and national disintegration seemed imminent by the late 1960s and early 1970s in such leading countries as Argentina, Brazil, Chile, and Uruguay. Again, as in the nineteenth century, it was the army that stepped into the vacuum.

The collapse of the older oligarchic order in 1930 had left a political lacuna that neither the old elites nor the new ones seemed capable of filling more than temporarily or with anything resembling majority support. Meanwhile, social and economic changes continued to transform underlying realities. The 1930s were a decade throughout all of Latin America of rapid, albeit uneven, industrialization; the pace of change quickened.

Heavy industry—steel, manufacturing, petrochemicals—was built up during this period. Domestic production accelerated further during World War II, both because of the difficulty of receiving goods from abroad and because of the demand for Latin American products occasioned by the war itself. Although in the postwar period the political instability seemed generally unrelieved, economic growth continued, in many countries pushing ahead at unspectacular but often steady rates. The share of gross domestic product (GDP) generated by industry and manufacturing gradually rose. Other social transformations, often un-dramatic but nonetheless cumulative, occurred: Literacy rates rose, as did life expectancy; new communications and transportation grids penetrated deeply into the interior; the middle sectors continued to grow; organized labor increased in strength; the population grew and empty areas were filled; production expanded; peasants migrated in droves to the cities; rural elements were organized for the first time; social problems multiplied; and workers and members of the middle class became impatient for larger numbers of goods and services.

As social and political pressures continued to mount in the 1950s, 1960s, 1970s, and the 1980s, the possibilities for a genuinely revolutionary transformation increased. Conflicts and divisions within the middle sectors and among the various groups (army, political parties, businesspeople, students) deepened. At the same time the struggle between some of these groups and the emerging labor and reformist movements took on aspects of class warfare. Peasant elements were by now sufficiently mobilized in some countries to constitute a force to be reckoned with, particularly in situations where peasant violence was accompanied by workers' strikes, student unrest, and middle-class discontent.

In seeking to break out of the immobility and conflict of the traditional system, the revolutionary alternative began to appear more attractive. In 1952 in Bolivia, a revolution destroyed the power of the traditional landed elites and mining interests and brought to prominence a movement dedicated to transforming the prevailing social and economic patterns. In Argentina, Perón had come to power in 1946 as a populist and on the basis of working-class support. On January 1, 1959, Fidel Castro ushered in his revolution in Cuba, transforming that society into the first socialist nation in the Western Hemisphere.

In Guatemala in 1944–1954 and the Dominican Republic in 1965, social revolutions took place as well, but these were frustrated by U.S. military intervention. In Chile, the Socialist-Communist Popular Unity government of Marxist Salvador Allende was overthrown in 1973 with the connivance of the United States. But in Peru in 1968, a revolutionary military regime successfully destroyed the power of the traditional landed oligarchy, and nationalist military regimes took power for a time in Ecuador, Bolivia, Honduras, and Panama. Nicaragua had a revolution that ended in 1979 with the fall of Anastasio Somoza Debayle, and revolutionary upheaval threatened to spread throughout Central America. Meanwhile, in some of the most important nations of the area—Argentina, Brazil, Chile, and Uruguay—authoritarian military regimes took over in the 1970s, determined to eliminate by brutal means if necessary the challenges from the left and from below. Argentina, Brazil, Uruguay, and Peru returned to elected governments in the early 1980s, and Chile did likewise in March 1990. The Dominican Republic restored democracy in 1978, and in several of the Central American countries (El Salvador, Honduras, Guatemala) an uneasy balance was struck—better than the repressive regimes that had gone before—between elected civilian governments on the one hand and the military, which often remained the power behind the throne, on the other.

THE CONTEMPORARY REVOLUTION IN LATIN AMERICA

Although the preceding discussion has of necessity focused on the political elites of Latin America, on the efforts of various regimes to control and manage the development process, and on what is (with perhaps three or four major revolutionary exceptions) still a predominantly conservative to middle-of-the-road political order, attention must now be given to the newer revolutionary currents sweeping over the area.

These often operate below the surface and do not get the headlines that major events occurring at the top do, but their importance is real and is certain to increase. The changes under way are so immense and far-reaching that they add up to a situation of genuine social revolution.

When we speak of the contemporary revolution in Latin America, we are not referring to the usual palace revolts and military *pronuncia-mientos* ("pronouncements against the government") but of deep-rooted social changes whose cumulative effects add up to full-scale, long-term social transformation. We discuss these basic changes under six broad headings: changes in values and political culture, the economic transformation of the area, changes in social structure, the emergence of new political forces and movements, the new policies and institutional arrangements fashioned by governments in response to new demands, and changes in the international context. These measures provide not only a working definition of development in Latin America but also a list of key indicators to watch for in measuring the relative strength of the forces of change in the country chapters.

Changes in Values and Political Culture

Latin America was founded upon a value system that stressed authority, hierarchy, and elitism. Although these values are still often strongly present throughout the area, in many countries the traditional beliefs that undergirded the social and political system for so long are undergoing transformation or are being fused with new values: social justice, democracy, participation, development, socialism, and the like.

It is no longer so easy as in the past to convince a peasant that one must be poor because poverty is good for the soul or that one must accept a low station in life as part of the natural order. The old myths simply do not wash anymore. Instead of the fatalistic rural worker who is resigned to his or her lot because Saint Thomas or the church said this is the way things must be, the countryside is now full of increasingly restless people who are questioning traditional values for the first time and who are impatient for change. Challenging new ideas are filtering in.

The agents of these changes are modern transportation and communications, particularly the transistor radio and now television as well. Whereas before, the rural peasant lived with almost no contact with the outside world, today it is practically impossible to go anywhere in Latin America where the transistor radio is not heard broadcasting news, sports, and a wider conception of the outside world. New roads have also brought the rural elements into contact with urban markets. Party organizers, U.S. officials, government agencies, and young revolutionaries have fanned out into the countryside, carrying with them new concepts of how to order one's life. The historic isolation of the *patria chica* is breaking down.

But even though the old values are being undermined and new ideas are being introduced, one cannot be sure of what the long-term meaning of these changes will be, for the new values—democracy, socialism, communism, capitalism—are also frequently in competition with each other. Not only do Radio Havana and the Voice of America come in loud and clear, but other competitors for the listener's ear are the government station, the church station, the voice of the armed forces, and various political parties. Hence, while the old assumptions are challenged, the new values are still inchoate and at best incompletely digested. There are too many ideas to be absorbed all at once. The value and belief systems of most transitional persons represent a mixture of old and new. There is no clear-cut or unilinear progression from traditional beliefs to modern ones.

A good number of efforts are also under way on the part of conservative interests and governments to control these changes or to manipulate the educational system so as to preserve the historical institutions. Education and social mobilization can be manipulated to produce conservative results as well as revolutionary ones. At this point, it is not clear whether one should expect increasingly sharp breaks with the past, whether the traditional elites will succeed in their quest to control the process of change, or whether, as seems most likely, Latin America will continue to represent a mixture of old and new—although always in a dynamic and changing relationship.

Economic Transformations

Latin America is also being transformed economically, but here, too, the outcome of the process remains in doubt. Along with the acceleration of the industrialization process, which began in the 1930s and continued in most countries through the 1970s, has come a steady rise in per capita income and standards of living. Two-thirds of the Latin American countries have now passed the threshold, arbitrarily put at US$1,000 of income per person per year, that separates the underdeveloped nations from the more developed. Although the standards of living are still not comparable to those of the United States, the countries of Western Europe, or Japan, neither are the Latin American nations basket cases. By most indices, the Latin American nations are intermediate systems, neither fully developed nor wholly underdeveloped.

A comparison of present-day per capita income in Latin America with the situation in 1960 or 1950 shows significant change. In most cases, per capita income has doubled and in some it has trebled or quadrupled in the preceding forty years. These figures are impressive, but they do not tell the whole story since they fail to indicate how income is distributed. Most of the income is still concentrated in upper- and middle-class pockets while the standard of living of the urban and rural poor remains abysmally low. In many areas, the standard of living of the poor, especially for the rural peasants and the subsistence farmers, has actually declined. But the general picture, obviously varying from country to country, is one of gradual improvement, although as shown

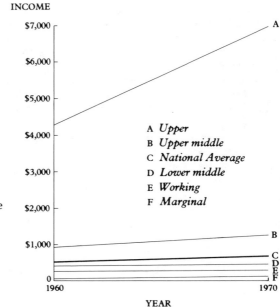

Figure 3.2 Average Income in Brazil by Social Strata, 1960 and 1970 (constant dollars)

Source: Based on Albert Fishlow, "Brazilian Size Distribution of Income," in Alejandro Foxley, ed., *Income Distribution in Latin America*, Cambridge University Press, Cambridge, 1976, pp. 61, 72.

in Figure 3.2, which uses data from Brazil, the rates of improvement for the distinct social strata are highly uneven.

The Brazilian case, which was fairly typical for the countries of Latin America through the 1970s, shows some interesting patterns. Most obvious is the steep rise in the income of the upper classes. The middle sectors also profited significantly from the recent economic growth, and skilled workers similarly improved their lot. The so-called marginals managed to achieve some improvement (though in many Latin American countries that was not the case), but for many lower-class Brazilians, living standards went down even under conditions of "miracle growth" on the national level.

Three points bear emphasizing in Figure 3.2. First, the income levels of the major organized groups showed improvement over the years. Second, it is clear that middle- and upper-class income and living standards improved far faster and more disproportionately than those of the working class (and, hence, the gaps between the classes widened, not narrowed). Third, the marginal elements, rural and urban, were left behind. Hence, although the general pattern in most countries has been economic growth, the *distribution* of income in Latin America is among the worst in the world and is actually getting worse.

At issue in Latin America, except for the poorest, unorganized, and marginal elements, was not so much sheer poverty—as in Ethiopia or Bangladesh, for example—as the relative deprivation of some classes vis-à-vis others. Most of the class groups improved their station in life, but some more than others. Most Latin American governments sought to channel sufficient benefits to their lower classes, at least to those organized elements that constituted a potential threat, to head off revolution. In this effort, most succeeded. Thus, while organized working-class elements often gained salary increases, the very poor, who were not seen as a threat, continued to have a difficult, hand-to-mouth existence. However, since the distribution of income is so uneven and these lower-class elements are now being organized and mobilized for the first time, there may be future revolutionary troubles looming for some of the Latin American systems.

This system of growth and some political stability have been severely threatened by the economic crisis that began in Latin America in 1979 and deepened thereafter. The crisis was first felt by the oil-importing countries of Latin America because of the two shocking oil-price increases of the 1970s. Next, the changed nature of the post-OPEC world negatively affected the Latin American countries because of changes in the importing capacities of the industrialized countries of the world (inflation also affected imports needed by Latin American countries) and because the world economic recession diminished demand in the industrialized countries and also resulted in lower prices for other primary-goods products. Both the inflation and the recession were caused in large part by the OPEC price increases. Finally, the "oil glut" of 1982, and the decline of petroleum prices, negatively affected the Latin American members of OPEC (Venezuela and Ecuador) and the other oil exporters (especially Mexico) because they had planned their economies on the assumption of both rising petroleum prices and constant, or even increasing, production levels.

By 1982, in the midst of a global recession, many Latin American countries were recording zero or negative growth. Their economies had turned stagnant or even shrunk. Throughout the region, a major economic crisis set in, and it was made worse by the stupendous debts at high interest rates that almost all the Latin American countries had earlier contracted. In large part these increased debts were the result of loans, to both public and private sectors in Latin America, from private banks in the industrialized countries, which were recycling the petrodollars invested in them by the oil-exporting nations. As the threat of default on these debts was faced by various Latin American governments, they increasingly turned to the International Monetary Fund (IMF) for standby loans. The IMF's formula was clear: Loans would be made available if the governments froze wages; cut employment in the public sector; cut down on deficit spending and inflation; ended subsidies, which were designed to especially benefit the lower- and middle-income sectors;

devaluated the national currency; and cut down on foreign imports while encouraging additional exports.

The economic crisis not only made many Latin American lower- and some middle-class elements worse off but also threatened political stability. At a time of rising expectations, there were fewer pieces of the pie to hand out, and discontent spread. Not only were many governments throughout the area faced with threats of destabilization but the whole Latin American system of gradualist, accommodative, evolutionary politics (described in Chapter 7) was undermined as well.

The continuing debt crisis has further compounded Latin America's persistent economic troubles and is a very complicated problem. Some Latin American countries plainly cannot pay all their outstanding international debts (approaching US$500 billion for the region as a whole at the end of the 1980s); on the other hand, the private foreign banks cannot admit that the loans are uncollectable (or their balance sheets will be in bad trouble and their stockholders very angry); and the U.S. government (meaning U.S. taxpayers) is unwilling to bail out the banks or the Latin American governments. What to do? The answer so far has been to "manage" the crisis: Play for time, hope the world economy remains solid so Latin America can grow out of the crisis; provide some financial shots in the arm from the U.S. Treasury in genuine crisis situations but on an ad hoc and individual country basis; and meanwhile provide a menu of approaches so the banks can reduce their exposure and the Latin American countries can avoid bankruptcy. But the problem has not been solved so far, and meanwhile quite a number of Latin American countries are sliding further toward financial ruin. A few are still doing relatively well economically, but for the rest it seems likely that some form of U.S. relief will be necessary.

There are other changes in the area's economic structure to be aware of when reading the country chapters. One involves the role of the government in the economy. Through the 1970s there was a growth of increasingly state-directed economies throughout Latin America, whether socialist economies or capitalist ones. The debt crisis, however, led to a movement toward a larger role for the private sector, and through "privatization," economic entities owned by many Latin American governments were sold to the private sector. The second change concerns the spread of the big multinational corporations (MNCs) throughout Latin America and their capacity to shape internal markets and governments—although with the deepening of Latin America's economic troubles, many MNCs have withdrawn their capital from the area. Although the countries endeavored to control the MNCs during the 1960s and 1970s, these constraints were loosened during the crisis of the 1980s. The third change relates to the growing interrelationships between the Latin American economies and outside market prices (such as the price of oil) and forces. More than ever, the Latin American economies are dependent on worldwide economic pressures over which they have little control.

Changes in Social Structure

With long-term economic development have come changes in the social structure. The Latin American societies are no longer the simple lord-and-peasant societies of the past. Rather, they are now much more complex systems with a far greater differentiation among social groups. Many aspects of the two-class system have been retained, but that should not blind one to the changes.

Industrialization helped give rise to new social forces. A new larger middle class has emerged, but it is split into upper, middle, and lower substrata and is additionally divided along vertical lines: clerics, army officers, university students, government workers, shop owners, small farmers, small-business people. The middle sector is also divided politically, so that if we say the army officer corps or the political party executive committees are dominated by middle-sector representatives, that may be insufficient to tell us their political ideologies. Indeed, it could be said that since 1930 virtually all institutions in Latin America—armed forces, church, political parties, universities, bureaucracy—have come to be dominated by the middle sectors and that, hence, politics in much of Latin America is essentially middle-class politics. But given the divisions within the middle sectors, a great variety of developmental solutions—ranging from far left to far right and all positions in between—are possible.

The trade unions have also shown themselves to be a significant new social force that must be discussed in any consideration of Latin American politics. Peasants and Indians have similarly been mobilized and partially organized, however unevenly, in most countries of the area. Urban marginals, the recent peasant arrivals in the major cities, who are generally underemployed and as yet not organized, have also emerged as a new social force.

Change has occurred not just within the newer social groups but within the more traditional sectors as well. Members of the military and the church hierarchies are not recruited from upper-class ranks anymore but from the middle sectors, and this change has had some important implications in terms of the political behavior of these institutions. Neither the church nor the army can any longer be depended on as automatic defenders of the status quo. Rather, both of these institutions are severely divided internally, and particularly within the army, nationalist and developmentalist ideologies are strong and cut across the traditional ideological divisions. Within the church, the large number of foreign-born clergy (French, Spanish, North American) has also acted as a stimulus to new ways of thinking about society and participation and so have changes in the church's theology, which has been dramatically altered as a result of Vatican II and liberation theology (see Chapter 4). Similarly, the oligarchy no longer consists of just a landed aristocratic class tracing its origins to colonial times but of a business-commercial elite, of old-rich and new-rich elements, and frequently now of powerful foreign communities. To understand the dynamics of contemporary Latin American politics, one must come to grips with these new complexities.

New Political Groups

Along with accelerated social change has come a host of new political associations and movements, and the old Liberal and Conservative elite factions have lost their monopoly on power. Beginning in the 1920s and 1930s and continuing into the post–World War II period, a variety of new middle-class and worker movements emerged to challenge the historical dominance of the old elites. Often led by charismatic, populist political leaders, these movements were able to break the monopoly of power that the upper class had long maintained, and they helped make the political situation much more fluid—and unstable—than it had been.

The first Communist and socialist parties were organized during this period, led usually by middle-class intellectuals and with a strong base in the emerging trade unions. Parties that called themselves Radical, patterned after the French Radicals but ultimately not very radical, had grown up earlier in Argentina and Chile, based on middle-class support. A variety of social-democratic or Aprista-like parties (named after the Peruvian APRA—American Popular Revolutionary Alliance) began to challenge the established order starting in the 1930s and in some cases came to power. New Christian-Democratic movements were organized, and a variety of agrarian, worker, peasant, anarchist, and other organizations added to the party potpourri.

But not just parties were organized; indeed, an entire associational vacuum began to be filled. Many of the new associations called themselves nonpartisan, but they frequently acted like partisan groups. The new trade-union movements—split into Communist, socialist, Christian-Democratic, and anarcho-syndicalist groups—often favored direct political action over collective bargaining. There were new associations of students, businesspeople, peasants, and women; military lodges, sometimes secret, were formed; landowners began to band together to protect their interests. The organizational void that had always plagued Latin America began to be filled, either through free association or by government fiat. The state frequently created its own official associations, trade unions, and the like as a way of heading off possible revolutionary change that a genuinely independent and pluralist associational life posed.

New Policies and Institutional Arrangements

A fifth area of major change involves the greater complexity of governmental institutions and the policies flowing from them. With the "revolution of rising expectations," government was called upon to provide a host of new services and carry out a variety of new programs. Government (almost always at the national level and not at the state and local levels as in the United States) was expected to deliver social security programs, health care, housing, rural electrification, roads, dams, water supplies, and a great number of other services. Moreover, with the Great Depression, World War II, and growth of the economy, the government's regulatory role was vastly expanded.

The result, in all the countries of the area, was the creation of many new ministries, agencies, and institutes to carry out the new programs. New ministries of labor, commerce, industry, planning, and social security were set up, and hundreds of other agencies to administer agrarian reform, community development, water resources, and the like came into existence. Moreover, to administer the new programs, bureaucratic behavior had to change. No longer could the line between the public and the private domains be so easily blurred. New norms of honesty, rationality, and effectiveness in public administration were called for. The patrimonialist conception remained strong, but it was no longer the only method of operating. Graft, family favoritism, political payoffs, and special privileges still provided the grease that helped turn the wheels of government, but real programs and not just paper ones had to be carried out—or else! Although traditional bureaucratic behavior remained strongly in evidence and was widely tolerated up to a point, the success of any government came to be judged on its capacity to effectively implement programs for social and economic development.

One result of this new thrust was the enormous growth of the public sector. The Latin American state assumed the roles of national patron, industrialist, and chief capitalist, and the government became the largest employer in the country. Even greater power than before was concentrated at the central state level, but local and regional authority and that of the local caudillos were undermined. The historical tendency to look to the central government to solve all of society's ills was greatly strengthened. These changes in the structure and the increasingly central role of the state resulted in some major transformations, probably equal in importance to the other social and political changes discussed earlier. The enormous power and funds concentrated at the central state level made the competition to capture these higher stakes that much more intense. Some blame this government control for the debt crisis. The privatization movement, of course, has had the effect of lessening the role of the government in the economy, but it has not ended its role completely.

Changes at the International Level

Latin America's traditional isolation, not only internally in terms of its separate *patrias chicas* but also externally in terms of its relations with the outside world, is breaking down. Latin America is no longer an isolated backwater but is being increasingly integrated into world trade patterns, communications networks, alliances, and the like. There has also been a major change in the way Latin America sees itself and relates to the rest of the world.

Modern communications and transportation networks are making all nations interdependent in ways they never were before, and markets and trade patterns have also become increasingly international. Latin America must sell its coffee, sugar, minerals, tobacco, and bananas, as well as its manufactured goods, abroad at favorable prices, or its entire economic (and political) structure will be threatened with collapse. At the same time, most of Latin America is absolutely dependent on the importation of oil at reasonable prices.

The web of dependent and interdependent relations is complex and difficult to sort out. The Latin American economies are heavily dependent on international markets, and they are particularly dependent on their trade with the United States. Economic dependence has often been translated into political dependence, i.e., the capacity of the United States to use its control over markets and international lending agencies to manipulate the internal politics of Latin American nations. Many nations are now trying to break out of this historical dependence by diversifying their economies and increasing their trade and contacts with Western Europe, Eastern Europe, Japan, the Soviet Union, and other areas, but these strategies have not been altogether successful, and dependency upon the United States is still the situation for many countries.

Latin America is also tied into a web of international political and defense arrangements similarly dominated by the United States. The cold war altered the face of Latin America's internal politics and made several countries (such as Cuba, Chile, Guatemala, and the Dominican Republic) pawns in the worldwide rivalry between the superpowers. Latin America's communications media are also closely tied to U.S. news agencies. The big multinationals gained immense power throughout the area, often with the ability to manipulate Latin American governments and their policies, and some people argue that even Latin American culture is becoming heavily Americanized as the "Coca-Cola-ization" and the consumer culture of the continent go forward. But in more recent years many of the big companies, fearing instability and tired of extensive regulation by the governments of the area, have begun pulling out of Latin America and investing elsewhere, and because of the debt crisis, private banks have stopped giving new loans to most Latin American countries.

Latin America is thus breaking out of its historical isolation, but in some areas that change has had decidedly mixed results. Latin America has become more a part of a modern and interdependent world, but that fact has frequently also meant accepting increased dependence.

CONCLUSIONS AND IMPLICATIONS

The pace of change has accelerated throughout Latin America. In the past four decades new and revolutionary transformations have begun to sweep across the continent, and these changes, taken together and cumulatively, add up to a profound social transformation in Latin American society and polity. The changes have generally been gradual but nonetheless profound. Since the 1930s new social and political forces have fundamentally altered all areas of Latin American life.

Still, the power of traditional forces has also remained strong, and the question must be raised as to whether the changes have been rapid and thorough enough. Has Latin America experienced fundamental change, or is it still engaged in a holding action? Have the changes noted affected basic power relationships, or is the essentially elitist, hierarchical, and authoritarian structure still in place? To what extent have the new groups gained genuinely independent bargaining power? Conversely, have the benefits channeled to them served to co-opt them into the older pattern of elitist rule and to prevent more fundamental changes? Is the democracy present in most Latin American countries in the late 1980s a sign of a lasting change, or is it just another cycle that will be replaced with military governments in the 1990s? These are critical issues; they lie at the heart of the Latin American political process—and of the analyses presented in this book.

4
Interest Groups and Political Parties

The Latin American political tradition differs in many ways from that of the United States and Western Europe. The distinct political tradition of Latin America is reflected in the composition and interrelationships of the political groups in the area. There is considerable disagreement as to whether Latin America has a politics of interest-group struggle comparable to that of the United States. Of course, there is competition among various groups and factions throughout Latin America, but whereas in the United States group politics is looked upon as a natural, generally wholesome aspect of the political system, in Latin America the emphasis is often on creating an administrative state that is above party and interest-group politics. Another difference is that in the United States the major groups, religious agencies, and the like are assumed to be independent of the government, whereas in Latin America such agencies as the church, the army, the university, and perhaps even the trade unions are often more than mere interest groups: They are a part of the state system and inseparable from it. There are degrees of government control over these groups, ranging from almost complete control to almost complete freedom. But the usual pattern involves considerably more state control over interest groups than in the United States, and this control helps put interest- (or what some people prefer to call corporate-) group behavior in Latin America in a framework different from that in the United States.

Latin America, as Charles Anderson has suggested,[1] never experienced a definitive democratic revolution—that is, a struggle resulting in agreement that mobilization of votes is the only legitimate way to obtain public power. In the absence of such a consensus, political groups do not necessarily work for political power by seeking votes, support of political parties, or contacts with elected representatives. Such groups might seek power through any number of other strategies, including coercion (the military), economic might (upper-class groups and foreign enterprises), technical expertise (bureaucrats), and controlled violence (labor unions, peasants, and students). Any group that can mobilize votes is likely to do so for an election, but since that is not the only legitimated route to power, the result of any election is tentative. The duration of any government is uncertain, given the varying power of the competing groups and the incomplete legitimacy of the government itself. Without a definitive term of office for any government, political competition becomes a constant, virtually permanent struggle and preoccupation.

Further, group behavior in Latin America is conditioned by a set of unwritten rules, leading to what Anderson has called the "living museum" effect. Before a new group can participate in the political system, it must tacitly demonstrate both that it has a power resource and that it will respect the rights of already existing groups. Until a new group has demonstrated that it has some capacity to challenge or even overthrow a government, there is little reason for the established groups to take it seriously. Equally important, this potential participant in the political process must give assurances that it will not use its power to harm or eliminate the groups that already exist. The result is the gradual addition of new groups under these two conditions but seldom the elimination of the old ones. The newest, most-modern groups coexist with the oldest, most-traditionalist ones.

A related factor is the tradition of co-optation or repression. As new groups emerge as potential politically relevant actors, already established groups (particularly political parties or strong national leaders) sometimes offer to assist them in their new political activities. The deal struck is mutually beneficial to both: The new group gains acceptance, prestige, and some of its original goals, and the established group or leader gains new support and increased political resources. The co-opted group drops some of its original goals, which leads many observers to be critical of the system as not providing for enough change. But those leaders and observers who prefer stability to more fundamental change see the co-optation system as beneficial to the political system.

Sometimes new groups refuse to be co-opted and fail to accept the rules of the game. Instead, they take steps that indicate—at least to the established groups and leaders—they might act against the interests of the established elites. In the case of a group that violates the ground rules by employing mass violence, for example, an effort is made by the established interests to repress the new group, either by refusing it legal standing or in some cases through the use of violence. The army or hired thugs are employed to suppress the group that ventures outside the system. Most commonly, such repression has proved successful, and the new group, at least for the time being, disappears or atrophies without accomplishing any of its goals. The general success of repression makes a co-optation strategy seem more desirable to new groups, since obtaining *some* of their goals through co-optation is preferable to being repressed.

In a few cases, the result is quite different. The established political groups fail to repress the emergent groups, and the latter come to power through revolutionary means and proceed to eliminate the traditional power contenders. These cases are known as the "true," genuine, or social revolutions in Latin America, and so far only the Mexican Revolution of 1910–1920, the Bolivian Revolution of 1952, the Cuban Revolution of 1959, and the Nicaraguan Revolution of 1979 are examples. Examples of the reverse process—utilization of violence and repression to eliminate a new challenging group and to secure the power of the more traditional system—are Brazil in 1964 and Chile in 1973. In both of the latter cases, power groups consisting of independent political parties, student associations, and labor and peasant unions were eliminated.

It is in this context of an often patrimonial, corporative, and co-optive tradition, now overlaid with the trappings of liberalism (and in some countries more than mere trappings), and of a set of elaborate though unwritten rules of the game that we should view the politically relevant groups of Latin America. After independence three groups, often referred to as the "nineteenth-century oligarchy," were predominant: the military, the Roman Catholic church, and the large landholders. These groups were once staunch defenders of the status quo; now they are more heterogeneous. As a result of economic growth and change, new groups became organized: first commercial elites; later industrial elites, students, and middle-income sectors; most recently industrial labor unions and peasants. Political parties have existed throughout the whole process. Particularly since the end of the nineteenth century the United States has also been a politically relevant force in the domestic politics of the Latin American countries, both the U.S. government and U.S. private businesses. The U.S. embassy is a leading actor, not only in terms of Latin America's trade and diplomatic relations but also in terms of internal affairs, comparable in importance to such major forces as the church, the oligarchy, and the army.

THE ARMED FORCES

During the wars for independence the Spanish American countries developed armies that were led by a great variety of individuals, including well-born criollos, priests, and people of more humble background. The officers did not come from military academies but were self-selected or chosen by other leaders. Few of the officers had previous military training, and the armies were much less professional than today's armies.

Following independence the military was one of the first important power groups. The national army was supposed to be preeminent, and in some countries national military academies were founded during the first quarter century of independence. Yet the national military was often challenged by other armies. The early nineteenth century was a period of limited national integration, and the *patrias chicas* or regional sub-divisions of the countries were often dominated by local landowners or caudillos—men on horseback who had their own private armies. One aspect of the development of Latin America was the struggle between the central government and its army on the one hand and the *patrias chicas* and local caudillos on the other, with the eventual success of the former.

The development of Brazil varied somewhat because of the different colonizing power and because of the lack of a struggle for independence. The military in that country first gained preeminence during the Paraguayan War (1864–1870), and until 1930 the Brazilian states had powerful militias, in some cases comparable in strength to the national army.

Although Latin American militaries varied in the nineteenth century, a study of them reveals two general themes. First, various militaries, including the national one, became active in politics. At given times they were regional or personal organizations; at others they were parts of political parties that were participants in the civil wars which were frequently waged between rival factions. Second, the national military often played the role of a moderating power—staying above factional struggles, preferring that civilians govern but taking over power temporarily when the civilians could not effectively rule. Although the military did not act as a moderating power in all countries, it did so in most, and in Brazil, the military became the chief moderator after the abdication of the emperor in 1889.

As early as the 1830s and 1840s in Argentina and Mexico and later in the other Latin American countries, national military academies were established. Their goal was to introduce professionalism into the military, and graduation was required for officer status. Aided in the first decades of the twentieth century by military missions from Germany and France and later by Chilean missions, these academies were for the most part successful in making entry into and promotion in the officer corps proceed in an established manner. No longer did individuals become generals overnight; rather, they were trained in military tactics and procedure. By the 1950s a Latin American officer would become a general, and thus have potential political power, only after a career of some twenty years.

Through professionalization, a military career was designed to be a highly specialized one that taught officers the skills for warfare but to eschew interest in political matters. Officership would absorb all the energy of its members, and this functional expertise would be distinct from the expertise of politicians. Civilians were theoretically to have complete control over the military, which would stay out of politics. Yet this model of professionalism, imported from Western Europe and the United States, never took complete root in the Latin American political culture. The military continued to engage in politics and to exercise its moderating power, and coups d'état continued.

By the late 1950s and early 1960s a change had occurred in the nature of the role of the military in Latin America and in the developed countries of the West. The success of guerrilla revolutions in China,

Indochina, Algeria, and Cuba led to a new emphasis on the military's role with respect to counterinsurgency and internal defense functions. In addition, Latin American militaries—encouraged by U.S. military aid—began to assume responsibility for civic-action programs, which assisted civilians in the construction of roads, schools, and other public projects. This activity led to a broader responsibility for the military in nation building.

The new professionalism of the past three decades is more in keeping with the Latin American political culture than the old professionalism was. Military skills are no longer viewed as separate or different from civilian skills—management, administration, nation building. The military was to acquire the ability to help solve those national problems that might lead to insurgency—which is, in its very essence, a political rather than an apolitical task. The implication of the new professionalism is that besides combating active guerrilla factions, the military will see to it that social and economic reforms necessary to prevent insurgency are adopted if the civilians prove incapable of doing so. Although this new professionalism also exists in the developed Western world and in other parts of the Third World, it has been particularly prevalent in Latin America, where it coincided with the moderating-power tradition. Professionalism in Latin America, therefore, has often led to more military intervention in politics, not less.

The end result of this process has been called "bureaucratic authoritarianism,"[2] that is, the rule of the military institution on a long-term basis. Developed especially in Argentina, Brazil, Chile, and Uruguay, this new form of military government was of the institution as a whole—not an individual general—and was based on the idea that the military could govern better than civilians. This type of military often governed repressively and violated human rights. The bureaucratic-authoritarian period lasted from the mid-1960s through the late-1970s when military rule was replaced by elected civilian governments in many countries.

It is difficult to compare the Latin American militaries cross-nationally, and trying to distinguish "civilian" from "military" regimes is also a meaningless task sometimes or at best a difficult one. Often military personnel temporarily resign their commissions to take leadership positions in civilian bureaucracies, and frequently they hold military and civilian positions at the same time. In some cases, an officer might resign his commission, be elected president, and then govern with strong military backing. In almost all instances, coups d'état are not purely military affairs but are supported by civilians as well, and it is not unheard of for civilians to take a significant part in an ensuing military government. Sometimes civilians actually draw the military into playing a larger political role. In short, Latin American governments are often coalitions of certain military factions and certain civilian ones.

Few people would argue that all Latin American governments are exactly alike with respect to the degree of military influence exercised, and various attempts have been made to categorize military intervention in politics. Although this chapter is not the place to present a definitive classification, we suggest that several dimensions be considered in the country chapters that follow.

1. How often does the military forcefully remove chief executives, either elected ones or the victors in previous military coups? For example, Colombia has had only two successful coups in this century, Ecuador has had many more, and Bolivia had almost 200 in its first 150 years of independence.
2. How often are military men elected to the presidency? And if they are elected, to what extent do they govern like "civilians" and to what extent is this a way to bring the military to power and yet remain "democratic"?
3. To what degree do military officers occupy key positions in the civilian bureaucracy, having resigned their commissions with the expectation of being recommissioned, at the same level and without losing seniority, when their civilian days are over?
4. To what extent do the leaders of the military have a say in nonmilitary matters, issues other than the size of the military budget and the nature of defense?
5. In what way does the moderating power of the military obligate it to step in and unseat an incompetent president or one who has violated the rules of the game?

Besides the degree of military influence in the political system, several other interrelated questions should also be kept in mind.

1. Why is the military active in politics? Is this normal behavior in a particular country, or does it occur only during times of severe crisis?
2. Whom does the military represent? Is it acting in its own corporate interests, for the perceived good of the entire nation, or in the interests of the middle class, from whose ranks most members of the officer corps come?
3. Is the result of military rule conservative, maintaining or returning to the status quo, or is the military the handmaiden of social change?
4. How is the military divided? In no country does it seem to be a monolithic entity. Splits have occurred between service branches (the more upper-class navy against the middle-class army), between age groups of officers (the young colonels against the old generals), between factions with different perceptions of the military's role in society (officers who prefer civilian rule versus those who like military government), and between groups with various ideologies (the traditionalists versus the radicals).

The military is one of the traditional pillars of Latin American society, with rights (*fueros*), responsibilities, and a legal standing that can be traced back to colonial times. This history means the military will and must play a different role than it does in the United States, and it is advisable to look at the military's role in any country in the context of the interaction of these traditions with the problems that each individual country faces. For newly established democratic regimes in Latin America, the question of how to deal with the military is a critical one—how to subordinate it to civilian control without provoking a coup. Little is gained from blanket condemnation or blanket approval of military intervention; rather, we need to understand Latin American civil-military relations in their own political context.

THE ROMAN CATHOLIC CHURCH

All Latin American countries are nominally Catholic, although the form of that religion varies from country to country. The Spanish and Portuguese came to "Christianize the heathens" as well as to seek precious metals. In areas with large Amerindian concentrations, religion became a mixture of pre-Columbian and Roman Catholic beliefs. To a lesser degree, Catholicism later blended with African religions, which also exist on their own in certain areas, especially Brazil, Cuba, and Haiti. Religion in the large cities of Latin America is similar to that in the urban centers of the United States and Western Europe, but in the more isolated small towns, Roman Catholicism is still often of fifteenth-century vintage.

The power of the church hierarchy in politics also varies. Traditionally, the church was one of the main sectors of Spanish and Portuguese corporate society, with rights and responsibilities in such areas as care of orphans, education, and public morals. During the nineteenth century the church was one of the three major groups in politics, along with the military and the landed interests. Yet, during the same century, some lay people wanted to strip the church of all its temporal power, including its lands. Generally speaking, the conflict over the role of the church had ended in most countries by the first part of the present century, with some exceptions.

Today the church is changing—especially if by church one means the top levels of the hierarchy that control the religious and political fortunes of the institution. Transformations have been occasioned by the new theologies of the past hundred years, as expressed through various papal encyclicals, Vatican II (early 1960s), and the conferences of the Latin American bishops at Medellín, Colombia (1968) and Puebla, Mexico (1979). A significant number of bishops (and many more parish priests and members of the various orders) subscribe to what is commonly called "liberation theology," which stresses that the church is of and for this world and should take stands against repression and violence, including the "institutionalized violence"—life-demeaning and life-threatening—experienced by the poor. Liberation theology also stresses the equality of all believers—lay people as well as clerics and bishops—as opposed to the former stress on the hierarchy. The end result has been, in some parts of the area, new people's churches, with lay leaders and only a minimal involvement of priests.

It would be a mistake, however, to assume that all, or even most, members of the Latin American clergy subscribe to liberation theology. Many of them believe that the new social doctrine has made the church more involved with politics than it should be, and some are concerned about the loss of traditional authority that the erosion of hierarchical power has brought. The various countries of Latin America differ substantially with respect to church authority and the adherence of the bishops to liberation theology, and additional information is given in the country chapters.

As a result of the changes, the clergy is no longer uniformly conservative, and its members differ on the role that the church should play in socioeconomic reform and on the nature of hierarchical relations within the church. At one extreme of this conflict is the traditional church elite, usually with social origins in the upper class or aspirations to be accepted by it, whose members are still very conservative and have close connections to other supporters of the status quo. At the other end of this intraclergy conflict are those priests, of various social backgrounds, who believe that the major objective of the church is to help the masses obtain social justice. In some cases, these priests are openly revolutionary, fighting in guerrilla wars. Other priests fall between these two extremes of political ideology, and still others favor a relaxing of the rigid hierarchy and giving more discretion to local parish priests.

The church still participates in politics to defend its material interests, although in most cases its wealth is no longer in land. Certain church activities are still the traditional ones: giving religious instruction in schools; running parochial high schools and universities, the cost of which has generally made higher education possible only for people of middle income or higher; and occasionally attempting to prevent divorce legislation and to make purely civil marriage difficult. At times the church has been a major proponent of human rights, especially when military governments deny them. A touchier issue is that of birth control, and in most cases the Latin American church hierarchies have fought artificial methods. However, in the face of the population explosion, many church officials have assisted in family-planning clinics, turned their heads when governments have promoted artificial methods of birth control, and occasionally even assisted in those government efforts.

Nominally, Latin America is the most Catholic area of the world, although many individuals are not active communicants. The general religious ethos that permeates some of the Latin American countries gives the church an indirect power, making it unnecessary for the archbishop or the clergy to lobby actively for or against legislation or to state the formal position of the church on a traditional issue. Decision makers usually have been exposed to religious education at some point and know perfectly well what the church's position is.

Some analysts feel the church is no longer a major power contender. They argue that on certain issues its sway is still considerable but that the church is no longer as influential politically as the army, the wealthy elites, or the U.S. embassy. Other analysts, pointing to the people's churches, argue the contrary, that the church or individual clerics connected to it are more powerful than ever before. These contradictory hypotheses will be examined in the studies of the various countries.

One of the most interesting phenomena in Latin America in recent decades is the explosive growth of Protestant religious groups. In some countries, Protestants make up 15 percent or more of the population; in Guatemala, a Protestant general even became president for a time. The fastest growing of these sects are the evangelical Christians, not the older, mainline churches. Protestantism is associated with the middle class, which makes it socially attractive. Also, Protestantism is identified with a strong work ethic, obliging its members to work hard and save. The Protestant groups, however, are generally not politically powerful.

LARGE LANDOWNERS

In all of the countries of Latin America, save Costa Rica and Paraguay, the colonial period led to the establishment of a group of large landowners who had received their lands as royal grants. With the coming of independence, these *latifundistas* (owners of large land tracts called latifundios) became more powerful than before and developed into one of the three major groups of nineteenth-century politics. They did not operate monolithically, however; in some cases, they were divided against each other.

In recent times such rifts among the large landowners have continued, usually along the lines of production. For example, they might disagree on a government policy favoring livestock raising to the detriment of crop planting. However, the major conflict has been between the people who have large tracts of land and the many landless peasants. In those circumstances, the various groups of large landowners tend to coalesce, burying their differences. In some countries, there is an umbrella organization to bring all of the various producer organizations together formally; in other cases, the coalition is much more informal.

In the 1960s the pressures for land reform were considerable, both from landless peasants and from foreign and domestic groups who saw this reform as a way to avoid Castro-like revolutions. In some countries, such as Mexico, land reform had previously been achieved by revolution; in others, such as Venezuela, a good bit of land had been distributed to the landless; in still others, the power of the landed, in coalition with other status quo groups, had led to the appearance of land reform rather than to the reality. More and more of the landless moved to the cities. In many of the Latin American countries, especially those in which the amount of arable land is limited and the population explosion has led to higher person-to-land ratios, the issue of breaking up large estates will continue for the foreseeable future. Given the power of the landed, such a change is likely to be slow in the absence of something approaching a social revolution.

One failure of the land reforms of the 1960s was that they did not achieve the vision, about which U.S. Agency for International Development (AID) officials and sociologists waxed poetic, of countries of middle-class farmers reflecting all of the Jeffersonian virtues of tilling the land and encouraging liberal democracy. Only three countries in Latin America have significant numbers of family farms—Costa Rica, Colombia, and Mexico—and these predate the 1960s. In the absence of wholesale land reform (and even with it, if the policymakers decide that the economies of scale call for collective or state ownership of land), the development of a middle-class farmer group seems very unlikely.

COMMERCIAL AND INDUSTRIAL ELITES

Commercial elites have existed in Latin America since independence, and one of the early political conflicts was between those people who wanted free trade (the commercial elites and allied landed interests producing crops for export) and those who wanted protection of nascent industry (industrial elites and allied landed groups not producing for export). Although the early industrial elites were important in this conflict, the real push for industrialization in Latin America did not come until the Great Depression and World War II, when Latin America was cut off from trade with the industrialized world. Before those crises, industrial goods from England and the United States were cheaper, even with transportation costs and import duties, than locally produced goods. The one exception to this generalization was the textile industry.

Since the end of World War II, the Latin American countries have experienced industrialization of the import-substitution type—that is, producing goods that formerly were imported from the industrialized countries. This type of industrialization has occurred for light consumer goods; some consumer durables, including assembly plants for North American and European automobiles; and some other heavy industries such as cement and steel. Because import substitution necessitates increased foreign trade in order to import capital goods, there no longer is much conflict between commercial and industrial elites: Expanded trade and industrialization go together.

Much of the industry that exists in Latin America today is of a subsidiary nature—consisting of parts of large multinational corporations based in the United States, Western Europe, and Japan—which lessens the industrial elite's status as an independent power contender in the political process (although the multinationals have their own power). Likewise, private local industry does not form as strong a group as it might, since Latin American governments themselves have developed or nationalized many of the industries that traditionally are private in the United States: steel, railroads, and petroleum, among others.

Another complicating factor is the relationship between the industrial elite and the landed elite. In some countries, such as Argentina, the early industrialists were linked to the landed groups; later, individuals who began as industrialists invested in land. The result was two intertwined groups, a marriage of older landed and newer industrial wealth, with only vague boundaries separating them and some families and individuals straddling the line. Although this situation is not the case in all Latin American countries, the interrelationship of the two groups has been offered as a reason for industrialist opposition to land reform. The land to be received by the campesinos (those living on the land) might belong to an industrialist, his family, or his friends.

Industrialists and commercial elites are highly organized in various chambers of commerce, industrial associations, and the like; they are strategically located in the major cities of Latin America; they generally favor a status quo that profits themselves; and they are seen as the driving forces in Latin American economic development. For these reasons and because they are frequently represented in high official circles, no matter what government is in control, they are very powerful.

STUDENTS

Student activism in politics is a long-standing tradition in Latin America, not only at the university level but at the high-school level too. University students are an elite group in Latin America in that they have the leisure to study rather than work. Although the figure varies from country to country, it is estimated that only about 3–5 percent of the university-age population has the opportunity to pursue postsecondary education.

University students tend to have power beyond their numbers. They are a highly prestigious group, traditionally held in high regard in Spanish and Portuguese culture and seen as the leaders of the coming generation. They are often looked to by workers and peasants as their natural leaders. Major universities are located in the capitals and other large cities, and since much of Latin American politics is urban politics, the students are in the right place to have maximum input by participating in street demonstrations and, sometimes, urban guerrilla activities. The traditional autonomy of university campuses means that the military and police cannot enter to make an arrest, even when they are in hot pursuit of urban guerrillas.

Although most students are of various leftist persuasions, political parties of all ideologies have attempted to include the students in their ranks. Each party tends to have its own student branch, and parties also sponsor "professional students," who dedicate more of their time to organizing on the campus than to studying. This attempt to organize students is based on their proven ability in politics, although students tend to be more successful in opposing than in supporting the government.

Yet the students as a group are not as strong as the groups discussed in the preceding sections. Deep political divisions among the students militate against their exercising greater power, as does the fact that students are a transitory group, with nearly 100 percent turnover every five or six years. This latter point is a disadvantage because recruitment to political activity and training must be constant. Finally, students have less influence than they might since some are much more concerned with education as a means of social mobility or preserving their social status than they are with politics.

Students can be expected to remain a politically relevant group, especially if economic growth is slow or nonexistent. In alliance with workers or a faction of the military, they can play an important role in making or breaking a government. Latin American universities, although they train a relatively small percentage of the population, are producing more potential white-collar workers than there are places for in government bureaucracy and private enterprise. Students who see slight possibilities of a professional career after college are likely to be drawn into politics because of frustration and insecurity. It is telling that most guerrilla leaders in Latin America have been university students.

THE MIDDLE SECTORS

Although the Latin American countries began independence with a basically two-class system and that situation still exists today, there have always been individuals who fall statistically into the middle ranges, neither the very rich nor abjectly poor. During the nineteenth century these few individuals were primarily artisans and shopkeepers; later they were doctors and lawyers. More recently the number of these middle elements has grown significantly.

The emergence of a larger middle sector has been a twentieth-century phenomenon associated with urbanization, technological advances, industrialization, and the expansion of public education and the role of the government. All of these changes necessitated a large number of white-collar, managerial workers. Teachers and government bureaucrats constitute part of this sector, as do office workers in private businesses. In addition, more small businesses have developed, particularly in the service sector of the economy, and many of these nonmanual professions have been organized into teachers' associations, small-business associations, lawyers' associations, organizations of government bureaucrats, and so forth. Frequently these and other new groups such as labor and student organizations have adopted liberal and socialist values that are at odds with the older hierarchical, Thomistic notions.

The people who fill the new middle-sector jobs are the product of social mobility—some came from the lower class; others were "fallen aristocrats" from the upper classes—and they lack a common historical experience. This fact, together with their numerous and heterogeneous occupations, has temporarily impeded the formation of a sense of common identity as members of a middle class. Indeed, in some of the countries of Latin America this identification has yet to emerge—and may not emerge. In the United States, there has always been an idealization of the middle class; in Latin America, in contrast, the ideal is to be a part of "society," preferably high society.

In those countries of Latin America in which a large middle-sector group has emerged, certain generalizations about its political behavior can be made. In the early stages, this group tends to unite with groups from the lower classes against the more traditional and oligarchic groups in power. Major goals included expanded suffrage, the promotion of urban growth and economic development, a greater role for public education, increased industrialization, and social-welfare programs. The principal means of accomplishing these goals was through state intervention.

In the later political evolution of the middle sectors, the tendency has been to side with the established order. In some cases, the middle-class movements have allied with landowners, industrialists, and the church against their working-class partners of earlier years; in other cases, when the more numerous lower class has seemed ready to take power on its own, the middle sectors have been instrumental in fomenting a middle-class military coup to prevent "premature democratization." Over the years, then, the political behavior of middle-class movements has changed dramatically.

Yet this transformation is sometimes more apparent than real. All the original goals of the middle-sector movements had as their effect, if not their intention, the creation of new white-collar, nonmanual jobs for teachers, government bureaucrats, and bureaucrats in private industry. When the middle-sector movements have taken political control, they have not completely replaced the traditional elite; they have come to terms with that elite, entered into compromises with the members of it, and in the process, become identified with the same elite institutions that they had planned to take over.

This general introduction, based largely on the more industrially advanced countries of the Southern Cone of South America, raises a number of questions that should be considered in reading the country chapters.

1. How large are the middle-income sectors of the country?

2. To what extent do the middle sectors tend to act together politically? Do they generally combine in one or several political parties, or are they split among parties on the basis of loyalties that predate the emergence of the middle class?
3. To what degree do the members of the middle sectors identify themselves as such? Is there a perceived commonality of interests? Or alternatively, although objectively they have the same class interests, do they fail to see them?

Many people writing about Latin America used to assume that there was a kind of progressive spirit inherent in the individual members of the middle class and that this spirit could be defined in terms of a desire for economic development and political democracy. This assumption was based on an idealized vision of what the middle classes had done in the United States and Western Europe. The evidence now suggests that in some cases, certainly not all, the growth of middle-class movements in Latin America might retard economic development and impede liberal democracy, encouraging military rule instead.

Until recently it could be safely concluded that the growth of the middle sectors did not necessarily lead to democracy. José Nun, writing in the 1960s, pointed out the middle sectors' fear of "premature democratization,"[3] that is, a democratic procedure that the middle sectors could not control. In some cases—certainly in Argentina, Brazil, Chile, and Uruguay—this fear led the civilian middle-sector members to call on the military for a coup to keep the lower-income sectors out of power. But by the late 1980s the military rulers had been replaced by civilian governments, in part because of the growth and frustration of the middle sectors. Only time will tell if the middle sectors will act differently because of the years of bureaucratic authoritarianism: whether the middle sectors will serve as a new, invigorated social base for democracy or whether they will continue to ape and imitate the upper class and thus perpetuate an essentially two-class and polarized social structure.

LABOR UNIONS

Organized labor in Latin America has always been highly political, and virtually all important trade-union groups of the area have been closely associated with a political party, strong leader, or government. Sometimes labor unions have grown independently until they were co-opted or repressed. In other cases, labor unions have owed their origins directly to the efforts of a party, leader, or government.

Two characteristics of the Latin American economies have favored partisan unionism. First, Latin American unions were organized relatively early in the economic development of the countries, in most cases earlier than in the United States and Western Europe. Second, in Latin America the labor pool of employable people is much larger than the number of relatively well-paid jobs in industry. An employer, therefore, can almost always find people to replace striking workers unless they are protected by a party or by the government. In addition to these two characteristics, inflation has been a problem in Latin America in recent decades, making it important for unions to win the support of political groups in the continual renegotiation of contracts to obtain higher salaries, which often need government approval.

The Latin American legal tradition requires that unions be officially recognized by the government before they can collectively bargain. If a group cannot obtain or retain this legal standing, it has little power. Further, close attention must be paid to labor legislation. In some countries, labor codes mandate that labor organizers be employed full time in the industry they are organizing; these and other restrictions make it very difficult for unions to organize and carry out their functions in Latin America.

Labor groups of some kind have long existed in Latin American industry. Before the early years of this century they tended to be mutual-benefit societies, collective insurance and Catholic charity agencies formed in the absence of government social security programs. Labor movements moved to the next stage with the arrival of large numbers of Europeans in the early years of this century, especially in Argentina, Uruguay, Brazil, and Cuba. Anarcho-syndicalism was the dominant philosophy of this period, with Marxism its main competitor. From the countries mentioned, the labor movement and its competing ideologies spread to the other countries of Latin America.

The influence of anarcho-syndicalism waned after World War I, when factory industry grew and with it the need for collective bargaining, which the anarcho-syndicalists did not accept as a tactic. Various national parties entered into the labor field, including the socialists and Communists with their international connections. Since World War II the older, international-type organizations have lost influence, and in most countries of Latin America the major labor federations now have few international ties, although some do belong or have belonged to Catholic associations and others have received support from the American Federation of Labor and Congress of Industrial Organizations (AFL-CIO). Attempts to convert Latin American labor unions into something more like the nonpolitical unions in the United States have generally not been successful.

Yet the co-optation-and-repression system has by no means taken over the labor unions of Latin America. Even though some union organizations have been co-opted, others remain outside the system. In the country chapters that follow, certain questions are relevant.

1. To what extent are industrial (and middle-class) workers organized?
2. How is the labor code used to prevent or facilitate labor organization?

3. What is the nature of the relationship between labor and political parties or between labor and government? Who has gained what from these associations?
4. To what extent are there labor unions that have not been co-opted or repressed? Is there a potential for new labor federations with new leaders outside of the unions themselves?
5. When labor has allied with political parties, has it done so with only one party or with several parties?

PEASANTS

The term *peasants* refers to many different kinds of people in Latin America. Some people prefer the Spanish word *campesinos* (people who work in the *campo*, the countryside) rather than the English word with its European-based connotations. The major groups of campesinos, which vary in importance from country to country, include the following:

1. Amerindian groups, who may speak only their native language or who may be bilingual in that language and Spanish;
2. workers on the traditional hacienda, tilling the fields in return for wages or part of the crops, with the owner as a *patrón* to care for the family or, more frequently, a manager-*patrón* who represents the absentee owner;
3. workers on modern plantations, receiving wages but remaining outside of the older *patrón*-client relationship;
4. persons with a small landholding (*minifundio*), legally held, of a size that makes a bare existence possible;
5. persons who cultivate small plots to which they have no legal claim, perhaps moving every few years after the slash-and-burn method of farming and the lack of crop rotation deplete the soil; and
6. persons who are given a small plot of land to work by a landowner in exchange for work on the large estate.

What all of these campesinos have in common, in the context of the extremely inequitable distribution of arable lands in Latin America, is a marginal existence because of their small amount of land or income and a high degree of insecurity because of their uncertain claims to the land they cultivate. It was estimated in 1961 that over 5 million very small farms (below 30 acres [74 hectares]) occupied only 3.7 percent of the land while, at the other extreme, 100,000 holdings of more than 1,500 acres (3,704 hectares) took up some 65 percent of the land. Some three decades later, the situation has changed little. At least 80 million people still live on landholdings too small to yield a minimum subsistence or they work as agricultural laborers with no land at all. For many of these rural masses, their only real chance of breaking out of this circle of poverty is by moving to an urban area, where they face another—in some ways even worse—culture of poverty. For those who remain on the land, unless there is a dramatic restructuring of ownership, the present subhuman existence is likely to continue. Moreover, as commercial agriculture for export has increased in many countries, the campesinos are more and more being shoved off fertile lands onto the infertile hillsides where their ability to subsist has become even more precarious.

Rural peasant elements have long been active in politics. The traditional political structure of the countryside was one in which participation in national politics meant taking part in the patronage system. The local *patrones*, besides expecting work on the estate from the campesino, expected certain political behavior. In some countries, this situation meant that the campesino belonged to the same political party as the *patrón*, voted for that party on election day, and if necessary, served as cannon fodder in its civil wars. In other countries, the national party organizations never reached the local levels, and restrictive suffrage laws prevented the peasants from participation in elections. In both situations, there was no such thing as national politics, only local politics, which might or might not have national-party labels attached to the local person or groups in power.

These traditional systems still exist in many areas of Latin America, but since the 1950s signs of agrarian unrest and political mobilization have been more and more evident. In many cases, major agrarian movements have been organized by urban interests—political parties, especially Marxist ones—and some of these peasant movements have been openly revolutionary, seeking to reform and improve the land tenure system and to reform significantly the entire power structure of the nation. They have employed strategies that include the illegal seizure of land, the elimination of landowners, and armed defense of the gains thus achieved. These movements could be called ones of revolutionary agrarianism. Less radical are the movements that seek to reform the social order partially, through the elimination of a few of the most oppressive effects of the existing power structure that weighs on the peasant subculture, without threatening the power structure as such.

The peasants, numerically the largest group in Latin America, remain politically weak basically because the peasant sector is largely unorganized—a situation that people with wealth and power have a vested interest in maintaining. Because of the diversity of land and labor patterns, the dispersed nature of the countryside, and the high rate of illiteracy there, it is difficult to mobilize a strong peasant movement. The distance from the urban centers of power also makes it hard for peasants to effect change. Hence, they remain subjects of the political system rather than participants in it, despite the activities of revolutionary agrarian movements.

The country chapters show there is a wide spectrum of peasant organizations and a wide variation of peasant success in Latin America.

In some countries, one or two political parties have been instrumental in organizing the peasants, who have received a fair degree of land as a result. In other cases, governments have facilitated the organization of peasants but have not given them private land titles. In still other instances, the landed elites have been successful in preventing significant agrarian reform. The variation is so great (and the issue so constant) that the reader is referred to the country chapters for individual cases.

THE UNITED STATES

Another important power element in Latin American politics is the United States. The influence of this country has been effected by at least three interrelated groups: U.S. government representatives, U.S.-based private businesses, and U.S.-dominated international agencies. Some people would deny the validity of this separation. The United States, they would argue, presents a common front, either by design or by effect. Their position is partly substantiated by the following statement made by Maj. Gen. Smedley D. Butler, U.S. Marine Corps:

> I helped make Mexico and especially Tampico safe for American oil interests in 1914. I helped make Haiti and Cuba a decent place for the National City Bank boys to collect revenue in. . . . I helped purify Nicaragua for the international banking house of Brown Brothers in 1909–1912. I brought light to the Dominican Republic for American sugar interests in 1916. I helped make Honduras "right" for American fruit companies in 1903.[4]

The general concern of this section is the activities of all the various U.S. groups in the Latin American political process. At times these groups work in harmony, and at times they operate at cross-purposes.

The U.S. government has been interested in the area since Latin America's independence. The country's first concern, that the new nations not fall under the control of European powers, led to the Monroe Doctrine of 1823. Originally a defensive statement, this doctrine was later changed through various corollaries to be more aggressive, telling the Latin Americans that they could not sell land to nonhemispheric governments or businesses (if the locations were strategic) and that the United States would intervene in Latin America to collect debts owed to nonhemispheric powers (the Roosevelt corollary). At various times the U.S. government has set standards that must be met before full diplomatic recognition is accorded to a Latin American nation. This de jure recognition policy, most memorable in the Wilson, early Kennedy, and Carter administrations, favors elected democratic governments, exclusion of the military from government, and a vision of human rights that should be applied in Latin America. At other times the United States has pursued a de facto recognition policy, according full diplomatic standing to any government that effectively controls its nation's territory.

Whichever recognition policy is followed, the U.S. ambassador to a Latin American country has impressive powers. One ambassador to pre-Castro Cuba testified that he was the most influential individual in the country, second only to the president. This ambassadorial power has typically been used to support or defeat governments, to focus the government policies of the Latin American countries in certain directions, and often to assist U.S.-based corporations in the countries. In Central America recently, a number of U.S. ambassadors have played this strong proconsular role.

From their early beginnings, particularly in agribusiness (especially sugar and bananas), U.S.-based corporations in Latin America have grown dramatically. Corporations have also entered the extractive field (petroleum, copper, iron ore), the retailing sector (Sears, Roebuck, among others), the services industry (accounting firms, computer outfits), and the field of communications (telephones, telegraphs). The most recent kind of U.S. corporation in Latin America is the export-platform variety—that is, a company that takes advantage of the low wages in Latin America to produce pocket calculators in Mexico or baseballs in Haiti for export to the industrialized world.

U.S. corporations in Latin America often enter into the politics of their host countries. Some of the instances are flagrant: bribing public officials to keep taxes low or threatening to cut off a country's products if certain policies are approved by its government. But most of the political activities of these corporations are much less dramatic. Almost always Latin Americans in the host countries buy stock in the U.S. corporations and hold high managerial positions in them. In many cases U.S. corporations purchase Latin American corporations, and their leaders then work for the new owners. The result is that a U.S. corporation develops contacts and obligations like those possessed by Latin American industrialists and commercial interests. In the 1980s there were some indications that the era of large U.S. corporate holdings, and hence their influence, in Latin America might be in decline. Many U.S. corporations pulled up stakes, withdrew their capital, and moved on to more profitable and stable areas. Yet by the end of the 1980s the business climate had improved because some Latin American governments had rescinded restrictions on maximum profits and repatriation, so it is premature to discard U.S. businesses as a power contender in the area.

Most foreign-aid and international-lending organizations are dominated by the United States. These agencies, which have been especially active since the early 1960s when aid to Latin America began in large quantities, include the U.S. Agency for International Development, which administers most U.S. foreign aid; the World Bank; the International Monetary Fund; and the Inter-American Development Bank (IDB). The World Bank and the IMF are international agencies, results of post–World War II agreements between the countries of the West. However, the representation of the United States on the governing boards of both is so large (based on the amount of money donated to the agencies) and the convergence of interests of the two with those of the U.S. government is so great that they can be considered U.S.-oriented agencies. So can the Inter-American Development Bank. Although urged by Latin American leaders who wanted a lending agency that was less dominated by the United States, in effect the IDB cannot lend to countries if the U.S. government does not want it to. Since economic development has been a central goal of the Latin American states for the past twenty years; since loans for such development come predominantly from AID, the World Bank, and the IDB; and since those loans are often contingent on having a monetary policy that is judged healthy by the IMF, the officials of these four groups have a great deal of influence on the day-to-day policies of the governments of the area.

This power of the lending agencies was probably greatest during the 1960s, and AID had its greatest leverage or "conditionality" during the Alliance for Progress. This foreign-aid program, initiated by the Kennedy administration and terminated by Nixon's, attempted to change Latin America dramatically in a decade. Even though it failed, it did lead to large loans from the U.S. government, substantial progress in some fields, and along with it much influence for the local AID head on the domestic politics of some Latin American countries. Some AID representatives sat in on cabinet meetings and wrote speeches for and gave advice to the local officials with whom they worked, and others largely ran the agencies or even the ministries of the host government to which they were assigned.

The power of the World Bank waned in the wake of the crisis of the industrialized economies of the West following the Arab oil embargo of 1973–1974 and with the growing power of OPEC. For a while the private banks, recycling petrodollars, filled many of the needs of the Latin American countries. However, after the debt crisis of the 1980s the IMF, and its Bretton Woods partner the World Bank, regained much of their lost power.

The economies of Latin America are undergoing crisis, and the importing nations have passed protectionist measures. The Latin American nations are clamoring for access to U.S. markets, and they are likely to be partially successful in that quest. The U.S. government has also initiated a new massive assistance program for Central America and the Caribbean that is designed to restore solvency and preserve stability.

The influence of U.S.-directed and U.S.-oriented groups—diplomatic, business, foreign-assistance—in Latin America is considerable. This is not to say that the power is equal in all Latin American countries. One might venture the hypothesis that U.S. influence is greater for security reasons in those countries that are closer to the continental United States and/or where U.S. private investments are larger. When a Latin American country is important strategically to the United States and when U.S. private investors have a large interest in the economy (for example,

Cuba before Castro), U.S. elements are extremely powerful in that country's domestic politics. This hypothesis does not mean that the United States cannot have considerable influence in the domestic politics of more-distant countries with relatively little U.S. private investment, as the example of Allende's Chile has shown.

POLITICAL PARTIES

In Latin America, political parties are oftentimes only one set of groups among several, and they are probably no more (and perhaps less) important than the army or the economic oligarchy. Elections are not the only legitimate route to power, nor are the parties themselves particularly strong or well organized. We do not want to denigrate the place of parties in Latin America, for they are important in the political process and in some of the more democratic countries they represent the chief means to gain high office. But neither do we want to give parties a significance they do not have, since frequently the parties are peripheral to the main focal points of power and the electoral arena is considered only one arena among several.

General elements of the groups previously discussed have often combined into political parties in their pursuit of government power. One must be careful with the term "political party" as the Spanish *partido* has a much more general application than the English equivalent. For example, *el partido militar* is used in the press of the Dominican Republic and other countries to refer to the military, although clearly the officers do not use electoral tactics like those normally associated with a U.S. political party. Further, some civilians belonging to political parties have been known to plot with factions of the military to take power through a coup d'état.

There have been a myriad of political parties in the history of Latin America; indeed, someone once quipped that to form a political party all you needed was a president, vice president, secretary-treasurer, and rubber stamp. (If times were bad, you could do without the vice president and the secretary-treasurer!) Nevertheless, certain characteristics are common to parties, although the country chapters indicate there is great national variation.

Groups calling themselves political parties have existed from the early years of independence. The first parties were usually founded by some elite groups in competition with other factions of the elite. Mass demands played only a small role, although campesinos were mobilized by the party leaders, often to vote as they were instructed or to serve as cannon fodder. In many cases, the first cleavage was between individuals in favor of free trade, federalism, and anticlericalism (the Liberals) and those who favored protectionism for nascent industry, centralism, and clericalism (the Conservatives). In most countries, these original party divisions have long since disappeared and been replaced by other cleavages; in some countries, they are still very much alive.

With social and economic change in most countries of Latin America, the emergence of new social strata led to the founding of new political parties. Some of these attracted the growing middle sectors, who were quite reformist in the early years but later changed as they became part of the system. In other cases, the new parties were more radical, calling for a basic restructuring of society and including elements from the working classes. Some of these originally radical parties were of international inspiration; most of the countries have had Communist and socialist parties of differing effectiveness and legality. Other radical parties were primarily national ones, albeit with an ideological inspiration that was traceable to Marxism.

One such party, founded in 1924 by the Peruvian Víctor Raúl Haya de la Torre while in exile in Mexico, was the American Popular Revolutionary Alliance (APRA). Although APRA purported to be the beginning of a new internationale of like-minded democratic-left individuals in Latin America, this goal was never fully reached. An inter-American organization was established, but it never had great importance. At the same time, inspired by Haya and APRA, a number of national parties were founded by young Latin Americans. The most successful Aprista-like party has been Democratic Action (AD) in Venezuela, but the same programs have been advocated by numerous other parties of this type, including the National Liberation party (PLN) in Costa Rica and the National Revolutionary Movement (MNR) in Bolivia as well as parties in Paraguay, the Dominican Republic, Guatemala, Honduras, and Argentina. Only in Venezuela and Costa Rica did the APRA-like parties come to power more than temporarily, and when they did, twenty years after the founding of APRA, they were no longer extremely radical. They favored liberal democracy, rapid reform, and economic growth. In most cases, the APRA-like parties were led by members of the middle sectors and received much of their electoral support from middle- and lower-class ranks. APRA came to power in Peru in 1985, but its founder, Haya, was no longer living.

A newer group of political parties are the Christian-Democratic ones, particularly successful in Chile, Venezuela, and El Salvador. These parties call for fundamental reforms but are guided by church teachings and papal encyclicals rather than Marx or Engels, even though they are nondenominational and open to all. The nature of the ideology of these parties varies from country to country.

Other parties in Latin America have been based on the leadership of one or a few persons and, hence, do not fit into the neat party spectrum just described. Quite often the "man on horseback" is more important than the program of a party. This tradition of the caudillo is seen in the case of Brazil, where Getúlio Vargas founded not one but two official political parties; in Ecuador, where personalistic parties have been strong contenders for the presidency; and in Communist Cuba, where in the 1960s the party was more Castroist than Communist.

The system of co-optation further complicates the attempt at classification. How is one to classify a political party traditional in origin that includes at the same time large landowners and the peasants who are tied to them as well as trade-union members organized by the party with the assistance of parts of the clergy? How does one classify a party, such as Mexico's Institutional Revolutionary party (PRI), that has made conscious effort to co-opt and include all politically relevant sectors of the society?

Even further complicating the picture is the question of party systems—that is, how many parties are there in a country and how often does power pass from party to party (or for that matter, from a party to the military)? All parties are coalitions, but is a party still a single party if it offers more than one candidate for president or more than one list of candidates for congressional seats? Both situations have occurred in recent years in the only Latin American countries with a two-party system—Colombia and Uruguay. These kinds of things do not happen by accident; they are the result of electoral laws drawn up by political elites with various goals in mind.

As in the case of the military, the literature on parties in Latin America is replete with contradictions, misleading classifications, and misunderstandings. We suggest keeping in mind the following questions in reading the country chapters.

1. How many major parties are there? What are their historical origins, their formal programs as enunciated by candidates and platforms, and their policies when in power?
2. Do the electoral laws favor or impede parties? Is the fact that proportional representation, with its countless variations, is the most common system a reflection of societal circumstances when the electoral laws were written, or does unwitting legislation change party systems?
3. What is the electoral behavior in each country? Do voting patterns indicate regionalism, urban-rural dichotomies, class voting, or some combination of the three?
4. What kinds of contacts are there between the political parties and the military? Are the two groups friendly and cooperative or hostile? The military is still the ultimate arbiter of a nation's politics, and political parties must take care not to go beyond the "dikes of military opinion," to paraphrase Harvard professor V. O. Key's statement about U.S. politics.
5. How often in a nation's history have civilian political parties been in power? If they are weak, is it because the military institution so quickly monopolized power after independence, or did the military do so because the parties were weak? No matter which

is the chicken and which the egg, is this a situation that can be changed in Latin America, or is the area likely to follow historical patterns for the near future?

6. What roles do parties play, and how do those roles vary from country to country? Is it their function to devise platforms and run candidates in elections, or are they really just another giant patronage agency? Are they independent of government or simply mechanisms of the state? Do they serve a public interest, or are they merely a means by which the ambitious may gain status and a following?

On two notable occasions in the past three decades, students of Latin America have been told to study political parties. Perhaps the time has come to change this advice, to urge not just a study of parties per se but, more important, a study of the relations between parties and the military, the state, and the system as a whole.

CONCLUSIONS AND IMPLICATIONS

The preceding discussion indicates that there are many politically relevant groups in Latin America and that they use various means to secure and retain political power. Yet at least two other themes should be introduced that tend to complicate the picture.

First, it should be noted that the urban and rural poor—those outside the labor unions—have not been included in the discussion. This deficiency shows one of the biases of the system. Preceding the first step in attaining political relevance is another—being organized. This means that some potential groups, especially poorly educated and geographically dispersed ones like the peasants and the urban poor, face difficulties in becoming politically relevant since they have difficulties in organizing themselves or being organized from the outside. Peasants have become increasingly organized, but the same is not true for the urban poor and those people who work in cottage industries, as street vendors, or not at all. Their numbers are swelling rapidly, with the growing exodus from the countryside to the cities. Although to this point the urban poor have not been organized, political party leaders are increasingly aware of their large numbers and are beginning organizational attempts that employ, not surprisingly, co-optation or repression tactics common to the Latin American practice. As campesinos were increasingly organized in the 1960s, perhaps the urban poor will be the next addition to the "living museum" in the 1990s.

Second, not all politically relevant groups fall into the neat categories of this chapter (which, of course, are familiar to both liberals and Marxists of the European and North American traditions). Anthony Leeds's research in Brazil has shown (at least in the small towns and probably in the larger cities, even perhaps the whole nation) a politically more relevant series of groups to be the *panelinhas* ("little saucepans").[5] These are composed of individuals with common interests but different occupations—say, a doctor, a large landowner, surely a lawyer, and a government official. A *panelinha* at the local level controls and endeavors to establish contacts with the *panelinha* at the state level, which might have contacts with a national *panelinha*. Of course, at the local level there are rival *panelinhas*, which might have contacts with rival ones at the state level, and so on. As is generally the case with such patrimonial kinds of relations, all interactions (except those within the *panelinhas* themselves) are vertical, and a lower-level *panelinha* must take care to ally itself with the winning one at the next higher level if it wants to have political power.

Similar research in other countries has revealed a parallel pattern of informal, elitist, patronage politics. Whether called the *panelinha* system in Brazil or the *camarilla* system in Mexico, the process and dynamics are the same. An aspiring politician (almost always a man) connects himself with an aspiring politician at a higher level, who is connected with an aspiring . . . and so forth on up to an aspiring candidate for the presidency (who might be a civilian or a military officer). If the person in question becomes president, the various levels of *camarillas* prosper; if he remains powerful without becoming president, the *camarillas* continue functioning in expectation of what will take place in the next presidential election; but if the aspiring candidate is disgraced, dismissed from the official party or dies, the whole system of various levels of *camarillas* connected with him disintegrates. Although this *camarilla* phenomenon is also known in the United States and the Soviet Union, it is more common in the personalistic politics of Latin America. The *camarilla* system operates outside, while overlapping with, the formal structure of groups and parties described earlier.

This discussion of *panelinhas* and *camarillas* raises the question again of whether U.S.-style interest groups and political parties operate and are important in Latin America. The answer is, They are and they aren't. In the larger and better-institutionalized systems, the parties and interest groups are often important and function not unlike their North American or European counterparts. But in the less-institutionalized, personalistic countries of Central America (and even behind the scenes in the larger ones), it is frequently networks that are more important—a fact that is often disguised behind the appearance of partisan or ideological dispute. One must be careful, therefore, not to minimize the importance of a functional, operational party and interest-group system in some countries while recognizing that in others it is the less formal network through which politics is carried out.

NOTES

1. Charles W. Anderson, *Politics and Economic Change in Latin America: The Governing of Restless Nations* (Princeton, N.J.: Van Nostrand, 1967), especially Chapter 4.

2. See David Collier, ed., *The New Authoritarianism in Latin America* (Princeton, N.J.: Princeton University Press, 1979).

3. José Nun, "The Middle Class Military Coup," in Claudio Veliz, ed., *The Politics of Conformity in Latin America* (London: Oxford University Press, 1967), pp. 66–118.

4. Quoted in John Gerassi, *The Great Fear in Latin America* (New York: Collier Books, 1965), p. 231.

5. Anthony Leeds, "Brazilian Careers and Social Structure: A Case History and Model," *American Anthropologist* 66 (1964):1321–1347.

5
Government Machinery and the Role of the State

Neither the classic Marxian categories nor the theory of liberalism gives more than secondary importance to the role of the state. In the Marxian paradigm, the state or governmental system is viewed as part of the superstructure shaped, if not determined, by the underlying structure of class relations. In the liberal model, the state is generally conceived of as a referee, umpiring the competition among the interest groups but not itself participating in the game, a kind of "black-box" intermediary into which the "inputs" of the system go in the form of competing interests and pressures and from which come "outputs" or public policies. Neither of these two classic models adequately explains the Latin American systems.

In Latin America, the state has historically held an importance that it lacks in the classic models. The state is viewed as a powerful and independent agency in its own right, above and frequently autonomous from the class and interest-group struggles. Whether in socialist regimes such as Cuba's or capitalist ones like Brazil's, it is the state and its central leadership that largely determine the shape of the system and its developmental directions.

The state not only reflects the class structure but, through its control of economic and political resources, shapes the class system. The state is viewed as the prime regulator, coordinator, and pacesetter of the entire national system, the apex of the Latin American pyramid from which patronage, wealth, power, and programs flow. The critical importance of the state in the Latin American nations helps explain why the competition for control of it is so intense and sometimes violent. Determining who controls the pinnacles of the system is a fundamental, all-important, and virtually everyday preoccupation.

Related to this is the contrasting way citizens of North America and Latin America tend to view government. In North America government has usually been considered a necessary evil that requires elaborate checks and balances. Political theory in Iberia and Latin America, in contrast, views government as good, natural, and necessary for the welfare of society. If government is good, there is little reason to limit it or put checks and balances on it. Hence, before we fall into the trap of condemning Latin America for its powerful autocratic executives, subservient parliaments, and weak local government, we must remember the different assumptions on which the Latin American systems are based.

It is around these issues concerning the role of the state that much of Latin American politics revolves. The following list provides some keys as to what to look for in the discussions that will come later: (1) the fundamental issue of who controls the state apparatus and the immense power and funds at its disposal; (2) the constant efforts historically of the state or strong presidents to expand their power, versus the efforts of others (university students, peasant or Indian communities, municipalities) to resist; (3) the requirement that governments have to somehow reconcile theory and constitutionalism, which are often liberal and democratic, with the realities, which are frequently authoritarian and elitist; and (4) the issue of whether and when a strong government oversteps the bounds of permissible authoritarianism and becomes an outright tyranny, thus justifying the "right of rebellion." After a successful coup the cycle may begin all over again.

THE THEORY OF THE STATE: CONSTITUTIONS AND LEGAL SYSTEMS

After achieving independence early in the nineteenth century, the Latin American nations faced a severe legitimacy crisis. Socialism had not yet produced its major prophets and therefore was not an alternative. Monarchy was a possibility (and some nations did consider or experiment briefly with monarchical rule), but Latin America had just struggled through years of independence wars to rid itself of the Spanish imperial yoke, and monarchy had been discredited. Liberalism and republicanism were attractive and seemed the wave of the future, but Latin America had had no prior experience with liberal or republican rule.

The solution was ingenious, though often woefully misunderstood. The new nations of Latin America moved to adopt liberal and democratic forms of government while at the same time preserving many of the organicist, elitist, and authoritarian principles of their own tradition. The liberal and democratic forms provided goals and aspirations toward which society could strive; they also helped present a progressive picture to the outside world. But the liberal and republican principles were circumscribed by a series of measures authoritarian in content that were truer to the realities and history of the area and to its existing oligarchic power relationships. The ongoing challenge of Latin American politics has been to blend and reconcile these conflicting currents.

Virtually all Latin American constitution have provided for the historical, three-part division of power among executive, legislature, and judiciary. But in fact, the three branches are not coequal and were not intended to be. The executive is constitutionally given extensive powers to bypass the legislature, and judicial review is largely outside the Latin American legal tradition. Knee-jerk condemnation of a Latin American government that rules without giving equal status to the legislature or courts often reveals more about our own biases, ethnocentrism, and lack of understanding than it does about the realities of Latin America.

Similar apparent contradictions exist in other areas. Although one part of a constitution may be devoted to civilian institutions and the traditional three branches of government, another may give the armed forces a higher-order role to protect the nation, preserve internal order, and prevent internal disruption. In this sense, the military may be considered a fourth branch of the state. Military intervention, therefore, should not necessarily be condemned as an extraconstitutional and illegitimate act since it is often provided for in the constitution and is an implied prerogative of the armed forces. The military thus generally sees itself as the defender of the constitution, not its usurper—although it is the military leaders who decide when the constitution needs defending.

The same situation exists for human rights. Even though all the Latin American constitutions contain long lists of human and political rights, the same constitutions also give the executive the power to declare a state of siege or emergency, suspend human rights, and rule by decree. The same applies to privilege. While one section of a constitution may proclaim democratic and egalitarian principles, other parts give special privileges to the church, the army, or the landed elites. Although representative and republican precepts are enshrined in one quarter, authoritarian and elitist ones are legitimated in another.

Pointing out these contradictions is not meant to imply approval of human rights violations or overthrows of democratic governments but to indicate how these actions are often perceived differently in Latin America. Hence, the real questions may concern, not the right of the armed forces to intervene in politics or the executive to prorogue the legislature (since those rights are often givens of the system), but the degrees of military intervention or limits on legislative authority and how and why these actions are taken. It is not simply a matter of the military usurping the constitution, since it is often the constitution itself that gives the military the right, even obligation, to intervene in the political process under certain circumstances. Similarly, when human rights violations are reported, we must understand this within the Latin American constitutional and legal traditions rather than within our own. Human rights are not conceived of as constitutional absolutes, and frequently there is a constitutional provision for their suspension. When, however, torture is practiced or, as in Paraguay, a state of siege is in effect and human rights suspended for a long period of time, one may legitimately suspect that basic rights are being violated, even in terms of Latin America's view of those rights.

The most important issues of Latin American politics, therefore, revolve, not around haughty condemnations from the point of view of some "superior" political system, but around the dynamics of change and process from the Latin American perspective. North Americans and others cannot understand the area if they look only at the liberal and republican side of the Latin American tradition and ignore the rest; nor should one simply condemn some action from the point of view of the North American constitutional tradition without seeing it in the Latin American context. If the civil and military spheres are not strictly segregated, as in the U.S. tradition, then what are their dynamic relations in Latin America and what are the causes of military intervention? If strict separation of powers is not provided for in Latin America and if the branches of government are not equal, what are their respective powers and interrelations? If hierarchy, authority, and special privilege are legitimate principles along with democratic and egalitarian ones, then how are these different principles reconciled, glossed over, or challenged, and why?

The fact that Latin American countries have generally each had a number of constitutions is also frequently misunderstood. People in the United States frequently smile condescendingly on Latin America because of its many constitutions (thirty-odd in Venezuela, Ecuador, and the Dominican Republic), but in doing so they ignore the fact that in Latin America a new constitution is generally promulgated whenever a new amendment is added or when a major new interpretation requires official legitimation. The situation is comparable to the United States' proclaiming a new constitution every time an amendment is passed or a major judicial reinterpretation decided upon. The facts are first, the Latin American constitutional tradition has been far more stable than the number of constitutions implies, and second, in most countries of the area only two main constitutional traditions, one authoritarian and the other liberal and democratic, reflect the main currents of Latin American politics. The many constitutions signify the repeated alternations between these two basic traditions, with variations.

These perspectives on the constitutional tradition also provide hints as to how the legal tradition in Latin America differs from that in the United States. Whereas the U.S. laws and constitution are based upon a history and practice derived from British common law, those of Latin America derive from a code-law tradition, a difference that has several implications. The U.S. legal system is founded on precedent and reinterpretation; the Latin American codes are complete bodies of law that allow little room for precedent or judicial reinterpretation. The codes, like the Latin American constitutions, are fixed and absolute; they consist of a comprehensive framework of operating principles; and unlike the common-law tradition, with its inductive reasoning based upon cases, enforcement of the codes implies deductive reasoning. One begins not with facts or cases but with general truth (the codes or constitution) and deduces rules or applications for specific circumstances from that truth.

Although the point should not be overstressed and although mixed legal forms exist throughout Latin America, an understanding of the code-law system and its philosophical underpinnings can carry one a considerable distance toward understanding Latin American behavior. The truths embodied in the codes and constitutions and the deductive method have their origins in and reflect the Roman and Catholic-scholastic traditions. The authoritarian, absolutist nature of the codes is also reflected by (and helps reinforce) an absolutist, frequently authoritarian political culture. The effort to cover all contingencies with one code and the almost constant constitutional engineering to obtain a "perfect" document tend to rule out the logrolling, compromise, informal understandings, and unwritten rules that lie at the heart of the U.S. and British political systems. And because courts and judges, in their roles as appliers and enforcers of the law rather than creative interpreters of it, are bureaucrats and bureaucratic agencies, they do not enjoy the respect their counterparts do in the United States, thus making judicial review and even an independent judiciary difficult at best.

EXECUTIVE-LEGISLATIVE-JUDICIAL RELATIONS

The tradition of executive dominance in Latin America is part of the folklore. Power in the Latin American systems has historically been concentrated in the executive branch, specifically the presidency, and terms like *continuismo* (prolonging one's term of office beyond its constitutional limits), *personalismo* (emphasis on the person of the presidency rather than on the office), to say nothing of *machismo* (strong, manly authority) are all now so familiar that they form part of the political lexicon. The noted Latin America scholar Frank Tannenbaum has argued that the power of the Mexican president is comparable to that of the Aztec emperors; it can also be said that the present-day Latin American executive is heir to an imperial and autocratic tradition stemming from the absolute, virtually unlimited authority of the Spanish and Portuguese crowns. Of course, modern authoritarianism has multiple explanations for its origin (a reaction against earlier mass mobilization by populist and leftist leaders, the result of stresses generated by modernization, and the strategies of civilian and military elites for accelerating development) as well as various forms (caudillistic and more-institutionalized arrangements). In any case, the Latin American presidency is an imperial presidency in ways never dreamed of in the United States.

The formal authority of Latin American executives is extensive. It derives from a president's powers as chief executive, commander in chief, and head of state and from his broad emergency powers to declare a state of siege or emergency, suspend constitutional guarantees, and rule by decree. The presidency in Latin America is such a powerful position that the occupant of the office can rule almost as a constitutional dictator.

The powers of a Latin American president are far wider than is implied in the provisions of the constitutions. The presidency has been a chief beneficiary of many twentieth-century changes: among them, radio and television, concentrated war-making powers, broad responsibility for the economy. In addition, many Latin American chief executives serve simultaneously as head of state and president of their party machine; if the leader's route to power was the army, the president also has the enormous weight of armed might for use against foreign enemies and domestic foes. Considerable wealth, often generated because the lines between the private and the public spheres are not so sharply drawn as in North American political society, may also be an effective instrument of rule.

Perhaps the main difference lies in the fact that the Latin American systems, traditionally and historically, are more centralized and executive oriented than in the United States. The president is the focal point of the system. It is around the person occupying the presidency that national life swirls. The president is responsible not only for governance but also for the well-being of society as a whole. A Latin American president is the symbol of the national society in ways that a U.S. president is not. Not only is politics concentrated in the office and person of the president, but it is by presidential favors and patronage that contracts are determined, different clientele are served, and wealth, privilege, and social position are parceled out. The president is the national *patrón*, replacing the local landowners and men on horseback of the past. With both broad appointive powers and wide latitude in favoring friends and people who show loyalty, the Latin American president is truly the hub of the national system. Hence, when a good, able executive is in power, the system works exceedingly well; when this is not the case, the whole system breaks down.

Various stratagems have been used to try to limit executive authority, but none has worked well. They range from the disastrous results of the experiment with a plural (nine-person government-by-committee) executive in Uruguay to the various unsuccessful efforts at parliamentary or semiparliamentary rule in Chile, Brazil, Cuba, and Costa Rica. Constitutional gimmickry does not work in limiting the power of the executive because such power is an area-wide tradition and cultural pattern, not just some legal article.

The role of the congress in such a system is not generally to initiate or veto laws, much less to serve as a separate and coequal branch of government. Congress's functions can be understood if one begins, not with the assumption of an independent branch, but with the concept of an agency that is subservient to the president and, along with the executive, a part of the same organic, integrated state system. The congress's roles are thus to give advice and consent to presidential acts (but not much dissent), to serve as a sounding board for new programs, to represent the varied interests of the nation, and to modify laws in some particulars (but not usually to nullify them). The legislature is also a place to bring some new faces into government as well as to pension off old ones, to reward political friends and cronies, and to ensure the opposition a voice while guaranteeing that it remains a minority.

Except in a handful of countries, only a very brave or foolhardy legislature would go much beyond these limited functions. Legislatures that do are often closed, and their members are sent home. Most legislative sessions in Latin America are of relatively short duration, since to fulfill the limited functions listed above requires little time. Because of the legislative restrictions and short sessions, few legislators see their jobs as being full-time ones. Nor do their limited functions and part-time role demand elaborate staffs and offices.

If the president in Latin America is the heir of royal absolutism, then the congress is in a sense a descendant of the old royal curia or cortes. The curia, which generally represented the major estates or elites, was a body of royal advisers to the Spanish and Portuguese crowns, and it evolved into the cortes. But the cortes never had the independent budgetary and law-making capacities of the British Parliament, nor did the supremacist doctrines put forth by the British Parliament ever become a part of Spanish or Portuguese public law. The king remained the focus, not the cortes. In all these ways, the modern-day Latin American congress is a direct descendant of the cortes. Moreover, in some countries it was determined early on not only that the congress would be just an advisory body but that it would chiefly represent society's major corporate groups— army, church, hacendados, industrialists, and perhaps some middle sectors and labor groups (though generally only those recognized and legitimated by the state). Popular representation—the idea of one person, one vote— has only recently been institutionalized in Latin America, and only partially and not altogether enthusiastically. Many countries have combined systems of geographic, political, and functional representation.

Still, one cannot say that the legislatures of Latin America are worthless. Their functions are sometimes important ones; and in some countries (Chile in the past, Colombia, Costa Rica, Venezuela), the congress has come to enjoy considerable independence and strength. A few congresses have gone so far as to defy the executive—and gotten away with it— and some have strong staffs and do important committee work. The congress may serve additionally as a forum that allows the opposition to embarrass or undermine the government, as a means of gauging who is rising and who is falling in official favor, or as a way of weighing the relative strengths of the various factions within the regime.

Many of the same comments apply to the courts and the court system. First, the court system is not a separate and coequal branch—nor is it intended or generally expected to be. A Latin American supreme court would declare a law unconstitutional or defy a determined executive only at the risk of embarrassment and endangering itself, something the courts have assiduously avoided. Second, within the prescribed limits, the Latin American court systems do manage to function; particularly in the everyday administration of justice they are probably no worse than the U.S. system. Third, the courts, through such devices as the writ of *amparo* (Mexico and Argentina), popular action (Colombia), and *segurança* (Brazil), have played an increasingly important role in controlling and overseeing government actions, protecting civil liberties, and restricting executive authority even in dictatorial regimes.

The court system has its origins in the Iberian tradition, has had French and Anglo-American practices superimposed on it, and has also been shaped by indigenous influences and national variations. The chief influences historically were Roman law, Christianity and the Thomistic hierarchy of laws, and the traditional legal concepts of Iberia, most notably the Siete Partidas of Alfonso the Wise. In Latin America's codes, lists of human rights, and hierarchy of courts, the French influence is pronounced, and in the case of a supreme court passing (in theory at least) upon the constitutionality of executive or legislative acts, the U.S. inspiration is clear.

It should be remembered, however, that what makes the Latin American political systems work is not the legislature or the judiciary but the executive. The former two meet or sit largely at executive discretion, and they have no delusions that they are independent and coequal branches. The modern Latin American president is thus still a man on horseback, although the means of transportation is now likely to be a helicopter. The formally institutionalized limits on executive power in terms of the usual checks and balances are not extensive and frequently can be bypassed. More significant is the informal balance of power within the system and the set of generally agreed upon understandings and rules of the game beyond which even the strongest of Latin American presidents (like a Trujillo, Somoza, Stroessner, or Pinochet) goes only at severe risk to his regime's survival.

LOCAL GOVERNMENT AND FEDERALISM

There have been four full-fledged federal systems in Latin America: in Argentina, Brazil, Mexico, and Venezuela. Federalism in Latin America emerged from exactly the reverse of the situation in the United States. In the United States in 1789, a national government was reluctantly accepted by thirteen self-governing colonies that had never had a central administration. In Latin America, by contrast, a federal structure was adopted in some countries that had always been centrally administered.

It is difficult to judge where federalism works best or least. In the United States, the federal principle survives, however inefficiently and precariously at times, in the face of a long-term trend toward the gradual centralization of power in the national government. In Latin America, the principle of unitary government has survived, also precariously at times, despite such weak central power sometimes that regionalism and an almost de facto form of federalism exist whether specified in the constitution or not.

The independent power of the states in those few Latin American countries organized on a federal basis was greatest in the nineteenth century when the central government was weak. For a long time Mexico, Argentina, and Venezuela were dominated by caudillos operating from a regional base that often corresponded to federal boundaries. In Argentina, the disparity of wealth and power between Buenos Aires and the interior was so great that the adoption of federalism seemed eminently sound. Brazil was so large that the federal principle also made sense there.

Although these nations were federal in principle, the central government reserved the right to "intervene" in the states. As the authority of these central governments grew during the 1920s and 1930s, their inclination to intervene also increased, thereby often negating the federal principle. These major countries have since been progressively centralized so that virtually all power is now concentrated in their national capitals. Nevertheless, the dynamics of the relations and tensions between these central governments and their component states make for a most interesting political arena.

Local governments in Latin America may be described by employing many of the same caveats. The Latin American countries are structured after the French system of local government. Virtually all power is concentrated in the central government. Authority flows from the top down, not from the grass roots up. Local government is ordinarily administered through the ministry of interior, which is also responsible for administering the national police. Almost all local officials are appointed by the central government and serve as its agents at the local level.

Local governments have almost no power to tax or to run local social programs. These activities are administered by the central government according to a national plan. Centralized rule is, of course, a part of the entire Iberian and Latin American tradition; it is also a means of concentrating power in oftentimes weak and uninstitutionalized nations. Only outsiders entirely unfamiliar with the area would try to impose a decentralized New England town-meeting style of local government on a system that has always been highly centralized.

And yet, even though the theory calls for a centralized state, the reality in Latin America has always been somewhat different. Spanish and Portuguese colonial power was concentrated mostly in coastal enclaves, and the vast hinterland was subdued but only thinly settled. The Spanish and Portuguese crowns had difficulty enforcing their authority in the interior, which was far away and virtually autonomous.

With the withdrawal of the colonial powers early in the nineteenth century, centrifugal tendencies were accelerated. Formerly large vice-royalties and captaincies general fragmented into smaller nation-states, and within the new nations, decentralization proceeded even further until the local region, parish, municipality, or hacienda became the focal point of the system. Power drained off into the hands of local landowners or regional men on horseback, and these people competed for control of the national palace. With a weak central state and powerful centrifugal tendencies, a strong de facto system of local rule emerged in Latin America, despite what the laws or constitutions proclaimed.

Thereafter, nation building in Latin America consisted of two major tendencies: populating and thus "civilizing" the vast empty interior and extending the central government's authority over the national territory. Toward the end of the nineteenth century national armies and bureaucracies were created to replace the unprofessional armed bands led by the local caudillos; national police agencies enforced the central governments' authority at the local level; and the collection of customs duties was centralized, thereby depriving the local strongmen of the funds for their *pronunciamientos*. Authority became concentrated in the central state, the regional isolation of the *patrias chicas* broke down as roads and communications grids were developed, and the economies were similarly centralized under the direction of the state. In most of Latin America the process of centralization, begun in the 1870s and 1880s, is still going forward. Indeed, that is how development is often defined throughout the area.

A developed political system is one in which the central agencies of the state exercise control over the disparate and centrifugal forces that make up the system. In many countries this process is still incomplete, and in the vast interior, in the highlands, in diverse Indian communities, and among some groups (such as landowners, large industrialists, the military, and big multinationals), the authority of the central state is still tenuous. Even today there is little government presence in isolated areas (especially those in the rugged mountains or tropical jungles), and local strongmen—sometimes guerrillas or drug traffickers—may be more powerful than the national government's representatives. This situation also constitutes one of the main arenas of Latin American politics: the efforts of the central government—any government—to extend its sway over the entire nation and the efforts of the local and component units (be they regions, towns, parishes, or Indian communities) to maintain some degree of autonomy.

A FOURTH BRANCH OF GOVERNMENT:
THE AUTONOMOUS STATE AGENCIES

One of the primary tools in the struggle to centralize power has been the government corporation or the autonomous agency. The growth of these agencies, which in many ways has paralleled that of the regulatory "alphabet agencies" in the United States, has given the central governments a means to extend their control into new areas. These agencies have become so large and so pervasive that they could be termed a separate branch of government, and some Latin American constitutions even recognize them as such.

The proliferation of these agencies means that in some countries they number in the hundreds. Many are regulatory agencies, often with far broader powers than their North American counterparts, with the authority to set or regulate prices, wages, and production quotas. Others administer vast government corporations: among them, steel, mining, electricity, sugar, coffee, tobacco, railroads, utilities, and petrochemicals. Still others are involved with social programs: education, social security, housing, relief activities, and the like. Many more participate in the administration of new services that the state has been called upon to perform: for example, national planning, agrarian reform, water supplies, family planning.

The reasons why these agencies have been set up are diverse. Some, such as the agrarian-reform or family-planning agencies, have been established as much to please the North Americans and to qualify a country for U.S. and World Bank loans as to carry out actual agrarian reform or family planning. Others have been created to bring a recalcitrant or rebellious economic sector (such as labor or the business community) under government control and direction. Some have been intended to stimulate economic growth and development; to increase government efficiency, and hence its legitimacy; or to create a capitalist structure and an officially sanctioned entrepreneurial class where none had existed before. They also enable more job seekers to be put on the public payroll.

But a common feature of all these agencies is that they tend to serve as agents of centralization in the historic quest to "civilize" and bring order to what was, in the past even more than now, a vast, often unruly, nearly empty territory with strong centrifugal propensities. The host of official agencies, bureaus, boards, commissions, corporations, offices, directorships, and institutes that are now part of the state structures are all instruments in this process.

The growth of these agencies, specifically the government corporations, has meant that the degree of central government control and even ownership of the means of production has increased significantly as well. It is a fundamental mistake to think that the Latin American economies are private enterprise–dominated systems. It is not just socialist Cuba that has a large public sector; in fact, all the Latin American economies are heavily influenced by the state.

If one asks who "owns" Brazil, for example, the answer will not be Coca-Cola, General Motors, or International Telephone and Telegraph (ITT) but the Brazilian government. The Brazilian national government, either by itself through the ownership of major public corporations or through joint ventures with private entrepreneurs, generates 35–40 percent of the total gross national product (GNP). The second-largest generator of GNP in Brazil is not Ford or Volkswagen but the Brazilian state governments, and the third-largest, municipal governments. Between these three levels of government, roughly 55–60 percent of the GNP is generated by the public sector. It is only after these three levels of public ownership that one can begin talking about General Motors, Chrysler, and other multinationals. The situation is similar, although the percentage of public ownership varies somewhat, throughout Latin America. Contrary to the popular notion, these countries do not have free-enterprise, capitalist economies but state-capitalist ones (state-socialist in Cuba) with a very high percentage of the GNP generated by the public sector.

This fact has important implications. It means the stakes involved in the issue of who controls the central government, with the vast resources involved, are very high. It belies conservative economist Milton Friedman's advice to the governments of Latin America to privatize their economies, because that advice is posited on the assumption of a free-market system, which the Latin American economies are not. It is also based on the assumption that very rapid structural change in Latin America is readily possible. Actually, it has usually been the case that moving to greater statism is relatively easy, but the reverse process is very difficult. In the Latin American countries where between 40 and 60 percent of the GNP (far higher than in the United States) is generated by the public sector and where so much power is already concentrated in the central government, the transformation from a state-capitalist to a state-socialist system is relatively easy and can happen almost overnight (as in Cuba and Peru). All that is required is that a leftist or socialist (instead of the usual rightist or middle-of-the-road) element assume control of these highly centralized systems.

The growth of all the centralized state agencies has another implication that deserves mention. Although established as autonomous and self-governing bodies, the state corporations have in fact become highly political agencies. They provide a wealth of sinecures and places for many people on the public payroll. They are giant patronage agencies by which one rewards friends and cronies and finds places for (and hence secures the loyalty or at least neutrality of) the opposition. Depending on the country, 30–50 percent of the gainfully employed labor force now works for the government. Many of the agencies are woefully inefficient, and the immense funds controlled by them means there are nearly endless opportunities for private enrichment from the great public trough. Because of these patronage and spoils functions, the state agencies have been instruments to preserve the status quo, since large numbers of people, indeed virtually the entire middle class, are dependent upon them for their livelihood and opportunities for advancement. It is not surprising that a significant part of the debt problems faced by many Latin American countries is the result of foreign loans made to state agencies—not the national governments.

ARMY, CHURCH, BUREAUCRACY: FIFTH, SIXTH, AND SEVENTH BRANCHES OF GOVERNMENT?

As noted in the previous chapter, the army, the church, and the vast bureaucracy in Latin American countries are sometimes more than mere pressure groups in the North American sense. Historically, they have constituted the backbone of nearly every Latin American regime and have been inseparable from it. Many scholars argue that these agencies should be considered not as private pressure groups that are distinguishable from the institutions of government but more accurately as part of the central state apparatus. They deserve brief mention here as perhaps the fifth, sixth, and seventh branches of government.

The army is the most clear-cut case. Although most Latin American constitutions proclaim that the government should be civil and republican and that the armed forces are to play an apolitical role, they also give certain special functions to the army that make it constitutionally the ultimate arbiter of national affairs. The army not only plays a moderating role but is frequently given the power to defend national integrity and preserve order. If these functions are not mentioned in the constitution, they are often given full expression in the organic law of the armed forces, literally a separate constitution that both establishes the internal structure of the military and defines its relations with the state.

All this is foreign to the U.S. experience. The usual distinction implied by the term *civil-military relations* is inapplicable in Latin America. There the distinction between the military and the civilian spheres is blurred, and in fact most regimes are coalitions, albeit in varying degrees, of civil and military elements. Not only do the armed forces have the right and obligation to intervene in politics under certain circumstances, but they are urged and expected to do so by the rest of the population. In this sense, the army is an integral part of the central state apparatus, and it functions almost as a separate, perhaps even coequal, branch of government. Although often internally divided, the army may still act as a monolith to protect itself when its own institutional interests are threatened.

Some of the same comments apply to the church, although in most Latin American constitutions church and state are now officially separated. Still the church, like the military, has its organic law, usually in the form of a concordat, signed by the government and the Vatican, that defines the rights and obligations of both. The concordat may give the church certain privileges in the areas of education, social services, charity, health care, and the like; it may obligate the state to aid the church with public funds; and it may grant the church autonomy in the appointment of ecclesiastic authorities.

In addition, the church can participate in a variety of quasi-official ceremonies (openings, blessings, and dedications of bridges, highways, and public buildings) and take quasi-official stands on a variety of matters that are undefined in any official document—for example, stands on abortion, divorce, family planning, or unofficial advice proffered the president or the voting population. In this more secular age, the church is not as strong or as influential as it once was, and it is certainly not as powerful as the army or the business elites. But its position remains more than that of a mere pressure group. In this way, the church could also be said to function as a distinct branch of government, no longer of first-rank importance but probably at least as influential as the legislature or the judiciary.

The third major corporate pillar deserving mention in this context is the bureaucracy. It too has its organic law, which carefully defines its powers and responsibilities and the relations of its members to the state. Whereas the church may be a declining power, the bureaucracy, thanks to the growth of the autonomous agencies and government corporations, is a rising one. Because of the strategic position of its members within the state system, its role (like the army's) is particularly critical in the making or breaking of existing governments.

There are other quasi-branches, discussed in the previous chapter as "interest groups," that merit brief mention in this context. The tendency in many Latin American countries to create and structure official trade-union organizations and official peasant associations—to say nothing of the university community, which has its own separate charter or organic law—adds still other branches to the state system. Such a categorization is not merely fanciful but may reflect more accurately the structure of power in Latin America than the Montesquieuian three-part division into which many of the analyses of Latin America are locked. One important study found there were no fewer than sixteen "powers" or "branches" of government in Latin America, each with its own carefully defined functions and responsibilities. That may be a more realistic and fruitful line of approach than the usual efforts, which involve gauging the success of Latin American governments by using criteria that stem largely from the North American constitutional tradition.

CONCLUSIONS AND IMPLICATIONS

In numerous places in this chapter it is suggested that in the organization of power the Latin American systems differ fundamentally from the U.S. system. These are not so much "underdeveloped" political systems as ones with philosophical underpinnings and cultural traditions distinct from our own. What also emerges from this study is a sense of the considerable variation that exists among the Latin American nations themselves. Throughout the country chapters, the reader should be thinking both of these variations within Latin America and of the even more fundamental differences between these systems and that of the United States.

Certain hints also surface as to what we should look for in the upcoming country chapters. Five critical areas may be identified:

1. the relations among the various branches of government within each system, including not only executive-legislative relations in the U.S. mold but also, in the Latin American mold, executive-military and other relations;
2. the competition among the rival elites, interest groups, factions, and mass organizations to capture the pinnacles of political power and thus control of the state system;
3. the relations between the central state apparatus and the various components of the system, particularly the constant struggle of the state seeking to expand its power and the efforts of such agencies as universities and trade unions to maintain their autonomy;
4. the relations of the central state with federal, regional, and local units and the effort of the state to extend its suzerainty over distant areas; and
5. the historical process of the expansion of state power, including the growth of new national agencies such as armies and bureaucracies, the emergence of a plethora of regulatory agencies and public corporations, the growth of public ownership in all levels of the economy, the issue of whom the emerging systems of state capitalism are to benefit, and the growth of the public bureaucracy and its political implications.

These are some major domestic political areas. To them must now be added the issue discussed in previous chapters of how the Latin American nations cope with the international forces that affect them—the pressures from the United States, the conditions of loan arrangements, the influence of the big multinational corporations and of such major international agencies as the World Bank and the IMF, and the effect of world market forces—as well as how these international pressures affect domestic policymaking.

6
Public Policy and the Policy Process

Before focusing on the major issues and problems of public policy in Latin America, several analytical distinctions should be made. By public policy, we mean the actions of groups in authority to implement their decisions. These policies are attempts by the relevant actors in a political system to cope with and to transform their environment by deliberate measures. These measures may involve the commitment of physical or symbolic resources. Alternatively, these measures include non-acts, decisions not to respond or even take up an issue. These nondecisions are extremely difficult to study because often they are not even detected.[1]

No political system is completely successful in accomplishing what it wishes. This is certainly the case in societies that are underdeveloped politically and economically, such as the Latin American countries in varying degrees. Further, there are certain uniquely Latin American traits, over and above the area's underdeveloped character, that militate against effective public policies. For this reason, it is analytically useful to distinguish between a policy output, which is a deliberate act or non-act of the ruling coalition to allocate resources for a determined purpose, and a policy outcome, which reflects the impact of a policy.[2] Although the output and the outcome are related, they are not the same. Output is much easier to study than outcome and is the subject of most studies of Latin American public policy.

Any government has a large number of policy outputs. Philippe Schmitter, in his ground-breaking study of public policy in Latin America, measured in quantified form eighteen policy outputs and nine policy outcomes. All of these were allocative policies, decisions that confer direct material benefit upon individuals and groups. Left out of his analysis (as well as most other studies) are those allocations of symbolic benefit and structural and regulatory policies, which establish structures or rules to guide future allocations.[3] These symbolic, structural, and regulatory policies, though important, are as yet little examined for Latin America because they are more difficult to study than the allocative policies.

MAJOR ISSUES OF PUBLIC POLICY

Most of the historic issues of the nineteenth-century—the role of the church, centralism or federalism, free trade or protectionism—have been resolved or at least placed on the back burner in post–World War II Latin America. Although from time to time these old issues reemerge in some countries, the newer issues of economic development, agrarian reform, urban reform, and population growth have largely replaced them.

Economic Development

Economic development is one goal of almost all sectors in the Latin American political process, although they disagree on its nature and the way to obtain it. For some groups, economic development means no more than growth of the national economy, with a resulting larger gross domestic product. In this conception, the nature and structure of the economy would not change at all, only the size. The kinds of products would remain the same; and the nature of trade relations with the outside world would vary only slightly, albeit expanded in amount.

Other Latin Americans, and probably the majority of the political leaders, define economic development as the industrialization and diversification of the economy. Traditionally, Latin American countries have produced agricultural or other primary goods, and these have been traded with the more developed countries of the North for industrial goods. Many Latin American countries have concentrated on only one primary good. Although they might have comparative advantage in those primary products, the national economy suffers when there is a world oversupply of a product, and the countries are also vulnerable because of crop failures and quotas fixed by the industrial nations. By the early 1960s it had become evident that there was a general decline in the terms of trade for all of these primary goods. The long-term trend was for the prices of industrial articles to go up more rapidly than those of primary goods. Although a frost in Brazil might mean a short-term increase in the price of Colombian coffee, a tractor imported to Colombia from the United States in the 1960s cost more bags of coffee beans than it had twenty years before. Although this situation did not pertain to Venezuelan oil before 1982, almost all other Latin American countries lost income as a result of the declining terms of trade.

The middle position on economic policy, then, would call for two major policies of an economic nature: industrialization and diversification. The former would be for the purpose of import substitution. Rather than importing industrial goods, a Latin American country imports capital goods and technology, which it then uses to produce the goods that formerly were imported. Further, in order to lessen the dependence on one crop, a government makes tax and credit decisions that will encourage production of goods other than the traditional one for export.

The vision of the new, economically developed society is one in which more goods of greater variety are produced for export while fewer manufactured goods are imported. Increased trade is an important facet of this policy, since hard currency is needed for the purchase of the capital goods.

A more radical position, held by most socialists and Marxists and by some people who fit into neither of those categories, also posits industrialization and diversification as goals. But this position further calls for a wholesale restructuring of society, with redistribution of income from the rich to the poor and from the cities to the countryside. At the same time, proponents of this position call for all kinds of social reforms: ending stratification on the basis of the manual-nonmanual distinction; terminating the subservient position of women; and building a whole series of government programs to deal with health, housing, and other problems. The reformist, slower, and parliamentary-democratic version of this position is exemplified by the Democratic Action party in Venezuela and the National Liberation party in Costa Rica. The more radical, rapid, and total transformation of this type has taken place in Castro's Cuba, Allende's Chile, and Sandinista Nicaragua.

An even more radical economic policy espoused by some intellectuals, and as yet untried in Latin America, is to cut a nation off completely from trade with the industrialized world. This policy option is based on the observation that most industrial development by Latin Americans themselves has occurred during those three periods of recent history— the first and second world wars and the Great Depression—when industrial goods were not available from the developed countries of the North. The argument is that autonomous Latin American development will happen only when most trade ties have been severed with the industrial world and Latin Americans are forced to generate their own capital and develop their own technologies. These people argue that the technology now imported is too capital intensive, calling for much machinery and little labor, and that industrialization in Latin America should be labor intensive and thus employ more people.

The more radical proponents of autonomous economic development are likely to continue to voice these opinions, and in some cases their ideas might be partially adopted. However, two of their key assumptions, which cannot be verified or disproved a priori, make any complete acceptance of this route to economic development unlikely, even in revolutionary situations. First, the autonomous development model assumes that the political leaders can convince or coerce the inhabitants of a Latin American country to forgo consumption of industrial goods until the nation's industry emerges. Second, this policy assumes that the individual Latin American countries can generate capital and develop technologies on their own. Both assumptions are tenuous, the first in all countries of Latin America, and the second in all but those large countries that are the most endowed with natural resources.

These four positions are ideal types, and the government's economic policy in all the countries of Latin America tends to be a combination of elements of the four. But economic policy is much more complex than this discussion has indicated. What to do about inflation? Latin American countries experienced stagflation (the combination of a stagnant economy and high inflation) for at least three decades before it reached its most acute form in the first half of the 1980s. Is this problem to be solved by monetary measures (printing less money, balancing budgets, maintaining a balance of trade between imports and exports), or is the real cause for the inflation a structural one, based on the declining terms of trade and the concentration of economic power in the small group at the top in most of the Latin American countries? If the reason is structural, more dramatic public policies are needed.

Another key question is, Who is to develop industry? Will national enterprise do it (and if so, will it be the government or private investors)? Or, alternatively, will laws be written to encourage foreign multinational corporations? How will the generally negative balances of payment be redressed? What kinds of laws are needed to encourage the importation of capital goods and infrastructure materials while discouraging the purchase of consumer goods from foreign countries? If national industry is to be developed, how is capital to be generated? By stopping capital flight, by reducing consumption on the part of the lower and middle classes through forced savings, or by some combination of techniques?

After October 1973 a new economic issue arose concerning the value of petroleum. For the oil-exporting countries, the question became how best to use their new wealth while keeping inflationary pressures at a minimum and protecting national industry. For the petroleum importers (the majority of the Latin American countries), the question revolved around how to keep economic growth going while using more of the scarce hard-currency export earnings and reserves to purchase needed oil.

In the early 1980s, whether these policy issues had been successfully resolved or not, the question changed to how the debt crisis could or would be resolved. This crisis was stimulated by the energy crisis in two ways. First, all Latin American countries had found, by the late 1970s, that private banks, recycling petrodollars invested by OPEC members, were willing to lend money at real interest rates (corrected for inflation) that were near zero. The debts were impossible to repay, however, because recession in the industrial world in the early 1980s meant that fewer Latin American exports were bought. Second, the oil-exporting countries (especially Mexico and Venezuela) contracted debts under the assumption that the price of petroleum would continue increasing. By 1982, however, the oil glut had led to much lower prices for their exports.

Almost all Latin American groups agree that economic development and growth are desirable, because only in that way can incomes be raised, social services increased, and the revolution of rising expectations dealt with or managed satisfactorily. There is much disagreement on what policy should be adopted to obtain these goals and on who should be the beneficiaries.

Agrarian Reform

A second major issue is that of the ownership of land. Land is very inequitably distributed, with a small number of very large landholders and a great number of landless, illegal squatters and owners of very small holdings. Only in a few countries are there substantial numbers of middle-class farmers. During the 1960s, in large part because of the influence of the United States and the fear of an agrarian revolution (such as the Cuban Revolution was perceived to have been), many countries of Latin America set up agencies to deal with the problems of land. Yet in only Venezuela and Mexico were there significant land reforms. Even though land reform was not the issue in the 1970s that it had been in the 1960s, the problem still existed: Land ownership was very unevenly distributed, and at least 80 million Latin Americans lived in the countryside under subhuman conditions. Guerrilla movements took root in many Latin American countries because of the land problem, and in Nicaragua, the agrarian problem was one of the reasons for the victory of the Sandinistas in July 1979. Since then Latin American elites and the U.S. government have once again seen land reform as a way to prevent revolutions.

One very important reason why more dramatic land reforms have not occurred is that the large landowners are powerful enough to prevent such an attack on their property—although in some countries, the landowners have given up a little land to avoid giving up a lot. Another reason for the failure of land reform is the lack of reliable information about who owns what land and what it is being used for. If the land were divided among peasants, would production go up or down? What would be the best crops? Which kinds of seeds and fertilizers would be best? What does the peasant need in addition to land?

Further, there are economic reasons for not breaking up the large tracts of land. The latifundios, or large estates, vary greatly in their use and economic output. If a sizable estate is not used or is being used very inefficiently, any granting of the land to campesinos would lead to increased agricultural production for either national consumption or export. If, however, an estate is being effectively utilized by the large landowner, the goals of land reform and increased agricultural production are, at least for the short run, in conflict. Evidence from many countries shows that breaking up well-run latifundios decreases agricultural production for at least the better part of a decade. Moreover, there are certain agricultural products that have economies of scale—that is, they cannot be successfully grown on a family-sized farm. In this case, agrarian reform means long-term lower production unless the land holdings are held collectively. There are both Spanish (the *ejido*) and Amerindian traditions of collective ownership of lands, and in Peru, such traditions have resulted in some communal ownership. The Cuban case shows that state farms—those owned by the government with campesinos receiving wages for work—can be another alternative.

Urban Reform

One reason that agrarian reform is a slightly less important issue than it was earlier is that many people have left the countryside to seek a better life in the cities. There are both push and pull factors for this internal migration. Some campesinos are pushed off the land, either because there are more children than the land can support or because the large landowners have mechanized production. Others are pulled to the cities by the better life they believe will be found there. The movement has been dramatic: It is estimated that every year from 1970 to 1985 some 8.75 million people were incorporated into the cities of Latin America; it is further estimated that in the 1985–2000 period the figure will increase to between 11 million and 12 million a year. Caused by both internal migration and the area's high birthrate, this urban growth affects the major cities, many of which doubled or tripled in size in the 1970s.

Cities in Latin America were not prepared for such rapid growth as U.S. cities were not during similar growth periods at the end of the last century and the beginning of this one. But there are important differences. Unlike the United States and Western Europe, Latin American urbanization has not been accompanied by a surge of industrial growth. Not many of the new urbanites receive jobs in industry; many have to settle for hand-labor construction work, and many more are underemployed or unemployed. The political dimension is also different in Latin America, given the greater centralization of the state, so policies to meet the new problems of the cities are more likely to come from national than city governments.

The problems that these national governments face are numerous and difficult. One is housing. Although some of the urban migrants rent rooms in large old houses where certain public utilities already exist, even more build makeshift homes in the open areas around the cities. Called different names in different countries (*callampas* or mushroom towns in Chile, *favelas* in Brazil, *barrios* in Peru, *tugurios* in Colombia), most of these new slums are built illegally on private or state-owned land and are completely devoid of such urban services as water, sewers, electricity, roads, and effective police or fire protection. Some studies have shown that the life expectancy is lower for the dwellers of these shantytowns than for the campesinos.

One author suggested at the beginning of the 1970s that the decade would be one of urban reform as the 1960s had been one of agrarian reform. Perhaps he was correct, since urban reform efforts have been no more successful than agrarian reform ones were earlier. One key reason for the lack of urban reform so far, although there has been progress in some of the countries, is that the urban dwellers have yet to organize into effective political movements. There are no doubt many explanations for this lack, and the following reasons have been mentioned in the literature:

1. The new urban poor are too busy in the day-to-day attempt to make enough money to feed themselves and their children. They work fourteen to sixteen hours a day and thus have little time for political activities.
2. In the shantytowns, people often develop a sense of community that seems to provide considerable security and often engenders resentment against government interference in their internal affairs.
3. Additional security is received from the extended family (one survey indicated that a typical resident of a São Paulo *favela* can identify by name anywhere from 30 to 500 relatives, many of whom live in the same city or even in the same *favela*) and from the ceremonial kinship relationship in which friends or people slightly higher in the social structure are godparents of another person's children.
4. Close contact is maintained between the urban poor and the rural areas from which they came. If things get extremely bad econom- ically, they can return.
5. A high percentage of the urban poor are engaged in service work and petty commercial activities such as street vending. Such people tend to form an atomized labor force, and their lack of association with others like themselves makes organization difficult.
6. Many who do obtain factory jobs work in very small factories, often of the cottage variety. The owner fulfills the traditional *patrón* function, dispensing all the benefits and liabilities, and thus prevents other forms of organization.
7. Businesspeople, industrialists, and governments participate in stra- tegic activities designed to give the urban poor a bit of what they want, but of course not all that they really need.
8. The same elite groups can participate in sanctions against the urban poor. The poor often have jobs in which they can be easily replaced by the unemployed if they engage in political activities, and many have illegally built houses from which they could be removed if the government saw fit.
9. Whether they will live longer or not, the new urban poor perceive themselves to be better off—or at least that their children will be better off—than they would be if they had remained in the country.

One does not have to accept all of these arguments, and the causes vary from country to country and among individuals. Yet the conclusion seems clear that the urban poor do not have the power yet that their numbers would indicate. They do have the advantage of being in the center of Latin American politics, which has always been essentially urban. Some governments and political parties have begun their co-optation-or-repression techniques (see the introduction to Chapter 4), and it seems likely that the urban poor will eventually become organized. With organization will come increased power for the urban poor and, as a result, some policy outputs favoring a better life for them.

Population Policy

The fourth modern issue of Latin American politics, at least for some groups, is population growth. Latin America has the highest growth rate in the world. Although the birthrate is higher in certain parts of Asia and Africa, death rates are lower in Latin America, and the result is a population growth rate for the area of roughly 3 percent per year. Of course, the rate varies from country to country: Argentina and Uruguay both increase in population at about 1.0 percent a year, roughly comparable to the United States. But other countries, such as Mexico, increase between 3 and 4 percent a year, which means that the population doubles every eighteen to twenty-four years.

Population growth is related to another issue area previously discussed. Economic growth must be at least equal to population growth if a country is just to stand still in per capita income terms. If an increase in per capita income is a target, then economic growth must be greater than the population growth rate. The Alliance for Progress of the 1960s led to impressive growth in the GDPs of many Latin American nations, but the GDP per capita gained only slightly because of population growth. Likewise, agrarian reform was an issue, in part because of the increasing numbers of rural inhabitants. And of course the population growth rate, as well as internal migration, is what led to the relatively recent issue of urban reform.

One of the key reasons for the high population growth rates is the increasing life expectancy and the lower infant mortality rates, both of which have changed dramatically since World War II. These improved rates are the result of better health care, more doctors, better sanitary conditions, and the eradication of some diseases, such as smallpox and malaria, through public-health programs. Meanwhile, the birthrate, with the exception of the countries of the Southern Cone of South America, has not decreased dramatically. Few would suggest that the solution to the growth problem lies in lowering life expectancy, so the way to slow this growth has to be through some control of the high birthrate.

Some people believe that if the population problem can be resolved, so can other public policy issues. In many cases, the people taking this position are not Latin Americans but officials of international population agencies. Whereas in the 1960s a precondition for foreign assistance was having an agrarian-reform program in place, in the 1970s the precondition was to have a program of family planning. Part of the motivation for requiring this type of program was humane: If Latin America could not adequately feed its current population, how could it expect to feed a doubled population in twenty-four years? But there were also other motivations related to U.S. strategic and economic needs. A growing population in Latin America would lead to nations in which there was so much human misery that there would be radical revolutions, whose protagonists were likely to ally themselves with the international enemies of the United States and take over the U.S.-based multinationals in the area.

Some groups in Latin America agreed with this reasoning, particularly those upper-class groups who would lose in a radical revolution. But the traditional ally of the secular status quo groups—the church—saw the matter differently. As the papal directives were against all artificial forms of birth control, in those places where the church was strongest, its hierarchy tended to oppose anything more than family-planning clinics and natural birth-control methods. Yet even church officials were split on the issue. Some, either for the humane reasons of caring for the flock or for fear of what a radical revolution might do to them, quietly supported artificial birth control.

In this particular policy area, the church found itself in the unusual position of taking the same stand as radical, nationalistic, and even Marxist groups. These argued that population growth was desirable either because the nations could absorb more people, and in the process would become more powerful in relation to the United States, or because with increased population, things would get so bad as to ensure revolution, which the radical groups considered desirable.

It is not entirely clear where the majority of the poor Latin Americans—those who are having the large families—stand on the matter. If they are practicing Catholics, they have been taught that artificial methods of birth control are wrong. But if they are finding it increasingly difficult to feed, clothe, educate, and house their growing families, their perception might be different.

Although it is among the poor that the population growth rates are highest (the middle and upper classes have no difficulty obtaining contraceptives), this is precisely the group least organized to lobby for an effective program of family planning. And with the ruling elites divided on the issue, population policy has largely been ineffectual, piecemeal, and often shifting because of changing government coalitions. The only constant proponents of birth control have been those international agencies that use their power and the leverage of foreign assistance to push toward their goal.

Some countries (even strongly Catholic Colombia) have developed family-planning programs. Further it has become evident that the birthrate has begun to fall even in the countries that lack effective programs. This decline seems related to increased urbanization, education, and knowledge concerning ways to limit family size, not necessarily to organized family-planning programs. After all, it may make some sense for a rural peasant to have lots of children, both to help in the fields and to take care of the parents in their old age (particularly in nations that have few effective social security programs). But for the urban poor the argument for more rather than fewer children makes less sense, and it is precisely in the urban areas that the birthrate has begun to fall.

CONSTRAINTS IN LATIN AMERICAN POLICYMAKING

Having considered some of the major issues of Latin American public policy, the aim of this section is to outline some of the constraints—conditions that affect political decisions as well as those that impede effective transition from policy outputs to policy outcomes. These constraints are divided into three areas: (1) those that come from economic underdevelopment, (2) those that stem from the nature of the Latin American political system, and (3) those that are owing to the position of these countries in a hemisphere dominated by the United States and to their position in the international political economy. Although the three are clearly related, for the purpose of analysis they are discussed separately.

Underdevelopment

The key feature of economic underdevelopment is that even a government that wishes to change many things does not have the revenue to do so. All allocative policies cost money. If the governing coalition of a Latin American country decides that economic development (through government ownership of industry), agrarian reform, urban reform, and birth control are desirable, there might not be enough money to fund all four policies adequately. Similar restraints might plague the more specific levels of policies. For example, Castro's policies have included government construction of schools, hospitals, rural housing, and urban housing. Yet the reality of underdevelopment in Cuba is that there are not enough construction materials for all four kinds of projects. In some instances in Latin America, policymakers honestly cannot do all that they would like; in other cases, legislatures create programs that are never funded. Government policy in Latin America, therefore, should be analyzed not only by studying established law but by looking at the actual expenditures of government revenues.

Yet another feature of underdevelopment, more political than economic, is the lack of bureaucratic expertise. Bureaucracies in Latin America have one very important purpose: to provide white-collar, nonmanual employment for the members of the middle sectors, especially those who, in the absence of such employment, would be likely to join the political opposition. Because of this co-optive function, the bureaucracies of the area are often not efficient in the day-to-day running of government programs. They contain people who have jobs only because of personal connections, people who do not have the necessary educational background, and people who hold multiple bureaucratic jobs, working only briefly or not at all in any one.

Because of this lack of expertise, some governments in Latin America have set up decentralized agencies for specific policies in an attempt to insulate them from the more corrupt regular bureaucracy. But in many countries even this method has failed to produce effective results. Therefore, even in the case of a policy that is accepted by the ruling coalition and adequately funded, the policy consequence might not be what was intended.

The Political System

The rules of the Latin American political game have been described in Chapter 4. Here it is sufficient to repeat that a new group entering into the accepted circle of power groups must tacitly demonstrate that it will not do anything to harm the existing groups. This system means that many public policy alternatives are not possible because of the rules of the game. How can there be agrarian reform—even one supported by international groups, the campesinos, and perhaps by organized labor—if the governing coalition includes the large landowners and their industrialist friends? How can there be urban reform when governing coalitions generally include those real-estate interests that would be adversely affected?

In most countries of Latin America, there are two possible ways to solve this dilemma. First, government policies will work in such a political system if the economy is expanding and increasing the government's income. In such a case, new revenues can be allocated to public policies in a distributive fashion—that is, by dividing up the bigger pie. Governments still have difficulties with such distributive policies, since industrialists, for example, would prefer that the new revenue used for urban reform, which doesn't benefit them very much, be employed for infrastructure improvements (roads, railroads) that would help them economically. However, the controversy over distributive policies is much smaller than that over redistributive ones—that is, policies that take something away from one group and give it to another. For this reason, land reform has generally encountered many difficulties. It is not surprising that Venezuela has had one of the most successful reform governments in Latin America, made possible by government taxes on foreign oil producers (and after 1976 by profits made by the government oil enterprise), and one of the most successful agrarian reforms, using land that the government already owned. Yet not all the governments in Latin America have the luxury of carrying out only distributive policies. If an economy is stagnant, and even worse if it is shrinking, there may be no government policy.

So the second possibility is a case-by-case, eclectic policy situation in which one group wins on one policy issue, another group on another issue, and so forth. Although politically this is a good short-run strategy, the long-term results might be contradictory, with detrimental ramifications for the economy, the people, and even the political system.

This dilemma of policymaking in the Latin American context is most evident in those countries where almost all individuals have organized into groups that have accepted the rules of the game. This situation (well documented for Mexico by Raymond Vernon,[4] with Argentina the only other example to date) results at worst in almost complete governmental stalemate or at best in very eclectic and contradictory policies. Since all groups are politically relevant and involved, and since all groups have agreed not to harm the interests of others, practically no agreed-upon policy is possible.

Still another feature of the Latin American political tradition that affects public policy implementation is the tentative nature of the political system. One question just beginning to be researched is whether public policies change when military governments replace civilian ones and vice versa. Early evidence suggests that policies do change with regime shifts, at least in most cases.[5] Furthermore, one might speculate that during the crisis periods of very tentative regimes—ones likely to fall at any time—policy implementation suffers. Why should a bureaucrat (who might be jockeying for a more powerful position in a new government) spend time trying to carry out a policy that might be reversed by a new regime? This aspect of public policy applies only in the most "tentative" systems and not so much in stable ones, be they military or civilian.

The United States and the International Political Economy

The third set of constraints on Latin American public policymaking relates to the position of these countries in a hemisphere dominated politically and economically by the United States and to their position in the international political economy. Some of these constraints on policymaking are dramatic and appear on the front pages of newspapers. In 1954 Guatemala found that a Central American government could not enact a dramatic land reform that adversely affected U.S. business interests or launch a general social revolution backed and participated in by the Communist party, as either would result in U.S. intervention. Eleven years later, the case of the Dominican Republic showed that the U.S. government might intervene militarily even if a coalition that is about to come to power only appears to be dangerous to certain U.S. security interests. In the 1970s Chile discovered that no matter how geographically remote and economically unimportant a country might be to the United States, the "giant of the north" can intervene through both government and private business agencies. The lesson of Chile for public policymakers in the rest of Latin America seems to be, "Thou shalt not institute a socialist economy, call it that, nationalize U.S. businesses, and follow a foreign policy independent of U.S. government interests."

There are certain things that Latin American governments cannot consider. The obvious exception to these generalizations is Cuba, where certain issues were raised and the U.S. opposition was foreseen, but by planning and a lot of luck the revolution survived. In Peru and Venezuela, major U.S. properties were nationalized without provoking a marine intervention. So far, however, these cases are the exceptions and not the rule. Nicaragua is the latest case of a country's being constrained in its policy options by the U.S. government, and especially after the March 1990 election of the U.S.-backed opposition candidate, the future of the Sandinista revolution is far from clear.

There are other more-subtle ways in which the United States manipulates Latin America's affairs. The Agency for International Development of the U.S. government has used its leverage to push certain programs: land reform in the 1960s, birth control in the 1970s, private-sector initiatives in the 1980s. Within these areas and elsewhere, AID officials assist the Latin American governments in operational plans. Likewise, international agencies dominated by the United States, such as the World Bank, the International Monetary Fund, and the Inter-American Development Bank, traditionally encourage the Latin American governments to make certain economic and fiscal policy decisions. For example, the IMF might push a Latin government to devalue its currency. If the country refuses, World Bank and IBD loans become unlikely, AID will be hesitant to offer credit to the country, and even the private banks of the United States and Western Europe will be reluctant to extend credit.

Other issues never arise and fall into the nondecision category because of the position of Latin America in the world political economy. Increasing national wealth means, in large part, obtaining higher prices for goods exported to the industrial world, which, in turn, leads to higher costs and less wealth for those industrialized countries, something they resist. There are many examples of the fact that industrialization in Latin America often means products that are more expensive in the short run than those that can be imported from the industrialized world. The major point is that because they are small, poor, and weak countries, the Latin American nations are severely constrained in their public policy options by the international political economy.

This situation has led to one school of thought—the dependency approach—whose basic premise is that Latin American underdevelopment is due not to the attitudes and institutions inherited from the Spanish and the Portuguese but, rather, to the dependent position of Latin America in the world economy. Although there are many kinds of dependency theorists, two basic strains of thought are predominant.

One group of these theorists sees the separation of an industrialized North from a primary-product-oriented South as the result of a conspiracy in which international capitalism works through trusts whose various holdings are intentionally meant to complement, not compete with, each other. If one subscribes to this conspiracy theory of capitalism, then the devils can be identified, perhaps eliminated, and presumably the plight of the poor can be ameliorated.

Other theorists of dependency see it more as a natural and an inevitable happening instead of a conspiracy. They argue that the development of the North and the underdevelopment of Latin America and the rest of the Third World go hand in hand. They say that Latin America has been and is financing the development of the United States and the nations of Western Europe, since those countries take more out of the region than they put in. Further, these theorists argue that dependency began when the European nations started their capitalist and mercantilist development in the sixteenth and seventeenth centuries.

Viewing the economic development of the world in this way, the dependency theorists reject certain theses often advanced by North American and Latin proponents of U.S. investment. The underdevelopment of Latin America was not caused by general backwardness or by the traditionalism of the area. Rather, underdevelopment in Latin America results from development in other parts of the world. As a corollary, the countries in Latin America have at no time paralleled the United States and the nations of Western Europe in their development, and this lack of similarity is owing to the northern countries having developed at a time when there were no other advanced countries. Further, the dependency theorists add that real economic development of Latin America will not come from import substitution. Although this technique might help the balance of payments in the short run, in the long run dependency on the industrialized North is even greater because of the need for continuing importation of technology, replacement parts, new machinery, and foreigners to run the industries.

Real economic development in Latin America will come, the dependency theorists argue, only when the influence of foreign capital and culture has been ended. The empirical evidence demonstrates that the years of the two world wars and the Great Depression were the only times that Latin Americans developed their own technologies and industries on a large scale. The prescription for the future, this school of thought suggests, is that the Latin Americans should divorce themselves from the industrialized countries once again.

For Latin American public policymaking, it is irrelevant whether dependency is the result of a conspiracy or is inevitable. The fact remains that industrial goods can frequently be imported more cheaply from the developed world than they can be produced in the nascent industries of Latin America. The dilemma, then, is how to convince the present generation to abstain from buying such goods so that future generations will have a better life. Further, in the smaller countries of Latin America, relatively autonomous development might be impossible, even if a generation or two of potential consumers make sacrifices. Some countries simply do not have the natural resources or the market size to make this goal possible. For this reason, one policy during the 1960s and 1970s called for the smaller countries of the area to join in common markets, such as the Central American Common Market and the Andean Pact. In such cases, public policymaking decided against purely national development and opted instead for economic development through cooperation and division of labor. By the 1980s, however, these common markets had, in effect, disappeared or were in decline. Having had only mixed results at best, the individual countries had decided, once again, to stress individual development.

In addition, and regardless of the arguments of the dependency theorists, most Latin American governments recognize they must deal realistically with the United States. For better or worse, the United States is the major political and economic power in the hemisphere, and Latin America is stuck in a dependency position. Hence, the real question is not whether Latin America can dispense with the United States but whether the Latin American countries can reap some advantages from this relationship. Can they get the capital and help that are necessary from the United States without losing their sovereignty? That is the trick. To try to achieve that goal, clever Latin American presidents as adeptly manipulate the U.S. embassy as the embassy does the politics of the Latin American countries—particularly if their country has commodities that the United States must have, or if it is of political or strategic importance to the United States.

CONCLUSIONS AND IMPLICATIONS

In this chapter, we have generalized about the issues and constraints of public policy in Latin America. Although there are great commonalities among the Latin American countries on these matters, there are also notable differences. We suggest that the following questions be considered as the country chapters are read:

1. What are the major issues of public policy in the individual Latin American countries? Are they the same as those analyzed in this chapter, or are there others of equal or greater importance?
2. Which issues lead to government policies and which do not and why?
3. What kinds of policies are designed? Are they distributive or redistributive?
4. What does the nature of the governing coalition suggest about which issues become policies? What variations exist among the several countries?

5. How effective is the bureaucracy in translating official policy outputs into policy outcomes? What are the ramifications, from a policy standpoint, of having or not having an effective bureaucracy?
6. In the case of each country, what are the major constraints on policymaking?
7. Who benefits from public policy: elites? the public?

We should warn that definitive answers to these questions should not always be expected. Study of public policy in Latin America has primarily occurred only since the mid-1970s, so the authors of the individual chapters have been hindered by a lack of empirical studies on which to base their conclusions. It is hoped that this problem will soon be rectified.

NOTES

1. Philippe C. Schmitter, "Military Intervention, Political Competitiveness, and Public Policy in Latin America: 1950–1967," in *Armies and Politics in Latin America,* ed. Abraham Lowenthal (New York: Holmes and Meier, 1976), p. 120.
2. Ibid., pp. 121–122.
3. Ibid., pp. 113–161.
4. Raymond Vernon, *The Dilemma of Mexico's Development* (Cambridge, Mass.: Harvard University Press, 1963).
5. Schmitter, "Military Intervention."

7
The Latin American Political Process and Its Present Crisis

North Americans often have difficulty conceiving of a Latin American political process or system. Because of frequent coups and repeated violations of constitutional precepts, the Latin American nations are instead thought of as having no system and only chaotic political processes. Such a view is myopic and mistaken and is based on a North American conception of what constitutes a political system and the proper political processes. Politics in Latin America is every bit as systematic as in North America, but the system is obviously quite different from what North Americans are used to.

It is not that Latin America has failed to develop a political system of its own but that residents of the United States have seldom attempted to understand either it or how it functions. A close examination reveals that the Latin American political systems are as rational (given the distinctiveness of Latin American political society), as complex, and as interesting as the North American ones. In this chapter, we shall be pulling together the various ideas and threads developed in earlier chapters to show the nature of the Latin American political system, broadly conceived, its various component parts and their interrelationships, and the system's present crisis.[1]

THE LATIN AMERICAN POLITICAL PROCESS

As a product of the Spanish and Portuguese political traditions, the Latin American political process is distinct from that of the Anglo-American nations. It often rests on different assumptions regarding the nature of humankind and how best to order social and political institutions. These differing traditions make Latin American politics distinct from North American politics, not necessarily less developed.

The Latin American political process is grounded historically on a set of assumptions and characteristic features that emphasize hierarchy, authority, personalism, family and kinship ties, centralization, the need for organic national unity, elaborate networks of patron-client relations, patrimonialism, and a pervasive pattern of vertical corporate organization. Many of these assumptions and concepts derived originally from Catholic precepts, particularly the Thomistic notions of hierarchy and authority, and to a large extent the givens of historic Catholic political culture still undergird the workings of the Latin American systems. But since the nineteenth century, many of these same assumptions have been given republican and/or secular bases, although in their basics they may not have changed very much.

Centralized, almost imperial rule is one of the chief characteristics of the Latin American political process. Much of Latin American history can be studied in terms of the effort to develop a centralized state capable of asserting its authority over distant territories and the diverse groups that make up each national society.

The president is the center of national political life. In theory and constitutionally, the president is the focus of decision making. The legislature, courts, and local governments are subordinated to the principle of strong, personalistic, executive-centered rule. It makes little difference whether one speaks of authoritarian right-wing regimes like Brazil's from 1964 to 1984 or revolutionary regimes like Cuba's; what is important is the system of executive-centered rule. The president is the focus of the system to an extent unknown in the United States. Presidential charisma, strength, and personality (or the lack thereof) are what make the system work or fail.

In nineteenth-century Latin American society, the three main societal groups were the church, the army, and the large landowners. These three constituted an impregnable system of power and were closely joined. In the absence of other organized centers of power, these three groups were the main corporate pillars of a traditional, agrarian, elite-dominated, and status quo–oriented society.

But toward the end of the nineteenth century and in the first decades of the twentieth century, new groups began to demand admission to the system. These included the business-industrial bourgeoisie, the new middle class, and eventually trade-union members and peasants. In other societies, such as Great Britain or the United States, the emergence of these new groups tended to give rise to a more liberal, pluralist, and democratic polity. In Latin America, the process was frequently different.

Although one should not understate the degrees of liberalism and republicanism present in Latin America (as demonstrated by the number of elected governments in the 1980s), and though some countries evolved in a pluralistic fashion, historically the more common pattern involved efforts to structure and control the admission of new groups to the system. Voting and the franchise were often carefully restricted, and political party activity was similarly controlled. Rather than allowing the free-wheeling, tumultuous pluralism of North American interest-group competition, the Latin American nations tried to regulate the process. They either policed closely the already existing groups or created official, government-run trade-union federations and peasant associations. In this way, they sought to co-opt the emerging middle sectors through the provision of government jobs and other benefits, and characteristically fashioned some strongly corporate (as distinct from pluralist) structures so as to keep the group struggle—particularly labor relations—under control. They also sought to maintain the unity of state and society, to forge links between workers and employers, and thus to avoid class struggle and the potential for revolutionary upheaval.

New groups could be admitted to the system and some change could go forward, but only under government and elite auspices and regulation. The hierarchical, structured, and elite-dominated system of the past was thus generally retained. Two conditions were necessary for the admission of a new power contender into the system. The first was that the group had to demonstrate a power capability: that it was strong enough to challenge the system and therefore deserved to have its voice heard. This factor helps explain why organized labor was admitted to the system in the 1930s and 1940s and the peasants only in the 1960s and 1970s—if at all. The second condition was that the group had to agree to abide by certain rules of the game. It was not permitted to destroy other groups in the system by revolutionary means, and those that tried to do so were often suppressed. Each group had to agree to accept its place in the system, which meant that it was not allowed to put forward what were considered exorbitant demands.

This system, which allows the gradual absorption of new groups into the political process without destroying the old ones or upsetting the basic hierarchical structure of society, had several important implications. It tended to concentrate power in the hands of the state and its growing administrative apparatus. It was the state that regulated the entire process by which new groups were admitted, licensed, and given juridical personality—that is, recognition and the right to bargain in the political process. In the country chapters, it is interesting to see the different patterns by which these new groups in Latin America were admitted to the system (for example, through the populist corporatism of Cárdenas in Mexico, the rigid controls of Trujillo in the Dominican Republic, the earlier liberalism of Chile, the authoritarian systems of Vargas in Brazil or Perón in Argentina), as well as to contrast these patterns with some parallel phenomena in the United States.

The state is now the great national *patrón*, replacing the local landowners and oligarchs of the past. It is from the state and its head that jobs, patronage, money, and favors flow. Political disputes tend to be handled administratively and bureaucratically, rather than through the open competition of party politics. The oft-stated goal of both leftist and rightist regimes is to have a technocratic administration that is devoid of divisive party squabbling and conflict-prone interest groups. That goal helps explain why political parties in Latin America have seldom enjoyed the importance they do in U.S. politics, since it is the state system and administration—and who controls them—that are critical and not the political parties. It also explains the effort oftentimes to incorporate the interest groups directly into the state apparatus as direct creations of the state or appendages of it.

Politics in Latin America revolves not just around ideological and class issues but around patronage, kinship, and friendship—except that now the patronage networks are larger and more elaborate than ever before. Who controls the presidential palace and its patronage opportunities is a matter of critical importance. A group of officials, and sometimes entire trade unions or peasant leagues, may tie themselves to one person to whom they are often related by blood or marriage and ride with this individual to the pinnacles of power—or crash down in the event of failure. In return for loyalty and support, the group or individual expects jobs and favors. It is a classic patronage pattern now greatly elaborated in a complex network of national, often highly institutionalized *patrón*-client relations.

Elections in such a system are important, but they do not always carry the definite legitimacy that elections have in the Anglo-American democracies. Elections may be genuinely competitive, but they also may serve to ratify the authority of a *patrón* (president, labor leader, or the like) who is already in power rather than to give the voters a clear choice. When elections are competitive, they are often manipulated to ensure that the government candidate wins. And even when the ballots are honestly counted, elections are viewed as providing only a tentative mandate. There are other routes to power that also enjoy legitimacy: the general strike, the coup d'état, the heroic guerrilla struggle. This situation makes the entire Latin American political system more tentative, more unstable, more open to rapid changeovers than is true in the United States. It also makes the job of the Latin American president, who must juggle all the contending forces without losing control of any of them, difficult and complex. In the shifting quicksands of Latin American politics, a president's power base may be eroded, a president's clientela will go elsewhere if they feel they have not received certain goods and favors, and there is always the potential for a president to be ousted from power at almost any time.

The accommodative, co-optive nature of the Latin American systems has also tended to rule out revolutionary transformations. That statement may sound strange, for there have been many revolutions in Latin America. But these have generally been revolutions in the palace guard, implying the substitution of one elite for another, and full-scale social revolutions have been rare. Only in Mexico, Cuba, and Nicaragua, and to a more limited extent Bolivia and Peru, have genuinely social revolutionary transformations occurred, and even in some of those cases (Cuba constituting the major exception, followed by Nicaragua), the restructuring that resulted showed considerable continuity with the past. Co-optation, the gradual absorption of new groups, the creation of official agencies of the state to meet the challenge of rising new groups, and the elaboration of larger patronage networks have helped militate against the possibility of violent revolution from below.

The role of the United States in this regard is interesting. Not only is the United States the most important external actor with which the Latin American nations must deal, but the U.S. embassy is one of the most influential internal forces as well. Most of the considerable amount of U.S. assistance over the last few years has been oriented toward support of the existing order in Latin America and the defense of the status quo. Although many U.S. officials are liberals and interested in change, the changes they have proposed have been gradual, piecemeal, evolutionary, and in support of the accommodative, nonrevolutionary politics described earlier. U.S. aid has also been based on the assumption of a fundamental commonality of interests between the United States and Latin America. These assumptions and policies have served to support the system in Latin America; by the same token, U.S. aid and influence have been employed to frustrate revolutionary challenges to that system.

These brief comments cannot do full justice to the richness and complexity of the Latin American political system and processes, or to the variations within the several countries. But they do serve to indicate some of the main features of the system and how it operates.

THE BIASES OF THE SYSTEM

All political systems have biases of one sort or another, biases that favor certain class, regional, or political interests at the expense of others. Let us look at the biases that are built into the Latin American system.

It should be said first that, contrary to numerous popular prejudices, many of the Latin American systems, with their distinct institutions, have proved to be quite effective in managing the twentieth-century change process. Economic growth and industrialization have been greatly stimulated, sometimes (as in the cases of Brazil or Mexico) at almost miraculous rates; per capita income and living standards have risen; social services and programs have been vastly expanded; and rising social forces have been progressively admitted as new participants in the system. Under the right circumstances, the centralized, technocratic, executive-centered, elite-directed, corporatist-controlled, frequently authoritarian and hierarchical, national patronage-dominated systems of Latin America can be quite efficient and responsive, which makes a great deal of growth and modernization possible.

But there are also biases within these systems that command attention. This section deals with the value, class, political, and economic assumptions that undergird the system, showing both how it has worked historically and why it is now being so strongly challenged.

First, the system is based on the assumption of a wide community of interest within the nation and shared popular values and outlooks, but such a community of interest was probably stronger in the sleepier, more Catholic nineteenth century than it is now. In the countries where those traditional values still hold or have been successfully secularized and popularized, the Latin American system will probably continue to function as before. But where newer values and concepts have been strongly felt, where Marxist and other revolutionary ideologies have gained mass appeal, and where groups have organized on bases other than those previously considered to be the only legitimate ones, the challenges are no longer simply a way of demonstrating power capability (and, hence, the desire to be admitted to the system), but they may be aimed at toppling the system altogether and replacing it with an alternative form. In addition, the assumed community of interest between the United States and Latin America is being increasingly questioned.

Second, within the Latin American system there is a strong bias in favor of the political status quo. This is not to say that change never occurs, but the changes tend to be within carefully defined boundaries and according to the rules of the game. The accommodative nature of the politics outlined earlier means that although new groups are assimilated into the system, old ones cannot be disposed of. Hence the army, the church, and the landed elites in Latin America continue to enjoy power and a privileged place out of proportion to their numbers. The persistence of many anachronistic groups and practices has given rise to a certain "mausoleum effect," whereby Latin America retains features of its semifeudal past that have been confined to the ash cans of history in other nations but serve in Latin America to perpetuate the status quo.

Third, there is a class bias built into the Latin American system. New groups are admitted but only on the condition that they accept the rules of the game established by the older wielders of power, the elite and the rising middle sectors. A patron-client system similarly involves a two-way give-and-take, but it is the patrons who receive most of the benefits while their clients are obligated to accept their station in life and the usually meager rewards that come their way. The trade unions may gain certain benefits, but these are generally doled out paternalistically. The government, dominated by the elites and the bourgeoisie, controls the process by which labor participates in the system, and the unions themselves tend to be headed, not by rank-and-file members, but by officials acceptable to the elites and often appointed by them. Peasants, Indians, and marginal laborers may be wholly excluded from participation. Similarly, the economic growth that has occurred has benefited the lowest classes very little, raised living standards somewhat for organized workers, profited the middle sectors to a greater extent, and enriched the elites most of all. Although much development has occurred throughout Latin America, it is the elites and upper bourgeoisie who have continued to control the entire process and who have been its prime beneficiaries.

Finally, there is the necessity for and assumption of sustained economic growth if this accommodative, co-optive political process is to work. In order to provide more pieces of pie to the newer groups, without depriving any of the older groups of their share, the pie must be steadily enlarged. During the 1930s, 1940s, 1950s, 1960s, and early 1970s (precisely the heyday of the system here described), economic growth occurred at a steady, if seldom spectacular, rate. Because their economies were expanding, the Latin American countries could afford to give more benefits to labor and to peasants—indeed, to all groups in the system. The model of the political process described here—involving the gradual assimilation of new groups, greater benefits, and rising living standards— was predicated on continued steady growth rates and, hence, more and more funds to buy off revolutionary challengers. But what if, as in recent years, the Latin American nations should be confronted with a situation in which the pie is no longer an expanding one but a stagnant or, in the case of some nations, a contracting one? Then how long could the political model outlined here—a relatively peaceful, stable, consensual, and accommodative one—be expected to last? These are the questions the Latin American nations must now face.

THE PRESENT CRISIS

The Latin American political systems are not the entirely rigid, static, unchanging systems of popular stereotype. Up to a point, in fact, they have proved to be quite flexible, adaptive, and accommodative, and many of the countries have recently taken important steps by electing civilian presidents. The nations of the area have accepted and assimilated a great deal of modernization, but without undergoing much change in their basic order or power relationships. The question now is whether they have reached the point where the old assumptions no longer hold, where the older model is no longer effective, where it is being increasingly challenged and in some cases superseded by alternative conceptions.

Sustained economic growth is an absolute requirement for the maintenance of the system, but such growth can no longer be taken for granted. Brazil's economic "miracle" is over, as is Mexico's; both countries are now being riven by severe economic and political tensions and conflicts. Sugar and coffee prices were up for a time but are down again, and, in any case, such boom-and-bust cycles cannot be the basis for steady, sustained growth. U.S. economic assistance is way down since the high point of the 1960s, there is little new investment, and the terms-of-trade imbalance between the commodity-producing nations of Latin America and the industrialized countries of the North is tipped disastrously in favor of the latter. Many Latin Americans are therefore questioning their situation of dependence vis-à-vis the United States: whether Latin American economic interests are not at loggerheads with those of the United States instead of being compatible with them; whether U.S. prosperity is in part based on keeping Latin America underdeveloped.

In the early 1980s most of the Latin American nations faced a stagflation far worse than that of the United States. The GDP rates leveled off and in some countries actually went into a decline. Some countries have recovered subsequently, but most have remained stagnant. Inflation runs from 30 percent to over 1,000 percent per year; unemployment and underemployment affect between 20 percent and 50 percent of the work forces. In the 1970s the price most Latin American countries had to pay for oil almost ruined them and led to huge balance-of-payments deficits and immense foreign debts. Argentina, Brazil, and other countries may have to default on their outstanding debts, and several other nations of the area are on the brink of financial disaster. It is clear that a political order based on the absolute necessity of an expanding pie cannot last long when the pie stops expanding or shrinks.

Coupled with the economic crisis is a rising popular challenge. This challenge has taken on strong class overtones and is increasingly the source of mass discontent, violence, and sporadic upheaval. The students are often in revolt; guerrilla movements remain active; workers are taking direct action; peasants are seizing private lands. In the past such protest movements could be contained through either mild authoritarianism or else partial acquiescence to the demands. But now the protests have grown into genuine class disputes, and in some areas they are getting out of hand; the response to them has therefore grown fiercer and more brutal. These protests have sometimes been exacerbated by the Soviet Union and Cuba because of their desire to advance their own interests in the region.

Finally, the historical model is being questioned by a variety of political actors who were once its staunchest supporters. As Juan Velasco Alvarado, former president and general of Peru, has stated:

> Our revolution is not interested in the false participation demanded by traditional politicians of the old system. The legitimacy of this Revolutionary Government cannot rest on the respect for the rules of a politically decadent game which only benefits the privileged groups of the country. Our objectives have nothing to do with the traditional form of politics, of a political system which is rotten to the core because it has never served to defend the authentic interests of the Peruvian people.[2]

In short, even the armed forces in Latin America, or some factions thereof, have come to believe that the traditional co-optive model is inadequate for today's needs. As Fidel Castro once neatly put it, "The fire has spread to the firehouse." Similar splits have occurred within the once monolithic church, the divisions within the middle class over the continued relevance and appropriateness of the older pattern have also widened, and the present student generation is strongly oriented toward nationalism and socialism. There is among all groups a general sense of malaise and discontent, of uncertainty and impending change, of the unraveling and even disintegration of society—a feeling that one epoch and pattern of rule may have ended and that another, although ill defined, may be about to begin. These changes indicate that interpretations of Latin America must be based not just on the traditional patterns of patronage and co-optive politics but on other interpretations as well: class analysis, dependency analysis, and the political economy of the international system.

REVOLUTION AND REACTION: THE NEW ALTERNATIVES

In a period of economic stagnation and downturn, the competition for the few available pieces of pie has accelerated, and throughout Latin America violence has increased. At the same time, the conflict among the various participating groups in the Latin American political process has in some countries produced a situation of paralysis and immobility, of spiraling discord and conflict. With no one group able to command a majority or rule by itself; with power often more or less evenly shared among eight or nine leading power contenders (army, church, oligarchy, business elites, middle sectors, bureaucracy, professionals, labor, universities); and with deep internal divisions and fragmentation present within each of these groups, decision making and policy implementation have been stymied. Not only have the problems multiplied of late, but Latin America's historic way of resolving them seems no longer to work.

These challenges and crises have increasingly brought into question the capacity of the traditional Latin American system to respond as in the past. One should not underestimate the ability of the traditional elites to survive the present crisis as they have others previously, to fashion new formulas designed to co-opt the newest challengers to their rule while keeping the historic structure intact. But there is no doubt that this traditional system is being challenged, questioned, and undermined to a degree never before experienced.

At least nine major alternatives seem possible at present, with a high likelihood of continued experimentation with new formulas or the borrowing from several to form new permutations. These alternatives, the reasons for them, and the distinct national variations should be kept in mind as one reads the country analyses in Parts 2 and 3. The nine alternatives are these:

1. the maintenance of traditional, authoritarian, almost nineteenth-century politics and society in a country largely unaffected by the revolutionary currents described (Paraguay, at least until recently)

2. a situation in the more advanced nations of recurrent crisis, breakdown, and fragmentation with seemingly no formula available to successfully resolve the national malaise (Argentina since the 1930s and perhaps Brazil)

3. a full-scale socialist revolution (Cuba under Castro, Sandinista Nicaragua)

4. a situation of revolution or social transformation frustrated through U.S. intervention (Guatemala, the Dominican Republic [now recovering from that intervention], Chile, and perhaps El Salvador)

5. a pattern of societal mobilization, conflict, paralysis, and endemic civil war so severe that the military is compelled to step in, restore order forcefully, and suppress groups such as workers and peasants who had previously been mobilized (primarily Bolivia, Peru; formerly Argentina, Brazil, Chile, Uruguay)

6. a democratic breakthrough (Costa Rica, Venezuela, and perhaps Argentina, Peru, Ecuador, Honduras, Chile, and Brazil—all of which democratically elected presidents during the 1980s for the first time in many years)

7. a single-party regime combining elements of both mass mobilization and control (Bolivia, for a time, and Mexico)

8. a military regime that takes a leftist rather than a rightist approach, stakes out a nationalist position, and ushers in revolution from above before it occurs from below (Peru during the military government between 1968 and 1973; some aspects of this pattern were also present for a time in Bolivia, Ecuador, El Salvador, Honduras, Panama)

9. a hodgepodge regime combining elitist features with democratic ones and continuing to muddle along largely in the historical pattern (Colombia and the Dominican Republic; perhaps Honduras, Paraguay)

NOTES

1. This discussion and that in the following section derive from Charles W. Anderson, "The Latin American Political System," Chapter 4 of his *Politics and Economic Change in Latin America* (Princeton, N.J.: Van Nostrand, 1967).

2. Quoted in David Scott Palmer, *"Revolution from Above": Military Government and Popular Participation in Peru, 1968–1972,* Cornell University Dissertation Series, Latin American Studies Program (Ithaca, N.Y.: 1973).

SUGGESTIONS FOR FURTHER READING

Adams, Richard N., et al. *Social Change in Latin America Today.* New York: Vintage, 1961.

Adie, Robert F., and Guy E. Poitras. *Latin America: The Politics of Immobility.* Englewood Cliffs, N.J.: Prentice-Hall, 1974.

Alba, Victor. *Politics and the Labor Movement in Latin America*. Stanford, Calif.: Stanford University Press, 1968.

———. *The Latin Americans*. New York: Praeger, 1969.

Alexander, Robert J. *Organized Labor in Latin America*. New York: Harper and Row, 1965.

———. *Agrarian Reform in Latin America*. New York: Macmillan, 1974.

Anderson, Charles W. *Politics and Economic Change in Latin America*. Princeton, N.J.: Van Nostrand, 1967.

Blackman, Morris J., and Ronald G. Hellman. *Terms of Conflict: Ideology in Latin American Politics*. Philadelphia: Institute for the Study of Human Issues, 1977.

Blasier, Cole, ed. *Constructive Change in Latin America*. Pittsburgh: University of Pittsburgh Press, 1968.

Boxer, C. R. *Four Centuries of Portuguese Expansion*. Berkeley: University of California Press, 1969.

Burnett, Ben G., and Kenneth E. Johnson, eds. *Political Forces in Latin America*. Belmont, Calif.: Wadsworth, 1970.

Burns, E. Bradford. *Latin America: A Concise Interpretative History*. Englewood Cliffs, N.J.: Prentice-Hall, 1977.

Cardoso, F. H., and E. Faletio. *Dependency and Development in Latin America*. Berkeley: University of California Press, 1978.

Cespedes, Guillermo. *Latin America: The Early Years*. New York: Knopf, 1974.

Chalmers, Douglas A. "The Politicized State in Latin America." In *Authoritarianism and Corporalism in Latin America*, edited by James Malloy, pp. 23–46. Pittsburgh: University of Pittsburgh Press, 1977.

Chalmers, Douglas A., ed. *Changing Latin America*. New York: Academy of Political Science, Columbia University, 1972.

Chaplin, David, ed. *Population Policies and Growth in Latin America*. Lexington, Mass.: Lexington Books, 1971.

Chevalier, Francois. *Land and Society in Colonial Mexico*. Berkeley: University of California Press, 1970.

Chilcote, Ronald H., and Joel C. Edelstein, eds. *Latin America: The Struggle with Dependency and Beyond*. Cambridge, Mass.: Schenkman, 1974.

Cockcroft, James D., et al. *Dependence and Underdevelopment: Latin America's Political Economy*. Garden City, N.Y.: Doubleday, 1972.

———. *Neighbors in Turmoil*. New York: Harper and Row, 1989.

Collier, David, ed. *The New Authoritarianism in Latin America*. Princeton, N.J.: Princeton University Press, 1979.

Cortes Conde, Roberto. *The First Stages of Modernization in Spanish America*. New York: Harper and Row, 1974.

Cotler, Julio, and Richard Fagen, eds. *Latin America and the United States: The Changing Political Realities*. Stanford, Calif.: Stanford University Press, 1975.

Davis, Stanley M., and Louis Wolf Goodman. *Workers and Managers in Latin America*. Lexington, Mass.: Heath, 1972.

Dealy, Glen C. *The Public Man: An Interpretation of Latin American and Other Catholic Countries*. Amherst: University of Massachusetts Press, 1977.

Duncan, W. Raymond. *Latin American Politics: A Developmental Approach*. New York: Praeger, 1976.

Duncan, W. Raymond, and James N. Goodsell. *The Quest for Change in Latin America*. New York: Oxford University Press, 1970.

Einaudi, Luigi R., ed. *Beyond Cuba: Latin America Takes Charge of Its Future*. Russak, N.Y.: Crane, 1974.

Elliot, J. H. *The Old World and the New, 1492–1650.* Cambridge: Cambridge University Press, 1960.

Erickson, Kenneth Paul. *The Brazilian Corporative State and Working-Class Politics.* Berkeley: University of California Press, 1977.

Feder, Ernest. *The Rape of the Peasantry.* Garden City, N.Y.: Doubleday, 1971.

Fitch, John Samuel. *The Military Coup d'Etat as a Political Process: Ecuador, 1948–1966.* Baltimore, Md.: Johns Hopkins University Press, 1977.

Freyre, Gilberto. *The Masters and the Slaves.* New York: Knopf, 1964.

Gibson, Charles. *Spain in America.* New York: Harper and Row, 1966.

Glade, William P. *The Latin American Economies: A Study of Their Institutional Evolution.* New York: Van Nostrand, 1969.

Gott, Richard. *Guerrilla Movements in Latin America.* London: Nelson, 1970.

Graham, Lawrence, and Clarence E. Thurber, eds. *Development Administration in Latin America.* Durham, N.C.: Duke University Press, 1973.

Greenfield, Sidney M. "The Patrimonial State and Patron-Client Relations in Iberia and Latin America." Occasional Paper no. 1, University of Massachusetts, Program in Latin American Studies, 1976.

Halperin Donghi, Tulio. *The Aftermath of Revolution in Latin America.* New York: Harper and Row, 1973.

Haring, Clarence. *The Spanish Empire in America.* New York: Harcourt Brace, 1963.

Harris, Louis K., and Victor Alba. *The Political Culture and Behavior of Latin America.* Kent, Ohio: Kent State University Press, 1974.

Heath, Dwight, and Richard Adams, eds. *Contemporary Cultures and Societies of Latin America.* New York: Random, 1965.

Herring, Hubert. *A History of Latin America.* New York: Knopf, 1968.

Hirschman, Albert O. *Journeys Toward Progress: Studies of Economic Policy-Making in Latin America.* Garden City, N.Y.: Doubleday, 1965.

Horowitz, Irving L. *Masses in Latin America.* New York: Oxford University Press, 1970.

James, Preston. *Latin America.* New York: Odyssey, 1969.

Johnson, John J. *Political Change in Latin America: The Emergence of the Middle Sectors.* Stanford, Calif.: Stanford University Press, 1958.

————. *The Military and Society in Latin America.* Stanford, Calif.: Stanford University Press, 1964.

Kantor, Harry. *Patterns of Politics and Political Systems of Latin America.* Chicago: Rand McNally, 1969.

Karst, Kenneth, and Keith Rosen. *Law and Development in Latin America.* Berkeley: University of California Press, 1975.

Kirkpatrick, F. A. *The Spanish Conquistadores.* New York: World, 1962.

Landsberger, Henry A. *Latin American Peasant Movements.* Ithaca, N.Y.: Cornell University Press, 1969.

Landsberger, Henry A., ed. *The Church and Social Change in Latin America.* Notre Dame, Ind.: Notre Dame University Press, 1970.

Lewis, Oscar. *The Children of Sanchez.* New York: Random, 1961.

Lieuwen, Edwin. *Arms and Politics in Latin America.* New York: Praeger, 1961.

Lipset, Seymour, and Aldo Solari, eds. *Elites in Latin America.* New York: Oxford University Press, 1967.

Lowenthal, Abraham F., ed. *Armies and Politics in Latin America.* New York: Holmes and Meier, 1976.

Lynch, John. *The Spanish-American Revolutions, 1808–1826*. New York: Norton, 1973.

McCoy, Terry, ed. *The Dynamics of Population Policy in Latin America*. Cambridge, Mass.: Ballinger, 1974.

McDonald, Ronald H. *Party Systems and Elections in Latin America*. Chicago: Markham, 1971.

————. "Nación y Estado en América Latina." *Estudios Andinos* 10 (1974–1975).

Malloy, James, ed. *Authoritarianism and Corporatism in Latin America*. Pittsburgh: University of Pittsburgh Press, 1977.

Mander, John. *The Unrevolutionary Society: The Power of Latin American Conservatism in a Changing World*. New York: Knopf, 1969.

Martz, John, ed. *The Dynamics of Change in Latin American Politics*. Englewood Cliffs, N.J.: Prentice-Hall, 1971.

Mecham, J. Lloyd. *Church and State in Latin America*. Chapel Hill: University of North Carolina Press, 1966.

Mercier Vega, Luis. *Roads to Power in Latin America*. New York: Praeger, 1969.

Moreno, Francisco J., and Barbara Mitrani, eds. *Conflict and Violence in Latin American Politics*. New York: Crowell, 1971.

Morison, Samuel Eliot. *The European Discovery of America*. New York: Oxford University Press, 1971.

Mutchler, David E. *The Church as a Political Force in Latin America*. New York: Praeger, 1971.

Needler, Martin. *Political Development in Latin America*. New York: Random, 1968.

Needler, Martin, ed. *Political Systems of Latin America*. New York: Van Nostrand, 1970.

————. *The Problem of Democracy in Latin America*. Lexington, Mass.: Lexington Books, 1987.

O'Donnell, Guillermo A. *Modernization and Bureaucratic Authoritarianism*. Berkeley: Institute of International Studies, University of California, 1973.

Paz, Octavio. *The Labyrinth of Solitude*. New York: Grove, 1961.

Petras, James. *Politics and Social Structure in Latin America*. New York: Monthly Review, 1970.

Petras, James, and Maurice Zeitlin, eds. *Latin America: Reform or Revolution?* New York: Fawcett, 1968.

Pike, Frederick B. *Spanish America, 1900–1970*. New York: Norton, 1973.

Pike, Frederick B., and Thomas Stritch, eds. *The New Corporatism*. Notre Dame, Ind.: University of Notre Dame Press, 1974.

Powelson, John P. *Latin America: Today's Economic and Social Revolution*. New York: McGraw-Hill, 1964.

Sarfatti, Magali. *Spanish Bureaucratic Patrimonialism in America*. Berkeley: Institute of International Studies, University of California, 1966.

Sheahan, John. *Patterns of Development in Latin America*. Princeton, N.J.: Princeton University Press, 1987.

Sigmund, Paul. *Multinationals in Latin America*. Madison: University of Wisconsin Press, 1980.

Sigmund, Paul, ed. *Models of Change in Latin America*. New York: Praeger, 1970.

Silvert, Kalman H. *The Conflict Society: Reaction and Revolution in Latin America*. New York: American Universities Field Staff, 1966.

Sloan, John W. *Public Policy in Latin America*. Pittsburgh: University of Pittsburgh Press, 1984.

Smith, T. Lynn, ed. *Agrarian Reform in Latin America*. New York: Knopf, 1965.
Stavenhagen, Rodolfo, ed. *Agrarian Problems and Peasant Movements in Latin America*. Garden City, N.Y.: Doubleday, 1970.
Stein, Stanley J., and Barbara H. Stein. *The Colonial Heritage of Latin America*. New York: Oxford University Press, 1970.
Stepan, Alfred. *The State and Society: Peru in Comparative Perspective*. Princeton, N.J.: Princeton University Press, 1978.
Stycos, J. Mayone. *Human Fertility in Latin America*. Ithaca, N.J.: Cornell University Press, 1968.
─────── . *Ideology, Faith, and Family Planning in Latin America*. New York: McGraw-Hill, 1971.
Tannenbaum, Frank. *Ten Keys to Latin America*. New York: Vintage, 1962.
Vallier, Ivan. *Catholicism, Social Control, and Modernization in Latin America*. Englewood Cliffs, N.J.: Prentice-Hall, 1970.
Van Niekirk, A. E. *Populism and Political Development in Latin America*. Rotterdam: University Press, 1974.
Veliz, Claudio. *The Politics of Conformity in Latin America*. New York: Oxford University Press, 1967.
─────── . *The Centralist Tradition in Latin America*. Princeton, N.J.: Princeton University Press, 1980.
Veliz, Claudio, ed. *Obstacles to Change in Latin America*. New York: Oxford University Press, 1965.
Wagley, Charles. *The Latin American Tradition*. New York: Columbia University Press, 1968.
Wauchope, Robert, ed., *The Indian Background of Latin American History*. New York: Knopf, 1970.
Wesson, Robert G. *Democracy in Latin America*. New York: Praeger, 1982.
Whither Latin America? New York: Monthly Review, 1963.
Wiarda, Howard J. *Corporatism and Development in Latin America*. Boulder, Colo.: Westview Press, 1981.
─────── . *In Search of Policy: The United States and Latin America*. Washington, D.C.: American Enterprise Institute, 1984.
Wiarda, Howard J., ed. *Politics and Social Change in Latin America*. Rev. ed. Amherst: University of Massachusetts Press, 1982.
─────── . *Rift and Revolution: The Central American Imbroglio*. Washington, D.C.: American Enterprise Institute, 1984.
Willems, Emilio. *Latin American Culture*. New York: Harper and Row, 1975.
Williams, Edward J. *Latin American Christian Democratic Parties*. Knoxville: University of Tennessee Press, 1967.
─────── . *The Political Themes of Inter-American Relations*. N. Scituate, Mass.: Duxbury, 1971.
Williams, Edward J., and Freeman Wright. *Latin American Politics: A Developmental Approach*. Palo Alto, Calif.: Mayfield, 1975.
Worcester, Donald E., and Wendell G. Schaeffer. *The Growth and Culture of Latin America*. New York: Oxford University Press, 1970.
Wynia, Gary W. *The Politics of Latin American Development*. New York: Cambridge University Press, 1984.
Zea, Leopoldo. *The Latin American Mind*. Norman: University of Oklahoma Press, 1963.

Part 2

The political systems of South America

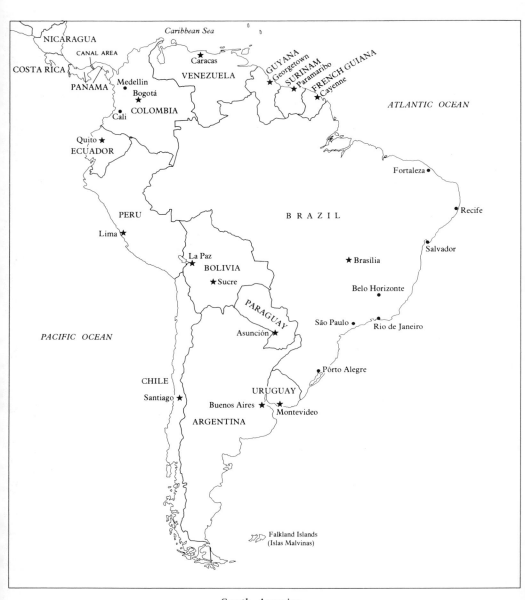

South America

8
Argentina: Politics in a Conflict Society

PETER G. SNOW
GARY W. WYNIA

Argentina is one of the most highly developed nations in the world—if development is thought of in exclusively social and economic terms. The people of Argentina are literate, urban, and relatively prosperous. And, in spite of the nation's image as a beef and wheat producer, three times as much of the gross domestic product comes from manufacturing as from agriculture. There is a large middle class, and a huge part of the urban working class belongs to powerful trade unions.

The political side of the picture, however, is quite different. During the last half century, there has been very little political stability. (Thirteen presidents have been removed from office by force; not a single civilian president has served a full term.) And, during the last quarter century, the level of political violence and repression has been higher than in any other Latin American nation (during the 1970s, perhaps as high as anywhere in the world).

Since economic, social, and political development are often thought of as going hand in hand, the vast disparity in Argentina between political development and social and economic development seems paradoxical. A great deal of time and effort has been expended in an attempt to find an intrinsically Argentine explanation for this apparent paradox. Only recently have scholars begun to question the very existence of the paradox and to examine the possibility that the high levels of social and economic development are the cause of political instability.

Samuel Huntington has written that violence and instability are "in large part the product of rapid social change and the rapid mobilization of new groups into politics coupled with the slow development of political institutions."[1] It is not at all difficult to make the case that this is exactly

---

Professor Wynia has updated Snow's chapter for this edition.

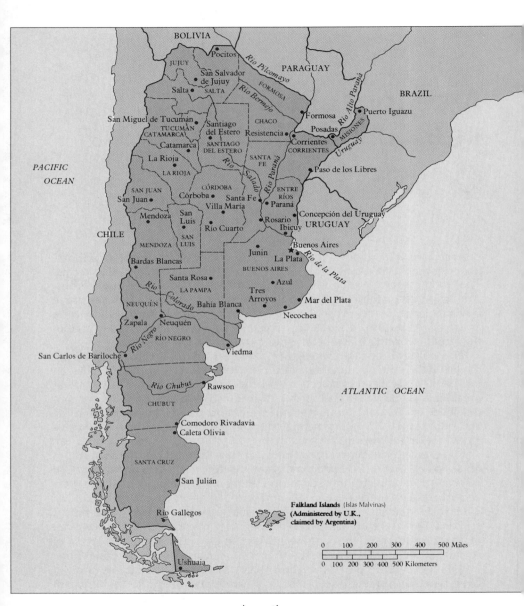

Argentina

what has occurred in Argentina. New social groups there were politicized earlier, more thoroughly, and more rapidly than in any other Latin American nation. The dramatic increases in political participation in 1912 and again in 1945 were not fully accepted by the older elites; the political system that allowed first the middle class and then the working class to gain an important voice in the government lost much of its legitimacy in the eyes of the upper class, and yet no new system was created to replace it. The result was that political groups began to confront each other nakedly, for there were neither institutions nor leaders that were recognized as legitimate intermediaries.[2] This problem, unfortunately, is one for which there are no simple solutions.

THE SOCIOECONOMIC BACKGROUND

Of all the nations of Latin America, Argentina is the one furthest removed from the stereotypical impressions held by many North Americans. In Argentina, one finds 28 million highly literate, well-fed people almost uniformly of European ancestry, who inhabit the world's eighth-largest nation, virtually all of which lies in the Temperate Zone. Almost a third of these people live in metropolitan Buenos Aires, one of the world's largest and most cosmopolitan cities. Even those living outside Buenos Aires fail to conform to the stereotypical image that sees them as poverty-stricken peasants working someone else's land. Certainly there are landless peasants in Argentina, but not nearly as many as might be expected. Almost three-fourths of the non–Buenos Aires population lives in urban centers, a fourth in cities of over 100,000 people.

For many years now Argentina has been an almost completely "white" nation. The Indian population has steadily decreased, not just relatively but also in absolute numbers. Today there are probably no more than 100,000 Indians in Argentina, and these are concentrated near the northwestern frontier. In the nineteenth century, when most of the Indians were killed in order to push the frontier to the south, the mestizos (a mixture of Indian and European) were absorbed by waves of European immigrants. Presently about 10 percent of the population is classified as mestizo, and these people appear to be concentrated in rural areas near the northern and western borders. There are virtually no blacks in Argentina. Although numerically significant at the time of independence, they have been rapidly assimilated into the general population until their number has dropped to about 5,000.

In spite of the swift move toward urbanization and industrialization, agriculture still provides the livelihood for about a fifth of the economically active population. Another third is engaged in the industrial sector of the economy, with the largest number working in food-processing, construction, textiles, and metallurgical industries. The remaining 45 percent is engaged in commerce and services. The largest groups within this sector are businesspeople and their employees, public officials, and domestic servants. It is the tertiary sector that is growing in relative size while the percentage of the population engaged in agriculture is declining and the industrial sector remains relatively constant. A major part of the growth of the tertiary sector is a result of the ever-increasing size of the bureaucracy, which now employs almost one out of every ten economically active citizens.

The often-repeated bromide about the lack of a middle class in Latin America simply is not true of Argentina, where about half of the population can be so classified (at least in terms of being neither upper class nor working class). However, this middle class—or, more appropriately, middle sector—is in almost no way a cohesive group. Wealthy businesspeople, members of the liberal professions, and clerks in government offices have little in common and certainly lack a single coherent world view that could be translated into political action.

PRE-1930 POLITICAL HISTORY: THE PERIOD OF DEVELOPMENT

The area that is now Argentina was originally settled by two separate streams of colonization. The first, coming from Peru, entered from the northwest and founded the towns of Mendoza, San Luis, Tucumán, San Juan, and Córdoba during the last half of the sixteenth century; the second, coming directly from Spain, settled along the Río de la Plata estuary. Throughout most of the colonial period the people of Buenos Aires and those of the interior lived quite separate existences. The interior was developed primarily to provide food, livestock, and textiles for the mining areas of Peru while Buenos Aires remained oriented toward Europe.

Prior to 1776 Argentina was part of the viceroyalty of Peru. The area was of little importance to Spain, largely because of its lack of precious metals. However, as the population increased and as the Portuguese in Brazil came to be seen as a threat, a new viceroyalty was created with its seat in Buenos Aires. Nevertheless, peninsula-born Spaniards continued to monopolize all high political offices, while those born in the colony were denied any appreciable influence in political affairs. Of greater significance, perhaps, is the fact that effective political control of the region was exceptionally difficult if not impossible. Although the lines of authority (running from the king of Spain, through the viceroy, to the local intendants) were clear, a number of factors militated against the uniform implementation of policy. Among these factors were (1) the great distance between population centers; (2) the overall scarcity of population (at the end of the colonial period there were fewer than 500,000 inhabitants in an area half the size of the United States); and (3) a largely rural, almost nomadic population. These factors led to deep-seated feelings of regional loyalty that later increased greatly the difficulty of creating a nation.

In 1808, Spanish authority in the New World was weakened immeasurably by the French invasion of Spain and the overthrow of King Ferdinand VII. Two years later, when the last vestiges of Spanish authority on the Iberian peninsula were gone, the lines of legitimacy were blurred, at best, and the viceroys found themselves in virtually untenable positions. On May 25, 1810, the Buenos Aires city council deposed the viceroy and assumed control of the city. This was the beginning of the independence movement, although independence was not formally declared for another six years.

Between 1810 and 1819 the Argentines fought not only the Spaniards but also the Paraguayans, Uruguayans, Brazilians, and, most frequently, each other. Although the southern part of the continent was free from Spanish control by 1819, a series of juntas, triumvirates, and supreme directors came and went without any success in the quest for national unification. Although the level of violence declined after 1819, until 1862 very little progress was made toward the creation of a single nation. During this period there existed only an amalgamation of autonomous provinces. Seldom was there even a semblance of a national government, and even in the provinces, if political order existed it was usually forcibly imposed by a local caudillo.

In 1852 most of the provincial governors agreed to attempt to form a national union, and the following year a constitution was written that, except for the interval between 1949 and 1955, has been Argentina's fundamental law ever since. Buenos Aires, however, boycotted the constitutional convention and maintained a separate existence. A single nation could not be created until the bitter struggle between the interior provinces and Buenos Aires was resolved.

Politically, this conflict was over the kind of national government to be established. The political leaders of the interior, referring to themselves as Federalists, tended to equate federalism with democracy and liberty. They remembered the intense centralization of the colonial period and wanted no part of a continuance of the unitary system. They recognized the economic and social differences among some of the provinces, especially between those of the interior and Buenos Aires, and felt that federalism was the best way to reconcile these differences. On the other hand, the Unitarians of Buenos Aires were convinced that only a unitary system could weld the warring provinces into a single nation; they were afraid that if federalism were adopted, there would be no nation.

In the realm of economics, the conflict revolved around the fact that the dominant source of income for the new nation was the import duties collected in Buenos Aires, which had the nation's only developed port. During and immediately after the war for independence, most of the interior provinces were in extremely bad shape financially. They were cut off from their traditional markets in Peru, and all their goods entering or leaving the country through the Río de la Plata estuary were taxed in Buenos Aires, with the revenue going into the treasury of that province.

In very general terms, the Buenos Aires Unitarians wanted to form a strong national government run by and for the people of Buenos Aires. To many of the political leaders of the interior, federalism meant provincial autonomy and the right of the local caudillo to exploit his province as he saw fit.

This conflict increased in intensity until it came to civil war in 1858 and again in 1861. In 1861 the forces of Buenos Aires, under the leadership of Bartolomé Mitre, defeated the provincial army at Pavón. After the adoption of relatively minor constitutional amendments, Buenos Aires agreed to join the union, and the next year Mitre became Argentina's first truly national president.

The inauguration of Mitre in 1862 marked the beginning of a new era in Argentina. For half a century the country had endured chaos and anarchy, interrupted only by the dictatorship of Juan Manuel de Rosas (1835–1852); the next seven decades were characterized by peace and stability and by rapid economic and political development.

Mitre and the two presidents who succeeded him concentrated most of their efforts on pacification and the creation of the institutions of government. The Congress was moved from Paraná to Buenos Aires and began meeting regularly. A national judiciary was created and staffed with extremely competent people. The city of Buenos Aires was removed from the province of that name and converted into a federal district, much like Washington, D.C. And, most important, general acceptance was gained for the existence of a single national government.

Beginning in 1880 emphasis shifted from politics to economics, and the next group of presidents set out to increase production by importing Europeans and European capital. At the time there were barely 1.5 million Argentines occupying 1 million square miles (2.6 million square kilometers). The majority of those people were rural, and most were engaged in subsistence agriculture. Infrastructural development was accomplished primarily through British financing; the rail system, for instance, was British owned until World War II. When Mitre took office there were perhaps 2,000 miles (3,200 kilometers) of track: fifty years later there were 20,000 (32,000 kilometers). During the same period the amount of cultivated land was upped from less than 1.5 million acres (0.6 million hectares) to more than 60 million (24.3 million hectares), and the amount of land devoted to grazing was increased almost as dramatically. These and similar factors changed Argentina from having a subsistence agricultural system to being a major exporter of primary products, and the transformation took place with amazing rapidity. By the time of World War I, Argentina was exporting 350,000 tons (317,450 tonnes) of beef and 5 million tons (4.5 million tonnes) of cereals annually.

During this same period there were important changes in the nature of Argentine society, largely as a result of massive immigration. The author of the 1853 constitution had said, "To govern is to populate," and the dictum was taken to heart by the country's nineteenth-century rulers. A concerted effort was made to attract Europeans to Argentina, an effort that was incredibly successful. Immigration began in the 1850s as little more than a trickle but increased at an astronomical rate during the next forty years. In 1870, 40,000 immigrants arrived; in 1885, 110,000; and in 1890, 200,000. Between 1869 and 1929, 60 percent of the nation's population growth came from immigration.[3]

Although a great many Argentines attained some degree of economic well-being between 1862 and 1916, the average person remained almost completely removed from the political process. Government machinery revolved around the person of the president. In the provinces the legislatures were subservient to the governors, to whom most members owed their election. The governor was also quite influential in the selection of congressional representatives from the province. The provincial legislature chose the members of the upper house, and the governor and the Conservative party had control over the electoral machinery so that "safe" representatives were returned to the lower house. The governors, in turn, were virtually the personal agents of the president, who could keep the governors in line with the use or just the threat of his presidential power to remove them from office. The system was self-perpetuating, as the president and the governors kept each other in office through the use of fraud and, when necessary, force. A number of political parties were active during this period, but until the turn of the century all were essentially conservative organizations representing different sectors of the aristocracy—primarily the large landowners of the interior and the commercial and livestock interests of the city and province of Buenos Aires.

This political system was perhaps appropriate for Argentina as long as its society was composed almost exclusively of a small landowning elite and a large politically inarticulate mass; however, such ceased to be the case when the nation's social structure underwent fundamental alteration. The most important of the societal changes was the rapid formation of a middle class composed largely of immigrants and their offspring.

It was this newly emerging middle class that formed the base for the Radical Civic Union (UCR) founded in 1890. During the first forty years of its existence this party was dominated by a single enigmatic politician named Hipólito Yrigoyen. Convinced that UCR participation in elections supervised by the Conservatives would only serve to place the party's stamp of approval on inevitable electoral fraud, Yrigoyen saw to it that the Radicals boycotted all elections prior to 1912. Instead, they attempted to come to power by force, instigating rebellions in 1890, 1893, and 1905. When these revolts proved unsuccessful, the Radicals still did not nominate candidates for office or write specific programs; rather, they contented themselves with denunciations of the oligarchic nature of the government and insisted that it be replaced by a "national renovation" led by the UCR.

In an effort to bring more people to the polls and thus increase the legitimacy of the regime, the Conservatives wrote a new election law in 1911. The law provided for universal and compulsory male suffrage, a secret ballot, permanent voter registration, and minority representation in Congress. Within five years, the honest administration of this law cost the Conservatives their monopoly on public office.

In 1916, in what may have been the country's first truly honest presidential election, Hipólito Yrigoyen became Argentina's first non-Conservative president. Unfortunately, the Radicals, still lacking a definite program, had no clear idea how to put into effect the national renovation they had so long promised. The UCR held power for fourteen years, but even though relatively minor reforms were enacted, no fundamental changes were even attempted and the economic power of the Conservatives remained intact. It may be that the Radicals had lost their revolutionary zeal and their goal had become simply recognition of the right of the middle class to participate fully in the economic, social, and political life of the country—or at least recognition of its right to a share of the spoils of office.

In 1912 the Conservatives had been willing to share power with the Radicals, although certainly not on the basis of equality. The former apparently saw the provision in the new election law guaranteeing minority representation in Congress as a means of co-opting their middle-class opponents. (The congressional debate on the law made it clear that the Conservatives did not envision the possibility of their becoming the minority party.) What the Conservatives were unwilling to do was to relinquish power to the Radicals, yet that is exactly what happened. Voter participation increased dramatically (from 190,000 in 1910 to 640,000 in 1912 and 1,460,000 in 1928), and as it grew so did the percentage of the vote obtained by the Radicals. By 1930 it was clear that the Conservatives were quite unlikely to win any national elections in the foreseeable future. Although the policies adopted by the Radicals had not been particularly disadvantageous to the nation's elite, the large and growing Radical electorate meant that this situation was a definite possibility at any time in the future. The institutions of liberal democracy that had served the elite in the past were called into question.

In September 1930 an economic crisis, ever-increasing corruption in the government, President Yrigoyen's senility (at the age of seventy-two he was serving a second term), recognition by the Conservatives that the rules of the game had to be changed if they were to return to power, and widespread popular disillusionment with the Radicals led to their overthrow and the establishment of Argentina's first military government.

POST-1930 POLITICAL HISTORY: THE PERIOD OF STAGNATION AND FRAGMENTATION

The 1930 military coup marked the beginning of a new era in Argentina. The preceding seventy years had been characterized by a degree of political stability almost unknown in Latin America and by a level of economic development that led to the attainment of a standard of living comparable to that of southern Europe. The years since 1930, on the other hand, have been characterized by exactly the opposite: economic stagnation and an incredible degree of political instability.

Following the overthrow of Yrigoyen, the armed forces retained power for less than two years before returning control of the government to the Conservatives by means of elections as fraudulent as those conducted prior to 1912. In fact, the period between 1932 and 1943 is frequently referred to as the era of patriotic fraud. According to the Conservatives, it was their patriotic duty to engage in electoral fraud, for otherwise the Radicals would hoodwink the immature voters, return to power, and once again lead the country down the road to ruin.

The social, economic, and political elite that governed Argentina between 1862 and 1916 had been dedicated to national development. Such was decidedly not true of the elite in power following the 1930 coup. The government did lead the country out of the depression and restore a degree of prosperity; however, it also saw to it that this prosperity was distributed even more inequitably than before. Argentina was run almost exclusively for the benefit of the landed aristocracy.

At about the same time, there occurred a profound change in the character of the urban working class. During World War I the majority of the urban workers had been recent immigrants, almost none of whom had become naturalized citizens; by World War II they were primarily recent migrants from the countryside or, to a lesser extent, the children of immigrants. During the 1930s and early 1940s the wave of migration to the cities was of truly incredible proportions. For example, it has been estimated that in one four-year period alone one out of every five rural dwellers moved into an urban center, most into greater Buenos Aires.[4] Politically, this new urban working class differed from its earlier counterpart in at least one important way: Its members were citizens and, hence, potential voters.

Unfortunately, the nation's political institutions were not equipped to handle large new groups of political participants. Neither the structures, nor the programs, nor the leaders of the existing political parties were able (or willing, perhaps) to offer anything of value to this working class. Until 1940 the Congress was dominated by the Conservatives, who seemed totally uninterested in the plight of the workers; for the next three years the Radicals used their congressional majority to harass the president and to prevent the enactment of any sort of program.

Such was the scene in 1943 when the leaders of the armed forces again assumed the role of keeper of the national conscience and deposed the Conservative government. In the military administration that followed the coup, power gradually came to be concentrated in the hands of a colonel who was to dominate the course of Argentine politics for the next thirty years: Juan Domingo Perón.

Perón was the one army officer who appears to have seen the political potential of the labor movement. Content with a quite secondary position in the revolutionary government, that of secretary of labor, he almost immediately began an active campaign for working-class support. He saw to it that wages were raised substantially and that existing ameliorative labor legislation was enforced for the first time. He presided over the formation of new trade unions and the enormous expansion of existing unions that were friendly to him. For example, under his influence, membership in the Textile Workers Union grew from 2,000 in 1943 to over 84,000 in 1946; the Metallurgical Workers Union grew from 2,000 to 100,000 in the same period.[5] By 1945 his labor secretariat was the nation's sole collective-bargaining agency, and unions utilizing its auspices were virtually certain to obtain whatever they sought.

In the presidential election of February 1946, Perón was the candidate of the hastily formed Argentine Labor party. Although opposed by a single candidate representing all the nation's traditional political parties, Perón won. In 1916 it had been the newly emerging middle class that was largely responsible for the election of Yrigoyen; thirty years later it was the new urban working class that could claim most of the credit for the election of Juan Perón.

As president, Perón continued to do a great deal for the working class, both materially and psychologically. The process of unionization was continued, wages and fringe benefits were dramatically increased, and a modern social security system was created. To an appreciable extent, there was a redistribution of income that favored the wage earners. At least as important in the long run was the thorough politicization of the working class, which came to realize its potential political strength. Nevertheless, the material benefits obtained by the workers during the Perón administration were essentially gifts from above rather than the result of working-class demands. The Peronist party (the name given the former Labor party) functioned primarily as a vehicle for mobilizing working-class support for the regime; it did not, in fact, participate in the governing of Argentina.

Although honestly elected in 1946 and reelected in 1951, Perón moved steadily in the direction of authoritarian rule. Freedom of the press was virtually destroyed, the judiciary was purged as were the universities, and opposition leaders were harassed, exiled, or imprisoned. Perón originally came to power with the support of the church, the armed forces, and organized labor. By 1955 his labor support had declined somewhat, and the church had moved completely into the opposition. Most important, an appreciable sector of the armed forces had decided that he must go.

In September 1955, Perón was deposed; he went into exile, from which he did not return for eighteen years. It was relatively simple to get rid of Perón, but it was much more difficult to rid the country of Peronism. For two and a half years Gen. Pedro Aramburu presided over a provisional regime dedicated to destroying Peronism and returning the country to civilian constitutional rule. With regard to the first goal, there was almost a total lack of success; in fact, the extreme anti-Peronism of the military government seems to have served only to convince Perón's followers that they must remain united in support of their exiled leader or see the political clock turned back to pre-1946. The second goal met with only limited success, for although elections were held, as far as the military was concerned the wrong man won.

The 1958 elections were swept by the faction of the old UCR calling itself the Intransigent Radical Civic Union (UCRI). Its leader, Arturo Frondizi, attained the presidency owing largely to a deal with Perón, who traded the votes of his followers for a promise of legality for the Peronist party. This bargain gave Frondizi the presidency, but it cost him the ability to govern effectively. The anti-Peronist sector of the population and especially the leaders of the armed forces considered his election tainted and his administration illegitimate.

For four years Frondizi made a concerted effort to accelerate the nation's rate of economic development and to integrate the Peronists back into political life. By 1962 his economic policies appeared to be on the verge of success, but his political maneuvers cost him his job. Restored to legality, the Peronist party emerged victorious in the congressional and gubernatorial elections held in March 1962. This was the last straw as far as the anti-Peronist military leaders were concerned, and Frondizi was deposed.

After a year of near total chaos and virtual civil war within the military, elections were held once again. This time they were won by the People's Radical Civic Union (UCRP), the faction of the old UCR that had lost the 1958 elections to Frondizi's Intransigent Radicals. Elected to the presidency was Arturo Illia, a mild-mannered country doctor who received only a fourth of the popular vote. (Peronists were denied the right to nominate candidates for executive office.) The three years of the Illia administration were characterized by lack of action. In 1962, Frondizi had been overthrown because the leaders of the armed forces disapproved of his action; in 1966, Illia was deposed because he refused to act.

By 1966 the military had witnessed the failure of two civilian administrations to resolve the Peronist problem and to bring about an acceptable rate of economic growth—and these were the administrations of the only two political parties with popular support approaching that of the Peronists. The military this time closed the Congress, dissolved all the nation's political parties, and granted almost complete authority to a retired general, Juan Carlos Onganía.

General Onganía was put in power to bring about a fundamental restructuring of the nation's political system. The leaders of the armed forces seemed to realize that the existing system was incapable of adapting to the myriad of demands placed on it. However, there was little in the way of consensus as to the form a new political system should take, and thus very little was accomplished during the seven years of military rule. An attempt was made to exclude the working class from the political process and to depoliticize groups such as the unions and the student organizations. However, unlike their Brazilian counterparts, whom they emulated to some degree, the Argentine military were unwilling to resort to extreme levels of repression, and thus these attempts were doomed to failure. Student organizations were banned by law, yet students engaged in violence to a greater degree than ever before. The labor movement was not depoliticized, and the working class refused to accept passively a reduction in its standard of living.

By 1970 it was clear that Onganía was accomplishing very little, that the public acquiescence he had originally enjoyed had almost vanished, and that the nation was experiencing a completely intolerable level of political violence. The leaders of the armed forces appear to have decided that they had no choice but to hold elections and return to constitutional government. (There was evidently some hope that a return to constitutionalism would relieve frustrations contributing to the violence and that even if constitutionalism failed, the armed forces would not be to blame.) When Onganía refused to go along with this decision, he was deposed, as was his successor a few months later when he too showed no signs of moving toward holding elections. Finally, the army commander in chief, Gen. Alejandro Lanusse, assumed the presidency and announced that he would hold office only long enough to stop the violence and hold elections.

It was obvious to all that if a newly elected government were to have any claim to legitimacy, the Peronist movement would have to be given complete electoral equality. Yet, since many military leaders opposed the prospect of a Peronist government, changes were made in the election law to require a runoff election if no presidential candidate received an absolute majority of the popular vote. (There was general agreement that the Peronist candidate, whoever that might be, would win a plurality of the vote but would be defeated in a runoff by a coalition of non-Peronist parties.) Moreover, a number of complicated maneuvers effectively prevented Perón himself from being a candidate.

When the elections were held in March 1973, the Peronist candidate, Héctor Cámpora (whose slogan was Cámpora to the Presidency; Perón to Power), received 49.6 percent of the vote, more than double that of his nearest competitor. In violation of his own regulations, Lanusse decided that the results were close enough to the required absolute majority to cancel the runoff. Upon Cámpora's inauguration, all political prisoners received amnesty, the universities were turned over to the far left, and in general the government took on a vaguely leftist tint. However, after only fifty days in office Cámpora and his vice president resigned, necessitating new elections—this time with Juan Perón himself a candidate.

Eighteen years and eighteen days after he was forced into exile Perón once again became the president of Argentina. Now the government moved decidedly to the right. In the universities, the Marxist administrators were replaced with neofascists; several leftist governors were removed from office; and most important, Perón openly sided with the relatively conservative labor sector of the Peronist movement against the leftist youth sector. On July 1, 1974, Perón died, leaving his widow, María Estela Martínez de Perón (Isabel) as the nation's chief executive.

The political violence, which had abated while Perón was president, reached an incredible level shortly after his death. Inflation, which was already high, increased until it approached 1 percent per day. Corruption became rampant. And quite predictably, the armed forces once again assumed power (in 1976). Isabel was arrested, and the army commander in chief, Gen. Jorge Videla, was inaugurated as president.

The major goals of the new military government were the elimination of antiregime terrorism and the achievement of economic recovery. With regard to the former, appreciable success was attained within three years, but at a very high price as the government itself resorted to terrorist tactics. Thousands of people were subjected to arbitrary arrest, imprisonment, and torture, and many more just disappeared. The nation's economic problems, on the other hand, proved far more difficult to resolve. In spite of some short-term successes, such as the rapid accumulation of foreign currency, seven years of military rule left the country in even worse shape than it had been in 1976. During this period the exchange rate for the peso went from 80 to 260,000 to the dollar, and the foreign debt increased equally astronomically to $43 billion.

By 1982 the military government was very much in disrepute. This situation changed quite rapidly, but equally briefly, on April 2 with the invasion of the Islas Malvinas (Falkland Islands). Although virtually all Argentines were delighted at the "recuperation" of the islands, they were also totally disillusioned with the loss of the war with Great Britain that followed. This rather ignominious defeat led almost immediately to the creation of a provisional government whose only purpose was to arrange for the holding of elections and the return to constitutional government.

On October 30, 1983, Argentines went to the polls for the first time in more than a decade, and to the amazement of most observers, they chose as their new president a Radical, Raúl Alfonsín. For the first time since the party's formation in 1946 the Peronists had lost a presidential election—and lost decisively, as their presidential candidate, Italo Luder, received only 40 percent of the popular vote while Alfonsín obtained 52 percent.

Alfonsín's inauguration was a time for celebration throughout Argentina. As skeptical as many Argentines were of their ability to govern themselves democratically, they cherished personal freedom and welcomed the military's retreat. The Radicals' defeat of the Peronists also gave democracy its best chance ever by invalidating the Peronists' claim to being the nation's only legitimate majority party. If the Peronists were to govern again, they would first have to convince the Argentine electorate that they could function without Juan Perón and within the democratic process as a loyal opposition party.

Governing Argentina is not easy, as Alfonsín quickly discovered. He was a conscientious and popular democrat who calmed the nation at home and earned it new respect abroad because of his prudent foreign policies. But as before, the economy proved unwieldy. When inflation soared to a rate of over 1,000 percent in 1985, Alfonsín imposed wage and price controls, and prices fell dramatically, earning him new praise. But they gradually rose again, from 90 percent in 1986 to nearly 400 percent in 1988, and wages did not keep pace, so the working class had 25 percent less real income when the president's term ended in 1989. The nation's foreign debt was equally frustrating. Alfonsín's military predecessors had borrowed far too much, accumulating a record $40-billion debt, and had left the debt for their civilian successors to pay. Consequently, Argentina had to send between 25 and 50 percent of its export earnings to foreign banks rather than investing them at home.

Economic woes usually benefit the opposition in democracies, and Argentina proved no exception. In the 1985 congressional elections the Peronists had done poorly, finishing second with less than 35 percent of the vote, but when congressional and gubernatorial elections were held in September 1987 they won handily by reminding the electorate that Alfonsín had failed to generate the prosperity that was supposed to accompany democracy. Then in May 1989 Argentines went to the polls once more, this time to select Alfonsín's successor. Remarkably, it was the first time since 1928 that they had an opportunity to elect a president to replace another elected one, no small achievement in a nation that had always found it so hard to discipline its politics with democratic rules.

Eduardo Angeloz, governor of Córdoba province, was the Radicals' candidate—an industrious, no-nonsense administrator who had put the province's finances in order and had rejuvenated Córdoba's economy by attracting private investment. A technocrat and lacking in great rhetorical skills, Angeloz knew that it would be hard to replicate Alfonsín's 1983 margin, even if he attracted nearly everyone who did not want a Peronist president. The Peronists chose Governor Carlos Menem from La Rioja province. The son of Syrian immigrants who had prospered in commerce, he had spent nearly five years in jail when the military governed during the late 1970s. A populist in the Peronist tradition, Menem was also quite pragmatic in his pursuit of power, willing to compromise with almost anyone. His interest in ideology was minimal, and he did all that he could to incorporate rich as well as poor Peronists into his campaign.

Menem benefited from Alfonsín's failure to prevent the economy's decline during the last three months of the campaign as well as from his own popularity within the working class. He won the presidential election on May 14 with 47 percent of the popular vote (compared to 37 percent for Angeloz). The Peronists also picked up several seats in the Chamber of Deputies, giving them a bare majority to match the one they already had in the Senate. Moreover, the presidential inauguration, which was scheduled for December, was moved up to July when it became obvious that Alfonsín had lost too much public support to govern as a lame-duck president for six more months. Menem started swiftly by appealing to conservative politicians and business leaders for help, promising that he would postpone his populism for the time being if they would assist in rebuilding the nation's battered economy. Menem wanted the Peronists to become more restrained, although he knew that such changes would be resisted by the working-class rank and file.

POLITICAL GROUPS

As in most nations, a large number of groups, institutions, and associations have played prominent political roles in Argentina. In terms of relative importance, three stand out above all others: the political parties, the armed forces, and the trade unions.

Political Parties

During this century a great many political parties have attained legal recognition, but only the Radicals and the Peronists have gained sufficient popular support to hope to win an honest national election.

The Radicals

Formed in 1890, the UCR was Argentina's first nonaristocratic party and the first with a grass-roots organization. Unlike the Radical party in Chile, however, it has seldom formulated a coherent program. Instead, it has demanded adherence to constitutional norms and promised change of an unspecified nature. Allegedly a middle-class organization, it has never effectively challenged the prerogatives of the nation's economic elite, nor has it appreciably alleviated the plight of the poor. For example, Peter Smith has shown that between 1916 and 1930, the period during which the Radicals first controlled the national government, ninety bills that benefited the nation's livestock producers were introduced in that Congress; 60 percent of these bills were introduced by Radicals, 29 percent by Conservatives.[6] Even the rather bland reformism of the Radicals seems to have died in 1933 with Yrigoyen. Shortly thereafter, the party's right wing gained control and retained it until 1957.

Throughout much of the party's history the catchwords of the UCR have been *nationalism* and *intransigence*. Radical nationalism has been, to a large degree, rhetorical. When out of power the party has often espoused greater control of multinational corporations, a more independent foreign policy, and freedom from the strings frequently attached to loans by the International Monetary Fund or the World Bank. With one major exception, however, the Radicals have failed to do very much that could be labeled nationalistic. That exception lies in the area of petroleum policy. In 1919 President Yrigoyen declared that petroleum was the property of the nation and thus no longer open to private exploitation. Three years later a government corporation was given a monopoly on the production of all petroleum products. Since then, petroleum policy and especially foreign oil concessions have been major issues in Argentine politics—and the number-one symbols of economic nationalism.

Intransigence, a word used constantly by Yrigoyen and repeated by most Radical politicians ever since, in practice means opposition to electoral alliances, to coalition governments, to any relationship with other political groups that might endanger "the purity of Radical ideals." (This messianism is itself characteristic of the Radicals, who deny that the UCR is a political party, instead insisting that it is a movement of national regeneration.) Although intransigence may have been a successful tactic for the UCR at times, it has rarely been beneficial to the political system. It was most detrimental in 1973 when in all probability the leader of the Radicals, Ricardo Balbín, could have been Juan Perón's running mate in the September presidential election. The party evidently refused to permit this, and the vice presidential slot was filled by Perón's third wife, who was unable to govern effectively when her husband died less than a year after his election. Although one cannot be sure that things would have been different with Balbín as president, the possibility exists that Radical intransigence contributed to the 1976 military coup.

In 1957 the followers of Arturo Frondizi left the main body of radicalism to form the UCRI. These Radicals departed from both the tactics and the program of the traditional UCR. The direction of this change may be described in terms of two words constantly repeated by this group: *integration* and *development*.

Integration was an attempt to reincorporate Peronism into national political life, preferably by attracting individual Peronists to the banner of the UCRI. Although most Radicals maintained their opposition to electoral alliances and Peronism, Frondizi's supporters made a deal with Perón. Perón told his followers to vote for Frondizi in the 1958 presidential election (thus ensuring his election) in return for a promise of legality for the Peronist party. With the legality granted by President Frondizi, the Peronists won the gubernatorial and congressional elections of 1962; Frondizi was deposed by the armed forces eleven days later.

The economic counterpart of integration was the attempt at total industrialization based on the creation of heavy industry. Directly contrary to the economic nationalism of the UCR, Frondizi's economic policies included free convertibility of the peso, loans from the International Monetary Fund, and the granting of petroleum concessions to foreign oil companies. In addition to being a political liability, *desarrollismo* (developmentalism) was less than successful from an economic point of view. Some progress was made toward the goal of total industrialization—steel production was increased dramatically, and the nation became virtually self-sufficient in petroleum—but during the period of *desarrollismo* the cost-of-living index went up more than 300 percent, and the value of the peso declined from 28 to 140 to the U.S. dollar.

After Frondizi was overthrown in 1962 the electoral success of his party declined steadily. Frondizi received 42 percent of the vote in the 1958 presidential election; his UCRI could manage only 25 percent in 1962, 16 percent a year later, and 10 percent in 1965. The Frondicistas were little more than a junior partner in the Peronist coalition that swept the 1973 elections, and ten years later their presidential candidate received less than 2 percent of the vote. Instead, it was the UCR that triumphed in 1983 behind the victorious Raúl Alfonsín.

Peronism

The Peronists, like the Radicals, have failed to develop a clear ideological position. This failure might be attributed to the party's originally heterogeneous social composition and to the fact that until 1974 it was dominated almost totally by Juan Péron. Between 1946 and 1955, while Perón was president, the party was essentially an alliance of three socioeconomic sectors: the urban working class, especially in and around the federal capital; the dependent middle class of the poorer interior provinces; and the newer industrialists, who had prospered during World War II but needed government protection soon thereafter. After 1955, although much of the party's middle-class and industrialist following was won over to the Intransigent Radicals, leaving Peronism a more clearly working-class movement, it still failed to develop a coherent program. In the industrial areas of the country, Peronism resembled a European labor party, but elsewhere it was closer to being a social-Christian party, a Catholic nationalist organization, or, in many rural areas, simply a personal vehicle for the local caudillo.

For several years following the overthrow of Perón, his movement was divided into two main sectors: a hard-line syndicalist group centered in Buenos Aires and its industrial suburbs and a soft-line or neo-Peronist group whose strength was concentrated in several of the interior provinces. The former was by far the more important in terms of the number of votes it could deliver. Its leaders dominated the General Confederation of Labor (CGT) and its vast financial resources. Calling for nothing more than a return to the "good old days" of 1946–1955, the hard-line group played an essentially negative political role. It was vehemently opposed to both the Frondizi and the Illia administrations and was overjoyed by the fall of each (even though neither the 1962 nor the 1966 coup worked to its immediate advantage).

The neo-Peronists formed an appreciably more moderate group. Without strong ties to the CGT, this sector of the Peronist movement was essentially a loose alliance of virtually autonomous provincial parties, most of which were more willing than their syndicalist counterparts to work within the system. The neo-Peronists showed a degree of independence from Perón, even to the extent that some of their leaders spoke of "Peronism without Perón." They lacked the class consciousness of the hard-liners, and in many provinces the party was more personalist than ideological, with the personality involved often a local political leader, not Juan Perón. It should not be surprising that neo-Peronism tended to be strongest in the least-developed provinces, where caudilloism plays an important role in the political process.

Many neo-Peronist leaders accepted positions in the military government of 1966–1973, thus abdicating to the syndicalists the role of the Peronist opposition. However, at this time a far more significant cleavage within the Peronist movement became apparent; it pitted the working-class sector of the party (whether urban or rural) against the increasingly radical youth sector. One of the country's leading urban guerrilla groups, the Montoneros, was in effect the Peronist youth movement. Given a good deal of moral support by Perón (then in exile in Madrid), the Montoneros were quite useful to Peronism as long as it was an *opposition* party. Their bombings, kidnappings, and assassinations were instrumental in persuading the leaders of the armed forces to hold elections and return to civilian rule. That same Montonero movement was very much a thorn in the side of Peronism when it returned to power. To most of the nation's union leaders, a Peronist election victory was first a means of attaining greater political power and second a means of raising the standard of living of their rank-and-file union members. To the Peronist youth, on the other hand, Perón's election was to be the beginning of a socialist revolution.

The bitterness of the labor-youth cleavage became apparent to all the day Perón returned from exile. Hundreds of thousands—perhaps a million—Argentines made their way to Ezeiza International Airport to cheer his return. However, shortly before his plane was scheduled to land a gun battle broke out between the labor and youth sectors. Twenty people were killed and hundreds wounded. There is still controversy over which side began the shooting, but the episode left no doubt as to how far each side would go to impose its brand of Peronism.

With the election of a Peronist president in March 1973, the Montoneros ceased, or at least drastically reduced, their terrorist activities. However, soon after Perón's inauguration in October, he openly sided with the trade-union sector of the movement. In 1975–1976 the Peronist youth movement was openly at war with the Peronist government—a war replete with atrocities by both sides.

With the death of Perón in 1974 and the overthrow and arrest of Isabel two years later, Peronism was left virtually leaderless. After Isabel was allowed to go into exile in Spain she remained completely aloof from the party's internal struggles; she even refused to take part in the process of nominating candidates for the 1983 elections. The selection of candidates for most major offices seems to have been dictated by a few Peronist labor leaders, who later had to assume responsibility for their defeat.

The Minor Parties

Completely dominant on the political scene prior to 1916 and again between 1932 and 1943, the Conservative party disintegrated rapidly during the first Peronist period. Although still an important force in two or three provinces, at the national level the Conservatives pose no electoral threat to the Radicals and Peronists. In 1983 there were two Conservative presidential candidates, neither of whom received as much as 2 percent of the popular vote.

The Socialist party, which received a great deal of electoral support during the 1930s when the Radicals were boycotting all elections, also lost most of its importance soon after Perón came to power. The Communist party has never been an important force at the polls; it made an enormous tactical error in the 1940s when it vehemently opposed Perón, who was considered simply another fascist dictator. In the 1983 presidential election there were four Marxist candidates, none of whom received as much as 1 percent of the vote.

The Lack of a Loyal Opposition

Although political parties in Argentina are susceptible to indictment on a number of counts, the one that has proved especially detrimental to the political system is their failure to form a loyal opposition. Given the nature of the Argentine political system, which concentrates power in the hands of the president, the losing parties seldom have accepted electoral defeat as definitive. To accept defeat at the polls and agree to act as a loyal opposition would mean almost complete impotence for at least six years. Thus, opposition parties traditionally have turned to other means of attaining power, most often a military coup. If the leaders of the armed forces can be convinced of the necessity to overthrow the government, the opposition parties might be able to gain power in the revolutionary government, or failing in this, they might fare better in new elections—especially if the party overthrown is denied participation at the polls.

All of Argentina's military governments have been supported, at least initially, by most of the major parties in opposition to the deposed government. In many instances, opposition parties have also been active in revolutionary conspiracies. Generally speaking, only the party removed from power has condemned the armed forces for breaking the constitutional order; the other parties have praised the removal of an "illegitimate" regime. In 1930 the Conservatives, unable to win honest elections, supported the coup that deposed Yrigoyen and soon inherited the government. The Radicals applauded the 1943 coup and moved into the opposition only when they realized that the military was not going to install them in power. Both Conservatives and Radicals were deeply involved in plots against the Peronist government, and each supported the revolutionary government. After the Peronist electoral victories in 1962, the Radicals might have been able to save the Frondizi administration by agreeing to serve in a coalition government; instead, they joined the chorus of those demanding that Frondizi resign. Frondicistas reciprocated four years later when they were influential in persuading the military to depose the Radical government. The single important exception to this rule came in 1974 and 1975 when the Radicals, and especially their leader, Ricardo Balbín, played a very responsible opposition role, thus helping to forestall, temporarily, the overthrow of Isabel Perón.

The military's defeat in the Falklands/Malvinas War in June 1982 and its government's collapse a few months later gave Argentines another chance to practice democratic politics. Equally important, when the Peronists lost to Alfonsín and his Radical party in a free election in 1983, they had no choice but to become the loyal opponent of the new government. And without General Perón to lead them anymore, they also had to reorganize their movement to compete more effectively in the electoral process. Consequently, during the next six years they played by the constitutional rules and took on the appearance of a conventional political party eager to take its turn at governing the nation. This strategy soon paid off, with Peronist victories in gubernatorial and congressional elections in 1987 and Menem's victory in the presidential election in 1989. This was no small achievement in a nation where the opposition had traditionally tried to destroy incumbent governments rather than defeat them at the polls.

The Armed Forces

With regard to the armed forces, the major questions to be answered are, What sorts of political roles do they play? Why have they become so deeply involved in politics? and Why have they been so unsuccessful in governing the country?

Types of Political Activity

The political activity of the Argentine armed forces has not been limited to deposing civilian presidents. One can discern four distinct political roles played by the military during this century: (1) a simple pressure group with limited objectives (1922–1930, 1932–1943, 1963–1966, and 1973–1976); (2) a governmental partner or, as many put it, "a cogovernment" (1946–1955 and 1966–1970); (3) a wielder of veto power (1958–1962); and (4) a national ruler (1930–1932, 1943–1946, 1955–1958, 1962–1963, 1970–1973, and 1976–1983).

When the military establishment has acted as a simple pressure group, its behavior has not placed great strain on the stability of the political system; its goals have been limited in scope, and its demands have dealt almost exclusively with military affairs. The armed forces played a more forceful role during the Perón and Onganía administrations, when they served as a partner of the government. In each government, the president was a retired army officer dependent to a great extent, but not exclusively, on the support of the military. During the Frondizi administration, the armed forces seem not to have actually formulated policy but rather to have insisted that major presidential policy decisions be submitted to the leaders of the armed forces for their approval. The last role is that of actually running the country. What factors lead the military leaders to take this most drastic final step?

Major Causes of Military Coups

The Argentine armed forces are frequently accused of assuming control of the government to maintain the status quo and to prevent any meaningful change, yet the reasons given by military leaders for their revolutionary actions rarely include complaints about the major policy decisions of the deposed governments. Instead of being criticized for their actions, these governments are more frequently criticized for their lack of action. It is impossible to find a single factor to explain any of Argentina's coups, much less all of them. Nevertheless, there are three or four factors that collectively help explain most of the coups.

Contributing to the first three military coups was the manner in which the government dealt with the armed forces. Particularly unacceptable was political interference in what the military considered its internal affairs. For example, both Yrigoyen and Perón promoted officers with little regard for military regulations such as time in grade; they also rewarded military personnel for past services and promised further benefits for future services. Frondizi was accused of playing off one faction or branch of the armed services against another and of capitulating to officers who were in rebellion against civilian and military authorities while disciplining those who were attempting to maintain legality. It is more than slightly ironic that this sort of action angered precisely the segment of the military that ordinarily would be most inclined to support constitutional government.

In the case of each military coup, the leaders of the armed forces claimed that they simply acceded to popular demands. It is true that all deposed presidents faced widespread civilian opposition and that at the time of the coups, only one, Perón, had any appreciable popular support (and his support was very definitely on the decline). An important feature of the popular opposition is that its leaders were not willing to await its manifestation at the polls but instead went to the military in an effort to convince it of the necessity of revolution. As one Argentine sociologist put it, "Although they must all deny it publicly, Argentine politicians cannot ignore the fact that at one time or another during the past quarter century they have gone to knock at the doors of the barracks."[7]

Within all but possibly the last of the revolutionary governments there has been a group of military leaders intent on changing the very nature of the political system. Many of those responsible for the 1930 coup were interested in replacing liberal democracy with some form of corporatism; in 1943 several army colonels wanted to establish a neofascist state; in 1966 there was near unanimity among military leaders that the political system had to be modified substantially; and in 1955 and 1962 several military leaders were intent on not only eliminating Peronism as a political force but changing the system that had allowed the rise of Peronism.

The last four coups have, to varying degrees, been a result of anti-Peronism. When first inaugurated in 1946, Perón certainly had the support of most of the leaders of the armed forces; however, by 1951 this support had begun to wane, and in 1955 it was the military that forced his removal from office. The first source of friction between the two seems to have been Perón's wife Evita. As the illegitimate child of a poor provincial family and later a radio and movie actress, she was not considered fit to be the wife of a high-ranking army officer, much less a president, and her openly antimilitary attitude did not improve the situation. Another source of friction was the extreme anticlerical stance taken by Perón in 1954 and 1955. Legalization of divorce, abrogation of religious instruction in the public schools, and the jailing and deportation of clergymen caused divided loyalties in the Catholic officer group. After 1952, when economic problems forced Perón to abandon his nationalistic posture, he lost the support of those military men who had been attracted by his economic nationalism. Also, government corruption during the Perón administration became so rampant that it began to cast suspicion on the honesty of the armed forces, which have always been eager to protect their reputation.

Above all, the major source of friction almost certainly was Perón's relationship with the organized labor movement. Many upper-middle-class military personnel were never prolabor (although certainly they were not opposed to using the labor movement for their own ends). The conflict intensified in the early 1950s when the CGT adopted an increasingly arrogant attitude toward the armed forces. Particularly galling was the fact that the CGT managed to have the death penalty reinserted into the Code of Military Justice. The last straw came in 1955 when Perón appeared to be considering the establishment of armed workers' militias.

Military opposition to Peronism between 1955 and 1983 was based partly on the fear that a return of the Peronists to power would mean a resurrection of the issues mentioned earlier. Military anti-Peronism became self-perpetuating. The bitterly anti-Peronist generals of 1955 were responsible for promoting the next generation of generals, and so on; many officers must have feared that a relaxation of their anti-Peronism would leave them open to widespread purges by their fellow officers or by the Peronists, should they return to power. Still, the most important reason for the anti-Peronism of the leaders of the armed forces between 1950 and 1970 was an unwillingness to accept any regime with power to deprive the military of its role as an arbiter or to eliminate it as *the* decisive power factor. Only Peronism, with its mass following centered around organized labor, was a potential threat to the continued hegemony of the armed forces.

There is one additional factor to be mentioned as a rationale for military intervention. This is the new national-security doctrine. National security is thought of as not only connected to but also dependent on economic development. Although there is some disagreement on what form economic development should take, there is a broad consensus that it must involve total industrialization. Since the maintenance of national security is clearly the responsibility of the armed forces and since national security is conceived of as an unobtainable objective without economic development, it is a short step to the conclusion that if civilian governments are not doing an adequate job in this realm, it is the duty of the armed forces to assume responsibility for economic development. Many military leaders are willing to go a step further and claim that the military is uniquely qualified to direct the development process. According to this perspective, not only does the military have the necessary hierarchical organization and discipline, it is, unlike most civilian groups, not tied to any specific economic interest and thus is able to represent the interests of the nation as a whole. (In this connection, it is frequently pointed out that the armed forces have done a better job of developing the steel industry than the state corporation has done developing the petroleum industry.)

Factionalism and the Failure of Military Regimes

Ever since 1930, when the armed forces became deeply involved in the nation's political life, the military has been plagued by the existence of antagonistic ideological factions. The problem seems most serious (and certainly most obvious) following military coups. Lack of agreement within the armed forces as to goals and the means of achieving them severely limits the ability of a military regime to carry out a coherent program.

In 1930 one group of officers thought of the military coup simply as a means of removing an inefficient, corrupt administration and of returning the government to more responsible elements—meaning the Conservatives; another group looked on the coup as the beginning of a revolution that would replace liberal democracy with a neofascist corporate state. Following the 1943 coup a group of young ultranationalistic officers believed the urban working class as a group was capable of legitimating a revolutionary regime; a far more conservative faction was as opposed to such a military-labor alliance as to the civilian administration just deposed. After the overthrow of Perón in 1955 military leaders were separated only by the degree of their anti-Peronism. In 1962 and 1963 the extreme anti-Peronists and their somewhat more moderate opponents within the armed forces quite literally went to war. The first battle, involving only army units, was won by the moderates, who immediately imprisoned or forcibly retired their opponents; the next year they put down an attempted putsch by the navy, whose leaders were almost uniformly extremists. As a result of the second battle all the nation's admirals were forced into retirement, and the naval marine corps was reduced to nearly insignificant size. The military regime of 1976–1983 appears to have been less subject to factionalism than its predecessors; nevertheless, the palace coups of 1981 and 1982 show that something less than complete consensus reigned within the armed forces.

The Labor Movement

Throughout much of Latin America, organized labor has recently attained a position of some political importance; this situation is especially true in Argentina, where the labor movement is very large, relatively wealthy, quite well organized, and thoroughly politicized. The leader of a large union in Argentina is almost automatically considered a prominent national politician; the secretary-general of the CGT holds potential political power equal to that of a major political party leader. This political prominence of the labor movement is a relatively recent phenomenon, and thus before examining the current political role of labor it is necessary to review the development of the movement.

Tomás R. Fillol has written that "the history of Argentine trade unions is largely an account of internal strife, of disunity, struggle and rancor."[8] Prior to the mid-1940s this internal struggle was among the anarchists, syndicalists, socialists, and Communists, who all had radically different ideas about the ultimate goals of the labor movement and the proper means of attaining those goals. In the decade 1945–1955 organized labor was relatively well united under Peronist control, but with the fall of Perón the movement split once again.

Before 1910 the dominant ideological faction within the union movement was that of the anarchists, who looked upon political authority as unnecessary and undesirable. Preferring solidarity strikes, general walkouts, and sabotage to negotiation, the anarchists resorted frequently to violence and assassination. Largely because of government repression, the anarchists lost control of the labor movement in 1910, and for the next quarter century dominance passed into the hands of the syndicalists. Theoretically apolitical, Argentine syndicalists accepted the Marxist analysis of class struggle but denounced political action on the part of the proletariat. About 1935 control of the labor movement passed into the hands of the socialists, who differed from the anarchists and syndicalists in that they were willing to work within the existing political system; they insisted that improvement of the conditions of the working class could be attained by legislative action.

The development of an effective union movement was opposed not only by employers but by the government. Prior to 1916 both looked on unions as inherently subversive. This attitude changed somewhat after the Radicals came to power. Yrigoyen protected both the right to organize and the right to strike, but the UCR had no specific labor program, and very little labor legislation was enacted. The administrations of the second Conservative era (1930–1943) were somewhat less hostile toward labor than their predecessors of 1862–1916, probably because by this time the labor movement was under the control of socialists willing to abide by the rules of the game. During this period some labor legislation was enacted, largely through the initiative of Socialist deputies, but the Conservative governments were quite willing to look the other way when employers ignored it.

A great deal changed during the 1943–1955 period. For the first time the labor movement had an ardent supporter in the government. Perón began his appeal to the workers as secretary of labor in the 1943–1946 government and continued it throughout his term as president. Wages, fringe benefits, and working conditions all improved appreciably; however, none of this was the result of pressure from below but was essentially a gift from Perón, and the price paid by the labor movement was near-total subservience to Perón. The Labor party was dissolved, non-Peronist unions were subjected to government intervention, and personal friends of the president were appointed to the top positions in the CGT. The constitution of the CGT was amended to declare that the fundamental purpose of the organization was to support Perón and to carry out his policies.[9] The labor movement benefited considerably during the Peronist administration, but given the means by which these benefits were obtained, they were certain to cease when Perón was overthrown.

Shortly after that happened, the military government intervened in all the nation's unions, replacing Peronist leaders with military men. However, when union elections finally were allowed, a majority of the unions reverted to Peronist leadership; a few were captured by the Communists, while others elected radical, socialist, or anarchist leaders as they had in the pre-Perón period. These political sectors soon came to be called by the number of union elections won at this time: The 62 organizations referred to the Peronist-dominated group; the 19 was the Communist group; and the 32 was the non-Communist, anti-Peronist sector. Most of the unions of white-collar workers (*empleados*), such as the commercial employees and government workers, belonged to the 32, and those of blue-collar workers (*obreros*)—the metallurgical and textile workers, for example—most often affiliated with the 62.

In 1963 the General Confederation of Labor held its first national convention since the fall of Perón. The Peronists regained effective control of the national apparatus of the trade-union movement, but the 62 also began to experience internal dissension. A so-called orthodox faction, unconditionally loyal to Perón, was in violent opposition to the administrations of Presidents Frondizi and Illia. A more moderate group, while claiming loyalty to Perón, preferred negotiation over open confrontation with the government. Also at about this time the conflict between the Peronist and non-Peronist unions intensified, further diluting the political strength of the union movement.

The methods employed by the Argentine labor movement have varied a great deal, depending largely on two things: the ideological faction in control of the labor movement and the type of government in power. During the period of anarcho-syndicalist domination, when the national government considered the very idea of labor organization to be subversive, there was an attempt by labor to destroy the state completely through general strikes, widespread violence, and assassination. During the period of socialist control, when the national administrations were less hostile to labor, emphasis was placed on legislative enactment, which failed almost as completely as had the violence of the earlier period. Between 1943 and 1955, when the government was openly sympathetic to the aspirations of labor, there was almost exclusive reliance on the good will of the president. Since that period labor has been badly split ideologically, giving rise to a number of different political methods.

Following the 1943 coup, labor began to flex its muscles at the polls. In the presidential elections of 1946, 1951, and 1973, the bulk of the Peronist votes came from the urban working class, and labor provided much of the margin of the Radical victories in 1958 and 1963. In 1958 the workers voted en masse for Frondizi—in accordance with orders from Perón—and in 1963 a large number of workers voted for Illia in an attempt to defeat General Aramburu. After the overthrow of Perón in 1955, however, the electoral strength of labor lost much of its significance as the armed forces refused to give Peronism any opportunity to regain executive power. Thus, while the votes of labor certainly were influential in 1958 and 1963, the workers were forced to choose between lesser evils as Peronist candidates were prohibited. In 1962, when the Peronists were given full electoral freedom, their victories were ephemeral since they led to a military coup and an annulment of the election results. With its electoral strength thus virtually nullified, the labor movement was forced to turn to other means of political expression.

Labor attempted to intimidate President Frondizi by means of a number of politically motivated strikes and sporadic violence, but the 1964 Plan de Lucha is the best example of post-1955 political bargaining. Shortly after his inauguration Illia was faced with labor demonstrations, inflammatory public speeches, and a general strike. Then in May 1964 the executive committee of the CGT decided to adopt a plan of systematic seizure of industrial plants. The country was divided into eight zones, each of which was subjected to a twenty-four-hour demonstration of labor's ability to seize control of the sources of industrial production. Within a month, 11,000 plants were occupied by over 3 million workers.

The ostensible purpose of the Plan de Lucha was to show labor's disapproval of the economic policies of the Illia administration. In actuality, its basic goal was to demonstrate the government's intrinsic weakness and to invite a military coup. The nation's labor leaders hoped the government would react either by applying massive repression, thus making martyrs of the workers, or by doing nothing. President Illia chose the latter course, refusing to call out the army to dislodge workers from the factories. Under different conditions, this response might have been the proper one, but in the Argentina of 1964 it satisfied no one. It failed to placate labor, it angered the business and industrial community, and it infuriated the leaders of the armed forces.

The military governments of 1966–1973 were harassed by the labor movement in much the same manner, although less successfully. When Perón returned to power in 1973 organized labor was once again rewarded for its support, but certainly not to the extent it had been between 1943 and 1955. Following the 1976 military coup the government intervened in all the nation's larger unions, not only removing the elected leaders but also barring them from future election. And, once again, the unions split on the question of how best to deal with a military government.

Other Groups

The Church and Catholic Lay Groups

Throughout most of Latin America, nineteenth-century politics was dominated by a bitter conflict over the proper relationship between church and state, just as the original cleavage between the Conservative and Liberal political parties was in large part a conflict between Catholic and anticlerical forces. Such was not the case in Argentina, where relations between church and state were relatively serene until the 1880s when religious instruction in the public schools was abolished and civil wedding ceremonies required. These laws were bitterly resented by the church and by many of the country's more devout Catholics, who formed a very short-lived confessional party. This party was completely unsuccessful at the polls, and religious issues soon disappeared from the political agenda.

It was not until 1943 that religious issues again attained a degree of political importance. In December of that year the military government reestablished religious instruction in the public schools, and this and other similar measures led the church to support not only the revolutionary government but also its candidate—Juan Perón—in the presidential election of 1946. Shortly before the election a pastoral letter forbade

Catholics to vote for candidates who supported separation of church and state, secular education, or legalization of divorce. Since Perón's single opponent was in favor of all these items, the nation's Catholics were told, in effect, to vote for Perón or to stay home on election day. In what turned out to be a relatively close election, it is quite possible that the church swung enough votes to put Perón in office.

Although Perón had the near-total support of the church in 1946, by 1951 its position had changed to neutrality and by 1955 to complete opposition. By 1955 the Perón administration had legalized divorce and prostitution and discontinued religious instruction in the schools. Also, a number of churches had been sacked and several clergymen imprisoned. In June 1955 Perón was excommunicated by Pope Pius XII, and since that time the Argentine church as an institution has remained relatively aloof from partisan politics. However, this behavior does not carry over to all Catholic groups.

One organization of Argentine clergymen that has attracted a great deal of attention is the Movement of Third World Priests. In mid-1967 eighteen bishops from several nations issued a statement entitled "A Message from Bishops of the Third World." Stating that the primary duty of the church is to aid the poor and the oppressed, this document called for the immediate implementation of the encyclical *Populorum Progressio*. This statement was immediately countersigned by 270 Argentine priests, who soon formed the Movement of Third World Priests. This group called for a Latin American brand of socialism (without explaining exactly what it meant). The Third World Priests supported peasant organizations, union demonstrations, and strikes and were accused of aiding, if not taking part in, terrorist organizations.

During the last half century a number of extreme nationalist organizations have been founded by militant Catholics who tend to equate liberalism with anticlericalism. The Argentine Catholic nationalists are especially opposed to formal structures of liberal democracy such as political parties and legislative bodies. The alternative they propose is most frequently referred to as communitarianism, which is essentially Catholic corporatism similar to that described in the encyclicals *Rerum Novarum* and *Divini Redemptorus*. Communitarianism is based on the assumption that society is not a cluster of individuals or social classes but an organic body composed of natural parts that must cooperate for the good of the whole. Thus, politics should not be organized on the basis of participation by individuals, political parties, or social classes— for this form of organization will lead to conflict, anarchy, and class warfare—but on the basis of confederations of workers and employers in each branch of economic activity. Catholic nationalist organizations have been most prominent and influential during the military governments of 1930, 1943, 1955, and 1966. They have not been able to attain any appreciable popular support, however, and have been of negligible importance during periods of civilian rule.

The only Catholic political party to attain any real significance was the Christian Democratic party founded in 1956. Although it elected a few congressional representatives in 1963 and 1965, the party was never able to obtain as much as 5 percent of the national vote. Roughly two-thirds of its votes came from women, most of whom appear to have been members of the upper and upper-middle classes. In 1973 the Christian Democrats split into separate parties: One supported Perón; the other joined the Communists and some Intransigent Radicals in a coalition of the moderate left. In 1983 a reunited party elected only one congressman.

Economic Groups

It is much easier to identify those economic groups that possess considerable political authority than it is to explain exactly how much authority is exercised and by what means. Most students of Argentine politics would agree that there are three associational groups of land-owners, businesspeople, and industrialists that traditionally have influenced the course of Argentine politics: the Rural Society, the Argentine Industrial Union (UIA), and the General Economic Confederation (CGE).

Since its founding in 1866 the Rural Society has spoken for the nation's largest and wealthiest agricultural interests. Although no longer quite as elite an organization as formerly, it still has only about 10,000 members, including almost all the rural elite of the pampas. The potential influence of the Rural Society may be seen in the fact that during the course of the last century, most ministers of agriculture have come from its ranks. The minister of economics between 1976 and 1981, previously minister of agriculture, was a former president of the Rural Society, as were his father and great-uncle; his great-grandfather was one of the founders and the first president of the organization.

Of the two important associations of industrialists and businesspeople, the older and more powerful of the two is the UIA, founded in 1887. It tends to represent the nation's largest industries, especially those centered in and around Buenos Aires. The CGE, founded in 1951, represents the smaller businesses and industries of the capital and interior provinces. Very much committed to free-trade policies, the UIA was bitterly opposed to the first Perón administration, which allowed it very little political influence. The CGE enjoyed a good deal of political say from the time of its formation until Perón was overthrown; it then suffered a dramatic decline in power until 1973 when the Peronists returned to power and it became the official voice of the business community.

Guerrilla Movements

Argentina's first guerrilla movements began operations in isolated rural areas of the northwest in the early 1960s; however, the rural guerrillas were never much of a menace and were rather quickly wiped out by the nation's security forces. A much more serious threat was the urban guerrilla movements that came to prominence about 1970. There were a large number of such groups, but by far the most important were the Montoneros and the People's Revolutionary Army (ERP).

The Montonero group was organized in 1968 by a number of young Peronists who saw in Peronism a means of national liberation within a neo-Marxist framework. The Montoneros first gained widespread attention in June 1970 when they kidnaped Pedro Aramburu, president from 1955 to 1958. In a series of well-publicized communiqués, it was announced that Aramburu had been tried, convicted, and executed for crimes against the Argentine people; his crimes were evidently the anti-Peronist measures taken while he was provisional president.

The ERP was the armed wing of the Trotskyite Revolutionary Workers party (PRT). Formed in 1970 the ERP was active in kidnappings and assassinations. Among its more prominent assassination victims were an army general, two navy admirals, the president of Fiat, and a secretary-general of the General Confederation of Labor. An enormous sum of money has been paid to ransom several ERP kidnapping victims; Esso allegedly paid more than US$14 million for the return of one of its executives, and a large landowner may have paid much more than that for the return of his sons.

The ideologies of these two groups were extremely eclectic. That of the Montoneros was a curious blend of Marxism, Catholicism, and Peronism. The ERP claimed to have taken from Lenin its ideas about the vanguard party, from Trotsky the concept of permanent revolution, from Mao the idea of a party army, and from Che Guevara the belief that the objective conditions for revolution can be created. Despite their common desire to overthrow the government, to destroy the liberal, capitalist system, and to create some form of national socialism, the Montoneros and the ERP were unable completely to coordinate their actions because of strategic differences and differing attitudes toward Juan Perón and Peronism. The Montoneros were ardent supporters of Perón until 1973 when he openly sided with their opponents in the labor movement; even then, they found it very difficult to attack the government as long as Perón was president. The ERP, on the other hand, never identified with Peronism and thus was not as confused by Perón's adoption of an essentially rightist stance upon his return to power.

During the administrations of Juan and Isabel Perón right-wing terrorist groups entered the fray. The best known of them was the Argentine Anticommunist Alliance (AAA), which assassinated a number of leftists, including politicians, intellectuals, and union leaders.

Following the 1976 coup the role of the AAA was assumed by groups organized by, or actually part of, the government. In the so-called dirty war, the armed forces themselves adopted terrorist tactics, and by 1979 antiregime terrorism was virtually at an end, the Montoneros and ERP members having been killed or forced to flee.

The Role of the United States

Many people are convinced that the United States plays an important role in Argentine politics, which may be true, but it is extremely difficult to demonstrate. Private investments from the United States amount to about US$1 billion (roughly two-thirds of it in manufacturing), and this amount represents almost half the total foreign investment in Argentina.[10] Still, it is virtually impossible to determine the degree of political influence exercised by the U.S. business community. Most U.S. business enterprises in Argentina are affiliated with the Argentine Industrial Union, and it is probably through the UIA that their interests are articulated, although from time to time they may use diplomatic channels.

The amount of political influence exerted by the U.S. government is likewise difficult to measure. In those few cases in which it is known that the U.S. government attempted to influence the course of events in Argentina, the results were quite unsuccessful. The most blatant intervention (and also the best known) occurred during the 1946 election campaign. Spruille Braden, the U.S. ambassador to Argentina, made a series of speeches denouncing the military government and most of its officials. Later, when Braden became assistant secretary of state, he continued his scathing denunciations of Perón, and just two weeks before the election he issued a blue book that called Perón a "Nazi-fascist." This attempt to destroy Perón's bid for the presidency was a marked failure. Equally unsuccessful was the effort of the U.S. embassy to prevent the military coup of 1966.

The preceding paragraphs should not be taken to mean that the United States plays no role in Argentine politics; rather, the role played is marginal and thus difficult to assess. It may well be that the more U.S. influence is out of public view the more successful it is, for no Argentine government, whether civilian or military, Radical or Peronist, can afford to be thought of as subservient to foreign interests.

GOVERNMENT MACHINERY
AND THE ROLE OF THE STATE

The organizational structure and the formal powers of most government institutions in Argentina closely resemble their counterparts in the United States. Political authority is divided between a national government and twenty-two semiautonomous provinces, each of which has a constitution that allocates power among the various branches of the provincial government. At the national level, there is a president chosen for a fixed term of office by an electoral college, a bicameral Congress composed of a Senate and a Chamber of Deputies, and a judiciary headed by a Supreme Court. Nevertheless, in practice there is a great deal of difference between the two countries.

To begin with, Argentina has long been a highly centralized state. Ever since the federal district was created in 1880 there has been near-total hegemony on the part of the national government, which now dominates the allegedly autonomous provinces both politically and financially.

All the constitutional provisions to ensure provincial autonomy are easily negated by the power of the national government to intervene in any province to guarantee a republican form of government. The fact that it is the national government itself that is empowered to define republicanism means the national government may assume total control of a province at any time; however, more often than not, the mere threat of intervention is sufficient to obtain provincial compliance.

As mentioned earlier, the only major source of government income during most of the nineteenth century was the import and export duties collected at the Buenos Aires port. With the nationalization of Buenos Aires, that revenue was monopolized by the national government. Then, with the passage of time, Buenos Aires became the commercial and industrial center of the nation, further increasing the disparity of wealth between that city and the remainder of the nation. For at least half a century the provincial governments have been dependent upon financial assistance from the national government. Because the provinces have lacked political and fiscal autonomy, decision making has come to be concentrated almost exclusively in the federal capital.

The centralization of authority does not stop there, for within the national government the president holds most power. Except for a brief period between 1912 and 1930, the Congress was a preserve of the Conservatives, who appear to have seen their function as that of rubber-stamping the proposals of the chief executive. Decisions tended to be made by the president and a small group of friends and advisers; some of the members of this group may have been congressional representatives, but it was their socioeconomic status that made them members of the political elite, not the offices they held. Between 1912 and 1930 the Congress did gain a degree of political influence, because after the election of Radical and Socialist representatives to the Congress, it became an open arena for conflict and, to a lesser extent, for conflict resolution. This short-lived situation ended with the 1930 revolution, and by the late 1930s "representative institutions like the Congress were discredited and useless."[11] Once again it was the president who was almost completely dominant.

The Argentine judiciary has never played a prominent political role. Although possessing the power of judicial review, the Supreme Court has used considerable restraint in its exercise. Like its U.S. counterpart, it has always refused to hear political questions, and it has defined as *political* any issue that might lead to a major conflict with the executive branch—a conflict that all justices realize they would certainly lose. Damaging to both the power and the prestige of the court is the fact that in spite of constitutional guarantees of life tenure for its members, there were major purges in 1946, 1955, 1966, and 1976. Also detrimental to its public image is its tradition of formally recognizing the de facto status of revolutionary governments. (In fact, during periods of military rule, the court seems to limit itself to attempting to protect individual liberties.) Although it would be an overstatement to claim that the Argentine judiciary has no political power, it is certainly true that all the courts are exceptionally weak in comparison to the president and even in comparison to their counterparts in the United States.

Political power, then, is concentrated to an enormous degree in the hands of a single individual, the president of the Argentine Republic. This situation is well understood not just by politically active groups and individuals but also by the average citizen (who quite frequently refers to the president as the government). In a presidentialist system such as this, in which the president is considered both omnipotent and all-responsible, there is a tendency for all political demands to be brought to him (or, between 1974 and 1976, to her). The people speaking for most groups are well aware that the president can meet their demands by issuing an executive decree, by bringing pressure to bear on the bureaucracy, or, if necessary, by obtaining the enactment of legislation by the Congress.

The president is constantly faced with a range of demands that far exceed the resources at his disposal and by sets of demands that are mutually incompatible. It is the president who must decide which to grant and which to deny. Most politically active groups, unwilling to leave this decision entirely to presidential discretion, back up their demands with threats. Wheat farmers may threaten to cut down on the number of acres planted, or cattle raisers to slaughter their breeding stock, thus reducing the exportable surplus and aggravating the balance-of-payments problem; students may threaten violent antigovernment demonstrations, or the General Confederation of Labor a general strike. Since the military is best equipped to threaten the president, many groups try to find a sector of the armed forces willing to articulate their demands. Since the participants in this game assume, probably correctly, that the president will accede only to those demands accompanied by the most dire threats, the level of the threats is ever increasing.

In such a situation, the president becomes powerful only in comparison to other individuals and institutions within the government. The government itself, buffeted by a myriad of unsatisfied (and in large part unsatisfiable) demands, is relegated to a position of weakness.

This position of relative government weakness is somewhat paradoxical considering that the state traditionally has played a very active role in Argentina. In the realm of economics, for example, the state performs a multitude of functions. It is actively involved in the collective-bargaining process, even to the point that in recent years the General Confederation of Labor has bargained first with the Labor Ministry, with the bargaining between individual unions and industries proceeding only after general guidelines had been established. Foreign trade is controlled to a great extent through the use of a complicated multiple exchange rate; and for a while during the first Peronist administration, foreign trade was monopolized by a government agency. The state is responsible for the licensing of all professions, for the legal recognition of political parties and trade unions, and so forth. It was actively engaged in the political mobilization of the working class during the late 1940s and in an attempted demobilization during the late 1960s and 1970s. The concept of limited government, so dear to the hearts of the framers of the U.S. Constitution, is virtually unknown in Argentina, where the state is considered virtually all-responsible.

PUBLIC POLICY

Given the preceding discussion of Argentine politics, it should not be surprising that there has been relatively little continuity of public policy in Argentina, especially during the last sixty years or so, largely because major political issues have usually been defined by the administration in power. Prior to 1916 the Conservatives were intent upon creating a modern nation, and most public policies were intended to attain that aim. On the other hand, between 1916 and 1930 the Radicals appear to have had no clearly defined goals and thus no consistent policies. Policies then seem to have been ad hoc reactions to events rather than part of an overall framework. Although the Yrigoyen administration was often prolabor, in 1919 the army was used to put down a strike of the metal workers; the 1918 university reform was not part of a larger educational policy but simply a reaction to a student strike. Such examples could be given indefinitely, but everything changed back when the Conservatives regained power in 1932. Once more, public policies appear to have been aimed at a single goal, but this time that goal was the protection of the economic interests of the landowning elite.

During the first Peronist period (1946–1955), public policy was designed primarily to maintain working-class support. There was a dramatic redistribution of income, with the percentage of the gross national product going for wages and salaries increasing from 45 percent to almost 60 percent.[12] However, except in relative terms this shift was quite painless for the nation's economic elite, for the bulk of the increase in wages was a result of the government's spending most of the credits built up during World War II when Argentina had a favorable balance of trade. Rather than investing this money in an industrialization process, the government used it to raise the standard of living of the working class without appreciably reducing the standard of living of the middle and upper classes.

A concerted policy of industrialization, especially the creation of heavy industry, did not come until the administration of Arturo Frondizi. Lacking sufficient domestic capital for the massive scope of industrialization envisioned, Frondizi was forced to seek foreign investment (even in the previously sacrosanct realm of petroleum) and to borrow large sums of money from international lending agencies. Some of the strings attached to loans by the International Monetary Fund reversed the income redistribution that had taken place during the Perón administration, although this result was not intended by the government. Despite extensive planning and four years of concerted effort, not a great deal of progress was made; in 1962 total industrial production was not appreciably greater than in 1958. The economic policy priorities of Frondizi were turned upside down during the Illia administration (1963–1966), which seemed unconcerned with industrialization and instead tried to stimulate agricultural production (an area virtually ignored by Frondizi).

When Perón returned to power in 1973 the Social Pact became the keystone of economic policy. This pact was an attempt to obtain both labor (CGT) and management (CGE) approval for a very general policy to increase production, reduce unemployment, and raise wages and profits—while maintaining social harmony. There was an initial wage increase and a freeze on many prices, with the understanding that future wages and prices would be determined by a commission representing the General Confederation of Labor, the General Economic Confederation, and the government. The social harmony did not last long as an ever-increasing inflation rate soon destroyed any possibility of labor-management cooperation.

The military administrations of 1976–1983 returned to a liberal, free-market economy and emphasized increased foreign investment. Such a policy was clearly something less than a panacea, and the return to civilian government almost certainly will mean a more statist economic policy. Raul Alfonsín was less eager to open up the nation's economy when he became president in 1983 for fear that it would offend the voters that he had just attracted to the Radical party. But his populism proved disastrous, and with inflation rising by an annual rate of more than 1,000 percent in 1985, he changed course, adopting measures aimed at forcing Argentines in business and labor to rely less on government for their maintenance. He was only briefly successful, however, and his popularity quickly fell when prices rose rapidly again in 1988, causing losses of income, especially among the working and middle classes. Once more it was left to the next president to deal with the economic obstacles that his predecessors failed to overcome.

FUTURE PROSPECTS

Democracy does not solve problems; it only provides a way for citizens and their leaders to make attempts to solve them. Argentines know that, of course, but that does not make their economic frustrations any easier to bear. Everyone knows what the problems are: a public sector that is too expensive and very inefficient, a debt that siphons away dollars which are desperately needed at home, and citizens who prefer to collect dollars and send them abroad rather than invest them in new Argentine enterprises. Everyone waits for good times before risking anything, but without taking those risks, good times are not likely to return. And defaulting on foreign debts or raising wages rapidly cannot solve everything either.

Sadly, social conditions deteriorated between 1976 and 1990 in this once-affluent nation, first swiftly under the military, when wealth was redistributed upward and industrial employment reduced by almost 30 percent in the late 1970s, and then more slowly in the 1980s as a result of a program of economic austerity. The Alfonsín administration tried to soften the impact of adversity with new housing and food programs, but the effects of these programs were minimal. There is no easy way to change the situation in the 1990s, since better services will cost far more than the government can hope to collect in taxes and paying more for services remains as unpopular as ever.

The armed forces are still a force to be reckoned with. Alfonsín tried to assert civilian control over the three services, sending the generals and admirals who had conducted the war against civilians to jail, reducing the military budget, and rewriting defense legislation. But the task is far from over as occasional military revolts demonstrate. Lt. Col. Aldo Rico led a small rebellion at Eastertime in 1987, and as a result, Congress passed legislation that limited prosecution of military officers who had killed civilians during the "dirty war" a decade previously only to officers at the highest ranks. Rico tried rebellion again in January 1988 but with less success. Then in December 1988 rebellious troops joined Col. Mohamed Ali Seineldin when he took over a military base and demanded the release of officers already convicted and higher military wages. The officers were not released, but wages were raised after Seineldin withdrew. Such mini-revolts are not military coups, but they do serve to remind civilians that their control over the armed forces is far from complete.

The army's leadership was divided in 1990 between conservative officers who were unwilling to forcefully challenge civilian authorities and a few romantic ones who gained much gratification from doing so. Many of the officers still believed that they were more dedicated than civilians to preserving order and security in the nation, but nearly all of them knew that they were in no condition to govern again given the many deficiencies in their own chains of command that remained from the Malvinas (Falklands) debacle. They also recognized how unpopular they were with the public and how much that fact hindered their ability to run the country. Still, there is no guarantee that President Carlos Menem will be able to subordinate them effectively before the armed forces regain what they need to govern once more.

It was the economy that absorbed most of Carlos Menem's attention after he became president in July 1989. His election was immediately followed by record inflation as everyone bought dollars to protect themselves against whatever might follow. In June alone, prices rose 114 percent. With a nearly bare treasury, huge debts to foreign banks that the armed forces had accumulated during the *Proceso*, and no new investments to revive the economy, Menem knew that populism would have to wait. With prices going out of control in June, he took the conservative path, administering conventional solutions in huge doses. The currency was devalued drastically, prices of public services were raised to keep them up with other prices, and all of the new prices and wages were frozen. Moreover, Menem insisted that the size of the government be reduced by selling off several of its enterprises, from the telephone company to the railways that Juan Perón had expropriated from the British almost forty years before. It was a bold move that astonished nearly everyone, even though it was obvious that drastic reforms were needed to revive an economy that had stagnated throughout the 1980s. Of course, that did not make it popular with workers who feared that they would lose their jobs when the government sold its enterprises. Despite their election of a Peronist president, neither the business people nor the workers who had come to rely on the government for their protection were willing to see it taken from them. But that is exactly what Menem said he intended to do.

NOTES

1. Samuel P. Huntington, *Political Order in Changing Societies* (New Haven, Conn.: Yale University Press, 1968), p. 4.
2. This is almost exactly the situation Huntington describes in *Political Order*, p. 196.
3. David Rock, *Politics in Argentina, 1890–1930: The Rise and Fall of Radicalism* (London: Cambridge University Press, 1975), p. 11.
4. Carlos F. Díaz Alejandro, *Essays on the Economic History of the Argentine Republic* (New Haven, Conn.: Yale University Press, 1970), p. 95.
5. Roberto Carri, *Sindicatos y poder en la Argentina* (Buenos Aires: Editorial Sudestada, 1967), p. 27.
6. Peter Smith, "Los radicales argentinos y la defensa de los intereses ganaderos, 1916–1930," *Desarrollo Económico* 7 (April-June 1967):826.
7. José Luis de Imaz, "Los que mandan: Las fuerzas armadas en la Argentina," *América Latina* 7 (October-December 1964):68.
8. Tomás Roberto Fillol, *Social Factors in Economic Development: The Argentine Case* (Cambridge, Mass.: MIT Press, 1961), p. 76.
9. Robert J. Alexander, *Organized Labor in Latin America* (New York: Free Press, 1965), p. 36.
10. Juan Eugenio Corradi, "Argentina," in *Latin America: The Struggle with Dependency and Beyond*, ed. Ronald H. Chilcote and Joel C. Edelstein (Cambridge, Mass.: Schenkman, 1974), p. 406.
11. Peter H. Smith, *Politics and Beef in Argentina: Patterns of Conflict and Change* (New York: Columbia University Press, 1969), p. 246.

12. Peter H. Smith, *Argentina and the Failure of Democracy: Conflict Among Political Elites* (Madison: University of Wisconsin Press, 1974), p. 104.

SUGGESTIONS FOR FURTHER READING

Baily, Samuel L. *Labor, Nationalism, and Politics in Argentina.* New Brunswick, N.J.: Rutgers University Press, 1967.
DiTella, Guido. *Argentina Under Peron, 1973–76.* New York: St. Martin's Press, 1983.
Fraser, Nicholas, and Marysa Navarro. *Eva Peron.* New York: W. W. Norton, 1980.
Gillespie, Richard. *Soldiers of Peron: Argentina's Montoneros.* London: Oxford University Press, 1982.
Goldwert, Marvin. *Democracy, Militarism, and Nationalism in Argentina.* Austin: University of Texas Press, 1972.
Imaz, José Luis de. *Los que mandan.* Albany: State University of New York Press, 1964.
Kennedy, John J. *Catholicism, Nationalism, and Democracy in Argentina.* Notre Dame, Ind.: University of Notre Dame Press, 1958.
Kirkpatrick, Jeane. *Leader and Vanguard in Mass Society: A Study of Peronist Argentina.* Cambridge, Mass.: MIT Press, 1971.
O'Donnell, Guillermo A. *Modernization and Bureaucratic Authoritarianism.* Berkeley: University of California Press, 1973.
Page, Joseph. *Perón: A Biography.* New York: Random House, 1983.
Pion-Berlin, David. *The Ideology of State Terror: Economic Doctrine and Political Repression in Argentina and Peru.* Boulder, Colo.: Lynne Rienner, 1989.
Potash, Robert A. *The Army and Politics in Argentina, 1928–1945.* Stanford, Calif.: Stanford University Press, 1969.
———. *The Army and Politics in Argentina, 1945–1962.* Stanford, Calif.: Stanford University Press, 1980.
Rock, David. *Politics in Argentina, 1890–1930: The Rise and Fall of Radicalism.* London: Cambridge University Press, 1975.
Smith, Peter H. *Argentina and the Failure of Democracy: Conflict Among Political Elites.* Madison: University of Wisconsin Press, 1974.
Snow, Peter G. *Political Forces in Argentina.* New York: Praeger Special Studies, 1979.
Timerman, Jacobo. *Prisoner Without a Name, Cell Without a Number.* New York: Alfred A. Knopf, 1981.
Waisman, Carlos. *Reversal of Development in Argentina.* Princeton, N.J.: Princeton University Press, 1987.
Walter, Richard. *Student Politics in Argentina.* New York: Basic Books, 1968.
Wynia, Gary W. *Argentina in the Postwar Era: Politics and Economic Policy Making in a Divided Society.* Albuquerque: University of New Mexico Press, 1978.
———. *Argentina: Illusions and Realities.* New York: Holmes and Meier, 1986.

9
Brazil: The Politics of Order and Progress?

IÊDA SIQUEIRA WIARDA

Brazil is a great country, both in physical terms and in terms of its potential. It is unique and distinct, sometimes but not always a part of the Third World. Politically, it defies easy definitions. "The system," as Brazilians like to call their political arrangements, is often contradictory and torn between very traditional and ultramodern aspects. Brazilians seldom doubt that theirs will be a great future, yet they are just as quick to wonder if that future will ever arrive. Popular, long-lived proverbs express a Brazilian fatalism that is tempered by messianic hope and a pervasive sense of humor. "God is a Brazilian" and "Brazil is a country of the future and always will be" are only two of the many versions of this mixture of faith and skepticism.

Brazil is big and diverse, its regions are distinct, and Brazilians enjoy touting their state of origin as being the best in the country. Historically, Brazil contains populations living at the level of the Stone Age all the way to those who are comfortable in the great metropolises of the world. Going beyond the diversities and the regionalisms is the common language, Portuguese. Throughout this largest Portuguese-speaking country in the world, the language is surprisingly uniform. Different accents are detectable, but Brazilians of all classes, all colors, and all regions understand each other. Thus, while Brazil faces many and complex problems as it approaches the twenty-first century, a high degree of basic cultural integration among the overwhelming majority of its citizens is a major positive source of strength.

This massive country occupies the east-central portion of South America and spreads over nearly half of the continent. The fifth-largest country in the world (3,290,000 square miles [8,521,000 square kilometers]), it shares borders with all other South American countries except Ecuador and Chile. Its Atlantic coast is over 4,500 miles (7,240 kilometers) long, and more than 90 percent of its population of over 149 million (1989) live on 10 percent of the land, in a 200-mile-wide

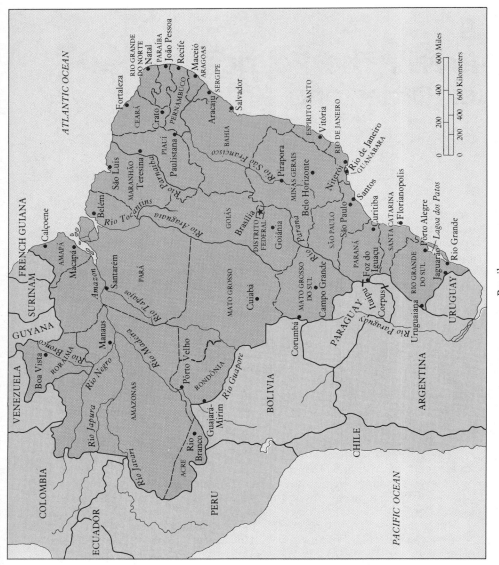

Brazil

(320-kilometer) zone bordering the Atlantic from south of Fortaleza to the Uruguayan border. The most populous country in Latin America and fifth in the world, it is now growing at a 2.2 percent rate annually.

Brazil has the world's eighth-largest market-based economy, booming during the "miracle" years from the mid-1960s to the mid-1970s until the "economic disaster" of the 1980s. Economic growth has been spectacular but erratic, but inflation has been a constant plague as it seldom drops below triple-digit rates. It is the largest less-developed-country debtor, owing about $110 billion (1989) to foreign and official creditors. Yet, in spite of these severe economic problems, Brazil is now a major trading nation, with a $5.2 billion bilateral trade surplus with the United States in 1989. Brazilian soybeans, orange juice, and shoes fill many store shelves, and its commuter airplanes link many cities in the United States. Arms and ammunitions manufactured in São Paulo state are found around the world, in Communist and non-Communist countries, and Brazilian engineers and technicians supervise and complete major construction projects in Africa and the Middle East.

Brazil has been criticized for not opening its own markets to other traders while it has been increasing its exports of manufactured goods and has become a strong contender in U.S., European, African, and Middle Eastern markets. The country has often attempted to soften this criticism by making small adjustments, but its traditional protectionism is now enshrined in the 1988 constitution, which gives Brazilian companies privileged access to finance and an exclusive right to operate in broadly defined key strategic sectors.

In spite of retrograde protectionism, in spite of negative consequences of energy and debt crises, and in spite of the burdens of inflation and continuing political uncertainties, Brazil's economy averaged a 7 percent yearly growth in the 1960s and 1970s, with the GDP reaching $270 billion in 1986 and a per capita GDP of $1,972 that same year. The state of São Paulo alone, with a population larger than that of Argentina, has a GDP similar to that of Belgium and thus ranks second in Latin America, after Mexico.

But while it is undeniable that Brazil has made impressive gains toward becoming a major power and a major industrialized nation, social, political, and international problems continue to fester and, in some cases, worsen. Even the official report *Brazil 2,000* indicates that nearly one-third of all Brazilians live in poverty and that in this food-exporting country, people literally starve to death.

Overall, Brazil struggles with huge problems, and this fledgling democracy is facing the challenges of unmet promises, cynicism about the value of a democratic system, and a conviction that, at least in the short run, no matter what form the political leadership takes, most Brazilians will face a deteriorating quality of life. In the mixture of hope for the future and current despair, much depends on the resilience of the country's cultural traditions and the ability to forge more-responsive government structures under the aegis of the 1988 constitution. It is clear that government policymaking is likely to continue to be ad hoc rather than deliberate, still inchoate and often capricious and nationalistic, no matter what the immediate consequences. Internationally, Brazil sends conflicting signals as to where its core interests lie, whether it is fully a First World partner or whether it should continue to receive the benefits of being classified with other Third World countries. Where will Brazil's alternative futures lie—in a continuing, if uneasy, accommodation of First and Third worlds, tradition and/or modernity? It is to an examination of these major underlying issues that this chapter is devoted.

HISTORY AND POLITICAL CULTURE

Brazil, bigger than the forty-eight contiguous states of the United States, stretches across three time zones, and the Atlantic island of Fernando de Noronha Territory lies in a fourth. Most of the country's land mass lies east of the United States, the equator crosses Brazil's northern border, and the portion south of Rio de Janeiro is outside the Torrid Zone. Mountains, geologically old and not very high, do moderate the climate, and nights are relatively cool. Rainfall is generally plentiful, but precipitation in the Northeast is irregular and that region, plagued by droughts, is the poorest in Brazil.

Some twenty mountains are above 5,000 feet (1,520 meters), but none is as high as 10,000 feet (3,050 meters). Half of the country is a plateau running from 500 to 3,000 feet (150 meters to 900 meters) above sea level. Geologically old, Brazil is not subject to earthquakes. The Amazon carries more water into the ocean than any other river in the world, its waters can be plied by oceangoing vessels as far as Peru, and many of its tributaries are also navigable by major ships. Without any great lakes, the country's rivers are numerous and powerful enough to assure that Brazil contains one-fifth of the world's fresh water. For a country that has had problems finding much oil, it is fortunate that Brazil has a great hydroelectric potential and that it now commands the world's largest hydroelectric power plant at Itaipú.

Brazilians usually divide their country into five regions. The North, stretching across the northern third of Brazil, is the largest and the least populated region. It is dominated by the Amazon and is an area of legendary wealth and potential, mostly still unproved. Manaus and Belém are the major cities in the largest rain forest in the world.

The Northeast occupies the eastern bulge and has become notorious in recent years for recurring droughts and human hardships. It is tropical in climate and does have a narrow coastal plain where traditional crops such as sugarcane and cacao have been grown for centuries. It is a region of old Portuguese names and proud political traditions, but it is also labeled "Brazil's Bangladesh"—poor and hopeless.

The densely populated East region goes from the states of Sergipe to Rio de Janeiro and includes the interior and politically important state of Minas Gerais, birthplace of presidents and a major industrial center. Unlike the Northeast, the East usually enjoys abundant rainfall. The highlands, rugged and mined for gold and precious and semiprecious stones in colonial days, are now mined for high-grade iron ore and other minerals.

The South, which includes the state of São Paulo, is the fastest growing center of Brazil's industry and agriculture. During years of severe drought Northeastern Brazilians seek haven and jobs in this bustling area, and this region has also received the largest number of immigrants, among them Germans, Italians, Lebanese, and Japanese—the last forming the largest Japanese enclave anywhere outside of Japan. The climate is mild, but occasionally frost occurs, damaging the coffee crop.

The Central West region includes the states of Mato Grosso (North and South), Goiás, and the federal district. This region has grown tremendously since the establishment of Brasília as the country's capital in 1960 and since becoming the site of lucrative agribusinesses. Rainfall is sometimes sparse, and the climate is tropical to mild in the highlands of the region. In the north, the region resembles the Amazon area, with dense forests and heavy rains, but its savannas are ideal for cattle raising. Some rivers flow north toward the Amazon while others run south to join the Plata Basin.

The East and the South regions have been the undisputed economic and political heartland for decades while the Northeast is the proverbial land of history, poverty, and drought. The North is the Amazon land of jungle and promise, and the Central West region is the brash political and growing agribusiness center. What links these varied regions is the same language and, progressively, the national communications grid. Railroads are scarce, highways are somewhat less so, rivers are used when not interrupted by falls, and the airplane now links most cities throughout the country, as do television, the telephone, and radio communications.

Just as Brazil has several distinct regions, its history sets it apart from Spanish America. It can be said that Brazil actually existed before it was formally discovered by the Portuguese explorer Pedro Alvares Cabral in 1500. In 1494 the pope, in an attempt to avoid subsequent disputes between the then-major empires of Spain and Portugal, divided the South American continent into an eastern portion, to belong to Portugal, and the larger western portion, to belong to Spain. Before long, it was clear that the Pope's Tordesilhas line would be breached and that the Portuguese would proceed to colonize the Brazilian landmass and impart to it their own Iberian traditions and their unique language.

The Tordesilhas line had granted Portugal only the easternmost bulge of today's Brazil, but Portuguese and later Brazilian explorers pushed the line westward until they reached the present borders. Seldom did land wars erupt between the Portuguese and the Spanish colonizers and their heirs. Often expansion occurred naturally as Brazilian pioneers went beyond the Tordesilhas line—in fact, most of them had never heard of such a line—to settle new land and to populate new areas, and their offspring moved even further west. Thus, from the beginning of its history, Brazil's concept of a "living frontier" has been a major aspect of its existence as a nation and has defined the character of its relations with other South American countries.

In the very early decades, however, the Portuguese seldom ventured beyond a few scattered primitive outposts on the Atlantic shore. Portugal, in contrast to Spain, was more interested in its lucrative trade with India than in exploring a primitive land where early promises of gold and precious stones had been disappointingly dashed. The only attraction of the new colony, in fact, seems to have been a red wood that produced a brilliant red dye. From this red wood—the color of glowing coals, and thus *brasil* wood in Portuguese—came the name of Brazil.

In the middle of the sixteenth century the French twice tried to settle near present-day Rio de Janeiro and were driven off, but their bold challenge proved to be the catalyst to Portugal's interest, and João III finally decided he needed to secure Cabral's discovery. The king parceled out the coastline in the form of fifteen royal grants (*capitanias*) to wealthy Portuguese. The *capitanias* gave Brazil its first formal shape and laid the basis for the country's enduring federalist traditions.

The *capitanias* grew very slowly, and only later in the sixteenth century did they become less stagnant as the Portuguese started raising sugarcane. But sugar, a highly prized commodity in Europe, required a great deal of labor in its production. Brazilian Indians were not suited to this strenuous labor (they preferred to die than to work as slaves), so at trading posts along the African coast, the Portuguese captured blacks and took them to tend the sugarcane fields and refineries. For the next three centuries, over 3 million young blacks were forcibly brought to the colony. Intermarriage between Portuguese, Indians, blacks, and the growing number of Brazilians (i.e., Portuguese subjects born in Brazil) was not uncommon, and the basis for Brazil's racial mixture was set.

Jesuit missionaries attempted to protect the Indians by gathering them into villages organized around a church, with the aim of Christianizing and educating them. Although the missionaries' intentions might have been good and did save Indians from enslavement and slaughter, most of the Indians died from strange diseases they had no immunity against, such as smallpox, measles, tuberculosis, and even the common cold. Their simple and unique culture was largely lost or slowly blended with the culture of the far more numerous blacks and whites. Today, only around 200,000 Indians remain in Brazil.

A sense of Brazilian national identity first emerged with the expulsion of the Protestant Dutch. For two decades they had controlled the northeastern coast, but Portuguese and Brazilians drove them out in

1654, a triumph for the Catholic church and for a Portuguese Brazil. But the event that brought about the opening of the interior was the discovery of good and plentiful gold and precious and semiprecious stones just before the onset of the eighteenth century. In Minas Gerais (literally, "general mines"), the development of the interior was given a major thrust by the exploits of the daring *bandeirantes*, mostly pioneers from São Paulo. These descendants of Portuguese and Indians traveled in bands and brought along flags (*bandeiras*), families, cattle, and Indian slaves. If confronted by the Jesuits, they were likely to pillage the missionaries' villages. Cruel and energetic, they ventured far from the coast and established the first settlements of present-day Goiás and the states of Mato Grosso. Diamantina in central Minas Gerais, now almost unknown outside of Brazil, was at one time considered the diamond capital of the world. It was also in these early mining towns that the first stirrings toward independence from Portugal took place, tragic and abortive attempts to emulate the North American independence movement and the republican form of government.

But Brazilian independence occurred in a distinct form from that of its Spanish neighbors. The other South American countries rebelled against Spain and eventually formed themselves into nine separate republics, but Brazil stayed intact, and its "war" of independence does not merit that label. Historically speaking, Brazil owes its independence to the facts that Napoleon's army invaded Portugal in 1807 and, under British pressure and protection, the Portuguese court moved to Brazil. Once in Brazil, João VI enjoyed the colony so much that he raised it in rank to a kingdom within the Portuguese empire, and even more significantly, he stayed in Rio de Janeiro long after the Napoleonic threat was past. When the British finally persuaded him to return to Lisbon, he left his son Pedro I as his regent. Shortly afterward, in 1822, Dom Pedro proclaimed Brazil's independence, and this Portuguese prince became Brazil's first monarch.

After this rather uneventful independence, Brazil experienced minor civil wars, slave rebellions, and secessions—including some in the south in favor of a republican form of government—but the former Portuguese colony somehow managed to survive all these struggles intact. The best explanation goes back to the fact that Brazil, in contrast to the rest of Spanish America, did not struggle through a protracted and divisive war of independence. The Portuguese House of Bragança ruled until 1889, and even today there are Bragança pretenders to the Brazilian government (and the newest constitution even allows voters to choose a monarchical form of government, if they wish, in the 1990s!).

The easy separation from the colonial power and the long period of relative stability gave Brazil a strong feeling of national unity and nearly a century of enlightened rule. In fact, it can be argued that it was the enlightened policies of Brazil's second emperor, Pedro II, that brought his reign to a close. His approval of the abolition of slavery in 1888 robbed him of the crucial support of the landed gentry, and shortly thereafter a republic was proclaimed and the heartbroken Brazilian king was sent into exile. But there were other forces that brought about the advent of a republic, many of which were nurtured by the king's policies themselves. A greater opening to the world made it possible for Brazilian elites to become familiar with democratic and republican forms of government elsewhere, and a trip by the emperor to the United States was fully reported back home so that educated people became familiar with the thriving republic to the north. In the meantime, especially during Pedro II's prolonged reign, the people in the southern portion of the country felt neglected by the government in Rio de Janeiro. Of even greater significance, younger military men were becoming increasingly politically involved yet restless under the emperor's rule. Brazil's war against Paraguay, which lasted from 1864 to 1870, was fought with a mixture of pride and shame since it pitted a giant against a determined but extremely weak opponent. Paraguay was ruined for decades by the consequences of the war, and even though Brazil and its allies, Argentina and Uruguay, were victorious, the war had been expensive and divisive for them too. This war debt was to be a burden for the rest of the Brazilian emperor's reign.

The debt, the doubts about the war itself, a desire to have a greater determination in the form of government, and the abolition of slavery converged to make the likelihood of change a foregone conclusion. Yet Pedro II was himself respected, and when the monarchy was overthrown, that action came as a surprise to most Brazilians. Benjamin Constant and Marshal Floriano Peixoto, who represented the disaffected military elements, engineered the overthrow with the crucial blessings of Marshal Deodoro da Fonseca, a longtime friend and supporter of Pedro II. On November 15, 1889, the Republic of Brazil was proclaimed. The emperor departed for Europe with his family and a few friends, refusing to accept the large compensation the revoultionaries offered. His wife died shortly thereafter, and Pedro himself died two years later.

The long reign had provided Brazil with decades of stability, but at the turn of the century the country was still almost empty, and its scarce population was mostly illiterate and divided into a miniscule rich elite, a large poor class, with an almost nonexistent middle class. The freed people were hardly better off than they had been as slaves. No universities had been established. Wealthy Brazilians sent their sons to Europe, mostly to France, to get an education because Pedro II's legendary love of learning had not been translated into the establishment of even a basic educational system. The few schools that did exist were run by the Catholic church, and most offered only a rudimentary education to the sons of the elite.

From 1889 to today the form of government has been that of a federal republic, but Brazil has never had a truly federal system. The president has traditionally been incomparably stronger than governors or mayors, checks and balances do not really apply, and the republican system itself has been tempered by degrees of authoritarianism. The 1988 constitution attempts to give greater powers to Congress, but it is still too early to know if these powers will go unchallenged.

The military, which was a power behind the throne during the monarchy, is still very influential, and between 1964 and 1985 actually governed the country. Revealingly, the latent powers of the military to intervene have not been fully removed in the most recent constitutional charter.

The middle class has expanded, especially since the 1930s, but it cannot compete in terms of sheer political and economic power with the military and economic elites. The poor still form the largest group, but they have gained some welfare protection since the 1930s. The 1988 constitution extends and expands many of their protections and welfare entitlements, but again, time will tell whether the country and the politicians have the will—and the money—to implement these more generous provisions.

In fact, Brazil in the 1980s was still spoken of as containing two civilizations, the "Belindia" of sophisticated Brazilians, who like to joke that their country is a juxtaposition of Belgium and India. The new constitution contains the promise of a less disparate Brazil, but even the most optimistic Brazilian politicians do not believe that the gap will soon be closed.

This lingering economic gap is somehow bridged, even transcended, by Brazil's vibrant culture. Television viewers worldwide are familiar with the spectacular pageant of carnival in Rio de Janeiro, in which the most daring and imaginative (as well as expensive) displays are staged by slum dwellers. Popular music, similarly highlighted during carnival, reaches many countries in toned down versions of the samba and bossa nova and finally, the all-pervasive Muzak. Brazilian movies have competed well in world festivals and in box office appeal; television shows are technically advanced and innovative; and a great many *novelas* (soap operas) that are first seen in Brazil are routinely seen in Portugal, in former Portuguese colonies in Africa, and even throughout Spanish America.

From an international perspective, it is not farfetched to consider Brazil as the cultural center of the Portuguese-speaking world, because of its vastly superior number of writers, actors, painters, and artists in comparison to other Lusophone countries. Jorge Amado, whose works fictionally depict life in Bahia and the Northeast, has had seveal of his novels become best-sellers in the United States and made into movies, among them *Gabriela* and *Dona Flor*. The visual arts are also noteworthy, and some of its best known interpreters reflect the ethnic mix of the country. Candido Portinari's murals in São Paulo portray the suffering of Northeastern migrants and urban poor, and Manabu Mabe, also of São Paulo, has paintings viewed around the world. The cities of Salvador and Ouro Preto feature some of the hemisphere's best examples of Baroque architecture by early artisans. Brasília is well known for its futuristic design, and its architecture has been emulated on all continents.

Sports, particularly soccer, occupy an important position in all Brazilians' lives. Life seems to come to a stop when the world soccer competition takes place every four years, and politicians vie with each other to show their devotion to a winning team. Volleyball, water sports, track and field, basketball, and car racing are other major sports in which Brazilians have done well in international meets.

A love of *novelas*, a penchant for emotional and earthy sambas, a cynical approach to religion and other ponderous matters, and a perennial sense of optimism in the face of daily disappointments seem to characterize the Brazilian personality. In the words of Elizabeth Bishop, the Pulitzer-prize-winning writer who made Brazil her home for many decades,

> Brazilians are very quick, both emotionally and physically. Like the heroes of Homer, men can show their emotions without disgrace. Their superb futebol players hug and kiss each other when they score goals, and weep dramatically when they fail to. Brazilians are also quick to show sympathy. One of the first and most useful words a foreigner picks up is *coitado* ["poor thing"]. . . . [There is the great] Brazilian belief in tolerance and forbearance . . . [with] the greatest tolerance . . . extended to love, because in Brazil that is always the most important emotion. Love is the constant element in almost every news story, street scene, or familiar conversation.[1]

Few Brazilians would quarrel with the poet's understanding of their psychology!

That psychological profile, even though written a number of years ago, still is fairly accurate for today's 149 million Brazilians. Theirs is now the most populous Latin American country. Most Brazilians live in the south-central part of the country, which includes the industrial and political centers of São Paulo, Rio de Janeiro, and Belo Horizonte. Brasília, whom many thought would never amount to more than a backwater capital, now has a population approaching 2 million and is a major magnet in the central-west area. Porto Alegre, approaching 3 million inhabitants, is the major center in the deep south. Urban growth has been spectacular; still mostly rural up to the 1950s, Brazil in 1984 had an urban population that included more than two-thirds of all the citizens. At the same time, while urbanization aided economic development and brought more people to work in the great and expanding industries, it also created serious social and political problems. The major cities are chronically short of funds to provide even the most rudimentary services such as water and sewer facilities. Still, various half-hearted attempts to lure the peasants back to the land have been dismal faiiures.

Overall, four major groups make up the Brazilian population: the indigenous Indians; the Portuguese, who began colonizing in the sixteenth century and who again came in large numbers after their own "revolution" in the 1970s; Africans, brought as slaves to work on the plantations and in the mines; and various European, Middle Eastern, and Oriental immigrants who have settled since the middle of the nineteenth century, particularly in the south-central area to make São Paulo one of the most cosmopolitan cities in the world. The states of Santa Catarina and Rio Grande do Sul have been havens for waves of German immigrants, prompting the unfounded scare that they might subvert Brazil to Hitler's cause. Altogether, it is conservatively estimated that about 5 million Europeans settled in Brazil between 1875 and 1960, and millions of Japanese and Middle Easterners have come to Brazil to find a land of opportunity. Many of these immigrants struggled for a long time but eventually succeeded beyond all expectations. Many highly placed politicians, professionals, and entrepreneurs are second and third generation hyphenated Brazilians. Most immigrant families have by now become fully integrated, having adopted the Portuguese language and often the Catholic religion as well. The sense of being Brazilian is strong, ethnic strife is minor, and when it does occur openly, it is not condoned officially and is ridiculed and condemned by the media.

The Portuguese explorers usually came without their families and often intermarried with the Indians and later with the African slaves. Thus, although the basic ethnic stock of Brazil was once Portuguese, miscegenation and the subsequent waves of immigrants have resulted in a rich ethnic and cultural heritage. Traditionally, Brazilians are adamant in denying any racial or ethnic prejudice. It is true, however, that the further one progresses up the socioeconomic and political ladder, the whiter one is likely to be (though not necessarily carrying a Portuguese name as presidential candidate Paulo Maluf and Presidents Juscelino Kubitschek and Ernesto Geisel attest). By the same token, attempts to organize black movements have not been very successful, and perhaps revealingly, the labels used in these attempts are not Portuguese but imported from abroad and the leadership is as likely to be foreign as it is Brazilian.

The Indians have been far less fortunate than the blacks or the immigrants. Located mainly in the northern and western border regions and in the upper Amazon Basin, there are now only around 200,000 Brazilian Indians, and they are considered an endangered group. Their numbers have been declining for years, but recently increased contact with the outside world, the expansion of agribusiness, and road projects have accelerated the Indians' disappearance. Although the government has had programs to establish reservations and to provide assistance, it has also promoted or at least condoned the expansion of roads, mining, and commerce onto hunting and tribal lands, with disastrous results for the dwindling numbers of indigenous people. Tragic stories of farmers and miners despoiling Indian villages are not unusual. Meanwhile, the efforts of private groups and the Catholic church to help the Indians survive are subject to controversy, and most Brazilians feel that the Indians should "integrate"—or else.

The fact that the few Indians who have survived often cannot communicate in Portuguese has not helped their cause because the Indian languages are wholly foreign to the vast majority of Brazilians. In fact, Portuguese is one of the main strands that holds the overwhelming majority of Brazilians together, of whatever region, class, or ethnic background. It is true that Brazilians who live near the borders can usually communicate in Spanish and that educated Brazilians know English, but Portuguese, with its regional accents, is the language of Brazil. North American–Brazilian cultural centers are very popular, and a knowledge of English is avidly sought as an essential key to professional, business, and social betterment. In São Paulo and Rio de Janeiro, British, French, and German cultural centers also exist and even maintain some schools, but in number and popularity they do not approach the draw of the North American–Brazilian cultural centers, almost all of which are now sponsored by private groups. It should be stressed, however, that even though ambitious young Brazilians do try to learn English and even to obtain *bolsas* (grants, scholarships) to study in the United States, brain drain is not a major problem.

Another main cultural strand is the Roman Catholic church, but this largest Catholic country in the world is also one in which Catholic tenets have been traditionally lightly respected and in which the number of religious vocations has never been high. Protestant sects, especially charismatic and fundamentalist ones, have grown tremendously in recent years, especially among the poorer urban dwellers, and many Brazilians, even if nominally Catholic, have great devotion to various spiritualist and voodoo rituals. There are also important Jewish groups in Rio de Janeiro and São Paulo, and Moacyr Scliar, a well-known novelist and essayist from Porto Alegre, has written extensively on Brazil's Jewish community and its role in national life. Overall, religious tolerance is the norm, and persecution for one's beliefs has been rare, although the Catholic church is accorded a special place in religious festivals, family traditions, and everyday life.

MAJOR INTEREST GROUPS, POLITICAL PARTIES, POLITICAL ORGANIZATIONS

With its size and economic, political, and regional diversity, it is not surprising that Brazil has always had a variety of major interest groups, parties, and organizations, but this variety has become more pronounced in recent decades. Since Pedro II's empire represented stability and provided for a great deal of freedom, the transition from monarchy to republic in 1889 did *not* bring about an outcropping of popular groups overnight. Indeed, the republic emerged as a continuation of oligarchic rule, one in which the landed interests were the most powerful, the states of São Paulo and Minas Gerais continued their preeminence, and the top military officers exerted the moderating power (*poder moderador*) that the emperor had represented. Outstanding civilians such as the great jurist Rui Barbosa were sometimes brought to the fore, and it was he, rather than the military leaders, who wrote the decree that brought about the separation of church and state in 1890.

World War I brought the first major challenge to the new Brazilian rulers. The loss of European markets was disastrous as the Brazilian farmers were unable to sell their crops, and only toward the end of the European conflict did trade improve somewhat as the warring nations needed to import foodstuffs. Brazil officially opted to side with the Allies in 1916, and this choice helped the country's trade situation. But even this improved trade was not enough to cure festering problems. The coffee plantations, which had supplanted the sugar plantations as the major export activity, were overproducing, and prices continued to drop. More ominously, the southern states, which long had felt alienated from Rio de Janeiro, were becoming more restless, and the old dream of secession still persisted.

Issues of civilian-military relations were a constant source of aggravation to people in and out of government. Although civilians managed to keep the military out of the presidency, discontent within the army made all presidents concerned. The impact of the Great Depression was acutely felt early on in Brazil as exports continued to drop. Influential Brazilians, powerful farmers, and young military officers began to look for a forceful president as the 1930 elections approached. The incumbent president further exacerbated these issues by favoring a presidential candidate from his own state of São Paulo, even though an informal alternation had prevailed in which presidents from the states of São Paulo and Minas Gerais had taken turns. The incumbent's failure to observe this informal tradition proved to be the catalyst for *mineiros* to support an alternative candidate, Getúlio Vargas, a popular governor from the southern state of Rio Grande do Sul.

When the 1930 elections took place and the official candidate won, many Brazilians felt that Vargas had been deprived of a legitimate triumph, and he was urged to rebel. Feeling that he had enough military and popular support to succeed, Vargas and his followers moved by train toward the capital. Vargas's support grew as he traveled north; by the time he reached Rio de Janeiro, the president had fled and Vargas could assume power with a minimum of force.

Between 1930 and his resignation in 1945 Vargas ruled with a combination of wiliness, forever changing political coalitions, a vaguely corporatist Estado Novo concept, and a brand of populism that endeared him to many Brazilians who got used to calling him "the father of the poor." With little regard for rules, Vargas instituted extraconstitutional policies and programs and was not averse to ruthlessly suppressing people who opposed him. Power was centralized, and federalism, already weak, was practically abolished when Vargas used his powers to intervene in the states, appointing his own governors. Education became centralized and controlled, censorship was imposed, and the legislative assembly was not convened.

But while many of Vargas's decrees and measures were more often than not softened in their application, other policies instituted by him were to have lasting effects. His social security system, a novelty in Brazil that made him very popular with workers, still forms the core of today's social welfare system. He also garnered a great deal of support from nationalists of different political stripes by carrying out extensive nationalization of economic institutions and natural resources. Characteristically calling himself "apolitical," Vargas's regime lacked a coherent ideology and even political parties. He counted on the support of labor but made sure it had little independent strength.

During World War II, after some initial hesitation, Brazil joined the Allied side in 1942 and even contributed troops and officers who saw action in Italy alongside U.S. forces. The United States was allowed to use Brazilian bases in the Northeast, and the country prospered because of the great demand for its products. Yet World War II, fought for the preservation of democracy, had the unsurprising effect of calling into question Vargas's authoritarianism. In October 1945 military officers, responding to popular demands for a freer system, stepped in and sent Vargas home to Rio Grande do Sul. The second republic, with a former minister of war, Gen. Eurico Gaspar Dutra, as president, was ushered in on January 1946.

In September 1946 a new constitution was adopted, and though it included guarantees of free elections and civil liberties, it preserved the greatly enlarged executive built up by Vargas and his centralized institutions. President Dutra continued investments in public works and a greater expansion of the health and transportation systems. Inflation, however, was a constant menace. Brazil expected greater trade and economic help from the United States, especially in view of Brazil's role in World War II, but these expectations were disappointed. Even more disappointing was the fact that the massive European Marshall Plan for economic reconstruction was not paralleled in Latin America.

Vargas was popularly elected to the presidency in 1951 as the candidate of the Labor party, but he no longer commanded the respect or the affection he had enjoyed during his earlier years in power. He had lost much of his popular appeal and was unable to deal with economic problems any more successfully than Dutra. Charges of corruption involved some of his closest associates, and when one of his aides appeared to have been directly involved in an assassination attempt against an opposition journalist and the death of an air force major, the armed forces seemed to be prepared to push Vargas to resign. Faced with the possibility of a military coup or perhaps in an effort to avoid possible bloodshed, Vargas committed suicide.

The election of 1955, in which Juscelino Kubitschek was chosen president and former Vargas minister of labor João Goulart vice president, was made possible by the military's willingness to play its *poder moderador* role to the hilt and serve as the guarantor that the duly elected officials could take office. Kubitschek, who had been one of the most popular governors of Minas Gerais, vowed to give Brazil "fifty years of progress in five"; and in many ways he succeeded in this promise, but at a heavy price. He pushed for the hasty completion of hydroelectric plants and a variety of public works, the establishment of several new universities and medical schools, the opening of major highways and airports. He launched Brazil's automobile and airplane industries, and he finally succeeded in building the long-planned new capital, Brasília, in the central state of Goiás. All of these projects could be justified as serving as the building blocks for a modern Brazil, but they were pushed too hastily, and practically all involved tremendous cost overruns. By the time he left office Juscelino, as he preferred to be called, was still a very popular man, but inflation had become a major burden. The successful presidential candidate in 1960, former mayor and governor of São Paulo, Jânio Quadros, ran on a pledge to balance the budget, end inflation, protect Brazil from foreign greed, curb corruption, and launch an independent foreign policy. Quadros was elected with the largest plurality in the history of Brazil.

He soon ran afoul of Congress and alienated even some of his strongest supporters by his aloof and erratic manners. He did push for measures designed to reform exchange controls, end consumer subsidies, and curtail the printing of worthless money, but these measures took away much of his support among the poor people and others most negatively affected by his policies. He publicly praised the Soviet Union, even though little trade was possible between the two countries and a communist system held little appeal for most Brazilians. He pinned a medal on Fidel Castro, even though it was common knowledge that the Cuban dictator had presided over a period of terrorism and indiscriminate deaths at the infamous *paredon* ("wall").

Quadros became an even more enigmatic figure as he exhibited a number of eccentricities, among them wearing a uniform and requiring others around him wear one too to ward off "germs." His economic measures did not seem to be working, his popularity evaporated, and his peculiarities led people to believe he was unstable. No longer adulated as a savior and being aloof and eccentric, he resigned abruptly and left Brazil before completing a year in office. His irresponsible tantrum was to cost Brazil dearly.

Quadros's vice president, João Goulart, had been picked for that position almost as an afterthought and mostly because it was felt he would bring to the ticket whatever remained of the old Vargas machine. Goulart, like Vargas, was from the south, a landowner and a politician with close ties to labor. At the time of Quadros's unexpected resignation,

Goulart happened to be in the People's Republic of China. Politicians favorable as well as unfavorable to him counseled that he return to Brazil by a long route so that the military, Congress, and other influential groups could work out a compromise that would enable him to become the president. The eventual compromise created the post of a prime minister who would share power with Goulart—and probably be closer to the people who most objected to him as president.

The compromise worked out, and Goulart became the president. But almost from the very start the relations among the president, the military, and the old-line politicians were strained. Goulart prevailed in getting rid of the prime minister, but this was a Pyrrhic victory. For the people who were already suspicious of his intentions, this action confirmed their fear that Goulart wanted to become a second Vargas, only more so—more populist, more to the left, and more demagogic.

Goulart's erratic economic policies proved to be far more inflationary than able to create new opportunities and greater development. Unable or unwilling to control his one base of support, the unions, Goulart let strikes and threats of strikes become a daily occurrence. For most Brazilians, who traditionally always opt for their flag's motto *Ordem e Progresso* (Order *and* Progress), the spectacle of a demagogic president unable to provide at least a measure of economic and political certainty engendered revulsion and a longing for a more stable government.

Much has been written about the U.S. involvement in the coup that eventually pushed Goulart from the presidency. A fair appraisal would conclude that North Americans, like most Brazilians, felt uneasy about the turn of events. This uneasiness was compounded by Goulart's inflammatory and vague threats against "foreign powers" and by his more radical advisers, some of whom may have had links to Brazil's small Communist party. But to conclude that the United States "made" the coup or even caused it is to be blind to the realities of Brazilian traditions and politics in 1964. The United States probably knew about and did not discourage a coup. The U.S. embassy was supportive of the people who wanted to get rid of Goulart and reform the country. After all, a number of highly placed North Americans in Brazil were close friends of influential Brazilians who were active in the opposition, especially those in the military.[2]

The actual unraveling is beyond dispute. The final catalyst came from Goulart himself when he seemed to undermine military discipline by siding with groups of mutinous soldiers. This was the last straw. With the growing middle class already bitter because of inflation and the daily uncertainties caused by strikes, the military was urged to fulfill its constitutional duty to act as the *poder moderador* and to make sure that progress *and* order, as well as discipline, prevailed. Unhappy governors of powerful states such as Minas Gerais joined with generals in insisting that Goulart resign or be faced with the prospect of a protracted civil war.

The "revolution" of March 31, 1964, was virtually bloodless. There was practically no support for Goulart, and even his earlier supporters, the labor unions, failed to rise in his favor. Most political leaders regarded military rule as the only alternative to strikes fomented by the president as well as mutinies and daily chaos. The army chief of staff, Marshal Humberto Castelo Branco, who had seen combat duty in Italy alongside U.S. forces, was chosen president. A quiet, intellectual man, he sincerely believed that his term in office would be a mere transition to another, more-reliable civilian president. But Castelo Branco was in the minority among his fellow officers, most of whom—as well as a great many civilians in Brazil—felt otherwise and thought that the country needed a strong "apolitical" government. The military was destined to rule Brazil for over twenty years, and even in the 1988 constitution their traditional power as a moderating force has not been eliminated.

Castelo Branco himself never doubted that he had acted constitutionally. The 1946 constitution had given the armed forces the responsibility of maintaining law and order and ensuring the normal functioning of government. In the military men's eyes—as in the eyes of most Brazilians—the civilian president had violated his own mandate. He had trampled on the constitution and had violated the military's code of conduct by siding with mutinous troops against their officers.

Whatever the debate about the constitutionality of the military takeover, there was little anticipation of what came after the coup. Instead of a transitional regime, the military consolidated its power. Even those politicians who had initially sided with the officers were banned from politics or sent into exile. The still-popular Kubitschek was among those who were proscribed. At first political parties were considered unnecessary or nuisances, and thus the thirteen that did exist were abolished. Eventually the military saw the need to promote a more "popular" image, and two political organizations, the progovernment National Renovating Alliance (ARENA) and the opposition Brazilian Democratic Movement (MDB), were formed under government auspices. As their names indicate, they were coalitions of parties and ideological factions rather than political parties in the U.S. sense.

For a time, especially between 1968 and 1972, the military leaders in power were prone to disdain any effort at democratization. The idea seems to have centered on providing an economic miracle that would, in turn, expand the economic pie and eventually also the number of pieces that could be given away to the populace. The emphasis was on technocratic rather than political advice, on economic development rather than preparation for democracy and popular participation. Censorship was the order of the day, and the regime in power was not hesitant to show who was boss, to use threats and outright brutality if it felt that was what was needed to "sanitize" the system.

As long as the economic expansion continued and inflation was kept fairly low, demands that the military give up power were muted. But the oil shock of 1973 changed the situation. Coming from outside and completely outside the control of the government, the skyrocketing of oil prices meant a drastic reduction of the economic forecasts. The economic miracle was no more, the pie was no longer growing, and the people who were demanding more than the merest of crumbs were becoming less intimidated and more vocal. With the economy faltering, the military leaders saw the wisdom of starting toward the eventual resumption of democratic forms.

Under an administration-sponsored bill, Congress abolished the two-party system, and a multiparty system was now contemplated. Five parties were recognized under the party reorganization law; two of them were actual continuations of those allowed previously. The opposition party Brazilian Democratic Movement (MDB) became the Brazilian Democratic Movement party (PMDB), and its basis was partly the old Brazilian Labor party (PTB) and a few smaller political groupings, as well as whatever remained of the more progressive elements of President Dutra's Social Democratic party (PSD). In its new incarnation, the PMDB counted among its supporters the expanding urban middle class, intellectuals, and workers. Its program called for greater control of the economy, income redistribution in order to help the disadvantaged groups in society, full political democracy, and direct elections.

The former government party, ARENA, itself went back to the old National Democratic Union (UDN), which, in turn, had been the main opposition to Vargas in the 1940s and early 1950s and had backed Quadros's successful presidential campaign in 1960. Most of ARENA's members had supported the 1964 coup, and many of its leaders had served in military administration cabinets. In its new guise, ARENA became the Democratic Social party (PDS). It tried to appeal to the urban middle class, but its greatest strength continued to be in the rural areas.

The pre-1964 Brazilian Labor party (PTB) suffered much infighting in its attempt to regain its preeminence, and out of the struggle emerged the Democratic Workers party (PDT), which was most active in the state of Rio de Janeiro where it was led by Governor Leonel Brizola. The governor, closely associated by family, state, and political ties to the deposed Goulart, sought to model the party on the European social-democratic parties, but most observers saw the PDT as a personalistic vehicle for the ambitious governor rather than an ideological one. Another party in search of the labor vote was the Workers party (PT), which competed primarily with the PMDB and the PDT for the votes of industrial workers and for the ideological backing of urban intellectuals.

The Liberal Front party (PFL) was led by former Vice President Aureliano Chaves of Minas Gerais, who split from the PDS in the 1984 presidential campaign to support the PMDB and fellow *mineiro* presidential candidate Tancredo Neves. In fact, most of the PFL, which in 1985 became a junior partner in President José Sarney's democratic alliance, was composed of politicians who had been elected in 1982 on the Democratic Social party ticket but who had subsequently broken away from that party in order to support Neves. With capable young leaders, the PFL nonetheless fared poorly in the 1986 election, giving rise to the joke that it was a party of great leaders and a tiny following. Its modest strength lay in small and rural enclaves, and this support worked to its disadvantage in a country that is increasingly urban and urban oriented.

President Sarney himself had been one of the original PFL leaders before he formally joined the PMDB to become Neves's running mate. The PMDB-PFL coalition enabled Neves to upset most predictions and to defeat the military government–backed PDS opponent, Deputy Paulo Maluf of São Paulo, in 1984. Neves commanded a wide margin in the electoral college and was a popular, grandfatherly figure. He had accomplished the nearly impossible tasks of assembling a disparate variety of ideological groups intent upon replacing the military and launching a democratic system. For its part, the military had stacked the game to favor Maluf but, faced with the popularity of Neves, opted to accept Neves as someone too politically shrewd to attempt too much democratic progress without a good measure of order. All prognostications came to naught when Neves fell fatally ill on the eve of his inauguration.

With Neves near death, the possibility of a military coup or the passing of the presidency to Ulysses Guimarães, the congressional leader, were only two of many possibilities. But Guimarães, a longtime opposition leader, could not count on the goodwill of the military, and the vice president–elect Sarney had, after all, been a former president of the promilitary Democratic Social party. After a great deal of political maneuvering, Sarney was confirmed as the new president. He had the support of the PDS and the PFL, but he was not a popular figure. The military did not fully trust him because he had switched sides instead of supporting its candidate, Maluf; the democratic forces that had so enthusiastically supported Neves could not forget that Sarney had been added to the ticket as a last-minute gesture toward people who had supported the military but were now willing to jump onto the civilian bandwagon.

Opposition to Sarney came mainly from the left, from the Democratic Workers party (PDT) of Rio de Janeiro and the Workers party (PT) of São Paulo. The PDT mixed populism and machine politics as part of Leonel Brizola's perennial struggle to attain the presidency; the PT, on the other hand, has really been an umbrella for a variety of socialist groups, often based on unions and on the Catholic church's liberation theology wing. Both the PDT and the PT assumed that worsening economic problems would bring them victory.

Their calculations, however, initially backfired because of the short-term maneuvers of the president and his supporters. The early success of the economic Cruzado Plan, launched in February 1986, buoyed

Sarney's popularity and ensured an easy victory for those people who were aligned with him. It mattered little in the election campaign that the Cruzado Plan proved to be an ephemeral respite and that it had to be abandoned shortly after the 1986 elections—in fact, cynics said that the plan worked only long enough to assure the socialists' loss in those elections.

By 1988, however, Sarney no longer could hide the economic debacle or even buy or influence many voters. In the November election for mayors and municipal assemblies, Sarney's policies were overwhelmingly rejected. Sarney and the old-line politicians, including presidential hopefuls Maluf and Guimarães, were the great losers, and the undisputed great winner was the Workers' party (PT), closely followed by Brizola's Democratic Workers party (PDT). It could also be said that the 1988 election, in which an unpopular and arguably illegitimate government paid the price for an inflation rate of more than 700 percent in the preceding year, reestablished populist Brizola and socialist Luis Ignácio da Silva (better known as Lula) as serious candidates for the presidency in 1989. The possibility of either man winning the elections was viewed with deep misgivings by the armed forces and the conservative business establishment, but the other alternatives were not much more reassuring for an orderly transition to democracy and to a renewal of "progress."

As it turned out, the 1989 contest proved the volatility of a large, young, and inexperienced electorate. More than twenty candidates waged a vigorous campaign. Some of them were old political names—not only Brizola but also Maluf, Guimarães, and former Vice President Aureliano Chaves. Others represented the new forces of organized labor and liberation theology; Lula probably found his greatest strength here. Just days before the elections, all polls were rendered meaningless when a popular television star announced his candidacy and immediately became one of the front runners. In a twist of the proverbial *jeito*, the supreme electoral court found him ineligible to run. That left Lula and Brizola as the major contenders, along with a young former governor of one of Brazil's smallest states, Fernando Collor de Mello.

Disdaining to affiliate with any major party, Collor came out of nowhere to lead the race. He survived the first ballot contest and narrowly edged out Lula in the runoff elections in December 1989. Collor had come to prominence when he led a campaign, as governor of Alagoas, against highly paid civil servants. He turned this campaign into a national crusade against corruption and incompetence. His vigorous denunciation of Sarney struck a responsive chord among Brazil's poorest, the rural population, and businessmen fed up with the state's dominance in the economy. With the backing of the powerful Globo news network, Collor successfully undermined Lula's appeal. Most of Brazil's intellectuals supported Lula and agreed with his Marxist prescription to cure the country's ills. Collor called for a vague Thatcheresque restructuring of the economy.

The young president (40 years of age) has promised to bring back some order and progress to his economically troubled nation. His program includes cutting the inflation rate, which ran at a record 1,800 percent in 1989, prosecuting tax evaders, cutting the number of ministries in half, and selling money-losing state companies. He hopes that foreign creditors will swap their debt titles for shares in Brazilian companies and that the debt can be renegotiated such that service payments are capped at $5 billion a year. But to enact even a portion of this ambitious plan, Collor needs the cooperation of a powerful and hostile Congress. Lula, Brizola, and other disappointed presidential hopefuls count on *increasing* their supporters' share of the congressional seats in the October 1990 elections. To those bitterly frustrated by Collor's victory, the goal is not greater order and progress but more chaos and confrontation.

Of course, the specter of a coup lurks just below the surface. The military, some of whom opposed both Lula and Brizola, are uneasy over Collor's proposal to abolish the National Information Service (SNI), Brazil's foreign and domestic intelligence agency. "If he wants to abolish the Service, let him send a bill to Congress," said Gen. Ivan Mendes, the current head of the SNI.[3] At the other end of the spectrum, two small Communist parties, illegal during the military regimes, are now openly poised to discredit the new president. A small Green party objects to Collor's development plans, and, one must not forget, many Brazilians, on nationalistic grounds, firmly oppose more foreign investments.

But all this political ferment has had some positive results. Since 1985 Brazilians, regardless of their ideological leanings, have fully participated in vigorous partisan politics, informed by a wide range of media reporting that expresses a broad range of political views and ideologies. One can speculate, however, that the two dozen or so political parties will eventually coalesce into three or four major fronts or umbrella organizations that fit into the pattern of right, center, and left—with Brazil's political center being considerably to the left of the U.S. political center.

In addition to the political parties, there are a number of interest groups that vie for popular support. Some of these groups predate the latest democratic opening and even go back to the Vargas era, when the president subsidized and assisted such groups in exchange for political support. Among them is labor, whose members first banded together in mutual aid societies in the very early years of industrialization. It was not until Vargas's first term as president, however, in the late 1930s and early 1940s, that these workers were organized into unions, which would receive benefits from the government while avoiding strikes and other destabilizing tactics. In effect, labor rights and social security provisions were provided at the price of collaboration or, at the very least, apathy.

After the 1964 coup the military abolished the largest labor confederation, the General Workers Command (CGT), which had been a major supporter of President Goulart, himself a former labor minister under Vargas. Under all the military administrations, the labor unions were strictly controlled and placed under government intervention. Union leaders were picked by the government to ensure industrial peace because it was essential, in the military's plan to attract more domestic and foreign investements, that labor did not agitate for raises or go out on strike.

While the economy was booming in the late 1960s and early 1970s, coinciding also with the most stringent military controls, the system of state-imposed industrial peace worked almost as predicted. After the downturn in the late 1970s labor was not as easily tamed, and also about this time, the military itself was beginning to question the wisdom of remaining in power for an indefinite period. Eventually, new unions and new leaders emerged outside of government control or, at the very least, with tacit acceptance by the military administration. After the democratic opening (abertura), which also began in the late 1970s, it was possible to strike even though strikes could still be ruled illegal. In 1980 metalworkers in São Paulo managed to shut down the powerful automobile industry there for several weeks. Their leader, Luis Ignácio da Silva, was finally jailed, but the strike showed that workers were again willing to take risks (from this fairly successful strike action emerged the new PT party).

In contrast to the CGT, Brazilian businesspeople, either as individuals or through their organizations, encouraged and welcomed the 1964 coup. They had had reason to fear Goulart's increasing alignment with labor's demands, and they had also disliked the general economic and political uncertainty, which made investment planning difficult, if not impossible. Their euphoria over getting rid of Goulart, however, proved short-lived because the military proceeded to further consolidate the government's role in the economy. Military and civilian technocrats moved into various new economic areas without consulting the private sector, and the old tradition of having the government protect weak companies was rendered obsolete by the government's determination to attain economic growth as fast as possible. Foreign companies were lured to invest in Brazil, often at the expense of less-efficient Brazilian enterprises, and the lowering of tariffs made it easier to import certain items than to produce them at home. Tax collection was tightened, and thus another traditional way of financing business was removed.

The growing disappointment and even resentment on the part of the business sector toward the military made the businesspeople, for their own reasons, ready to welcome and support abertura just as the workers and old-line politicians were doing. Business support for an end to the military regime coalesced with that of other groups that had challenged the authoritarian system for years. One of these groups was the Catholic church.

Brazil is the most Catholic country in the world, in terms of the number of church members, and the church has a special position as an interest group. In contrast to many Spanish-speaking countries in Latin America, Brazil has not experienced bitter and long fights in relation to the church. The first republican constitution in 1891, under the inspiration of positivism, took away the church's special privileges without causing major trauma.

For decades after the advent of the republic the Brazilian Catholic hierarchy concentrated on running schools for the Brazilian elite and on stressing theological and pastoral duties. Vatican II, between 1962 and 1965, moved the church toward greater involvement in social and political matters, but this was not a radical departure because, especially in the 1940s and 1950s, a number of lay and Catholic groups had become active among students, workers, and even clearly political organizations. Vatican II did give a new impetus to this refocusing of the church, however, and it also gave Brazilian theologians the opportunity to advocate liberation theology and greater attention to the poor.

In the early 1960s this refocusing coincided with President Goulart's call for populist measures, such as agrarian reform and expansion of the welfare system. At the time of the 1964 coup the church was deeply divided, with some members of the clergy supporting Goulart and others seeking to undermine him. Some supported his populism, but others saw it simply as a demagogic appeal. Many people feared that the church's growing political involvement would entangle it in matters that were not crucial to it as an institution and as a church. Large parades in the major cities often had the tacit approval and support of the church, with parishioners calling for moral renewal and decrying the chaos of everyday life. In the Northeast, priests were among those who helped landless peasants take over large and often unused tracts of land. The possibility of a divided church did not help Goulart's cause.

After the advent of a military regime in 1964 this split continued. At first many people continued to be wary of what they perceived as the politicization of the church. Others, however, increasingly denounced government repression and accused the government of failing Brazilian traditions by refusing to return to the barracks and give power back to civilians. By the 1970s most of the Brazilian church hierarchy was behind the effort to organize popular Catholic base communities in order to obtain greater social justice and respect for human rights, and the churches were providing fairly safe havens for striking workers who were being chased by the soldiers. With the *abertura*, church leaders and lay people alike were involved in the formation of political parties and eventually in the drafting of the new constitution. Perhaps not by coincidence, the greater political involvement of the Catholic church occurred simultaneously with a growing challenge to Catholicism by a variety of Protestant sects, especially the more charismatic and evangelical ones and those focusing their greater proselytizing efforts among the poor, the illiterate, and the displaced in the urban areas.

Besides the churches, the unions, the military, and the political parties, a number of other organizations act as pressure groups, with varying degrees of success. Thus, the Brazilian Order of Lawyers was active during the military regimes in seeking the restoration and enforcement of legal protections. The Brazilian Press Association opposed censorship and publicized, especially abroad, the plight of persecuted journalists. A number of women's organizations emerged, particularly after the 1975 International Women's Year. The National Student Union, abolished at the time of the coup, continued to operate underground and sometimes even fairly openly. With *abertura* and the holding of elections, literally hundreds of issue-, policy-, and candidate-focused groups emerged and began to compete, though most of them were transitory.

One organization that has exerted and continues to exert influence is the Superior War College (Escola Superior de Guerra [ESG]). Founded in 1949, the ESG has been a center for training military *and* civilian elites. Somewhat similar to a think tank, except that it is sponsored and subsidized by the government, it has trained several presidents, including Castelo Branco and Ernest Geisel, and the outstanding presidential adviser Golbery do Couto e Silva.

The ESG's slogan, Security and Development, became a banner for anticommunism during the military regimes, but the organization goes far beyond pure anticommunism. It has been at the forefront of a great deal of sophisticated economic and strategic planning, and because it stresses that it aims to better educate and inspire leaders, whether military or civilian, it is likely to remain a formidable institution. Its extensive network of alumni serves as a recruiting source for both government and private enterprises, and no matter what government structure evolves under the 1988 constitution, many male and female ESG alumni will be in key positions.

GOVERNMENT STRUCTURES AND POLICYMAKING

Russell H. Fitzgibbon, one of the most astute observers of Latin America, has stated that "the organization of the Brazilian political system is largely distinguished by its federalism, which provides a backdrop for the performance of various political functions."[4] It has also been said that Brazil is the most federal of Latin America's federal regimes, but these statements do not mean that it is "really" federal in terms of the U.S. model.

Given the size and diversity of Brazil, federalism made sense to the people who drafted the first republican constitution in 1891. The Rio de Janeiro government was weak and unwilling to challenge powerful regional centers, and while the central government remained vulnerable, for the next three or four decades, the states had a great deal of freedom. São Paulo, Minas Gerais, and Rio Grande do Sul showed so much independence that they maintained diplomatic relations with foreign governments, displayed their state flags above the national one, and even called their state governors "presidents."

The Vargas era lessened these centrifugal pulls. The 1934 constitution clearly gave preeminence to the national executive, state flags and anthems were abolished, and most economic functions were now handled by the national government. Vargas's Estado Novo strengthened and reinforced centralization to the extent that even after his departure in 1945 the national government's powers far outpaced states' rights. Only during the turbulent and short Goulart years did some states again act on their own, perhaps secure in the knowledge that the federal government had enough other problems and would not worry about states' initiatives. Governor Leonel Brizola of Rio Grande do Sul, without a clear mandate to do so, expropriated U.S.-owned utilities in that state, and an economic development organization in the Northeast, SUDENE, managed to receive funds directly from the USAID organization. Military units based in Rio Grande do Sul, Minas Gerais, and São Paulo were also crucially involved in the civilian-military coup that deposed President Goulart in 1964.

From 1964 to 1985 the military regimes revised the constitution with institutional acts and decrees, and sometimes these gave the national executive carte blanche in the restructuring of the government and in the proclamation and implementation of all types of policies. The taxing powers of the federal government ensured that all governors and mayors, even those of powerful states and metropolises, would comply with the wishes of the president if they hoped to get any funding for essential services. The 1988 constitution is still untested. It promises greater freedom and power to states and local administrations, but few Brazilians believe it will reverse the decades-old trend toward centralization.

The new constitution does give Congress greater power than ever before and strengthens civil liberties, labor rights, and social benefits. Its proclamation, in October 1988, abolished the authoritarian charter of 1967. Under the new constitution, Brazilians elected a president by direct popular vote in November 1989, for the first time since 1960. The constitution also provides for the right to strike, sets the voting age at sixteen, abolishes censorship, and gives more power and income to state and municipal governments.

In what may turn out to be a major source of all sorts of domestic and international wrangles, questions concerning the international debt will be debated by the entire Congress, and the president and the minister of finance will no longer be able to settle on a course to resolve Brazil's mammoth international obligations. Many businesspeople also contend that restrictions on foreign investment will prove harmful to the country's long-term development, and an editorial in the British *Financial Times* labeled the new charter "utopian."[5] The constitution does nationalize exploration for the extraction of oil and minerals, and the nearly 500 foreign companies in these sectors were given four years to adjust, though the rules are somewhat flexible for those operations that process the raw material in Brazil.

The Constitutional Assembly did not discard the presidential system, but the president, who will now hold office for five years, has been made accountable and in some instances subordinate to Congress. The legislature, composed of a Chamber of Deputies and a Senate, can sanction the president, alter the national budget, and determine international treaties. The text of the constitution is sufficiently ambiguous concerning the power of Congress that it is possible the legislative branch will assert itself against a president, or vice versa.

A similar ambiguity surrounds the role of the military as the guarantor of the constitutional order, the old *poder moderador* concept, but the armed forces retain their claim of being the ultimate arbiter of political life in Brazil. Land reform, on the other hand, one of the most controversial issues in Brazil and practically as old as the *poder moderador* question itself, is not resolved in the new constitution. Not surprisingly, the left complains that the constitution protects large private landowners and further weakens the sputtering efforts to distribute plots to landless peasants, at a time when 4 percent of the country's population owns half the arable land.

The new constitution is one of the world's longest with a total of 245 articles. Its length and detail ensure that it does not fully please or irritate all Brazilians. Some provisions are impractical, and they are the likeliest to be the first to be modified or ignored. Among them is an article that sets a ceiling of 12 percent on interest rates. It is widely assumed that a *jeito* (practical twist) will be found to cover the difference in a market where interest rates in real terms are now close to 22 percent. Perhaps the people who drew up the constitution realized the inevitability of having to modify the overly ambitious charter, because the document itself provides that amendments for the next five years will require only a simple majority.

Regardless of the tinkering to which the new constitution is already being subjected, some structural mainstays are not likely to change. Thus, traditionally, Brazilian ministries have been very large bureaucracies with a plethora of subcabinets, councils, and other agencies, many of them powerful in their own right, plus institutes, autonomous agencies, and the like attached directly or indirectly to the ministries themselves. In this bureaucratic maze, personal and political linkages are of great importance and often override considerations of merit, efficiency, or organizational rationalism. With so many people involved, many of them moving toward contradictory goals and policies, it is not surprising that Brazilian bureaucracy is notorious for its red tape (*papelada*) and unpredictability. Antibureaucratic czars have been appointed, to no avail. It is not corruption that is pervasive; what is, at all levels, is the sheer dead weight of myriad legal rules and enacted codes that long ago outlived their usefulness. About the only saving grace is the proverbial ability of the Brazilian bureaucrat to bend the rules just a little, apply a little humor or a *jeito*, so that some business can be transacted daily and the whole machinery of government does not come to a grinding halt.

A very conservative estimate places the federal civil service at three-quarters of a million people. This figure is practically meaningless as it does not take into consideration the countless independent and semi-independent bureaucracies or those many civil servants who have more than one full-time job. The Foreign Ministry (Itamaraty) is one of the better-run ministries with a reputation for well-trained career officers, some continuity, and a relative insulation from political vagaries. Interestingly, it is also the ministry that is least popular and least liked, with Brazilians and foreigners alike complaining about its inflexibility and its mind-numbing respect for the most minute and meaningless detail.

Brazil has traditionally had a bicameral legislature, and this tradition is respected in the 1988 constitution. Although the number of legislators has varied, the usual provision calls for three senators from each state and the federal district. The Chamber of Deputies, chosen on a population basis, has in fact favored the least-populated rural states. The chambers have legislative committees, but their staffing patterns vary a great deal, and thus their ability to draft legislation is hard to predict. Throughout history the president has been the chief legislator, and the legislation proposed by the executive branch almost always used to be approved by Congress by overwhelming margins. The newest constitution, however, does give far greater powers to the Congress and denies the presidency its former wide decree powers. By the same token, under the 1988 charter it will no longer be possible for a strong or a dictatorial president to dismiss the legislature—as had been done several times in the past.

Both federal and state courts exist in Brazil, and the federal Supreme Court has usually enjoyed a reputation for judicial learning and impartiality. The federal system is made up of the Supreme Court, the Court of Appeals, and the specialized military, electoral, and labor courts. The size of the Supreme Court has varied, as military presidents have added members in an effort to obtain more favorable judgments.

Finally, it should be added that the 1988 constitution, in spite of or perhaps because of its length and detail, is still untested. Its 245 articles cover nearly every aspect of daily life, and most Brazilians are speculating that it will soon prove unworkable and will have to be amended—a fairly easy procedure now—or even discarded. Brazilians voted for a new president in 1989 and in 1993 will decide whether they prefer that a monarch, a prime minister, or a president run the country. The government structure and the policymaking up to 1993 will be subject to many daily and long-term adjustments. If one relies on history and tradition as guides, this constitution, like those that preceded it, will be "reformed" through its daily encounters with Brazilian realities just as policymaking, regardless of the mountains of regulations and decrees, will remain ultimately at the mercy of the most skilled bureaucrat or the most imaginative Brazilian's *jeito*.

INTERNATIONAL ARENA

Even in colonial times Brazil's relations with its neighbors were characterized by accommodation and expansion: accommodation in the sense that Brazil seldom went to war with its neighbors, the major exception being its war with Paraguay, and expansion in the sense that through natural population expansion and government indifference or lukewarm encouragement, Brazil's borders, which initially were marked off by the Tordesilhas line, now contain more than twice as much territory as originally envisaged by the pope who drew that imaginary line. In more recent years Brazil has been a leader among the Latin American nations and has played a prominent role in security efforts and in economic cooperation within the Western Hemisphere. During World Wars I and II Brazil aligned itself with the Allies, and in the 1940s Brazilian soldiers played a distinguished and decisive role in the Allied victory at Monte Castelo, Italy. Many of the generals behind the 1964 coup were involved in that campaign and formed close professional and personal relations with their North American counterparts. A man who was later to be president, Castelo Branco, shared a tent with the American Vernon Walters, and the two men continued to be lifelong friends.

Brazil is a signatory of the Rio Treaty, the Inter-American Treaty of Reciprocal Assistance, and the Organization of American States (OAS), which is sometimes headed by a Brazilian diplomat. Brazilian career foreign officers have distinguished themselves in international bodies, and some of them have been chosen to head such organizations, as was the case in the World Health Organization a few years ago. More recently Brazil has given priority to strengthening its ties with other South American states and has become a member of the Amazon Pact and the Latin American Integration Association (ALADI). President Sarney and Argentine President Raúl Alfonsín overcame the traditional enmity between their two countries with several understandings and protocols to ensure cooperation in a number of areas, including nuclear armaments and research. Brazil is a charter member of the United Nations and has been an active participant in several of its specialized agencies. It has contributed troops to UN peacekeeping efforts in the Middle East, in the former Belgian Congo (now Zaire), and in Cyprus.

Brazil's booming economy, trade, and enormous debt have pushed it to become increasingly involved in international politics and economics. It is a member of the General Agreement on Tariffs and Trade (GATT), the Committee of the Twenty of the International Monetary Fund (IMF), the World Bank, the Inter-American Development Bank (IDB), and several international commodity agreements. The United States, Western Europe, and Japan are the primary markets for Brazilian exports and the main sources of foreign lending and investments. In value, Brazil is the third leading trade partner of the European Economic Community (EEC).

Brazil's dependence on imported oil has forced it to strengthen its ties with the oil-producing nations in the Middle East, and a number of technical barter arrangements have been worked out whereby Brazilian technicians and laborers have exchanged their expertise and their work for oil from Middle Eastern countries, especially Iraq. In a pragmatic if not in a principled way, Brazil has often voted with Arab countries rather than with Israel in international organizations.

Beginning in the 1970s Brazil began to greatly expand its relations with black African countries. In 1986 it introduced a proposal at the UN General Assembly to establish a zone of peace and cooperation in the South Atlantic. Because of its own large black population and its long-standing integrationist record, Brazil has consistently voted for resolutions calling for the end of apartheid in South Africa.

As an indication of Brazil's broader international role, trade with other developing countries increased from 9 percent of the total in the 1970s to nearly 30 percent in 1983. Private entrepreneurs and government officials have been imaginative in bringing about a great deal of trade with the Middle East (for example, major poultry exports to Arab countries and Israel) and Lusophone Africa.

Brazil presently has diplomatic relations with most countries in the world, among them the USSR, China, all the Eastern European countries, and Cuba, but not with Vietnam, Cambodia, or North Korea. But the country's relations with the United States are unique. The United States was the first country to recognize Brazil's independence in 1822. Dom Pedro II admired Abraham Lincoln and visited the United States during the 1876 centennial. President Eisenhower was given a hero's welcome when he visited Brazil in 1960, and Presidents Roosevelt and Truman were also cordially received. President Carter visited in 1978, but at the time there were major strains between the two countries on questions of human rights, and Brazilians were incensed by the attempts of the United States to interfere in Brazil's nuclear program. President Reagan visited Brazil in 1982, and Brazilian president Sarney was in the United States in 1986.

In the 1950s and 1960s Brazil received about $2.4 billion in U.S. economic assistance through the U.S. Agency for International Development, PL480 (Food for Peace), and the Peace Corps. During the military administrations the Peace Corps and the Inter-American Foundation (IAF) were accused of interfering in domestic affairs and were told to leave the country; IAF has since resumed its large program there.

After 1972 the U.S. aid efforts emphasized the training of young Brazilian technicians and social scientists in graduate schools in the United States. In view of Brazil's economic development and its ability to obtain loans and technical assistance from private and multilateral sources, the U.S. assistance programs were phased out in the 1970s. Major AID activities ceased in 1979, and the Peace Corps ended its work in Brazil in 1980. Presently AID has a small contingent in Brazil that collaborates in science and technology projects; responds to endemic diseases, emergencies, and natural disasters; and may be of technical assistance in family-planning efforts.

The United States is still Brazil's most important commercial partner, although the U.S. share of Brazilian trade dropped from a high of about 26 percent in the 1970s to about 21 percent in 1985, when the two-way trade amounted to $9.6 billion. The trading relations have become less friendly as Brazil has actively sought other partners as well as refusing to open its markets to certain U.S. products, particularly certain types of computers. Nationalism and simple tradition reinforce Brazil's insistence on continuing export subsidies and on protectionism; nowhere are these clearer than in the 1988 constitutional provisions that actively discriminate against foreign investors and, in effect, close certain industries to foreign firms.

The more-formal agreements between Brazil and the United States include a treaty of peace and friendship; an extradition treaty; a joint participation agreement on communication satellites; and scientific cooperation, civil aviation, and maritime agreements. The two countries exchange academic personnel under Fulbright and other scholarly programs and carry out university cooperation projects. Under the popular Partners of the Americas program, several U.S. states have active exchanges with their counterparts in Brazil. Increasingly, Brazil has also sponsored artistic and other groups to enable them to visit the United States and other countries in order to promote better relations and publicize Brazil's cultural achievements.

Overshadowing all of these efforts at better relations is the enormous foreign debt that continues to damage Brazil's standing in the international arena. With respect to this debt, there are both encouraging signs and those that do not seem to augur well. On the plus side, in September 1988 President Sarney formally ended the country's nineteen-month-old moratorium on payments on its $121-billion foreign debt. At the time the Brazilian president warned that Brazil could not permanently export capital and called on creditors to do their part as Brazil was doing its. Brazil's return to orthodox strategies and its rapprochement with the IMF marked the end of a roller-coaster period of economic experiments that included a wage and price freeze, a promising boom, and the moratorium on payments enacted shortly after the 1986 elections.

On the more worrisome side is the fact that Brazil is likely to continue its tradition of failing to meet IMF economic targets—since 1983 it has broken six agreements. In order to obtain a green light from the IMF for an economic package that would ease the country's debt burden slightly, Brazil then promised to limit its public deficit to about 2 percent of the size of the economy and acceded to a 600 percent limit on annual inflation. But even at the time of the IMF agreement it was already clear that Brazil would not be able to live up to those commitments. The 1988 constitution further complicates the picture by giving Congress wide powers to decide on external payments and policies affecting Brazil's relations with international banking institutions.

These developments are but the most recent chapters in the long-simmering dispute between Brazil and its creditors. The second oil shock of 1979 and the world recession that followed were keenly felt in Brazil because of its heavy dependence on foreign oil and its crucial need to maintain ever-higher levels of exports in order to finance its economic development. The oil shocks of 1973 and 1979 confirmed Brazil's continuing vulnerability to the vagaries of international markets over which it has little or no control. Brazil sought to work out mutually satisfactory banking relations that would, in effect, let the country stretch its payments on the interest and, in the meantime, count on an eventual forgiveness for the huge principal. Not surprisingly, U.S. banks feel they are hostages to Brazil's economy and, worse, Brazil's deepening nationalism. For now, Brazil is probably ahead of this game because it has not been declared an economic pariah like Peru. In effect, U.S. banks and even the U.S. government have become guarantors of Brazilian solvency—ironically, at the very time that Brazil has proclaimed a constitution that is very specific in its restrictions on foreign entrepreneurs and lenders.

In a broader sense, the United States misread Brazil's willingness to pay a diplomatic price for a U.S. bailout. It seems clear that U.S. officials for a time thought that their willingness to help Brazil in its dire economic situation would in turn make Brazil more open to U.S. products and more supportive of U.S. initiatives in Latin America. These expectations were dashed as the United States has had little, if any, success in linking debt negotiations to Brazilian support for U.S. strategic interests in the Caribbean.

Brazil's relations with other American countries have their own uniqueness. Brazil and Mexico agreed in 1983 to complete a barter deal that would provide for the exchange of up to $1 billion of goods each way. Brazil has also successfully concluded agreements for hydroelectric dam systems in the Plata Basin, and the Itaipú Treaty, signed with Argentina and Paraguay, makes Brazil the owner of the largest hydroelectric dam in the world. Better relations now exist between Argentina and Brazil after decades of suspicion on both sides. President Sarney advocated a common market between the two countries, and while this idea is probably far from realization, Brazil and Argentina are trading much more than before, with Brazil exporting a wide variety of manufactured goods in exchange for agricultural products. Nearly one-quarter of Brazil's capital goods exported to Latin America in the late 1980s went to Argentina.

Brazil is not a major partner with the Soviet Union but talks continue between the two countries with the idea of sending more Brazilian goods to that market. The Soviet Union has been quite active in promoting cultural exchanges at all levels, and a number of young, promising Brazilians have been provided with scholarships to study in Moscow.

Overall, Brazil has been pragmatic in the conduct of its foreign affairs. Unless a clear benefit can be derived, Brazilians seldom take the lead. Brazil is content with and comfortable in pursuing its own interests without antagonizing unnecessarily those countries it deeply depends on, but it will stand firm when it feels its nationalism and sovereignty are not being given the attention they deserve. The best case, in this instance, was Brazil's strong stand in obtaining nuclear technology from West Germany in spite of President Carter's insistent and eventually counterproductive pressures.

It is still too early to speculate on the extent to which the overly specific and detailed provisions in the 1988 constitution will affect Brazil's conduct of foreign policy. It is clear that for the time being and in the period of transition, Congress will have much more to say in this area than was previously the case. Once a popularly elected president comes upon the scene, the pendulum may swing again toward the executive as the major player. Last but not least, more nationalistically inclined congresses and presidents can be expected to be less amenable to compromise and more insistent upon being treated on a more equal footing when dealing with the U.S. or the Russian envoys, with representatives of international banks or international lending agencies.

CONCLUSION

Brazil's growing sense of importance and impact on the world scene goes beyond mere posturing. If Brazil were not as diverse, as potentially rich and culturally integrated, its assertiveness would be empty indeed. A longtime observer of Brazil put it best in an issue of the *Economist:*

> Brazil is the unstoppable colossus of the south; a major regional power already; the first big third-world country knocking on the door of the club of developed democracies; and a potential United States in the next century.
>
> . . . Brazil's long-term prospects are glowing; its very bravado is one of the main reasons why it can look forward to the future much as, say, the United States did in the 1890s. If this view is right, then foreign bankers, investors, potential migrants and, not least, governments ought to be looking at Brazil as carefully as their precursors did at the United States in its early maturity. . . .
>
> Brazil has reached major power adulthood, although not yet the responsibility—and caution—of middle age.[6]

In fact, most careful observers usually echo this correspondent's conclusions. They agree that despite Brazil's present economic and political problems, it is not too rash to predict that the next decades will witness Brazil's rise, first to an unchallenged status within Latin America, then to a predominant status within the South Atlantic community, and finally, to some form of major-power status.

The potential is there, but there too are the burdens of a chaotic and overly bureaucratized system, a new constitution still untried, and a fragile and fevered democracy. One military president expressed his misgivings, "The country is doing well, the people not so well." In spite of democracy, this assessment is still very true. If anything, *because* it is now a democracy, more is expected of Brazil, of its leaders and its system, by the average Brazilian. Will potential and reality finally meld into one? Will Brazilians no longer be, at one and the same time, among the poorest and the richest people in Latin America? Time alone will tell.

NOTES

The Brazilian flag has carried the motto *Ordem e Progresso* since the inception of the republic in 1889. The foremost sociologist of Brazil, Gilberto Freyre, used that motto as the title of one of his books, but the motto's actual author was a much earlier social scientist, the French Auguste Comte. Comte's positivism was very influential in Brazil and in many ways coincided with the Brazilians' attachment to tradition, their sense of optimism, and their faith that Brazil is destined for great power status. Brazilian history and politics exemplify and challenge Comte's philosophy.

1. Elizabeth Bishop, *Brazil* (New York: Time, 1963), pp. 12–13.
2. Much has been written on this issue. One of the best and shortest pieces is the analytical article by Glaucio Ary Dillon Soares, "The Rise of the Brazilian Military," *Studies in Comparative International Development* 21:2 (Summer 1986):34–62.
3. As quoted in James Brooke, "Bad Times, Bold Plans for Brazil," *New York Times* (January 7, 1990).
4. Russell H. Fitzgibbon and Julio A. Fernandez, *Latin America: Political Culture and Development* (Englewood Cliffs, N.J.: Prentice-Hall, 1981), p. 270.
5. "Brazil's New Constitution," *Financial Times* (London), September 13, 1988.
6. Robert Harvey, "Brazil: Unstoppable," *Economist* (April 25, 1987), pp. 3–26. The quotation appears on p. 3.

SUGGESTIONS FOR FURTHER READING

Assembléia Nacional Constituinte, 1988. *A Constituição do Brasil*. Rio de Janeiro: Bloch Editores, S.A., 1988.
Burns, E. Bradfdord. *A History of Brazil*. 2d edition. New York: Columbia University Press, 1980.
Chacel, Julian M., Pamela S. Falk, and David V. Fleischer, eds. *Brazil's Economic and Political Future*. Boulder, Colo.: Westview Press, 1988.
Coniff, Michael L., and Frank D. McCann. *Modern Brazil: Elites and Masses in Historical Perspective*. Lincoln: University of Nebraska Press, 1989.
Daland, Robert T. *Exploring Brazilian Bureaucracy: Performance and Pathology*. Lanham, Md.: University Press of America, 1981.
Freyre, Gilberto. *Order and Progress: Brazil from Monarchy to Republic*. Berkeley: University of California Press, 1986.

McDonough, Peter. *Power and Ideology in Brazil.* Princeton, N.J.: Princeton University Press, 1981.

Mainwaring, Scott. *The Catholic Church and Politics in Brazil.* Stanford, Calif.: Stanford University Press, 1986.

Patai, Daphne. *Brazilian Women Speak: Contemporary Life Stories.* New Brunswick: Rutgers University Press, 1988.

Roett, Riordan. *Brazil: Politics in a Patrimonial Society.* Rev. edition. New York: Praeger, 1984.

Selcher, Wayne A., ed. *Political Liberalization in Brazil: Dynamics, Dilemmas, and Future Prospects.* Boulder, Colo.: Westview Press, 1986.

Stepan, Alfred. *The Military in Politics: Changing Patterns in Brazil.* Princeton, N.J.: Princeton University Press, 1971.

Trebat, Thomas J. *Brazil's State-Owned Enterprises: A Case Study of the State as Entrepreneur.* Cambridge: Cambridge University Press, 1983.

Wesson, Robert. *The United States and Brazil: Limits of Influence.* New York: Praeger, 1981.

Wesson, Robert, and David V. Fleischer. *Brazil in Transition.* New York: Praeger, 1983.

Wirth, John D., Edson de Oliveira Nunes, and Thomas E. Bogenschild, eds. *State and Society in Brazil: Continuity and Change.* Boulder, Colo.: Westview Press, 1988.

10
Chile

PAUL E. SIGMUND

What is it about Chile that is so fascinating to the foreign observer? A long (2,600-mile [4,200-kilometer]) "stringbean" of a country of 12 million inhabitants squeezed between the Andes and the sea, it is one of the most important copper producers in the world. It exports fine fruits and wine and has a literate, relatively large middle class. Evidence of its cultural sophistication is the substantial number of world-class Chilean writers and poets including two Nobel prize winners. Its topography is varied, ranging from deserts in the north to a fertile 600-mile (966-kilometer) Central Valley, not unlike the valley of the same name in California, to heavily wooded mountains and fjords in the farthest southern regions. Chile's strategic value is limited, except for its control of the Strait of Magellan. It has had long-standing border disputes with its neighbors (Argentina, Peru, and Bolivia), but the Andes provide a strategic buffer from all except Peru. None of these factors accounts for the foreigners' extraordinary fascination with the country.

Chilean politics is the reason for the great interest in that country. Until the 1973 coup it was one of the oldest constitutional democracies in the world. Since 1833, with only two interruptions—a short but bloody civil war in 1891 and a period of military intervention between 1925 and 1932—its political system had followed regular constitutional procedures, with civil liberties, the rule of law, and periodic contested elections for a bicameral legislature and a directly elected president.

In recent decades, successive governments have attempted to implement a variety of approaches to Chilean underdevelopment. Between 1958 and 1964 a conservative government headed by President Jorge Alessandri tried to resolve Chile's problems of inflation, unemployment, and slow growth by emphasizing market incentives along with government programs in the areas of housing and a limited agrarian reform. The Christian Democratic government of Eduardo Frei (1964–1970) initiated a Chileanization program for a partial government takeover by purchase of the U.S.-owned copper mines, adopted a much more radical agrarian reform law, promoted programs to benefit peasants and "marginalized"

202

Chile

sectors, and cooperated actively with the U.S.-sponsored Alliance for Progress in attempting to carry out what Frei called a "Revolution in Liberty." A three-way election in 1970 led to the victory of Salvador Allende, the candidate of the Marxist-dominated Popular Unity coalition. Allende tried to initiate a "transition to socialism" involving income redistribution, takeovers of industry and agriculture, and accelerated class polarization.

In 1973 the three armed services and the national police (*carabineros*) overthrew Allende, and what had begun as an institutional coup to save democracy from Marxism soon became a personalist dictatorship under Gen. Augusto Pinochet, the head of the army. Pinochet closed down the political system but allowed a group of free market–oriented economists, many of whom (known as "los Chicago boys") had been trained at the University of Chicago, to open up what had been a highly protected economy and to drastically reduce government intervention in a controversial experiment in economic—but not political—libertarianism. In 1980 Pinochet appealed to Chilean legalism and constitutionalism to legitimate his power by calling and winning a snap plebiscite on a constitution that enabled him to continue in office until 1989 but required the calling of a plebiscite on a new mandate for an additional eight years. On October 5, 1988, he lost that plebiscite by a vote of 55 percent to 43 percent, and Chile began the difficult process of returning to the constitutional civilian rule that it had known throughout most of its history before 1973.

The sharply contrasting approaches to development adopted by recent Chilean governments have produced a large and controversial literature. Conservatives, reformists, revolutionaries, and authoritarians have cited the accomplishments and failures of the various Chilean governments to defend or attack more general ideological approaches to Third World politics. The Allende experiment in particular has spawned an enormous literature—probably 1,000 books in many languages—but the Frei and Pinochet governments also have both their defenders and their critics.

Americans, in particular, have reason to be interested in Chilean politics because of the deep involvement of the U.S. government in that country since the 1950s. Because Chile has the oldest and, outside of Cuba, the largest Communist party in the Western hemisphere, the United States has taken a strong interest in its political life at least since 1958, when Salvador Allende, as the candidate of the Socialist-Communist coalition, came in a close second in the presidential election. The United States supported, overtly and covertly, the reformist Christian Democratic regime in the 1960s; opposed, overtly and covertly, the Allende government in the early 1970s; and was ambivalent about the Pinochet regime, repelled by its human rights violations (which led to a cutoff in 1976 by the U.S. Congress of all military aid and sales to Chile) even though supporting Chile's free-market approach to development and willingness to respect its international economic obligations. Beginning in the mid-1980s, for both ideological and pragmatic reasons the Reagan administration began to promote a democratic transition in Chile and an end to the Pinochet dictatorship. Before the 1988 plebiscite the U.S. Congress went even further, appropriating a million dollars to support free elections in Chile.

The interest in Chile thus revolves around three general questions. First, how is it that, in contrast to most other Latin American countries, Chile has been able to develop and maintain pluralist civilian constitutional rule throughout most of its history? Second, why did what appeared to be a strong stable democracy give way to repressive military rule in 1973? And, third, what are the lessons of Chile for those interested in the future prospects of programs that try to combine democracy and development?

POLITICAL HISTORY TO THE 1973 COUP

To answer the first question, we must look at Chile's history and political culture and at the self-image held by the Chileans themselves. Most accounts of the origins of Chile's constitutionalism begin with the early postindependence struggles for control of the government between the conservative *pelucones* ("bigwigs") and the more liberal *pipiolos* ("upstarts"). After the autocratic ways of "the Liberator," Bernardo O'Higgins, had led to his resignation in 1823, a period of conflict ensued that ended with the triumph of the *pelucones* in the Battle of Lircay. The 1833 constitution adopted under their auspices created a strong role for the president, elected by property holders for a five-year term with the possibility of reelection for a second term, but it also gave the Congress a role in approving the budget. To this day Chilean conservatives look back to the 1830s, when Diego Portales established a strong centralized state operating under the rule of law, as a governmental ideal that is still valid. They argue that the strong presidency and state not only continued cultural patterns inherited from the Spanish monarchy but also maintained the rule of Castilian-Basque landowners in a way that prevented the breakdown of authority and military intervention that characterized many other newly independent Latin American states. Others maintain that the development of civilian constitutionalism owes more to the presidency of Manuel Bulnes (1841–1851), the hero of the 1837 war with Peru and Bolivia, than to Portales. Bulnes sharply reduced the size of the army and built up a civilian-based National Guard as a counterweight to it, while strengthening the state bureaucracy so that it provided effective administration and loyalty to the institutions of the state. In addition, he was willing to work with Congress even when it opposed his plans; he relied on changes in his cabinet to keep in touch with elite opinion; and, most important, though still personally popular, he left office in accordance with the constitutional timetable.[1]

In the two-term ten-year presidency of Bulnes's successor, Manuel Montt (1851–1861), the Liberals reemerged, now reinforced by the influx of progressive ideas from the Europe of the liberal revolutions of 1848. As in other Latin American countries, the Liberal-Conservative split focused on centralism versus federalism and the relations of church and state. The federalist tendencies of the Liberals reflected the opposition of the mining interests of the north and the medium-sized landholders of the south to the political dominance of the large landowners of the Central Valley around the capital, Santiago. Revolts against Santiago domination in 1851 and 1859 were put down, but what Chileans call the Oligarchic Republic (1830–1861) gave way to the Liberal Republic (1861–1891), in which factions of the elite combined and recombined in the Congress and the presidency to open the system by limiting the presidency to five years (1871) and abolishing the property requirement for voting (1874). A small but expanding middle class found political expression in the founding in 1861 of the Radical party, which was committed to Freemasonry, reducing church influence, promoting public education, and establishing universal male suffrage. However, Conservative control of elections in the countryside in what was still largely a rural country meant that the large landowners were able to use electoral democracy to maintain their dominance rather than resorting to military intervention to stem the effects of increased popular participation. Church-state issues, such as who should control clerical appointments, cemeteries, and education, still divided the political class; but after 1859 all groups now agreed on elections and peaceful competition rather than on the use of force to resolve their differences.

The Liberal-Conservative split was papered over during the War of the Pacific (1879–1883) against Peru and Bolivia. Chile's victory gave it a one-third increase in territory involving the rich copper and nitrate areas of the north, but it also led to border disputes with Peru (which were resolved as late as 1929) and with Bolivia, over its access to the Pacific (still an issue today). The victory vastly increased government revenues from export taxes and produced not only a period of economic prosperity but also the beginnings of an inflation problem that was to continue for almost a century. When President José Manuel Balmaceda (1886–1891) began to take measures to end currency depreciation, promote small landholding, and establish state control over the largely British-owned nitrate deposits, he encountered fierce resistance from landowners and foreign interests. When Congress refused to approve his budget, he attempted to rule alone, and a civil war ensued in which 10,000 Chileans died, including Balmaceda himself, who committed suicide after his forces were defeated.

A large body of literature has been written on the role of economic factors in the 1891 Civil War. Balmaceda in particular has been seen by writers on the left as a champion of economic nationalism and state-sponsored development who was defeated by the forces of British imperialism and its domestic allies. Others have argued that the conflict was more institutional (president versus the Congress) than ideological or that there were strong domestic reasons for the opposition to Balmaceda that were more important causes of the war than his opposition to British ownership of the nitrate industry. Chilean and foreign historians have also been divided on a more general assessment of the country's development in the nineteenth century. The traditionalist right sees the emergence of anticlerical liberalism as the cause of the destruction of the Hispanic-Catholic consensus that had produced national greatness in the days of Portales. Others cite the immigration of European merchants and entrepreneurs from Britain, France, and Italy (although they were easily absorbed into the ruling elite) or the arrogance of the scions of the landowning families (*la fronda aristocratica*) in opposing the expansion of the state as the causes of the 1891 breakdown. In turn, the left blames the same groups for not maintaining the vigor and expansion that had characterized the Chilean economy before the War of the Pacific—and for being content to leave the economic initiative to foreigners as long as the revenues from mineral development enabled the government to keep property taxes low.

All are agreed, however, that the Chilean constitutional system was fundamentally transformed as a result of the 1891 Civil War. During the period of the Parliamentary Republic (1891–1920), power passed from the president to the Congress, and the center of political attention shifted to the local bases of the notables who ran for Congress. National governments (a total of 121 cabinets between 1891 and 1924) rose and fell depending on shifting congressional majorities, while weak presidents presided over unstable coalition governments.

Following the end of the War of the Pacific in 1883, a Prussian captain, Emil Körner, was invited to organize the Chilean Academy of War, and he began a program to professionalize the army along Prussian lines. (The goose step and the army's strict hierarchical sense and professionalism mark the continuing effects of the original Prussian influence.) So effective was Körner that Chilean military missions were subsequently invited to train armies in Colombia and El Salvador.

In the economy, nitrate, coal, and copper mining expanded (in the last case, under U.S. auspices), and labor agitation increased. Labor began to organize, and the massacre of 2,000 nitrate workers and their families at Iquique in 1907 became a part of the collective memory of the labor movement. Luis Emilio Recabarren, a labor leader, was elected to Congress in 1906 but was not allowed to take his seat. In 1912 Recabarren founded the Socialist Workers party, which in 1921 became the Communist party of Chile. The expanding middle class found its political expression in the Radical party, which, in addition to its traditional endorsement of the separation of church and state, began to adopt programs favoring social welfare legislation.

The development of cheap synthetic nitrate during World War I dealt a serious blow to Chilean prosperity, which had been based on mineral exports, and the election of 1920 brought to the presidency a new populist leader, Arturo Alessandri Palma. Although Alessandri's supporters secured a majority in the congressional elections of 1924, the Congress resisted his proposals for social legislation and labor rights. These proposals were adopted only under pressure from young reformist military men in the galleries—a case of the so-called rattling of the sabres. Alessandri left the country in protest against military intervention but returned in 1925 to preside over the writing of the 1925 constitution, which was in effect until the 1973 coup. That constitution allowed for a strong, directly elected president to serve a six-year term but denied the president the possibility of succeeding himself. Members of Congress were elected at a different time and for different terms (four years for the Chamber of Deputies and eight years for the Senate), and Congress was obliged to choose between the top two presidential candidates if no single candidate received an absolute majority in the popular election. Congressional members were elected according to a system of proportional representation that accentuated the proliferation of parties that had already begun to take place. Church and state were separated, and labor and social welfare guarantees were included in the constitution. Chile was thus well ahead of most other Latin American countries in the establishment of the welfare state.

Alessandri resigned three months later, and his successor was forced out by Col. Carlos Ibáñez, who ruled by plebiscite and decree until 1931. Following a series of short-lived military governments, Chile returned to civilian-elected governments in late 1932. The military withdrew from politics, and four decades of civilian rule ensued.

One of the many unstable governments in the period from 1931 to 1932 was a military-dominated "socialist republic" that lasted 100 days from June to September 1932. Marxist intellectuals, students, and military men then joined to form a new leftist party, the Socialist party of Chile, which was formally established in April 1933. In late 1932 Arturo Alessandri returned as president, but he now followed a much more conservative policy than earlier. The period that followed has been described by some Chilean writers as *el Estado de Compromiso* ("the compromise state")—i.e., one in which there was something for everyone and no interest group was directly threatened. The combination of staggered elections and proportional representation meant that it was difficult to get a stable majority for any program, especially if it involved fundamental reforms.

In 1938 Pedro Aguirre Cerda, the candidate of a Popular Front coalition of Radicals and Socialists with Communist support, won the presidential elections. He faced a hostile legislative majority, and the coalition lasted only two years. The Popular Front succeeded in securing the passage of a few social welfare laws, but its principal accomplishment was the establishment of the Chilean Development Corporation (CORFO), which provided the legal basis for a larger state role in the economy. The period from 1938 to 1952 was characterized by the dominance of the Radical party, which governed through shifting coalitions and policies along with generous patronage to the party faithful. One such shift was from an alliance with the Communists in 1938 to the outlawing of the party by the Radical-sponsored Law for the Defense of Democracy in 1948. (The Communists were legalized again in 1958.)

When the country looked for an alternative to the Radical party in 1952, it turned to none other than the old military strong man, Carlos Ibáñez, who won by a landslide under the symbol of a broom to sweep out the corrupt and ineffective Radicals. Ibáñez did not deliver on his promises, however, and the traditional parties returned to the fray in 1958. A new party, the Christian Democrats, which had been formed by successive reformist splits from the Conservatives, put in a surprising showing in the 1958 elections. The Christian Democrats divided the centrist vote with the Radicals, while the leftist alliance of the Socialists and Communists came close to electing Salvador Allende as president. Allende was narrowly edged out (by 33,000 votes) by Arturo Alessandri's son, Jorge, the candidate of the Liberals and Conservatives. (There were no longer any significant differences between the Liberals and Conservatives since the church-state issue had been settled in 1925, and overlapping rural and urban interests in both parties rendered the old divisions between the landowner and merchant classes no longer valid.) The 1958 election, with its three-way split between left, center, and right, marked the beginning of a recurrent problem in Chilean politics— how to get majority support for presidents and parties when the electorate was divided into "the three-thirds" (los tres tercios).

When it looked as if the 1964 presidential elections might give Allende a chance to win by a plurality in a multicandidate race (and thus, by tradition, to be elected in the congressional runoff), the right threw its support to the charismatic Christian-Democratic candidate, Eduardo Frei, whose program for a Revolution in Liberty was offered as a democratic response to the challenge of the Cuban Revolution. Frei won the popular election with the first absolute majority in modern Chilean history— 55 percent to Allende's 39 percent. But when he began to implement his program of agrarian reform, expanded welfare legislation, and higher taxes, the right withdrew its support.

Frei's reforms had strong U.S. backing inasmuch as they coincided in aims and methods with the Alliance for Progress, but they ran into congressional opposition (because of staggered elections, the Christian Democrats never controlled both houses) and created inflationary pressures. After a successful first three years, Frei faced an increasingly hostile Congress, and in 1969 he had to put down a local military revolt, the first since the 1930s. The right was optimistic that it could win the 1970 presidential elections with Jorge Alessandri, now eligible to run again; the Christian Democrats had lost some support and did not put forward a strong candidate. On the left, meanwhile, the Socialist-

Communist alliance backing Salvador Allende was broadened to include a left splinter group from the Christian Democrats as well as the main body of the Radical party (which had also split).

The result was a narrow victory by Allende (36.2 percent, lower than his vote in 1964) over Alessandri (34.9 percent). The Christian Democratic candidate was a distant third with 27.8 percent. Chile was thrown into a constitutional, political, and economic crisis as Congress, which was over two-thirds non-Marxist, was asked to elect a Marxist as president in the constitutionally mandated runoff between the top two candidates. The crisis was intensified by U.S. covert efforts to create turmoil in the economy as well as by unsuccessful CIA efforts (documented in a 1975 U.S. Senate investigation) to promote a military coup. It is a testimony to the legalism and constitutionalism of the Chilean military and people that the constitutional tradition was followed, and in November 1970 Salvador Allende became president.

In the case of the Allende government, the pattern of three good years followed by three bad ones that had characterized previous administrations was telescoped into eighteen months for each period. In 1971 the U.S.-owned mines were completely nationalized by a widely supported constitutional amendment (although the compensation procedures, which in most cases amounted to confiscation, immediately got the Allende government into trouble with the United States and the copper companies); a boom produced by the granting of large wage raises, while price controls were strictly enforced, buoyed the economy; and the Allende coalition received nearly 50 percent support in the municipal elections of that year. However, by 1972 runaway inflation had set in, violence was increasing in the countryside as leftist groups seized landholdings, shortages of foodstuffs and essential goods occurred, and class polarization, encouraged by a government that was trying to broaden its base of support among the lower classes, exacerbated personal and political relations. Using among other "legal loopholes" the legislation from the 1932 Socialist Republic, the government took over and "intervened" (or "requisitioned") 500 firms; agricultural and industrial production dropped. Chilean professional and occupational groups (gremios) called strikes that paralyzed the country in October 1972 and again in July 1973.

Despite several attempts at negotiations with the Christian Democrats, Allende was not able to work out any agreements with the opposition-dominated Congress. (The left wing of his Socialist party opposed any agreement, as did the right wing of the Christian Democrats.) By the time the congressional elections of March 1973 had rolled around, the three-thirds had become two intransigent pro- and anti-Allende blocs. The center-right Democratic Confederation won 55 percent of the congressional vote, compared to 43 percent for Allende's Popular Unity Federation, but the division of the country only intensified. Violence increased as extremists on both sides (the Movement of the Revolutionary Left [MIR] and the rightist *Patria y Libertad* [Fatherland and Freedom]) carried out assassinations, blackouts, and bombings. To the concerns of the military over the collapse of the economy and the breakdown of law and order (symbolized by a widely circulated picture of a policeman being beaten by a masked and helmeted revolutionary) were added fears of Marxism as the government announced that all schools would be required to give government-mandated courses in socialism.

Yet the army still considered itself to be "professional, hierarchical, obedient, and non-deliberating," as required by the 1925 constitution. The armed forces did not move until the Supreme Court had written open letters to Allende protesting his government's refusal to carry out court orders to return seized property, the Congress had passed a resolution accusing the government of "habitually" violating the constitution and the laws, and the other army generals had forced their constitutionalist commander-in-chief, Carlos Prats (who was later assassinated in exile by Chilean intelligence agents), to resign. On September 11, 1973, the army, air force, navy, and national police overthrew the Allende government in a one-day coup that included the bombing of the presidential palace (the traditional symbol of civilian rule) and the death of Salvador Allende, probably by his own hand (following the example, which he had often cited, of President Balmaceda in 1891).

Despite reports, never proven, of CIA involvement in the coup (the 1975 U.S. congressional investigation indicated that between 1971 and 1973 CIA money supported the opposition media, some of the strikers, and one extreme-right group), the coup was an authentically Chilean product. The armed forces moved only when it became clear that the civilian politicians were unable to run the economy or to maintain a constitutional consensus, and that the military monopoly on the instruments of coercion was being threatened by armed groups. Allende had been able to use the constitution to defend himself against military intervention so long as the economy was functioning and law and order prevailed. But once it appeared to the military that the legality and constitutionalism that Allende had proclaimed to be essential to the *via chilena* to socialism no longer existed, the armed forces broke with their tradition of nonintervention. Many factors contributed to the breakdown of constitutional democracy—but the most important ones seem to have been the sharp increase in violence and polarization, and the collapse of the economy.[2]

MILITARY RULE

Most observers had assumed that if the armed forces intervened, it would be for a short period during which they would outlaw the Marxist parties, stabilize the economy, and call new elections. They were wrong. It is now clear that 1973 was a turning point in Chilean history. The leaders of the coup—especially Gen. Augusto Pinochet, who used his position as head of the senior branch of the armed services to centralize political power in his hands—were determined to change the pattern of Chilean politics. They spoke of eradicating the "cancer of Marxism," of creating a "protected democracy" that would not be subject to the demagoguery of the politicians, and of making sure that the breakdown of law and order as well as the threats to national security that occurred during the Allende administration would never be repeated.

Yet as clear as their determination to change Chilean political culture might have been, the specifics of how to do so were not evident at the outset. The leftist parties were outlawed, the Communist party headquarters was burned, and the other parties were declared "in recess." Thousands of suspected leftists were rounded up, tortured, and in many cases killed. (The best-known case is that of Charles Horman, a U.S. citizen. It is the subject of the book and film, *Missing*, which accurately portray the atmosphere of post-coup Chile, although the basic thesis of *Missing*, that Horman was killed because "he knew too much" about the U.S. role in the coup, is incorrect.) Many of the leaders of the left went into exile or took refuge in foreign embassies. Those who did not were transported to Dawson Island in the frigid south and were later allowed to go into exile as well. The constitution, in the name of which the coup had been carried out, was simply ignored as the government began to function in accordance with a series of decree-laws that gave legislative and constitutional power to the four-person junta and executive power to its head, Augusto Pinochet. (At the time of the coup there had been discussion of rotating the presidency of the junta among the armed forces, but it was soon clear that Pinochet intended to stay in that post, and a decree-law in June 1974 made him President of the Republic and Supreme Chief of the Nation.) The judiciary remained in place and supinely recognized the legal validity of the decree-laws, refusing to issue writs of habeas corpus (*recursos de amparo*) for people who were arrested or detained. A committee of conservative jurists was appointed to revise the constitution, but it worked very slowly and did not report out a draft until five years later.

The effort to remove what the military viewed as the sources of subversion meant not only that the parties that were members of Allende's Popular Unity coalition were outlawed but also that the universities were put under military rectors and leftist professors were purged, the newspapers and magazines of the left were closed (along with the theoretical journal of the Christian Democrats), labor unions, many of which had been Marxist led, were dissolved, and peasant organizations were disbanded. Foreigners who had been assisting the Allende government were expelled and, in a few cases, tortured or killed. Diplomatic relations were broken with Cuba and the Soviet Union (but not with China, a principal customer for Chilean copper).

The most important change, in terms of its lasting impact on Chilean society, was the opening of the economy carried out under the auspices of "los Chicago boys." Departing from the usual statist tendencies of the Latin American military, the junta decided to entrust economic policy to a group of free market–oriented civilian economists who had developed an alternative economic program during the Allende years. In reaction to the socialist interventionism of the Allende years, that program called for opening Chile to internal and external competition by relying on private enterprise, competition, and market forces. It removed price controls, reduced tariffs dramatically, expanded exports, moved toward the establishment of flexible exchange rates, and returned landholdings and businesses that had been illegally seized. (The copper nationalization was not reversed both because it had been carried out by a constitutional amendment and because copper foreign exchange earnings were partially earmarked for military purposes.) At first, the program was adopted in a gradual fashion; two years later, it was applied in a drastic "shock treatment."

The junta's Declaration of Principles, published in March 1974, spoke of organizing "a great civilian-military movement based on decentralized vehicles of participation." However, no effort was made to create a government party or movement, inasmuch as the regime's main aim was the depoliticization of Chile—and Pinochet may have seen such a movement as a possible rival center of power. The declaration spoke of property rights as an example of the principle of subsidiarity endorsed by Catholic social thought, ignoring the substantial limits that the papal social encyclicals place on property rights. It also stated that although the government respected human rights, it could not allow that "in the name of a misunderstood pluralism, a naive democracy could permit organized groups within it to promote guerrilla violence or, pretending to accept the rules of democracy, support a doctrine or morality whose objective is the construction of a totalitarian state. Consequently Marxist movements and parties will not be admitted again to civic life."

Of course, human rights were not being respected. Military missions moved to the north and the south to carry out summary trials and executions of leftists. The number of people killed after the coup has been estimated at between 1,300 and 4,000. The Catholic church, which has also kept records of documented cases of "disappearances," lists the total as 672, with possibly several times that number killed without a record.

Cardinal Raúl Silva of Santiago created an ecumenical Committee of Cooperation for Peace to care for the families of those being persecuted and to defend human rights. When the government dissolved the committee in 1976, he turned its work over to the archdiocesan Vicariate of Solidarity, which continues to be active in the defense of human rights. The effort to secure church legitimation for the Pinochet regime, evident in the Declaration of Principles, was never successful. Instead, the Catholic church offered shelter to victims and opponents of the regime, and even established a research institute, the Academy of

Christian Humanism, for some of the academics who had been removed from universities.

Human rights violations in Chile also led to a serious deterioration in relations with the United States, and in 1976 the United States imposed a ban on Chilean arms aid and purchases—the ban was still in place in 1989. Relations worsened after 1976, when President Jimmy Carter made human rights a central element of U.S. foreign policy. In the United Nations, reports to the General Assembly about Chile were prepared each year by a special rapporteur, and the UN Human Rights Commission continued to discuss Chilean abuses.

Within Chile, Pinochet managed to transform what had been an institutional coup by the four services into a personal dictatorship. The system of promotions and retirements was altered so that his protégés could remain beyond retirement age while those who were a possible threat to his power could be retired. The intelligence branches of the armed services were consolidated into a single National Intelligence Service (DINA), which established computerized files and conducted a national system of terror. DINA killed General Prats, in exile in Argentina, and wounded Bernardo Leighton, a Christian Democrat with good relations with the left, in Rome. Its most heinous crime was to blow up the car of Allende's former ambassador to the United States, Orlando Letelier, in the heart of Washington, D.C. This act led to a U.S. investigation, which led to the extradition and conviction of the immediate perpetrator, a rightist U.S. citizen who had been living in Chile, and continuing pressure on Chile to extradite the higher-ups involved.[3]

As a result of the Letelier investigation, Pinochet removed the head of DINA and reorganized it as the National Information Center (CNI), which wielded less independent power than DINA had exercised. He promised that there would be a new constitution in 1980, and in January 1978 he called a plebiscite in response to a hostile UN vote, cosponsored by the United States, that condemned Chilean human rights abuses. In the 1978 plebiscite Pinochet won 75 percent approval for a vote of confidence that endorsed "the legitimacy of the government of the Republic to lead sovereignly the process of institutionalization." When Gen. Gustavo Leigh, the air force member of the junta, began to call for more rapid progress toward civilian rule, Pinochet removed him and appointed a low-ranking air force general as his successor. This action led to the resignation or forced retirement of eighteen air force generals. With his triumph over Leigh, Pinochet's personal control of the armed forces was complete.

Meanwhile, the economy, which had suffered a drastic contraction as a result of the shock treatment, was now beginning to be described as the "Chilean economic miracle." From 1977 until 1981 it expanded at rates of 6 to 8 percent a year. With tariff rates down to 10 percent (from an average of 100 percent during the Allende period), cheap foreign imports flooded the country. The exchange rate was fixed at 39 pesos to the dollar, and nontraditional exports such as fruit, lumber, and sea food reduced the share of copper in earning foreign exchange from 80 percent to 40 percent. It was possible to take out dollar loans at what was an overvalued exchange rate, and Japanese cars and scotch whiskey could be purchased more cheaply in Chile than in their countries of origin. It was in this heady atmosphere that another snap plebiscite was held on the 1980 constitution.

THE 1980 CONSTITUTION

In late 1978 the Committee for the Study of a New Constitution produced a draft that was submitted to the advisory Council of State created by Pinochet in 1976. (The council was headed by ex-president Jorge Alessandri. Ex-president Frei had refused to serve on it.) On July 1, 1980, the council submitted a revised draft of the constitution to Pinochet and the junta. It proposed a five-year transition, with an appointed Congress until 1985 and a full return to civilian rule at that time. In the next month Pinochet and his advisers completely rewrote the transitional provisions of the draft to produce a quite different timetable that would enable Pinochet to remain in power until at least 1990. With only one opportunity for public criticism—a public meeting at which Frei spoke and leftist slogans were chanted (by CNI agents, some said)—the draft was submitted to a vote on the seventh anniversary of the coup, September 11, 1980, and the government-controlled media announced that it had been approved by a 67 percent vote. Later there were charges that the vote had been artificially inflated in the more remote areas, with more votes reported than there were voters. The voting rolls had been destroyed after the coup, and there were no independent poll watchers to check on the voting.

One of the transitional provisions added in July 1980 was that approval of the constitution also constituted election of General Pinochet for an eight-year presidential term beginning March 11, 1981. During that time, the junta continued to act as the legislature, but in order to maintain an element of the separation of powers, the army representative on the junta was the general next in seniority to Pinochet. The transitional articles also called for a plebiscite in late 1988 on an additional eight-year term from 1989 until 1997 for a presidential candidate nominated by the junta. In the event that the junta candidate lost the plebiscite (as in fact happened), competitive elections for the presidency and for Congress were to be held in late 1989, with winners of both elections taking office on March 11, 1990.

Transitional Article 24 also gave the president power to declare states of emergency, expel persons from the country, detain them for twenty days in places other than prisons, or subject them to internal exile for three months without any court appeal. The armed forces commanders were also exempted from the new constitution's four-year limit on their terms of office.

The main body of the constitution attempted to remedy the defects of the 1925 constitution by providing for the simultaneous election of the president and the Congress (thus removing the adverse effects of staggered elections) and establishing a two-round runoff system for the popular election of the president (so that he would have the mandate of a popular majority—a system that almost certainly would have led to the election of Jorge Alessandri in 1970). The constitution also created a strong Constitutional Tribunal with the power to "control" (that is, review) the constitutionality of all important laws and to make definitive judgments on all constitutional disputes. The Chamber of Deputies was to have 120 members elected for four-year terms, whereas there would be 26 senators elected for eight years, half of them elected every four years. In addition, all ex-presidents were to be senators for life, and other appointed senators would include two former members of the Supreme Court and one ex-controller general, one university rector, and one ex-cabinet member. Each of the four armed services would also be represented in the Senate by one of its former commanders. Thus, in addition to 26 elected senators, there were to be 9 or more *ex officio* or appointed senators.

The representatives of the armed forces in the Senate were not the only instances of the institutionalization of military influence on policy. More important was the creation of a National Security Council made up of the four current military commanders plus the president and the heads of the Senate and the Supreme Court. In a constitutional plebiscite in July 1989, the number of elected senators was increased to 38, and a fourth civilian was added to the National Security Council. Aside from naming two members of the Constitutional Tribunal and advising the president on matters of national security, the council was authorized to give its formal opinion to any government body concerning matters that might adversely affect "in a serious way the bases of the institutions of government or compromise national security." To some critics, the National Security Council was likely to constitute a fourth branch of government, dominated by the military, that could review all government actions on vaguely defined national security grounds.

Another controversial provision of the constitution was Article 8 authorizing the Constitutional Tribunal to punish "any action of a person or group aimed at propagating doctrines that attack the family, advocate violence or a concept of the state and juridical order which is of a totalitarian character or based on the class struggle." Individuals sanctioned under Article 8 were also to be banned from positions in public office, education, political parties, professional groups, and the media. (This article was repealed in 1989.)

In the Declaration of Principles, the junta had announced its commitment to administrative and governmental decentralization and had reorganized the country into numbered regions that replaced the provinces as intermediate governmental bodies. The regions were governed by a presidentially appointed *intendente* (usually a military man), and the mayors of the local municipalities were replaced by presidential appointees. However, the new constitution called for the establishment of Regional Development Councils (Coderes) made up of the *intendente*, the provincial governors, representatives of the "principal public and private organizations" in the region, and a representative of each of the four armed forces. On the local level there were also to be Communal Development Councils (Codecos) consisting of the mayor and representatives of "territorial and functional organizations." Among other responsibilities, the Codecos were to propose a list of three mayoral candidates to the Regional Development Council, from which it was to select the mayor. Representation by functional organizations instead of the direct election of municipal council members (*regidores*), as provided by the 1925 constitution, was one of the few areas in which the corporatist orientation of some of the original members of the constitutional committee had any effect. (The system was never fully implemented, and there was a consensus in the Congress, elected in 1989, to return to the earlier system of direct elections.)

THE "MODERNIZATIONS"

The struggles in the immediate post-coup period between the corporatists (those who felt that direct elective democracy should be replaced by a system of indirect representation through functional, professional, and specialized groups) and the libertarians (those who supported the maximization of individual choice) were generally won by the libertarians. This was certainly true in the case of economic policy, in which the promotion of consumer choice in a competitive market was the principal guideline of policy. With the apparent success of the government's economic policy, Pinochet's advisers began to extend the principle of free choice to the area of social policy by means of "modernizations." Labor unions were now permitted, but they were restricted to the local firm or factory; in addition, the right to strike was limited, and several unions could operate in a single firm. The National Health Service was reorganized and decentralized, and private health services were authorized to receive payments from the compulsory health insurance checkoff, leading eventually to the enrollment of about 12 percent of Chileans in private health plans. Private universities and educational institutions were authorized, and tuitions were raised, which could be financed by low-interest loans that were immediately payable if a student failed or was expelled from the university (e.g., for political activities). Local education was reorganized on the basis of contracts between the municipality and private educational corporations, so that teachers ceased to be civil servants and lost tenure rights. Housing policy was reoriented to encourage private contractors to build low-cost housing, and the government provided low-interest loans and grants to the poor to pay for them. The most fundamental shift was a complete reorganization of the complicated and essentially bankrupt social security system to induce Chileans to place their compulsory social security deductions in publicly regulated but private and competitive pension funds resembling the investment retirement accounts (IRAs) in the United States. Unlike IRAs, however, the pension funds largely replaced rather than supplemented the public social security program. The government still maintained a basic social security "safety net" for those people who, for reasons such as poor health, could not participate in the system; over the next several years, however, the government's responsibility for most of the social security program ended.

The "modernizations" and the opening of the economy to internal and external market forces were part of a broader view that was influenced by neoconservative (Latin Americans would call them "neoliberal") thinkers in the United States and Europe. Friedrich Hayek and Milton Friedman visited Chile, and think tanks and publications began to project a vision of a new Chile with a consumer-oriented and prosperous economy, like those of South Korea and Hong Kong, gradually moving toward a democratic and decentralized politics that would replace the statism and socialism of the past. The fact that this libertarian vision was just as utopian as the visions of the Marxists in the 1970s and the Christian Democrats in the 1960s was not recognized.

In March 1981, when Augusto Pinochet entered the newly reconstructed presidential palace as "constitutional" president of Chile, he was able to feel secure. The original legitimation of the coup (the prevention of a Marxist takeover) was no longer viable, but it had been replaced by a constitution that had the support of the armed forces and of many members of the upper and middle classes—and the new prosperity of the "economic miracle" was even beginning to trickle down to the lower classes as employment and wages began to rise and inflation declined. A state of emergency in various degrees and a limited curfew were still in force, and police roundups in the poor areas and occasional political murders of leftists still occurred. But some opposition magazines and books (although not newspapers or television) were tolerated, and the more visible aspects of the repression were no longer evident.

THE PROTESTS

The sudden collapse of the Chilean economy in 1982 shattered this optimistic view of the prospects of the regime. External factors such as excessive indebtedness at rising interest rates and a low price for copper exports, combined with internal weaknesses such as an overvalued exchange rate and the existence of underfinanced paper financial empires involving interlocking banks and industries, led to a wave of bankruptcies and widespread unemployment. As unemployment figures rose to include nearly a third of the work force (including those enrolled in the Minimum Employment Program), Chileans began to engage in public protests against the government for the first time since 1973. Beginning with the copper workers union in May 1983, and soon joined by the illegal but newly revived parties, the protests escalated monthly until August 1983, when President Pinochet had to call out 17,000 members of the regular army to keep order. Labeling itself the Democratic Alliance, an opposition coalition ranging from a few conservatives to a wing of the old Socialist party but centered mainly on the Christian Democrats, pressed for Pinochet's resignation and immediate elections. Pinochet authorized a few rounds of negotiation but held fast. Partly because of a fear that the protests would lead to a Nicaragua-style polarization that might be dominated by the Communists, the United States began to press the Pinochet government for an orderly transition to civilian rule. The fact that such transitions were taking place in most other South American countries also added to the pressure. In August 1985 the newly appointed cardinal of Santiago, Juan Francisco Fresno, a known conservative, sponsored a National Accord for a Transition of Full Democracy, and this document was signed by a broad spectrum of political leaders from known conservatives to democratic socialists.

Pinochet, however, was able to keep his hold on power by pointing to the timetable outlined in the constitution and appealing to fears of disorder and violence. (The Manuel Rodríguez Patriotic Front [FPMR], a terrorist movement associated with but more committed to violence than the Communist party, had begun to engage in acts of sabotage, bombings, and blackouts.) Pinochet's position was strengthened in 1986 when large arms deposits destined for the FPMR were discovered in August, and that group carried out an unsuccessful assassination attempt against him in September.

As a result of the protest movement, the political parties—though still technically illegal—began to be active. The threefold division of the pre-coup period was still evident, but there was an important difference in that there had been a significant broadening of the center. The right-wing National party was unenthusiastic about Pinochet's continuation in power after 1989, the leader of another conservative group had signed the Accord, and on the left, a significant group of socialists began to work with the Democratic Alliance. The Communists were specifically outlawed by the Constitutional Tribunal, but they allied themselves with another socialist sector to form the Popular Democratic Movement (MDP), which was later rechristened the United Left and broadened to include Catholic leftists and part of the Radical party. With the recognition that protests alone could not force Pinochet out of office, particularly as the economy began to rebound from the crash of the early 1980s, the party leaders were compelled to decide whether or how to participate in the plebiscite scheduled for late 1988.

THE 1988 PLEBISCITE

In contrast to the snap plebiscites of 1978 and 1980, the 1988 plebiscite was organized well in advance. Laws were published concerning electoral registration, recognition of political parties, and the method of carrying out the plebiscite itself. The problem for the opposition was to decide whether, by participating, they would give implicit recognition to the 1980 constitution, the legitimacy of which they had always questioned. The Communist party, which since 1980 had favored "all forms of struggle" (including violence), called for a boycott—but later, under pressure from its membership, it permitted its adherents to register. The Christian Democrats eventually complied with the legal requirements for party registration, and the socialists had it both ways by refusing to seek recognition while registering a Party for Democracy (PPD) open to all who opposed the regime.

The rightist parties had already been recognized, and they urged their members to register and vote. The government pressured the military and public employees to do the same. At the beginning of 1988, when it was rumored that Pinochet was urging the junta to call a plebiscite in March, it looked as if he could get a new eight-year term without difficulty. Several factors turned the situation around, however.

First, sixteen opposition parties from the center and the left (minus the Communists) formed a unified Command for the No, published a program calling for a return to democracy and an end to ideological proscriptions, and insisted that a democratic government would respect private property and the economic rules of the game. Second, several church-related groups conducted massive registration drives throughout the country, resulting in the registration of 92 percent of the eligible voters by the time the electoral registries were closed. Third, the Constitutional Tribunal ruled that the opposition must be given access to the state-owned television—and fifteen minutes of prime time was given free of charge to the opposition for twenty-seven days. With the assistance of the OAS Center for Free Elections (COPEL) and the U.S. National Endowment for Democracy, the opposition developed an effective television campaign as well as poll-watching and vote-counting techniques that made fraud almost impossible. The result was that, despite massive government propaganda arguing that a "no" vote would mean a return to the chaos and communism of the Allende period, Pinochet was defeated by a vote of 55 percent "no" to 43 percent "yes" on his continuation as president until 1997.

On December 14, 1989, Chile elected a president (Patricio Aylwin) and a Congress to take office on March 11, 1990. (Aylwin will serve four years, and his successors will have eight-year terms.) Pinochet continued on as president until that date, and he is constitutionally empowered to remain as army commander for eight years—an exception to the constitutional requirement that service chiefs retire after four years. As army commander, he will have a seat on the National Security Council, and as an ex-president, he can be a senator for the rest of his life.

As Chile moves toward redemocratization, can one look at the sixteen-year period of Pinochet's rule as a merely temporary interruption in the country's constitutional continuity? Or have the regime and the society been permanently altered? To answer these questions, we must look at the major interest groups as they were before 1973 and as they are likely to be in the foreseeable future.

POLITICAL PARTIES

The Right

Before 1973 the right was dominated by the National party, which had been formed in 1966 by a fusion of the old Liberal and Conservative parties. The Nacionales declared their party dissolved after the coup and reemerged only in the mid-1980s. The party was split on the plebiscite and seems to have been replaced as the principal rightist group by the National Renovation party, which includes one of the most important leaders of the earlier National party, Sergio Onofre Jarpa, as well as the most appealing of the new generation of rightist political leaders, Andrés Allamand. Renovación wishes to keep what it considers to be advances made under Pinochet—protection of private property, a decrease in the scope and activity of the state, and opposition to Marxism. ·A similar position has been adopted by the Independent Democratic Union (UDI), which is dominated by a former Pinochet adviser, Jaime Guzmán. It differs from National Renovation in the intensity of its anticommunism and in having significant lower-class support.

The Center

The most significant centrist party is the Christian Democratic party of Chile. The government party in the 1960s, it has maintained its internal structure and youth, student, labor, and women's branches. In the 1980s internal elections were held regularly, usually pitting center-right candidates against center-left ones for party office. Drawing its welfare state–human rights–mixed economy political philosophy from Catholic social thought, the party is supported by about 40 percent of the Chilean electorate. Having abandoned the policy of going it alone (*camino propio*) that it pursued in the 1960s, the party is strongly committed to working together with other parties to its left and right. The Christian Democrats were the most important group in bringing about the Democratic Alliance in 1983, the signing of the National Accord for a Transition to Full Democracy in 1985, the formation of the sixteen-party Command for the No in 1988, and the creation of the Coalition (Concertación) of Parties for Democracy in 1989. A long-time Christian-Democratic leader,

Patricio Aylwin, was the successful candidate of the Concertación in the December 1989 presidential election, winning 55 percent of the vote against two other candidates.

The Christian Democratic party is supported by the Chilean middle class, but it has an important labor component as well as support in the urban shantytowns (*poblaciones*). Moreover, women tend to vote for the Christian Democrats in larger proportions than men. During the Pinochet period there were a number of foreign-financed think tanks with a Christian Democratic orientation in Chile, and they worked out alternative programs in many areas. The party has long since abandoned the communitarian socialism with which it briefly flirted during the Allende period, and it now accepts the importance of the market as an allocator of resources while criticizing the regressive effects of the economic policies of the Pinochet regime. The Christian Democratic government of Eduardo Frei adopted a strong agrarian reform law, but the party now advocates other means (e.g., technical assistance and access to credit) to raise living standards and production in the countryside. It does not favor nationalization, and it is not opposed to foreign investment, but it has been critical of the excessively favorable terms granted to foreign investors by the Pinochet government.

The Radical party was once the fulcrum of the Chilean center, but it has been weakened by frequent splits on the left and right. The main leadership of the party is allied with the Christian Democrats in the center; but some Radicals, who were most active in the Popular Unity coalition, have formed a separate Radical Socialist Democratic party, which has joined various left coalitions. Although there are still Radical supporters in the provincial towns and rural areas, and the Radical party has international recognition as, for example, a member of the Socialist International, it no longer plays the pivotal role in the formation of governments that it exercised between 1938 and 1964.

The Humanist party was the first party to secure the signatures required for formal legalization under the Political Parties Law. Since it is a new party composed primarily of young people, it is uncertain as to what kind of electoral following it will attract. Its political programs are vague except for concern about the environment and opposition to traditional Chilean politics. It cooperates actively with the new Green Party, which is concerned with environmental issues as well.

The Left

In the past the left has been dominated by the Socialist and Communist parties, which were allied in the Popular Action Front (FRAP) between 1957 and 1970 and formed the core of Allende's Popular Unity coalition from 1970 to 1973. In the late 1960s the Socialists adopted an increasingly radical position such that, during the Allende period, they represented the most "revolutionary" party in Allende's coalition, often taking positions to the left of Allende himself. After the coup, most of the

Socialist leaders went into exile in Europe. By the late 1970s a split had emerged between those (mainly in Western Europe) who favored a more moderate position similar to the positions of the French and Spanish socialists and those (mainly in Eastern Europe and the Soviet Union) who favored continued close cooperation with the Communists and a commitment to Marxism-Leninism. With the opening of politics within Chile and the return of the exiles in the 1980s, this split was reflected in the differing alliances of the two groups. One wing, under Carlos Briones and later Ricardo Núñez, gave varying degrees of support to the broad anti-Pinochet opposition coalitions such as the National Accord; the other, associated with Clodomiro Almeyda (Allende's former foreign minister), allied itself with the Communists in the Democratic Popular Movement. (In late 1989 the two groups united to reestablish the Socialist Party of Chile.)

When the more moderate wing of the Socialists decided to form the Party for Democracy as an "instrumental" party to defeat Pinochet, its president, Ricardo Lagos, achieved national prominence in the pre-plebiscite debates. When Almeyda returned to Chile, he was tried and imprisoned under an antiterrorist law. Immediately after the 1988 plebiscite, a court shortened his sentence, and he was released.

The Communist party has been formally declared an unconstitutional party, but despite government persecution and the murder of many of its principal leaders who did not go into exile, it continues to be active among workers and in the shantytowns. Although it endorsed the *via pacífica* to power between 1957 and 1973, it has advocated "all forms of struggle," including "acute forms of violence," since 1980. For this reason, the centrist parties have been unwilling to work with the Communist party, although they endorse its right to participate in the democratic process by nonviolent means. Since the 1989 election in which its candidates, running on another party ticket, made a poor showing, it has decided to seek legal recognition—which presumably would involve abandonment of the 1980 policy of "all forms of struggle."

The left also includes several groups that originated as split-offs from the Christian Democrats. The most important is probably the Christian Left headed by Luis Maira, although it does not have a large electoral base. The Movement of the Revolutionary Left (MIR), which engaged in revolutionary activity in the late 1960s, has been the particular object of government repression in the Pinochet period. It moved closer to the Communist party—in the past one of its most bitter critics—and was internally divided on the advisability of the use of violence to overthrow the Pinochet government. Most, but not all, of the violent actions by the left in the 1980s (killing of policemen, attacks on police stations, blowing up of electricity towers) have been the work of the Manuel Rodríguez Patriotic Front (FPMR).

Balance in the Spectrum

Many other would-be political parties and political groups exist in Chile; at one point a Santiago newspaper counted over fifty of them. However, as the Political Parties Law has strict requirements for registration and the holding of internal elections, many of them will not achieve (or even seek) official recognition, while other recognized parties may have recognition withdrawn for failure to receive the required 5 percent of the vote in the 1989 election. Yet the classic three-thirds division has reemerged, although with significant differences. The center habitually works with part of the right and of the left; and the center and the left, with the exception of the Communists, have been cooperating closely in promoting a transition to democracy. Patricio Aylwin's first cabinet, although dominated by the Christian Democrats, included a number of Socialists in important positions as well as several representatives of the center-right.

THE ARMED FORCES

Gen. Augusto Pinochet was able to remain in power for over sixteen years because he appealed to the legalism and constitutionalism of the military by legitimizing his rule through the adoption of the 1980 constitution. Strict application of the provisions of the 1980 constitution also led to his defeat in the 1988 plebiscite, but the constitution continues to give the armed forces an important political role. The armed forces "guarantee the institutional order of the Republic" (art. 90); their representatives comprise half of the powerful National Security Council, and an organic law regulates promotions and prevents reductions in the defense budget.

There are differences in the orientation and social composition of the officers of the armed forces. (It has been said that Chile has a British navy, a U.S. air force, and a Prussian army.) The navy has an aristocratic tradition, the army and air force draw many of their officers from the upper middle class, and members of the national police (*carabineros*) often come from lower-middle-class backgrounds. There were tensions among the services within the junta, especially over Pinochet's dominance and even concerning the advisability of his candidacy in 1988, but he was able to use his control of the army to maintain a facade of unity and support. He also doubled the number of army generals, thus diluting the possibility of opposition, and at the end of his term was nineteen to twenty-five years more senior than all of the generals in a system that very much depends on seniority and retirement after thirty years of service. The Pinochet-controlled intelligence agency, the National Information Center (CNI), was dissolved in January 1990, but many of its members and activities were transferred to Army Intelligence, thus remaining under Pinochet's command.

BUSINESS AND AGRICULTURE

Chilean industry and agriculture were fundamentally altered by the policies of the Pinochet government. Inefficient companies protected by high tariffs went bankrupt, while new export-oriented businesses in everything from kiwis to rosehips tea flourished. Ownership became concentrated in a few financial-industrial *grupos* after the selloff of state enterprises following the coup. Some of the largest groups went bankrupt and were taken over by the government in 1982 (along with many other state enterprises, their holdings have since been privatized), but new or restructured conglomerates have emerged. Chilean industry and business are formally organized into the Society for the Promotion of Manufacturing (SOFOFA) and the Confederation for Production and Commerce.

In agriculture, too, a process of restructuring has occurred. Seized lands were returned to their owners after the coup, and the land that had been legally distributed into cooperatives under the 1967 agrarian reform law was divided into individual holdings. Many of the small holdings were later sold to agrobusiness entrepreneurs, resulting in a process of reconcentration—though often under different owners than the traditional landowner families. The rival Christian Democratic and Marxist-influenced peasant organizations that developed after peasant unionization was legalized in the 1960s were suppressed after the coup, but they may reemerge after redemocratization. The landowners are organized into the National Agricultural Society (SNA), one of Chile's oldest interest groups. Other groups such as shopkeepers, truckers, and so on, are represented by organized occupational groups—as are lawyers, doctors, nurses, and architects. In keeping with the government's individualist philosophy, however, their legal right to set rules for their professions was withdrawn in the late 1970s and their leaders were forbidden to take part in politics.

THE CHURCH

Between 75 and 80 percent of Chileans claim to be Catholics, although the percentage of Chileans who actively practice their faith is much lower. There are also significant numbers of Lutherans descended from earlier German immigration, a small Jewish colony, and a growing number of evangelical and fundamentalist Protestants. Although church and state have been separated since 1925, the Catholic church retains considerable national influence. Several of the elite private secondary schools are church related, and the Catholic universities in Santiago and Valparaiso are important educational institutions. (They were taken over by the military after the coup but have since been returned to the church; both are heavily dependent on government funding.) Church publications (especially *Mensaje*, published by the Jesuits) are influential, and the declarations of the Chilean Bishops Conference are given wide publicity by the media. The bishops have repeatedly criticized human rights abuses of the Pinochet government, and the church-sponsored Vicariate of Solidarity has actively assisted the victims of repression. The bishops' statement before the 1980 plebiscite outlining the conditions for a free vote cast doubt on the legitimacy of the election. In contrast, the bishops hailed the free and fair character of the 1988 plebiscite and after the plebiscite called for dialogue between the two sides to achieve consensus. A progressive majority has dominated the Bishops Conference, but recent Vatican appointments have increased conservative influence.

The most important social activity of the church during the Pinochet period was its effort to promote human rights and to give spiritual and physical sustenance to the poor. It also sheltered persecuted intellectuals through the Academy of Christian Humanism and co-sponsored the Latin American Faculty of Social Science (FLACSO) after the government had withdrawn its support. Polls have shown that the church is the most respected institution in contemporary Chile.

LABOR ORGANIZATIONS

The Marxist-dominated Unitary Labor Central (CUT) was dissolved after the coup, and its leaders were persecuted; the Christian Democratic labor leaders were treated less severely. In the late 1970s union activity was renewed, and in the early 1980s a Christian Democratic–oriented and anti-Communist Democratic Workers Confederation (CDT) was created, although not legally recognized. This was followed by the establishment of a National Labor Command (CNT), which, along with the Copper Workers Union, called the first antigovernment protests in 1983. In 1988 the CNT, led by a Christian Democrat but with strong Marxist influence, was reorganized as the CUT. It continued to be subject to government harassment, however. Since industry-wide collective bargaining and country-wide union confederations were forbidden under the 1979 Labor Plan, organized labor has been seriously weakened in comparison with its pre-coup power; but in a democratic Chile its power should increase.

STUDENTS AND INTELLECTUALS

One of the signs of the political opening in the 1980s was the reemergence of student political activity. Once again, university elections were watched for their political impact, and student protests forced the modification of university policies and appointments. Despite the government takeover of the universities, students have tended to be strongly antigovernment. Moreover, student leaders (most of whom are Christian Democrats although some are supporters of the left) are publicized in the national media. Chilean intellectuals—writers, artists, poets, and playwrights—have also been anti-Pinochet, and they played a significant role in the opposition television programs before the 1988 plebiscite. Two Chilean novels—*La Casa de los Espíritus* (The house of the spirits), by Isabel Allende, the niece of the former president, and José Donoso's *Desesperanza* (Curfew)—are international best-sellers highly critical of the Pinochet dictatorship.

FOREIGN INFLUENCES

Chileans have always tried to overcome their geographical isolation by keeping up with developments in Europe and the Americas through the media or, if they can afford it, foreign travel. Chileans tend to be more sensitive than others—the Argentines, for example—to what is said about them in other countries. The Pinochet government was concerned about its bad international image, and any good reports were widely publicized in the press, whereas critical reports such as those of the United Nations were answered at length. There are significant foreign colonies in Chile as well as English, French, and German schools. U.S. policy toward Chile is an important consideration in the formulation of Chilean policy. With the expansion of the Chilean economy in the late 1970s, foreign banks and financial institutions opened up branches in Chile. In addition, the purchase of discounted debt instruments by foreigners to invest in Chile was encouraged by the Pinochet government, specifically as part of its accelerated program of privatization of state-owned enterprises. There are major UN regional offices in Chile, the most important of which is the UN Economic Commission for Latin America and the Caribbean (CEPAL is its Spanish acronym), and particularly since the opening of the economy, foreign influences and trends have been readily accepted. The existence of foreign-financed think tanks of the left, center, and right during the Pinochet period also meant that Chile was aware of, and receptive to, the latest thinking in the social sciences and the humanities. As a result, the Chilean left in particular was an active participant in the rethinking of radical, especially Marxist, ideology that occurred in Europe in the 1970s. During the same period the Chilean right, also influenced by international ideological currents, moved from a traditionalist hierarchical corporatism to more modern libertarian and economically oriented modes of thinking. These changes should influence the prospects for a democratic consensus since both right and left are now more receptive to democratic ideas and practices than in the past.

GOVERNMENTAL STRUCTURE

On March 11, 1990, the transitional provisions of the 1980 constitution, which vested legislative and constitutional power in the military junta and executive power in General Pinochet, ceased to be in effect. The constitution's permanent provisions, however, have shifted the governmental balance of power in significant ways. For instance, the Chilean Senate includes nine senators named by Pinochet before he left office. Along with an electoral system that produced an overrepresentation of the conservative vote, the appointed senators will make it more difficult for the victorious Concertación to amend the constitution and to adopt reforms opposed by the right.

The constitution is clearly designed to limit the power of Congress. The president can call a plebiscite on constitutional amendments rejected by the Congress. Presidential budgets must be voted on within sixty days, or they automatically go into effect. New expenditures must be matched by new taxes, and the Central Bank may not borrow money. All takeovers of property must be compensated in cash at full value. The Constitutional Tribunal automatically reviews important legislation, and its decision is final. The National Security Council can address messages to the Congress on national security matters, which may (or may not) amount to peremptory commands to take action. And, to reinforce the Pinochet government's intention to keep Congress out of the way, a new Congress building has been constructed in Valparaiso, an hour and a half from Santiago.

More generally, the constitution, laws, and policies of the Pinochet government have been designed to limit the power of the central government. The regional and municipal councils have been strengthened, taxing power has been given to the *comunas*, education and health care have been decentralized and partially privatized, and social security has been turned over to private pension funds. Regional political parties have been recognized, and regional universities created. The number of state enterprises has been reduced from 500 at the time of the coup to 20, and there is discussion of privatizing the state railroads, the Santiago subway system, and the government-owned television chain.

GOVERNMENT POLICYMAKING

The scope of government policymaking has been significantly reduced during the Pinochet years. The opposition parties, with the exception of a few groups on the left, have recognized the importance of the market as an efficient allocator of resources and have reaffirmed their willingness to respect property rights. But disagreement will occur over new laws to mitigate the regressive nature of some of the Pinochet social policy changes, particularly in the areas of health care and limits on the rights of labor. The opposition has indicated that it plans to orient its programs to satisfy basic needs through public works, housing, and the promotion of employment. It has also announced that it may reexamine some of the enterprises involved in the recent wave of privatizations of public enterprises—in particular, the Pacific Steel Company (CAP), which was founded by the government and recently privatized. (The difficulty here, as in other recent cases, is that the company employees and workers have been encouraged by loans and tax benefits to buy shares of the enterprise—and they now own one-third of CAP's shares.)

Significant by its absence in the opposition program is any reference to nationalization or the extension of agrarian reform. The only likelihood of debate in these areas would be over the ownership of the vast new copper holdings that are being developed by foreign companies. (For reasons mentioned earlier, the copper mines that were nationalized in 1971 have not been part of the privatization program.) Thus the main differences between the left and the center seem to be over matters of degree rather than of kind. No group except the Communists is recommending a radical transformation of property relations.

TOWARD THE FUTURE: THE LESSONS OF CHILE

Many, often contradictory, lessons have been drawn from the Chilean experience. An obvious conclusion is the importance of rebuilding the institutional and constitutional consensus and the willingness to compromise that characterized Chile for so many years. As neighboring Argentina has demonstrated, once the armed forces begin to intervene in the political process, it is difficult to persuade them to return to the barracks. There is evidence that Chile's civilian political leaders have learned from the sad recent history of their country the desirability of avoiding the ideological dogmatism of the right, left, and even of the center that characterized the politics of the 1960s and early 1970s and ultimately led to military intervention.

On March 11, 1990, Chile joined the rest of South America with a democratically elected government, thus ending its international isolation. Economically it is in a better condition than most of its neighbors, and although democracy will place new demands upon the economy, it has skilled and educated political and economic elites that are capable of steering a moderate course in economic and social policy. There are still leftist extremists capable of carrying out acts of violence that might provide an excuse for military intervention. There are also problems to be resolved with an inflexible and not wholly legitimate constitution. However, precisely because it has taken so long to come back to democracy, the political class has learned to cooperate in ways that were not possible before the 1973 coup. The question for the future is whether Chile will follow either the Venezuelan example of continued cooperation in defense of democracy by previously hostile political actors or the pre-1983 Argentinian model of a self-defeating alternation between civilian and military rule. Short of a worldwide economic collapse or an army revolt against human rights prosecutions, the odds are for a return to the constitutional stability and spirit of *convivencia* that Chile has known for most of its history.

NOTES

1. On Bulnes, see the forthcoming book on the origins of constitutional democracy in Chile, by Arturo and J. Samuel Valenzuela. Its conclusions are summarized by the Valenzuelas in Chapter 10 of the second edition of *Latin American Politics and Development*.

2. See Paul E. Sigmund, *The Overthrow of Allende and the Politics of Chile, 1964–1976* (Pittsburgh: University of Pittsburgh Press, 1977), and Arturo Valenzuela, *The Breakdown of Democratic Regimes: Chile* (Baltimore: Johns Hopkins University Press, 1978).

3. For the details of this real-life James Bond tale, see Taylor Branch and Eugene M. Propper, *Labyrinth* (New York: Penguin Books, 1983).

SUGGESTIONS FOR FURTHER READING

Angell, Alan. *Politics and the Labor Movement in Chile*. London: Oxford University Press, 1972.

Arriagada, Genaro. *Pinochet: The Politics of Power*. Boston: Unwin Hyman, 1988.

Blakemore, Harold. *British Nitrates and Chilean Politics, 1886–1896*. London: Athlone Press, 1974.

Branch, Taylor, and Eugene M. Propper. *Labyrinth*. New York: Penguin Books, 1983.

Davis, Nathaniel. *The Last Two Years of Salvador Allende*. Ithaca, N.Y.: Cornell University Press, 1985.

De Vylder, Stefan. *Allende's Chile: The Political Economy of the Rise and Fall of the Unidad Popular*. Cambridge: Cambridge University Press, 1976.

Edwards, Sebastian, and Alejandra Cox Edwards. *Monetarism and Liberalization: Chilean Economic Policy, 1973–1986*. Cambridge: Cambridge University Press, 1987.

Falcoff, Mark. *Modern Chile, 1970–89: A Critical History*. New Brunswick, N.J.: Transaction Books, 1989.

Fleet, Michael. *The Rise and Fall of Chilean Christian Democracy*. Princeton, N.J.: Princeton University Press, 1985.

Foxley, Alejandro. *Latin American Experiments in Neoconservative Economics*. Berkeley: University of California Press, 1983.

Garreton, Manuel Antonio. *The Chilean Political Process*. Boston: Unwin Hyman, 1989.

Gil, Federico. *The Political System of Chile*. Boston: Houghton Mifflin, 1966.

Hauser, Thomas. *Missing: The Execution of Charles Horman*. New York: Touchstone Books, Simon and Schuster, 1983.

Kaufman, Edy. *Crisis in Allende's Chile*. Westport, Conn.: Praeger Publishers, 1988.

Kaufman, Robert. *The Politics of Land Reform in Chile, 1950–70*. Cambridge: Harvard University Press, 1973.

Kinsbruner, Jay. *Chile: A Historical Interpretation*. New York: Harper and Row, 1973.

Loveman, Brian. *Chile: The Legacy of Hispanic Capitalism*, 2d ed. New York: Oxford University Press, 1988.

Mamalakis, Markos. *The Growth and Structure of the Chilean Economy: From Independence to Allende*. New Haven, Conn.: Yale University Press, 1976.

Moran, Theodore. *Multinational Corporations and the Politics of Dependence: Copper in Chile.* Princeton, N.J.: Princeton University Press, 1974.

Muñoz, Heraldo, and Carlos Portales. *Elusive Friendship: A Survey of U.S.-Chilean Relations.* Boulder, Colo.: Lynne Rienner, 1990.

Nunn, Frederick. *The Military in Chilean History.* Albuquerque: University of New Mexico Press, 1976.

Politzer, Patricia. *Fear in Chile.* New York: Pantheon Books, 1989.

Remmer, Karen. *Party Competition in Argentina and Chile, 1890–1930.* Lincoln: University of Nebraska Press, 1984.

Sigmund, Paul E. *The Overthrow of Allende and the Politics of Chile, 1964–1976.* Pittsburgh: University of Pittsburgh Press, 1977.

Smith, Brian H. *The Church and Politics in Chile.* Princeton, N.J.: Princeton University Press, 1982.

Stallings, Barbara. *Class Conflict and Economic Development in Chile, 1958–1973.* Stanford, Calif.: Stanford University Press, 1978.

U.S. Senate. *Staff Report on the Select Committee on Intelligence Activities: Covert Action in Chile.* Washington, D.C.: Government Printing Office, December 18, 1975.

Valenzuela, Arturo. *The Breakdown of Democratic Regimes: Chile.* Baltimore: Johns Hopkins University Press, 1978.

Valenzuela, Arturo, and J. Samuel Valenzuela, eds. *Chile Under Military Rule.* Baltimore: Johns Hopkins University Press, 1986.

Whelan, James R. *Out of the Ashes: Life, Death, and Transfiguration of Democracy in Chile, 1833–1988.* Washington, D.C.: Regnery/Gateway, 1989.

Winn, Peter. *Weavers of Revolution: The Yarur Workers and Chile's Road to Socialism.* New York: Oxford University Press, 1986.

Zeitlin, Maurice, and Richard Ratcliff. *Landlords and Capitalists: The Dominant Class of Chile.* Princeton, N.J.: Princeton University Press, 1988.

11
Colombia:
The Struggle Between
Traditional "Stability"
and New Visions

HARVEY F. KLINE

During the 1980s the Colombian political system experienced one of the major crises of its history. In contention were two views of how politics should be carried out. On the one hand, the "traditional" system was one of stability, albeit with exceptions and defined in a particular Colombian way. On the other, new power contenders—especially guerrilla groups and narcotics interests—were attempting to build a different system, with new structures and rules of the game.

Traditional Colombian politics was graphically reflected in the presidential election of 1974. There was little doubt that the winner of the election would be the next president; though there have been certain military rumblings in recent years, Colombia in its own way has a liberal democratic record equaled by few other countries in Latin America (there has been only one military dictatorship in this century and only two successful military coups d'état). Two major parties were involved in the election, but there was a third candidate from a splinter party. The existence of a party other than the historical Conservatives and Liberals was unusual; the fact that the election was no simple contest between two candidates for the presidency was typical. Although the country is termed one of the few two-party systems in Latin America, only two presidential elections in this century have been contested by only one representative of each of the two parties.

Finally, the parentage of the three major candidates illustrated the traditional domination of the nation's politics by the same families. The winner, Alfonso López Michelsen, was the son of the former president Alfonso López Pumarejo. Coming in second was Alvaro Gómez, son of

Colombia

another former president Laureano Gómez. And finishing third was María Eugenia Rojas de Moreno Díaz, daughter of the only military dictator of the century. This election thus demonstrated that democratic Colombia, albeit in a different way than in other Latin American countries, had a stable and very small group of people at the very top and that this group monopolized meaningful political power and the children followed their fathers' careers.

Since that symbolic election of 1974 some apparent changes have taken place. The third party of 1974 disappeared but was replaced by another; in three presidential elections, only two of the candidates have been the sons of former chief executives—Alfonso López Michelsen when he sought reelection in 1982 and Alvaro Gómez when he ran again in 1986. The basic Colombian state structure has remained the same.

The challenges to this traditional system have come from two sources and have led to a "dirty war" that has been going on since the mid-1980s. Four major guerrilla groups, formed in the 1960s and 1970s, have attempted to overthrow the government. Although the government of Belisario Betancur Cuartas (1982–1986) negotiated cease-fires with them, by the end of his presidency the relative peace had ended. Drug dealers, especially groups centered in Medellín and Cali, have established an illicit trade that the government is incapable of ending and have used bribes, threats, and assassinations to live above the law. Numerous right-wing death squads have appeared in reaction to the radical left and to the drug dealers. The public order apparatus of the state has been unable to end this dirty war—and sometimes at least, some of its individual officers participate in it. Law enforcement agencies have little time to deal with "common crime," and in 1988 it was estimated that 90 percent of the crimes in the country were not solved. Homicide is the leading cause of death for males between twenty and forty. And leading politicians—including Liberal Senator Luis Carlos Galán, odds-on favorite to win the 1990 presidential election—had been assassinated by the drug dealers.

In this chapter, the "traditional" Colombian political system and the "different" challenges to it are described. In the end, however, one is not able to conclude which of the two (or more) visions of the future will prevail.

BACKGROUND

Colombia is a country of great geographic diversity. It is crossed by three ranges of the Andes Mountains, includes a part of the plains of the Orinoco River and seemingly limitless expanses of Amazonian jungle, and has coasts on the Caribbean Sea and the Pacific Ocean. Of the national territory, the fifth largest in Latin America, the one-third lying in the Andean region contains 75 percent of the population and all the

major centers of economic and political activity, with the exceptions of
Barranquilla and Cartagena on the Caribbean.

Yet the Andean region itself demonstrates much regional diversity.
Transportation difficulties led to little interaction between areas before
the advent of the airplane. There is a great diversity of climate, based
on altitude. Bogotá, at 8,530 feet (2,600 meters), has cold nights and
brisk days. Medellín, at 4,852 feet (1,479 meters), calls itself the "city
of eternal spring," with temperatures the year round in the sixties at
night and low eighties during the daytime. Cali and Bucaramanga, being
slightly lower, have hot climates. The hottest cities, however, are at sea
level, either on the coasts of the Caribbean and the Pacific, on the
Orinoco Plains, or in the Amazon jungles.

Agricultural products vary by elevation, the highest areas being most
productive in the cultivation of grains and potatoes, medium altitudes
in coffee, and the low altitudes in the tropical crops, such as sugarcane
and bananas. These tropical products are also common in the lowlands
of the coasts, whereas the llanos of the Orinoco River are most suitable
to ranching (and in recent years for growing coca leaves and refining
them into cocaine). The Amazon region, formerly a center of rubber
production, is now economically important only insofar as tourists can
be convinced to visit it.

The diversity of Colombia's geography is matched by the diversity of
its people, who number 30 million, making the country the third largest
in population in Latin America. The chief Indian group at the arrival
of the Spanish, the Chibchas, had reached a level of civilization that
was relatively high but below that of the Aztecs of Mexico or the Incas
of Peru. As a result, Spanish colonization led to a nearly complete
incorporation of the Chibchas, although more so culturally than racially.
The direct descendants of the Chibchas, living in the central Andean
region, dress no differently from people of Spanish or mixed background
of the same social standing, and they speak Spanish. Only in the southern
departamentos (provinces) of Nariño and Cauca, to which the Incan
empire reached, and in certain parts of the isolated areas of the country,
such as the Amazon jungles and the Guajiran peninsula, are there sizable
groups of people of Indian background who speak a language other
than Spanish.

In other parts of Colombia, especially the coastal areas and the Cauca
Valley region, large numbers of African slaves were brought in to work
on sugarcane plantations. In the areas of Antioquia and Chocó, slaves
were imported for mining because of the small number of Indians. These
regions are characterized by societies quite different from those in the
Spanish-Indian areas. Not only is race visibly different, but so are social
relations, religion, and indeed, politics.

Today Colombian society demonstrates a great racial diversity. One
meets in the "right circles" Colombians of pure Spanish ancestry, speaking
what is reputed to be the best Spanish of the hemisphere and taking

great pride in their *abolengo* ("pedigree"). Quite often they have social prominence, economic wealth, and political power. On the other end of the racial spectrum are those individuals of pure Indian or black descent, speaking a Spanish that is not so technically proficient (but at least speaking Spanish, as is not the case in some other Latin American countries). Most often they have neither social, political, nor economic wherewithal. In the middle are the majority (although it is difficult to be more precise, since no recent Colombian census has included "race" as a question) of individuals who are a mixture of white and Indian (mestizo), white and black (mulatto), black and Indian (zambo), or of all three great racial currents. Race is not the salient issue that it is in the United States, but clearly it is better to be white, and there is a great correlation between race and socioeconomic status.

The country, especially in the Andean area, is marked by strict stratification along class lines. The most basic division is between those people who have manual jobs and those who have nonmanual (or mental) occupations. Within the nonmanual groups, further stratification is decided by the criteria of wealth, race, and *abolengo*. At the very top are the people with the "best" of all three criteria, although there are notable cases of "fallen aristocrats," who no longer have the extensive wealth of the past, and of the *nuevos ricos* (recently including the *narcotraficantes*, the drug dealers), who have no pedigree but do have a great deal of wealth. Within the manual group, stratification follows the same criteria (it's better to be a fairly white individual with a relatively high degree of income), but *abolengo* does not enter into the equation, and there appears to be much less stability in the social order. Yet there are notable differences, in the cities, for example, between the members of a labor union and someone living in a hut illegally constructed on someone else's land.

In foreign trade, Colombia has less of a one-crop economy than it used to. Although coffee is still the largest export earner, by the late 1980s it was followed closely by petroleum and coal. In 1964 coffee contributed 79 percent of the export earnings, 42 percent in 1975, and 32 percent in 1987. The trend varies, however, such as when coffee prices and Colombia's share of the world market increased after there was a frost in Brazil in 1975. By 1978 the percentage of export earnings coming from coffee had reached a zenith of 66 percent; the figure declined afterward as Brazilian production recovered. A coffee "bonanza," such as that of the 1970s, is not an unmixed blessing. The increased foreign exchange led to a higher value for the Colombian peso, making it easier for foreign imports to enter, thus damaging local industry, and making it more difficult for exports other than coffee to be sold, also damaging local industry.

This damage to local industry was exacerbated in the 1970s when a new illegal commerce began, especially dealing with marijuana and cocaine. It was estimated that by 1979 the drug trade plus other contraband brought some US$3.2 billion into the country, greater than all legal export earnings combined.[1] Nothing changed the magnitude of the drug trade in the following ten years.

Coffee production affected the kind of dependency Colombia developed. Although it is certain that the country suffered from the vagaries of world market prices for coffee and that the buyer of the product has predominantly been the United States, there is one characteristic of some dependent agricultural economies that does not pertain in Colombia: the presence of foreign owners of the lands. Colombian coffee has traditionally been shade-grown on lands owned by the Colombians themselves. The myth is that coffee is in the hands of independent family farmers working their own land—the case in some instances, but increasingly the product is picked by tenant farmers who own little or no land of their own. Indeed, the issue of land reform, both in the coffee areas and elsewhere, has been a salient one for decades, but one that is largely unsolved.

Colombia has chronically suffered from a negative balance-of-payments problem. It appeared in the mid-1970s that the problem would become worse when the country stopped being an exporter of petroleum and became an importer of that essential product. Government policymakers, projecting growing consumption and increased prices as well as declining production trends, concluded that by the mid-1980s the country would import about US$1.5 billion worth of petroleum a year, more than twice the value of the unusually high coffee exports of the coffee bonanza years. Such a crisis did not eventuate, because of the coffee and drug bonanzas and because more favorable terms for the foreign multinational corporations resulted in the discovery of new oil fields. By 1985 Colombia was once again a petroleum exporter, and there are other new exports, particularly coal.

Before the bonanzas of the 1970s one of the strategies to meet the trade imbalance was import-substitution industrialization (ISI). Many manufactured goods, especially food products and clothing and even some consumer durables such as cars, stoves, and refrigerators, were produced in Colombia—some by Colombian industry, others by U.S.- and European-based multinational corporations. The "cheap" dollar that came with the bonanzas dealt a serious blow to ISI. By the early 1980s the Colombian government was keeping the peso at artificially low exchange rates, which allowed the importation of all kinds of consumer goods and lessened inflationary pressures but seriously damaged the Colombian manufacturing industry. At the encouragement of the International Monetary Fund, the Betancur government began a series of mini-devaluations, and by the end of his presidency the peso had a more realistic value.

Inflation is another part of this mixed economic picture. By the mid-1970s the consumer price index was in the low thousands (1954 = 100). With the coffee and drug bonanzas, the yearly inflation rate between

1976 and 1981 was between 17.8 percent and 26.5 percent (leading to, by the end of 1982, a consumer price index of 1,122 [1970 = 100]). Inflation would have been much higher if the government had not freed imports.

The Colombian economy is an intermediate one in Latin American terms. The gross domestic product per capita is estimated at US$1,684 per year, and the country's GDP grew at an average of 6 percent a year between 1970 and 1979. Although the 1980s were years of slow growth, Colombia maintained creditworthiness with international lenders and received new loans, without an International Monetary Fund standby loan. Indeed, the Inter-American Development Bank, in a report released in 1988, stated that in the previous five years Colombia had had the lowest rate of inflation in Latin America, one of the five highest per capita GDP growth rates, and the lowest foreign debt per capita.

One reason for many of the country's problems before the 1980s was the growth of the Colombian population—2.3 percent per annum after 1973, down from about 3 percent a year during the previous two decades. This rate made Colombia one of the fastest-growing countries in the world, and its population increased from 17.5 million in 1964 to 27.3 million in 1980. This growth, as well as massive urban immigration, led to the meteoric growth of the cities. Bogotá's population increased from 1.5 million in 1968 to 5 million in 1980, and other major cities, especially Medellín and Cali, had similar growth rates. This situation has led to a whole series of new problems and political issues.

HISTORY TO 1930

During the Spanish colonial period Colombia was neither a backwater nor a center as important as Mexico or Peru. The quantity of precious metals was less, although there was a substantial amount of gold. For most of the period Colombia was part of the viceroyalty of Peru, but in 1739 Bogotá became the center of a new viceroyalty, which also included the present countries of Venezuela, Panama, and Ecuador.

The struggle for independence in Colombia came from those criollos of the very highest standing. The battles were fierce, highlighted by various reversals and historic treks through the rugged mountains on horseback. Independence finally came after the Battle of Boyacá (1819), and the victorious army, led by Simón Bolívar, went south and played an instrumental role in the liberation of Ecuador, Peru, and Bolivia.

The first ten years of national independence were ones of confederation with Venezuela and Ecuador in Gran Colombia. Yet regional differences among the three countries had already appeared. Bolívar himself once remarked that Venezuela was a military garrison, Ecuador a convent, and Colombia a debating society—an assessment of "national character" that demonstrated a certain validity in the following years. In 1830 the countries went their own ways, and Colombia (called Nueva Granada and including a distant province that later became Panama) was alone.

Although in the first years the chaos that was so prevalent in newly independent Latin America also existed in Colombia, by 1850 the new country had settled into patterns that, in large part, continue today. For some reason, about which historians disagree, the norm became civilian partisan politics, a sharp departure from the experiences of most other Latin American countries. By 1849 there were two political parties, one calling itself Liberal and the other Conservative, and the public programs of each were not dramatically different. These were elite-instigated parties (as most in Latin America were at that time) rather than ones coming from popular demands. Ideological differences soon developed between the two parties, at least at the leadership level. The Liberals favored federalism, free trade, and a restricted role for the church in politics. The Conservatives favored centralism and protectionism for nascent industries and were proclerical.

During the nineteenth century constitutional structure changed when one party replaced the other, and some public policies, most obviously in the realm of trade and the position of the church, were altered with a change in the majority party. Furthermore, competition was not restricted to the ballot boxes; there were six civil wars between the two parties, some of which were lengthy and led to many deaths. In these wars the elites of the parties mobilized as their troops the people who were economically and socially dependent on them—largely the peasants. A campesino became a Liberal or Conservative because of the affiliation of his *patrón*, not because of his "own" interests. Because of the many civil wars, the peasants developed strong, intense loyalties to their parties. The wars left "martyrs" in many peasant families—relatives who had been killed by members of the other party. As a result, Colombians began to be "born with party identification cards attached to the umbilical cord," as one Colombian sociologist has expressed it.[2] Not only were they born into the party of their parents, they learned to hate the other party. This socialization, combined with the religious nature of the conflicts—the Conservatives using the Catholic religion to mobilize its followers against the "atheist Liberals"—led to a division of the Colombian population into two closed worlds—one Liberal and the other Conservative.

The results of this intense party socialization have been numerous, beginning in the nineteenth century and continuing into this one. Other cleavages—in social class, the economy, and region—have been secondary in importance to the overwhelming importance of political party. It is difficult to organize third-party movements, and later socioeconomic changes did not lead to new parties.

The peasant and lower-class masses took these party differences seriously. The elite elements of the parties gained the benefits and governed. Sometimes there were periods of hegemony of the parties, the Liberals monopolizing power from 1861 to 1886 and the Conservatives from 1886 to 1930. Sometimes the elites of the two parties disagreed violently, and civil war resulted. But in nine instances before 1930 (and three other instances afterward), all or part of the elite of one party formed electoral and/or governing coalitions with part of the elite of the other party. In roughly twenty-eight of the eighty years between 1850 and 1930 there were such coalitions,[3] and they usually formed in response to a strong, antiparty executive after a civil war or at the end of a period of party hegemony.

Before 1930 Colombia's economic development was slow, which led a few new social groups to seek entry into the political system. The few new middle-income people, who came with the growth of government and private industry, never banded together into a group to form a new political party. Rather, the importance of the party cleavage continued: New middle-income people were first Liberal or Conservative in identification, based on family loyalties, and only second members of the middle sector. Their political importance was in the traditional parties, not in the formation of parties of their own.

POLITICAL HISTORY SINCE 1930

Toward the end of the 1930s the Conservative party hegemony ran into difficulties, in part because of the Great Depression, in part because of the apparent bankruptcy of the party itself, and in part because of its repressive tactics in relation to a growing labor-union movement. The Conservative hegemony was replaced by a Liberal one in 1930, but many of the themes stayed the same as before, although with new variants. The new Liberal president, Enrique Olaya Herrera, was elected by a coalition of Liberals and Conservatives. A civil war that broke out between Liberal and Conservative peasants was only in part called for by the elite elements of the party, also being caused by the increasing land pressures on the campesinos.

Yet there were important contrasts with the previous period. A significant faction of the Liberal party had become identified with a new liberalism, in which the state was to take an active role in social reform (including agrarian reform). This group of Liberals held most of the power during Alfonso López Pumarejo's "Revolution on the March" (1934–1938) when various reform programs were attempted, albeit unsuccessfully in most cases. In reponse to this new Liberal thrust, one part of the Conservative party, led by Laureano Gómez, took a reactionary stance, evoking as a model the Spain of Ferdinand and Isabella, that is, of traditional Spanish corporatism. The "middle" part of the spectrum, made up of both "moderate" Liberals and Conservatives, wanted to maintain the status quo. The coalition of moderates of both parties and Gómez Conservatives was successful in delaying the social legislation of the López Liberals, which finally led to López's early retirement during his second term as president (1942–1945).

Yet neither party could or was willing to stop social change. An organized labor movement was first legalized by López, who was also instrumental in the creation of the first national labor federation, the Confederation of Colombian Workers (CTC), in 1935. The Conservatives, in 1946, reacted favorably when the church formed the Union of Colombian Workers (UTC). Hence, in the normal way of politics in Colombia, organized labor entered the political scene in two groups, one basically Liberal and the other predisposed to the Conservatives.

An important chapter of modern Colombian history began with the election of 1946, in which two Liberals were opposed by a single Conservative, Mariano Ospina Pérez. Following Ospina's election, rural violence broke out between the followers of the two parties. In large part, the violence was elite instigated: by the Conservatives to consolidate their new presidential power and to win a majority in the congressional elections of 1948 and by the Liberals to avoid the same things. At the same time, Conservative peasants took over land that had been taken from them by the Liberals sixteen years earlier, believing correctly that the government in Bogotá would support them.

The civil war that began in 1946 was so dramatically different from the past ones that Colombians call it *la violencia,* which indicates its scope and intensity. Aggravated by the April 9, 1948, assassination of Jorge Gaitán—a populist Liberal who had lost the 1946 election but had later become head of the party and odds-on favorite to win the 1950 presidential election—the violence covered the entire Andean region (save southernmost Nariño) and the llanos of the Orinoco region. It was less intense but existed in the Caribbean coastal region. During the next ten years at least 200,000 Colombians (in a country of some 10 million) lost their lives fighting in the name of party loyalty. The war largely began as Liberal versus Conservative, apparently was most grave in those areas of land pressures, and eventually disintegrated into banditry and some leftist movements. In the final analysis, an entire generation of Colombian peasants grew up thinking that violence was the normal way of life.

One result of the violence was the only military dictatorship of the century, that of Gustavo Rojas Pinilla from 1953 to 1957. Rojas came to power promising to end the violence and with support from all major factions of the two traditional parties, except the Gómez Conservatives (it was the presidency of Laureano Gómez [1950–1953] that the coup d'état ended). The Rojas government was only partially successful in ending the violence at first, and although Rojas talked about social reform and carried out a good many economic infrastructure improvements, he began to show signs of wanting to continue in power and grew increasingly repressive.

Two motivations—the "nontraditional" group in power and the continuing violence in the countryside—led leaders of the two historic parties to plan a coalition to replace Rojas and to institutionalize bipartisan government. Rojas also lost the support of various other power groups, including the church, the students, and most important, the military itself. In 1957 he was overthrown and replaced by a caretaker military regime for a year. This regime was followed by the most dramatic bipartisan coalition government in Colombian history—the National Front.

The National Front, approved by the people of Colombia in a plebiscite and by the National Congress in a constitutional amendment, was basically the creation of two men—Alberto Lleras Camargo, a Liberal who had been president in 1945–1946 (completing López's second term), and Conservative ex-president Laureano Gómez. The basic stipulations of the National Front amendments for the sixteen-year period from 1958 to 1974 were the following:

1. The presidency would alternate every four years between the two traditional paties (*alternación*).
2. All legislative bodies (National Congress, departmental assemblies, municipal councils) would be divided equally between the Liberals and the Conservatives regardless of the electoral results within a district (*paridad* ["parity"]). Within each of the traditional parties, seats would be assigned by a list form of proportional representation.
3. The same rule of party parity would apply to all high administrative appointments, such as the president's cabinet, governors, governors' cabinets, and mayors.
4. No new political parties could participate in elections during the period, only the Liberal and Conservative parties.
5. The lower-level, nonappointive bureaucrats would be chosen, not on the basis of partisan affiliation, but on merit in a proposed civil-service system. This stipulation was to end the pre–National Front practice of complete changes of bureaucrats with changes of the party in power.
6. All legislation in the National Congress had to be passed by a two-thirds majority.

In sum, the National Front was a legal mechanism designed to divide political power equally between the two traditional parties. Thus, a limited democracy was established. Political competition was legally restricted to the two traditional parties, and indeed, they would not compete with each other in elections.

Although many people thought that the National Front would not last, in the final analysis it did. Two Liberals were president (Alberto Lleras Camargo, 1958–1962; Carlos Lleras Restrepo, 1966–1970), and so were two Conservatives (Guillermo León Valencia, 1962–1966; Misael Pastrana Borrero, 1970–1974). New groups participated in elections, but they did not call themselves "political parties" until a constitutional reform in 1968 made it possible for them to do so. Parity prevailed, until the same constitutional amendment reopened competitive elections for departmental assemblies (roughly the equivalent of state legislatures in the United States, but with considerably less power) and town councils in 1970. The violence was ended, but it had taken at least six years for the government to accomplish this feat.

On August 7, 1974, the National Front ended with the inauguration of freely elected Alfonso López Michelsen, who gained 56 percent of the popular vote. Yet this Liberal was restrained by certain aspects of the dismantling (*desmonte*) of the National Front, as provided for by the constitutional reform of 1968. During López Michelsen's entire four-year term all cabinet ministers, governors, mayors, and other administrative positions not part of civil service were divided equally between Liberals and Conservatives, a continuation of parity.

After the end of López's term the same offices were divided between the parties "in such a way that gives adequate and equitable participation to the major party distinct from that of the president" (as called for in the constitution). However, if that party decided not to participate in the executive, the president would be free to name the officials in any way that he chose.

Both President Julio César Turbay Ayala (Liberal, 1978–1982) and President Belisario Betancur Cuartas (Conservative, 1982–1986) offered what they considered "adequate and equitable participation" in the appointive positions to the other party. But in 1986 the Conservatives refused to accept the three cabinet positions offered by newly elected Liberal President Virgilio Barco, who had called for a party government during the campaign. Rather, the second party entered into "reflexive opposition," as it was called. Hence, for the first time since the fall of Rojas Pinilla in 1957, the Colombian regime was a government-opposition one rather than a coalition.

TRADITIONAL SOCIAL AND POLITICAL GROUPS

During the years of the National Front and since, new socioeconomic groups have appeared. The traditional Colombian system has demonstrated a great deal of resiliency, with two predominant (and factionalized) political parties being most important. Large landowners, industrialists, and other upper-income groups are very organized and effective. Labor unions are organized in both political parties (and elsewhere), but the campesinos and urban poor are only in the process of being organized.

Political Parties

The most important Colombian power contenders have traditionally been the Liberal and Conservative parties. Going back over a century, these traditional parties are strong in emotional terms but not organizational ones. The parties do not approach the "mass party" model, nor indeed, do they need such a structure to mobilize votes.

But one should not be overwhelmed by the appearance of a two-party system. The leaderships of the Colombian parties have generally been split into various factions, sometimes along ideological lines, other times on more personalistic lines. The majority of Colombian voters, although the proportion has declined in recent years, remain identified with the party only, not, it seems, with the various factions.

Today the ideological differences of the party elites are about as great (or meager) as those of the Democratic and Republican parties in the United States. The Liberals have their internal divisions, but as a whole this party tends to be more welfare-state oriented, more anticlerical, and less private-property oriented than the Conservatives. The latter, although having their own internal divisions, tend to take opposite positions on these ideological dimensions.

One key fact of present Colombian partisan life is that the Liberal party is the majority one. All public opinion polls indicate that a majority of the electorate identifies psychologically with this party. Throughout the National Front period, more people voted for Liberals for Congress than for Conservatives (although, of course, parity meant that each of the parties received 50 percent of the seats). López Michelsen, in his successful 1974 presidential campaign, received 56 percent of the vote in a contest against two principal opponents and several minor ones. Turbay Ayala received a smaller majority over Betancur in 1978.

Although a Conservative president was elected in 1982, even that election seems to reinforce the conclusion that the Liberal party is the majority one. The Liberals presented two candidates—Alfonso López Michelsen and Luis Carlos Galán—which allowed Conservative Belisario Betancur to win with 46.6 percent. Betancur thus became the first Conservative elected in a competitive election since 1946, and in so doing reinforced the historical tradition of a minority party winning when the majority party was split between two candidates. In 1986, with the Liberals once again united, Virgilio Barco won overwhelmingly.

Furthermore, third-party movements of the early 1970s have now failed. In 1961 ex-dictator Gustavo Rojas Pinilla founded the National Popular Alliance (ANAPO) in an attempt to vindicate himself. ANAPO did not declare itself to be a new political party; that would have made it ineligible for elections before the constitutional reform of 1968. Rather, it was a "movement" that offered both Liberal and Conservative candidates for Congress, departmental assemblies, and town councils. Since the electoral system within parties was one of proportional representation, Anapistas (members of ANAPO) were elected at all three levels. The movement had its greatest success in 1970 when the Liberal Anapistas garnered 14 percent of the national Liberal vote, and Conservative Anapistas collected 21 percent of the national Conservative vote. The same year, Rojas lost the presidential election by about 3 percent to

Conservative Misael Pastrana, a coalition candidate agreed to by the Liberals and a significant group of the Conservative party.

Since then ANAPO's fortunes have declined. In 1971 the movement dramatically declared itself a party, which was perhaps a logical step since the parity restrictions no longer pertained in town council and assembly elections, but ill considered since all evidence suggests that Colombian voters still predominantly considered themselves to be Liberals or Conservatives. In addition, with the end of the National Front, votes once again became more meaningful. Although in 1970 a Liberal might vote for Conservative Rojas since all the candidates for president had to be Conservatives, this situation no longer applied in 1974 when once again Liberals and Conservatives (and additionally Anapistas) were contesting the elections. In addition, ANAPO had always been a personalistic party, with little organization or leadership from outside the Rojas family. As Rojas's health declined, leadership was more and more centered in his forceful daughter, María Eugenia Rojas de Moreno Díaz, who was a presidential candidate in 1974. Hampered by the return of partisan conflict between Liberals and Conservatives, as well as by being a woman in male-dominated politics, María Eugenia received only 9.4 percent of the popular vote, finishing a poor third to both López and the Conservative Alvaro Gómez.

The other notable case of a third party came in 1986 when the left presented a coalition candidate for the first time, under the "democratic opening" of the Betancur government. Called Patriotic Union (UP) and founded by the legal Communist party and one group of guerrillas, the Armed Forces of the Colombian Revolution (FARC), this movement's candidate, Jaime Pardo Leal, received only 4 percent of the vote. It did elect twelve members to Congress, however. But Colombia continues to have a two-party system in which the two parties are factionalized, in part because the electoral system does not discourage factionalization.

Other Traditional Groups

There are a variety of other political groups of importance in Colombia. The most powerful of these tend to be those representing or allied to the upper classes.

Founded in 1944, the National Association of (Large) Industrialists (ANDI) has become the leading advocate of free enterprise among the Colombian organizations. ANDI has more than 500 of the largest industrial enterprises affiliated with it throughout the entire country, and its power in Colombian politics is owing to the wealth of its members, their social prestige, and the common overlapping of this group with the agrarian interests. Furthermore, industrialization has been a goal of half a century of Colombian presidents, especially those during the National Front period and since.

If Colombian development in one part depends on industrialization, it also has depended on exporting coffee to earn foreign exchange to purchase capital and other goods. Therefore, it is not surprising that another important group is the National Federation of Coffee Growers (FNCC). Founded in 1927, this private association is open to all people interested in developing the coffee industry, but the association tends to be dominated by the larger coffee producers and/or exporters. The relations between the coffee growers and the government are close.

The Roman Catholic church of Colombia is probably the strongest politically in Latin America. This strength is in part because of the religious fervor of the Colombian people and in part because of church landholdings in the past century and alliances with other upper-class groups.

During the nineteenth century there was a close relationship between the church and the Conservative party. At various times, even quite recently, bishops have threatened to excommunicate anyone who voted Liberal, and during *la violencia* some parish priests refused sacraments, including burial, to Liberals. Perhaps this attitude is best exemplified by a quotation from some bishops who prohibited the faithful from voting for Liberal candidates in 1949 because they might "wish to implant civil marriage, divorce, and co-education, which would open the doors to immorality and Communism."[4]

When the National Front was organized, the partisan politics of the church ended. The church hierarchy strongly supported the concept of the front and in doing so, embraced Liberal presidents as well as Conservative ones. In turn, Liberal presidents treated the church well.

Today the church still has many functions and much power. Until the early 1970s the majority of secondary schools were parochial. Although government efforts have led to a current majority of state schools, even in them (and in public universities as well) a course of religious instruction is required. In addition, the church must approve textbooks. No major government project is opened without a bishop to bless it; no divorce legislation is introduced without the church mobilizing to fight it.

The church hierarchy is no longer a unified, monolithic friend of the status quo (if, indeed, it ever was). Although growing numbers of priests come from the middle-income sectors, the upper level of the hierarchy is still dominated by sons of the upper classes. But even these upper- and middle-class priests differ, often not along class lines. In recent years there have been cases of priests who are anything but status quo oriented. The most dramatic one is that of Camilo Torres, son of a Bogotá upper-middle-class family and a sociologist as well as a priest, who concluded that to be Christian in Colombia was to be a revolutionary. After his failure to change society as a priest, Camilo left the clergy and went to the guerrilla wars, where he was killed.

The first two labor federations were each connected to one of the traditional political parties. The Confederation of Colombian Workers (CTC) was founded in 1935, during the first presidency of Alfonso López Pumarejo, and flourished during the rest of the Liberal hegemony. The

Union of Colombian Workers (UTC) was founded in 1946, during the presidency of Mariano Ospina Pérez, and by the late 1950s had become the largest labor federation. But not all of the local labor unions in Colombia are organized into one of these national federations, and there are more locals not affiliated with any national federation than there are in any of the three major ones. The largest national federation by the 1980s was the Syndical Confederation of Workers of Colombia (CSTC), which at times causes more difficulties for the government than either the CTC or the UTC. Although the latter two owe much to their respective parties, neither is formally a part of those parties as such membership is prohibited by law.

Labor legislation has generally been unrestrictive. However, labor leaders are still required to be full-time workers in their industries, a requirement that if enforced (and it isn't) would mitigate against labor unions. Colombian political leaders are pleased to have active unions (at least usually, if they are members of CTC or UTC) but are not reluctant to have the law enforced more rigorously when a union is allied with Communist elements or if one takes actions that the government has prohibited. In 1985, for example, the CSTC lost its right to exist for six months for participating in a general strike previously declared illegal by the Betancur government.

The military has been one of the least interventionist in Latin America. Before the turn of the century there was little professionalism, with a "national army" supporting the party in power and another "army" of the party not in power. Only in 1907 were the Escuela Militar de Cadetes and the Escuela Naval founded, with the Escuela Superior de Guerra following two years later.

Colombian presidents cannot, of course, ignore the military, which jealously guards its share of the government pie (although that share is one of the lowest per capita in Latin America) and the integrity of the military institution. Moreover, the Colombian president must take care that the military does not oppose him for reasons of national politics. López Pumarejo, during his first term, transferred military officers who opposed him to remote posts and promoted those who supported him. During his second term, López Pumarejo was captured in a coup attempt in the southern town of Pasto, but the rest of the military supported him. During the Conservative years 1946–1953, both Ospina and Gómez took steps toward making the army an arm of the Conservative party, a process that politicized the military more than ever before (and was very likely a precipitant of the military coup of 1953).

One cannot categorically ignore the possibility of a military coup in the future. The National Front went a long way toward ending the partisan identification of the military, but beginning in 1962, with the aid of the U.S. government, the army began a program of civil-military action in which the army's personnel, equipment, and skills are used in social and economic projects. Furthermore, the military has developed expertise in a number of development areas, in some cases greater than that of the civilian bureaucrats. Further, during the "dirty war" of the 1980s it became clear that if public order degenerates too much, certain military officers are likely to take power.

The groups discussed thus far are probably the most powerful traditional ones in Colombia, but they are not the only ones. The society is replete with groups at the upper- and middle-income levels—merchants, large landowners, teachers (at all levels), doctors, and so forth. It is no exaggeration to state that anyone of middle or upper income fits into an occupational group that is organized (within limits stated by the laws), has *personería jurídica* (or a license to exist), and has at least some power in the political process. However, the great majority of the Colombian people—especially peasants and the urban poor—are not organized into such groups. There is some peasant organization through the National Association of Land Users (including about half a million small farmers who use the services of government organizations) and the National Agrarian Association (an affiliate of the UTC claiming to represent 100,000 peasants). Some of the urban poor are a part of Communal Action. But in all cases, these organizations are incomplete, elite instigated, and divided along traditional party lines.

The nature of group relations, with its middle- and upper-class bias, is the subject of some academic debate. Surely Colombia is not a purely corporatist society, with every group controlled by the political elite. But neither is it the "pure" pluralistic system in which groups are formed and operate almost completely free of government control. Rather, Colombia is somewhere in between.[5] The National Federation of Coffee Growers, for example, is quite tied to the government: Of the eleven members of the FNCC's national committee, five are ex officio ministers of foreign relations, finance, development, and agriculture and the government-appointed manager of the Agrarian Credit Bank. The superintendent of banking supervises the financial transactions of the federation; the manager of the federation is appointed by the president of the republic from a list of three names submitted by the federation, and the manager in turn acts as Colombia's representative in international negotiations pertaining to coffee. Although this is the extreme case, other economic associations have government-appointed members, usually cabinet ministers, on their boards and a concurrent influence of the government over internal policy. In addition, many groups receive money from the government, sometimes even in the millions of pesos. At the other extreme, some groups, such as ANDI, receive no money from the government and have no government members in their leadership groups. But ANDI, by law, does have representatives on half a dozen boards of government agencies, a situation that is very common in Colombia.

NEW GROUPS: GUERRILLAS, DRUG DEALERS, AND DEATH SQUADS

Three major new groups challenge the traditional Colombian system: the guerrillas, the drug dealers, and the death squads. The guerrillas desire a new system with more power and benefits for the common people; the drug dealers, one in which they can carry out their illicit trade with impunity—and surely without extradition to the United States; and the death squads, one without guerrillas or poor people making demands. All three groups use violence in seeking their goals; all three prefer to kill someone who is "innocent" (that is, not opposed to them) than to let a "guilty" person live.

Guerrilla Groups

The four main guerrilla groups are the Armed Forces of the Colombian Revolution (FARC), the 19th of April Movement (M-19), the Popular Army of Liberation (EPL), and the Army of National Liberation (ELN). By 1988, the last three were cooperating through the Coordinara Nacional Guerrillera (CNG).

At the beginning of the Betancur presidency an estimated 17,000 guerrillas were in combat with the government, but cease-fires were signed with all except the ELN. The "democratic opening" allowed the guerrilla groups to form political parties and offer candidates. Although those truces were falling apart, by the end of the Betancur administration it was estimated that 5,000 guerrillas had a truce with the government, with another 2,000 not observing a truce.

The FARC, the largest, most militant, best-equipped, and best-trained guerrilla group, has an estimated membership of about 60 percent of all the guerrillas. Beginning in the 1950s, the FARC has always had close ties with the Communist party, and it is still dominated by Marxists. The organization's goal is a popular revolution that destroys the existing social and economic order and establishes a Marxist-Leninist state. Operating through twenty-seven front groups, the organization is led by Manuel Marulanda Vélez, also known as Tirofijo. The FARC finances itself partly through agreements with illegal drug dealers. Some members of FARC accepted the 1982 government amnesty, but many later returned to guerrilla activity. A one-year cease-fire pact with the government went into effect in May 1984 and was extended indefinitely in 1985.

The FARC participated in the 1986 elections through the Patriotic Union. The presidential candidate, Jaime Pardo Leal, was later assassinated in 1987, allegedly by drug dealers concerned about the inequitable split of profits (some 500 UP members have met death since the party was established). The FARC continued the truce during the first year of the Barco administration and sought contacts with him. Yet some FARC fronts continued fighting, and in June 1987 one ambushed an army road-building crew, killing twenty-seven. By the end of the year the truce had ended, in fact if not formally.

During most of the years of its existence, the M-19 has been the second-largest guerrilla organization. Formed in reaction to claims of fraud in the 1970 elections, it has traditionally been viewed as less doctrinaire and less tied to Marxist-Leninist ideas and strategies than the FARC. Its membership includes doctors, lawyers, and other professionals, but in recent years hard-line Marxists have taken greater control, and the group has become increasingly radical. The leadership has been decimated by clashes with the army and police, especially since the July 1985 decision to break the truce negotiated with the Betancur government and return to open warfare. In November 1985, M-19 units seized the Palace of Justice in the center of Bogotá and took most of the Supreme Court hostage. After a brief attempt to negotiate, the military stormed the building, precipitating a battle that ended with the death of twelve justices and the bulk of M-19's leaders. In early 1986, M-19 lost more strength in its failed effort to undertake a major offensive around Cali. Afterward, in serious trouble, the group turned more toward isolated acts of terrorism. In 1989 the M-19 signed an agreement with the Barco government, whereby the guerrilla group would turn over its arms and demobilize, in exchange for reincorporation into civilian life.

The small EPL is active in the central valley of the Magdalena River and has connections with the Marxist-Leninist wing of the Communist party. Numbering less than 1,500, the EPL is strongly disciplined and criticizes the FARC for financing its operations partly through drug traffic. The EPL finances its activities through kidnappings and uses violence to gain power and liquidate the landed elite, while claiming to want peace. The EPL wants the military to leave the rural areas and end the state of siege. It joined the FARC in accepting the 1984 cease-fire.

The ELN, another Marxist movement, is about the same size as the EPL and also uses kidnappings and extortion to finance its operations. It now leads the CNG, and it has been particularly disruptive to the Colombian economy through bombing of the pipeline from the eastern plains to the Caribbean sea, through which most of Colombian export petroleum is sent.

Drug Dealers

One of the most powerful Colombian groups, but one of the most difficult to describe, consists of the drug dealers. There is little doubt that they include extremely wealthy individuals, with one estimate that there are 6 Colombian billionaires and about 150 millionaires as a result of this illicit trade. Three major groups are in conflict with each other: the Medellín cartel, the Cali cartel, and the Atlantic coast cartel.

There have been documented cases of drug dealers cooperating with guerrilla groups, and others of armed conflict between the two over division of the profits from the trade. There have been other documented cases of the diversion of drug earnings into legitimate business (including a professional soccer team), politics, and military and police forces. No one knows the degree to which the drug dealers are in legitimate Colombian life. It is known, however, that drug leaders have been involved in the assassinations of ministers of justice, attorney generals, and newspaper editors who openly oppose their activities.

In 1987–1988 the carrot-and-stick nature of the power of this group was clearly seen. In the first case, a known drug dealer, Jorge Luis Ochoa, was released from a Bogotá jail, although the U.S. Drug Enforcement Administration wanted his extradition, because there was no arrest warrant for him. The judge was later tried for taking a bribe. The "stick" aspect of their power was shown when a judge contemplated bringing a known drug dealer to trial in connection with the assassination of the editor of a Bogotá newspaper. The judge received the following message from "the extraditable ones":

> Having read the latest information in the newspapers . . . we have decided to write you again to tell you the following: We are friends of Pablo Escobar Gaviria and we are ready to do anything for him. We have the knowledge that you propose to bring him to trial in the case of Mr. Cano, bowing to the pressure brought by Mr. Mesa Márquez and by *El Espectador*. The most serious thing is that we know perfectly well that not even the slightest evidence exists against Mr. Escobar. We have also heard versions according to which, after the trial, you will be given a foreign diplomatic position. But we want to remind you that, in addition to perpetrating a judicial infamy, you are making a big error that will blemish your life and will make it cursed until the end of your days. You know perfectly well that we are capable of executing you at any place on this planet. You should also know that in the meantime you will see the fall, one by one, of all of the members of your family. We advise you to rethink it, since later you will not have time to be sorry about it. Be absolutely certain that in calling Mr. Escobar to trial you will remain without forebears or descendants in your genealogical tree.[6]

On August 18, 1989, the drug dealers assassinated Senator Luis Carlos Galán, leader in the preference polls for the 1990 presidential election who had often called for stronger actions against the *narcos*. The next day President Barco called for an all-out war against the *narcos*, soon to be supported by President Bush. Actions taken by the Colombian government included the confiscation of possessions of suspected drug leaders and the extradition of those indicted in the United States. The drug dealers responded with a massive bombing campaign, especially in Bogotá and Medellín. By the end of 1989 several middle-level *narcos* had been extradited and one of the leaders of the Medellín cartel, José Gonzalo Rodriguéz Gacha, had been killed during a battle with government troops. Yet it was far from clear as to which side would win this war.

The Death Squads

Even less is known about the death squads than about the drug dealers, but in 1988 the minister of justice stated that there were some 160 such squads operating in the country. Perhaps the best known is Death to Kidnappers (MAS), set up as a way for drug dealers to protect themselves from guerrillas who finance themselves by kidnapping dealers. But other groups have had the killing of "troublemakers" as their goal. The Patriotic Union party states that 500 of its members have been killed in recent years, peasants making demands for land or other goods are attacked, and students are killed. In short, the death squads appear to be diverse in their targets—but with the common tactic of a dirty war: If in doubt, kill.

Finally by the time the Barco administration began in 1986, Colombia was going through a second "partial breakdown of the state," as Paul Oquist called the same occurrence during *la violencia*.[7] Simply put, this breakdown means that with a high probability of impunity, an individual or group can attempt to achieve its goals (land, money, justice, and so on) through violence. There simply is little likelihood that the Colombian law enforcement system will catch criminals or that the court system will try them.

GOVERNMENT MACHINERY

Colombia's national government is very similar, in appearance at least, to that of the United States: three branches of government with separation of powers and checks and balances. There are some important differences, however. The executive is clearly the most powerful branch of government, with that power centered in the president, who is elected for a four-year term with no immediate reelection allowed. Congress is bicameral, with both chambers elected on the basis of population, and is clearly secondary in power. Legislation is rarely written by the Congress, but it is not merely a rubber stamp—projects initiated by the executive are often dramatically changed, or indeed blocked altogether, by Congress. In comparative terms, probably only the congresses of Venezuela and Costa Rica have more power than the Colombian one. The Supreme Court has the right of judicial review, and its members are appointed by the president, with approval of Congress, for fixed terms.

The Colombian system is an extremely centralized one. *Departamentos* have only slight independent taxation abilities, and their governors are appointed by the president. *Municipios* (townships) have even lower taxation abilities, and until 1988 the mayors (with the exception of the mayor of Bogotá) were appointed by the governors. In 1988, for the first time in the country's history, Colombians elected the mayors, despite the fear of some that this constitutional change would increase the power of the drug dealers. Although *departamentos* might have some independent bureaucracy, most bureaucrats are national employees and report back to officials in Bogotá.

The machinery of government has been purposefully manipulated by the party elites, as in the National Front, for certain goals. The same is true of the form of elections, so important in democratic Colombia. The electoral system (for both houses of Congress, departmental assemblies, and town councils) is a list system of proportional representation. Although this form is not uncommon in Latin America and elsewhere, there is a particular Colombian variant, which encourages factionalism in the parties. If a list does not receive one-half of the electoral quotient (which is equal to the total number of votes in a district divided by the total number of seats to be filled), then the votes of that list go to the list with the same label with the most votes. Thus, a party (or a group within a party) can safely offer more than one list of candidates in a legislative election with the security that there will be no "wasted" votes, since they will revert back to the list with the same label and the most votes. The results of this system have been a multiplicity of lists in most elections, both during and since the National Front, which makes the individual voting choice a difficult one for the average Colombian.

Colombians take pride in having a "mixed" economy—one that is not purely capitalist or socialist. Therefore, certain industries are government owned and run, such as communications, electricity, and natural resources. Others, especially in the area of consumer goods, are financed purely by private capital, either Colombian or foreign. In still others the government is one of several stockholders. The end result is a society in which the government plays a much larger part in the economy than it does in the United States, and government spending represents a larger percentage of the GNP.

One result of this government role is a large bureaucracy. Before the National Front governments, bureaucratic posts were one of the chief spoils of the political system, with the changing of the party in the presidency leading to a nearly complete bottom-to-top turnover in the bureaucracy. This practice ended with the National Front, but the principle of spoils did not, and the civil service grew rapidly. Bureaucratic posts are sought after as they give a decent salary, the chance not to work with one's hands, and the concurrent social prestige. However, the technical training of government bureaucrats is not one of the high points of Colombian government. The major purpose of the bureaucracy, even today, often is to give nice jobs to bright young people rather than to develop bureaucratic expertise. One study in 1969 concluded that of the 100,000 civilian employees of the national government, only 3,000 were part of the civil service. Seven years later the number had increased only to 13,000.[8] Whether or not to have a real career administration is still the subject of lively debate.

One way to avoid the spoils problem is through the *institutos descentralizados* ("decentralized institutes"), which have been set up to administer certain specialized programs and government industries. This form of bureaucracy has become predominant. In 1976, 36 percent of the government employees fell into this category, as compared to 26 percent who were teachers and 8 percent who were in agencies directly under the cabinet ministries. In 1975 fully 59.5 percent of the national budget was spent by the decentralized institutes. It is not at all clear if these decentralized institutes have been more immune than the regular bureaucracy to the politics of spoils or if they have developed more bureaucratic expertise.

PUBLIC POLICY

The Colombian public policy process is conditioned by a number of characteristics discussed in the preceding section. Bureaucracies are not very efficient in carrying out laws as proposed by the president and passed by Congress (a situation not uniformly condemned), and certain numerically large groups of peasants and urban poor are not yet among the major power contenders and, hence, do not have the power that their numbers would indicate. The political elite is far from being a microcosm of the society as a whole: A 1970 study showed that 87 percent of the members of Congress had had some university education, in a society in which only two out of every hundred university-aged individuals pursue post-secondary-school education.[9]

In addition, the National Front system (and the transition that followed) were not conducive to strong, innovative policies. National Front presidents had to preside over the policymaking process with half of their cabinets, half of Congress, and half of the governors and mayors being members of the other party—and with politicians constantly looking for the next president, who could not be the current one or even someone from the same party. This situation was worsened by the existence of personalistic factions within the parties, especially the Conservative one. As a result, presidents found it increasingly difficult to form a majority around any policy. When Virgilio Barco again led a party government in 1986, it was obvious that his Liberal party did not understand what that meant and that the Conservatives did not know how to be a loyal opposition.

I do not mean to imply that policy initiatives, even during the National Front years, were complete failures. Even before the United States started the Alliance for Progress, the Alberto Lleras administration had started a Colombian Agrarian Reform Institute (INCORA), and later a national development plan was written. Many new government agencies, both within the ministries and as decentralized institutes, were formed, and the verdict is still out on some of these. Others have had mixed results, but many appear to have been just paper agencies, the true purpose of which was to furnish white-collar jobs for the middle sectors and to comply with stipulations for U.S. aid.

Yet it would be unfair to condemn the Colombian government categorically. Agrarian reform has been a modest success, especially since most of the good lands were already occupied at the time the program was initiated so that redistribution was slight and most of the reform took place on public lands. Land titles were handed out to tens of thousands of families, but many more did not receive land. Schools and classrooms have been built, with the result that the state now enrolls more secondary students in public education than the church does in its higher-priced parochial schools. Health programs have led to more physicians and nurses and to lower death and infant mortality rates, and as a result, average life expectancy has increased. Public housing has been constructed, but not nearly enough for the masses of urban migrants; roads have been built; and kilowatt hours of electricity have increased. But in the process, the foreign debt has doubled in size.

Much still remains to be done to integrate fully the lower classes into national society, especially those in rural areas. President Barco has declared that he will end "absolute poverty" during his presidency. Defining that condition as not having sufficient income for food, clothing, and housing, it is estimated that 45 percent of the Colombian people live in absolute poverty. By the end of Barco's third year as president, it was clear that little progress had been made in this overly ambitious program. Land reform still remains an issue, although one probably should not look for very rapid reform given the power of the large landowners. Urban reform—housing and public services—is becoming more and more of an issue as the size of the cities increases dramatically every year. And basic public order recently has taken so much of the time of the executive branch of government that little time remains for the other issues.

Difficulties of an international nature continue. Although the Colombian economy is healthier than it was in the mid-1970s, since the dependence on coffee exports has declined, the balance of payments has typically been negative, and inflation has been rapid. Various sets of policies have been used to meet these problems. During times of foreign-exchange shortages, policies include taxes on consumer imports, tighter control of dollar exchanges, control of tourism, and encouragement of domestic manufacturing industries for both export and internal consumption. During times of foreign-exchange excesses, policies have been quite different: a loosening up of consumer imports, lighter dollar-exchange regulations, and discouragement of domestic industry.

Colombia has the possibility of becoming more economically stable because of new exports of petroleum and coal. Occidental Petroleum discoveries on the Orinoco Plains allowed Colombia to begin exporting oil in 1985. In 1982 the first coal was exported from the El Cerrejón coal fields in the department of La Guajira, and a larger northern area of El Cerrejón began export production in 1985. This production, which will reach a minimum of 16.5 million tons (15 million tonnes) annually, is the result of a joint venture between the Colombian state coal company, Carbones de Colombia (CARBOCOL), and International Colombia Resources Corporation (INTERCOR), a wholly owned subsidiary of Exxon. Although the El Cerrejón coal fields will not produce the bonanza projected by INTERCOR in 1980, the additional foreign revenues coming from their production will result in fewer balance-of-payments problems. Further, the coal will be used for thermoelectric generation.

Another way in which the Colombian government has attempted to solve some of its foreign-trade problems, as well as the problem of the multinational corporations (MNCs), has been membership in the Andean Pact. This pact, dating from 1969, was a cooperative effort of Colombia, Venezuela, Ecuador, Peru, Bolivia, and Chile. The six countries agreed (1) to eliminate all trade barriers among the member countries by 1980, (2) to establish a common external tariff on imports from outside the subregion by 1980, (3) to develop a mechanism to coordinate investment and encourage specialization rather than duplication of industry, and (4) to have a common foreign (non-Andean) investment code. The last was intended to place limitations on MNCs by requiring them to sell some of their stock to Andeans if they wanted to enjoy the benefits of the lower intraregion tariffs, by prohibiting MNCs from buying existing companies, and by not allowing additional investments of MNCs in public services and insurance. To date, the Andean Pact has had mixed results, complicated among other things by the abrupt changes of government in Chile. And in the 1980s the Colombians—as well as the other members of the pact—began new policies that relaxed the restrictions on MNCs. No longer is becoming a "mixed" company necessary unless an MNC intends to export within the pact countries, and even in that case they have a longer time period to attain that status.

With respect to the Latin American debt crisis, Colombia has been one of the least affected countries. Policymakers were conservative in accepting foreign loans during the late 1970s and early 1980s, and as a result, there has been no IMF standby loan to Colombia, although the country did accept IMF monitoring in order to be one of the few Latin American countries to receive new loans during the late 1980s. Colombia still enjoys the lowest per capita debt burden in Latin America.

PROSPECTS FOR THE FUTURE

In the past the resiliency of the Colombian system was remarkable. Party hegemonies came and went; civil wars, including the dramatic *la violencia*, appeared about to tear the social fabric apart; leftist guerrillas called for Cuban-like revolution; and Fidelist and Maoist groups of university students literally fought battles. The Colombian population doubled every twenty-four years or so (this rate has now "slowed" to every thirty), and thousands of landless peasants left the countryside for a life that was no better in the cities. Despite all these challenges, at its very essence Colombian politics remained the same: elitist, patrimonial, civilian, modified two-party, classist. Given the current "dirty war," it is no longer certain that these patterns can continue.

At least in part, this uncertainty is owing to an irony: While being one of the most "liberal democratic" of Latin American countries—albeit in its own way—Colombia has actually done less for the country's poor people than many other countries. In part, this situation is caused by the great problems and complexities of the country. But in another way, this irony is owing to the political system, which, whether by design or accident, has favored and continues to favor nondecisions. Of course, not making a decision favors the current situation, one that gives Colombians the "human right" of being able to vote every four years for unlimited numbers of candidates but does not give all Colombians the "human rights" of pan, techo, y tierra—"bread, a roof, and land."

As a result there are two possible scenarios for the 1990s. First, and perhaps most likely, Colombia will continue with its kind of liberal democracy, which makes the country a fine place for the middle and upper classes to live. Although "new" natural resources, such as petroleum and coal, might become economically important, it seems unlikely that their value will be such that it will be possible for politics to become significantly more distributive rather than redistributive. The current elite system will continue its attempts to co-opt emerging groups and individuals, with all the benefits and liabilities of that strategy. Second, during the 1980s it appeared increasingly likely that the traditional system might break down. It has been reported that even at cocktail parties of the elite, the common topic of discussion is when the military will take over. Former president Misael Pastrana agreed with this possibility when he stated in 1988 that the country was in an abyss. Although the guerrillas are unlikely to take power, the drug dealers already have power in many ways, and common crime can now be carried out with impunity. The speculation is that the breakdown of order might reach such a point that the military, as it did in 1953, will find it necessary to take power to save the country.

At this writing it appears to me that the two scenarios are equally likely. However, in most other Latin American countries, a situation like that in Colombia would have long ago led to a military coup, and if anyone in Latin America is likely to come up with a viable alternative, it is very apt to be that same Colombian elite (or its sons and daughters) that gave birth to the National Front.

NOTES

1. "Análisis del sector externo colombiano," Revista ANDI 48 (1980):55.

2. Eduardo Santa, Sociología política de Colombia (Bogotá: Ediciones Tercer Mundo, 1964), p. 37.

3. Harvey F. Kline, "The National Front: Historical Perspective and Overview," in Politics of Compromise: Coalition Government in Colombia, ed. R. Albert Berry,

Ronald G. Hellman, and Mauricio Solaún (New Brunswick, N.J.: Transaction Books, 1980), pp. 59–83.

4. Quoted in John D. Martz, *Colombia: A Contemporary Political Survey* (Chapel Hill: University of North Carolina Press, 1962), p. 84.

5. John Bailey, "Pluralist and Corporatist Dimensions of Interest Representation in Colombia," in *Authoritarianism and Corporatism in Latin America*, ed. James Malloy (Pittsburgh: University of Pittsburgh Press, 1977), pp. 259–302.

6. *El Espectador* (Bogotá), July 31, 1988.

7. Paul Oquist, *Violence, Conflict, and Politics in Colombia* (New York: Academic Press, 1980), Chapter 5.

8. Jonathan Hartlyn, "Consociational Politics in Colombia: Confrontation and Accommodation in Comparative Perspective" (Ph.D. dissertation, Yale University, 1981), p. 338.

9. Gary Hoskin, Francisco Leal, Dora Rothlisberger, and Armando Borrero, *Estudio del Comportamiento Legislativo en Colombia* (Bogotá: Departamento de Ciencia Política, Universidad de los Andes, 1975), p. 140.

SUGGESTIONS FOR FURTHER READING

Berry, R. Albert, Ronald G. Hellman, and Mauricio Solaún, eds. *Politics of Compromise: Coalition Government in Colombia*. New Brunswick, N.J.: Transaction Books, 1980.

Dix, Robert. *Colombia: The Political Dimensions of Change*. New Haven, Conn.: Yale University Press, 1967.

Fals Borda, Orlando. *Peasant Society in the Colombian Andes: A Sociological Study of Saucio*. Gainesville: University of Florida Press, 1955.

Fluharty, Vernon Lee. *Dance of the Millions: Military Rule and the Social Revolution in Colombia, 1930–1956*. Pittsburgh: University of Pittsburgh Press, 1957.

Hartlyn, Jonathan. *The Politics of Coalition Rule in Colombia*. New York: Cambridge University Press, 1988.

Hoskin, Gary, Francisco Leal, and Harvey Kline. *Legislative Behavior in Colombia*. 2 vols. Buffalo, N.Y.: International Studies Series, 1976.

Kline, Harvey F. *Colombia: Portrait of Unity and Diversity*. Boulder, Colo.: Westview Press, 1983.

———. *The Coal of El Cerrejón: Dependent Bargaining and Policymaking*. University Park: Pennsylvania State University Press, 1987.

Martz, John D. *Colombia: A Contemporary Political Survey*. Chapel Hill: University of North Carolina Press, 1962.

Morawetz, David. *Why the Emperor's New Clothes Are Not Made in Colombia*. New York: Oxford University Press, 1981.

Oquist, Paul. *Violence, Conflict, and Politics in Colombia*. New York: Academic Press, 1980.

Payne, James. *Patterns of Conflict in Colombia*. New Haven, Conn.: Yale University Press, 1968.

Urrutia, Miguel. *The Development of the Colombian Labor Movement*. New Haven, Conn.: Yale University Press, 1969.

12
Peru: Democratic Interlude, Authoritarian Heritage, Uncertain Future

DAVID SCOTT PALMER

Peru is a study in contrasts. A coastal desert gives way inland to imposing peaks of the Andes, which in turn fall off to the dense tropical rain forest of the Amazon Basin. The bustling, aggressively cosmopolitan coastal capital of Lima contains a third of Peru's 21 million people, including over half of its government employees, and generates at least two-thirds of the nation's gross national product (GNP). Lima seems worlds away from the sierra, where modern conveniences are often absent and centuries-old traditions still thrive. Irrigated coastal valleys cultivated with modern equipment for the export market coexist with small family plots and communally held lands on which a bare subsistence is eked out using the implements and practices of Indian ancestors. Procedures originating with the Spanish conquest can be found some 170 years after Peru's independence alongside the latest technological innovations from France and the United States.

Modern foreign and domestic investors extract oil and copper, produce cotton and woolen textiles, and employ tens of thousands of people. Government enterprises make steel and mine silver and employ other tens of thousands. The informal sector, based largely in metropolitan Lima, puts hundreds of thousands to work in everything from button selling to bus driving and may add an additional 60 percent to the GNP. The illegal sector, jungle based, refines and exports cocaine from the traditional home-grown coca leaf, involves many local peasants, and generates about $1 billion in foreign exchange annually.

Conservative, centrist, reformist, and radical political parties have competed for votes for both national and municipal offices several times since 1980, after a military regime ruled without elections for the twelve years before that, and at a time of the most burdensome foreign debt

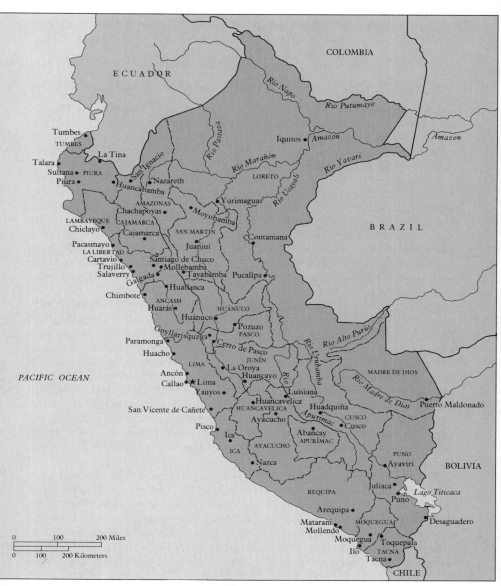

COLOMBIA

ECUADOR

Rio Napo

Rio Putumayo

Amazon

Tumbes
TUMBES

La Tina

Iquitos • Amazon

Talara

San Ignacio

Rio Marañón

Rio Yavari

Sultana • PIURA

Nazareth

Amazon

Piura

Huancabamba

LORETO

BRAZIL

AMAZONAS

Rio Ucayali

Chachapoyas

Moyobamba

Yurimaguas

LAMBAYEQUE
CAJAMARCA

Chiclayo

SAN MARTIN

Contamana

Pacasmayo
LA LIBERTAD

Cajamarca

Juanjui

Cartavio

Santiago de Chuco

Trujillo

Mollebamba

Salaverry

Tayabamba

Pucallpa

Galgada

Chimbote

Huallanca

ANCASH

Huarás

HUÁNUCO

Huánuco

Pozuzo

Rio Alto Purús

Goyllarisquzga

PASCO

Paramonga

Cerro de Pasco

Rio Urubamba

Huacho

JUNÍN

MADRE DE DIOS

Ancón

La Oroya

LIMA

Callao

★ Lima

Huancayo

Rio

Rio Madre de Dios

Yauyos

Luisiana

Puerto Maldonado

PACIFIC OCEAN

San Vicente de Cañete

Huancavelica

HUANCAVELICA

Huadquiña

Apurímac

CUSCO

Pisco

Ayacucho

Cusco

Ica

Abancay

ICA

AYACUCHO

APURÍMAC

PUNO

Nazca

Ayaviri

BOLIVIA

AREQUIPA

Juliaca

Lago Titicaca

Arequipa

Puno

Matarani

MOQUEGUA

Desaguadero

Mollendo

Moquegua

Toquepala

Ilo

TACNA

Tacna

CHILE

0   100   200 Miles

0   100   200 Kilometers

Peru

in modern Peruvian history. Emerging to coexist with the formal democracy are both rural- and urban-based guerrilla movements, defying the axiom that open politics and revolutionary ferment are incompatible.

Contrasts and contradictions abound, giving Peru, with its authoritarian heritage and recent democratic interlude, a most uncertain political future.

POLITICAL CULTURE AND HISTORICAL BACKGROUND

The political culture of Peru has been shaped by a number of factors, of which the most important is the almost 300 years of Spanish colonial rule. The main elements of Spanish control included authoritarian political institutions and mercantilist economic institutions, both of which gave colonialists little experience in handling their own affairs. The carryover into the postcolonial period was greater in Peru than in other Latin American countries not only because control was imposed more consistently but also because of the nature of the independence movement itself. The belated struggle for independence in this part of the empire was more a conservative reaction to liberalizing forces in Spain and elsewhere than a genuine revolution, and it was brought largely from outside. As a result, there was no real break in Peru with the colonial past after 1824, even though some liberal organizations and procedures were introduced at that time.

Not surprisingly, therefore, authoritarian rule continued long after independence. There was no elected civilian president until Manuel Pardo in 1872, although there were some enlightened military leaders such as Ramón Castilla (1845–1851, 1854–1862). Also continuing were neomercantilist economic policies as Great Britain replaced Spain as Peru's major trading partner and the source of most capital and investment. Few local entrepreneurs emerged in this context, and most who did acted as agents for British interests. Peru did experience its first economic boom during this period, based on the rich deposits of bird droppings, or guano, on islands off the coast. The economic benefits were short-lived, however, owing to the outbreak of the War of the Pacific (1879–1883).

The war forced a partial break with Peru's past. Chile wrested from Peru the coastal department of Tarapacá, with its immense nitrate deposits, and occupied a large portion of the country, including Lima. Politically, this disaster demonstrated the weakness of the existing institutions and contributed to the emergence of Peru's only sustained period of limited liberal democracy (1895–1919). Economically, the war left the country bankrupt, and because many of the country's basic resources were mortgaged, Peru became even more dependent on British interests.

This coincidence of sharply increased economic dependence and liberal democracy set the pattern for a limited state and private foreign enterprise that most Peruvian governments tried to follow until the 1968 military coup. With few exceptions, the Peruvian economic elite was dependent for its well-being on foreign trade and investment, predominantly British until the 1920s, largely U.S. since. It did not advance, by and large, on the basis of its own innovations and risk taking in productive domestic investment.

In addition, much of Peru's independent political life has been marked by a flamboyant leadership style that has tended to garner support on the basis of personal appeal rather than institutional loyalties and obligations. Many leaders have tended to place personal interests above obligation to any political party organization or even to the nation. As a result, most parties have been personalist vehicles, and most presidencies have involved tumultuous struggles among contending personalities, often ending in a military coup.

Furthermore, until very recently a large percentage of the national population was not integrated into national economic, political, or cultural life. The Indian subculture of Peru, though in numbers predominant until the 1970s, has participated in national society only in the most subordinate of roles, such as peon, day laborer, and maid. The way open, historically, for Indians to escape repudiation by the dominant society was to abandon their own heritage and work their way into that of the Spanish. Among the most important changes in contemporary Peru is large-scale Indian immigration to towns and cities, where Indians feel they—or their children—can become a part of the dominant culture: Catholic, Hispanic, Spanish speaking. In addition, the constitution of 1978 gave illiterates—predominantly Indian—the right to vote for the first time in national and municipal elections.

In Latin America, traditional domestic politics were challenged in fundamental ways between 1900 and 1930 by the emergence of new social and political groups, by post–World War I and depression price declines, and by such outside political forces as the Russian Revolution and Mussolini's corporatist state. Peru, of course, did not escape the effects of these various factors. However, politics did not change in any basic way until 1968, when a military coup ushered in a period of unprecedented reform.

Changes in Peruvian politics were delayed for a number of reasons: Domestic elites were willing to retain strong foreign economic control; the military was largely under elite dominance; political leadership kept its personalistic and populist character; a non-Communist, mass-based political party absorbed most of the emerging social forces; and the Indian cultural "barrier" slowed the flow of new elements into national society. As a result, the liberal model of the limited state and the open economy was retained with few modifications until 1968.

Peruvian political history may be divided into the following periods: consolidation (1824–1895), limited civilian democracy (1895–1919), populism and mass parties (1919–1968), reformist military rule (1968–1980), and fully participatory formal democracy (1980–   ).

Consolidation (1824–1895)

Peru took much longer than most Latin American countries to evolve a reasonably stable political and economic system. Because Peru had been the core part of a larger viceroyalty during the colonial period, it took some time just to define the country's national territory. The boundaries were roughly hewn out in 1829 (by the failure of Augustín Gamarra and José de la Mar to capture Ecuador for Peru), in 1839 (by the Battle of Yungay in which Andrés Santa Cruz lost his post as protector of the Peru-Bolivia confederation when defeated by a Chilean army), and in 1841 (by the Battle of Ingavi when Gamarra was killed in his attempt to annex Bolivia to Peru).

Once the boundaries were more or less settled, there remained the key problem of establishing reasonable procedures for attaining and succeeding to political office. Peru had at least fifteen constitutions in its first forty years as an independent country, but force remained the normal route to political power. Of the thirty-five presidents during this period, only four were elected according to constitutional procedures, and no civilians held power for more than a few months. Regional caudillos often attempted to impose themselves on the government, which by the 1840s was becoming an important source of revenue because of the income from guano.

Unlike much of Latin America during the nineteenth century, Peru was less divided politically by the conservative-liberal cleavage and more by the issue of military or civilian rule. By the 1860s partisans of civilian rule were beginning to organize themselves into the *civilista* movement. The War of the Pacific dramatically demonstrated the need for professionalization of the Peruvian military and helped provoke the formal establishment of the Civilista party, as well as a number of more personalistic contenders. The eventual result was Peru's first extended period of civilian rule, starting in 1895.

The War of the Pacific also more firmly embedded the tendency to depend on foreign markets, foreign entrepreneurship, and foreign loans. War debts of more than $200 million were canceled by British interests in 1889 in exchange for Peru's railroads, the Lake Titicaca steamship line, a large tract of jungle land, free use of major ports, a Peruvian government subsidy, and large quantities of guano.

Limited Civilian Democracy (1895–1919)

Peru's longest period of civilian rule thus far began in 1895. While the military reorganized itself under the guidance of a French mission, a coalition of forces from an emerging commercial elite gained control of the government. Embracing neopositivist ideals of renovation, modernization, and innovation, the civilians also advanced the classic liberal precept of a government that would serve to enhance the capacity of the private sector. Their main political objective was the very modest one of keeping civilians in power. This effort implied fostering a civilian state and a civilian society by increased government expenditures for communications, education, and health. These were financed by taxes on rapidly expanding exports, by revenues from new foreign investments (largely U.S.), and by new foreign loans after Peru's international credit was restored in 1907.

This civilian rule was somewhat tenuous even at its height. The Civilista party, although reasonably well organized, suffered periodic severe internal divisions. Other parties, such as the Liberal, the Democratic, and the Conservative, were personalistic and rose and fell with the fortunes of their individual leaders.

The civilian democratic interlude, ensured when Nicolás de Piérola (1895–1899) provided for the direct election of his successors, was undone by various factors. One was the severe domestic inflation precipitated by the international economic crisis accompanying World War I. Another was the growing unwillingness of elite-oriented parties to respond to a wide array of new political demands from beneficiaries of reforms in such areas as health, education, and urban conditions. To a certain degree, the elites had problems in responding to the longer-term political consequences of their own economic success. Also corrosive to civilian rule were the actions of some leaders themselves. In particular, Presidents Augusto B. Leguía (1908–1912; 1919–1930) and Guillermo Billinghurst (1912–1914) operated in self-serving and personalistic ways. Billinghurst, once elected, eschewed Civilista party support to make populist appeals to the Lima "masses." Although he was beholden to the commercial elite, Billinghurst did not try to work within the party or "the club" to try to bring about some quiet accommodation that might have avoided a confrontation. Elite dismay eventually drew that group to the military, which intervened in 1914 just long enough to remove Billinghurst from office. Leguía, after ruling constitutionally during his first presidency, ended once and for all the shaky civilian democracy in 1919. Rather than work out a behind-the-scenes accommodation with opposition elements in 1919, after he had won democratic election, he led a successful coup of his own and ruled without open elections until being ousted himself in 1930.

Certainly a different perception of reality and a different set of priorities guide such individuals to contribute to the discrediting of the set of political institutions and procedures that have facilitated their rise to political prominence. Among these must be a sense that the individual is more important than institutions, a distrust of organizations, and a reluctance to compromise a position or accommodate oneself to the view of others. These differences, although not unique to Peru, suggest the tension between some Latin American leadership styles and a well-institutionalized, routinized political system.

Populism, Parties, and Coups (1919–1968)

The populism of this period took two forms: civilian, exemplified by Leguía, and military, best illustrated by Gen. Manuel Odría (1948–1956). Both forms were characterized by efforts to discourage the development of political organizations and to encourage loyalty to the person of the president through favored treatment for the elites and by the distribution of goods, jobs, and services to politically aware nonelite segments. Both forms were also marked by very favorable treatment for the foreign investor and lender; thus, they maintained long-standing external dependence relationships.

The great advantage of the populist alternative is that it gains popular loyalty to government at very low cost as new sectors of the population are becoming politically active. The great disadvantage is that it operates best in an organizational vacuum and, thus, does not provide a long-term solution to relating citizen to system.

Both civilian and military populism had a number of important effects on the Peruvian political system. They permitted elites to retain control through their narrowly based interest-group organizations (the National Agrarian Society [SNA], the National Mining Society [SNM], and the National Industrial Society [SNI]) and their clubs (Nacional and La Unión). When confronted after 1930 with Peru's first mass-based political party, the American Popular Revolutionary Alliance (APRA), the elites were forced to rely on the military to carry out their political will because they had no comparable party to turn to. The military, in turn, found it could accomplish its own objectives by directly intervening in the political system rather than by working through organized intermediaries. Thus populism, by discouraging political parties, contributed significantly to continued political instability.

Between 1914 and 1984 Manuel Prado (1939–1945; 1956–1962) was the only elected civilian to complete a term (the first). Why he did so is instructive: He (1) was of the elite and accepted by it, (2) did not try to upset the status quo, (3) gained the military's favor by supporting its material and budget requirements, (4) reached an implicit modus vivendi with APRA, (5) happened to be president during a period when foreign market prices for Peruvian primary-product exports were relatively high and stable.

Perhaps the most important political event in pre-1968 Peru was the organization of APRA. Although founded in Mexico by exiled student leader Víctor Raúl Haya de la Torre in 1924, APRA soon became a genuinely mass-based political party in Peru with a fully articulated, if not completely coherent, ideology. By most accounts APRA was strong enough to determine the outcome of all open elections held in Peru after 1931. Until the 1980s, however, the military ensured that the party would never rule directly.

Although APRA has had a strong populist appeal through the years, the party's importance for Peruvian politics rests on its reformist ideology and its organizational capacity. With the exception of Lima, APRA absorbed most of the newly emerging social forces in the more integrated parts of the country between the 1920s and the 1950s, most particularly labor, students, and the more-marginal middle sectors. The party's appeal thus helped prevent the emergence of a more radical alternative. Furthermore, even though APRA was an outsider for most of the period from its founding to 1956, it never overthrew the system. At key junctures the party leadership searched for accommodation and compromise to gain entry even while continuing to resort to assassinations and abortive putsches in trying to impress political insiders of its power capabilities.

Between 1956 and 1982 APRA became a center-conservative party willing to make almost any compromise to gain greater formal political power. In 1956 APRA supported the conservative Manuel Prado in his successful bid for a second term as president and worked with him throughout his administration in what was called in Peru *la convivencia* ("living together"). When APRA won open elections in 1962 but was just shy of the constitutionally required one-third, the party made a pact with its former archenemy Odría to govern together. At this point the military intervened and ran the country for a year before facilitating elections, which its favored candidate, Popular Action's (AP) Fernando Belaúnde Terry, won. During the Belaúnde administration (1963–1968), APRA formed an alliance with Odría forces in Congress to attain a majority and block or water down many of AP's reforms. Although such actions discredited the party for many people during this period, APRA remained the best organized and most unified political force in the country.

The AP, founded in 1956, brought reformist elements into the system just as APRA had done before. AP's appeal was greater in the sierra and south, where APRA was weak. Thus, the two parties complemented each other by region, and between them they channeled into the system virtually the entire next wave of newly mobilized popular forces.

In spite of APRA-Odría political obstructionism, important reforms were carried out between 1963 and 1968, including establishment of various new agricultural programs; expansion of secondary and university education, cooperatives, and development corporations; and reinstitution of municipal elections. For all intents and purposes the extremist threat to Peruvian institutions remained stillborn. But the opposition in Congress often blunted initiatives or refused to fund them, and the U.S. government, anxious to assist Standard Oil Company's settlement of the investment-expropriation dispute between its Peruvian subsidiary International Petroleum Company (IPC) and the Peruvian government, withheld for more than two years Alliance for Progress funds badly needed by the Belaúnde administration to help finance its reforms. Growing economic difficulties in 1967 and 1968 eroded public confidence, and a badly handled IPC nationalization agreement sealed Belaúnde's fate. On October 3, 1968, with a bloodless coup, the armed forces began Peru's first long-term, institutionalized military rule.

The Military *Docenio* (1968–1980)

"The time has come," stated the new military regime's first manifesto, "to dedicate our national energies to the transformation of the economic, social, and cultural structures of Peru." The underlying themes of the military's major statements during the *docenio* ("twelve-year rule") included a commitment to change, national pride, social solidarity, the end of dependency, a worker-managed economy, and "a fully participatory social democracy which is neither capitalist nor communist but humanistic." Past governments had declared their intention to change Peru, but this one was prepared to act. True enough, the civilian government from 1963 to 1968 had been a reformist one, and in many ways it set the stage for continued change after the takeover. What was so surprising, given Peru's history of military intervention on behalf of the elites, was that the 1968 military coup occurred in large part because the civilian government had failed in its plans to carry out reform, not because it had succeeded.

An explanation can be found in a number of changes occurring over a number of years within the military, which led most of the officer corps, at least within the army, to the conclusion that the best protection for national security was national development. In their view, civilian politicians and political parties had taken on the development challenge in the 1960s and had failed. Many officers concluded that only the military, with its monopoly of legitimate force, was capable of leading Peru toward this goal. Helping to forge this reformist institutional perspective among the officers was their educational experience after the mid-1950s in the Center for Higher Military Studies (CAEM), a small but intense antiguerrilla campaign in 1965, U.S. military training from the 1940s through the 1960s, the U.S. government's decision in 1967 not to sell jet fighter planes to Peru, and a vigorous army-led civic action program after 1959.

Once in power, the military called itself revolutionary but practiced reform. Almost without exception, the 1968–1975 policy initiatives were based on the twin assumptions of continued economic growth, with improved distribution of this growth, and the willingness of economic elites to accept incentives to redirect their wealth toward new productive activities. The military's policies were not based on redistributing the existing pie.

A number of significant changes occurred. One of the most important was the rapid expansion of state influence and control. New ministries, agencies, and banks were established; basic services were expropriated, as were some large foreign companies in mining, fishing, and agriculture, with compensation and reinvestment incentives; and state enterprises or cooperatives were established in their place. Important areas of heavy industry were reserved for the state, new investment laws placed various controls on the private sector, and government employment mushroomed. At the same time Peru pursued the objective of enhancing development by becoming more diversified in its external relationships, thereby reducing the country's economic and political dependency. Another significant initiative was a large-scale agrarian-reform program, which effectively eliminated large private landholdings. About 360,000 farm families received land between 1969 and 1980, most as members of farm cooperatives. Commitment to cooperatives illustrated the regime's concern for popular participation at various levels. Neighborhood organizations, worker communities, and cooperatives of several types proliferated after 1970, as did various coordinating bodies. All of these changes represented substantial adjustments in past practices, and for a time appeared likely to succeed.

By 1971 the military's model for the future political system of Peru had emerged in more or less coherent form; subsequent statements, decrees, and practices tended to flesh it out. The official model was essentially corporatist in nature. It perceived Peruvian social and political reality in terms of an organic whole, organized naturally by functional sectors and within each sector by a natural hierarchy. Government was to serve as the overarching body to initiate, coordinate, and resolve disputes within or among sectors. In this context, established political parties and unions were perceived as being disruptive forces, and numerous decrees before 1975 were designed either to marginalize such groups or to provide competitors, though not to outlaw or expel them. It was apparently assumed that the new model would eventually replace the old because of the dramatic increase in the size and capacity of government and the incentives provided to popular sectors to relate to it rather than to parties and interest groups. For a variety of reasons, however, this assumption proved false.

Three major factors led to the regime's undoing. First and most fundamentally, success was premised on continued economic growth, which stopped after 1974 when economic difficulties multiplied rapidly. In part these were caused by overly ambitious projects and miscalculations of resource availability, in part by the military's desire for perquisites and equipment. With locally generated resources not available as expected, the military government turned to foreign loans, often short-term ones, to keep up the momentum. This policy produced a severe resource crunch by 1978, the first of what have become the endemic Latin American debt crises, and partly explains Peru's recurring economic problems to the present. Second, the people in power failed to consult openly and as equals with the citizens, the presumed beneficiaries of the reforms. This neglect contributed to popular resentment and mistrust as well as to a number of inappropriate policies, which did not benefit the periphery in ways the center expected. Third, the illness after 1973 of the head of state, Gen. Juan Velasco Alvarado, contributed to a loss of the institutional unity of the armed forces themselves, which his dynamic and forceful leadership had helped to instill. The eventual result was a mixture of old and new programs in yet another overlay, increasingly ill-financed, confusing to the citizens, and ultimately counterproductive.

An August 1975 coup led by Gen. Francisco Morales Bermúdez and supported by the military establishment gently eased out the ill and increasingly erratic General Velasco and ushered in the consolidating phase of the *docenio*. With the exception of the agrarian reform, initiatives were quietly abandoned or sharply curtailed. By 1977 the economic and political pressures were so great that the military regime decided to initiate a gradual return to civilian rule. The resulting Constituent Assembly elections in 1978 represented another political milestone, for they included participation by an array of leftist parties, which garnered an unprecedented 36 percent of the vote though APRA won the most seats. The Assembly itself was led by Haya de la Torre, another first. These elections marked the beginning of significant involvement in the system by the Marxist left. The Assembly produced the constitution of 1979, which set up national elections every five years, beginning in 1980, and municipal elections every three years, starting in 1981. The irony of these two elections was that they returned to the presidency the same Belaúnde (and to many local mayoralties his same party colleagues) who had been so unceremoniously unseated in 1968. The 34 percent inflation rate and $700-million debt that had contributed to Belaúnde's ouster had increased by 1980 to over 60 percent inflation and an $8.4-billion debt.

Civilian Rule (1980–)

This time Belaúnde's AP was able to forge a majority in Congress, in coalition with the small Popular Christian party (PPC), and won the first plurality in the 1981 municipal elections as well. But events conspired once again to make life difficult for the governing authorities. Inflation continued to increase; by 1984 it had reached a record of over 100 percent. The recession deepened so that in 1983 the GNP actually declined by over 10 percent, and real wages eroded during Belaúnde's second administration (1980–1985) by over 30 percent. World market prices for Peru's exports—copper, oil, sugar, fish meal, minerals—remained low or declined even further. Devastating weather accompanied the arrival in 1982 of the El Niño ocean current, and crops and communications networks in the northern half of Peru were destroyed because of rain and flood; in the south, crops withered as a result of drought. Given the unfavorable economic developments, the foreign debt burden became even more onerous—over $13 billion by 1985. International Monetary Fund (IMF) agreements provided new external resources and debt refinancing but also imposed restrictive domestic economic policies, which sparked much controversy. Belaúnde ultimately hedged on these requirements, thus provoking a breakdown in the IMF agreement and leaving a substantial burden for the next civilian administration of Alán García.

Another unanticipated problem for the civilian government was the growing violence associated with the activities of the Shining Path

(Sendero Luminoso). Originally based in the isolated south-central sierra province of Ayacucho, and headed by former professors and students from the local University of Huamanga, Shining Path advocated a peasant-based republic forged through revolution on the principles of Mao and José Carlos Mariátegui. After more than fifteen years of theorizing at the university and working in the Indian-peasant-dominated local countryside, the group's leaders moved to increasingly violent confrontations, first against symbols of authority and then against the authorities themselves.

The Belaúnde administration did not take the group seriously at first; only after almost three full years of Shining Path activity did the government declare an emergency zone in the Ayacucho area and send in the military to deal with the problem. Although the government committed itself to providing economic aid to the impoverished region as well, little was actually done before 1985. By the end of Belaúnde's term over 6,000 had perished in the violence, most in 1983 (1,977) and 1984 (3,587); human rights violations had skyrocketed; and over $1 billion in property damage had occurred. New guerrilla groups had appeared as well, particularly the Lima-based Tupac Amaru Revolutionary Movement (MRTA), and these contributed to spreading the perverse legitimacy of political violence.

These economic and political difficulties substantially weakened popular support for Belaúnde and for the AP in the 1983 municipal elections; in the 1985 presidential vote, the AP candidate was routed, gaining only 6 percent of the total. The largely Marxist United Left party (IU) garnered 23 percent for its candidate, and a rejuvenated APRA, with the youthful (thirty-six-year-old) Alán García as its standard bearer, won with 48 percent.

The García victory was doubly historic: APRA had finally gained the presidency after a fifty-five-year struggle (and a majority in both houses of Congress as well), and 1985 marked the first time in forty years that one elected civilian president handed power over to an elected successor (only the second time since 1912). The 1986 municipal elections also saw substantial APRA gains, including, for the first time ever, the mayorship of Lima.

Alán García's forceful, nationalistic leadership put the international banking community on notice that Peru would be limiting repayments on its debt (now over $14 billion) to 10 percent of export earnings, which contributed to a long overdue domestic economic stimulation leading to growth rates of 9 percent in 1985 and 7 percent in 1986. But the recovery ran out of steam in 1987, and the economy was further shaken by the surprise presidential announcement that year nationalizing domestic banks. By 1988 the economy was in a new tailspin, with international credit totally dried up, inflation for the year at 1,722 percent, more than five times Peru's previous high, and an 8.5 percent decline in GNP. García's popularity plummeted from an 80 percent favorable rating to under 15 percent, and rumors abounded of a possible coup.

Military spokesmen committed their institutions to upholding civilian rule, however, and parties across the political spectrum competed aggressively for support in the November 1989 municipal elections and the April 1990 presidential and congressional vote. In 1989 the left IU divided badly, squandering an historic opportunity. From virtual oblivion reemerged Peru's right, centered on the capacity of novelist Mario Vargas Llosa to galvanize popular concern over President García's failures. A new coalition, the Democratic Front (FREDEMO), was formed among conservative and centrist parties, including former President Belaúnde's AP, perennial conservative candidate Luis Bedoya Reyes's Popular Christian party (PPC), and Vargas Llosa's new Liberty Movement. To the surprise of many, FREDEMO captured a plurality of mayorships in the 1989 municipal elections, and opinion polls indicated that Vargas Llosa was most likely to be the next president of Peru. Even as electoral politics advanced, however, the guerrilla movements expanded their activities. By mid-1989 deaths attributed to guerrilla violence and the government response had exceeded 12,000, with damages in excess of $15 billion and no end in sight. The paradox of an open, formal democracy and growing terrorism was never more apparent than in Peru.

SOCIAL AND POLITICAL GROUPS

Organized social and political groups have played less of a role in Peruvian affairs than in most other Latin American countries. The reasons may be traced in part to the strong patterns of Spanish domination that inhibited growth long after the formal Spanish presence was removed. What emerged instead was a strong sense of individualism within the context of region and family for that small portion of the total population that was actually included within the nation's political system. In the decades following independence, governments were made and unmade by regional caudillos or officials whose power was based on control of arms, personal appeal, and family or regional ties. The best lands were increasingly controlled by non-Indians, who took advantage of postindependence decrees and constitutions that removed Indians and their preserves from state protection. The church also lost some of its land-based financial strength, and private beneficent societies (*beneficencias*) took over the ownership and administration of many church properties. Thus, political and economic power were quite fragmented in nineteenth-century Peru. The disastrous War of the Pacific abruptly ended the beginnings of economic consolidation based on the guano export boom.

With the consolidation of a limited civilian democracy in the 1890s, some of what were to become the country's most important interest groups were founded, including the National Agrarian Society (SNA), the National Mining Society (SNM), and the National Industrial Society (SNI). However, for a long time the important decisions affecting the country were usually made in the Club Nacional, formed much earlier

(1855) and the lone survivor of post-1968 reforms. Even the military operated between 1914 and 1962 largely as the "watchdog of the oligarchy." Thus, elites could determine policy outside the electoral arena when necessary and had limited incentives to operate within any party system.

Elections themselves were intermittent and tentative until 1980, and electoral restrictions historically kept most Peruvians out of the national political arena. Property ownership requirements were not lifted until 1931, when the secret ballot was also introduced. Women were not enfranchised until 1956, and literacy and age requirements remained in effect until the advent of universal suffrage in the 1980s.

The political party scene in Peru is quite fragmented as well. AP split into pro- and anti-Belaúnde factions, though it came back together with the Belaúnde victory in 1980, only to divide again after 1985. APRA divided after the death of Haya de la Torre in 1979, but the progressive faction regained control after the election of Haya's protégé, Alán García, as party head in 1982 and president in 1985. The García government's problems after 1987 contributed to new divisions within APRA. A small but influential Christian Democratic party (DC) also divided into a tiny leftist faction allied with IU and a larger conservative group (PPC), which by 1988 was a part of the new rightist group known as FREDEMO. A Marxist political movement (founded by the intellectual José Carlos Mariátegui in 1928) became the Communist party, which has retained its Moscow-oriented core while fragmenting almost endlessly into Maoist, Castroite, and Trotskyite splinters. All share pieces of equally divided urban and rural union movements, though the Moscow line controls the largest portion (about 75 percent). The military government's efforts in the 1970s to build a new corporatist structure of political participation compounded the confusion for a time but has now been largely put aside.

The public prominence of the Shining Path that began in 1980 and its recourse to guerrilla tactics evoked an almost universally negative response by Peru's Marxist left, suggesting that the core of the Communist movement is not inclined at this time to pursue its goals through violence. As long as most of its members are joined (however loosely) in the IU, the Communists have found that they can fare quite well in presidential, congressional, and municipal elections, with support ranging from 25 to 35 percent. Some people maintain that the rise of an organized left operating within rather than outside the political system is one of the positive legacies of the military *docenio*. The IU's problem is its tendency to divide, which sharply reduces its possibilities for success in the 1990 national elections.

The role of U.S. public and private participation has always been quite complex. Private investment in Peru grew rapidly in the early twentieth century but was almost exclusively in isolated enclaves on the north coast (oil and sugar, later cotton and fish meal) and in the sierra (copper, other minerals, later iron). Successive governments encouraged such investment. Even during the *docenio*, in spite of some expropriations and a conscious attempt to diversify sources of foreign investment, substantial new U.S. investment took place, particularly in copper (Southern Peru Copper Company) and oil exploration and production (Occidental Petroleum Company). The Belaúnde government's policy toward private investment was more open but only partly successful owing to international and domestic economic problems. The García administration's nationalistic posture in a context of growing economic and political difficulties has discouraged most new investment, domestic or foreign, since 1985.

However one may debate the issue of foreign dependence, in a very real sense U.S. investment and loans served in predepression Peru to balance the country's extreme reliance on Great Britain. The enclave nature of this assistance had both positive and negative impacts: reduction of economic-ripple effects on the rest of the Peruvian economy, provision of islands of relative economic privilege for workers in which unions could become established, and creation of small areas of virtual foreign hegemony within Peru.

With growing economic nationalism in Peru in the 1960s, the U.S. government collaborated closely with U.S. businesses to try to work out solutions satisfactory to "U.S. interests." The IPC case between 1963 and 1968 illustrates this policy in the extreme. One basis for Peru's desire to expropriate IPC rested on well-founded claims that the concessions giving Standard Oil of New Jersey subsoil rights in La Brea y Parinas (near Talara) in 1921 and 1922 were illegal. The U.S. government supported Standard Oil's position, and when negotiations bogged down periodically, U.S. government foreign assistance and loans under the Alliance for Progress were interrupted. The Belaúnde government, under duress, finally struck a bargain with the company, but the controversial terms generated public debate and turmoil and provided the immediate precipitant for the 1968 coup. Within a week after taking power the military nationalized IPC. This and subsequent periodic expropriations kept most new official U.S. aid suspended between 1968 and 1972, except for relief and rehabilitation assistance after a 1970 earthquake. Eventually, the military government found itself obliged to resolve expropriations with financial settlements that companies considered fair, in part as a result of U.S. government pressure but also because the Peruvian regime wanted and needed continued foreign private investment and loans.

Historically, the U.S. government presence in Peru was not a large one. Starting in 1938, however, because of U.S. concern about the threat of international fascism within the hemisphere and continuing after World War II because of the perceived menace of international communism, the U.S. government has been a major actor. Between 1945 and 1975 grants and loans to Peru totaled $1.107 billion, of which $194 million was military assistance. Aid funds during the Belaúnde years, when available, went primarily for projects in marginal sectors the opposition-controlled Peruvian Congress was unwilling to fund. A large-scale civic-action program for the military in the 1960s helped shape officers' views on the national development mission of the Peruvian armed forces. The U.S. government's refusal to permit the sale of jet fighters to Peru in 1967 also shaped the armed forces' perspectives—helping officers to realize that their own welfare, as well as that of their country, would be enhanced by diversifying their sources of supply and, hence, their dependence as well.

Actions and reactions by both the Peruvian and the U.S. government since 1968—including aid and loan cutoffs, the expulsion of most of the large U.S. military mission, and the end of the Peace Corps presence—have considerably lowered the official U.S. profile in the country. García's prickly relationship with the United States has limited U.S. programs to some modest economic aid and drug interdiction and eradication assistance. Since 1973 Peru has had a substantial military sales and assistance relationship with the Soviet Union—in excess of $1 billion—which involves the training in Peru and in the Eastern bloc of several hundred army and air force personnel each year and over 100 Soviet advisers in Peru.

GOVERNMENT MACHINERY

The Peruvian government, like many of its Latin American counterparts, may be largely characterized as limited, centralized, and personalistic. Until the 1960s government employees constituted a very small proportion of the work force and were usually selected on the basis of party affiliation, family ties, or friendship. Most ministry bureaucracies were concentrated in Lima, and for all practical purposes, the government's presence in the provinces was limited to prefects and their staffs, military garrisons in the border areas, small detachments of national police, local teachers, and a few judges. All of these people were appointed by the appropriate ministry in the capital.

A government monopoly of the guano industry and of tobacco, matches, and salt marketing were among the few official ventures before 1960. Until the 1960s the Central Bank was privately controlled, and even government taxes were collected by private agencies. Within the government the executive branch predominated. During periods when Congress was functioning, however, the executive's authority was subject to numerous checks, including Congress's powers to interrogate and censure ministers and to appropriate funds.

The government's size and scope increased considerably during the first Belaúnde administration, largely in the number of semiautonomous government agencies: for example, provincial development corporations, a national housing agency, a domestic Peace Corps (Cooperación Popular), a national planning institute, a cooperative organization, and squatter settlement organizations. Total government employment increased from 179,000 in 1960 (6 percent of the work force) to 270,000 in 1967 (7 percent of the work force), and the public sector's share of the gross domestic product grew from 8 percent to 11 percent during the same period.

However, the most dramatic changes in the size and scope of the state machinery occurred between 1968 and 1980, within an official ideological context of "statism." This ideology advanced the virtue of government involvement to accelerate development along nationalistic lines. Most existing ministries were reorganized, and numerous new ministries and autonomous agencies were created. By 1973 total government employment had increased by almost 50 percent over 1967 figures to 401,000 (9 percent of the work force) and by 1975 to an estimated 450,000 (11 percent of the work force). The public sector's share of the gross domestic product doubled between 1967 and 1975 to 22 percent.

Although a great deal of attention was given to the need to decentralize government activities to make them more accessible to a larger share of the population, in practice central government activities remained as concentrated in Lima as they had been historically. Much of the increase in government budget went toward construction, equipment, and white-collar employment in the capital rather than toward activities in marginal areas.

The political and financial crises of 1975 and the change of government brought to an end the dynamic phase of public-sector reforms. Resource limitations, financial and human; the continuance of prior modes of party, union, and interest-group activity; and the practical inability of the military regime to effectively act upon all decrees prevented the full implementation of the corporatist model articulated between 1971 and 1975. The second Belaúnde administration announced its intention to restore the dynamism of the private sector and to reduce the role of government, but continuing economic problems and substantial public resistance made these changes difficult to carry out. The García government moved quickly to implement long-standing APRA goals of regional development corporations and expanded agricultural credit while working simultaneously to win the confidence of the domestic entrepreneurial sectors. Initial successes were substantial, but by 1989 they had been overwhelmed by an ill-advised nationalization of domestic banks and Peru's worst economic crisis since the general collapse after the War of the Pacific.

PUBLIC POLICY

Historically, public policy in Peru may be characterized as limited. Laissez-faire liberalism applied from consolidation in the 1890s up to 1968 with few exceptions. Most services were privately owned, and the government's role was normally that of facilitator or expediter for the private sector, including foreign enterprises.

Unlike many Latin American countries, Peru did not respond to the challenge of the world depression after 1929 by sharp increases in public services and enterprise. This difference may have resulted in part from the simultaneous domestic challenge to the elites posed by APRA, with its advocacy of sharply expanded state control. By successfully keeping APRA from gaining control of the political system in the 1930s, the elites also retained the limited state. By the time APRA was finally permitted to enter the political arena as a legitimate force in 1956, its position on the role of the state was much more accommodating to elite interests.

The electoral campaigns of 1961–1962 and 1962–1963 raised more explicitly the need for a greater public-sector role. The ultimate winners, AP and Belaúnde, worked actively between 1963 and 1968 to make the state a more dynamic force and began numerous public initiatives. Some redistribution of income in favor of the less-privileged sectors did occur in the 1960s, although it is not clear just how much of the change was the result of government policies. Perhaps the most important legacy of the Belaúnde administration was to break down the long-standing aversion in Peru to the state as a dynamic force and to create a climate of increased popular expectations regarding what the state could and should do.

Between 1968 and 1980 the military government served as the major force for an unprecedented expansion of the state and its policies, in a country with one of the weakest public sectors in Latin America. Rapid state expansion was not without its problems, and in trying to do so much so quickly, the government spread itself too thin. Although providing new job opportunities for the middle class, the rapidly expanding bureaucracy often had difficulty delivering promised goods and services, especially in outlying provinces. Official announcements and periodic flurries of activity raised expectations and often turned government offices into "lightning rods" for popular demands that could not be met. Growing economic resource limitations compounded the problems.

The 1968 expropriation of IPC set all on notice that the military government was serious about its reform objectives. This action served simultaneously to unite the armed forces around the realization of a long-held aspiration, to establish the legitimacy of the new regime with the citizenry, and to demonstrate to the U.S. government and foreign investors that Peru would no longer accept the degree of foreign-participant influence that had prevailed in the country up to that point. Several subsequent expropriations of foreign enterprises took place, but with compensation. New foreign investment was welcomed under stricter regulation and occurred principally in copper mining and oil exploration. Foreign loans were avidly sought and were acquired at record levels.

Thus, even while adopting a radical posture in foreign economic relations, the military government recognized the necessity of continued foreign loans and investments to help accomplish national development goals. However, such heavy international borrowing after 1971, in part a result of the reluctance of the domestic private sector to invest in spite of generous incentives, came back to haunt the government. Prices for some Peruvian exports declined markedly, domestic production of others also declined, and optimistic forecasts concerning probable oil exports proved erroneous. A severe financial crisis resulted in 1978 and 1979. Consequently, many development objectives were compromised, and the very legitimacy of the regime came into question.

The subsequent civilian governments have had to face many of the same problems. Although no new nationalizations occurred under Belaúnde, efforts to sell some enterprises back into private hands and to encourage new foreign investment were largely thwarted by domestic depression, international recession, and large debt-repayment responsibilities. The García administration adopted a much more nationalistic and government-activist posture, with debt repayments tied to export earnings and some nationalizations, among other measures. However, over the last half of APRA rule, the economic crisis overshadowed other policy priorities.

The agrarian reform of 1969 was the most far reaching of all the military government's policy initiatives. However, without enough arable land to go around, the majority of the needy farmers did not benefit. The better-off coastal farmers received most of the reform's redistributive benefits, and the central government's major effort in the more isolated sierra was too little and too late. Part of the continuing problem is the center's limited ability to affect the periphery, even with the best of intentions. As a result many cooperative enterprises in the sierra never operated effectively, which contributed to a move back to private ownership in the 1980s. A by-product of the reform was a serious decline in agricultural production, which was overcome only partially by the Belaúnde government's sharp reduction in food subsidies and the resulting increase in food prices after 1980. The García administration sharply expanded agricultural credit until 1988, thus helping to boost production. But the same agrarian-reform problems that led Belaúnde to reprivatize a large number of the agricultural cooperatives also contributed to the ability of the Shining Path to expand its influence in the more-marginal Indian highlands. From the elections of 1980 onward, the sections of Peru with the highest levels of blank and spoiled votes and abstention rates were these very areas—Ayacucho, Apurímac, and Huancavelica in particular. There levels ranged from 30 to 50 percent, suggesting lower legitimacy of the central government and perhaps even support for or at least passive acquiescence in the Shining Path. In the 1989 municipal elections, blank and spoiled ballots and abstention exceeded 75 percent in 13 of 14 districts in Ayacucho's most populous province, Huomanga, thus forcing their annulment.

Another important area of reform by the military involved the rapid expansion of various types of "local units of participation." These included various cooperative forms in agriculture, neighborhood associations in the squatter settlements, and worker self-management communities in industry and mining. At their peak in the late 1970s these entities incorporated as many as 800,000 workers, often including families as well.

Such a proliferation of local-participation organizations gave the military government the advantage of providing an alternative for citizen participation, at the level of workplace and residence, at a time when normal participation by political parties at the national level was cut off. Although the benefits of membership in local-participation organizations were often significant, most members were by and large from the working-class elite. Since growth of these enterprises was predicated on profit generation, and since economic conditions in most years since 1975 have not favored such growth, the organizations have not developed as expected. Responsibility for organizing, coordinating, and controlling citizen participation was entrusted after 1971 to the National Social Mobilization Support System (SINAMOS), initially an "umbrella" agency incorporating several other government agencies, most of whose top leadership positions were held by military officers.

As SINAMOS became operative, its regional offices became a focal point of opposition to government policies, and some offices were sacked and burned in 1973 and 1975. These disturbances showed the limits of popular support for the government. As a result of a conflict between the national police and the military, large groups of citizens took to the streets of Lima and several provincial capitals and engaged in massive looting and burning sprees with antigovernment overtones. These events were a key precipitant of the August 1975 coup, and SINAMOS itself was phased out in 1978.

With the restoration of civilian rule in 1980, parties and unions regained their roles as transmitters of their members' concerns to government authorities, largely supplanting the structure so laboriously fashioned by the military regime. Vigorous political participation through a score of parties covering the entire ideological spectrum characterized the 1980s, with power alternating between center-right and center-left groups at the national executive level and substantial representation in Congress by the Marxist left. In municipal elections all major political organizations won their share of cities and towns at different times, with pluralities shifting from AP to IU to APRA and back to IU. An unanticipated legacy of long-term reformist military rule, then, was to usher in a historically unprecedented level of partisan politics, institutionalized to a degree that few people foresaw and proceeding apace in spite of profound domestic economic difficulties and a substantial, growing terrorist guerrilla movement.

Official combined unemployment and underemployment figures have ebbed and flowed between 50 and 65 percent of the economically active population. Overall real-wage statistics show a similarly variable pattern, with some improvement during the first half of the García administration, followed by a precipitous erosion in 1988 and early 1989, with average wage levels in late 1989 at 52 percent below those of 1970. Without the dynamic informal sector, an array of economic activities outside official purview and measurement, the average Peruvian might be even worse off. Estimates suggest that about 60 percent of the nation's economy and two-thirds of the jobs are to be found in this sector, and these figures do not include some 100,000 peasant families who live off the coca and cocaine-paste industry in the Upper Huallaga Valley 250 miles northeast of Lima, where it is believed that more than 50 percent of the world's production of "crude cocaine" originates. Although perhaps $800 million to $1.2 billion in foreign exchange filters each year back to Peru as a result of this industry, materially aiding the country's foreign currency reserves, the corrosive effects on society and political institutions are substantial.

Inflation rates stood at 8.2 percent per month for the first quarter of García's presidency and more than 100 percent per month by the same quarter three years later. At the end of 1985 nineteen provinces in Peru were under emergency law because of terrorist violence; by July 1989 that number had increased to 56. In 1988, 120,000 Peruvians emigrated abroad—four times the number emigrating in 1986. These indicators suggest that Peru's problems are severe indeed and threaten to undermine the substantial institutional development of the period.

FOREIGN AFFAIRS

Historically, Peru's foreign relations have been conditioned by boundary disputes, diverse natural resources, domestic political and economic objectives, and the Humboldt current. From independence into the 1980s, boundaries were a matter of dispute and a prime motivator of Peruvian diplomacy. Wars and armed conflicts have occasionally broken out. In the south, the loss of nitrate-rich Tarapacá and Arica to Chile in the War of the Pacific (1879–1883), ratified by the Tacna-Arica Treaty (1929), has conditioned relations with Bolivia and Chile for over a century and has given a certain defensive dimension to foreign policy. In the north, Peru ceded Leticia to Colombia in 1932, an unpopular move, but successfully pursued a brief war with Ecuador in 1941 to assert a claim to substantial lands in the northeastern Amazon Basin. Ecuador signed the Rio Protocol of 1942 accepting the new frontier but renounced it in 1960. Armed clashes have broken out periodically since, including a major incident in 1981 that required the mediation of the Rio Protocol guarantor powers (Argentina, Chile, Brazil, and the United States).

Peru's diverse natural resources include sugar, cotton, rice, fish and fish products, and minerals from copper to iron to gold and silver to oil. Historically, these natural resources have often served as a buffer to the vicissitudes of international economic forces as well as being the object of expanded government influence. Peru joined forces with Ecuador and Chile as early as 1952 to proclaim a 200-mile territorial limit in ocean waters, a claim to the rich fishing of the Humboldt current that eventually worked its way into international law in the 1970s as a 200-mile economic zone. The Peruvian government was also a driving force behind the Andean Pact, begun in 1969 to expand markets, diversify trade, and apply common foreign investment criteria among the Andean countries. Economic nationalism has joined political nationalism as a major component of Peruvian foreign policy for most of the period since 1968. Foreign holdings in agriculture, mining, and fishing have often been nationalized; remaining or new enterprises are subject to much closer regulation and tighter rules regarding profit remissions. Relations with a number of investing companies and their governments have been strained as a result, particularly U.S. ones.

The military government's stated objective in international affairs from 1968 to 1980 was the elimination of dependency, a call also taken to heart by the APRA administration of Alán García after 1985. This goal led to Peru's taking a number of steps to alter its international position to at least diversify, if not end, its dependence. Several Eastern European countries were recognized, as were some Arab oil states, China, and Cuba, and trade and barter arrangements and some loans were worked out with numerous countries of the socialist bloc. Important trade and loan agreements were arranged with such countries as Japan, Belgium, the Netherlands, Italy, and Spain. Foreign investment and loans continued to be avidly sought from individual countries and international institutions until the mid-1980s, but the government consciously diversified Peru's trade, investment, and loan assistance rather than depend on a few sources, as in the past. These policies continued during the Belaúnde administration and may have helped for a time to keep the severe economic problems from being even worse. García pursued a more nationalistic strategy, which contributed to economic growth in 1986 and 1987 before developing into a new, more severe crisis beginning in 1988.

From the 1968 military takeover onward, Peru attempted to strengthen its developing-nation position. It took on an important leadership role among the Third World nonaligned countries—hosting conferences, serving as a leading spokesperson at others, and generally asserting an independent position. Unfortunately, Peru's struggle to diversify its dependence and to achieve a position of Third World leadership was seriously compromised by the country's growing economic difficulties after 1975. In 1978, 1982, and 1984 Peruvian governments were forced to accept stringent IMF conditions for the continuance of economic and loan assistance.

Beginning with Alán García's inaugural address in July 1985, however, Peru committed itself to an independent debt-repayment position based on a maximum of 10 percent of export revenues. By the end of 1987

Peru was in arrears to governments, international agencies, and foreign private banks; by the end of 1988 economic nationalism had contributed to producing Peru's most severe domestic economic crisis in over 100 years. The elected reformist APRA government found itself as constrained by international forces as its reformist military predecessor, in spite of equally strenuous efforts to break with past patterns and move Peru along a more independent course in the foreign affairs arena. Domestic factors interfered with this goal as well. In June 1986 President García hosted the annual meeting of the Socialist International (SI) in a bid to reassert Peru's independent reformist credentials. However, a Shining Path assassination attempt on the Peruvian president during the meeting, followed almost immediately by a coordinated prison uprising of jailed guerrillas, brutally repressed with almost 300 inmate deaths, thoroughly embarrassed the Peruvian head of state and dashed any hopes García held for SI leadership.

CONCLUSIONS

Peru as an independent nation has had great difficulty in overcoming its authoritarian legacy. The Spanish colonial heritage was an important factor impeding the evolution of liberal democratic institutions in the nineteenth century. Additional considerations, including international market forces, the incorporation of more and more of the population into the national political and economic system, and political leadership perceptions and actions prevented the emergence of a stable institutional structure in the twentieth.

The country's ability to hold successive national democratic elections since 1980 in spite of many domestic and international problems— including world recession, falling prices for many of Peru's exports, floods and droughts, guerrilla insurgency, and a growing drug problem— is remarkable. Were circumstances more favorable, one might be more optimistic about Peru's political future within a democratic institutional context.

Most assessments of the post-1968 period conclude that military leaders erred in expanding public policy as quickly and across as many areas as they did. In attempting to do too much, government resources were stretched too thin and the quality of delivery suffered at the same time that public expectations were being raised. The post-1975 consolidation phase of the military government was an acknowledgment of failure. The election of Belaúnde in 1980 with over 45 percent of the vote in a multicandidate race demonstrated the level of popular dissatisfaction with the policies of the military *docenio*. However, the civilian government proved equally unable to sustain economic growth or to ensure domestic tranquillity. The García administration's adjustments provided short-term success and mid-term problems bordering on the disastrous, both eco-nomically and politically. Even though a new round of military intervention remains unlikely owing to the armed forces' difficult experience with long-term rule, it can no longer be ruled out.

Peru's recurring economic and political crises since 1975 are evidence of the failure of the reformist military and civilian governments and demonstrate the boundaries within which reformers must operate to accomplish national political and economic development objectives. In particular, the crises illustrate the degree to which policymakers in a middle-sized Third World country, with a long dependent tradition, are hemmed in by forces essentially beyond their control. Under the circumstances, what is remarkable is that the successive governments accomplished as much as they did, not that they failed to achieve all they set out to do.

Some of the difficulties of the succeeding civilian governments may be traced to the policies of their military predecessors, but the civilians have made their own share of mistakes as well. Perhaps the most important long-term legacy of military rule in Peru is the articulation of concerns by a new generation of Peruvians, mostly on the left and mostly within the political system. Democratic alternation has remained, in short, in spite of severe and growing problems. Even the right has been revitalized by the continuing crises of the 1980s and is another viable choice in the elections of the 1990s. Political uncertainty abounds, but democratic procedures and practices have remained in place under quite uncomfortable circumstances and might yet ultimately prevail.

SUGGESTIONS FOR FURTHER READING

Becker, David G. *The New Bourgeoisie and the Limits of Dependency: Mining, Class, and Power in "Revolutionary" Peru.* Princeton, N.J.: Princeton University Press, 1983.

Booth, David, and Bernardo Sorj, eds. *Military Reformism and Social Classes: The Peruvian Experience, 1968–80.* New York: St. Martin's Press, 1983.

Bourque, Susan C., and Kay Barbara Warren. *Women of the Andes: Patriarchy and Social Change in Two Peruvian Towns.* Ann Arbor: University of Michigan Press, 1981.

DeWind, Josh. *Peasants Become Miners: The Evolution of Industrial Mining Systems in Peru, 1902–1974.* New York: Garland Publishers, 1987.

Dietz, Henry A. *Poverty and Problem-Solving Under Military Rule: The Urban Poor in Lima, Peru.* Austin: University of Texas Press, 1980.

Dobyns, Henry F., and Paul L. Doughty. *Peru: A Cultural History.* New York: Cambridge University Press, 1977.

Figueroa, Adolfo. *Capitalist Development and the Peasant Economy of Peru.* Cambridge: Cambridge University Press, 1984.

FitzGerald, E.V.K. *The Political Economy of Peru 1956–1978: Economic Development and the Restructuring of Capital.* Cambridge: Cambridge University Press, 1980.

Gorman, Stephen M., ed. *Post-Revolutionary Peru: The Politics of Transformation.* Boulder, Colo.: Westview Press, 1982.

Klarén, Peter F. *Modernization, Dislocation, and Aprismo: Origins of the Peruvian Aprista Party, 1933–1970.* Austin: University of Texas Press, 1973.

Kuczynski, Pedro-Pablo. *Peruvian Democracy Under Economic Stress: An Account of the Belaúnde Administration, 1963–1968.* Princeton, N.J.: Princeton University Press, 1977.

McClintock, Cynthia. *Peasant Cooperatives and Political Change in Peru.* Princeton, N.J.: Princeton University Press, 1981.

McClintock, Cynthia, and Abraham F. Lowenthal, eds. *The Peruvian Experiment Reconsidered.* Princeton, N.J.: Princeton University Press, 1983.

Mörner, Magnus. *The Andean Past: Land, Societies, and Conflicts.* New York: Columbia University Press, 1984.

North, Liisa, and Tanya Korovkin. *The Peruvian Revolution and the Officers in Power, 1967–1976.* Occasional Monograph Series no. 15. Montreal: Centre for Developing-Area Studies, McGill University, 1981.

Palmer, David Scott. *Peru: The Authoritarian Tradition.* New York: Praeger, 1980.

Pike, Frederick B. *The Politics of the Miraculous in Peru: Haya de la Torre and the Spiritualist Tradition.* Lincoln: University of Nebraska Press, 1986.

Preeg, Ernest H. *The Evolution of a Revolution: Peru and Its Relations with the United States, 1968–1980.* Washington, D.C.: National Planning Institute, 1981.

Reid, Malcolm. *Peru: Paths to Poverty.* New York: Monthly Review Press, 1984.

Scheetz, Thomas. *Peru and the International Monetary Fund.* Pittsburgh: University of Pittsburgh Press, 1986.

Stein, Steve. *Populism in Peru: The Emergence of the Masses and the Politics of Social Control.* Madison: University of Wisconsin Press, 1980.

Stein, William W. *Peruvian Contexts of Change.* New Brunswick, N.J.: Transaction Books, 1984.

Stepan, Alfred. *The State and Society: Peru in Comparative Perspective.* Princeton, N.J.: Princeton University Press, 1978.

Thorp, Rosemary, and Geoffrey Bertram. *Peru 1890–1977: Growth and Policy in an Open Economy.* New York: Columbia University Press, 1978.

Uriarte, J. Manual. *Transnational Banks and the Dynamics of Peruvian Foreign Debt and Inflation.* New York: Praeger, 1985.

Weeks, John. *Limits to Capitalist Development: The Industrialization of Peru, 1950–1980.* Boulder, Colo.: Westview Press, 1985.

Werlich, David P. *Peru: A Short History.* Carbondale: Southern Illinois University Press, 1978.

13
Venezuela: The Politics of Liberty, Justice, and Distribution

DAVID J. MYERS

On the morning of January 23, 1958, *Caraqueños* (people of Caracas) shouting "Long live liberty" and "Down with torture and tortures" stormed and captured the national headquarters of Col. Marcos Pérez Jiménez's dreaded Seguridad Nacional (National Security Police). Within the hour, dazed and wounded political prisoners, some of whom had to be carried, emerged into the dazzling tropical sunlight. In other Venezuelan cities, this scene was repeated over and over again. Pictures of the abused, coupled with stories of prison torture, moved Venezuelans of all political persuasions to vow that never again would people in positions of authority be allowed to violate human rights. In addition, as the magnitude of corruption in the Pérez Jiménez dictatorship became known, the resolve grew that more effective means must be found for using Venezuela's great oil wealth to stimulate economic modernization and create a just society.

The international community was skeptical that Venezuelans could or would create a meaningful democracy. Their history did not augur well for political rules that respect basic human rights, foster social justice, and stimulate economic development. The country had experienced less than a single year of civilian elected government during its first century and a quarter of independence. Years of peace and prosperity had fostered periodic optimism, but in each instance hopes had been dashed by civil strife that decimated the population and destroyed the country's wealth.

At the beginning of the twentieth century this cycle of disillusionment and death led to the seizure of power by Gen. Juan Vicente Gómez, who orchestrated one of Latin America's longest-lasting and most primitively violent dictatorships (1908–1935). Two decades later, between

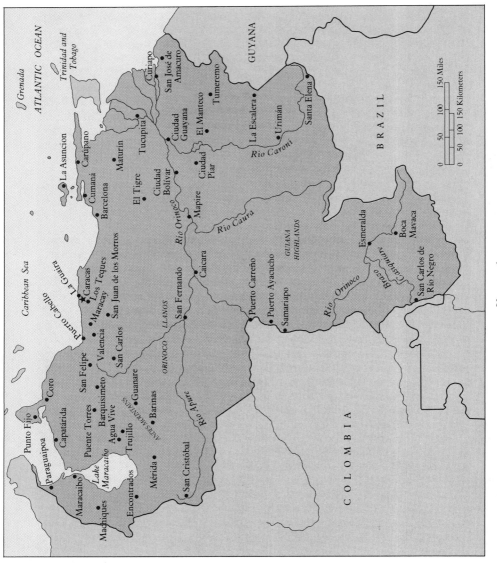

Venezuela

1952 and 1958, Col. Marcos Pérez Jiménez presided over an updated version of Gómez's barbarism. Thus, the odds on January 23, 1958, that a transition to democratic government would take place in Venezuela were no better than even. And even should the attempt to establish democracy succeed, the odds that the new regime would consolidate and develop were far longer.

Between May and December of 1988, Social Democrat Carlos Andrés Pérez, Social Christian Eduardo Fernández, and numerous minor-party candidates faced each other in Venezuela's seventh consecutive free presidential election campaign. Against all odds, democracy had taken root and flourished. Unanticipated, this turn of events is now taken for granted, and therein lies a fundamental reason for the importance of Venezuelan politics. They provide multiple clues as to how and why rules of the political game favorable to liberty and justice take root and flourish in soil that historically has fostered dictatorship, privilege, and human rights abuses.

Venezuela and Venezuelan politics are important for other reasons. Post-1958 elites have overseen a transformation from rural to urban society that avoided political breakdown and minimized the pain of transition. In addition, over the past decades, literacy rates have risen dramatically, indigenous heavy industry has been created, and Venezuelans have come to enjoy one of Latin America's highest standards of living. Income from petroleum was critical for these accomplishments; thus, Venezuelans pioneered international coordination in the pricing of petroleum by helping to create and manage the Organization of Petroleum Exporting Countries (OPEC). Concurrently, they developed an elaborate system for internal resource distribution. The centrality of this system in consolidating and developing the existing political regime remains controversial because there is disagreement over whether petroleum income has so distorted the country's political, economic, and social development that Venezuela's experience is of little relevance to understanding politics elsewhere in Latin America.

Finally, post-1958 Venezuela is important because of its activist foreign policy. Social Democratic and Social Christian leaders have long supported the United States in its Caribbean Basin competition with the Soviet Union; however, they become apprehensive when Washington projects military power into the region. New strains in U.S.-Venezuelan relations are appearing as Caracas joins with other Third World countries in demanding more favorable treatment from the industrial North (OECD countries). In their advocacy of the South's demands, post-1958 elites draw upon lessons learned from domestic politics. Especially relevant is their experience in building a coalition that undermined entrenched power and privilege. To summarize, not only does the Venezuelan democratic experience illuminate the processes of political change and regime maintenance, it also contributes to an understanding of North-South issues.

LAND AND PEOPLE

Geography and history have shaped contemporary Venezuelan politics. Nestled in the northeastern quadrant of South America, between 1 and 12 degrees north of the equator, Venezuela is hot and tropical. Cool temperatures predominate only at altitudes above 3,280 feet (1,000 meters). The country's 20 million (mid-1989 figure) inhabitants live in an area of 352,150 square miles (912,050 square kilometers), roughly the size of Texas and Oklahoma combined. Stretching for some 1,750 miles (2,816 kilometers) along the Caribbean Sea and the Atlantic Ocean, Venezuela extends south into continental South America. It encompasses snow-covered mountains rising to 16,427 feet (5,007 meters—Pico Bolívar), crosses broad plains (llanos), and reaches into the Orinoco and Amazon jungles. Some 3,000 miles (4,800 kilometers) of continental borders form frontiers with Colombia, Brazil, and Guyana. Four-fifths of the country is drained by the Orinoco River, one of the largest and most navigable rivers in the world. But the mountains, not the river or the plains, have historically been Venezuela's most influential geographical feature. The dominant colonial settlements, agricultural estates, and urban centers lie in cool mountain valleys, and until 1925, when petroleum extraction became Venezuela's most important economic activity, these valleys formed the unchallenged economic, administrative, and social heartland.

Geographers divide Venezuela into five regions: the Guyana Highlands, the Orinoco Lowlands, the Northern Mountains, the Maracaibo Basin/ Coastal Lowlands, and the numerous small islands along the Caribbean coast. These regions vary immensely in size, resources, climate, population, and historical input.

The Guyana Highlands, encompassing 45 percent of the national territory, is the largest region. Historically remote, poor, and sparsely populated, Guyana has become a symbol of the democratic regime's drive to industrialize and reduce dependence on imported manufactures from the North Atlantic countries. In addition, the discovery of new gold deposits suggest that this area may become a major producer of that precious metal. However, Guyana's industrial and mining centers remain oases of modern civilization surrounded by dense tropical forests. Ancient plateaus, some extending for 125 miles (200 kilometers), rise more than 3,280 feet (1,000 meters) above the jungle floor. From their heights tumble breathtaking waterfalls, including the world's highest uninterrupted one, Angel Falls. On these plateaus flourish flora and fauna that exist nowhere else on the planet. Until the late 1950s Guyana exerted little influence on national affairs; however, it is now the political base of several important leaders of the ruling Acción Democrática (AD) political party.[1]

Lying between the southernmost part of Venezuela and the coastal mountains are the great grassland prairies (llanos) of the Orinoco

Lowlands. They occupy 33 percent of the national territory and support 20 percent of the population. For six months of the year this vast, featureless plain, 620 miles (1,000 kilometers) long and 400 miles (645 kilometers) wide, is subject to rainfall so heavy that much of it lies under water. As the ensuing dry season progresses, mud turns to deep layers of dust, vegetation shrivels, the heat becomes intense, and streams dry up. Even the aboriginal Indians avoided this harsh area, and it remained for the Europeans and mestizos (individuals of mixed Indian and white ancestry) to settle and colonize it. Although the region is far from ideal for cattle raising, a type of culture based on that industry has grown up there and continues to be managed by a rough, and for many years lawless, breed of man (*llanero*) to whom cattle raising is a way of life. Forced by his environment to become a tough, self-reliant individual, the llanero played an important part in the war of independence and later uprisings. More recently, oil has been found in the area, and now the Orinoco Lowlands supply one-fourth of Venezuela's total crude oil production. Two presidents and one major presidential candidate have come from this region since 1958.

The Northern Mountains constitute the third major geographical region. Although they encompass only 12 percent of Venezuela's land area, they support roughly two-thirds of the country's population. The principal mountain chain consists of the coastal range and the Sierra Nevada de Mérida. In the coastal range are found the capital city of Caracas, the Valencia-Maracay industrial center, large coffee holdings, sugar haciendas, and rich farmlands surrounding Lake Valencia. Because of its agricultural importance, this region was for many years dominated by a rural oligarchy and large estates maintained by cheap peasant labor. Although coastal range political leaders have played a central role in Venezuelan history, they have often lost out to more aggressive rivals from less-favored regions.

The high and rugged Sierra Nevada de Mérida is a western spur of the Andes. With peaks rising to 16,400 feet (5,000 meters), its early inaccessibility discouraged great agricultural estates (latifundios); hence, the Venezuelan Andes were characterized by medium-sized landholdings and populated by small clusters of people, both mestizos and Indians. Despite the presence of an influential university in the city of Mérida, Andean Venezuela remained isolated until the rise of coffee as a commercial crop. It is a region where religion and family ties are strong, as are the historic values of Hispanic culture. Thus, Andinos hold personalism, hierarchy, and military power in high regard, which partly explains why so many Venezuelan leaders—from Cipriano Castro to Carlos Andrés Pérez—have come from this region.

Ten percent of Venezuela's national territory consists of a narrow, partly arid, partly swampy belt of lowland lying between the steeply rising coastal mountains and the Caribbean Sea. This region comprises the Maracaibo Basin and the Coastal Lowlands. Most of Venezuela's oil is found in the Maracaibo Basin, and the region's drained swampland has been transformed into rich farms and cattle ranches. However, over 80 percent of the basin's inhabitants are classified as urban. Most reside in Maracaibo, the country's second-largest city. Beginning in the 1920s oil exploitation transformed Maracaibo into a thriving commercial, industrial, and educational center. In contrast, tourism is the most important economic activity of the eastern Coastal Lowlands. Here are located the best Caribbean beaches, and the climate is clear and dry. Also, black influence is stronger in this region than anywhere else in Venezuela.

In addition to the mainland, there are seventy-two islands of varied size and description. The most important and best known is Margarita, in the state of Neuva Esparta. The site of some of the oldest Spanish settlements in Latin America, Margarita today is a thriving free port and tourist center.

Most Venezuelans are an amalgam of Caucasian, Indian, and black. They share a common culture, predominantly Hispanic but with important Indian and African strands. Overwhelmingly Roman Catholic (90 percent) and Spanish speaking, Venezuelans view themselves as members of a single ethnic mixture. The national census does not classify according to race or ethnicity (except for Indians in the Orinoco and Amazon jungles), so it is only possible to make educated guesses. Pure Caucasians make up between 10 and 15 percent of the total population. A small number belong to proud white families who trace their ancestry to renowned Spanish names, but most of the pure Caucasians immigrated to Venezuela from southern Europe during the 1950s. Perhaps 10 percent of Venezuelans are black, less than 3 percent are pure Indian, and between 70 and 80 percent are of mixed ancestry. Ethnic mixing has occurred at all social levels, and ethnicity does not serve to distinguish either separate groups or class. Large numbers of people with strong Indian and black ancestry have become leaders in politics, business, and culture. Nevertheless, Caucasian features are valued, and their predominance is greater among the higher social and economic strata.

Internal migration since World War II has transformed Venezuela from a rural society into one that is highly urbanized. First, peasants abandoned the countryside and rural villages for regional market towns. Second, townspeople subsequently moved to the large cities. Caracas received a disproportionate number of these migrants, mushrooming from a center of about 500,000 in 1945 to a diverse metropolis approaching 5 million in 1989. Two other cities, Maracaibo and Valencia, boast populations of more than 1 million. In contrast, large areas of rural Venezuela are depopulated. Census estimates in 1989 placed the total urban population at just over 80 percent. In addition, the cities have received most of the at least 2 million illegal immigrants from Colombia, Ecuador, and Trinidad. These *indocumentados* (literally, "undocumented" illegals) are concentrated in Maracaibo and Caracas, along the Colombian border, and in the eastern state of Sucre.

HISTORY AND POLITICAL ECONOMY

The history of Venezuela is one of progressive integration into the North Atlantic area. Integration began when Christopher Columbus landed in eastern Venezuela during his third voyage, in 1498. The Venezuelan mainland was the first area of South America to be explored by Spain, but the region proved a disappointment, especially when contrasted with the riches discovered in Peru and Mexico. Disappointment led to neglect, and Venezuela remained a colonial backwater until the last half of the eighteenth century. At that time Spain's Bourbon monarchs chose to update their imperial organization.

Pre-independence

The pattern that crystallized between 1750 and 1800 has exerted a strong influence on the course of Venezuelan history. Late-eighteenth-century Venezuela, the mature colonial society, revolved about Caracas, the region's central city. The creation of a captaincy general located in Caracas brought together under unified administrative control the region's semi-independent provinces. Power based in Caracas became the most important symbol of the colony's new maturity, and it tied Venezuela's other regions into a single management bureaucracy.[2]

Venezuela had little time to enjoy its new-found maturity. Napoleon's invasion of the Iberian peninsula in 1807–1808 led to twenty years of civil strife in Latin America, and fighting ended only after all of Spain's continental colonies had gained their independence.

Venezuela's Simón Bolívar, a criollo (Caucasian born in the colonies) and a landownder from Caracas, led the movement that liberated northern South America. Although discussion of the wars for independence is beyond the scope of this chapter, it must be kept in mind that Bolívar sought to create a continental empire. However, regional elites in Venezuela resented Caracas's assumption of leadership and rejected Bolívar's vision. As a result, the Caraqueño white elite found it necessary to reconquer its own territory before attempting Bolívar's grand design elsewhere. Not only was reconquest costly in terms of lives and property, it also modified the pattern of political control that had characterized the mature colonial society. Before the wars, conflicts and disputes at all levels were settled through an elaborate, formalized, and bureaucratic system. With few exceptions, Venezuelans accepted the constraints of this system and worked to maximize their advantages within its rules.

The war of independence destroyed Venezuela's colonial bureaucracy in a clash of bandit armies that confiscated and reallocated property. Old methods of defining legitimacy and right were replaced by a new system based almost entirely on force and favor with the people who controlled force. This modification of the colonial order came as a logical extension of the militarization of political authority. Militarization also confirmed the primacy of Caracas. After Venezuela separated from Gran

Colombia in 1830, control of Venezuela more than ever meant control of the capital city.

Consolidating Political Order

Between 1830 and 1920 Venezuela evolved into a commercial bureaucratic outpost of the industrializing North Atlantic. Beneath the confusion of civil strife, ideological conflict, and class warfare, Venezuela was experiencing the transformation of its mature colonial society. Political and economic elites struggled to cope with the new demands placed on the old organization by the country's gradual integration into international commerce. As a part of this commerce, which capitalists in Western Europe and the United States designed to nourish their domestic industries, Venezuela came to provide certain agricultural commodities in exchange for a mixed package of finished goods produced abroad. Control over this trade remained in the hands of entrepreneurs, financiers, and companies in Western Europe and the United States; thus, Venezuelan elites had to adjust to the requirements of the new relationships.

The increasing stability of the commercial bureaucratic pattern led to the consolidation of political order during the late nineteenth and early twentieth centuries. Crucial in this process were the pacification and development programs initiated by Gen. Antonio Guzmán Blanco (1870–1888) and consolidated by Gen. Juan Vicente Gómez (1908–1935). Gómez took the essential relationships inherent in Guzmán Blanco's programs for exploiting Venezuela's niche in the international arena and—by applying ruthless logic aided by a monopoly on technology and communications—developed them to their conclusion. Along with the brutality and repression of his regime, Gómez fixed the bureaucratic commercial pattern in its final form before Venezuela succumbed to the overwhelming pressure of what historian John Lombardi has labeled the "petroleum-based technological imperium."[3]

Caracas, measured by any set of variables, gained disproportionately from this consolidation of the commercial bureaucratic pattern. The city attracted the ambitious and wealthy who sought to partake of the benefits accompanying close ties with North Atlantic capitalism. As many amenities as could be afforded were imported, but because Caraqueños could afford very few, they seldom shared advantages with the rest of the country. University education, art, culture, social services, architectural and urban grandeur, whatever the North Atlantic imitation, Caracas monopolized it to an ever-growing degree. Thus, Caracas acquired the trappings of modernity while the rest of Venezuela remained much the same. The distance separating the capital city from the interior grew greater, until no other center could compare with it.

After 1925, in the final decade of Gómez's rule, the petroleum-based "technological imperium" overpowered the commercial bureaucratic system. This arrangement was and is the product of opportunities and complexities implicit in petroleum exploitation. Transformation involved creating a modern communications and transportation infrastructure, bringing Caracas up to the standards of comfort prevailing in the urban North Atlantic, and diffusing industrial technology into the interior. Transformation also facilitated the intervention of foreign interest groups and ideologies into Venezuela's internal politics. These influences shaped political developments during Venezuela's journey (1935–1959) from primitive dictatorship to liberal democracy; they have also influenced liberal democracy's consolidation and development (1958–present).

The example of North Atlantic democracy, coupled with the obvious inadequacy of the commercial bureaucratic structures to manage conflict, inclined post-Gómez leaders toward experimentation with political democracy. In October of 1945, however, power was seized by youthful military officers in alliance with middle-class reformers from the interior. When the reformers began using their mass-based political party, Democratic Action (AD), to create a regime intent on redistributing wealth, status, and power, the people with the most to lose abandoned the democratic experiment. In November 1948 they convinced the officer corps to overthrow the popularly elected president (Rómulo Gallegos) and outlaw the AD political party.[4]

The traditional elites justified their seizure of power as the only way to prevent another foreign ideology, communism, from derailing Venezuela's integration into post–World War II North Atlantic capitalism. Initially a benign dictatorship, anti-Communist developmentalism degenerated into a crude attempt to resurrect the pattern of status and power that had prevailed between 1830 and 1935. This effort, the ill-fated regime of Col. Marcos Pérez Jiménez (1952–1958), was nasty, brutal, and short. Its demise—the result of cooperation among a broad spectrum of classes, strata, and leaders—opened the way for a political regime founded on the reconciliation of competing interests.

Fair and open elections were held at the end of 1958, and reform-minded Rómulo Betancourt (AD) won the presidency with almost 50 percent of the total vote. AD also gained control of Congress, but the populist Democratic Republican Union (URD), the Social Christian party (COPEI), and the Venezuelan Communist party (PCV) elected significant delegations. The three major parties (AD, URD, and COPEI) agreed to share power, and partisans of each received posts in the bureaucracy and leadership positions in the most important interest-group organizations (e.g., the Labor Confederation, the Peasant Federation, and professional associations such as the Engineering Guild). In addition, while the leaders of the three political parties agreed that they would not abandon their commitment to equality, they opted to give precedence to fostering acceptance of pluralistic rules for conflict management. This agreement, the Pact of Punto Fijo, was critical in fixing the legitimacy of post-1958 democracy.[5]

Venezuela's technological-empire elites opted for the Punto Fijo reconciliation system because of their disastrous experience with authoritarianism under Pérez Jiménez and because they anticipated that distributive politics would predominate. They viewed the allocation of petroleum income as critical for gaining the loyalty of such new and previously excluded groups as workers and peasants. Labor Confederation and Peasant Federation leaders were to be positioned within the distributive political process to allow them increased resources for allocation to their clients. Traditional elites would be regulated but permitted to keep their fortunes and use them to create additional wealth. Thus, traditional and newly integrated interests had strong reasons for crafting and supporting a distributive process that would maintain social peace and tie Venezuela ever more tightly into the North Atlantic system. Thirty years after the Pact of Punto Fijo, a broad spectrum of Venezuelans still identified with its commitment to power sharing.

Economy Based on Petroleum

Central to the economic outlook of Venezuelan elites is the obvious but critical conviction that properly invested petroleum wealth holds the key to national control over the economy, to progress in the realm of social justice, and to achieving balanced economic development. Although the concept of using petroleum to create industry and modernize agriculture has received lip service since the early 1940s, little was accomplished until Betancourt's administration in 1959–1964. Indeed, an additional reason for the overthrow of Pérez Jiménez was his adoption of a policy of benign neglect toward such a use of petroleum. His advisers essentially viewed the growth of the oil industry, plus income from new concessions and sales, as a means to finance an ever-increasing volume of imports. Under his regime, oil represented as much as 98 percent of the total value of exports while occupying a mere 3 percent of the economically active population.

For a time, reliance on the oil industry's growth to facilitate economic development appeared to be working. The increase in the domestic product averaged an extraordinary 9.4 percent per year during the middle 1950s, and national income also grew rapidly, with Venezuela enjoying one of the highest rates of increase in the world—5.7 percent when adjusted for population growth. Petroleum constituted the basis for this expansion, as the country took advantage of a rapidly growing world market to increase exports of crude oil by 7.4 percent and petroleum products by 14 percent per annum. However, the condition of having a dynamic enclave petroleum economy surrounded by inefficient agricultural production, a dualism that intensified as the petroleum imperium developed, generated increasing tension. In addition, by late 1957 a host of grandiose public-works projects stood incomplete, especially in Caracas. They had been financed by short-term treasury bills that had pushed public indebtedness beyond the government's ability to pay. The situation became critical after Pérez Jiménez looted the treasury during his final weeks in power.[6]

The administrations of Rómulo Betancourt (1959–1964), Raúl Leoni (1964–1969), and Rafael Caldera (1969–1974) returned the government to solvency, reactivated the private sector, initiated and expanded a broad range of development projects, and improved the quality· of service delivery. During the second half of the Caldera administration, however, the import-substitution policies of the previous fifteen years seemed to be yielding diminishing returns. Venezuela's domestic market was small and geared to the middle classes and the elites. One obvious strategy for overcoming this limitation, entry into the Andean Pact, engendered active opposition from Venezuelan industrialists because they feared competition from their low-wage neighbors. FEDECAMARAS, the most important private-sector federation, argued that pact membership would discourage investment, introduce greater domestic inflation, and place difficult strains on the labor unions, whose members were paid far more than workers in Colombia, Ecuador, Peru, Bolivia, and Chile. Nevertheless, in February 1973 President Caldera convinced Congress (at that time controlled by AD) to approve pact membership. One factor that influenced Caldera's advocacy was his desire to unite Spanish South America in order to match Brazil's rapidly expanding economy. Also, over the long run, Caldera hoped to decrease Venezuelan dependence on the U.S. market.

Presidents Betancourt, Leoni, and Caldera managed Venezuela's political economy within the context of modestly increasing petroleum revenues. In contrast, benefiting from international events over which Venezuela had no control, their successors administered unprecedented wealth. During the terms of Presidents Carlos Andrés Pérez (1974–1979), Luis Herrera Campíns (1979–1984), and Jaime Lusinchi (1984–1989), Venezuela obtained more than 80 percent of its twentieth-century petroleum income. The quadrupling of petroleum revenue in the twelve months preceding Pérez's government enabled him to create a potpourri of state corporations and initiate a multitude of infrastructural development projects. He also nationalized, with mutually agreed upon compensation to foreign investors, the iron and petroleum industries. However, Pérez spent on many activities whose payoff would be only in the long range, and he proved unable to reduce agricultural imports. By the end of his tenure the state had yet to extend its economic largesse and natural resources on an equitable basis to large numbers of people. This failure largely explains why in 1978, despite general optimism and prosperity, voters entrusted the presidency for a second time to the opposition Social Christian party.

President Luis Herrera Campíns presided over an economic roller coaster. At the time of his inauguration, in February 1979, Venezuela appeared headed for a period of prolonged budgetary deficits. The infrastructural investment projects initiated between 1974 and 1979 were demanding additional capital, but the price of oil in constant dollars was declining. An era of scarcity loomed. Thus, the new president chose as his minister of finance Luis Ugueto, an advocate of the conservative Chicago school of economics. Before Ugueto's austerity programs could be implemented, however, increases in the price of petroleum almost doubled the government's income.

Unprepared for this favorable turn of events, the Herrera government was unable to take advantage of it. Pressures to spend stimulated corruption, capital flight accelerated, the economy stagnated, and unprecedented borrowing tripled the country's international debt to $35 billion. Thus, in early 1983, as world petroleum prices plunged, President Herrera was forced to devalue the currency. He opted for a three-tiered exchange system: A few "essential" goods continued to be imported at the rate of 4.3:1; nonessential goods at an intermediate rate of 6 to the dollar; and foreign travel and currency remittance at a floating rate of 7.5:1. By December the floating rate hovered around 13:1. An important reason for this upward spiral of the floating rate was that in February OPEC had reduced Venezuela's production quota by roughly 10 percent, to 2.02 million barrels per day. President Herrera had no choice but to implement an austerity program, even though his party was engaged in a hotly contested battle to retain the presidency. Again foreign events shaped Venezuelan politics: Jaime Lusinchi, the opposition AD candidate, soundly defeated the former president Rafael Caldera.

Management of Economic Crisis

The Lusinchi administration (1984–1989) assumed power amid an economic crisis of historic proportions. This government's management of the political economy focused on damage control and shrinking a distribution system because there were significantly fewer resources to distribute. The highest priorities of damage control were stemming capital flight (the IMF estimates capital flight from Venezuela between 1976 and 1984 at $30 billion) and renegotiating terms for repaying the huge public-sector foreign debt. Although improved regulation made the former problem manageable, the latter proved far more difficult. State corporations and individual ministries had contracted the lion's share of Venezuela's foreign debt, and neither the Finance Ministry nor the Central Bank had overseen this borrowing. President Lusinchi discovered that most funds were to be repaid within five years, an impossible condition given lower petroleum prices and Venezuela's reduced OPEC production quota.

Negotiating mutually acceptable terms for rolling over and stretching out repayment of the foreign debt remains a critical concern for Venezuela's democratic elites. Failure will jeopardize their domestic dominance and economic ties to the industrialized world. Debt management, however, has been complicated by falling oil prices and by the high political cost of implementing austerity. Only after three years of bargaining, in September 1987, did President Lusinchi and the banking consortium holding Venezuela's foreign debt sign an agreement that restructured

$20.34 billion of medium- and long-term public debts. This accord reduced the size of principal payments below $1 billion for 1987, 1988, and 1989. Tentative agreement had been reached in September 1984, but nothing was formalized because of differing views on the Venezuelan government's responsibility for repayment of the $8 billion owed to foreign creditors by the private sector. Nevertheless, following tentative agreement in 1984, President Lusinchi had lifted his predecessor's moratorium on debt repayment. Between 1984 and 1987 Venezuela paid more on its foreign debt than any other Latin American country: $4.24 billion on the principal and $13.03 billion in interest. The magnitude of this capital outflow forced an unprecedented contraction in the distributive network that had expanded so dramatically following the first oil shock in 1973.[7]

Jaime Lusinchi's strategy for shrinking the distributive network rested on economic and political calculations. He opted to make the most painful readjustments during his first years in office, gambling that during the second half the bitter medicine he had administered would restore economic health and assist his party's presidential candidate in the 1988 election. Shortly after assuming office, therefore, President Lusinchi implemented an austerity package. It included a minimum 10 percent cut in current expenditures for all government departments, designed to save 10 billion bolivars, and also provided for reorganization of the central government and liquidation of such public agencies as the Venezuelan Development Corporation (CVF) and the agricultural marketing agent, CORPOMERCADEO. Public employees displaced by the reorganization were guaranteed employment in other sectors, and the government promised 200,000 new jobs. President Lusinchi also devalued the bolivar by 75 percent, substantially increasing the cost of imported foodstuffs in a country that purchases 50 percent of its food abroad. In addition, government subsidies were eliminated on scores of foodstuffs, notably milk, the price of which rose by 120 percent. The blow was softened, however, by a monthly transportation bonus for low-income employees, a partial restoration of food subsidies, and a mandated 10 percent increase in the payrolls of private companies. Finally, in an attempt to stabilize the free market exchange rate, the Central Bank raised the commercial exchange rate by 10 percent, to 14.5 bolivars to the dollar.

The Lusinchi administration's economic performance was mixed; it remains difficult to evaluate. Retrenchment created the expected hardships in 1984 and 1985, but the economy subsequently stabilized. During the final three years of Jaime Lusinchi's presidency, rates of economic growth oscillated between 3 and 6.8 percent. The policies that produced growth, however, had consequences that cast doubts on what at first glance appeared to be a good record. Like so much else throughout Venezuelan political and economic history, Lusinchi's policies were hostage to international developments over which Caracas had little control. Most significant, the price for a barrel of petroleum received by the state oil company plummeted from $26.55 in 1985 to $13.90 in 1986. In 1987 the price recovered to $17.57, but in 1988 it fell to $3 below the disastrous levels that had prevailed in 1986. With petroleum exports of 1.52 million barrels per day in 1988, Venezuela's income from petroleum in that year was approximately $10.5 billion. This amount was insufficient to cover public expenditures, a mixture of imports ($8 billion), debt payments ($5 billion), and other obligations ($1.5 billion).

Expenditures for the presidential election year of 1988 were initially calculated under the mistaken assumption that the 1987 level of income would hold for two years. Reduced income, however, was not matched by reductions in expenditures. Determined to avoid an economic recession during the presidential election campaign, the government accepted a balance-of-payments deficit of $4 billion. A mixture of gold sales, sales of petroleum on the futures markets, loans, and multilateral credits covered $3 billion of this gap. The remainder came from a drawdown of reserves, including all but a token amount left in the coffers of the Venezuelan Investment Fund.

President Lusinchi's economic juggling helped Carlos Andrés Pérez retain the presidency for AD. It also allowed Lusinchi to depart from office as a popular figure, one who appeared to have performed competently under difficult circumstances. Upon assuming the presidency in February 1989, however, Carlos Andrés Pérez discovered that foreign exchange reserves had fallen to less than $3 billion, a level so low that Venezuela was handicapped in its conduct of normal international financial transactions. The new government had no alternative but to accept an International Monetary Fund austerity program. Implementation, three weeks after the presidential inauguration, dashed the hopes of millions who voted for Carlos Andrés Pérez because they associated him with the petrobonanza prosperity of the 1970s. Frustrations exploded in a week of urban rioting, the worst violence in Venezuela since the overthrow of Colonel Pérez Jiménez thirty years earlier.

Following the February riots, President Pérez, the U.S. government, and the international banks reassessed the political, social, and economic consequences of enforced austerity. All acknowledged that they had underestimated the magnitude of popular frustration produced by six years of declining living standards. Yet structural limitations precluded any drastic change in policy. President Pérez continued with the IMF austerity program. While warning creditors and friends in the OECD countries that belt tightening could lead to anarchy, he acquiesced to IMF guidelines, viewing them as Venezuela's best hope for obtaining debt reduction, fresh money, and new foreign investment. The U.S. government reiterated its commitment to Venezuelan democracy. However, responses to the dramatic events in Eastern Europe had a higher claim on Washington's limited foreign aid budget. Bush administration support did not go beyond lobbying Venezuela's creditors to use the Brady plan to forgive a portion of its debt and to stretch out repayment of the remainder.

The international banks holding Venezuela's foreign debt viewed its economic and political problems as less desperate than the situation portrayed by President Pérez following the February rioting. While the banks did agree to emergency funding to prevent a Venezuelan default, they balked at forgiving a significant portion of the $29 billion debt so long as Caracas was receiving billions of dollars from the sale of petroleum. Thus President Pérez did not get the 45 percent reduction that he described as "absolutely necessary." By the end of his first year in office, he was forced to pin his hopes for debt relief on a "twist" menu, similar to the programs implemented by Mexico and the Philippines. Venezuela's menu included the following: a buy-back option for some $2 billion worth of debt, at a 50 percent discount; low-discount (35 percent) and high-discount (50 percent) swaps, the latter backed by oil receivables; debt-for-equity swaps of $1 billion a year; and new lending. The amount of new lending sought would depend on how much funding could be obtained under the other options.

Venezuela's resort to this "twist" menu confirmed that debt repayment would remain a significant problem at least into the middle 1990s. It also suggested that, provided the petroleum market did not collapse, the debt could be managed. Prudent debt management would create the confidence necessary to stimulate savings, reverse the flight of capital, and attract new foreign investment. Whether this optimistic scenario will take place remains one of the most important unknowns in determining the quality of life Venezuelans will experience in the 1990s.

Foreign policy between 1984 and 1990 encountered difficulties that reflected economic decline. Because Venezuela needed to maximize its short-term income from petroleum, President Lusinchi found his government increasingly at odds with Saudi Arabia inside of OPEC. Thus, Saudi maneuvering focused (successfully in many instances) on undermining the Lusinchi administration's credibility with other oil producers. The problem was sufficiently serious that President-elect Carlos Andrés Pérez visited Saudi Arabia prior to his inauguration. The rift was closed, and with Saudi support the Pérez government obtained a small increase in its OPEC production allocation. However, although Venezuela possesses the largest proven petroleum reserves in the Americas (58.5 billion barrels), its influence within OPEC remains inferior to that of the major Middle Eastern producers.

Venezuela's status closer to home has also declined. During the 1970s oil wealth enabled Caracas to become a leading player in Caribbean Basin politics. But after 1983 Venezuela no longer had funds that could be channeled into development projects in neighboring states. What influence remained depended largely on the country's ability to sell petroleum and to interest nations (for example, Brazil) in bartering finished goods for petroleum. Venezuela also retained potential influence with other members of the Andean Pact. They had some hope that Caracas would reopen pact trade in nontraditional exports.

To summarize, Lusinchi's Venezuela experienced downward international mobility, and Carlos Andrés Pérez's efforts to regain lost ground were undercut by his inability to secure significant reductions in the foreign debt. Reduced petroleum income and crushing debt payments had dire internal consequences that, if unattended, threatened political stability. However, the loss of international status in and of itself had little impact on the course of internal political development and decay. The democratic regime, even given the February 1989 rioting, was able to draw upon the legitimacy cushion of three successful decades. Its distributive network, while much reduced, remained formidable. Venezuelans enjoyed more liberty than most other Latin Americans, and they persisted in the expectation that matters would improve.

POLITICAL PARTIES, ELECTIONS, AND INTEREST GROUPS

Political Parties

Political party and party system performance are as central to the continued viability of democracy in Venezuela as developments in the international petroleum market are. Venezuelan parties perform diverse tasks: They mobilize their supporters, recruit individuals to fill government positions, mediate the demands of competing interests, and create symbols that either strengthen or undermine regime support. Since 1958 the country's political leaders have skillfully and imaginatively institutionalized a competitive party system that is dominated by representatives of the democratic center, Acción Democrática (AD) and the Social Christian party (COPEI). Both parties have strong indigenous roots, but the former operates with a social-democratic perspective, and the latter advocates Christian democracy.

The electoral system that AD and COPEI dominate mandates voting for all citizens eighteen years or older. National elections are held every five years. Voting is secret, and military oversight of the electoral process has insured its honesty since the overthrow of Pérez Jiménez. Other election rules favor centralized control by Caracas-based party elites. For example, in national elections, voters cast only two ballots. The first, or "large card," is for president, and the candidate receiving the most votes wins. The second, or "small card," forces voters within each state to choose among statewide party slates for members of the Senate, Chamber of Deputies, and state legislatures. Election is by a modified system of proportional representation, and list position is critical to the chances of state and national candidates. Position and list composition are determined through complicated negotiations between state and national party leaders.[8]

Party organization is the key to political domination in democratic Venezuela. The most important political parties are controlled from Caracas, and they penetrate all sectors of urban and rural life. Maximum authority resides in the national party convention, which meets irregularly, usually every eighteen months. On a daily basis, however, Venezuelan political parties are controlled by a secretary-general, a secretary of organization, and assorted luminaries such as former presidents and others who have held high office in either the government or the party. Together they form the party's national executive committee (CEN). Each CEN meets weekly and includes the national secretaries of the party's societal organizations; for example, organizations for labor, peasants, professionals, educators, and women.

State and local party organizations re-create their national counterparts on a smaller scale. There are between twenty and twenty-five state or regional secretary-generals, secretaries of organizations, and executive committees. There are functional secretariats (for example, for labor, peasants, and professionals) in each state organization and in the most important local organizations. All organizations are linked to party headquarters in Caracas by a dualistic command structure; for simplicity, only the national-to-state command structure is discussed.

Within each state, the entire party organization is subject to the authority of the state secretary-general, who, in turn, reports directly to the national secretary-general. State secretaries of the functional organizations also report to their national counterparts as well as to the state secretary-general. Thus, parties maintain two channels through which authority can be exercised and information gathered about the needs and desires of the members and of the general population. These channels also enable party leaders to detect threats and take remedial action before situations get out of control.

Venezuela's political party configuration, from a structural perspective, may be characterized as a dynamic "two-and-a-sixth-plus" system. The "two," AD and COPEI, command between 75 and 80 percent of the total vote (in presidential voting, the two account for almost 90 percent). Although AD is clearly the stronger of the two parties, COPEI has elected two of the six post-1958 presidents; in 1978 COPEI even received a slightly larger congressional vote than AD. The party system's "one-sixth" is a collection of militantly leftist organizations ranging from the personalistic Democratic Republican Union (URD) to the ideologically orthodox Venezuelan Communist party (PCV). The most important party in this cluster is the Movement Toward Socialism (MAS), many of whose leaders participated in guerrilla insurrection during the 1960s. This movement coalesced after members of the PCV broke with their party over its backing of the 1968 Soviet invasion of Czechoslovakia. The decision to elect state governors in December 1989 opened new opportunities for MAS. Whereas many voters were reluctant to support the presidential candidate of a party with no chance of winning, MAS appeared to be competitive in a number of states. The party captured the governorship in the industrial state of Aragua and finished second to AD in several others.

Finally, the party system's "plus" encompasses several rightist and personalistic movements. Since the polarizing 1973 election, assorted rightist party slates have received up to 5 percent of the total congressional vote. At present, the most important of these groupings are the Democratic New Generation (NGD) and the evangelical party, the Authentic Renewal Organization (ORA).

Venezuela's political party system may also be described in terms of its four ideological families: the social democrats, the Christian democrats, the militant left, and the personalistic right (see Table 13.1). In the decade following the overthrow of Pérez Jiménez, only political parties espousing the social-democratic and Christian-democratic ideologies were unequivocally committed to a free and open multiparty democracy. Nevertheless, the system's strength and resiliency eventually won over both militant leftists and personalistic rightists. It remains an open question, however, whether those groups' public acceptance of liberal democracy constitutes a genuine change of heart from earlier authoritarian preferences or whether it is a tactic of expediency.

Presidential balloting in 1988, as in the previous four elections, was more polarized than voting for Congress. Carlos Andrés Pérez, with 54 percent of the total valid vote, became the first former president to be elected to a second term since the constitutionally mandated waiting period was enacted (two terms or ten years). Social Christian Eduardo Fernández had gotten off to a rocky start after wresting his party's presidential nomination from party founder Rafael Caldera, but he closed strong and received 41 percent of the vote. With just under 3 percent of the valid presidential vote, the Movement Toward Socialism's candidate, Teodoro Petkoff, finished a weak third, and no other presidential candidate received even 1 percent. Although the 1988 elections marked the first time since 1963 that the opposition failed to capture the presidency, AD lost its absolute majority in both houses of Congress.

Abstention was an important and unexpected feature of the 1988 elections. Venezuela's 1961 constitution makes voting obligatory, and in earlier elections more than 90 percent of the people eligible to cast ballots chose to participate. However, in December 1988 almost one in five eligible voters either failed to vote or deliberately spoiled their ballots. Subsequent polling revealed that these decisions reflected negative evaluations of the past and likely future performances of AD and COPEI governments. Polling also confirmed the widespread lack of enthusiasm for existing militant leftist parties or for such personalistic movements as Democratic New Generation (NGD). This alienation fueled the unexpected and violent demonstrations of late February 1989 that lashed out against the recently inaugurated austerity program of the Pérez government.

Table 13.1   Percent of Total Congressional Vote Received
by Ideological Family and Important Political Parties in the Venezuelan
National Elections on December 4, 1988

	Political Party	Ideological Family
SOCIAL DEMOCRACY		43.3
Acción Democrática (AD)	43.3	
CHRISTIAN DEMOCRACY		31.1
Social Christian party (COPEI)	31.1	
MILITANT LEFT		17.4
Movement Toward Socialism/Movement of the Revolutionary Left (MAS-MIR)	10.2	
Radical Cause (LCR)	1.7	
People's Electoral Movement (MEP)	1.6	
Democratic Republican Union (URD)	1.4	
Venezuelan Communist party (PCV)	.9	
Others	1.6	
RIGHTIST PERSONALISM		7.6
Democratic New Generation (NGD)	3.3	
Fórmula 1 (RHONA)	1.3	
Authentic Renewal Organization (ORA)	1.3	
Others	1.7	
UNCLASSIFIED MICROPARTIES AND MOVEMENTS	0.6	0.6
TOTAL	100.0	100.0

Source: Consejo Supremo Electoral, "Boletín Extra-Oficial No. 7" (December 1988), mimeo.

The December 1989 state and local elections were held against a backdrop of continuing austerity, recession, and disillusionment with the established political parties. President Pérez portrayed the elections as a fulfillment of his campaign promise to deepen democracy. He noted that in addition to the traditional balloting for municipal councilmen, voters would have their first opportunity to select governors and mayors. Abstention, however, was unprecedented: 53 percent nationally and approaching 70 percent in some states. COPEI candidates won six governorships, MAS secured one, and two others went to fusion coalitions, backing candidates from other militant left parties. Of the eleven governorships won by AD, most were in small rural states. AD lost a majority of the 269 municipal councils and, except for Caracas, went down to defeat in the most important mayoral races. These results led to the proclamation by COPEI Secretary General Eduardo Fernández of his Social Christians as victor. The Movement Toward Socialism announced that the elections marked the emergence of a three-party system in Venezuela. While the COPEI and MAS statements appeared selectively optimistic, President Pérez and AD clearly viewed the results with concern.

The frustrated abstainers of 1988 and 1989 hold the key to transforming the party system that crystallized in 1973. One option would have President Pérez effectively reaching out to the alienated and consolidating single-party dominance by the AD. A second rests upon the prospect that the COPEI state governors will exhibit a competence in governing that would return the Social Christians to the majority status that they enjoyed at the end of the 1970s. Another possibility is that MAS could emerge as a viable challenger for presidential power. Personalistic rightists, especially the Democratic New Generation's charismatic leader Vladimir Gessen, will also mount an appeal to the disaffected. However, COPEI's resilience under the leadership of Eduardo Fernández, and the party's proved capability to organize a broad range of societal interests, place the opposition Social Christian party in an excellent position to emerge as an umbrella for all people who want change.

Interest Groups

In addition to favoring mass-based political parties, Venezuelan democracy encourages institutional and associational interest groups. The armed forces and the church, both historically elitist, are the most important institutional interests. The business community, also elitist, operates in an associational mode, but the most important associational interest groups, labor and peasants, crystallized in the late 1930s and 1940s. Their formation was part of the strategy of reformist party leaders to wrest control of the government from the heirs of Gen. Juan Vicente Gómez. On occasion, the urban poor have also expressed themselves as an anomic interest group.

The military, along with the church and landed elite, generally dominated from independence until the revolution of 1958. Following the overthrow of Colonel Pérez Jiménez, a provisional government was formed with Admiral Wolfgang Larrazábal as president. Although the admiral promised a transition to democracy, many army generals hoped to establish a developmentalist preatorian regime, but their revolts against the provisional government in July and September of 1958 were suppressed. Even more important, massive national strikes—supported by business, labor, and other groups—clearly demonstrated the popular unacceptability of renewed military rule. Confused and dispirited, the army acquiesced to the election of its archenemy, Rómulo Betancourt, as president.

Events in 1962 presented an opportunity for Betancourt and the generals to work together toward a common goal. Castroites and Communists mounted a guerrilla insurgency with the expectation of preventing elections in 1963 and discrediting the fledgling democratic regime. The counterinsurgency struggle forged links between the armed forces and the democratic political parties and transformed historic fear and distrust into a relationship of camaraderie and mutual support. This relationship remains a formidable obstacle to extraconstitutional change.

The clerical hierarchy, once a focus of opposition to mass political mobilization, also has become a pillar of support for Venezuelan democracy. Clerics strongly opposed AD during the Trienio—a time when two AD presidents, Rómulo Betancourt (1945–1948) and Rómulo Gallegos (1948), oversaw rapid political, economic, and social modernization— and felt especially threatened by AD efforts to expand secular public education. Clerics supported the Social Christian party and remained silent when, in 1948, the military overthrew the elected Gallegos government.

The human rights abuses of dictator Marcos Pérez Jiménez and Rómulo Betancourt's election as president at the end of 1958 caused the church to rethink its opposition to AD. President Betancourt approached the church hierarchy on two issues of greatest concern to it. He assured Cardinal Quintero that AD and the government would continue state subsidies to the church, and he communicated his vision of an educational system in which Catholic schools played an important role. The hierarchy responded by adopting a policy of peaceful coexistence with AD, and subsequently, the church assisted in consolidating the democratic regime.[9]

Private-sector interests in Venezuela are diverse, ranging from local agribusinesses to multinational manufacturers. During the Trienio businesspeople were united in their opposition to AD's reformist Marxism, with its emphasis on regulation and state intervention in the economy, but like the military and the church, the business community has accommodated to party democracy as defined in the Pact of Punto Fijo. The most important private-sector organization, FEDECAMARAS, became a central player in the democratic politics of resource allocation. Composed of more than 200 individual groups, FEDECAMARAS is dominated by four key interests: industry, trade, cattle raising, and agriculture. Each interest possesses its own chamber: CONINDUSTRIA for industry, CONSECOMERCIO for commerce, FENAGAN for cattle raising, and FEDEAGRO for agriculture. Because these key interests have different and sometimes conflicting priorities, the single-interest or intermediate chambers are as important as centers of political demands as FEDECAMARAS. Finally, foreign business, especially since President Pérez's nationalization of the petroleum and iron industries, keeps its distance from indigenous private-sector politics, and multinational managers opt for a low-profile mode of political participation.

Two associational interest groups, labor and peasants, crystallized in the late 1930s and 1940s. Their formation was part of the strategy of reformist party leaders to mobilize the masses and wrest political power from the Andean elite backers of Presidents Eleazar López Contreras (1935–1941) and Isaías Medina Angarita (1941–1945). Labor and peasant leaders, and people in the more recently formed professional associations, have always been subject to party discipline: Failure to comply with the instructions of one's political party usually results in expulsion. Because interest-group members also belong to the same disciplined, mass-based parties, expulsion from the party usually entails loss of leadership within the interest-group organization. Using these prerogatives, the parties extended power sharing as defined in the Pact of Punto Fijo into worker and peasant organizations. Positions of authority within them were divided among ADECOS (AD militants), COPEYANOS (COPEI militants), and assorted minor party leaders. Worker and peasant organizations were structured to have five-member governing boards, and the number of positions allocated to each party depended on its showing in periodic federation elections. During the first year of the Pérez government, AD held three of the five leadership positions in most worker and peasant organizations.[10]

Workers have become more important than peasants as an organized interest. According to the census of 1988, peasants make up less than 5 percent of the total population; in contrast, the largest labor union, the Venezuelan Confederation of Labor (CTV), boasts 2.5 million members. Recent developments, however, have undermined the CTV's capability to obtain benefits for its members. Declining petroleum income has reduced the resources available for distribution, and the absence of strong CTV leadership has made it impossible to focus the demands of some 8,000 competing unions. Two other conditions tie organized labor's hands: Many of its members are public-sector employees and thus are forbidden by law to strike, and, with AD in power, the national executive has invoked party discipline to curb wage demands. Nevertheless, the CTV has convinced the government to grant several significant wage increases since 1982. The confederation also dominates the labor courts, which settle contract disputes, and it played a pivotal role in securing the 1988 AD presidential nomination for Carlos Andrés Pérez.

Two rival labor confederations, the Unified Center of Venezuelan Workers (CUTV—estimated membership 80,000) and the Confederation of Autonomous Unions (CODESA—estimated membership 60,000), provide alternatives to the CTV. Neither is organized in accord with the Pact of Punto Fijo, and both are of only marginal importance. The CUTV coalesced during the guerrilla struggle of the 1960s, after the CTV expelled Communists and members of the radical leftist Movement of the Revolutionary Left (MIR). CODESA is allied with COPEI.

Finally, the urban poor have lashed out on occasion to defend their interests. Outbursts were common during the 1958–1960 transition to democratic government, and squatter areas remained restive for almost a decade. Improved service delivery during the petroleum bonanza (1973–1983) defused opposition to AD and COPEI, and they expanded their organizations into the slums. Although these distribution networks contracted after 1982, they continue to channel sufficient resources to sustain existing services. The leverage of the urban poor in the interest articulation process, however, is less than that of the other groups, and if the distributive networks must be contracted further, slum dwellers will be among the first to suffer. The length of time that declining resources can preserve the loyalty of the urban poor with respect to the distributive norms and procedures of post-1958 democracy is an open question, but this uncertainty also applies to the allegiance of the more-favored groups.

GOVERNMENT STRUCTURE

Venezuelan state organization is specified in the constitution of 1961, the country's twenty-sixth. Twenty states, two federal territories, and a federal district interact in a system that is nominally federal. However, for reasons peculiar to the unitary, centralistic tensions in Hispanic and Roman Catholic constitutional development, the state and local governments are more closely connected with national political patterns and performance than is true in North American democracies. The national executive is by far the most important branch of government.

The 1961 constitution uses language that suggests the font of all lawmaking in the country lies with an autonomous Congress, which is one of the three coequal branches of government. Congress is composed of a Chamber of Deputies (199 members) and a Senate (44 elected members plus all former constitutional presidents). Electoral law stipulates that each body is elected at the same time, with the same congressional ballot, every five years and that a party list system of proportional representation is the method of selection for both houses. The feature of alternates (*suplentes*) allows for persons so designated formally to hold the position to which a principal has been elected should the latter be granted an excused absence. Public complaints about personal and party irresponsibility under this arrangement have grown to where both 1988 major presidential candidates promised changes that would allow for the direct election of senators and deputies by name.

Congressional organization is also a product of the historical decision at Punto Fijo to share power. Rules within each chamber specifically establish parallel committees of apparently functional utility, and committee leadership is allocated among the political parties. Since the polarizing election of 1973 members of AD and COPEI have chaired most committees. However, committee power pales in comparison with that of the *fracción* or party caucus. A *fracción* encompasses members of a party's elected delegation to the Chamber of Deputies and Senate, and while it is presided over by a chairman (*jefe*) who is nominally elected by members of the *fracción*, in fact the chairman has been preselected and approved by the party's national executive committee.

Throughout the democratic period Congress has performed four critical functions:

1. *Legitimation.* The discussion of public policy prior to its implementation helps to legitimate the policy in the eyes of the electorate.
2. *Political catharsis.* The rhetoric of often highly emotive debate allows for the pacific airing of grievances in an open, legal, more or less dignified, articulate manner.
3. *Delay.* Debate can force postponement of the implementation of executive decisions, and the delay can mean that the government will lose, as least psychologically, on a particular issue.
4. *Democratic socialization.* The effect of political adversaries cooperating or discussing issues openly provides an example to the electorate of the political party elites observing the norms of democratic pluralism.[11]

Thus, the importance of Congress for Venezuelan democracy does not lie in any autonomous decision-making capability but in its communicative and symbolic functions. Since 1958 all political parties have invested a great deal of effort to control and maneuver this institution to their own advantage. This fact suggests that it is the visibility of Congress that is viewed as being of critical importance, both to the political parties organizationally and to ambitious congressional members intent on advancing their own political careers.

Article 203 of the 1961 constitution seeks to guarantee the judiciary's independence from the legislative and executive branches. However, despite reaffirming that Venezuela is a federal state, the 1961 constitution contains no provision for state courts to adjudicate state law. Neither are there nonfederal police forces of any importance. Thus, all of Venezuela's major legal offices—arresting, prosecuting, and judging—are staffed by "federal" (that is, central) government officials.

The judicial system is capped by a Supreme Court, which theoretically has the same power of judicial review as that in the United States. At lower levels, the system is composed of several types of courts, all of which have been divided by the Venezuelan jurist, Juan Mayorca, into two major categories: special and ordinary jurisdictions. The ordinary jurisdictions are of three types—civil, labor, and penal—and each has a hierarchy of courts. The courts of special jurisdiction are also of three types: juvenile, fiscal, and military tribunals. The Castillian tradition of the military *fuero* ("right") has been incorporated into the Venezuelan legal system to protect members of the military from being tried by civilian courts, and tax and juvenile offenses constitute other types of special cases that the "ordinary jurisdiction" courts do not oversee.

The constitution mandates that the Supreme Court transact its business by organizing into three panels (*salas*) concerned with various facets of the law—politico-administrative, criminal, and civil law. Each panel is composed of no fewer than five members. Only when the Supreme Court decides constitutional issues does it meet as a body.

The Supreme Court has yet to make use of its official right to declare any legislative law or executive-decree law "unconstitutional." Several factors explain this failure. Venezuela's history of strongman rule has created a history of judicial subservience to the executive. The code-law tradition itself, which casts jurists in the role of confirmers of the written code rather than as finders or makers of laws, also constricts Supreme Court initiative. Finally, judges in the system are selected for short periods of time by the minister of justice (for lower civilian courts) or by Congress (for the Supreme Court), and they receive their salaries, not as a guarantee, but from a line item in the Ministry of Justice's annual budget request to Congress. Yet, to assume that the Supreme Court has not played a role in consolidating post-1958 democracy would be misleading. During the tense presidential election of 1968 the Supreme Court took dramatic action after the opposition's congressional coalition referred a case to it and ordered President Raúl Leoni, who appeared ready to intervene on behalf of maintaining AD's organizational control of the Senate, not to interfere.

In summary, democratic Venezuela's judicial system is not yet well established, and a comprehensive national-inspired body of law is lacking, although some is developing. The current judicial system is a melange of democratic political system ideas superimposed on a code background that evolved out of the country's Spanish colonial and dictatorial past.

The 1961 constitution, in keeping with tradition, makes executive power paramount and places it in the hands of a president who is ineligible for reelection until he has been out of office for two terms. Among the most important presidential powers and prerogatives are command of the armed forces; the right to call special sessions of Congress; and appointment of all cabinet ministers, state governors, and even some local officials, most without congressional approval. The president can also declare a state of siege and temporarily order the restriction or suspension of constitutional guarantees. Equally important, the president is empowered through his ministers to adopt all necessary regulations to bring laws into effect. Such regulations are not subject to the approval of either the Congress or the courts. In addition, several presidents (most notably Carlos Andrés Peréz in 1974) have been granted a Special Powers Law (Ley Habilitante) during their first year in office.

This law circumvents the need for congressional approval of key legislation.

The 1961 constitution assumes that executive decisions will be implemented by national ministries. Ministries are centered in Caracas and organized hierarchically. The physical and cultural disparities between Caracas and the rest of the country remain great, and given the capital's cosmopolitan life-style, this difference has had a negative effect upon national public administration. Ministerial leaders often lose perspective and come to view "the interior" as alien and backward, qualitatively different from the world of Caracas. The resulting mind-set hinders the transmission of information about state and local needs, especially because leadership is a prerogative traditionally exercised only by the head of an agency and because effective lines of communication to and from this leader are personal. Inefficiencies and delay resulting from blocked communication within existing national ministries have led post-1958 presidents to create new ministries on several occasions. They have also encouraged experimentation with decentralized public administration.

During the first decade of democratic government the number of ministries remained stable at thirteen. In 1984, at the end of Luis Herrera's administration, there were twenty-five ministers of state and twenty ministries. President Jaime Lusinchi reduced these numbers only marginally. These figures illustrate the extent to which, since the quadrupling of oil prices in 1973, the public payroll has expanded. Concurrently, there was a proliferation of the decentralized bureaucracy over which the president exercises even more tenuous control.

Venezuela's decentralized public administration (DPA) consists of a vast network of state enterprises, autonomous institutes, foundations, and other quasi-public entities on the periphery of the executive. This off-budget or "third" sector of the economy is often discussed as though it were a fairly uniform, coherent whole. Quite the contrary is true. These decentralized state organizations are extremely diverse as to type, legal status, linkage to the state, structure, autonomy, personnel systems, financing, size-control mechanisms, and so on. Complexity and diversity can be represented in several ways: in terms of ministerial ties (e.g., to the Ministry of Agriculture), organizational cluster (e.g., revolving about the Venezuela Guyana Corporation [CVG] or the state petroleum corporation), and sectoral organization (e.g., transportation or electricity).

One example, from the perspective of ministerial ties, suffices to illustrate the difficulties of controlling Venezuela's DPA. "Third" sector entities, while nominally attached to one or more ministries, are often connected very indirectly. Thus, a few shares in one state company may be owned by another state company, which in turn is ascribed to a ministry, which is partially owned by an autonomous institute, which in turn is attached to still another ministry. For example, before the 1982 intervention by public authorities in the Workers' Bank (BTV), of which about 45 percent of the stock was owned by the Treasury (the

BTV was formally attached to the Ministry of Labor), only three of five subsidiaries of the BTV appeared on public records. After the intervention the BTV was found to have a major share interest (usually through wholly owned subsidiaries) in eighty other enterprises. The fact that such DPA activities can be hidden makes it extremely difficult for the state to exercise oversight.

Decentralized public administration entities have shaped many of the central characteristics, positive and negative, of Venezuela's political economy. They have implemented rural electrification, developed the mineral-rich Guyana Highlands region, modernized petrochemical production, and expanded Venezuelan ports. Thus, after decades of controversy, the productive role of the state in basic industries and its promotive activities in small business and agriculture are now legitimate. DPA entities, on the other hand, have consumed a disproportionate amount of petroleum income—since the middle 1970s more money has been spent through DPA than by state, local, and national governments combined—and only a small number of DPA entities, even after a decade of investing, have generated any significant returns. Financial accountability remains generally inadequate, so Presidents Lusinchi and Pérez have been receptive to schemes that would privatize elements of the DPA. This idea reverses policy that for fifty years has underlain AD's reformist Marxist approach to government.

POLICYMAKING

Venezuelan policymaking is conditioned by a number of previously discussed characteristics. Critical is the limited but real pluralism, with its toleration of dissent, that has remained constant since 1958. Equally important has been the large per capita petroleum income available for distribution by the Venezuelan state, especially that income's dramatic expansion in the middle 1970s and contraction in the 1980s. Other influential characteristics include the Hispanic tradition of centralized and hierarchical authority, persisting North Atlantic influence on domestic political evolution, and efforts to industrialize by creating a decentralized public administration, especially state corporations. These characteristics have shaped policymaking in each of the four central policy arenas: service delivery policy, economic development policy, public order and safety policy, and foreign and national defense policy.

Service Delivery Policy

Service delivery impacts immediately and directly on quality of life, and its highly diverse components include housing, water, electricity, health, sanitation, food, environment, social security, education, urban development, culture, and transportation. Until the revolution of 1945 only the upper class had access to quality services, and one of the most attractive dimensions of the AD's early program was its promise to use the state to extend high quality services to all. Billions of dollars in petroleum revenue have enabled AD and COPEI to accustom Venezuelans to the highest level of service delivery available in Latin America, and their success is one reason why, in public opinion poll after public opinion poll, the overwhelming majority of Venezuelans answer that democracy is the form of government that best serves the interests of "all the people."

The making and implementing of service delivery policies, with a few exceptions, are controlled directly by the national government. The Ministry of Health and Social Assistance provides health care and administers social security programs; environment, education, transportation, urban development, and culture each have their own ministries. Sanitation, on the other hand, is a municipal service, and responsibility for delivering housing (Venezuelan National Housing Institute [INAVE]), water (National Institute of Sanitary Works [INOS]), and electricity (Autonomous Corporation for Developing Electricity [CADAFE]) lies with decentralized public administration entities. The last was also true of food until 1984 when corruption and inefficiency related to the storage and marketing of food persuaded President Lusinchi to experiment with privatization by abolishing CORPOMERCADEO (the responsible state enterprise) and transferring its activities to the private sector. Food production increased immediately, spoilage rates declined, and Venezuela was able to reduce agricultural imports. Supporters of the process labeled the turnabout an "agricultural miracle": others warned that should prices rise too much or shortages reoccur, the government would come under irresistible pressure to resume its direct role in managing food.

Electricity distribution is unique in that, despite CADAFE's competent performance, it is also delivered by private utility companies in Caracas, Maracaibo, and several other large cities. Indeed, ELECAR (the Caracas Electric Company) is one of the country's largest and best-run corporations. In 1964, however, militant AD socialists pressured President Raúl Leoni to place all electricity delivery in the hands of CADAFE, which created a major crisis between AD and the private sector. Businesspeople rallied to ELECAR's defense, warning that "statizing" ELECAR would be taken as confirmation that AD remained as hostile to entrepreneurial activity as it had been during the Trienio. President Leoni defused this thinly veiled threat to democratic consolidation by negotiating an informal agreement that conceded the distribution of electricity in several important cities to the private electric companies. In return, the companies promised to supply power for municipal lighting and to the urban poor at subsidized rates. This understanding, which remains in force, was viewed as extending Pact of Punto Fijo guarantees of pluralism into the economic sphere.

Economic Development Policy

Economic development, the second policy cluster, revolves about activities that expand capacity to produce goods and commodities for internal consumption and for export. Its impact on quality of life, while just as important as service delivery, is less immediate and direct. Like service delivery policy, economic development policy's issue areas are highly diverse and include mineral extraction, industry, commerce, finance, and planning. Venezuela's private sector has traditionally played a pivotal role in all facets of economic development policy. Thus, to a greater extent than in service delivery policy, AD decisions affecting economic development after 1958 were scrutinized by businesspeople for evidence that the party intended to continue with Pact of Punto Fijo pluralism.[12]

Although mineral extraction is almost exclusively a national government prerogative, the private sector remains pivotal for industrial activity. Venezuelan mineral extraction, despite the importance of gold, iron, and bauxite, revolves about petroleum. Nationalization of the $5-billion oil industry, the product of a broad national consensus, occurred on January 1, 1976. The multinationals for years had known that nationalization was a certainty. Thus, in hopes of minimizing their losses, they had shared technical expertise and management skills with their local employees. When nationalization came, the companies received compensation that they considered "fair and equitable." On the other hand, the industry's 23,000 workers were prepared to handle their jobs without assistance from foreigners. The multinationals, under contract, continued to participate in several technical aspects of the industry.

To manage and coordinate the newly nationalized petroleum industry, Venezuela created Petróleos de Venezuela (PDVSA), a state corporation attached to what is now known as the Ministry of Energy. PDVSA consolidated some forty foreign oil companies into four semi-autonomous operating divisions. Consensus existed initially that professional judgments by the managerial technocrats inherited from the multinationals should determine PDVSA policy. Executives in the newly nationalized industry urged that proved reserves be expanded and that heavy capital investment be made. These actions would enable PDVSA to remain at the cutting edge of oil industry technology. Also, in order to secure market stability for Venezuelan production, PDVSA purchased interests in Western European refineries and North American distribution networks.

With the decline of petroleum prices and the demands of debt servicing, the executive branch began to overrule PDVSA executives with increasing frequency. Important benchmarks are President Herrera Campíns's 1982 decision to transfer $8 billion in PDVSA reserves to the Central Bank and Minister of Energy Hernández Grisanti's withholding of approval for the company's 1988 investment budget at the beginning of the year. As a result, PDVSA budgets now depend as much on political perceptions of what the nation can "afford" as on technical assessments of PDVSA needs and capabilities. Although political interference has weakened the petroleum industry, the extent of the damage remains unclear.[13]

Industrial policymaking involves the government continually in setting boundaries between the public and private sectors. Many capital-intensive heavy industries—for example, steel (Siderurgía del Orinoco [SIDOR]), aluminum (Aluminio del Caroni S.A. [ALCASA]), and petrochemicals (Petroquimica de Venezuela [PEQUIVEN])—are organized as state corporations. Public-sector regional development corporations exist for all major regions, and the Ministry of Development has long been a source of capital for politically favored industrial activities. On the other hand, a broad range of other industries (for example, automobile manufacturing, construction, and cement) are in private hands.

Businesspeople remain uncomfortable with AD's reformist Marxism. They complain that during the petroleum boom AD orchestrated an expansion of the DPA that preempted private-sector involvement in many sectors of the economy. Nevertheless, entrepreneurs failed to respond when President Lusinchi spoke of the need to privatize a broad range of industrial activities, especially those requiring heavy capitalization. In theory, businesspeople would like to see many industries and commercial enterprises removed from the public sector; however, they have been unwilling to repatriate from abroad the sums of money necessary for large-scale transfers to private hands.

Finance and commerce are economic development issue areas that have an especially intensive public sector–private sector interaction. The Ministry of the Treasury and the Central Bank set the broad financial parameters within which economic development will be pursued. Throughout the Pact of Punto Fijo era the minister of the Treasury has come from the business community; the president of the Central Bank, in contrast, has belonged to the government party's cadre of financial experts. Foreign banks played a prominent role in Venezuela until 1970, when the government limited foreign ownership to 20 percent of a bank's capital. At present, the national banking community is divided among twenty-eight private banks, four mixed ownership (government and private sector) banks, and twelve savings and loan (*financiera*) institutions.

During the Lusinchi administration's final year AD introduced a bill into Congress that increased government control over the banks. It regulated profit distribution, protected minority stockholders, and increased the Central Bank's power to set minimum reserve requirements. Banking interests, and the private sector, objected on the grounds that the bill gave too much power to the central government and failed to address the more urgent problem of effectively enforcing regulations already on the books. Although AD refused to back down on banking reform, the enforcement of banking regulations is a major problem facing the government of President Carlos Andrés Pérez.

Finally, the Ministry of Planning (CORDIPLAN) has responsibility for coordinating economic development and service delivery planning.

CORDIPLAN receives plans from all the ministries and their ascribed institutes and state corporations and is charged with eliminating duplication and setting overall priorities. In practice, however, CORDIPLAN does little more than compile the plans it receives. In 1984, when President Lusinchi's first director of CORDIPLAN took seriously the charge to reorder the priorities of the other ministries, he was asked to resign. His successor returned CORDIPLAN to its less assertive orientation.

Public Order and Safety Policy

The third policy area cluster, public order and safety, is comparatively homogeneous and revolves about the Ministries of Interior and Justice. The minister of the interior serves as the president's right hand in exercising political control. He supervises each of the state and territorial governors (who are appointed by the president) in all matters concerning internal territorial administration. He also disburses the constitutionally mandated allocation of federal budgetary funds, which are an important increment to state income, and oversees the National Identification Service and the Office of Immigration. During a president's absence from the country, the minister of interior serves as acting president. Thus, the Interior Ministry is always in the hands of an individual in whom the president has complete trust and confidence.

Responsibility for public order leads to the Interior Ministry's being entrusted with operation of the General Directorate of Police (Dirección General de Policía [DIGEPOL]). The director of DIGEPOL, although under the minister of the interior's direct supervision, has unhindered access to the president. Popularly referred to as the political police, DIGEPOL is responsible for crime prevention, for the preservation of public order, for the supervision of foreigners within the country, and for narcotics control. This final responsibility has taken on increased importance as, in the wake of declining petroleum income, drug trafficking has increased and there is a growing fear that the country may change from being a corridor and consumer for drug shipments into being a major cocaine processor. Opponents of the two major presidential candidates in 1988 played on this concern when they accused both Carlos Andrés Pérez and Eduardo Fernández of ties to the Medellín drug cartel.

A second national police force, the Technical and Judicial Police (Policia Técnica Judicial [PTJ]), is under the Ministry of Justice. Founded in 1958, following dissolution of dictator Pérez Jiménez's Seguridad Nacional, the PTJ is charged with protecting the rights and liberties of citizens. It resembles the U.S. Federal Bureau of Investigation in purpose and has primary responsibility for criminal investigation and the arrest of suspects. The Ministry of Justice also oversees the penal system, allocates government subsidies to the church, and ratifies clerical appointments.

Foreign and National Defense Policy

Defense

Foreign and defense policymaking, a constitutionally mandated presidential responsibility, are centered in the Ministries of Defense and Foreign Affairs and the institutes and state corporations attached to them. The Ministry of Energy, because of Venezuela's heavy dependence on international petroleum markets, also plays an important role in foreign policy. Petroleum policy has been discussed earlier, so the focus here is on traditional national security and foreign policy concerns: defense of the frontiers, control of the national territory, relations with foreign powers, and an array of nonpetroleum international economic issues.

Despite substantial overlap in the assigned tasks of the Ministries of Defense and Foreign Affairs, coordination between them is minimal. The most important explanation for this shortcoming is that since independence the critical missions of the armed forces have been internal. Presidents Betancourt and Leoni strengthened relations between AD and the military during their successful campaigns against leftist insurgents, and since then a primary military mission has been to exercise control over the national territory in a manner that discourages dissidents from attempting guerrilla warfare. Thus, the armed forces have cultivated ties with those domestic groups that traditionally provide recruits for any insurgency. The national guard, Venezuela's fourth armed service, is especially active in this area.

The armed forces generally follow the lead of the United States in externally oriented defense. The air force boasts twenty-four U.S.-manufactured F-16 aircraft, and officers from the four services regularly attend military schools in the United States and the Canal Zone. A U.S. Military Assistance Group (MAAG) in Caracas advises on strategy and tactics, and Venezuelan military units participate in joint exercises with U.S. and other Rio Treaty military units. During the early 1980s the Venezuelan military shared the United States' concern about Soviet penetration in Grenada, especially after Maurice Bishop's murder and the seizure of power by the ruling political party's Moscow-oriented faction. Although Venezuelan forces did not participate in the October 1983 invasion of Grenada, they supplied the United States with valuable intelligence.

Recent border clashes between Venezuela's armed forces and Colombian guerrillas, coupled with perceptions that the United States is incapable of implementing a long-range policy for the Caribbean Basin, have prodded Caracas into adopting a more autonomous defense policy. Correspondingly, the armed forces are seeking increased coordination between the Ministries of Defense and Foreign Affairs.

Institutional coordination has involved efforts to strengthen the role of the National Council for Security and Defense (Consejo Nacional de

Seguridad y Defensa [CONASEDE]) and its permanent secretariat (SECONSEDE), which serve in an advisory capacity to the president of the republic. However, SECONSEDE remains outside the pyramidal structure of military authority and discipline, of which the minister of defense, at least nominally, stands at the apex.

The chief of the General Staff (Estado Mayor General) oversaw the military establishment until the 1958 revolution. During the Betancourt administration, the centralized General Staff was replaced by the Joint Staff (Estado Mayor Conjunto), which became an advisory rather than a centralizing organ. It no longer coordinates defense policies and budgets, and these tasks have been delegated to the individual services. Two factors played an important role in this change. First, the post-1958 party regime was searching for ways to control the military, and party leaders preferred to negotiate decisions with four actors rather than one. Second, interservice rivalry also favored decentralization, because the navy, air force, and national guard were looking to reduce the army's domination within the armed forces and that domination had been exercised through the General Staff system.

Each service chief now lobbies on behalf of his service. Thus, in matters in which the military has a high potential for influence—budget, promotions, and equipment—the internal organization of each sector stimulates competition. In the case of budgetary management, there is a division of interests among the army, navy, air force, and national guard. Concerning professionalization, the peak of the pyramid for promotions is relatively politicized. As José Antonio Gil observed, "Individual appetites for power within the sector motivate individuals to play the game from outside, which weakens the internal cohesion of the group and its potential for influence on other sectors."[14]

Foreign Policy

Foreign policymaking and implementation, also constitutionally mandated presidential responsibilities, revolve about the Ministry of Foreign Relations. Presidents Betancourt and Leoni gave the position of foreign minister to prominent independents as a way to build support within the professional community, and in 1969 Rafael Caldera appointed his close collaborator, Aristides Calvani, to the post. Subsequently, AD and COPEI each developed a cadre of foreign policy experts. The professional foreign service has been co-opted into these cadres, which manage the Ministry of Foreign Affairs and the Foreign Trade Institute (Instituto de Comercio Exterior [ICE]). Established during the government of Rafael Caldera, ICE oversees and stimulates nonpetroleum exports. As president, Carlos Andrés Pérez has stressed the importance of ICE in his plans to reduce the state's dependence on petroleum income.

Until the middle of the twentieth century commerce with the North Atlantic countries was the only truly important aspect of Venezuela's international relations, and ties with these countries are still central.

Primacy derives from, and is determined by, the composition of Venezuelan exports and imports. Traditionally, Venezuelan raw materials were exchanged for manufactured goods from Western Europe and the United States, but beginning in the 1960s, Venezuela has used petroleum revenue to purchase industrial machinery and technology. Both were most readily available from traditional suppliers in the North Atlantic countries.

Cooperation within OPEC to set the price of petroleum acquired great importance during the late 1960s; in the 1980s coordination with other debtor countries in negotiating repayment terms with OECD country banks became equally significant. Both issues present opportunities for Caracas to resurrect rhetoric associated with such anti-Anglo and anti-U.S. themes as Latin American unity, Bolivarian solidarity, and Hispanic cultural superiority. In 1982 Washington's backing of London over Buenos Aires in the Falkland Islands dispute created unprecedented strains on Venezuelan-U.S. relations, and elements long hostile to "Yankee imperialism" portrayed President Reagan's support for Great Britain as a vindication of their position that Washington was basically anti-Latin and anti-Southern. The validity of these allegations, however, proved irrelevant: Venezuela remained economically dependent on the North Atlantic countries, and relations between the OECD countries and the leaders of AD and COPEI returned to normal within eighteen months.

Relations with other Latin American countries have been rocky. The policy of refusing to recognize governments that came to power by force (the Betancourt Doctrine) isolated Venezuela from many of its neighbors during the first decade of democracy, and with the return of Carlos Andrés Pérez to the presidency, there is increasing talk of reactivating this earlier policy. Venezuela also has territorial disputes with two of its neighbors: Colombia (over maritime boundaries in the Gulf of Venezuela) and Guyana (over ownership of the Essequibo border region). In addition, growing Brazilian power, and especially efforts to integrate the Amazon Basin into Brazil's effective national territory, have intensified Venezuelan apprehensions. Three administrations, beginning with that of Rafael Caldera, committed themselves to countering Brazilian efforts by integrating Venezuela's own Amazonian periphery with coastal Caribbean population centers. Although Brazil's program far surpasses that of Venezuela, the vastness of the Amazon Basin makes both appear like drops in the bucket. Thus, this potentially explosive rivalry is of only secondary importance.

Another persisting concern of Venezuelan foreign policy involves integration of the Bolivarian republics' economies inside the Andean Pact. More than fifteen years of pact membership have confirmed that Venezuela's high-price industrial goods cannot compete with those manufactured in Colombia, Ecuador, Peru, and Bolivia, which vindicates the initial opposition of Venezuelan businesspeople toward lowering tariff barriers on imports from their Andean neighbors. In addition, the pact's initial vision of political unity is now dismissed as unrealistic. Thus, recent presidents have all but ignored this once-promising attempt at regional economic integration. However, President Carlos Andrés Pérez has provided a possible reason for renewed Venezuelan interest in the Andean Pact: its "utility" for coordinating and strengthening the economic bargaining position of its members with the OECD countries.

Finally, democratic era foreign policy has focused increasingly on the Caribbean Basin. Relations with the basin countries are viewed as less important than relations with other petroleum producers but considerably more important than intensifying ties with countries in Africa and Asia. Venezuela's pivotal basin policy, strengthening ideologically compatible elites, originated in the "island of democracy" siege mentality that characterized the years of democratic consolidation (1959–1969). President Rafael Caldera modified this policy by shifting emphasis away from supporting only those elites who were committed to political pluralism and giving priority to cooperation with all basin countries, regardless of their domestic political regime, toward the end of forcing a more equitable distribution of wealth between Latin America and the North Atlantic countries. This approach, the doctrine of international social justice, has characterized Venezuelan basin policy for two decades. It legitimated efforts to reintegrate Fidel Castro into the regional community, to reduce the capability of outside powers (especially the United States and the Soviet Union) to project military power into Central America, and to strengthen the economies of the Caribbean Common Market states.

Building bridges to Caribbean Basin neighbors is not unrelated to the broad strategy of strengthening ties with other Southern countries. Both seek additional leverage in bargaining with the industrial North, especially the United States. AD and COPEI leaders, however, are not blindly hostile toward Washington. They view Venezuela's complex relationship with its powerful northern neighbor as filled with contradiction: admiration underlain by antagonism and dependence in the face of efforts to control national destiny. If Venezuelan leaders were to appear to be surrogates for Washington, their domestic legitimacy would be undermined. Thus, AD and COPEI leaders downplay cooperation with the United States in public. Nevertheless, they will present Washington with important opportunities to work closely with Venezuela during the 1990s.

PROSPECTS FOR THE FUTURE

The most likely shape of Venezuela's political system through the remainder of this century will be some variant of the Pact of Punto Fijo's limited pluralism, retaining commitment to liberty and justice but modified by continuing austerity. It would be redundant and anticlimactic to discuss the pact's power-sharing system yet another time, but it seems useful to examine the possible changes that may occur because of the system's reduced ability to extract resources from the international environment and derivative difficulties within the distributive and regulative networks. Although a small but real possibility exists that belt-tightening might force a significant regime change, a transformation to either military authoritarianism or a Marxist-Leninist dictatorship appears unlikely.

The post-1958 democratic state, like its predecessors, has centralized resource management in order to consolidate political power and stabilize the regime. Consequently, most government decisions have been made by national elites rather than by leaders at the state and local levels. Demands to move political decision making closer to the people culminated in the 1989 electoral reforms. By providing for the popular election of governors and mayors, elites recognized that new cadres of popularly based regional leaders were needed to energize and further legitimate the democratic regime. In the economic sphere, however, debate continues over how to make inefficient state industries more productive. Disillusionment over the impact of existing patterns of party-bureaucracy relations on the performance of national ministries and decentralized public administration is widespread.

Pact of Punto Fijo power sharing, the great legitimizing myth of post-1958 democracy, encouraged political parties to distribute bureaucratic positions without demanding performance in return. Only party loyalty was expected. Although this policy strengthened AD and COPEI, it facilitated exploitation of a state that remained weak and inefficient. For the bureaucracy to function required an ever-increasing injection of resources. In the post-1982 environment, with diminished resources, continuation of the earlier operational style is not possible, and the bloated bureaucracy, crafted to distribute wealth coming from abroad, appears incapable of the innovations called for in times of scarcity. In its present incarnation, therefore, the bureaucracy threatens political stability.

The role of the political parties is being rethought in light of the reductions in government income. Between 1958 and 1984 a large number of vertical-access channels were created to link society's interests and government, and political parties—above all the government party—oversaw the allocation of goods and services from government to the interest groups. Few horizontal-communication channels developed among interest groups. Therefore, it was almost impossible for expressions of interest to take place away from the vigilance of party and government leaders. Interest groups, perceiving themselves as having no choice but to use the existing vertical channels, became captives of AD and COPEI. Private problem-solving initiative was stifled, which proved to be a mixed blessing for the political parties. They became so involved in the internal politics of particular groups that they neglected the task of interest aggregation. Like the government bureaucracy, the party bureaucracies attempt to act in so many diverse circumstances that it becomes difficult for them to perform efficiently, a situation that leads to political decay.

Individual Venezuelans remain positive about democracy and competitive party politics. Nevertheless, it is unclear how long the post-1982 economic stress can continue before either the masses or the political elites will attempt to change the system. Three days of widespread rioting during February 1989 may be a harbinger of democratic decay; more immediately, they suggest that the opposition Social Christian party has an excellent chance of capturing the presidency in 1993.

The most probable alternative to Venezuela's existing competitive party democracy is single-party pluralism, with AD as the hegemonic party and COPEI and MAS as subordinate but relevant components. In assessing the probability of this transformation, it is important to remember that the February 1989 riots occurred only three weeks after Carlos Andrés Pérez's inauguration and that Pérez, elected by an absolute majority, is AD's most popular leader. Also, AD has been voted out of office twice since 1968. It is no small matter to change from a competition in which the government has lost four of the past six elections to one in which the opposition has no realistic chance of taking power. Certainly, continuing economic difficulties and system performance problems will modify the Pact of Punto Fijo system, but during the remainder of this century (always keeping in mind the centrality of petroleum revenue in nurturing Venezuela's distributive network), revolutionary change is unlikely.

NOTES

1. Iêda Siqueira Wiarda, "Venezuela: The Politics of Democratic Development," in Howard J. Wiarda and Harvey F. Kline, eds., *Latin American Politics and Development* (Boulder, Colo.: Westview Press, 1985), pp. 293–296.

2. John D. Lombardi, "Patterns of Venezuela's Past," in John D. Martz and David J. Myers, eds., *Venezuela: The Democratic Experience*, rev. ed. (Westport, Conn.: Praeger/Greenwood, 1986), pp. 7–21.

3. Ibid., p. 19.

4. John D. Martz, *Acción Democrática: Evolution of a Modern Political Party in Venezuela* (Princeton, N.J.: Princeton University Press, 1966), pp. 49–80.

5. Judith Ewell, *Venezuela: A Century of Change* (Stanford, Calif.: Stanford University Press, 1984), pp. 124–127.

6. Gustavo Escobar, "El Laberinto de La Economía," in Moisés Naim and Ramón Pinango, eds., *El Caso Venezuela: Una ilusión de armonía* (Caracas: Ediciones IESA, 1985), pp. 74–80.

7. Robert Bottome, José Antonio Gil Yepes, and John Sweeney, *The Economic Outlook for Venezuela 1988–1993* (Caracas: Ven Economy, 1988), pp. 5–17.

8. Howard R. Penniman, ed., *Venezuela At the Polls: The National Election of 1978* (Washington, D.C.: American Enterprise Institute, 1980).

9. Daniel Levine, *Conflict and Political Change in Venezuela* (Princeton, N.J.: Princeton University Press, 1973), pp. 62–144.

10. Stuart I. Fagan, "Unionism and Democracy," in John D. Martz and David J. Myers, eds., *Venezuela: The Democratic Experience* (New York: Praeger Publishers, 1977), pp. 174–192.
11. R. Lynn Kelley, "Venezuelan Constitutional Forms and Realities," in Martz and Myers, *Venezuela*, rev. ed., pp. 35–37.
12. Janet Kelley de Escobar, "Venezuela: Letting in the Market," in Raymond Vernon, ed., *The Promise of Privatization* (New York: Council on Foreign Relations, 1988), pp. 57–90.
13. *Venezuela 1988: Annual Report on Government, Economy, and Business* (London: Latin American Monitor, 1988), pp. 60–62.
14. José Antonio Gil Yepes, "Political Articulation of the Military Sector in Venezuelan Democracy," in Martz and Myers, *Venezuela*, rev. ed., p. 174.

SUGGESTIONS FOR FURTHER READING

Alexander, Robert J. *Romulo Betancourt and the Transformation of Venezuela.* New Brunswick, N.J.: Transaction Books, 1982.

Baloyra, Enrique A., and John D. Martz. *Political Attitudes in Venezuela: Societal Cleavages and Political Opinion.* Austin: University of Texas Press, 1979.

Bigler, Gene E. "Professional Soldiers and Restrained Politics in Venezuela." In Robert Wesson, ed., *New Military in Latin America*, pp. 174–193. Stanford, Calif.: Hoover Institution Press, 1984.

Blank, David E. *Venezuela: Politics in a Petroleum Republic.* New York: Praeger, 1984.

Coronel, Gustavo. *The Nationalization of the Venezuelan Oil Industry.* Lexington, Mass.: Lexington Books, 1983.

Ellner, Steve. *Venezuela's Movimiento al Socialismo: From Guerrilla Defeat to Innovative Politics.* Durham, N.C.: Duke University Press, 1988.

Ewell, Judith. *Venezuela: A Century of Change.* Stanford, Calif.: Stanford University Press, 1984.

Gil Yepes, José Antonio. *The Challenge of Venezuelan Democracy.* New Brunswick, N.J.: Transaction Books, 1981.

Greenwood, Johnathan C. "Regional Planning in Venezuela: Recent Directions." *Third World Planning Review* (August 1984):239–253.

Herman, Donald L. *Christian Democracy in Venezuela.* Chapel Hill: University of North Carolina Press, 1980.

Levine, Daniel. *Religion and Politics in Latin America: The Catholic Church in Venezuela and Colombia.* Princeton, N.J.: Princeton University Press, 1981.

Lombardi, John V. *Venezuela: The Search for Order, the Dream of Progress.* New York: Oxford University Press, 1982.

Martz, John D., and David J. Myers. *Venezuela: The Democratic Experience.* Rev. ed. Westport, Conn.: Greenwood Press, 1986.

Myers, David J. *Venezuela's Pursuit of Caribbean Basin Interests: Implications for U.S. National Security.* Rand-R-2994-AF/1. Santa Monica, Calif.: Rand, 1985.

Powell, John D. *Political Mobilization of the Venezuelan Peasant.* Cambridge, Mass.: Harvard University Press, 1971.

Vallenilla, Luis. *Oil: The Making of a New Economic Order—Venezuelan Oil and OPEC.* New York: McGraw-Hill, 1975.

14
Uruguay:
Democratic Regeneration
and Realignment

RONALD H. McDONALD

Uruguay is the smallest of the South American republics, but the distinctiveness of its political experience and innovations far transcend its size. It is perhaps best known today as a traditional democracy that "failed," one now struggling to reestablish its democratic traditions. But it is also a country that in the nineteenth century created democracy out of chaos and translated its traditional corporatist values and realities into democratic institutions. It experienced a profound disillusionment with the modern premises of economic growth and stability and went through a period of increasing political instability and incremental military intervention.

Uruguay sometimes has been viewed as a historical exception to the general pattern of politics in Latin America, an isolated instance of enlightened pluralistic politics in a region of corporatist authoritarianism. Uruguayans, in fact, have shared the same corporatist values as most of their neighbors but, almost uniquely, have shaped them into distinctive democratic processes and traditions, borrowing selectively from the experiences of Europe and the United States and, as necessary, making innovations to suit their own environment. Today Uruguay is reestablishing its democratic heritage and revitalizing its historic values, and in the process it is cautiously exploring new forms of organization and reevaluating the failed premises that destroyed its traditional democracy.

The unique qualities of Uruguayan democracy have been little known, let alone understood, outside the country. Outwardly the country seems to have many similarities with other democracies, including regular and meaningful elections, a rule of law that respects and protects individual liberties and freedoms, and a policymaking process that is responsive to public opinion and scrutiny. Yet these qualities exist within a dis-

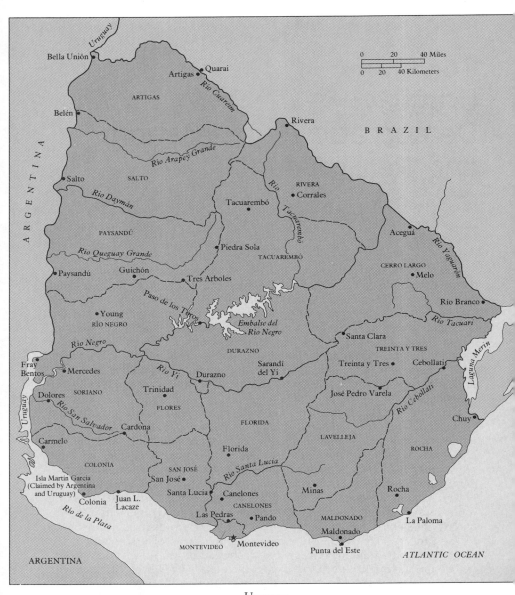

Uruguay

tinctively Latin American context, which recognizes and incorporates corporatist assumptions in the democratic processes, utilizing such familiar devices as co-optation, parity, coparticipation, and charismatic leadership. Many of the premises, the logic of the country's traditional democracy, proved unreliable, and in the mid-twentieth century Uruguay went through a period of sustained political and economic decay, violence, and ultimately, authoritarian military rule.

The establishment of Uruguayan democracy originally was the result of an armistice between contentious landowners and provincial caudillos who came to recognize the potential for significant profits from increased exports. The politicians also saw democracy as a way to create political stability and gain political support from a rapidly expanding urban middle class committed to consumerism, consumption, and the benefits of state-provided services and welfare. Uruguayan democracy was based on an important economic assumption: Economic growth was inevitable, irreversible, and largely a spontaneous process that could subsidize the expanding and increasingly costly demands of a democratic society—an assumption common to other liberal democracies, including the United States.

The political ideas that underlay Uruguayan democracy were forcefully and explicitly articulated by its most influential statesman, José Batlle y Ordóñez; namely, the belief that political stability was essential for prosperity and growth, that it could be achieved only by allowing free but balanced access to political power under a rule of law, that it could be sustained only by responding to the needs and demands of the masses, and that it must be protected from the pernicious influences of strong executives, politicians, and international opportunists. Batlle was strongly anticlerical; he believed that the church and Catholicism represented an organized threat to secular control and progress and that the church and state should be totally separated.

What is important about the Uruguayan experience is its relevance to other democracies whose processes, welfare, and stability are based on similar assumptions. The reexamination in Uruguay today of fundamental democratic premises and values within a contemporary context of economic stress has not been an easy task, and it is as yet unclear how much the result will borrow from the past, from neighboring societies in Latin America, or from new premises and new values. Uruguay has confronted crises and dilemmas that could threaten any democracy, and for that reason its experience, both the universal and the parochial dimensions of it, deserve careful evaluation.

ECONOMIC HISTORY AND SOCIAL CONTEXT

Uruguayan economic history is particularly important for understanding the country's politics and government. Early in the twentieth century Uruguay became a largely middle-class country with one of the highest standards of living in Latin America, but it subsequently experienced a protracted economic decline that challenged and eventually helped destroy its democratic politics. Uruguayan exports failed to remain viable and competitive internationally; its domestic economy became heavily dependent on service rather than agricultural and industrial activities; its dependency on imports, particularly for energy, created massive financial problems; and its commitment to consumption rather than productivity distorted national priorities and created an escalating international debt and uncontrolled inflation. Uruguay's economic success and its subsequent decay were both influenced by international economic realities, most of them beyond the country's control.

Uruguay's wealth was generated by the export of traditional commodities, principally wool, mutton, lamb, cattle, and grains. The economy was too small to industrialize rationally or efficiently, and the effort to do so encouraged import-substitution industrialization and protectionist trade policies, which in turn created inefficient monopolies, both foreign and domestic, along with equally inefficient state-owned enterprises. The domestic economic situation was complicated by high production costs and profit expectations resulting from high-risk industrial ventures. It was also complicated by modern but unrealistic economic expectations of workers, who effectively organized and created politically influential labor unions.

By the end of the nineteenth century the worldwide demand for Uruguayan exports had grown dramatically; traditional fibers like wool had not yet been challenged by synthetic ones, and by the mid-1870s the technology of refrigerated ships had made the export of fresh meat possible. The rural sector provided the capital on which the nation's development and wealth were based, subsidizing the industrial, commercial, and financial interests of the capital city, Montevideo. Export revenues allowed the importation of consumer goods demanded by the urban dwellers and helped supply the capital for Montevideo's own inefficient industrialization. Because the small-scale industrialization was inefficient, expensive, and monopolistic, industrial products could not compete in export markets or domestically in quality or price. But the workers whom the industries employed, concentrated in and around the capital city, grew in number and became more highly organized and politically active than their rural counterparts; for them the process of industrialization was popular. There was an inevitable conflict between the rural and urban interests in the country, one in which the capital city eventually prevailed by virtue of its greater population. The situation was a corrosive and dangerous one in which the affluence, the growth, and the consumption of the urban area were being subsidized by the rural areas, whose economy was slowly deteriorating.

By the end of World War II the demand for Uruguayan exports had begun to decline. Other supplies of fresh meat were available in international markets, particularly for Uruguay's largest trading partner, Great

Britain, and wool fibers were being replaced by synthetic ones. The traditional rural economy did not respond to these changes and continued producing the same export commodities, so export revenues decreased within a context of shrinking demand.[1] Uruguay's failure to renovate its export economy, to recognize and respond to major shifts in international demand and new technologies, set in motion a slow process of economic decay, which went largely unnoticed until after decades its cumulative effects were clearly visible. The eventual political implications were disastrous.

At the end of World War II neighboring Argentina and Brazil, not to mention Mexico, were effectively industrializing at rapid rates, but industrial growth in Uruguay had ground to a halt. The worsening imbalance between export revenues and import costs, an imbalance seriously aggravated by the sharp rise in the cost of imported energy in the 1970s, severely strained the country's financial solvency and encouraged two further and ultimately disastrous economic decisions. To sustain economic growth and financial liquidity, the civilian governments expanded the money supply, inducing rapid and at times rampant inflation, and the country increasingly borrowed money from international sources to subsidize its worsening trade deficit.

The first policy eroded the confidence of Uruguayan investors and encourged an accelerating capital flight and decline in investment. It also destroyed the ability of the urban middle and working classes to save or to maintain (not to mention improve) their living standards, which eventually alienated a substantial portion of the electorate and eroded confidence in the economic system. The second policy created a massive international debt, which today is per capita equal to about half the annual national income. In the decade from 1977 to 1986 the level of international debt in Uruguay increased by more than 400 percent, one of the highest rates in the hemisphere, and that was largely under a military government committed to economic austerity and willing to endure unpopular policies.

Economic decay was not an unpredictable, catastrophic experience that instantly devastated the living standards and economic activity. It was slow, incremental, and entirely predictable, but the difficult political decisions required to reverse it were not or could not be made, even by a military government. As economic conditions deteriorated following World War II, increasing demands were imposed on the government to provide compensatory services and subsidization, which in turn created more public spending and inflation, further discouraged domestic and foreign investment, and ultimately reinforced the general pattern of economic decline and the political problems associated with it. Although the country had achieved one of the highest standards of living in Latin America, Uruguay began to face apparently insolvable economic problems, which continue to frustrate the nation's politics and politicians even today.

The Uruguayan people are themselves a distinctive mixture. During the colonial period the country had virtually no indigenous population. Most of its people immigrated from southern Europe, primarily in the late nineteenth and early twentieth centuries. They were largely middle- and working-class people from urban areas, attracted to the then-prosperous and expanding Uruguayan economy, and they remained in the capital city of Montevideo. They brought with them European political attitudes and economic expectations, which were incorporated into the country's party politics. Today about half the national population resides in the capital city. Rural life, perhaps because of its historic economic importance, spawned a mythology of its own centered about the gaucho, but the reality of rural life has little in common with the myths. During the period of economic decay following World War II there was a substantial migration of urban Uruguayans out of the country, many of them to Argentina and Brazil, a process reinforced by the turbulent political conditions of the 1960s and the subsequent military dictatorship.

Uruguay was one of the first nations in Latin America to make a major commitment to public education, with the result that a high level of literacy was achieved in the country at a relatively early time. With that literacy came high levels of both political awareness, and participation, and modern socioeconomic expectations.

POLITICAL ORGANIZATION IN URUGUAY

Uruguay has a highly organized society, with clearly defined interest groups and complex political parties, but the society is organized in organic rather than pluralistic ways. The framework for this organization was devised by José Batlle to achieve political stability out of the chaotic experience of civil wars, international intervention, and party-organized conflict.

The nineteenth century produced two political parties, the Colorado party and the National party, more commonly known as the Blanco party (the parties originally were identified by the color of the brassards their adherents wore during armed confrontations). After generations of fighting for national hegemony, often with international provocation from Brazil, Argentina, and Great Britain, the possibility of economic prosperity, which came in the 1870s with the potential for a rapid expansion of exports, dramatized the advantages of cooperation rather than armed conflict for advancing the economic interests of both sides. The resolution of the civil conflict was promoted and eventually achieved by José Batlle.

Batlle was a descendant of a politically prominent and influential Uruguayan family that has produced many important political leaders in the country. He was elected president twice, in 1903 and 1911, and established the framework for modern Uruguayan politics and govern-ment. After defeating the Blancos in the last of the civil wars, he established a political compromise with them, based on the concepts of parity and coparticipation. Parity recognized the "legitimate" interests of the Blancos in the rural departments where they were strong, and Batlle all but ceded these departments to their control. He also accepted their participation in the national government, proportional to their share of the national vote, and allowed them a share of government patronage and revenues. The Blanco party won only three subsequent national elections, in 1958, 1962, and 1989, and became virtually a permanent minority. Batlle's Colorado party consistently attracted more voters nationally than the Blancos, but it was willing to share with the Blancos the exercise and benefits of power. The 1952 constitution went so far as to formalize coparticipation by awarding two of five positions on the boards of all state enterprises to the minority party.

Batlle designed an electoral system that incorporates parity and coparticipation both within and between the nation's political parties.[2] The Uruguayan electoral system regulates parties, elections, and the distribution of legislative seats, establishing "lemas" and "sub-lemas," which are equivalent to parties and party factions. Lemas are made up of sub-lemas, factions that are the followings or political machines of individual leaders. Anyone can form a sub-lema, acquire formal identification within a lema (or party), and in effect create a personal political organization with a separate identity. The electoral strength of a sub-lema and its leader adds to the total vote of a lema, which in turn determines both lema and sub-lema legislative representation. Ambitious political leaders are thereby permitted into the political system and can exercise political influence proportional to their ability to elicit votes. Their organizations are integrated into the larger lema, or party coalition, and they have a vested interest in the success of other sub-lemas, which they nonetheless campaign against since their representation is determined by their share of the cumulative vote for the lema. Elections have the effect of combining a primary election with a general election.

Sub-lemas in Uruguay form the nucleus of political organization and encourage a clientele relationship between the party leaders and the voters. Constituents with problems can request help from sub-lema leaders and their organizations, and in Montevideo sub-lemas maintain neighborhood clubs and organize campaigning. Through cross-endorsement, cross-listing, and a sharing of candidates, they form additional coalitions among themselves within the lemas or parties, coalitions that constantly shift from one election to another.

The lema system is formalized by proportional representation, which allocates legislative representation according to the size of the popular vote, and campaign costs are also subsidized for sub-lemas according to the size of their vote. For the voter, the system encourages a general identification with a lema and a personal identification with a sub-lema. The electoral system also reinforces the Colorado and Blanco parties, which benefit principally from it, and restrains the growth and success of new or smaller parties.

Batlle built the Colorado party into the majority political organization by mobilizing the urban classes of Montevideo and appealing to their interests. He proposed, and while president implemented, vast public programs of education, culture, welfare, and social security. He encouraged industrialization and resisted foreign penetration of the country's economy. He advocated abolishing the presidency as an institution and replacing it with a rotating collegial executive, an idea he borrowed from Switzerland. He reasoned that the dictatorships that were so common in Latin America were the result of an inevitable greed for power, and since one could not change human nature, the only way to prevent dictatorships was to abolish the presidency and replace it with an institution that dispersed power. Batlle was by profession a journalist (he founded *El Día*, the largest daily newspaper in Montevideo), and he used his journalistic interests to further his political objectives, a process that continues today in Uruguay. Opposition to his leadership arose within the Colorado party, and anti-Batllista factions (sub-lemas) were formed.

Batlle's ideas were visionary for their time; he initiated a modern welfare state in Uruguay long before it had been tried elsewhere. He was a consummate politician, but his political pragmatism was partially tempered by his idealism. Batlle believed he could eliminate instability and turmoil by expanding and organizing the political base of the country and by responding to the basic needs of the Uruguayan people.

In spite of his influence and success, Batlle's ideas were based on two vulnerable assumptions, both of which proved to be erroneous and eventually contributed to the decay of Uruguayan democracy. The first was the assumption of continued economic growth and prosperity, a common perspective among industrializing nations during the nineteenth century. This assumption was drawn from the experiences of large nations, specifically Great Britain, France, Germany, and the United States, and proved inappropriate for Uruguay. The second was the assumption that a collegial executive could prevent authoritarian governments. Uruguay did not experiment with the collegial executive until the 1950s, perhaps the worst possible time as the economy was in the process of decline and strong leadership was desperately needed. Ironically, the government was controlled for eight of the collegial executive years by the Blanco party, the first time in the twentieth century it had prevailed in national elections. The experiment with a collegial executive, combined with the economic dilemmas for which no answers could be found, contributed to the political paralysis that encouraged a revolutionary group known as the Tupamaros and, ultimately, military intervention. The Tupamaros did not succeed in taking power, but their actions provoked the military into doing so.

There have always been minor political parties in Uruguay. One of the oldest is the Civic Union (UC), a conservative Catholic organization that provides an alternative to the prevailing tradition of anticlericalism that Batlle sponsored. By the 1960s several small parties combined with a dissident liberal sub-lema of the Colorado party to form an electoral coalition, originally known as the Leftist Front of Freedom (FIDEL) and ultimately as the Broad Front (Frente Amplio). Included in the Broad Front were the Communist party of Uruguay, the Christian Democratic party, the Socialist party, and List 99 of the Colorado party established by Zelmar Michelini. By combining their strengths in the 1971 and 1984 elections, the coalition gave serious competition to the two traditional lemas, which in many ways are themselves political coalitions.

Like the political parties, economic interests have been well organized in Uruguay. The organizations include national associations of ranchers, business enterprises, and labor. Labor organizations emerged very early in Uruguay and were modeled after their European counterparts. The largest labor organization, the National Confederation of Workers (CNT), is Marxist, but its strength has not necessarily translated into votes for Marxist parties. Organized workers were a principal target for Batlle's policies, and a large proportion of them have been Colorado party supporters in spite of their union's orientation. The CNT was outlawed under the dictatorship, but a new organization, the Plenario Intersindical de Trabajadores (PIT), was formed in the early 1980s and subsequently merged with the CNT after the reestablishment of democracy.

The political scenario that eventually produced a military dictatorship is a long and complex one. Military intervention occurred gradually, although by mid-1973 the military was fully in control of the government. The Tupamaro revolutionary movement, specializing in urban terrorism in the capital city, became a highly destabilizing influence during the 1960s. The government retaliated with a state of siege, massive arrests, torture, suppression of political leaders and groups, and censorship, but these actions were ineffective and even counterproductive. The military gradually assumed responsibility for the Tupamaro threat, and in the process brought the civilian institutions under its control. It ruled directly from 1973 to 1985.

The military regime had both successes and failures in managing the economy, but the experience proved unpopular for Uruguayans and divisive for the military. No single military leader was able to consolidate his control, although one (Gregorio Alvarez) tried. The military response to the Tupamaros was brutal and, for Uruguay, unprecedented. Eventually the movement was effectively crushed, but at extraordinarily high costs to Uruguayan legal and political values.

By the early 1980s the military leaders had begun to recognize the inevitability of restoring civilian rule and began looking for a way to maximize their continuing influence and minimize any retribution to them, individually and institutionally, after leaving power. They looked for inspiration to Brazil, whose officers were methodically and gradually returning that country's government to civilian control, and they were aware of the chaotic experience occurring in Argentina, where the military was leaving power in disgrace and facing civilian retribution. The military regime decided to hold a referendum in 1980 on a new constitution that would protect the military's political influence, a referendum held under conditions of tight controls and censorship. Not only was the measure defeated, it was so decisively defeated that the regime had no choice but to acknowledge its failure. At that point, military officers began negotiating with civilian political leaders, at least those they were willing to talk with, about conditions for a return to civilian rule. This change was formally achieved in May 1985 after elections the preceding November in which two of the major presidential contenders, Wilson Ferreira Aldunate of the Blanco party and Liber Seregni of the Broad Front, were prohibited from being candidates. The victor was a Colorado party candidate, Julio Sanguinetti. Party voting and the resulting legislative representation were very similar to what they had been in 1971, the last election before the total military takeover.

GOVERNMENT STRUCTURE AND POLICIES

Uruguay has a centralized government and is divided into nineteen departments, including the capital city of Montevideo. Virtually all decisions in the country are made at the national level. The 1966 constitution allows departments to elect local legislatures comprising thirty-one members and an *intendente,* the departmental administrative officer.

The president is popularly elected for a five-year term, and all other elections in the country are held simultaneously. The legislature is bicameral, with ninety-nine representatives in the Chamber of Deputies and thirty in the Senate, all elected by proportional representation; the Senate is elected at large. The current constitution was adopted in 1966, following the twelve-year experiment with a collegial executive. The legislature has considerable power and is organized through a system of committees.

The Uruguayan economy is a distinctive mixture of private and public enterprises. Most of the economy is privately owned and managed, but about 20 percent of the gross domestic product (GDP) comes from state-controlled companies. The largest of the state-owned monopolies is the Asociación Nacional de Combustibles, Alcohol y Portland (ANCAP), which refines petroleum and manufactures alcohol and cement. That agency alone accounts for 4 percent of the GDP. In the 1970s there was an effort to encourage international banking in Uruguay, in order to provide "off-shore" benefits to foreign banks and investors and stimulate economic development by encouraging new investments in the country. The policy was partially successful and was supported by both the military and the subsequent civilian government.

What has given Uruguay the appearance of a welfare state historically has been not so much the direct participation of the government in the economy but the benefits provided by the government. Nowhere is this situation more apparent than in the social security system, which partially supports over 350,000 retired Uruguayans, a number almost equal to one-third of the active work force. Low population growth means Uruguay has the highest proportion of retired persons of any Latin American nation, and this fact, combined with state-provided retirement benefits, creates an enormous economic burden on the people who are economically active.

The economic problems facing the civilian government are formidable. They include a revitalization of the rural economy, both for export objectives and for food production; managing one of the highest per capita international debts in the region; stimulating national investment and economic growth; and dealing with a difficult foreign trade situation, in which exports cannot provide sufficient revenues to pay for the energy, resources, and manufactured goods the country needs to import as well as servicing its international debt obligations. The only course the government has available to it is economic austerity, not a policy designed to cushion the return to civilian, democratic government. Besides these economic problems, the erosion of public services and programs and a decline in real income and savings during the twelve years of military control have stimulated new demands, which are difficult for political leaders to ignore in the restored democratic environment but even more difficult for them to meet. Generally the performance of the economy during the Sanguinetti administration was far better than most observers had expected.

The Uruguayan military is professional by Latin American standards, and except for the recent dictatorship, it has stayed out of politics for most of the twentieth century. During the dictatorship the size of the military grew at least 400 percent, and defense expenditures rose appreciably to a percentage of the GDP far exceeding that of Brazil, Argentina, or Mexico. The military is now technically under the control of civilians, but it is not yet certain that its political influence has been totally contained.

After the restoration of civilian government a major issue arose as to how to deal with those military leaders who were responsible for the human rights violations committed during the dictatorship. The issue plagued the Sanguinetti government. In late 1987 the national legislature passed an amnesty bill, which prevented prosecution of military and police personnel for human rights violations during the dictatorship. The legislation was very unpopular and provoked a petition campaign to hold a referendum on the legislation and the question of immunity from prosecution for military officers charged with human rights violations. Public opinion polls consistently demonstrated that a large majority of Uruguayans believed that military personnel did commit human rights violations during the dictatorship and that those who did should be punished.

The petition campaign was successful, and a referendum was held on April 16, 1989. The effort to overturn the immunity legislation failed, by a vote of 53 to 40 percent, with 7 percent of the ballots either blank or spoiled; the majority of voters in Montevideo, however, voted in favor of the referendum. Many government leaders felt it was necessary to end the bitter recriminations of the dictatorship, concentrate on the tasks of economic development, and finesse an issue that might create a confrontation with the military and thus raise the possibility of another military intervention. The 1989 national election was to be the first truly open one since the end of the military dictatorship, and its results will be a significant indicator of the future of the nation's two traditional political parties.

National elections were held again on November 26, 1989, and produced a plurality victory (38 percent) for the National party. One of its candidates, Luis Alberto Lacalle, was elected president, and it was only the third time in the twentieth century that the National party had prevailed in a national election. The Colorado candidates received less than one-third of the vote, the Broad Front about one-fifth. The latter did, however, receive a plurality (34 percent) in the municipal elections for the city of Montevideo, electing a Socialist mayor and a bare majority of the municipal council. The national results were ambiguous, particularly on the question of electoral realignment, but they may imply a permanent three-way party competition in the country.

INTERNATIONAL AFFAIRS

Uruguay found itself isolated internationally during the years of the military dictatorship, and with the reestablishment of civilian rule, the country began to review and renovate its international commitments. It reestablished diplomatic relations with Cuba, supported efforts to achieve a peaceful resolution of the issues in Central America, and participated in regional economic conferences. It has pursued closer ties with Argentina, including a free-trade zone, and has become increasingly active in regional organizations and the United Nations. It also has actively sought new markets for its exports.

Uruguayan exports are now more diversified, and the largest share of them (26 percent) goes to Latin America. The country has also achieved considerable growth in exports to Western Europe, the Middle East, Eastern Europe, and other nontraditional markets. There has been a growth in nontraditional exports, including fruits, cereals, vegetables, fish, and some manufactured goods. The struggle to increase exports is a difficult one, but without significant increases in productivity, investment, and trade, the country's economic future is not encouraging. Apart from the domestic political and economic problems the civilian leaders face, the country's economic prosperity and survival depend on its agility in international affairs, particularly international finance and trade. The resolution of its international debt crisis is the most formidable issue facing the country's economy.

REGENERATION AND REALIGNMENT IN URUGUAYAN POLITICS

The reestablishment of civilian control in Uruguay has been an uncertain and difficult experience. It has been accomplished in a characteristically Uruguayan way, requiring political negotiation between civilian and military leaders and ultimately relying upon the resilient democratic values of the society. The task is one of innovation and reevaluation, ascertaining which traditional Uruguayan practices can be salvaged and what realignments will emerge. The future of the two-party system is one of the issues, but the results of the 1989 elections were ambiguous and failed to clarify the extent to which a third force may successfully challenge the traditional parties. Regeneration is occurring within the two major parties, and a new generation of leaders is emerging that may redefine their parties' roles in national politics. Electoral realignment could be a consequence of this process.

The national economic problems are challenging and potentially threatening to the process of regeneration. The country has faced serious economic challenges for at least a half century, and it has learned that the relationship between economic viability and growth and political stability is a fundamental one. The issue clearly transcends the borders of Uruguay; it is relevant for all democracies, including the United States. The violence and abuses from the mid-1960s until the democratic restoration in 1985 created a political hiatus, the consequences of which a new generation of Uruguayan politicians must now resolve. Their innovation and judgment, their successes and failures, will ultimately determine the viability of the restored democratic process.

NOTES

1. By comparison, Argentina has been reasonably successful in adjusting its rural exports—balancing cattle and grain exports—as international demand and prices have changed.

2. For a more extensive discussion, see Ronald H. McDonald and J. Mark Ruhl, *Political Parties and Elections in Latin America* (Boulder, Colo.: Westview Press, 1989), pp. 91–110.

SUGGESTIONS FOR FURTHER READING

Campiglia, Nestor. *Los Grupos de Presión y el Proceso Político.* Montevideo: Arca, 1969.

Gillespie, Charles G. "Activists and Floating Voters: The Unheeded Lessons of Uruguay's 1982 Primaries." In P. W. Drake and E. Silva, eds., *Elections and*

Democratization in Latin America, 1980–1985, pp. 215–244. San Diego, Calif.: Center for Iberian and Latin American Studies, Center for U.S.-Mexican Studies Institute of the Americas, 1986.

Handelman, Howard. "Uruguay." In H. Handelman and T. G. Sanders, eds., *Military Government and the Movement Toward Democracy in South America*, pp. 215–284. Bloomington: Indiana University Press, 1981.

_____ . "Prelude to Elections: The Military's Legitimacy Crisis and the 1980 Constitutional Plebiscite in Uruguay." In P. W. Drake and E. Silva, eds., *Elections and Democratization in Latin America, 1980–1985*, pp. 201–214. San Diego, Calif.: Center for Iberian and Latin American Studies, Center for U.S.-Mexican Studies Institute of the Americas, 1986.

Kaufman, Eli. *Uruguay in Transition*. New Brunswick, N.J.: Transaction Books, 1978.

McDonald, Ronald H. "Legislative Politics in Uruguay: A Preliminary Analysis." In W. H. Agor, ed., *Latin American Legislatures: Their Role and Influence*, pp. 113–138. New York: Praeger, 1971.

_____ . "The Rise of Military Politics in Uruguay." *Inter-American Economic Affairs* 28 (1975):25–43.

_____ . "Redemocratization in Uruguay." In G. Lopez and M. Stohl, eds., *Liberalization and Redemocratization in Latin America*, pp. 173–190. Westport, Conn.: Greenwood Press, 1987.

Rial, Juan. "The Uruguayan Elections of 1984: A Triumph of the Center." In P. W. Drake and E. Silva, eds., *Elections and Democratization in Latin America, 1980–1985*, pp. 245–272. San Diego, Calif.: Center for Iberian and Latin American Studies, Center for U.S.-Mexican Studies Institute of the Americas, 1986.

Taylor, Philip B. "The Electoral System in Uruguay." *Journal of Politics* 17 (1955):19–42.

_____ . "Interests and Institutional Disfunction in Uruguay." *American Political Science Review* 58 (1963):62–74.

Weinstein, Martin. *Uruguay: The Politics of Failure*. Westport, Conn.: Greenwood Press, 1975.

_____ . *Uruguay: Democracy at the Crossroads*. Boulder, Colo.: Westview Press, 1988.

15
Authoritarian Paraguay: The Personalist Tradition

RIORDAN ROETT
RICHARD S. SACKS

One of the oldest countries in the hemisphere and one of the most unique, Paraguay was isolated from the world for centuries, first by Spanish colonial neglect and then by postindependence economic autarchy. Its distinguishing traits of isolation, racial homogeneity, and authoritarian rule were set during its first years as a colony and reinforced under the Republic. The first independent nation in Spanish America, Paraguay was the only one to undergo a form of social revolution as a result of its struggle for independence. The country was experimenting with state control of the economy fully 100 years before the Bolsheviks stormed the Winter Palace in 1917.

An "island surrounded by land" in the heart of South America, Paraguay is about the size of California (157,047 square miles [406,752 square kilometers]) and has an estimated (1987) population of 3.8 million. Asunción, the capital and principal commercial center, is 1,000 miles (1,600 kilometers) from the Atlantic Ocean. Paraguay has access to international shipping lanes via the Paraguay-Paraná river system that flows south to Buenos Aires and by road to Paranaguá, a treaty port on the Brazilian coast.

Paraguay's verdant soil, lush forests, cool riversides, and natural beauty could make the country a paradise, but the gap between potential and reality in Paraguay has always been uncomfortably wide. Poverty, backwardness, ignorance of the outside world, and periodic military invasions from neighboring Brazil, Argentina, and Bolivia have exaggerated the nation's insecurity, its authoritarian politics, and its deeply ingrained nationalism. Paraguayans see themselves as a persecuted people who have had to defend their distinct ethnicity and national independence more than once against powerful enemies.

The country has had its share of bad luck: Paraguay was the battlefield for two of South America's three major wars since independence. Paraguay

Paraguay

is also a geopolitical anomaly. It is a country that under ordinary conditions would have been absorbed long ago by its giant neighbors—Brazil and Argentina. Had Paraguayans not fought so often and so well, their nation probably would not exist today.

Racially and culturally, Paraguayans are among the most homogeneous people in Latin America. About 95 percent of the population is mestizo. Almost all Paraguayans speak both Spanish (the official language) and Guaraní, making Paraguay the only country in the Western Hemisphere in which an indigenous language has wide currency. Government policies during the Francia era (1814–1840) discouraged the elitism that is characteristic of other Latin American nations by forbidding marriages between whites, banning European immigration, and forcing many upper-class families into prison or exile. The Triple Alliance War (1864–1870), arguably one of the greatest military disasters in modern history (in relative terms), killed most of the Spanish-descended males that remained. Demographics dictated that white women who wanted spouses had to accept mestizo suitors. Unable to preserve their racial identity or their socioeconomic privileges, the Spaniards failed to become a ruling class that monopolized positions of power and influence.

Dictatorship is to Paraguay what democracy is to Sweden or Great Britain: normal, traditional, and—for many Paraguayans—comfortable. With the sole exception of Francisco Solano López (1862–1870), dictators have brought economic prosperity, so many Paraguayans have learned to equate democratic politics with weakness and authoritarian politics with strength. Change traditionally comes from the top. Whenever authoritarian rule has been removed (such as during 1870–1936 and in 1947), politics have tended to become unstable and the state has functioned poorly.[1] Political instability has exacted a heavy price—Alfredo Stroessner's thirty-five-year dictatorship was a costly way to insure against coups d'état—and many Paraguayans believe that paternalism best serves the national interest. Regardless of what they may say about democratic principles, groups and individuals who achieve political power tend to repress their opponents. No Paraguayan government has ever been made or unmade because of an election.

Despite the country's solitude and paranoid nationalism, Paraguay has begun to enter the modern world. The giant Brazilian-financed Itaipú hydroelectric project has brought Paraguay wealth and new influence in international affairs. Ironically, by raising expectations and making its citizens more aware of world affairs, Itaipú has also helped shove Paraguay out of its age-old torpor. On the surface, the coup of February 2–3, 1989, that deposed Alfredo Stroessner and brought Andrés Rodríguez to power simply substituted one army general for another. Yet there are signs that the personalist tradition in Paraguay and the unique environment that engendered it are coming to an end.

HISTORICAL SETTING

Colonial Rule

The recorded history of Paraguay began with the arrival of Europeans looking for gold and silver in the wrong place. In 1524 a Portuguese named Aleixo Garcia marched through Paraguay to raid the Inca empire, and news of Garcia's exploits attracted the seagoing explorer Sebastian Cabot to the area in 1526. Cabot sailed up the Paraguay River, naming it Rió de la Plata[2] after sighting Indians with silver trinkets (possibly from Garcia's trove).

In 1536 Charles V of Spain dispatched Pedro de Mendoza to the Río de la Plata with over 1,000 men to find a route to Peru. They founded Asunción in 1537 after hostile Indians forced them to abandon their fort at Buenos Aires. Since Paraguay contained no precious metals at all, the colony soon became little more than a buffer against the Portuguese in Brazil and a transit zone for Bolivian and Peruvian silver shipments to Buenos Aires.

Overwhelmed from the start by Indians and mestizos and ignored by the outside world, the small Spanish population in Paraguay could not easily maintain its social and cultural identity. The only way the Spaniards could survive was by intermarrying with the sympathetic Guaraní Indians and making do with a standard of living based on subsistence agriculture. Under such conditions, they based authority on their personal power as Guaraní chiefs rather than on laws or institutions. Personalism in politics—the Paraguayan paradigm that emphasizes a leader's individual qualities and places little importance on ideology—thus emerges at the very start of Paraguayan history.

Asunción steadily lost its influence after 1616 when the seat of Spanish colonial rule was transferred to Buenos Aires. Meanwhile, *la provincia gigante*, as Paraguay was known because of its immense but undefined formal boundaries, lost two-thirds of its territory to the advancing Portuguese. Starting in 1609 the Jesuits chose the eastern hinterlands of Paraguay as a laboratory for what was probably the world's biggest experiment in communal living. By 1650 these enterprising men had organized 100,000 Guaraní Indians into twenty *reducciones* ("townships"), and these productive, self-sustaining, hierarchical Indian communities cultivated export crops, such as yerba maté (Paraguayan tea) and tobacco, and raised maize, mandioca (cassava), and livestock. Although the Jesuits treated their neophytes like children, the *reduccion* Indians were the most prosperous in Latin America. The experiment ended when Spain expelled the Jesuits from its colonies in 1767.

Nineteenth-Century Independence

Spanish colonial rule ended in 1811 when Paraguay defeated an Argentine invasion, deposed its Spanish governor, and declared its independence from Spain and Buenos Aires. Dr. José Gaspar Rodriguez de Francia, a theologian turned lawyer, emerged as the dominant personality in Asunción's revolutionary junta. One of the most educated men in Paraguay at that time, Francia was named dictator in 1814. Eliminating his opponents one by one, he was designated dictator for life by an 1816 Congress.

Known to the masses as *Carai Guazu* ("Great Señor"), this frugal, ascetic bachelor remained in power until his death in 1840. A man who admired the most radical leaders of the French revolution, Francia preserved Paraguay's independence, kept the country at peace, and was a controversial agent of social change. Yet "El Supremo Dictador" (his official title) was a harsh ruler who trusted no one. He defended his country's independence but failed to school Paraguay's citizens in democracy.[3] Opponents were exiled, imprisoned, tortured, or shot. The stability of the regime was due not only to repression but also to Francia's policy of building an imaginary "Chinese wall" around the country to restrict foreign contacts, especially with Argentina.

This draconian ban on travel and trade with the outside world had little effect on the masses, but it was a death sentence to Paraguay's creole elite. Naturally, some of the members of this elite rebelled. Following the discovery of an 1821 plot against his life, Francia destroyed the financial base of his elite opponents by taxing them and confiscating their property. Many were shot, imprisoned, or exiled. Francia destroyed the elite's social base by making marriages between whites illegal. He also imposed his total control on the church and the army, which were kept lean but moderately well equipped.

By 1840 Francia's class leveling had made Paraguayan nationalism hard to separate from Paraguayan racial identity. State lands confiscated from the rich and the church had been leased to the poor. State farms and factories for armaments, ironworks, and shipbuilding had been founded and ran at a profit. Income from expropriations, state monopolies on tobacco and yerba, and profits from state industries had allowed Francia's government to survive virtually without taxes, and surplus farm produce and livestock had been handed out to peasants. Francia left an independent, introspective, self-sufficient, and reasonably prosperous nation whose psychological, genetic, and linguistic foundations were unassailable. When he died, Paraguayans were probably better off than at any previous moment in their history. But they understood that they owed these things to Francia.[4]

After Francia's death a freely elected 1841 Congress of 500 delegates chose a mestizo lawyer named Carlos Antonio López as first consul. López ruled until his death in 1862. As under Francia, opposition was out of the question, and state regulations applied to all aspects of society. Unlike Francia, López enriched himself and founded a dynasty. He also strengthened national defense, got Paraguay international recognition, stimulated economic development, and built schools. By 1862 Paraguay had a reputation as being one of the most progressive countries in South America.

Raised as his heir-apparent, Carlos Antonio's son Francisco Solano López was named president by an 1862 Congress. The younger López set out to make Paraguay a regional power, aiming to forge a "third force" with Uruguay to counter South America's behemoths, Brazil and Argentina. Troubled by Brazilian meddling in Uruguay, López declared war on Brazil in 1864 and soon sent a 30,000-man army against the combined forces of Argentina, Brazil, and the latter's puppet, Uruguay.

The allies easily routed the invasion and soon went on the offensive. The hostilities became a war of attrition, a virtual holocaust that all but erased Paraguay from the map. The Triple Alliance War ended in 1870 when López died in battle. It had killed more than half of Paraguay's population (220,000 were left out of 525,000, including only 20,000–30,000 males), stripped over 60,000 square miles (155,400 square kilometers) of territory, and was responsible for an indemnity of nearly 19 million gold pesos.

The next chapter of the nation's history opened under conditions of defeat, devastation, and foreign domination. In 1870 the occupation forces (who stayed until 1876) set up a provisional government that imposed a constitution which was never more than a scrap of paper. Based on the U.S. and the Argentine constitutions, this liberal and democratic document was an alien imposition and unsuited to Paraguay's political culture. Caudillos used the militia as a private army; the government used fraud or violence to deter opponents; elections were farcical.

In 1887 the politically articulate coalesced into two parties: the Colorados, who claimed to be the political heirs of Solano López and branded their more-educated opponents as enemy collaborators for participating in the Argentine-sponsored Paraguayan Legion, and the Liberals, who professed to believe in representative government, free elections, private property, and minimum state intervention. In fact, both parties advocated the same free-trade, laissez-faire policies. Party loyalties in Paraguay are fierce but hereditary and not based on ideology. Former members of the Paraguayan Legion became prominent Colorados; former López officers became influential Liberals. Both groups—the Colorados (Reds) and the Liberals (Blues)—were personalist parties and engaged in violence, electoral fraud, and opportunism.

The economy was prostrate for many years after 1870. Foreign speculators, mainly Argentines, manipulated local finances and plunged the country into debt. During 1883–1887 the Colorado regime sold off vast quantities of state-owned lands in large parcels at low prices. Yet the Liberals had advocated the same policies. By 1935 nineteen companies owned over half the country, and peasants had been driven from plots their families had farmed for generations. For the first time, many Paraguayans began to emigrate. While politicians stole or squandered the revenue from land sales, Argentine, British, North American, French, and Italian business interests gained control of important segments of local industry and agriculture. Backed by Brazil, the Colorado party founder Gen. Bernardino Caballero dominated Paraguayan politics for thirty years, making and unmaking presidents.

The Twentieth Century

Crowned by the longest dictatorship in modern Latin American history, the twentieth century brought unparalleled disaster to Paraguay. Although some prosperity, trade, and intellectual life increased after 1900, the country endured three civil wars—in 1904, 1922, and the most serious, 1947. With help from Argentina, three decades of Colorado party rule gave way in 1904 to three decades of Liberal rule.

A new turning point came in 1932 when Paraguay and Bolivia went to war over the desolate, unpopulated Chaco region. Although Bolivia's German-trained and -equipped army enjoyed every paper advantage, the better-motivated Paraguayans soon advanced to the foothills of the Andes amid scenes of ferocious combat. A 1935 truce produced an international peace conference and a 1938 treaty that gave Paraguay virtually all the contested area (20,000 square miles [51,800 square kilometers]).

But the Chaco War unleashed a period of unprecedented social upheaval and political mobilization. In an event that plunged the military into politics, the army overthrew President Eusebio Ayala in February 1936 and installed war hero Rafael Franco as president, an act that virtually destroyed the Liberals as a political force.[5] An unstable amalgam of diverse and incompatible political tendencies—including communism, fascism, and liberalism—the revolutionary Febreristas gave Paraguayans an eight-hour day and the right to strike. They also expropriated about 500,000 acres (200,000 hectares) of land for distribution to peasant families. But this "socially conscious" government was overthrown by more-conservative sectors of the army (possibly with foreign encouragement) in August 1937.

Following a two-year interregnum dominated by "new" Liberals (with an authoritarian rather than a laissez-faire outlook), Paraguay endured eight years of despotism during 1940–1948 under the openly pro-Nazi regime of Higinio Morínigo.[6] Placing Paraguay's social and economic institutions under state control, Morínigo guaranteed military support by spending about half the national budget on the armed forces.

World War II brought prosperity to Paraguay as demand for its agricultural exports mushroomed and foreign funds became available. But the defeat of Germany and Japan introduced pressures for liberalization. In July 1946, after allowing exiles to return and the Liberal, Febrerista, and Communist parties to operate freely, Morínigo formed a Colorado-Febrerista coalition government. Six months later the Colorado party–military coup of January 13, 1947, ruptured the coalition. The Concepción garrison revolted against the coup, and about 80 percent of the officer corps defected to the rebels, setting the stage for a desperate and bloody civil war that raged for almost a year. Poor rebel leadership, timely help from Argentine dictator Juan Perón, and quickly organized units of armed Colorado peasants[7] saved Morínigo's government and defeated the only group in Paraguayan history willing to fight for democracy.

The Colorado party emerged from the civil war strong enough to depose Morínigo in 1948, which set the stage for a messy power struggle. While opposition Liberals and Febreristas were severely repressed and sent into exile, Colorado factions staged a series of coups and short-lived regimes. Some stability returned in September 1949 when Federico Chaves became president. But Chaves was just beginning his second term when the commander in chief of the armed forces, Gen. Alfredo Stroessner, dumped him on May 4, 1954. Backed by a Colorado party faction, Stroessner was elected president and inaugurated on August 15, 1954. He remained in power until February 3, 1989. Proving even more durable than Francia, he held power longer than any modern political leader in the Western Hemisphere (Fidel Castro is now the longest-ruling head of state in the region), and Stroessner won his eighth consecutive term of office in 1988 with 89 percent of the vote.

The Stroessner Regime

After a shaky start, Stroessner consolidated his power gradually, using carrots and sticks to seduce and divide the opposition. He was aided by a thoroughly purged Colorado party, which he put in charge of politics (under an amended version of the 1940 constitution); a privileged armed forces and secret police to guarantee the system; and timely support from Brazil and the United States. By 1960 Stroessner had silenced most of his domestic critics by throwing dissidents of every stripe into jail, suppressing internal revolts, and defeating invasions by Paraguayan exiles based in Brazil and Argentina.

The Stroessner regime eventually faced sharp criticism from abroad about its handling of human rights, including accusations of torture and murder. Journalists, peasants, workers, church officials, opposition party members, petty thieves—all were liable to be detained, imprisoned, or tortured at the whim of the police, without recourse to due process of law. Detainees were punched, kicked, beaten with clubs, immersed in tanks of filthy water, and subjected to torture by electric shock. By the 1970s Stroessner had made Paraguay a stereotype for human rights abuse and state terrorism. Yet the situation improved after 1979, when Stroessner, as a result of prompting by the United States, released hundreds of political prisoners from Paraguayan jails. After that time torture of political prisoners was rare.

Stroessner founded a system that seems capable of surviving his 1989 political demise. At its core is the party–armed forces–government triad. The military serves as the system's guarantor, the party is the primary instrument of patronage and social control, and the government regulates the system in favor of the regime's supporters. The triad's central element was Stroessner himself, the system's architect, who held all the strings, who alone was able to co-opt or repress internal opposition to his rule.

Although Stroessner successfully resisted any fundamental changes in the regime, the succession issue torpedoed him in the end. In 1987 the ruling Colorado party fractured during the run-up to the 1988 elections. With obvious covert support from Stroessner, the *militante* faction seized control of the party convention by using police to bar the *tradicionalistas* from entering the convention hall. Sickly and increasingly frail throughout 1988,[8] Stroessner evidently wished to surround himself with people who were 100 percent loyal to him.[9] The traditionalist "old guard" unsettled Stroessner because its members saw that Stroessner's interests and those of the Colorado party were not necessarily identical. Top army officers, including Gen. Andrés Rodríguez, disliked the militants, whom they viewed as usurpers.

General Rodríguez launched his February 1989 coup when the militants clumsily tried to force his resignation as commander of the Paraguayan First Army Corps to clear the way for the president's son, Gustavo Stroessner (who was eventually to succeed his father). But General Rodríguez preferred rebellion to resignation, and a brief battle at the Presidential Escort Battalion on the night of February 2–3 decided the issue. Rodríguez quickly consolidated his support within the Armed Forces and within the more modern wing of the Colorado party. He surprised many by promising political liberalization and reform. In a whirlwind presidential campaign in the spring of 1989, Rodríguez became a popular figure. He easily defeated five opposition presidential candidates in balloting on May 1 that was scrutinized by international observers and generally accepted as open and honest. Rodríguez was inaugurated on May 15 for a five-year term of office.

SOCIAL GROUPS AND POLITICAL OPPOSITION

Mass-based pressure groups organized for collective action are only just beginning to appear in Paraguay, where patronage and clientelism have always prevailed. Although independent trade and peasant unions started to show their strength in the mid-1980s, the country's only firmly entrenched institutions with a nationwide network of personnel remain the military, the church, and the Colorado party. Businesspeople and landowners either favor the regime or keep a low profile.

The electoral process gave Stroessner and the Colorados an effective way to legitimize their rule while repressing any true opposition. With a lock on the electoral apparatus, the Colorado party routinely racked up huge majorities in all parts of the country, Colorado candidates sometimes setting 100 percent or more of the vote in rural areas.[10] The political opposition in Paraguay is weak, fragmented, given to petty rivalries and caudillismo and is an uncertain vehicle for democratization. In 1979, with support from U.S. Ambassador Robert White, a vocal advocate of President Jimmy Carter's human rights policy, the major opposition groups banded together in the National Accord, an umbrella organization that attempts to coordinate opposition strategy. After the February 1989 coup Paraguay's opposition groups seemed more disposed to cooperate with each other, but Paraguay's electoral law forbids coalitions.

By promising "real democracy, not just a facade," by promising free elections and respect for human rights, President Rodríguez has transformed Paraguay's political landscape. Within days of the coup Rodríguez allowed banned opposition newspapers and radio stations to reemerge[11] and promised fundamental changes in Paraguay's electoral law and constitution.[12] It is widely accepted that the presidential campaign and May 1 election were the most honest in the country's history, with widespread participation and freedom of expression.

Under the leadership of Partido Liberal Radical Auténtico (PLRA) president Domingo Laíno, the Liberals are the Colorado party's most formidable opponents. As one of Paraguay's two traditional parties, the Liberals still retain a mass following in the countryside. Laíno is a former professor of economics and congressman whose antiregime speeches earned him Stroessner's wrath. The victim of torture and countless detentions (he was arrested at least four times in 1988), Laíno was allowed into Paraguay in 1987 after five years in exile. Within weeks he had launched an audacious and unprecedented political campaign, addressing about 140,000 people at mass rallies in country towns. Laíno's respectable second-place vote in the presidential elections in May 1989 assure him an important role in future political developments.

Unlike the PLRA, the Partido Revolutionario Febrerista (PRF) has been a legal party for the past twenty years. Confined mainly to the capital (membership is probably less than 5,000), Febrerismo is Paraguay's indigenous socialist party, similar in some ways to Aprismo in Peru. Its membership is still a diverse and somewhat inchoate ideological mixture that the party inherited from its early years, but the party's youth looks to European social democracy for inspiration. The PRF has more influence than its numbers imply because it has attracted accomplished professionals and intellectuals to its ranks. The PRF president is the youthful Euclides Acevedo, whom one retired U.S. diplomat has called Paraguay's "toughest, smartest" political operator.

Launched in 1960 the Christian-Democratic movement became a political party in 1965. Although this party maintains close ties with the church, its political following numbers a meager 2,000 but nonetheless contains some influential businesspeople. Its goals include agrarian reform and ending government control of the universities and labor unions. The Christian Democrats have undeniable growth potential because they are positioned to attract support from the church's lay organizations.

The rebel Colorado Popular Movement (MOPOCO) broke ranks with Stroessner in 1959 because of his dictatorial tendencies, and for thirty years MOPOCOs were treated like Paraguay's Trotskyites. As Stroessner's principal bugaboo, MOPOCO launched various unsuccessful guerrilla movements from exile and maintained a strong if shadowy presence within the Colorado party. A long-standing member of the National Accord, MOPOCO quickly abandoned its erstwhile opposition allies and joined the Colorado party's Junta de Gobierno (Governing Council) in a somewhat amazing flip-flop during Rodríguez's post-coup version of Paraguayan *glasnost*.

Other opposition groups include the Popular Democratic Movement (MDP), a left-leaning group of activist-minded students and young people that has emerged only since 1985. Caught in Paraguay's peculiar time warp, this group advocates the political ideology of the so-called Dependency School, which makes it circa 1968 in its thinking. Finally, the Communist party of Paraguay (PCP), founded in the 1930s with student and labor support, was legal for only nine months during 1946–1947. In 1984 its membership of about 3,500 lived mainly in exile in various Latin American and European countries, and PCP action within Paraguay is minimal.[13]

Another persistent opposition voice in Paraguay, in many ways the focal point of the opposition, is the Catholic church. In the late 1960s the church dropped its traditional political neutrality and began to work for social reform. It also began to criticize Stroessner's reelections, the regime's human rights violations and its treatment of political prisoners, the inequitable distribution of wealth, and official corruption. Opposed to the continued concentration of land holdings, the church organized Christian "land leagues" and peasant cooperatives to resist tenant evictions. Stroessner answered with repression, closing church publications and newspapers, expelling non-Paraguayan priests, arresting and sometimes shooting activists and peasants. The church has retaliated by excommunicating government officials accused of engaging in torture and corruption.[14] The church's cohesiveness strengthened its position despite repression, and the Stroessner regime played the uncomfortable role of host to Pope John Paul II during his May 1988 visit when he called for democracy and respect for human rights.

Paraguay's low level of industrialization has limited the political roles of labor and capital. Economic enterprises are small, class consciousness is low, and personal (not professional) relationships between employers and workers prevail. Business as a corporate group is also weak, partly because foreigners own many of the country's financial institutions and industries. In general, local businesspeople favor the regime and its political and monetary stability and collaborate with the government. Foreign absentee landlords and wealthier local landlords have consistently supported Stroessner and the Colorado party, and the extremely skewed landholding patterns that have prevailed since the 1880s work in their favor.

Until the mid-1980s the state preempted, co-opted, or suppressed any signs of independent labor-organizing activity, controlling organized labor directly through the government-sponsored Paraguayan Confederation of Workers (CPT) since 1959. During the 1960s and 1970s the CPT never organized a strike and was expelled from the International Confederation of Free Trade Unions (ICFTU) in 1979.

This repression-induced labor peace lasted only until the end of the Itaipú boom in 1981, when various groups began to secede from the CPT and new groups began to appear. The most important labor group in the country is the Movimiento Intersindical de Trabajadores (MIT), an umbrella organization for various unions representing about 6,000 workers who defected from the CPT.[15] Its birth around 1985–1986 was accompanied by street demonstrations and mass arrests. Still, less than 12,000 of Paraguay's 1.3 million wage earners are organized. No worker in Paraguay has the right to strike, and rural workers (40.4 percent of the labor force is engaged in agriculture) enjoy few of the benefits given urban labor.

University students traditionally have been the most outspoken critics of the Paraguayan government, although they reached the high-water mark of their political activism in 1959. Politically independent students issue publications, hold seminars on social issues, demonstrate against the regime, and often work with the church, but constant police harassment has prevented them from organizing effectively. The population of Paraguay is extremely young,[16] but decades of one-party rule have robbed many young people of their idealism.

GOVERNMENT MACHINERY

Since 1936 no Paraguayan president has remained in power without military support. In the absence of a genuine aristocracy based on wealth and birth, the armed forces have emerged as the nation's economic and social elite. Officers use their influence to secure government jobs for friends and relations, and senior officers hold top civil-service jobs as cabinet ministers and administrators of autonomous government agencies.

Since 1947 Colorado party members have been the direct beneficiaries of the political system. Practically all government and military jobs (including judgeships) require party membership. The Colorado party (like the other traditional party, the Liberals) is a patronage organization that has consistently restricted political participation when in power. Party membership is not based on ideology as much as on family ties and interpersonal relationships, and factional differences are often more important than party differences. Earlier in the century political leaders did not hesitate to form coalitions with factions from opposing parties, but the present electoral law forbids coalitions.

Paraguay's current constitution[17] is based on the 1940 document that President Félix Estigarribia wrote to ease his assumption of dictatorial powers, a constitution that reflected Paraguay's economic, social, and political realities. The liberal state was dead. Instead, a vaguely corporatist structure emerged that abandoned the pretense of equality between the executive, legislative, and judicial branches. The new constitution placed the state at the apex of a regime that regulated, controlled, penetrated, distributed. It also put the president unambiguously at the head of the state.

The president is elected by popular vote for an unlimited number of five-year terms. He appoints the cabinet, prepares the budget, conducts foreign relations, appoints government officials, and commands the armed forces.[18] In addition, the president controls local administration, having the power to appoint the head of each of Paraguay's nineteen administrative departments. The 1967 constitution provides for a bicameral Congress consisting of a Senate and a Chamber of Deputies, but Congress is little more than an appendage of the executive. The same is true of the judiciary. Although the constitution provides for a Council of State to render opinions on laws and matters of economic or international policy, the executive routinely ignores the council when making policy decisions.[19]

PUBLIC POLICY AND THE ECONOMY

Paraguay experienced a "miracle decade" during the 1970s when its gross domestic product (GDP) grew 8–10 percent a year, outpacing all other South American economies. The boom was sparked by the completion of a road from Asunción via Puerto Presidente Stroessner to duty-free port facilities at Paranaguá on the Brazilian coast and by rapid increases in the prices of Paraguay's main exports, cotton and soybeans. These facts, plus an abundance of cheap, fertile land near the Brazilian border, produced an agricultural land rush.

Yet the main economic influence during this period was the construction of the giant Itaipú hydroelectric project on the Paraná River between Paraguay and Brazil, which cost close to $20 billion. With an installed generating capacity of 12.6 million kilowatts, Itaipú is the world's largest hydroelectric generating plant. The Itaipú project employed thousands of Paraguayan campesinos who had never before held jobs and fundamentally altered Paraguay's status as a lethargic backwater.[20]

Corruption increased markedly during the 1970s and 1980s as the Itaipú bonanza pumped money into the economy and as Paraguay gained more access to the Brazilian economy (tenth largest in the world). Paraguay's proximity to Brazil and Argentina makes it an ideal smugglers' haven—the true *industria paraguaya* has always been contraband. The main items in this illicit trade (whose value probably exceeds that of legal trade) are agricultural produce from Brazil (particularly soybeans and coffee), liquor, perfume, consumer electronics, household appliances, cigars and cigarettes, stolen Brazilian automobiles, and drugs. Stroessner's frequent use of the phrase, El contrabando es el precio de paz ("Contraband is the price of peace") was a tacit admission that he was allowing his associates and underlings to get "a piece of the action" and reaping the political dividends.[21]

The same conditions that make Paraguay a smugglers' paradise also make it an ideal base for drug runners, and smugglers have sent an increasing amount of cocaine to Europe and the United States from there. The country's notoriety as a drug entrepôt began during the 1960s when Mafia operators used it as a privileged haven for a lucrative heroin smuggling business run from Marseilles, France, known as "the Latin Connection." Masterminded by August (André) Ricord, the drug ring used Paraguay as a transit point for heroin worth an estimated $2.5 million a year. In 1972, when Stroessner agreed to extradite Ricord after President Richard Nixon had threatened to cut off U.S. aid, Ricord's biggest defenders inside Paraguay were identified as chief of police investigations Pastor Coronel, Gen. Patricio Colmán, and Gen. Andrés Rodríguez.[22]

Cocaine smuggled across the Chaco from Bolivia and a thriving trade in bootlegged marijuana destined for Brazil have replaced heroin as the main concerns of U.S. officials. Cocaine is linked to the heroin problem of the 1970s but is probably more serious for several reasons. Unlike heroin, cocaine distribution follows well-established smuggling routes, and canny drug traffickers see Paraguay as a less sophisticated and less vigilant place to ply their trade. Although coca probably is not grown within the country, Paraguay's vast and unpatrolled Chaco provides an ideal base for processing plants and landing strips. And the enormous profits associated with drugs have provided some highly placed regime supporters with income to replace the rake-offs and graft that dried up when the Itaipú project was completed in 1982. With U.S. prodding, some of this situation has changed. Notably, Paraguay has sharply increased penalties for drug offenders and has agreed to an aerial marijuana-spraying program financed by the United States.[23]

Changes in Paraguay's economy overshadowed politics for much of the 1980s. As the boom faded after 1982 and as prices for Paraguay's commodity exports fell, growth declined, and inflation and unemployment increased.[24] In 1983 around 12 percent of the labor force was unemployed (three times the average of the preceding decade). The GDP fell 2.5 percent in 1982 and 5 percent in 1983. Growth at 3–4 percent returned in 1984 and 1985 but paused in 1986 as Paraguay suffered one of its worst recorded droughts; positive growth rates returned in 1987 and 1988. In 1986 the labor force comprised 37 percent of the population.[25]

The government plays a highly significant role in Paraguay's economy as a regulator and promoter of investment and exports. In Paraguay, economic controls cover prices, wages, banking, and insurance. Certain farm products (primarily sugar and meat) receive price supports, subsidies, and marketing quotas. Despite its role as a regulator, government revenue and spending were 8 percent of GDP in 1986, the lowest figure for South America and one of the lowest in the developing world, where government spending often dominates economies. Even so, control of jobs in the public and semipublic sectors provides the regime with an important source of patronage. The state is directly involved in banking; public utilities and telecommunications; air, sea, and rail transportation; and cattle ranching. Its stake in industry includes ship repair, furniture factories, quarries, sawmills, meat-packing plants, and alcoholic beverage marketing.

The state has dealt with Paraguay's inability to finance investment domestically by opening the country to foreign investors, at the price of increasingly denationalizing the economy. Government policy encourages foreign capital through liberal tax benefits and measures such as Law 550, which provides fiscal and other incentives to promote investment in export industries and the less-developed departments of Alto Paraná, Nueva Asunción, Chaco, and Boquerón. Brazilians are the biggest investors in Paraguay, followed by investors from West Germany, the United States, Argentina, Japan, France, and Italy.

Paraguay's net external debt remained a constant 15 percent of GDP until the early 1980s. Although it quadrupled from $200 million in 1972 to almost $850 million in 1980, Paraguay's debt did not grow faster than the GDP. After 1982, however, the debt spiraled to over $2 billion in 1988, more than 50 percent of the GDP, and debt servicing reached 78.7 percent of export earnings.[26] Expanded public-sector borrowing—mostly in the form of "soft" loans from other countries (notably Brazil) and multilateral institutions (such as the World Bank)—was largely responsible for these increases. Part of the debt problem is also owing to the regime's sponsorship of costly and inefficient public-sector projects to provide new sources of patronage during a period of economic stagnation.[27]

Largely because of the contraband trade, Paraguay's debt situation is not as dire as that of its more powerful neighbors. Despite an estimated 1988 trade deficit in excess of $100 million, the private sector (which has little debt) does not depend on the government for access to foreign exchange. Smugglers pay cash, so many of Paraguay's imports are unaffected by balance-of-payments problems. In addition, Brazil, which needs Paraguay's continued cooperation on Itaipú, would be unlikely to turn the screws too tightly.

Although differences in income and cultural levels are not as extreme in Paraguay as elsewhere in Latin America, Itaipú money made many fortunes, and conspicuous consumption—and the resentments it produces—is on the rise. A small, tightly knit group, the members of the elite owe their positions mainly to their ties with the chief executive and the ruling party. The middle class contains professionals, middle-ranking officials, and a few people who have achieved modest prosperity in administration or business. About 80 percent of the population of Asunción is lower class.

Paraguay has a rural society. About 58 percent of Paraguayans lived outside of cities in 1980, only 7 percent less than the 1950 figure.[28] Events in the capital traditionally have little impact on the countryside. Agriculture, cattle raising, and lumbering have long been the bases of the economy,[29] and particularly important to agriculture in the 1970s were cotton and soybeans, which enjoyed four- and fivefold production increases. One of the least-industrialized nations in South America, the country's major imports include foodstuffs, machinery, transportation, equipment, fuel, and lubricants.

The biggest problem facing rural Paraguayans continues to be land tenure. According to the 1981 agricultural census, 1 percent of Paraguay's 275,000 farms (average size, 18,000 acres [7,300 hectares]) account for 79 percent of all land under cultivation, but 35 percent of all farms cultivate only 1 percent of the land.[30] The land provides subsistence but little monetary return, and in Paraguay, economic development has not reached the rural population.[31] Despite some improvements in education (literacy is 80.5 percent) and life expectancy (sixty-eight years in 1987, up from fifty-six years in 1960), 1986 per capita income was barely $1,000 (GDP was $3.4 billion), the lowest in South America aside from Bolivia. The government's efforts to resettle landless peasants in the undeveloped northeast helped Paraguay avoid the rampant urbanization so prevalent elsewhere in South America.[32]

THE INTERNATIONAL ARENA

Paraguay always has been unduly dependent on its giant neighbors, but since the 1950s Brazil has clearly become more important than Argentina. As late as 1969 Argentina was Paraguay's only important regional export market because Paraguay's road, rail, and river links with the outside world all passed directly through Argentine territory. But Argentina's share of Paraguay's regional exports fell to less than half in 1982 while Brazil's share rose from nothing to 58 percent.

Brazil began to court the Stroessner government almost from the beginning. It has paid for new buildings at the University of Asunción, built a bridge between the two countries across the Paraná River, offered Paraguay an alternate export outlet by creating a free port on the Brazilian coast at Paranaguá, and built a road linking Paraguay to the coast. Brasília became Asunción's major international partner when the 1973 Itaipú hydroelectric agreement was signed. Yet the treaty is highly controversial. Even Colorado politicians and the military fear that the Itaipú Treaty may undermine national sovereignty by linking the two countries so closely that Brazil will gain hegemony over the entire Paraguayan economy. Some Paraguayans compare their relationship with Brazil to that of Panama and the United States, calling Itaipú "our Panama Canal."[33]

Yet Stroessner proved that Paraguay can adjust the momentum of its relations with Brazil by signing a separate agreement with Buenos Aires for construction of hydroelectric projects on the Paraná at Yaciretá (3.3 million kilowatts—due to be completed in 1990) and at Corpus. The electricity that Corpus and Yaciretá will generate is less important for Paraguay than pushing the diplomatic pendulum toward Argentina,[34] and the swing may be coming at a good moment for Paraguay. Brazil has begun to protest the rampant car thefts that have provided Paraguay with 90,000 of the 264,000 vehicles on the road. Brazilian drivers who resist thieves are often murdered, and the Brazilian police have complained that Paraguayan gangsters offer drugs to Brazilian thieves to steal cars "to order."[35]

Until the mid-1970s no country in the world was more responsible for the stability of the Stroessner regime than the United States. Relations between Paraguay and the United States since World War II have been conditioned by overlapping interests in security matters, trade, and investment and by Paraguay's desire for military and development assistance. Paraguay has voted with the United States more consistently than any other South American country in the Organization of American States and the United Nations. Since 1961 the United States has given Paraguay over $31 million in military aid, police training, and matériel; since 1954 Paraguay has received over $210 million in U.S. economic and technical assistance. Paraguay has also proved a safe and profitable market for U.S. foreign investment.

After the mid-1970s the repressive, pro-U.S., and staunchly anti-Communist Stroessner regime seemed less alluring to U.S. policymakers. U.S. policy about-faced under President Jimmy Carter among other things, and although Stroessner released hundreds of political prisoners, he remained indifferent to democratic niceties and was not easily threatened by Washington, particularly since U.S. influence and aid had declined. Calls by the Reagan administration and Ambassador Clyde Taylor (who ended his tour in mid-1988) for a democratic transition in Paraguay evoked only scathing hostility from the Stroessner regime. The Colorado party media insulted Taylor, calling him "a treacherous and caustic big mouth" and "a defamer and blasphemer with a diplomatic sinecure," and the ambassador was teargassed in February 1987 as he attended a meeting of a democratic women's group.

Because of Paraguay's continuing refusal to grant rights to organized labor, the United States withdrew trade benefits to Paraguay in 1987 under the Generalized System of Preferences (GSP)—worth about $2 million annually—and in 1988 the U.S. Congress almost decertified Paraguay as a recipient of aid from multilateral development banks because of allegations of noncooperation with U.S. drug enforcement efforts. In fact, although cocaine from Paraguay has been seized in Miami, Paraguay allowed the U.S. Drug Enforcement Agency to open an office in Asunción in 1988. Aside from the $125,000 Paraguay still gets for police training and the popular Peace Corps program (which has plans to sponsor around 200 volunteers in Paraguay), the United States wields only moral influence in Paraguay. But moral influence nonetheless remains a surprisingly potent force in the minds of ordinary civilians and soldiers and will be an important element in a democratic transition.

A notable feature of Paraguayan foreign relations in the 1980s is the country's growing ties with the Orient, especially South Korea, Taiwan, and Japan, a trend that threatens to undermine Paraguay's ethnic balance. Paraguay's retail trade is largely in the hands of its 12,000 Korean residents, Hong Kong Chinese are coming to Paraguay by the hundreds, and about 50,000 Paraguayans (1 percent of the population) are of Japanese descent. Japan's new multimillion-dollar cultural center in Asunción makes the U.S. center look like an outhouse.

PROSPECTS FOR THE FUTURE

Since the coup of February 2–3, 1989, and the elections of May 1, Paraguay is headed either for political democracy or for a more liberal version of Stroessner's regime. With the legalization of the PLRA and the Christian Democratic party (PDC), Paraguay's political lineup is out in the open. Improvements in freedom of speech and the press are startling, as is the general mood in Asunción. Paraguayans are glad to be rid of Alfredo Stroessner. How long this period of liberalization will last and where it will end are the main political questions in Paraguay today.

An observer of the post-coup political scene is struck by simultaneous and equivalent reasons for pessimism and optimism. For instance, many of the principal figures in Stroessner's government remained in jail at the end of 1989, awaiting trial for corruption. On the other hand, nearly everyone in Rodríguez's government once worked for Stroessner. The May 1, 1989, elections were the freest in Paraguay's history, but they were still run by the same team that used to run Stroessner's phony elections. And Paraguay's electoral law still bans coalitions and gives the majority party two-thirds of the seats in Congress. Rodríguez has allowed press freedoms that have no parallel in recent memory, but Rodríguez is a Paraguayan general who gained power in a bloody coup. Will he hesitate to restrict civil liberties if they start to cost him politically?

Yet the path before any would-be dictator is rough, for several reasons. Dictatorship, as practiced by Stroessner, is discredited in Paraguay, and popular expectations for civil liberties, democracy, and human rights are high. The entire South American continent is moving toward some form of democracy, and current international conditions are not favorable to dictatorships. Civil liberties, once granted, are hard to take back, so dictatorship, for the moment, is probably out.

Those comments do not mean that Paraguay is on the road to democracy. In the first place, there is no evidence that anyone within the ruling group wants to undo the armed forces–Colorado party–government triad that has ruled the country for forty years. Rodríguez, the winner of the May 1 elections, is the army's highest-ranking general and a Colorado party member. The army is not considering retiring from politics; the Colorado party is hardly mulling over getting a divorce from the army. No member of the government could remotely be classified as a "democrat."[36] Once again, change has come to Paraguay from the top, without the participation of Paraguay's citizens. Paraguay's ruling elite is used to doing business "the old-fashioned way" and may well find democratic forms annoying and inconvenient. Yet Rodríguez's political honeymoon may last for some time, particularly because the publisher of Asunción's largest independent newspaper, *ABC Color*, is favorably disposed toward his regime.[37]

Paraguay's connections with the Far East give Rodríguez a certain leeway. Japan was very generous with Stroessner in his last years of rule and seldom, if ever, protested Paraguay's lack of democracy. This uncritical support from Japan, and from South Korea and Taiwan, is likely to continue. In addition, the leaders of Brazil's armed forces are favorably disposed toward Rodríguez—yet Brazil's soldiers increasingly view the Paraguayan drug trade as a national security problem and may well conclude that more democratization will help Paraguay clamp down. The United States will continue to be democracy's cheerleader in Paraguay and may be able to expand its influence if it reinstates Paraguay in the GSP.

The best chance for democratic change (and for political instability) in Paraguay will come whenever a breakdown occurs in Paraguay's ruling triad. It may not prove as durable as it now appears. Stroessner's iron-fisted rule was as much directed against dissenters within the ruling group as it was against his political opposition, and the unity of Paraguay's ruling class was a condition that Stroessner imposed on it, not one it accepted voluntarily. Stroessner was a genius at keeping competing interests and individuals in line and loyal to him; Rodríguez may not prove as skilled. Competition and internal dissension may force a critical split between the military and civilians.

Another possibility is an increase in power and influence of the so-called institutionalist tendency within the armed forces, which would like to see the military play a more professional, more politically neutral, and less corrupt role in Paraguayan society. Stroessner gave this group no chance to develop, using corruption and official favors as a means of commanding personal loyalty from the people around him. But economic reality has already begun to force Paraguay to clean up its economic house. The scope for corruption and bonanzas like Itaipú and charcoal-burning steel plants will narrow, making professionalization an unavoidable option. Another possibility for change lies in the growth of the private sector, which will soon be larger than the public sector. Once private businesspeople (assuming they are not soldiers or officials) have more economic clout than the government, they will eventually be in a position to force a rewrite of Paraguay's "rules of the game."

NOTES

1. Paraguay had three rulers during its first sixty years of independence: José Gaspar Rodriguez de Francia (1814–1840), Carlos Antonio López (1842–1862), and Francisco Solano López (1862–1870). In contrast, the eighty years between 1870 and 1950 produced fifty rulers, six of whom completed their terms. The rest were deposed (with the exception of Higinio Morínigo, who was reelected) or did not finish their terms. One president, Bautista Gill, was assassinated in 1877.

2. Literally, "river of silver" or "river of money."

3. Francia probably did not think highly of Paraguayans, whom he once called *pura gente idiota* ("really stupid people").

4. See John Hoyt Williams, *The Rise and Fall of the Paraguayan Republic, 1800–1870* (Austin: University of Texas Press, 1979), p. 99.

5. The Liberals had produced reasonably good governments in the 1920s and 1930s, but its leaders eventually were widely seen as an effete elite of cosmopolitan lawyers who served foreign interests. In addition, the Liberals had the bad luck to be in power during the Great Depression, when the world economy was deteriorating and totalitarian ideologies were becoming more fashionable. The fatal error of the Liberals was to underestimate the power of Paraguayan nationalism.

6. Morínigo came to power suddenly and unexpectedly when the hero of the Chaco War, President José Félix Estigarribia, died in a plane crash.

7. The so-called *py nandi* ("barefoot ones").

8. Stroessner was hospitalized at least twice in 1988 for various ailments that required surgery, and his work schedule was severely reduced to a few hours a day.

9. The so-called *quatrinomio* (the militant "inner circle") included Sabino Augusto Montanaro (minister of the interior and president of the Colorado party), Mario Abdo Benítez (Stroessner's private secretary), Adán Godoy Jiménez (minister of public health and social welfare), and J. Eugenio Jacquet (minister of justice and labor). The last three were secretaries of state and vice presidents of the Colorado party.

10. See Virginia M. Bouvier, "Decline of the Dictator: Paraguay at a Crossroads" (Washington, D.C.: Washington Office on Latin America, July 1988), p. 18.

11. The most important independent Paraguayan daily is *ABC Color* (which closed in March 1984 and reopened in March 1989). *Radio Ñanduti* (forced off the air in January 1987) and the Febrerista weekly *El Pueblo* (closed in August 1987) went back into operation after the coup. Other independent news media in Paraguay are the Catholic church's *Radio Caritás* and its weekly *Sendero*. Asunción supports several dailies, including *Diario Noticias*, *Ultima Hora*, and *Hoy*. The PLRA has launched its own newspaper to counter the Colorado party's well-funded *Patria*.

12. For example, he promised to legalize Paraguay's unrecognized opposition parties and discussed the possibility of limiting consecutive presidential terms to one.

13. Richard F. Staar, ed., *Yearbook on International Communist Affairs* (Stanford, Calif.: Hoover Institution Press, 1984), pp. 162–163.

14. See Paul Lewis, *Paraguay Under Stroessner* (Chapel Hill: University of North Carolina Press, 1980), pp. 189–198; see also Robert Fraser, ed., *Keesing's Contemporary Archives* (London: Longman Group Limited, 1976), number 27976.

15. MIT represents bank and construction workers, journalists and typesetters, transport and theater workers, among others.

16. At least 40 percent of the population is under the age of fifteen (see James W. Wilkie, *Statistical Abstract of Latin America* [Los Angeles: UCLA Latin American Center Publications, 1987], p. 112), and some sources estimate that 70 percent of Paraguayans are under thirty. An overwhelming majority of Paraguayans were brought up under the Stroessner dictatorship and have little firsthand experience of any other political system.

17. The constitution was rewritten in 1967, but it retained most of the framework of the 1940 constitution. Amendments ratified in 1967 and again in 1977 allowed Stroessner to remain in office longer than the constitution had originally prescribed.

18. Stroessner took advantage of the constitution's provision for emergency executive powers to rule Paraguay under a state of siege, nearly without interruption, for thirty-three years.

19. Under the 1967 constitution, the Council of State includes the archbishop of Asunción, the rector of the National University, the president of the Central Bank, cabinet members, retired members of the three branches of the armed forces, and representatives of corporate groups such as farmers, stock raisers, manufacturers, and commercial and labor leaders. The two agricultural representatives (one for farmers and one for stock raisers) and the three people who represent manufacturing, commerce, and labor are selected from slates prepared by the three trade organizations and submitted to the president for consideration. The Council of State and the National Congress have the constitutional power to name a provisional president "in case of resignation, incapacity, or death" of the elected president. Yet General Rodríguez became provisional president of Paraguay without recourse to this cumbersome and inconvenient constitutional procedure.

20. See Daniel Seyler, "The Economy," in *Paraguay: A Country Study* (Washington, D.C.: Government Printing Office, 1989). See also Werner Baer and Melissa Birch, "The International Economic Relations of a Small Country: The Case of Paraguay," *Economic Development and Cultural Change* 35:3 (April 1987):601–627.

21. Some critics claimed that military officers oversaw the activities of smuggling groups to diminish the potential for unauthorized violence; see Gregorio Selser, "Paraguay: Octavo Mandato Presidencial de Alfredo Stroessner" (unpublished paper presented to the Latin American Studies Association conference in New Orleans, March 1988), p. 10.

22. Paul Lewis, *Paraguay Under Stroessner* (Chapel Hill: University of North Carolina Press, 1980), p. 136.

23. Worth $100,000, this program began in the spring of 1989. No evidence has ever been found to prove that coca is grown or processed within Paraguay's borders.

24. For more than twenty years Paraguay's currency was among the most stable in the hemisphere. Paraguay's exchange rate was fixed at 126 guaranies to the U.S. dollar in 1961 and was not altered until the 1980s. In 1989, with inflation running at 30–40 percent annually, the rate exceeded 1,000 guaranies to the dollar. Inflation is still much less of a problem in Paraguay than elsewhere on the continent.

25. Seyler, "The Economy."

26. See "Foreign Economic Trends and Their Implications for the United States," Paraguay, FET 88-114 (Washington, D.C.: Department of Commerce, November 1988), p. 9.

27. One example is an uneconomic charcoal-burning steel plant outside Asunción that will cost over $400 million in borrowed Brazilian funds. Iron ore for the plant will be imported from Brazil.

28. But urbanization is not negligible. Over 18 percent of the population lived in Asunción in 1983, and over 40 percent lived in cities or towns; Wilkie, *Statistical Abstract.*

29. Although agriculture accounted for nearly all (98 percent) of registered export earnings and employed almost half (48 percent) of the labor force in 1987, it produced only about one-quarter of the GDP. On the other hand, manufacturing mainly processes agricultural raw materials. Otherwise, industry consists of small factories and handicraft workshops.

30. Seyler, "The Economy."

31. Health and sanitation needs are particularly acute: As of 1980, indoor water supplies and sewerage services reached 18.4 percent and 6.5 percent of the population, respectively; see Anibal Miranda, *Desarrollo y pobreza en Paraguay* (Rosslyn, Va.: Inter-American Foundation; Asunción: Comité de Iglesias para Ayudas de Emergencia, 1982), p. 156.

32. The Instituto de Bienestar Rural helped resettle 41,000 peasant families to the sparsely populated eastern border region during the 1960s and 1970s. This figure may represent 225,000 Paraguayans; see Fran Gillespie, "Comprehending the Slow Pace of Urbanization in Paraguay Between 1950 and 1972," *Economic Development and Cultural Change* 31:2 (January 1983):355–375. Two other elements were at work: (1) Up to 1 million Paraguayans have emigrated, mainly to Argentina and mainly for economic reasons; (2) new road construction opened up previously inaccessible forest areas in eastern Paraguay during the 1970s, attracting new settlers and expatriate Paraguayans fleeing the Argentine economic downturn.

33. One obvious sign of growing Brazilian leverage is the 300,000–400,000 Brazilians who have moved to eastern Paraguay, where they now outnumber native Paraguayans. In this region, Portuguese has replaced Guaraní as the vernacular, and monetary transactions typically are conducted in Brazilian currency.

34. See Melissa H. Birch, "Pendulum Politics: Paraguayan Economic Diplomacy, 1940–1975" (Darden Graduate School of Business Administration, University of Virginia, 1988, Mimeograph).

35. Early in 1988 Paraguay acceded to Brazil's demand to expel the Paraguayan consul and Paranaguá port director Justo Eris Almada, a close associate of President Stroessner. The Brazilians had accused him of owning and operating a fleet of stolen Brazilian trucks.

36. Rodríguez himself has refused to call Stroessner a dictator, pointing out that he was reelected repeatedly by large margins and had the support of the people.

37. Aldo Zuccolillo, editor and publisher of *ABC Color*, has been quoted as saying that Rodríguez "is the general we've been waiting for to lead us to democracy."

SUGGESTIONS FOR FURTHER READING

Baer, Werner, and Melissa H. Birch. "Expansion of the Economic Frontier: Paraguayan Growth in the 1970s." *World Development* 12:8 (1984):783–798.

———. "The International Economic Relations of a Small Country: The Case of Paraguay." *Economic Development and Cultural Change* 35:3 (April 1987):601–627.

Bourne, Richard. *Political Leaders of Latin America*. Harmondsworth, Eng.: Penguin Books, 1969.

Bouvier, Virginia. "Decline of the Dictator: Paraguay at a Crossroads." Washington, D.C.: Washington Office on Latin America, July 1988.

Box, Pelham Horton. *The Origins of the Paraguay War*. New York: Russell and Russell, 1967.

Caraman, Philip. *The Lost Paradise*. London: Sidgwick and Jackson, 1975.

Chaves, Julio César. *El Supremo Dictador*. Madrid: Ediciones Atlas, 1964.

Corvalan, Grazziella. *Paraguay: Nación bilingüe*. Asunción: Centro Paraguayo de Estudios Sociológicos, 1981.

Graham, R.B. Cunninghame. *A Vanished Arcadia*. New York: Dial Press, 1924.

Grow, Michael. *The Good Neighbor Policy and Authoritarianism in Paraguay*. Lawrence: Regents Press of Kansas, 1981.

Latin American Bureau. *Paraguay Power Game*. Nottingham, Eng.: Latin American Bureau, 1980.

Lewis, Paul H. *Politics of Exile: Paraguay's Febrerista Party*. Chapel Hill: University of North Carolina Press, 1968.

———. *Paraguay Under Stroessner*. Chapel Hill: University of North Carolina Press, 1980.

———. *Socialism, Liberalism, and Dictatorship in Paraguay*. New York: Praeger, 1982.

Miranda, Anibal. *Apuntes sobre el desarrollo paraguayo 1940–1973*. Asunción: Universidad Católica "Nuestra Señora de la Asunción," 1980.

———. *Desarrollo y pobreza en Paraguay*. Rosslyn, Va.: Inter-American Foundation; Asunción: Comité de Iglesias para Ayudas de Emergencia, 1982.

Paraguay: A Country Study. Washington, D.C.: Government Printing Office, 1989.

Pastore, Carlos. *La Lucha por la Tierra en el Paraguay*. Montevideo: Editorial Antequera, 1972.

Pendle, George. *Paraguay: A Riverside Nation*. London: Oxford University Press, 1967.

Rivarola, Domingo M., et al. *La Población del Paraguay*. Asunción: Centro Paraguayo de Estudios Sociológicos, 1974.

Rout, Leslie B. *Politics of the Chaco Peace Conference, 1935–1939*. Latin American Monographs no. 19. Austin: Institute of Latin American Studies, University of Texas, 1970.

Service, Elman R., and Helen S. Service. *Tobati: Paraguayan Town*. Chicago: University of Chicago Press, 1954.

Warren, Harris Gaylord. *Paraguay: An Informal History*. Norman: University of Oklahoma Press, 1949.

―――――. *Paraguay and the Triple Alliance: The Postwar Decade.* Austin: Institute of Latin American Studies, University of Texas, 1978.

Washburn, Charles A. *The History of Paraguay.* New York: AMS Press, 1973.

Wilkie, James W., and David Lorey, eds. *Statistical Abstract of Latin America.* Los Angeles: UCLA Latin America Center Publications, 1987.

Williams, John Hoyt. *The Rise and Fall of the Paraguayan Republic, 1800–1870.* Austin: University of Texas Press, 1979.

Ynsfran, Pablo Max, ed. *The Epic of the Chaco: Marshal Estigarribia's Memoirs of the Chaco War, 1932–1935.* New York: Greenwood Press, 1969.

Zook, David H., Jr. *The Conduct of the Chaco War.* New Haven, Conn.: Bookman, 1960.

16
Bolivia:
Revolution and Reaction

EDUARDO A. GAMARRA
JAMES M. MALLOY

On April 9–11, 1952, Víctor Paz Estenssoro and the Movimiento Nacionalista Revolucionario (MNR) led Bolivian workers, peasants, and displaced middle sectors in one of the most profound social revolutions of twentieth-century Latin America. In a short time the new revolutionary regime had nationalized 80 percent of the nation's mining industry, declared universal suffrage, downgraded the armed forces, and approved a broad agrarian reform program that ended a system of Indian semi-servitude. Although the MNR destroyed the old order, it was incapable of establishing a new order; thus the revolution remained incomplete. In November 1964 a military coup ended twelve years of single-party rule; however, Bolivian political life during the next two decades was shaped by the dynamics unleashed by the revolution and the reactions of national and international groups. Moreover, the military regimes that ruled Bolivia until 1982 followed the basic contours of the state-led development strategy initiated by the MNR.

As in other nations in the region, beginning in the late 1970s the Bolivian military attempted an orderly withdrawal from politics, but civilian rule was not achieved until 1982 when Hernán Siles Zuazo, one of the founders of the MNR, was elected president. During a hapless three-year period, however, Siles presided over a 26,000 percent hyperinflation rate, the highest ever recorded in Latin America and the seventh highest in world history.

At age seventy-eight, Víctor Paz Estenssoro returned to the presidency in 1985 for the fourth time since 1952. His return to the presidency was dramatic. In what many people deem a major reversal of the revolution, Paz stabilized the economy and established the basis for the short-term survival of political democracy in Bolivia. Paz has ended the chapter begun by the revolution and has initiated one that will be written throughout the 1990s.

Bolivia

POPULATION, GEOGRAPHY, AND LOCATION

The political turmoil that has characterized Bolivia's history is partially rooted in its racial, geographic, and ethnic diversity. With 424,000 square miles (1,098,160 square kilometers), about the size of Texas and California combined, Bolivia is the sixth-largest country in South America. Relative to its geographic size, however, Bolivia has a very small population (in 1988, 6.5 million). Over one-half of the population (52 percent) is rural; over 50 percent of this sector is concentrated in the Andean departments of La Paz, Oruro, and Potosi. Less than one-fourth of the population lives in the eastern interior, which constitutes 59 percent of the national territory. In 1988 only three cities had a population of over 200,000 and only two, La Paz and Santa Cruz, surpassed half a million (La Paz, 1,049,800; Santa Cruz, 615,122; Cochabamba, 377,259).

Bolivia's heterogeneous population fragments along racial and cultural lines. Approximately 60 percent of the population is racially and culturally Indian; of these people, over 50 percent are Quechua and 40 percent Aymara speakers. In the eastern lowlands, a small proportion speaks Guaraní and other Indian languages. Around 30 percent of the population is racially mixed (mestizos). Although people of white extraction constitute less than 10 percent of the population, they have always dominated Bolivian political life. Racial and cultural hostility have consequently undercut any sense of national identity.

Geographic and regional diversity have exacerbated racial and cultural diversity. Bolivia divides into three distinct topographical regions. The core region is the high plain (altiplano) situated in the Andes Mountains at over 12,000 feet (3,657 meters). East of the Andean chain, a region of semitropical valleys called yungas descends eastward and spreads out into the third region, the llanos (or lowlands) of the Amazon Basin. Few railways or roads link these regions, and vast stretches of the country are accessible only by air.

Topographic diversity and economic realities have contributed to a strong sense of regional identity and intraregional rivalry in Bolivia. Historically, the residents of provincial cities such as Cochabamba (valley region) and Santa Cruz (llanos region) have viewed the capital city, La Paz (altiplano), as an alien force hostile to their regional interests. Thus, regionalists have resisted or tried to dominate the national government, and this regionalism has often been tinged with racial animosity. The people from Santa Cruz, for example, consider themselves white and proudly refer to themselves as Cambas. They look upon the Indian and mixed populations of the mountains and valleys with a mixture of fear and disdain and refer to them derisively as Kollas. This particular mode of regional-racial tension has been a crucial political factor in the last thirty years and has undermined the effectiveness of the national government.

PRELUDE TO REVOLUTION

Control over these diverse regions and peoples has always proved elusive to central governments. Although Bolivia's numerous constitutions have been based on U.S. and French traditions, the political structure reflects the Spanish tradition of bureaucratic patrimonialism, in which power rests in the executive branch. The historical trend, especially since 1930, has been toward an even greater role for the state in the economy and society. A great disparity has always existed, however, between the patrimonial pretension of the state and its effective power over the country's disparate regions and population.

Owing to this historical reality, Bolivia has always been characterized by an extremely unstable tenure of incumbent governments. Since 1825 no fewer than 190 changes of government have occurred. With the exception of 1952, most were the result of struggles among rival elite factions to control the central government and the largess that lay therein.

Before 1930 this process of intraelite factional struggle passed through two distinct stages. Between 1825 and about 1880 Bolivian public life, like that of most of the new Latin American states, was dominated by a series of quasi-military strongmen, known as caudillos, who emerged after the collapse of the Spanish Empire. In Bolivia, the collapse was particularly severe because of the exhaustion of silver as a resource and the country's subsequent lapse into economic stagnation and isolation. Effective power reverted to the fragmented and dispersed creole landed elite, which had led the fight against the Spanish. The semifeudal hacienda thus became the key economic, political, and social unit of the new nation. Indeed, the creole elite seized the opportunity to despoil most of the remaining free Indian communities and to convert their lands into haciendas upon which the Indians now labored in a system of semiservitude known as *pongeaje* for their white or mestizo masters.

In that context, the new republican constitution and the national government were little more than a prize for one or another regionally based alliance led by a prominent caudillo. These alliances, in turn, were based on personal loyalties to specific leaders and the patriarchal family structure of the creole landed elite. In fact, the patriarchal family structure, in which all power and authority inhere in the dominant male of the family, rapidly became the primary model of all authority relationships in the society. By far the most colorful, and at the same time horrific, of these strongmen was Mariano Melgarejo (1862–1871), who, among other depredations, abrogated the land titles of some 100,000 Indian peasants and occasionally sold off large slices of the national territory to Bolivia's neighbors as if they were his own personal property.

Perhaps the most crucial factor in understanding Bolivia's political structure is the nature of the country's economic links to the international capitalist system. Bolivia is one of the most extreme cases of the phenomenon of dependence in all of Latin America. Throughout the colonial period Alto Peru, as it was known then, was one of the principal suppliers of silver to the Spanish Crown. By the middle of the nineteenth century the silver mines were depleted and independent Bolivia was left without a viable export commodity.

At the end of the nineteenth century, however, mining activities in the *altiplano* revived because of a partial recovery of the silver industry and the first stirrings of the new giant, tin. Bolivia was integrated into the international system as a supplier of minerals to, and a consumer of goods made in, the advanced capitalist countries. Bolivia's period of isolation came to an end, and the country experienced a new process of externally stimulated economic development and modernization.

The end of caudillo politics was largely the product of the War of the Pacific of 1879–1883, in which the combined forces of Bolivia and Peru suffered a humiliating defeat at the hands of Chile's armed forces. As a result of the war a new mining elite, linked to the traditional oligarchy and oriented to a laissez-faire economic model that would assure the outward flow of minerals, appeared. Supported by external capitalist interests, the new elite struggled to suppress the unstable caudillo pattern of rule. In the rhetoric of the day, this group sought to impose a new civilian regime of "order and progress," aided by the complete discrediting of the Bolivian armed forces during the War of the Pacific.

In the 1880s the unfettered development of the private sector, especially in mining, gained the upper hand and ushered in a brief era of relative political stability and social peace. More important, Bolivia began to take on the outward accoutrements of a typical Western democratic political system; for example, the country had a functioning constitutional order, programmatically oriented political parties, and interest groups. At the same time, new social groups such as an entrepreneurial and commercial elite, a new urban middle class, and an embryonic working class also appeared.

At the elite level, the civil groups split into two party formations, Conservative and Liberal, which reflected competing regional and economic interests. The Conservatives were identified with southern silver-mining interests, the traditional elite, and the claim of the city of Sucre to continue as the capital. The Liberals, on the other hand, were associated with the tin interests, the emerging urban middle class, and the regional claims of La Paz. In 1898 the two clashed in a civil war won by the Liberals.

The Liberals rewrote the constitution and established a centralized unitary political order based on a standard Western separation-of-powers system, that is, executive, legislative, judiciary, in which the office of the president dominated. Bolivia entered a new era of political peace, rapid economic development based on the tin industry, and considerable modernization in the urban-based mining sector. But this development and modernization had no positive effects on the rural sector, where the mass of the Indian populace remained locked as *colonos* ("share-croppers") in the hacienda system. The new elite that had emerged with the tin industry quickly merged with the more-traditional landed elite to form a relatively coherent oligarchy that dominated the nation's political and economic life until the 1930s.

At that point Bolivia was a prime example of a formal democracy with legally limited participation. Literacy and property requirements excluded the Indian masses and most of the urban working class from participation in politics; formal political life was the preserve of a tiny upper class and a relatively small urban middle class. Public policy, in turn, reflected this fact; it was aimed at maintaining a stable rural order and pushing the growth of the export sector.

Superficially, Bolivia settled into a stable two-party political system in which the Liberals and a new Republican party did electoral battle. Behind this facade, however, was a new mode of intraelite factional politics in which cliques formed around dominant personalities who stood a chance of winning the presidential chair and the store of patronage jobs it controlled. Thus, although the armed caudillo bands had been supplanted by an ostensibly institutionalized political order, the essential reality of job- and office-oriented, personalistic, factional politics remained. Party labels and programs meant little. The real game was one of "ins" and "outs," with the latter, regardless of party affiliation, forming coalitions to harass and unseat the former.

This situation, in turn, was rooted in Bolivia's extremely skewed pattern of dependent, outwardly oriented economic development and in the gradual halt of growth in the 1920s. In that type of economic and political order (common to a number of Latin American countries), small landholding and exporting elites monopolized sources of hard wealth and especially excluded the new urban middle classes of the 1920s. The urban middle class was a very dependent group because of its reliance on salaries and fees paid by the elite, which controlled the hard wealth. The major sources of employment for the middle class were the liberal professions (particularly law and medicine) and public jobs. As growth leveled off, competition for the limited number of positions increased, and control of the executive branch of government became the key mechanism for the distribution of the coveted positions and contacts: A lawyer with no political contacts was of little use to fee-paying clients. Government, in effect, became a prized commodity struggled over by factions made up of leaders drawn from the elite and ambitious personal followers drawn from the middle class. A Bolivian saying captures this point well: La industria mayor de este país es la política (The major industry of this country is politics).

This underlying dynamic of job politics necessitated by a skewed and dependent economic structure proved to be one of the key structural weaknesses of the old order and contributed directly to the revolution of 1952. As the middle class grew, the static economic base could not generate sufficient jobs to absorb all of this important social stratum into the system. Hence, sectors of the middle class, especially the young, began to question the system.

Another key group was from the urban working class, primarily railroad workers, miners, commercial workers, and a few factory workers. The working class was small (never more than 100,000) but a strategic force in the economy. By and large, workers were excluded from the political process, their demands for better conditions were ignored, and their organizations suppressed. Not surprisingly, these groups began to turn toward more-radical organizations and ideologies that advocated the need to seize political power and destroy the existing order.

Even before the 1930s serious strains developed within the urban sector, which was rooted in the mining industry, and structural constraints generated disaffection with the existing order, not only among the working class but also among sections of the urban middle class. It was the Great Depression of 1930, however, and the disastrous Chaco War with Paraguay (1932–1935) that laid the base for sections of the middle class to coalesce with the working class and form a broad revolutionary movement.

From the mid-1930s to 1952 Bolivia was in a revolutionary situation in the sense that there was an almost continual open and violent struggle between groups oriented toward substantial change in the existing order and groups defending the status quo. As in most of Latin America, the most significant challenge to the old regime did not come from the Marxist left but from the MNR, the broad multiclass "populist" party that was officially formed in 1941. Contrary to the Marxist concept of class conflict, the MNR projected a conflict between the "nation" (middle class, workers, and peasants) and the "antination" (the local oligarchy and its imperialist allies such as the United States). Historically, the private sector in Bolivia has been small, yet over 80 percent of tin production fell under the control of three giant corporations: Patino, Aramayo, and Hochschild. The "big three" (commonly referred to as La Rosca) parlayed their control of tin into substantial control of banking, commerce, and transport, acquiring in the process a power base that dwarfed all other opponents, including the state. The MNR's objective, therefore, was to eliminate the power of this "antinational" oligarchy.

The stated aim of the MNR was to form a multiclass movement of the middle class, workers, and peasants to seize the state and use it to break the external power of the imperialist forces. The party also sought to destroy the local power of the oligarchy so as to liberate human and natural resources for the purposes of state-sponsored economic development and social justice. A key to these goals was the need to diversify the local economy so as to escape the economic dependence on a single export product.

By the late 1940s the MNR had built a fairly broad alliance among sectors of the urban middle class and key sectors of the working class such as railway, mine, and bank workers—before 1952 there was little direct mobilization of the mass of Indian peasants. The leadership of the MNR came overwhelmingly from the youth of the urban middle class, and its ties with the more Marxist-influenced workers' unions were tenuous and based on the pragmatic perception that working alone, neither had enough strength to seize power.

An important factor that paved the way for the revolution of 1952 was the extreme political and economic weakness of Bolivia's old elite, which, in turn, was rooted in the extremity of Bolivia's distorted and dependent economic structure. Some Latin American countries were able to traverse these difficult decades without a revolutionary upheaval because of their ability to generate economic growth within a new framework of import-substituting industrialization and subsequent accommodation of their urban middle and working classes. This time-buying strategy was not available to Bolivia, which lacked a substantial internal market. Moreover, the steady exhaustion of the country's tin mines weakened its ability to recoup in the export sector. The economic crisis of the 1930s persisted and worsened in the 1940s.

Other Latin American countries escaped revolution during this period because their incumbent elites had both the will and the means to suppress opposition forcefully. In neighboring Peru, the military remained the implacable foe of the American Popular Revolutionary Alliance (APRA), which in many ways was very similar to the MNR. The humiliating defeat of the Chaco War, however, demoralized the Bolivian armed forces, and they split into a variety of factions. Some of these factions supported the populists to the extent that three reform-oriented, civil-military regimes were attempted in 1936–1937, 1937–1939, and 1943–1946. Other military factions ousted these regimes, but nonetheless the military could not provide a stable source of power to end the status quo. The revolution of 1952 resulted more from the internal fragmentation and collapse of the old elite than from the organized and coherent strength of the MNR.

THE BOLIVIAN REVOLUTION

Since the 1950s Bolivian political life has been shaped by the dynamics unleashed by the revolution of 1952 and the reactions of national and international groups to the dilemmas posed by the revolution. The MNR middle-class elite persuaded peasants and workers to adopt fundamental structural changes that eliminated the power of *La Rosca*, the old oligarchy of tin barons, and of the large landowners. A momentous transformation of the nation soon followed: The largest tin mines were nationalized and reorganized into a new state mining corporation (Corporación Minera de Bolivia [COMIBOL]); the old hacienda system was destroyed through a land reform program formally sanctioned in 1953; for the first time universal suffrage enfranchised the majority of the population; and the national military was reduced in size, officers were purged, and the institution reorganized.

The MNR's task was to construct a new order that would simultaneously shape the social energies unleashed by the revolution and push forward the promises of economic development and social justice. Constructing a new social order was a difficult task plagued by three recurring problems of Bolivian political life. First, the MNR had to create a set of institutions that were capable of channeling and controlling the demands of the groups mobilized by the revolution. Second, there was a need to design and implement a macroeconomic strategy that could simultaneously spur economic growth and reduce social inequalities. Third, the achievement of these two goals depended on the formation of coalitions among the principal social sectors to sustain governments. These were the same problems that had been partially responsible for provoking the revolution in the first place.

The MNR took as its inspiration the great Mexican Revolution, particularly the corporatist strategies for social control of that country's Partido Revolucionario Institucional (PRI). Two obstacles, however, prevented the MNR from institutionalizing similar mechanisms. Labor, headed by Juan Lechín Oquendo, organized into the Central Obrera Boliviana (COB) and gained a *fuero sindical*, thus assuring it a semi-sovereign status over the working class. The MNR also gave in to COB's demands for cogovernment, a move that reinforced labor's autonomy from the party. As the party lost control over COB, a reorganized military won more power to deal with the potential threat of labor militias.

The second obstacle to consolidating power was internal to the MNR, which before and after the revolution drew support from the dependent middle class through the offer of state employment. Again a contrast to Mexico is illustrative. The PRI was able to contain factional disputes (at least until 1988) through the rotation of patronage every six years. In contrast, the MNR split into at least four visible factions headed by Víctor Paz Estenssoro, Juan Lechín Oquendo, Hernán Siles Zuazo, and Walter Guevara Arze. For three decades these leaders were to play crucial political roles: They are the titans of Bolivian politics.

Growing dissatifaction among factional leaders intensified as their demands for greater access to power and jobs were denied by the maneuvering of individuals such as Víctor Paz. Contrary to original expectations, Paz returned to power in 1960, following four years under Siles Zuazo, and a new constitution that permitted reelection was forced through Congress in 1961 as Paz moved to exert personal control over the party.

The political problems that bedeviled the MNR were intrinsically related to the issue of economic growth and development. Thus, factional strife also reflected debates surrounding the macropolitical and economic strategies that should be adopted. Labor and the left of the party favored populist redistribution, and the middle sectors leaned toward more pragmatic solutions. The pragmatists eventually succeeded. Bolivia reentered the international market, an IMF-sponsored stabilization program was adopted in 1956, and a state capitalist development strategy was implemented.

The state capitalist strategy inevitably meant a dramatic shift of the costs and the focus of the revolution. In the early 1960s Paz Estenssoro, backed by the Kennedy administration and the U.S. Alliance for Progress, moved to deepen the process of state capitalism by rationalizing the production of tin and promoting the development of agri-industry in eastern Bolivia. Conflict with labor soon ensued as the government attempted to restructure the tin industry through layoffs, wage adjustments, and the like, and enforced this restructuring through the use of the military to discipline labor. In mid-1963, for example, the armed forces surrounded and invaded mining camps whose workers refused to abide by government orders. A total rift between the MNR and COB resulted, and the consequences were long term: Every government since has had to deal with COB's demands for a greater and more equitable redistribution of wealth and power.

In 1964 Paz Estenssoro sought reelection, but labor and other factions of the MNR opposed Paz's new bid to consolidate his grip over the party. Undaunted, Paz rigged the party convention and had himself chosen as the party's candidate. To secure support from the military, he named René Barrientos Ortuño, a popular air force general, as his running mate. Although reelected, Paz lasted in office only three months; in November labor and opposing factions in the MNR recruited Vice President Barrientos to lead a successful coup.

MILITARY POLITICS

Between November 1964 and October 1982 the military was the dominant force in Bolivian political life, but the major contours of the nation's political economy were those established by the MNR. General Barrientos attempted to follow the same state capitalist strategy of the Paz government without the burden of labor, and Barrientos's control over the armed forces facilitated the enforcement of the economic development strategy as the military invaded the mines, destroyed unions and labor militias, and attempted to supplant COB. Through the Pacto Militar Campesino (Military Peasant Pact), Barrientos was also able to buy off major peasant unions, especially in his home department of Cochabamba, while others were squashed or outlawed.

Under still-mysterious circumstances, Barrientos died in a 1969 helicopter accident. After a brief (five-month) civilian interregnum, two military-populist generals (Alfredo Ovando [1969–1970] and Juan José Torres [1970–1971], who had been inspired by General Velasco in neighboring Peru) came to power. During this brief military-populist interlude labor and the left reemerged, invigorated by the nationalization of Gulf Oil, the expulsion of the U.S. Peace Corps, and the creation of the Asamblea del Pueblo, a soviet-type assembly.

Military populism ended abruptly in August 1971 in a bloody coup led by Col. Hugo Banzer Suárez. Banzer ruled until 1978, a period known as the Banzerato, the longest uninterrupted rule of any leader in twentieth-century Bolivia. By all accounts, the Banzerato was extremely repressive: Labor leaders and leftist politicians were exiled, jailed, and killed, and COB was again outlawed.

Banzer and his civilian allies, including Víctor Paz Estenssoro's wing of the MNR, continued the state capitalist strategy adopted in the early 1960s of rationalizing mining, shifting to agri-industry in eastern Bolivia, and opening the nation to foreign investment and borrowing. This strategy succeeded in the short run, and there were positive growth rates in 1975–1977; however, the costs of this development plan were long term, especially the significant levels of foreign indebtedness. Growth also came at the expense of key sectors of the economy, especially mining. Moreover, the growth was financed by heavy foreign borrowing and expectations that the boom in oil and natural gas prices would continue. As debt payments matured and the oil boom went bust, the true and sorry state of the Bolivian economy surfaced.

Politically, the military did not fare any better. Banzer and the military grew impatient with their civilian political allies and by 1974 had forced them out. Between then and 1978 Banzer attempted to emulate the Brazilian bureaucratic-authoritarian strategy, relying solely on the military and a few select civilian technocrats. In reality, Banzer only established a set of patrimonial ties to a few key individuals in the private sector, so the success of this strategy was brief. Contradictions in the regime's relationships with labor, the private sector, and the military, coupled with pressures because of the Carter administration's human rights policy, forced Banzer to call elections in 1978, long before he had expected to do so.

THE TRANSITION TO DEMOCRACY

Bolivia was about to enter into one of the darkest and most unstable periods in its history. Between 1978 and 1982 seven military and two weak civilian governments ruled the country, each lasting an average of only six months. The Bolivian experience during this period was by far the most dramatic of all Latin American democratizing countries.

When the military opened the electoral process, nearly seventy competing political parties emerged—the MNR alone had divided into at least thirty factions. Víctor Paz Estenssoro, Juan Lechín Oquendo, Hernán Siles Zuazo, and Walter Guevara Arze, the now-gray titans of Bolivian politics, reemerged as the principal electoral contenders. In short, the military had failed to resolve the dilemmas of development or to eliminate the politicians it had sought to control for two decades.

In a futile attempt to constitutionalize his regime, General Banzer initially attempted to run as the official candidate. Opposition from rival military factions, however, forced him to name Gen. Juan Pereda Asbun, an air force general, as the official candidate. Moreover, Banzer was forced to lift proscriptions on left-wing groups following a massive nationwide hunger strike.

Accusations of fraud against General Pereda, the official candidate, led to the annulment of the 1978 elections. Pereda refused to accept the annulment and retreated to Santa Cruz, Banzer's stronghold, where he launched a coup that ended Banzer's seven-year tenure. In November 1978 Pereda suffered the same fate at the hands of Gen. David Padilla, who, in turn, called for a new round of elections to be held in July 1979.

The campaign and elections of 1979 revealed the extent to which Bolivian institutional life had deteriorated. Because the military was unable to provide leadership at the center, civil society became engaged in a free-for-all as parties, factions, and other groups searched for a formula to carry them to the presidency. Hernán Siles Zuazo's Union Democrática y Popular (UDP), which included the Siles Zuazo Movimiento Nacionalista Revolucionario de Izquierda (MNRI), the Revolutionary Left Movement (MIR), and the Bolivian Communist party (PCB), was the principal leftist coalition. Víctor Paz Estenssoro led a centrist coalition, which included Walter Guevara Arze, the pro-Peking Communists (PCML), and a variety of other smaller groups. Of the myriad leftist parties only the Socialists (PS-1) were able to garner any electoral muscle. The right discovered a useful political mechanism in Acción Democrática y Nacionalista (ADN), a party founded in 1979 around General Banzer and a group of his civilian supporters. These groups were to become the most significant political contenders of the next decade; they were also the key players in the turbulent transition to democracy.

The voting of July 1979 was inconclusive, although the UDP outpolled Paz and Banzer (candidates must win 50 percent of the vote, otherwise Congress elects the president from the top contenders). As a compromise among Paz, Banzér, and Siles, Walter Guevara Arze, one of the four stalwarts of the MNR, was elected by Congress for a one-year interim period. In a bloody coup that led to the appointment of yet another interim president, Lydia Gueiler, Guevara was overthrown in November 1979. Gueiler presided over another weak caretaker government that barely managed to hang on through a new round of elections held in June 1980.

The UDP also obtained a plurality in the 1980 elections; however, Congress would not be able to convene to vote for president until October 1982, for on July 17, 1980, Gen. Luis García Meza overthrew Lydia Gueiler. The resulting regime was one of the most corrupt in Bolivian history because of García Meza's connections to cocaine traffickers, neofascist terrorists, and other groups. Faced with international isolation, especially nonrecognition from the United States, and the repudiation of nearly every political and social group, García Meza ruled with brutal repression.

In August 1981, one year after taking power and plunging Bolivia into a severe economic crisis, García Meza was replaced by a military junta that named Gen. Celso Torrelio to preside over its goals of stabilizing the economy, reestablishing relations with the United States, and holding a new round of elections in 1983. Following a series of disputes among rival officers and pressure from political parties and the private enterprise confederation (CEPB) to turn the government over to the Congress elected in 1980, Torrelio was replaced in July 1982 by yet another officer, Gen. Guido Vildoso Calderón.

A new round of elections, called by the military junta, was favored by COB and the UDP, who rejected the 1980 Congress since it would be controlled by the opposition. In September, however, Vildoso yielded to the parties and the CEPB and convened the Congress elected in 1980; it elected Hernán Siles Zuazo as president on October 10. By then, Bolivia was suffering its most profound political and economic crises since the revolution. Foreign debt servicing had reached nearly 50 percent of export earnings, and the production of tin and natural gas, the country's two principal exports, had declined to all-time lows.

Hernán Siles Zuazo ruled between 1982 and 1985. From the outset, his government was beset by a recurring split between the executive, controlled by the UDP coalition, and Congress, which was in the hands of Banzer's ADN and Víctor Paz's MNR. Siles faced a hostile Congress, and opposition legislators, as well as many from his own ostensible coalition, maneuvered to block and even subvert his government.

The central issue facing Siles was the deteriorating economy, which meant there was a need to enforce some type of stabilization program based on austerity. Enforcing such stabilization measures, however, brought to the fore the conflict that had surfaced in the 1950s among the government, COB, an emergent private sector represented by the CEPB, and regional civic committees. A basic pattern of political conflict ensued. The government would decree a stabilization package designed to satisfy the IMF and the private sector. Strikes and demonstrations, directed by COB and often backed by peasant road blockades, would follow. Incapable of satisfying any group, the government would modify the package to the point of undermining its effectiveness, thereby provoking the wrath of the IMF and the CEPB.

Lacking any authority to govern, as a result of the political conflict with parties in Congress and the confrontations with labor, private-sector, and regional groups, the Siles government reached the point of collapse. In the meantime the Bolivian economic crisis had reached unbelievable dimensions. According to some calculations, inflation in 1984–1985 reached 26,000 percent, a Latin American record and the seventh highest in recorded history. Siles also angered international creditors by unilaterally suspending debt-servicing payments in mid-1984 when they reached nearly 70 percent of export earnings. Bolivia's crisis had so intensified that in December 1984 Siles was pressured into giving power up one year earlier than expected. A new round of elections was called for July 1985.

The 1985 elections were indicative of Bolivia's vacillating electorate. General Banzer, who had retired in disgrace in 1978, was the victor with 28.5 percent to Víctor Paz Estenssoro's (MNR) 26.4 percent. Siles Zuazo's MNRI received less than 5 percent, an indication of his failure in office. A faction of MIR, which had formed part of the UDP, headed by Vice President Jaime Paz took a respectable third with 8.8 percent. Once again the outcome of the elections was to be decided by Congress. To block Banzer and seat Paz, the MNR moved quickly to mobilize an electoral coalition among the parties that had felt the brunt of Banzer's repressive regime. Winning over MIR was the key to the MNR's strategy. After a first round tally the coalition took hold, and Paz Estenssoro was elected president of Bolivia for the fourth time. He was two months short of his seventy-eighth birthday.

STABILIZATION AND DEMOCRACY

Resolution of the economic crisis was the main priority of the new Paz government. On August 29, 1985, Paz surprised the MNR and the leftist groups that had supported his election in Congress by announcing Decree Law 21060, hailed as the Nueva Política Económica (New Economic Policy [NPE]). The NPE represented a dramatic shift in the state capitalist development strategy established by Paz and the MNR and reinforced by subsequent military regimes. In our view, however, the NPE did not mark a rupture with previous policy as much as an extension of the logic of that policy to the new national and international realities.

The NPE sought three objectives that revealed a philosophical shift in Bolivian state capitalism. It called for the liberalization of the economy, the transformation of the private sector as the central participant in economic development, and the recuperation of state control over key state enterprises, such as the Bolivian Mining Corporation and the Central Bank, that had been appropriated by organized labor.

In policy terms, the NPE aimed specifically to stabilize the economy and end hyperinflation through a shock therapy of reducing the massive fiscal deficit, freezing wages and salaries, devaluing the currency, and drastically reducing employment in the public sector. Because it called for the dismantling of inefficient state enterprises such as COMIBOL and the privatization of others, Decree Law 21060 ended the era of state-led growth.

Implementation of the NPE, however, depended on the ability of the government to control labor. As expected, COB headed a movement to resist the new policy, but COB had been severely weakened by its struggles with Siles and had difficulty in mobilizing support for a general strike. Still, the new government required political support from Congress to deal with labor and implement the NPE.

In this vein, the most significant political development since 1985 has been the formulation of the Pacto por la Democracia (Pact for Democracy) between the MNR and Gen. Hugo Banzer's ADN signed on October 17, 1985. The pact did not establish a governing alliance, as in Colombia, but an agreement through which the two parties agreed to cooperate in Congress to push through Decree Law 21060 and other related legislation. By agreeing to enter into the political pact, Banzer and the ADN gained control of key public-sector corporations and the patronage that went with that control. The pact allowed ADN to consolidate its organizational base and to achieve an enviable position for the May 1989 elections.

The pact served the Paz government in two key ways. First, after its inception the pact enabled the government to impose two congressionally sanctioned states of siege that delivered a punishing blow to labor from which it has not yet recovered. Second, Paz used the pact to pass a far-reaching tax reform program, three budgets, and a new electoral law through Congress. In short, the pact resolved the structural impasse between executive and legislative authorities that had plagued the Siles government and ended the thirty-year threat of the COB to incumbent governments.

Many viewed the NPE and the pact as evidence of Paz's treason to the revolution. In our view, however, the NPE is an adaptation to a very difficult set of domestic and international realities. Resolution of Bolivia's crisis required a "new pragmatism" that only the old caudillo could manage to bring onto the political scene in Bolivia. In this sense Paz was no longer a politician with an eye on the next electoral round. Indeed, he pursued the NPE outside of, and even against, the old party structure and supported technocrats, such as Gonzalo Sanchez de Lozada, against old party bosses. This strategy, coupled with the absence of challengers to Paz's control over the MNR, threatened to bury the party with the old leader. But the outcome of the municipal elections in December 1987 revealed little support for the party's populist wing and a great deal of support for the younger generation led by Sanchez de Lozada.

Based on the growing popularity of Sanchez de Lozada, who as minister of planning became the principal architect of the NPE, the MNR selected him as presidential candidate for the May 1989 general election. Sanchez de Lozada's popularity, however, also constituted a threat to the presidential aspirations of former dictator Gen. Hugo Banzer. In February 1989, in the heat of the 1989 electoral campaign, tensions between the MNR and General Banzer's ADN led to the breakdown of the Pact for Democracy and to an intensely disputed election.

Gonzalo Sanchez went on to win the May elections by a very slim margin; as a result, Congress once again would determine the next president of Bolivia. General Banzer, who finished second, refused to support the MNR's candidate owing to the bitterness of the campaign and the breakdown of the pact with the MNR. In an unprecedented development, Banzer ordered his party to vote for Jaime Paz Zamora of the MIR, who had placed third, in the August 1989 congressional vote. The ADN and the MIR went on to establish a so-called National Unity and Convergence coalition, which provided political support in Congress in ways reminiscent of the Pact for Democracy.

On August 6, 1989, Víctor Paz Estenssoro became the first president to complete a full term in office since 1964. Under the watchful eye of six Latin American presidents, the outgoing president ended a political career that spanned five decades. Paz Estenssoro proudly read a detailed state-of-the-nation message and then handed the presidential sash to his nephew, Jaime Paz Zamora. As he departed he proclaimed "mission accomplished"—an eloquent manifestation of his success in rewriting his place in Bolivian history.

Significantly, the elections of May 1989, and their eventual outcome, revealed that the NPE had achieved a great deal of popular support. Consensus among the principal contenders had also been achieved as they vowed not to modify the key components of the NPE. Only labor and the Izquierda Unida (United Left) coalition actively campaigned against the NPE. In sum, Víctor Paz Estenssoro played a historic role in bringing Bolivia back from economic disaster; in so doing, however, he also put an end to the chapter that he and the MNR had begun in 1952.

Although the NPE faced opposition from labor and the left at home, international reactions to the program were mostly positive. International agencies such as the IMF and the World Bank, for example, were pleased with the NPE because it went beyond their own highest expectations. Furthermore, since 1985 debt arrangements with private banks—such as debt for equity swaps, debt for nature swaps, and debt buy-back schemes—have renewed Bolivia's creditworthiness.

The results of the NPE, however, have been mixed. Inflation was brought under control, a remarkable achievement if one considers the extremes it reached in 1984–1985. On the other hand, economic reactivation has been slow in coming, although positive GDP growth rates did appear for the first time in the 1980s. The economic model has also failed to bring Bolivia out of a deep recession; in fact, many entrepreneurs from the industrial sector who have been forced to compete on the open market with Argentine, Brazilian, and Chilean products have openly voiced their displeasure with the government. The record of the NPE in resolving labor's demands and reducing poverty levels has been dismal. According to many socioeconomic indicators, Bolivia now ranks below Haiti, and income levels have dropped to 1950 levels.

The success of the NPE depends almost entirely on Bolivia's ability to sell natural gas to Argentina and Brazil. Theoretically, economic reactivation will be financed through revenue from natural gas sales and loans from international agencies. Recently, however, Argentina has fallen behind on its payments and has hinted that future gas purchases may be ended since that country has vast reserves of its own, and the prospects of gas sales to Brazil are equally gloomy. Moreover, international agencies have been very slow to release promised loans and grants.

On another front, Bolivia has sought to establish close ties with the Reagan and Bush administrations, based on the assumption that U.S. economic support for the NPE was crucial to the survival of Bolivian democracy. Washington's principal interest, however, was not to underwrite Bolivia's economic recovery but to force its government to combat the growing narcotics trade. Since at least 1982, the United States has insisted on coca leaf eradication programs despite repeated warnings from the Bolivians about their social, political, and economic impact. The fact is that long before cocaine became a popular recreational drug in the United States, Bolivians cultivated the coca leaf for traditional and medicinal consumption, so eradication has been equated with the destruction of the Indian culture.

Because U.S. economic support is crucial to the success of the NPE, Bolivian governments have accepted many of the demands of the U.S. Drug Enforcement Administration (DEA). In July 1986, in a highly publicized but ineffective operation dubbed Blast Furnace, U.S. troops were sent to the northeastern department of El Beni to seek out and destroy cocaine labs. In July 1987 the Bolivian government signed a treaty with coca producers to limit the number of hectares used for coca production. In spite of widespread protests from coca producers, Víctor Paz signed the most far-reaching coca eradication program in Latin America into law in June 1988.

This apparent commitment to combating the drug trade did not impress the U.S. Congress, which imposed sanctions in 1986 and 1987. In particular, the United States was distressed by the refusal of the Bolivian government to use dangerous herbicides to eradicate coca plants. Moreover, revelations that politicians, military officers, and even a few government officials were linked to the drug lords raised questions about the dedication of the Bolivian government to the drug war. Finally, U.S. efforts were undermined by the fact that total coca leaf acreage under cultivation tripled after 1985. In contrast to Colombia, however, there is little concrete evidence that Bolivian politics are totally subverted by the cocaine lords.

But the United States has also been a weak, and often bumbling, partner in the Bolivian drug war. DEA drug busts have yielded little, and until the arrest of Roberto Suárez Gómez, the "king of cocaine," few major drug lords had been captured. The Bolivian government has pointed out that the United States has disbursed less than one-third of the aid promised and that Bolivia cannot be expected to go at it alone, especially given the magnitude of its economic crisis. During one visit, Secretary of State George Shultz highlighted and praised Bolivian efforts to combat the drug traffic; however, it became increasingly clear that the level of rhetoric in Washington about the drug war being waged in Bolivia exceeded the level of economic support given to the Bolivian government.

A final note should be made about the Bolivian military and the prospects for democracy. Because of Bolivia's experience with praetorian politics, the current absence of the military from the political scene is quite surprising. Although coup rumors have occasionally stirred unrest, the military has supported the democratic process since 1982. Perhaps because of the institutional fragmentation and corruption that led to its withdrawal from government in 1982, the military has rarely expressed a threat to the democratic process.

The military resolved internal disputes and was satisfied with the role assigned to it by Víctor Paz Estenssoro. This military satisfaction with its role was owing to several factors. First, Víctor Paz's government renewed military spending and training. Second, the armed forces played a key role in disciplining society. After August 1985 the military was charged with the enforcement of two congressionally sanctioned states of siege and was a key player in the narcotics war. Third, the military was not threatened by civilian investigations into its past behavior. In contrast to Argentina, where civilian courts indicted, tried, and convicted dozens of officers for their "dirty war" campaign, the trial of Gen. Luis García Meza by Congress and the Supreme Court on charges of human rights violations and corruption did not implicate other members of the armed forces. As a result, the military in Bolivia did not feel threatened by civilian inquiries and continued to support the Paz government. Finally, no attempt was made to restructure the military hierarchy as happened in Argentina.

THE PROSPECTS FOR DEMOCRACY IN BOLIVIA

Historically, threats to democracy in Bolivia have not come from discontented masses but from elite sectors forced to relinquish rights and privileges. Because of the support from key elite groups, the prospects for the survival of democracy in Bolivia are better today than in the recent past. The major sociopolitical actors have come to terms with democracy in Bolivia. For the moment labor, the private sector, political parties, and even the military realize that their group and class interests are best served by supporting political democracy.

It is clear to us, however, that the survival of political democracy in Bolivia depends greatly on the resolution of the economic crisis. Bolivia's extreme dependence on primary export products, such as tin and natural gas, reduces the likelihood of recovery from the current crisis. Moreover, political democracy has brought little relief to Bolivia's impoverished masses, who have been forced to pay the costs of stabilization and austerity. Unless their burden is alleviated substantially, the prospects for democratic consolidation will remain bleak.

SUGGESTIONS FOR FURTHER READING

Dunkerley, James. *Rebellion in the Veins: Political Struggle in Bolivia 1952-1982.* London: Verso Editions, 1984.

Gamarra, Eduardo A. "Political Stability, Democratization, and the Bolivian National Congress." Ph.D. dissertation, University of Pittsburgh, 1987.

Kelley, Jonathan, and Herbert S. Klein. *Revolution and the Rebirth of Inequality: A Theory Applied to the National Revolution in Bolivia.* Berkeley: University of California Press, 1981.

Klein, Herbert. *Parties and Political Change in Bolivia, 1880-1952.* Cambridge: Cambridge University Press, 1969.

———. *Bolivia: The Evolution of a Multi-Ethnic Society.* Oxford: Oxford University Press, 1980.

Ladman, Jerry, ed. *Modern Day Bolivia: Legacy of the Revolution and Prospects for the Future.* Tempe, Ariz.: Center for Latin American Studies, 1982.

Malloy, James M. *Bolivia: The Uncompleted Revolution.* Pittsburgh: University of Pittsburgh Press, 1970.

Malloy, James M., and Eduardo A. Gamarra. "The Transition to Democracy in Bolivia." In James M. Malloy and Mitchell Seligson, eds., *Authoritarians and Democrats: Regime Transition in Latin America*, pp. 93-119. Pittsburgh: University of Pittsburgh Press, 1987.

———. *Revolution and Reaction: Bolivia 1964-1985.* New Brunswick, N.J.: Transaction Books, 1988.

Mayorga, Rene, ed. *Democracia a la deriva.* La Paz: CERES, 1987.

Mitchell, Christopher. *The Legacy of Populism in Bolivia: From the MNR to Military Rule.* New York: Praeger Special Studies, 1977.

Morales, Juan Antonio, and Jeffrey Sachs. "Bolivia's Economic Crisis." Monograph presented at the National Bureau of Economic Research Conference on Developing Country Debt, Washington, D.C., September 1987.

Sachs, Jeffrey. "The Bolivian Hyperinflation and Stabilization." Working Papers no. 2073. Boston: NBER, 1986.

Whitehead, Laurence. "Bolivia's Failed Democratization, 1977-1980." In Guillermo O'Donnell, Phillipe Schmitter, and Lawrence Whitehead, eds., *Transitions from Authoritarian Rule: Latin America*, pp. 49-71. Baltimore, Md.: Johns Hopkins University Press, 1986.

17
Ecuador:
The Fragility of
Dependent Democracy

JOHN D. MARTZ

On August 10, 1988, a remarkably varied group of political leaders attended the presidential inauguration of Rodrigo Borja Cevallos in Quito. They ranged from Nicaragua's embattled Sandinista president, Daniel Ortega Saavedra, and the graying Cuban revolutionary, Fidel Castro, to the U.S. secretary of state, George Shultz. While these and other hemispheric figures debated issues of politics and revolution, Ecuador's fledgling democracy was witnessing the transfer of power between bitter enemies with pronounced policy differences. The second such constitutional exchange since the military withdrawal from power in 1979, it symbolized both the ambitions and the frustrations of Ecuador's fragile democracy.

In 1984 the accession of León Febres Cordero to the presidency had brought to office a wealthy businessman ardently committed to a free-market system. Claiming that Ecuador had nearly been destroyed by irresponsible free-spenders, Febres promised a renewal of the private sector in tandem with a divestiture of state-operated agencies. Free enterprise would be unshackled from statist chains, price controls would be lifted, and efficient management of government would reactivate the economy. Foreign investment would be stimulated and the foreign debt renegotiated. All of these were measures on which Febres was fundamentally opposed by his elected successor. Borja, while far from being the left-leaning radical depicted by Febres, espoused a democratic socialism that was anathema to Ecuadorean conservatives. The two men were long-standing philosophical and political combatants, with Febres having narrowly defeated Borja in the 1984 presidential contest. Their differences also sharply mirrored the deep-seated fissures between traditionalist and reformist currents in Ecuadorean society and politics.

378

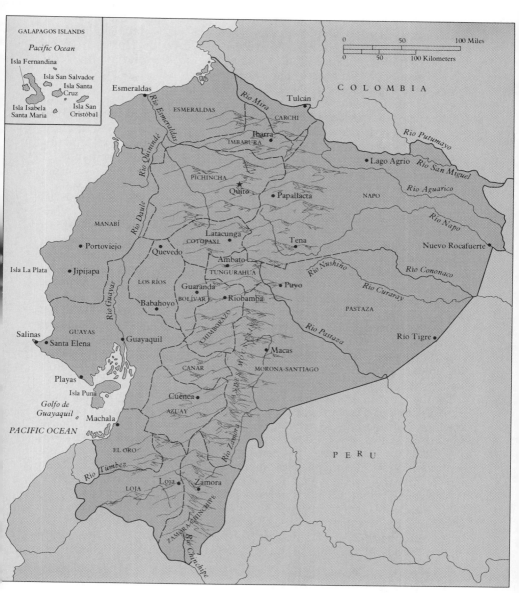

Ecuador

The years of formal democracy following the military retreat to the barracks in 1979 have been turbulent and unsettled. Jaime Roldós Aguilera had won a sweeping victory, only to lose control of his party and its congressional majority, see a renewal of armed conflict with Peru over the disputed border, and then die when his plane plunged into an Andean mountainside in 1981. Vice President Osvaldo Hurtado Larrea was permitted to replace Roldós, struggling to the end of his term against economic difficulties aggravated by a hostile Congress. When Febres edged past Borja in the 1984 elections, he too faced a legislature that was antagonistic to his policies. After negotiating a series of arrangements that produced a progovernment majority, it crumbled during the second half of his term. The president exercised authority in a high-handed and arbitrary fashion while suffering a crisis in civil-military relations, which even included his brief kidnapping at the hands of rebellious airmen in 1987.

Throughout this period Ecuador's economic condition was also on a downslide. The advent of the nation's petroleum boom in the early 1970s had reshaped the economy while feeding a rapidly expanding, consumption-oriented middle class. The military government of the period benefited from the bonanza years but, even before relinquishing power, conceded that the boom was finished. Ecuador's dependency on petroleum grew dramatically until, by 1987, over two-thirds of export earnings, 60 percent of government revenue, and 16 percent of the gross domestic product (GDP) were provided by that industry. When prices dropped sharply on the international market, the loss of an estimated $700 million in revenue forced the government in February 1987 to suspend interest payments to its 400 creditor banks. Ecuador's dependency was further underlined when the earthquake of March 5, 1987, destroyed over twenty-five miles of pipeline. There were no further payments to foreign creditors for the remainder of the Febres term.

By the time of Borja's inauguration, social and economic conditions were assuming crisis proportions. Petroleum earnings had dropped to less than half the nation's export income, the sucre had plunged in value 75 percent against the U.S. dollar in the span of eight months, there was a fiscal deficit greater than 10 percent of national output, capital flight continued, and the foreign debt approached $10 billion. Borja declared shortly after the elections that he saw five problems of particular urgency: (1) the foreign debt, (2) unemployment of more than 12 percent, (3) the fiscal deficit, (4) an annual inflation rate of some 60 percent, and (5) worsening income distribution and consequent social inequities. For the longer run, Ecuador faced a host of challenges emanating from its struggle to wrest modernity from a heritage of Latin American traditionalism.

A HISTORY AND CULTURE
OF TRADITIONALISM

From Ecuador's verdant Amazonian jungle to its snow-capped Andean mountain peaks and steamy tropical coastlands, the country has been deeply penetrated by Spanish values of authoritarianism and personalism. Long accustomed to strong paternalistic leadership, Ecuadoreans have never fully overcome the regional fragmentation between the highlands (*sierra*) and the coast (*costa*). Although the population of 10 million is divided almost equally between the two, the *serranos* are predominantly Indian or mestizo while the people on the coast include the mixed-blood *montuvios* as well as a sizable African component in the northern Pacific region. Geography, climate, economic activity, and sociopolitical attitudes are all marked by sharp contrasts, nowhere more sharply depicted than in the differences between the mountainous capital city of Quito and the tropical port of Guayaquil.

These differences also suggest a political and cultural disunity, and even today such disunity constitutes an obstacle to development of a true sense of national identity. This quality of fragmentation can be traced back virtually to the founding of Quito and Guayaquil in 1534 and 1537, respectively. Long before the enfeeblement of the Spanish monarchy and the independence struggle of the early nineteenth century, the traditions of authoritarianism and personalism had become strongly entrenched. Military victory by independence forces at the Battle of Pichincha on the slopes above Quito on May 24, 1822, assured the ouster of the royalists, and the breakup of independent Gran Colombia (present-day Ecuador, Colombia, Panama, and Venezuela) in 1830 brought the Venezuelan-born general Juan José Flores to Ecuador's presidency. A dominant figure for fifteen years, he was later followed by other authoritarian leaders, most notably Gabriel García Moreno for the Conservatives and the Liberals' Eloy Alfaro.

The first came to power in 1861 as the apotheosis of Conservative rule. A religious zealot who assigned the Jesuits responsibility for national education while officially dedicating Ecuador to the Sacred Heart of Jesus in 1873, García Moreno also stimulated a concerted drive to diversify the economy, provide an economic infrastructure, and organize efficiently the functions of the state. Assassinated on the steps of the government palace in 1875, García Moreno nonetheless had erected a vigorous theocratic system that survived another twenty years. Only in 1895 did the Liberals seize power under Alfaro, the "old campaigner," and their rule endured for the next half century. While Alfaro occupied the presidency from 1895 to 1901 and 1906 to 1911, the power of the church was curbed, foreign investment was encouraged, and further public works were undertaken. Unwilling to relinquish power, Alfaro was killed by a Quito mob in January 1912, but the Liberal hegemony continued. Only in 1944 did their long dominance draw to a close.

By this time the ineffable José María Velasco Ibarra had emerged on the scene. A charismatic figure who combined demagogic oratory with moralistic austerity, Velasco overshadowed Ecuador's national politics for nearly fifty years. He ultimately reached the presidency five times (first in 1934–1935 and for the last time in 1968–1972), but only once did he serve out his constitutional term. Whether exercising power or planning his return from exile, Velasco remained a force until his death in 1979 at the age of eighty-four. A gifted personalistic leader but disastrously unskilled as an executive and administrator, he effectively assured a high degree of systemic instability while retarding the institutionalization of political parties, which he loathed. Meanwhile, Ecuador experienced twenty-one different governments between 1925 and 1948. After an unusual interim of three successive constitutional periods, there was a return to more familiar patterns. From 1960 to 1979 there were eight different governments, including the last two of Velasco, while 1970 to 1979 constituted a dictatorial decade under first a civilian regime, then two consecutive military ones.

The armed forces eventually decided to leave power, but it was nearly three years before the so-called democratic restoration took place with the 1979 inauguration of Jaime Roldós. At that juncture, Ecuador was at the forefront of Latin American returns to democracy. A new generation of leaders was emerging with Roldós and his running mate, Osvaldo Hurtado—as well as several rival candidates—still being in their thirties, while Velasco had died and other former presidents had retired from politics. The political party system was still far from institutionalized, but it did number several new entities and enjoyed an organizational structure and programmatic orientation that had customarily been absent. The same tended to be true of other sociopolitical forces and, while basic values and attitudes had not been altered, it could be hoped that a new era might be looming ahead.

PARTIES AND DOMESTIC POLITICAL FORCES

By the 1970s Ecuador's historical Conservative (PCE) and Radical Liberal (PLR) parties had faded into the background, and the oft-resuscitated *velasquista* movement faded away after the collapse of his fifth and final administration in 1972. What gradually emerged were new, more programmatically oriented organizations, accompanied by modernizing movements consistent with well-established populist traditions. Thus, the elections of 1978–1979, the first since 1970, reflected the political changes then in progress. Traditionalistic forces were fragmented, and the Izquierda Democrática (ID)—originally formed by dissident Liberal reformers—was joined by the Christian-Democratic Democracia Popular (DP) as a representative of distinguishable doctrinal beliefs. The Marxist left was marked by several splinter groups, but it also shared in the emergence of a new generation of leaders. Ecuadorean populism was epitomized by the Concentración de Fuerzas Populares (CFP), a Guayaquil-based party long controlled by Assad Bucaram, a charismatic if controversial figure who rose from an impoverished background to become the nation's single most popular mass leader.

The outgoing military, fearful of the Bucaram temperament as well as his antiestablishment rhetoric, succeeded in annulling his candidacy, after which the CFP named the youthful Jaime Roldós, whose wife was a niece of Bucaram. Alliance with Democracia Popular produced the Roldós-Hurtado ticket, which unexpectedly led the field in a six-candidate race. Defying traditionalist efforts to annul or otherwise bar them from office, Roldós and Hurtado won a subsequent runoff between the two leading slates when, on April 28, 1979, the reformists steamrollered the conservative candidacy of Sixto Durán Ballén with 68.5 percent of the vote. Also elected was a solid CFP congressional majority under the iron-fisted control of Bucaram. From the very outset, however, the struggle for power between Roldós and Bucaram (who regarded the electoral victory as his) weakened the government and underlined the fragility of the nascent democracy.

The CFP was at the point of division when Roldós's plane crashed; Assad Bucaram died of natural causes in November 1981, leaving followers and relatives of both men to fight for control. The regionally based populism personified by Bucaram and his CFP later reemerged with his nephew Abdalá Bucaram, who ran a strong race in the 1988 presidential contest as part of the Partido Roldosista Ecuatoriano (PRE). The organizational remnants of the CFP by then were being contested by two of Assad's sons, and his widow attempted to mediate. It was with Abdalá Bucaram and the PRE, however, that the nondoctrinal, opportunistic, and mass-based populism of Guayaquil and the coast was finding expression by the close of the 1980s. In the meantime, more-structured and self-consciously programmatic politics were being exemplified by the ID and the DP. The first was notable in that it created a nationwide party organization, although it lacked popular strength with the Guayaquil masses. Rodrigo Borja guided the work while also developing the Ecuadorean vision of social democracy. The Democracia Popular party (Christian Democrats) remained smaller and less well organized, although building toward the future while their founder occupied the presidency.

The adolescence of the party system was underlined when seventeen organizations contested the January 1984 elections. Among nine presidential candidates, Rodrigo Borja presented the reformist option against León Febres Cordero, standard-bearer of the traditionalist alliance, Frente de Reconstrucción Nacional (FRN). With illiterates voting for the first time—a major shift in electoral custom—a record high of 2.5 million citizens participated. Borja won narrowly, with 28.4 percent to 27.5 percent for Febres, only to be upset in the second-round runoff on May 6, 1984, by 46.6 percent to 43.8 percent. The combative Febres had run a vigorous personal campaign, scattering promises in the best tradition of Ecuadorean populism. When he entered office, however, he did so with an economic approach frankly derived from the Chicago school theories. Furthermore, a reformist bloc known as the Frente Progresista controlled the unicameral Congress.

During Febres's tumultuous term in office, the party system continued to be stretched and twisted by the enduring conflict between traditionalist and reformist sectors. By 1988 the unpopularity of the Febres administration left the conservative parties weaker than ever. In contrast, Izquierda Democrática was prepared to lead the reformist drive, seconded at least indirectly by the Christian Democrats. Populism also retained its place in party politics under the aegis of Abdalá Bucaram and the PRE. In the January 1988 contest, Borja and Izquierda Democrática led; with some 20.8 percent, Borja headed a field in which Bucaram surprised observers with his 15.6 second-place finish. Sixto Durán, as the conservative candidate, could not overcome Febres's unpopularity, finished third, and failed to reach the May 8 runoff. On that date, after a campaign marked by Bucaram's remarkably colorful, often scatalogical rhetoric, Borja on his third attempt won the presidency with a margin of some 47 percent to 40 percent. He also entered office with a congressional majority—twenty-nine members of the ID plus Democracia Popular and other sympathizers initially provided at least forty votes in the seventy-one-member body.

The party-based strength of the new Borja administration did not contradict the relative fragility of the system. For the decade of the 1990s it appeared that the ID and the DP would continue to be moderate options for reform; the ever-fragmented left would offer varied forms of more radical change; personalism would be most evident in the populism of an Abdalá Bucaram; and traditionalist forces, while powerful and well-financed, would have difficulty in mounting and maintaining a significant party organization. In short, the undeniable successes of the national party system in recent years were tempered by the frequent outbursts that still rocked the body politic. Many of these came from other domestic interest groups, especially labor, students, and business. The first two have the potential for temporary interruptions or for some adjustment of public policy, and the third still enjoys sweeping influence on the broad direction of public policy.

Organized labor has historically been weak and poorly organized, a condition that has been slow to change. Three self-styled "national" confederations have been increasing their collective action as the Frente Unitario de Trabajadores (FUT). The first effective twenty-four-hour general strike was called by the FUT in October 1985, and the tempo of similar antigovernment protests mounted throughout the remainder of the Febres government. The domination by the Communist party of the Confederación de Trabajadores del Ecuador (CTE), the oldest and most important FUT member, combined with declining workers' wages and worsening living conditions through the 1980s to augment labor's impact. The inauguration of Rodrigo Borja did not mean a quieting of labor activism, although it was true that many Ecuadorean workers were still unorganized while others belonged to groups outside the FUT. Even so, organized labor enjoyed somewhat greater cohesion than the university student movement.

The highly politicized students respond swiftly and angrily to arbitrary government, viewing themselves as the major defenders of the poor and the oppressed. Their leadership is often fragmented by bitter internal rivalries and ideological strife, but nonetheless, the students constitute an interest group that is an important political participant. Meanwhile, the array of business groups and chambers of commerce that formalize the interests of Ecuadorean industrialists, entrepreneurs, and agriculturalists exercises far greater and more constant authority in the setting of the national policy. Although far from monolithic, the private sector constitutes a powerful force, which generally sees the task of government as being the protection of its own interests rather than representing all socioeconomic sectors. In this orientation the nation's business leadership is often joined by the ranking hierarchy of the church, although internal debate occasionally dilutes the inherent conservatism of the religious leaders in Ecuador.

GOVERNMENT STRUCTURES

The operating style of government in Ecuador has customarily been authoritarian, whether the regime is civilian or military. Constraints on executive power depend more on political dynamics than on formal government structures. A president relies far more on individual prestige, oligarchic approval, and military support than on Congress or the courts. The judicial system in particular has been subject to manipulation by the executive, as happened frequently during the Febres years. The same was true of the Supreme Electoral Tribunal and even the Tribunal of Guarantees, which is assigned responsibility for guarding the constitutionality of government actions and regulations. In contrast, the legislative branch has gradually been expanding its role and impact since the 1979 restoration of elected government.

The 1978 constitution gave Ecuador a unicameral system, as embodied in the Cámara Nacional de Representantes (CNR). The role of this body has sometimes been as irresponsible and destructive as others in earlier times; in the early 1980s there was still occasional reliance on side arms, and galleries were packed by either pro- or antigovernment mobs. Even so, the enlarging vistas of democratic government have contributed to greater congressional authority. If presidents have tilted angrily with the CNR, they have also sought to deal with it as a legitimate arm of constitutional government. During the 1979–1984 period Roldós first confronted the personal animosity of Asaad Bucaram's majority forces; after both men died in 1981, Osvaldo Hurtado confronted a fragmented body, which included the vitriolic attacks of the Febres-led traditionalist opponents. When Febres became president, he spent nearly two years turning the majority from its initial opposition. Persuasion, browbeating, and behind-the-scenes maneuvering brought temporary success, but this fell apart as Febres's popular fortunes deteriorated. His plans for constitutional tinkering led to a plebiscite in 1986, but a resounding "no" assured the maintenance of existing structures. Febres subsequently lost control of the CNR and eventually finished his term with a bitter Congress opposing his every move. The fate of Borja, who began with a progovernment majority, should permit further progress toward a responsible and responsive CNR. In the short run, however, CNR contributions to the body politic remain erratic in substance and in impact.

If the executive remains the dominant branch of national government, the authority of the state is relatively weak. For all practical purposes the system is decentralized; Guayaquil often challenges the national leadership while small towns and communities sometimes lie beyond the effective reach of the Quito government. It is not coincidental that Guayaquil's mayor is the second-most-powerful elected official in the country or that power in the rural areas is still controlled by the *teniente político* (political lieutenant). Although appointed by the executive, the *teniente* enjoys considerable freedom of action, especially in Indian highland regions. In addition, authority in policymaking and policy implementation can be diluted by the bureaucracy, which, since the administrative and fiscal reforms of the late 1920s, has grown by leaps and bounds. This growth was further stimulated during the 1970s under the military. The increase in petroleum earnings encouraged a new surge of agencies and personnel, and the number of government employees doubled in a mere three years.

The inclination toward a proliferation of state-related agencies and their staffs is unlikely to be reversed. The prevalence of *palanqueo*— employment derived through influence and personal connections—has united with irresponsible bureaucratic autonomy to undermine further effective presidential authority. As was noted in the second edition of this book, "Ecuador's governmental machinery combines features of the worst possible world: a personalistic chief of state . . . shackled in his policymaking by diluted authority in the countryside and a swollen, self-indulgent bureaucracy independent of both his will and that of the ordinary citizen." Even more fundamental to the authority of the state, however, is the military, for its political role continues to extend beyond its constitutional responsibility for maintaining order and the security of national sovereignty.

Although less professionalized than the armed forces of neighboring states, the Ecuadorean military has undertaken serious efforts at modernization in recent years—particularly during the military governments (1972–1979), and the trend has continued since that time. Even as the armed forces were planning their withdrawal from power, it was with the conscious intention of maintaining and deepening the military's institutional advances as well as being significant levers of power. Guayaquil's well-informed weekly newsletter, *Análisis Semanal*, noted that after seven years in government, the military was leaving with greatly enhanced perquisites and prerogatives. Among these were 23 percent of annual petroleum revenues, the power to appoint members to boards of directors of major state corporations, a near-monopoly of transportation through control of air and sea transport, investments by the Directorate of Army Industries, and even direct participation in the appointment of the defense minister. Furthermore, linkages with civilian elites had been forged by the growing practice of retired officers entering business at high management levels.

Military loyalty to constitutional procedures was tested when Jaime Roldós was killed, but after a few hours' uncertainty the decision to support Osvaldo Hurtado was reached. Institutional patience was more severely tested during the next administration as President Febres, constantly attacked by the political opposition on grounds of high-handed rule, also followed a capricious path with the military. Scornful of institutional autonomy, Febres frequently overrode existing procedures and practices while indulging in favoritism toward his own favorite officers. There were numerous incidents, the most serious of which nearly provoked his ouster.

Controversy over charges of high-level corruption by Gen. Frank Vargas Pazzos, chief of the Joint Command, led to his arrest in March 1986 and, shortly thereafter, a brief armed rebellion at Quito's air base. Months of complicated maneuvering, bargaining, and broken promises led to Febres's seizure by pro-Vargas paratroopers on January 16, 1987. The release of the president after a few hours was followed by a new exchange of charges in which military loyalty was again severely tested. Vargas, a distinguished pilot and military figure, subsequently launched a presidential bid, finishing fourth in the 1988 contest. The question of military loyalty to constitutionality was also raised when Abdalá Bucaram, an outspokenly hostile critic of the military, reached the presidential runoff. Had he won, the presidential relationship with the armed forces would have been gravely taxed. In systemic terms, all of these events merely underline the fragility of Ecuadorean democracy and the immaturity of civil-military relations.

GOVERNMENT POLICY

The functioning of government structures has helped only marginally to alter the essentially elitist and discriminatory distribution of national wealth. Traditional attitudes of dominant social groups, mediated through authoritarian patterns, have mitigated against the realization of reforms in such major policy areas as health, housing, and education. Furthermore, the loosely redistributionist inclinations of several past governments proved only modestly different in impact from the distinctive free-market approach of León Febres Cordero and his collaborators. The latter approach involved a concerted effort to reduce government regulation, promote private enterprise, encourage foreign investment, reschedule the foreign debt, and employ petroleum earnings as the base on which to build economic growth. As the government's official plan stated, it was committed to stabilizing the economy and restoring its capacity for growth through control of inflation while simultaneously strengthening output growth, income, employment, savings, exports, domestic and foreign investment and regulating imports and rationalizing the distribution of vital products.

Febres enjoyed early success in seeking more favorable terms for debt servicing. Eased investment regulations were adopted, and a new series of oil exploration contracts also brought an infusion of fresh funds. Nontraditional exports increased, and there was some progress in housing and generally with public works—although there was marked regional favoritism toward Guayaquil and the coast. At the same time, by the close of Febres's term there had been a deterioration in the areas of manufacturing and industry. Perhaps the single policy area of greatest effectiveness was preventive medicine and health, thanks in some part to the efforts of the president's wife on behalf of a national program of free infant medicine. On balance, however, the decidedly mixed record of the administration said less about the capacities of the free-market system and more about government ineffectiveness in the face of unanticipated economic calamity.

Until 1987 Febres's policy relied substantially upon an overproduction of oil. Consistently exceeding the quotas established by OPEC, Ecuador was nonetheless a slave to world prices. In this respect, its experience was consistent with that of earlier governments. In 1986, for example, the national budget was pegged on prices of $24 per barrel of petroleum; it was later readjusted to the $19 level, and the ultimate drop to less than $15 per barrel was understandably devastating. This factor alone cut GDP growth from 3.8 percent in 1985 to 1.1 percent in 1986. When the March 1987 earthquake destroyed much of the pipeline and totally halted production for more than six months, economic plans were further shattered. These factors contributed to the gravity of economic and social conditions when Rodrigo Borja assumed office, and his own predilection for reformist programs and adjustments did not obviate the magnitude of the policy problems. All of these factors testify to the endemic obstacles to productive policymaking that governments of very different economic and doctrinal outlooks must share. The difficulty for the immediate future in "sowing the petroleum," as oil-rich Venezuela put it felicitously some four decades earlier, remained a critical but at the same time intimidating challenge for government planners.

As the nation moved into the final years of the century, the basic policy issues were constant, and the configuration that faced the Borja administration when it took power in 1988 was scarcely unique. Thus, the foreign debt loomed over the economy, and the degree of state regulation, including control of exchange rates and price-wage ratios, was a subject for both partisan and patriotic debate. Social welfare needs required funds that were hard to identify; even the minimum wage was hard to maintain in the face of the inflationary spiral. The level of public spending was similarly problematic, from both political and economic perspectives. To avoid an enlargement of the public deficit required a restructuring of public finances, which could only stimulate opposition from the private sector.

THE INTERNATIONAL ARENA

The major international actor affecting Ecuador over the years has been the United States. Over the past three decades the U.S. embassy in Quito has periodically exerted conscious pressure on the government. This tendency is exemplified by both covert and overt opposition to the Carlos Julio Arosemena Monroy administration in the early 1960s and by subsequent encouragement of the 1963–1966 military junta. More than a decade later the determination of the Carter administration to encourage the spread of civilian governments in Latin America was reflected by relentless pressure on the Ecuadorean military to convene national elections. Washington later worked behind the scenes to support constitutionality at the time of Jaime Roldós's death and later made evident its desire that the Febres administration serve out its term of office. From the Ecuadorean perspective, the role of the United States through the years, whatever the intention, has been manifested through old-fashioned power politics and diplomatic arm-twisting. Only occasionally, as with León Febres Cordero, has an Ecuadorean chief executive deliberately sought to tighten the relationship with Washington.

This effort was consistent with Febres's belief that additional loans and foreign investment would result from more cordial ties with the United States. His first encounter with Ronald Reagan actually preceded his own inauguration by some six weeks, and there were subsequent trips to the United States during his term. President Reagan, in turn, approved of Febres's advocacy of free enterprise and his commitment to greater stimulation of foreign investment. In 1986, barely one week after having joined the Contadora Support Group on behalf of Central American peace, Febres calculatedly provoked an angry exchange of epithets with Nicaragua's Daniel Ortega and broke off diplomatic relations with that country. Febres's government continued to support the U.S. approach to the Nicaraguan and other Central American issues until the very end.

Febres's overt pro-U.S. posture also triggered acrimonious debate in 1987 with his acceptance of some 6,000 U.S. troops (rotated in contingents of 600 on a biweekly basis from May through October) to help post-earthquake reconstruction efforts in the Amazon Basin. Operation Blazing Trails involved the use of unarmed troops to repair bridges and roads in the devastated province of Napo, at a cost of some $7 million. Both Marxist and centrist leaders denounced the action as endangering national sovereignty, and there were frequent charges that Washington was in fact seeking a new military-training base. In July a congressional resolution was passed calling for an immediate troop withdrawal. When the departure finally took place in October, very little road building had been accomplished, and anti-U.S. attitudes had been fanned.

The accession to power of Rodrigo Borja brought a restoration of more-customary relations with the United States. The new president supported the Arias peace plan for Central America, advocated closer regional collaboration, and promptly extended diplomatic recognition to Nicaragua. Although there was no hostility per se toward Washington, there was a willingness to maintain some distance. Meanwhile, relations with Ecuador's other neighbors were consistent with existing patterns. To the south, Peru was still the nation that had militarily seized territory in the 1941 border war, and Ecuador staunchly continued its refusal to accept the loss. There was warmer friendship with Colombia to the north, including some collaborative efforts against drug traffickers and smugglers.

Multilateral ties have not generally received high priority from Ecuadorean governments, although León Febres Cordero was more unenthusiastic than Rodrigo Borja. The Andean Pact has not lived up to the country's initial expectations, and its provisions are often viewed as taking too little account of Ecuador's economic conditions. Ecuador's role in OPEC, at first very active, has gradually declined, although the country continues to participate in the cartel's meetings. Historically, Ecuador has in some ways pursued a somewhat solitary path, isolated from the mainstream of regional and global affairs. This tendency has certainly marked its behavior in the international arena, although the pattern is likely to be altered in the years to come. Among other factors, the existence of party-based ties with international political movements cannot be discounted. The Izquierda Democrática is an active member of the Socialist International, and Democracia Popular, and especially Osvaldo Hurtado, enjoy prominence within the Christian-Democratic movement.

The rise of drug trafficking and of regional terrorism has also driven Ecuador toward more active cooperation with its neighbors. This policy concern became an important one for the Febres administration and will continue into the indefinite future. The magnitude of the drug industry, especially in light of conditions in Colombia, virtually guarantees that Ecuador cannot avoid having its territory being used for transshipments as well as the growing of crops. The Febres government, in conjunction with Colombian and U.S. authorities, incorporated the armed forces into the effort. Over 1,800 acres (700 hectares) of coca fields were destroyed, some 2,000 people were arrested for related crimes, and Interpol seized 553 tons (502 tonnes) of chemicals used in the refining of cocaine. The problem will continue to demand international and regional collaboration.

The same may well be true for political terrorism. The subversive Alfaro Vive, Carajo group was responsible for a chain of robberies and kidnappings in the 1980s, and it was also linked with Colombia's M-19 subversives and had contacts with the Shining Path in Peru. Fierce opposition by the Febres government severely damaged the group, although another shadowy guerrilla organization took shape as the Montoneros Patria Libre (MPL). Ecuador, traditionally one of South America's more tranquil states, was thus moving toward the destabilizing conditions that were so prevalent in the two closest neighboring republics. There is little likelihood that the country can stand aloof from such challenges to internal security and domestic order.

CONCLUSION

Ecuador inaugurated its third successive democratic government in August 1988. Rodrigo Borja enjoyed the initial benefits of a congressional majority, support of other centrist groups, and the organizational capacity of his country's leading party. Public sentiment in favor of constitutional order was on the rise—especially after the system had survived the political excesses and rancorous exchanges of the Febres years. Such positive signs of a growing commitment to democracy were counter-balanced, however, by the magnitude of socioeconomic problems, which stubbornly resisted solution. Petroleum, the cornerstone of the economy, was being steadily diminished, and world market conditions were un-favorable. The bonanza of the 1970s had been dissipated, and in the process of attempting to maintain new consumer habits, Ecuador had amassed a foreign debt that could not realistically be repaid.

During his first year in office, Rodrigo Borja labored to renegotiate the debt, a process that was long and tortuous. Even by early 1990 there were details to be worked out, while the economy continued to be wrung out by a series of austerity measures. Protests were frequent, especially on the part of organized labor, but the government eschewed the strong-arm tactics of the Febres administration. The tenuous alliance between Izquierda Democrática and Democracia Popular broke down some months before the off-year congressional elections, but Borja succeeded in retaining an effective legislative majority. Even so, the legacy of economic stagnation and recession proved difficult to overcome.

At the same time, the nation's wrenching struggle to move toward modernization was either opposed or complicated by deeply rooted traditionalism. Notwithstanding the new generation of political leaders, Ecuador was sharply divided over means, methods, and basic development policies. The democratic system therefore is fragile and strongly dependent upon international economic forces, powerful foreign influences, and even acts of nature over which there can be no control. For the majority of Ecuadoreans, conditions of life and society will remain difficult, and change will continue to come only slowly and haltingly.

SUGGESTIONS FOR FURTHER READING

Blanksten, George I. *Ecuador: Constitutions and Caudillos.* Berkeley: University of California Press, 1951.

Conaghan, Catherine M. *Restructuring Domination: Industrialists and the State in Ecuador.* Pittsburgh: University of Pittsburgh Press, 1988.

Cueva, Agustin. *The Process of Political Domination in Ecuador.* Translated by Danielle Salti. New Brunswick, N.J.: Transaction Books, 1982.

Fitch, John Samuel. *The Military Coup d'Etat as a Political Process: Ecuador, 1948–1966.* Baltimore, Md.: Johns Hopkins University Press, 1977.

Handelman, Howard, and Thomas G. Sanders. *Military Government and the Movement Toward Democracy in South America.* Bloomington: Indiana University Press, 1981.

Hurtado, Osvaldo. *Political Power in Ecuador.* Translated by Nick D. Mills, Jr. Albuquerque: University of New Mexico Press, 1980.

Icaza, Jorge. *Huasipungo: The Villagers, A Novel.* Translated by Bernard M. Dulsey. Carbondale: Southern Illinois Press, 1964.

Martz, John D. *Ecuador: Conflicting Political Culture and the Quest for Progress.* Boston: Allyn and Bacon, 1972.

———. *Politics and Petroleum in Ecuador.* New Brunswick, N.J.: Transaction Books, 1987.

———. *The Military in Ecuador: The Policy and Politics of Authoritarian Rule.* Albuquerque: Latin American Institute, University of New Mexico, 1988.

Miller, Tom. *The Panama Hat Trail: A Journey from South America.* New York: William Morrow and Company, 1986.

Needler, Martin C. *Anatomy of a Coup d'Etat: Ecuador 1963.* Washington, D.C.: Institute for the Comparative Study of Political Systems, 1964.

Rodriguez, Linda Alexander. *The Search for Public Policy: Regional Politics and Government Finances in Ecuador, 1830–1940.* Berkeley: University of California Press, 1985.

Schodt, David W. *Ecuador: An Andean Enigma.* Boulder, Colo.: Westview Press, 1987.

Thomsen, Moritz. *The Farm on the River of Emeralds.* Boston: Houghton Mifflin, 1978.

Part 3

The political systems of Central and Middle America and the Caribbean

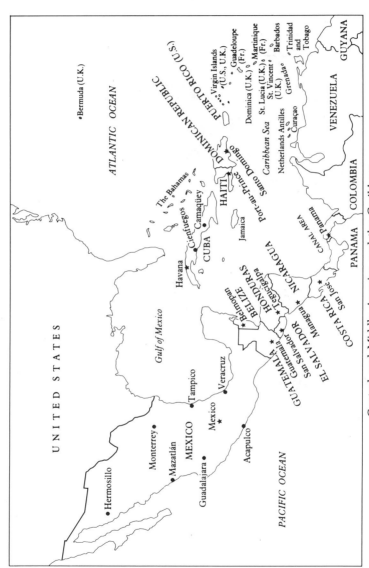

Central and Middle America and the Caribbean

18
Mexico

SUSAN KAUFMAN PURCELL

Until very recently Mexico was one of the few countries in Latin America that appeared to have found a formula for achieving both political stability and economic growth. Under the aegis of a dominant official party, today known as the Partido Revolucionario Institucional (PRI), it had succeeded in forging a national consensus around an economic development strategy that produced growth rates averaging 6–8 percent during the 1960s and 1970s. The fruits of the economic expansion admittedly were distributed very unevenly, yet social unrest was generally avoided since most Mexicans experienced at least an absolute improvement in their living standards during this period.

The onset of the debt crisis in August 1982 spelled an end to Mexico's continued economic growth and threatened to undermine the "peace of the PRI" as well. In order to ensure continued political stability, the leaders of the PRI decided to put Mexico's economic house in order by adopting a severe austerity program that would require the country to stop spending more than it was producing. Such a decision implied short-term risks in the form of economic hardship and rising popular discontent, but it was expected that as a result of the austerity program, economic growth would soon resume, thereby allowing Mexico's unique system of dominant party rule to remain intact.

By 1985 it had become clear that the new strategy was not working. Three years of austerity had produced zero or negative growth while the population had continued to expand by nearly 3 percent annually. This combination had translated into a severe decline in living standards for most Mexicans. Realizing that such a situation could lead either to an unprecedented defeat of the PRI's candidate in the 1988 presidential election or, possibly, to the breakdown of the political system, the government decided to shift course. Instead of attempting to revive the pre-1982 economic strategy, the president and his advisers embarked on an ambitious and risky attempt to restructure the Mexican economy.

The decision to restructure the economy ultimately produced a split within the dominant political party. If Mexico is lucky, the result could

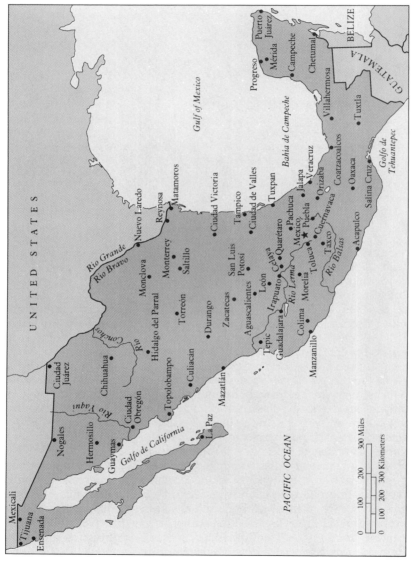

Mexico

be a peaceful transition to a competitive, multiparty democratic regime. More pessimistic scenarios, however, cannot yet be ruled out. These include the breakdown of the political system which would usher in a period of chronic instability, or a reassertion of the PRI's authority through the use of force and repression. Both the PRI and the people who have left it favor a peaceful transition to democracy. They still need to agree, however, on how to achieve their common goal.

POLITICAL BACKGROUND

The current political system in Mexico was itself not the result of a peaceful transition from one kind of regime to another. Instead, it resulted from the breakdown early in this century of a personalistic dictatorship that had proved incapable of incorporating new political groups produced by a modernizing economy and society. The end of the dictatorship ushered in a period of violent civil war that came to be known as the Mexican Revolution.

The Porfiriato

Porfirio Díaz, who first assumed power by means of a military coup, governed Mexico from 1876 until 1911. Initially, his one-man system of rule was welcomed by many Mexicans who had tired of or suffered from the chronic violence and instability that had plagued Mexico throughout most of the nineteenth century.

The absence of peace preceding the Porfirian era had reflected the absence of an elite consensus over the kind of country Mexico was to be in the aftermath of its successful war of independence against Spain between 1810 and 1822. The split had basically pitted Conservatives against Liberals. Conservatives had favored a more traditional, authoritarian, and centralized political system, characterized by a large government role in the economy. They also believed in the unification of church and state. Liberals, in contrast, had wanted power to be decentralized in a more democratic federal system of government. They envisioned a relatively small role for government in the economy and supported the separation of church and state.

Porfirio Díaz managed to combine elements of the two approaches in the system of personalized rule that he established. Although nominally a Liberal, he set up a highly centralized political system. Order was maintained by the military and the rural police, known as the *rurales*. Díaz kept these groups loyal to him, rather than to regional strongmen or caudillos, by continuously rotating their leaders throughout the country. He used the military and the police to implement his policy of *pan o palo* ("bread or the stick"), by means of which supporters were rewarded and opponents crushed.

Beneath the centralized facade, however, an important degree of decentralization was tolerated. As long as the regional strongmen accepted

Díaz's rule and did not resist his policies, they were allowed substantial autonomy at the local level. Mexico under Díaz thus came to resemble a kind of feudal system, with the various caudillos ruling over their own personalized fiefdoms.

The ideology of the Díaz period was best summed up by the positivist slogan, "Order and Progress." The order maintained by the selective use of force and repression was reinforced by a rapidly expanding economy, which provided benefits and payoffs to the people who lived under the system's rules. Political stability, combined with generous incentives for foreign investors, enabled Díaz to attract considerable foreign capital, principally from Great Britain and the United States. Eventually, Díaz's critics began to allege that during his rule, Mexico became "the mother of foreigners and the stepmother of Mexicans."

In the meantime, however, Mexico began industrializing. Financed by foreign capital, the railroad system expanded, opening vast new tracts of land to cultivation for export. Díaz's removal of trade barriers among the states gave foreign investors access to a larger internal market, helped develop new areas of the country, and helped create a larger and more diversified sector of Mexican large and small businesspeople.

Unfortunately, Díaz's emphasis on economic development was not accompanied by an equal concern for the modernization of the political system. Economic decisions remained in the hands of an aging group of technocrats known as the *científicos*. Political power was not shared with important sectors of the emergent middle class. Elections were held throughout the Díaz period in order to provide a veneer of political legitimacy to the prolongation of one-man rule but did not allow new interests to attain representation or to share in the distribution of power.

Eventually, the disgruntled middle class, particularly in the north, demanded "effective suffrage and no reelection," and rallied around the candidacy of Francisco Madero when the aging dictator told a foreign reporter that he planned to step down in 1910. When Díaz subsequently changed his mind, Madero's supporters took up arms against the regime. At about the same time peasant groups in central Mexico, under the leadership of Emiliano Zapata, also began to rebel against the dictator. Unlike the northern middle-class rebels, who wanted to reform the national political system, the essentially conservative peasant leaders asked for the return of their traditional landholdings that the Díaz regime had allowed foreigners to take from them.

To the surprise of the insurgents, the Díaz military forces quickly collapsed. Their numbers had been inflated. In addition, many of the soldiers were prisoners who had been pressed into military service, and they quickly deserted when presented with the first opportunity to do so. Unable to stem the growing insurrection, Díaz resigned in May 1911 and left the country. His departure plunged Mexico into the civil war that has come to be known as the Mexican Revolution.

The Mexican Revolution

The first revolutionary president, Madero, was not very revolutionary. He had never been interested in broad social and economic reforms but, instead, had focused mainly on bringing honest elections to Mexico. He soon found that this goal was not enough to quell the growing unrest in the country. As peasant mobilization continued, Madero sought to strengthen his government by allying with groups that had been dominant under Díaz. Madero failed to implement the kinds of reforms that would have won him peasant support. His efforts to control the growing organized labor movement also failed. Never completely trusted by the old guard and opposed by the growing mass rebellion, Madero's brief presidency eventually ended with his murder in 1913.

The force behind the conspiracy, Gen. Victoriano Huerta, attempted to restore the old Díaz alliance, but he was opposed by Gen. Venustiano Carranza, who enjoyed significant backing from peasant and labor organizations. Carranza's Constitutionalist Army succeeded in overthrowing Huerta in 1914, whereupon Carranza set up a new government and emerged as its head. He was unable to win the support of the peasant leaders Francisco Villa and Emiliano Zapata, who were more concerned with local issues than with forging a new national consensus. Over the next several years, Carranza strengthened his military forces and brought new middle-class representatives of regional and other interests into his provisional government. At the same time he began promulgating a series of economic and social reforms to win over the supporters of Villa and Zapata.

Perhaps Carranza's most lasting contribution to modern Mexico, however, was his calling of a constitutional convention to draft what became the Mexican constitution of 1917, which is still in effect. Middle-class representatives dominated the proceedings, which explains the liberal cast of the document. At the same time the need to win the support of labor and peasant groups led to the adoption of several articles that provided a legal basis for a strong national government and a large state role in the economy. Most noteworthy in this regard are Article 27, which defined different types of property and provided a rationale for agrarian reform, and Article 123, which established a series of labor rights and bestowed upon the state the role of mediator in disputes between workers and employers.

The combination of elements of liberal and radical thought in the new constitution represented the first successful attempt since the fall of Díaz to forge a new political consensus in Mexico. Both strands of thought had coexisted uneasily since Mexico's independence from Spain, but neither had been able to become the dominant ideology. When adherents of both views had been able to compromise, as was the case during the Porfiriato, Mexico enjoyed political stability; in the absence of compromise among Mexico's ideologically divided elites, the country had suffered from chronic instability and violence. Carranza, as the first revolutionary leader to recognize the importance of ideological compromise and embody it in the new constitution, laid the groundwork for the institutionalization of a new political system that was to give Mexico decades of peace and stability.

Carranza occupied the presidency of the new constitutional regime only three years before he, too, was murdered. During that time he made some progress in linking local caudillos to the new national government by means of a system of co-optation that closely resembled the one Porfirio Díaz had successfully used. Specifically, he offered regional strongmen official positions in the new government, thereby buying their loyalty and increasing their dependence on the state. It remained for his successors, however, to take the more radical steps that would institutionalize the new political system along lines that departed in important ways from those that had characterized Díaz's.

With Carranza's death, the so-called Sonora dynasty of northern revolutionary generals took control. Gen. Alvaro Obregón, a powerful and charismatic figure, governed from 1920 to 1924. During this period he began forging alliances with a number of worker, peasant, and middle-class organizations, thereby broadening the base of political support for the new regime. He also laid the groundwork for the eventual subordination of the military to civilian rulers by reducing the size of the military by 50 percent. Finally, he successfully defeated a major rebellion from within the ranks of the "revolutionary family" of generals, that of Adolfo de la Huerta, who had contested Obregón's choice of a successor. By so doing, Obregón strengthened the office of the presidency.

He was followed in office by Gen. Plutarco Elías Calles. During his four years in office (1924–1928), the Bank of Mexico was established, together with a number of other financial institutions; the highway system was expanded; and the state's role in electricity, oil, and other industries important for the economic development of the country grew. Agrarian reform was accelerated, and the hacienda lands that were given to peasants to exploit collectively made them loyal to the revolutionary government. Perhaps most important in terms of the country's future political stability, Calles professionalized the army and further reduced its size, thereby reinforcing civilian control over the government.

Calles was to be succeeded by Obregón, who had decided to run for a second term, but his murder left a political vacuum and raised the possibility of a rebellion by Obregón's supporters. Calles resolved the problem in 1929 by creating a multiclass political party that would integrate all important organized groups in the country while allowing him to retain de facto control of the government. Known as the Partido Nacional Revolucionario (PNR), the party also represented Calles's attempt to institutionalize the revolutionary government by moving Mexico beyond the era of caudillos to that of institutions and laws.

The new party was eclectic in its organizational base—allowing membership based on region and on membership in organized groups.

The only politically important groups excluded from the party were the private sector, which was obliged to join semiofficial chambers of industry and commerce; the church; and landowners, many of whom, by this time, were former revolutionary generals. Those people who were incorporated into the party did not do so on their own initiative but, rather, in reaction to a government initiative. This fact explains why the party, from its earliest days, was never an institution for the free and independent representation of the interests of its members but, instead, an organization that the government used essentially to co-opt and control its members.

By creating this party, Calles "modernized" authoritarian rule in Mexico. One of the major weaknesses of the Díaz system of rule had been the absence of institutionalized mechanisms that allowed, expanded, and controlled popular participation. The PNR was designed to correct this problem, with its incorporation of the most important organized groups in Mexico and its top-to-bottom flow of authority. That the party differed from its counterparts in traditional democratic societies was evident from the fact that its founders conceived of it from the beginning as the party of the government, not as one party that would ultimately compete for and relinquish power to competing parties.

Calles was able to retain de facto control of both the new party and the government by selecting three weak men to serve as provisional presidents of Mexico between 1928 and 1934. He was unable, however, to get his preferred candidate elected to the presidency in 1934. Instead, Gen. Lázaro Cárdenas, who had his own power base within the new party, was named the party's presidential candidate. Within two years of his election he forced Calles into exile.

Cárdenas was the first revolutionary president to govern for six years and with the benefit of a plan for introducing broad political, economic, and social reforms. He felt strongly that in order to further consolidate the revolution, and increase the revolutionary regime's legitimacy and support, it was necessary to strengthen Mexico's political institutions, encourage economic growth, and distribute the fruits of that growth to the peasant and working classes in particular.

In order to achieve these goals, he restructured the official party. In 1936 he integrated all important labor unions into the newly created Confederación de Trabajadores Mexicanos (CTM), and peasant unions were restructured in 1938 into an umbrella organization known as the Confederación Nacional Campesina (CNC). Two new sectors were created: the popular sector, composed of the still small but growing middle class, and the military sector. In order to reflect and emphasize the reorganization of the party along more corporatist lines, its name was changed. In 1938 the PNR became the PRM (Partido de la Revolución Mexicana).

Cárdenas's presidency also saw the expansion of the state's role in the economy. Cárdenas himself was faced with a double challenge: to bring about an economic recovery in the aftermath of the depression as well as to create the infrastructure that would allow a sustained government role in promoting economic growth. During his six years, therefore, he established numerous state enterprises, which he used to help foster and finance economic activity, particularly in rural areas. Exports were also promoted. Perhaps most symbolic of both his commitment to a large state role in the economy and his nationalism was his nationalization of the petroleum industry in 1938, followed shortly thereafter by his nationalization of the railroads.

These populist actions did not go unopposed. Leaders of the private sector formed the Mexican Employers Confederation (COPARMEX) to protect their interests against both the government and the labor unions allied with it, and middle-class conservatives, mainly in northern Mexico, launched an opposition party, the Partido de Acción Nacional (PAN), in 1939. Neither organization was able to reverse the reforms of the Cárdenas years, although they did succeed in slowing the pace of those reforms during the final year or two of his presidency.

Cárdenas's presidency marks the end of the period during which the structure of the modern Mexican political system was put in place. By 1940 the "revolutionary family" had consolidated its power over its opponents, by both military and political means. A single party had been created to incorporate the lower classes, which had been excluded from participation in the benefits of the prerevolutionary Porfirian era. Its restructuring along corporatist lines integrated and linked all important groups and organizations to the presidency and facilitated their control by the government. The economy had been restructured in such a way as to strengthen the state's involvement in the economic development of the country, thereby giving the political heirs of the revolution the ability to put their ideas into practice.

When today we speak of the ideology of the revolution, we refer mainly to individuals and events of the 1910–1940 period. Social justice, agrarian reform, nationalism, and the developmental state were all concepts that began to achieve some concrete reality during this period. It is important to remember, however, that the Mexican Revolution did not have a coherent or unified ideology. The above concerns were not those of all who fought against the Díaz dictatorship. Many of the middle-class revolutionaries in particular had considerably more conservative goals, and many others initially limited their concerns to political issues such as effective suffrage and no reelection. At first, these groups lost out to their more radical compatriots, but their turn to help determine the shape of modern Mexico finally came during the 1940s.

The Institutionalized Revolution

The ascent of the middle class began during the presidency of Manuel Avila Camacho, whose views were considerably more conservative than those of his predecessor. Unlike Cárdenas, who had linked economic growth with redistributive policies in order to improve the living standards of the peasantry, the new president realized that Mexico was entering a new phase of development, one that would require closer cooperation with the growing urban middle class, particularly its professionals and entrepreneurs. Cárdenas's populist policies had alienated precisely those groups, which explains why Avila Camacho decided to shift the emphasis during his presidency.

Mexico's new opportunities for development arose mainly because of World War II, which had begun shortly before Avila Camacho took office. The war made it difficult for Mexico to continue importing consumer goods from Europe and the United States, and this fact, combined with the growing internal demand from the expanding middle-class urban population for such goods, encouraged Mexico to start producing such products. The war therefore served as a kind of de facto protective tariff that allowed Mexico to begin developing an industrial base without having to compete with established and more efficient industries in the more advanced countries.

At the same time, and again because of the war, demand in the United States for Mexican exports rose, and Mexico's increased export earnings were invested in the new domestic industries. The abandonment of many of Cárdenas's populist policies also made Mexico more attractive for foreign and domestic private-sector investment, which Avila Camacho made a point of encouraging. His support of Fidel Velázquez over the Marxist Vicente Lombardo Toledano to lead the main labor confederation is an example of the new pragmatism that characterized his presidency.

On the other hand, Avila Camacho did not break entirely with the policies of Cárdenas. He continued to expand the role of the state in the economy, creating numerous new public enterprises to build up the infrastructure in rural as well as urban areas. He also laid the groundwork for a more stable political relationship between the government and the private sector by setting up separate semiofficial organizations, known as CONCAMIN and CONCANACO, for private-sector members involved in industry and commerce, respectively.

The transition to a new development model became even clearer during the administration of Miguel Alemán (1946–1952), the first president since the revolution who had not fought in it. A lawyer rather than a general, Alemán represented the transition of the political system to a new generation of political leaders. The ascent of this group was further reflected by still another change in the name of the government party, which from then on was known as the PRI or Partido Revolucionario Institucional. The name, which in English is the Revolutionary Institutionalized party, is a contradiction in terms but aptly reflected Mexico's new reality: The revolution, by becoming institutionalized, had also become considerably less revolutionary.

Under Alemán's predecessor, Mexico's economy had grown at the impressive rate of 6 percent annually, in great part owing to the war.

With the end of the war, Mexico had to work harder to attract the capital needed to further industrialize the country. To this end, the Alemán administration invested heavily in infrastructure—expanding the country's network of roads, highways, and railroads—and implemented repressive labor policies that made it difficult and costly for workers to protest and strike. These policies, combined with the purge of left-wing labor leaders and the strengthening of labor leaders who were loyal to the government, created a relatively low-cost and docile labor movement, which made it easier for the private sector to operate and earn substantial profits. To stimulate investment in agriculture, agrarian-reform policies were put on hold, and Article 27 of the constitution was amended to allow the retention or creation of large landholdings for commercial farming and cattle raising.

These policies generated an economic boom as well as high inflation and rampant corruption. They also produced growing discontent on the part of elements of the working class and rural poor, who resented the unequal distribution of the fruits of the economic "miracle." Finally, the neglect of social policies particularly alienated the so-called Cárdenista wing of the "revolutionary family," a situation that, if allowed to continue, could have threatened the continued stability of the country's political institutions.

In order to avoid such a development, Alemán's preferred choice for his successor was rejected, and instead, Adolfo Ruiz Cortines, a consensus candidate, was chosen as the PRI's standard-bearer. Having inherited an overheated economy, he was obliged to implement an austerity program. This required him to reduce government spending, devalue the peso, and keep the exchange rate undervalued in order to reduce imports and increase exports. At the same time, under Ruiz Cortines, who governed between 1952 and 1958, the private sector continued to receive incentives for investment so that the economy would continue to grow. Wages were kept down as an anti-inflationary measure, although some social expenditures were approved in order to dampen growing signs of unrest. These included land invasions in the countryside and increased strike activity in urban areas, led by more-radical and independent labor leaders chosen by the rank and file over incumbents who were considered too subservient to the government.

The growing labor unrest explains the selection of Adolfo López Mateos to govern Mexico between 1958 and 1964. As Ruiz Cortines's secretary of labor, he had managed through negotiations to avoid thousands of strikes. Nevertheless, the labor situation was far from resolved, and within months of taking office, López Mateos decided he had no alternative but to stem the escalating labor unrest by imprisoning the radical leader of the railroad workers as well as the leaders of other striking unions. Once order was restored, however, López Mateos implemented a series of labor reforms, including profit sharing and an expansion of social security.

His whole presidency, in fact, was a carefully calibrated balancing act. Sometimes he appeared to favor the left wing of the party, as with his labor reforms and his significant increase in the amount of land distributed to peasants during his administration. His outspoken support of the Cuban Revolution and his initial hostility toward the United States further reinforced this image. On the other hand, although he frightened the private sector with these kinds of policies, he also won its loyalty and support by virtue of his continuation of the policy of "stabilizing development," which kept government investment in infrastructure high, taxes low, and labor unrest to a minimum, despite relatively low wages.

López Mateos's talents as a negotiator and balancer of conflicting interests made Mexico's growing social, economic, and political problems seem less urgent than they really were. For some time now the population had been growing faster than productivity, causing an increase in unemployment and a general decline in lower-class living standards. The middle class, in contrast, had continued to prosper economically but came to resent the restricted democracy that limited its political participation in the decisions that affected its members' lives and fortunes. Finally, the political system that developed between 1929 and 1934 had been designed for a different Mexico, one whose population was not only smaller but also less complex and more rural. Since the late 1940s, however, Mexico had become increasingly urban, with a strong and important private sector and a multitude of groups, associations, and interests that were not represented adequately, or at all, by the official party.

EARLY SIGNS OF CRISIS

The implications of these changes became clear during the presidency of Gustavo Díaz Ordaz (1964–1970). The new president had assumed that the policy of stabilizing development would continue to produce enough economic growth to meet the needs of Mexico's increasingly urban population. Instead, in the late 1960s it became apparent that the development strategy was in trouble. Agricultural exports, which until then had generated the foreign exchange necessary to sustain investment and growth, began to decline—the result of increased domestic consumption and an inability to maintain a competitive edge abroad. This situation translated into a declining ability on the part of the government to meet the needs of the growing numbers of urban poor.

The increasingly important urban middle class also began to express its unhappiness. For some time middle-class elements had resented the authoritarian nature of the political system, which denied them a political role commensurate with their abilities and wealth. As long as the government's policies had produced economic growth, however, they had been content to remain on the political sidelines. Once the economy began to flounder, they began to demand more participation in the decisions that affected their lives.

Student demonstrations in 1968 were initially a reflection of this middle-class discontent. The students peacefully organized a march in support of greater democracy and social justice. The government over-reacted, in part because of the impending Olympic games that Mexico was hosting, and fired on the demonstrators, killing at least several hundred of them, mainly young people. This incident undermined the already-weakened legitimacy of Mexico's political and economic systems and caused Díaz Ordaz's successor, Luis Echeverría Alvarez (1970–1976), to shift course radically.

The events of 1968 had divided the governing elite and made it impossible for this elite to agree on a successor to Díaz Ordaz. This fact allowed the outgoing president to reward his minister of government, Luis Echeverría, for his loyalty. Echeverría, therefore, took office without the strong base of elite support that his predecessors had enjoyed. He also had never before been elected to a political office, a situation that set him apart from other successful presidential candidates of the ruling party.

In order to reestablish consensus within the governing elite, Echeverría decided he needed to aim for both economic growth and social justice, or so-called shared development, in contrast to the stabilizing development of his predecessors. When he tried to reform the tax system in order to redistribute income, however, he was blocked by vested interests. Instead of persevering in his reform effort, or abandoning one of his two goals, he reaffirmed his commitment to both growth and distribution and resorted increasingly to deficit financing to fill the growing gap between government revenues and expenses.

The results proved disappointing, though predictable. Inflation grew to unprecedented levels, and the private sector, lacking confidence in Echeverría's economic policies, curtailed investment and began sending capital abroad. Instead of reducing government spending in order to restore business confidence, Echeverría decided that the solution to his and Mexico's problems lay in further increasing both state spending and the role of the state in the economy. In this decision, he was influenced by so-called dependency theory, in vogue at the time among Mexican intellectuals. Distrustful of private enterprise, whether foreign or domestic, dependency theorists advocated a statist development strategy to enable Third World countries to achieve both greater independence from in-dustrialized countries and greater social justice.

Under Echeverría, therefore, the number and role of state enterprises expanded. Such a policy constituted a change in the rules of the game between business and government. More disturbing was the demagogic populist rhetoric and behavior of the administration. In order to restore the "revolutionary" legitimacy of the political order and offset private-sector resistance to his policies, Echeverría encouraged trade-union militancy and attacked foreign and domestic businesspeople for exploiting the country. Capital flight intensified and eventually forced the government to devalue the peso in 1976.

Echeverría's growing frustration at the unraveling of his economic and political policies ultimately led him, in the final weeks of his presidency, to expropriate vast tracts of private agricultural land for distribution to landless peasants. This action triggered rumors of a military coup for the first time in recent Mexican history. By the time the next president (José López Portillo) took office, Mexico was in crisis, both economically and politically.

The new president promised a return to normalcy and adopted a conciliatory approach toward the private sector.[1] His term of office, however, coincided with a period of escalating oil prices and the discovery in Mexico of vast petroleum reserves. This combination enabled López Portillo to postpone indefinitely any plans for the restructuring of the economy and, instead, to continue the expensive statist policies of his predecessor.

Mexico's great oil wealth, however, led the new president to adopt an even more ambitious plan than that of his predecessor. He decided to use Mexico's oil to borrow additional capital in order to transform Mexico from a Third World to a First World country during his six-year term (1976–1982). The strategy made sense initially. Petroleum prices were expected to rise well into the 1980s. High rates of inflation abroad meant that debts could be repaid with greatly inflated dollars, and low interest rates, combined with that inflation, meant that the funds could be borrowed at negative real interest rates. Finally, commercial bankers in other countries were eager to lend Mexico money in an attempt to recycle the billions of petrodollars that Arab governments had placed on deposit.

López Portillo's strategy worked for a number of years. Huge investments were made in roads, ports, and industries such as oil and steel. The economy boomed, hundreds of thousands of new jobs were created, and unprecedented spending occurred in areas such as health and education. Unfortunately, the greater availability of resources also translated into astronomical increases in waste and corruption.

The international context, however, changed dramatically in 1981. Oil prices began to fall in response to the economic recession in the United States and other industrialized countries, and oil conservation efforts in oil-importing nations began to produce results. The Mexican president refused to adjust Mexico's oil prices downward, believing that the oil-price decline was temporary. Nor did he alter Mexico's ambitious development plans. Instead, he tried to replace what he thought was Mexico's "temporarily" lost oil revenues with foreign borrowing.

This failure to adjust to the new economic reality generated a growing lack of confidence in the administration's economic policies and in the peso. The government, unwilling to pay the political costs, refused to devalue the currency, and because the peso was overvalued, imports surged; at the same time a growing belief that a massive devaluation was imminent triggered billions of dollars of capital flight. The government was thus increasingly forced into short-term borrowing at ever higher, and floating, interest rates.

The bubble finally burst in August 1982, when Mexico was unable to obtain enough loans to service existing debts and ran out of money. With his term drawing to a close, López Portillo made a desperate attempt to stem capital flight and refurbish his historical image by nationalizing the Mexican banking system. He achieved neither aim. Like Echeverría, he left it to his successor to find a solution to the increasing disintegration of Mexico's economic and political systems.

Initially, the approach adopted by President Miguel de la Madrid (1982–1988) did not differ greatly in its goal from that of his two immediate predecessors. Like Echeverría and López Portillo, he tried to close the yawning gap between government income and expenditures. Unlike them, however, de la Madrid could not resort to foreign borrowing to bridge the gap, since private commercial banks were willing to lend money to Mexico only for the servicing of its approximately $85 billion debt. Nor could de la Madrid close the gap with oil revenues because petroleum prices continued to plummet, from approximately $40 a barrel when he took office to a low of approximately $10 a barrel in 1986.

To deal with the situation, de la Madrid imposed an economic austerity program to oblige Mexico to begin living within its means. Imports were cut, and the government announced plans to reduce government expenditures by decreasing the number of government employees, selling off or closing unprofitable state-owned or state-run enterprises, and reducing government subsidies to all groups.

The resulting improvement in Mexico's economic situation was not sufficient to keep the PRI from losing twelve important mayoral contests in northern cities during elections in 1983. The sense of the increasing political costs of continued austerity eventually led the government to relax its austerity program in 1984, prior to important gubernatorial elections scheduled for 1985 and 1986. But the relief generated by the loosening of the government's tight rein on the economy was short-lived. Inflation soared, and economic growth proved elusive.

Until 1985 the president's top advisers still generally believed that Mexico's economic health could be restored mainly by reducing imports and decreasing government spending. In 1985 they concluded that Mexico could no longer hope to prosper by isolating itself from the international economy and focusing almost exclusively on producing for a captive domestic market. Instead, the economy would have to become more export oriented, which meant that productivity and efficiency would have to improve so that Mexican products could compete successfully in international markets.

Even before 1985 the government had taken a number of steps in this direction. Import licenses had been gradually removed, tariffs had been reduced, foreign investors had been made to feel relatively more welcome, and a number of state enterprises had been sold to the private sector or closed down. But these actions had resulted from ad hoc decisions rather than a carefully reasoned change in development strategy. Once the decision was made to shift course in mid-1985, the de la Madrid administration stepped up its efforts in all these areas.

Mexico's decision to enter into the General Agreement on Tariffs and Trade (GATT) in 1986 best symbolized its new commitment to a more open economy and a liberal development strategy. A more realistic exchange rate policy adopted after 1985 was still another indication. In 1987 the government negotiated a bilateral agreement with the United States for trade and investment, which set up a consultative mechanism for resolving disputes and negotiating the reduction or removal of remaining barriers to bilateral trade. The administration also continued to eliminate import-license requirements and to sell off state companies. In December 1987 it implemented an Economic Solidarity Pact with business and labor designed to bring down Mexico's unprecedented triple-digit inflation.

DIVISION OF THE DOMINANT PARTY

President de la Madrid's moves to liberalize the Mexican economy were not paralleled by equivalent efforts in the political sphere. Early in his administration he launched an anticorruption campaign and committed his administration to free and fair elections. Both actions were motivated by a desire to restore confidence in the PRI and to rebuild the legitimacy of the political system in general, and both failed. Corruption was so pervasive that any real effort to eradicate it would divide and weaken Mexico's political class. And the combination of a sick economy and a divided political elite could ultimately undermine the stability of the entire political system. The president was therefore forced to limit his efforts to imprisoning the former head of Petróleos Mexicanos (PEMEX) and to extraditing the highly corrupt former chief of Mexico City's police force.

On the electoral front, de la Madrid's support for free and fair elections produced a string of victories for the main opposition party, the Partido de Acción Nacional (PAN), in mayoral elections throughout northern Mexico. The administration therefore decided to postpone its democratic opening until there was sufficient economic growth to produce majority votes for the PRI. In the meantime, the government tried to offset the loss of political support caused by the absence of economic growth with a number of ad hoc reforms aimed at eliminating the more egregious shortcomings of the political system. It began to select more popular and qualified candidates to run on the PRI ticket, in the hope that doing so would reduce the need to resort to electoral fraud in order to "win" elections. It also allowed opposition candidates relatively greater access to the media.

These limited reforms failed to produce the desired results. Instead, the PRI continued to lose support throughout de la Madrid's presidential term and went into the 1988 presidential election severely weakened by a split within the official party that led to the defection of important leaders of the PRI's left wing.

The problem began when a dissident group within the PRI, known as the *corriente democrática* ("democratic current"), decided to challenge President de la Madrid's right to choose his own successor. Led by Porfirio Múñoz Ledo and Cuauhtémoc Cárdenas, the *corriente* pressed for an open election within the PRI to choose the party's presidential candidate. Democracy, however, was not the only issue. The *corriente's* leaders and supporters were highly critical of President de la Madrid's efforts to restructure the Mexican economy along more liberal lines. Instead, they advocated an end to economic austerity, a repudiation of the debt, and a return to the kind of statist, redistributive development strategy that Echeverría had unsuccessfully tried to implement.

The *corriente's* strength within the PRI was not allowed to be tested. Instead, President de la Madrid's candidate, former planning and budget minister Carlos Salinas de Gortari, was named the PRI's standard-bearer. The meaning was clear: President de la Madrid was doing all he could to ensure that his restructuring efforts would be continued after he left office by naming as his successor the person most identified with those efforts.

When Cuauhtémoc Cárdenas refused to support Salinas, he was expelled from the party. Subsequently, he decided to challenge both the PRI's candidate and its authority by running for president as the candidate of a coalition of minor opposition parties. He did better than expected, receiving 33 percent of the vote according to the government; Cárdenas himself claims to have defeated Salinas. As the son of Mexico's most popular president since the 1910 revolution, Cárdenas attracted support among the rural and urban poor who had benefited from the land, labor, and other reforms implemented by his father in the 1930s. He also received the votes of Mexicans who had a vested interest in the maintenance of a statist development strategy, which includes government bureaucrats as well as laborers employed in government enterprises such as PEMEX, the state petroleum company. Cárdenas's message of a return to better days also had broad appeal among voters tired of economic austerity and the hardship it had brought.

At the same time that Cárdenas challenged the PRI from the left, the PAN ran a charismatic candidate, Manuel Clouthier, who siphoned off support for the PRI on the right. Clouthier demanded an even greater liberalization of Mexico's economic and political systems than President de la Madrid was willing to implement. Charging the PRI with being corrupt and undemocratic, he argued that its continued rule was keeping

Mexico from realizing its economic and political potential. Like Cárdenas, the PAN candidate objected to the outflow of capital to service the debt and claimed that the money should be spent to alleviate the suffering of the Mexican people.

Although de la Madrid was able to transfer the presidency to his preferred candidate, it remains to be seen whether President Salinas will succeed in completing the economic and political reforms that his predecessor could only begin. Salinas's weak electoral mandate initially led to expectations that he would have to compromise with the forces represented by his electoral challengers. He began by doing no such thing. Instead, he announced his intention of intensifying efforts to divest the state of inefficient and unproductive enterprises and to liberalize the Mexican economy so as to enhance the country's ability to compete abroad. He continued to welcome foreign investment and to explore ways of enhancing Mexico's trade, with the United States and Japan in particular.

To the surprise of many people, he also asserted himself politically by imprisoning the corrupt and powerful leader of Mexico's most powerful union, that of the petroleum workers. In the process, he increased his political support by his show of courage and his imagination. At the same time he helped undermine the position of Cuauhtémoc Cárdenas, who enjoyed strong support from the petroleum workers and their leader because of his commitment to a statist development strategy. Salinas's indictment of a number of wealthy business leaders charged with fraud in the collapse of the stock market in October 1987 also sent a strong signal against corruption and increased his popularity with ordinary Mexicans. Finally, he accepted the defeat of the PRI's candidate for governor in Baja California Norte, thereby allowing an opposition party (the PAN) to take control of a state for the first time since the Mexican Revolution.

It is still too early to tell whether President Salinas will succeed in his efforts to modernize and revive the economy and to increase the legitimacy of Mexico's political system. But there is little doubt that he intends to do his best to achieve what many people thought impossible in the aftermath of the debt crisis—a peaceful modernization of Mexico's economic and political systems.

POLITICAL AND SOCIAL GROUPS AND THE STATE

The Mexican political system has generally been classified as authoritarian by those people who have studied it extensively. This definition does not mean that the state is all-powerful and governs by force. Instead, it describes a relationship between the state and organized groups in which political pluralism, or the independence of groups from the government, is limited. Stated differently, power tends to flow from the top down rather than from the bottom up. In contrast to the situation in democratic political systems, groups are often organized at the initiative of the state or, in those cases in which there has been a grass-roots initiative, the state has managed either to co-opt or select the group's leaders. As a result, interest-group leaders have tended to serve two masters, the state and the members of the group, and have been more dependent on the former for their continued power.

Because a single party, the Partido Revolucionario Institucional, has governed Mexico since 1929 (though under a number of different names), it is difficult to separate the party from the state. This blurring of lines between the two has helped maintain the limited pluralism of organized groups. The party itself has a corporate or group structure, in which member organizations are affiliated with one of three sectors—the labor, peasant, or so-called popular sector that joins together a variety of middle-class groups. These groups constitute the electoral base of support of the political system. In return for their support, representatives of the various sectors are given the opportunity to run for political office on the PRI label, which until recently has generally guaranteed them an electoral victory.

As Mexico has become more urbanized, the relative power and influence of the peasantry and organized labor have decreased. Without the sectoral organization of the party, both labor and the peasantry would find their ability to elect representatives to national office severely diminished. The sectoral basis of organization of the PRI, therefore, has been a key element in maintaining a strong and dependable base of support for the government. Another key element has been the co-opted group leaders. Without their willingness to work with the government in delivering the support of their followers in return for electoral office and other benefits, the top-down structure of authority that has characterized the Mexican political system would collapse.

The sector that has been the easiest for the government to manipulate and control has been the peasantry. Its members have the least access to independent resources and are the least educated. The popular sector has been the most independent. Its members are more homogeneous, relatively wealthy, and educated. The strongest organized group within the popular sector has been the government employees' union (FSTSE), whose support has been crucial to the PRI's ability to maintain its dominant place in the political system. The most powerful unions within the labor sector are those of the oil workers and the teachers. Like the government employees' union of the popular sector, these unions group together all the workers in a particular industry. Their refusal to support the government could create severe problems for the PRI, which helps explain why their members have been the best rewarded by the government for their loyalty and support.

Although it is difficult to distinguish between the government and the PRI because the same party has always controlled the presidency, the PRI is not really a policymaking body. That function has increasingly been performed by the government bureaucracy, which is dominated by technically trained professionals. Instead, the PRI has mainly functioned as a kind of ministry of elections, in the sense that its principal function has been to mobilize electoral support for the PRI during presidential, state, and local elections. As already noted, its role in maintaining limited pluralism has also been crucial.

As the majority party, the PRI has been able to win most of the elections honestly, particularly on the national level. Many Mexicans have long identified the PRI with the government and have given their vote to the party either because of tradition or because of a belief that the government has served their interests relatively well. The PRI has also received support from less contented voters who have seen no better alternative. On the other hand, electoral fraud has occurred, particularly in rural areas where there are no opposition parties to oversee the honesty of electoral procedures. Sometimes such fraud has been blatant, as in the state and local elections in northern Mexico in the early 1980s.

Until the 1970s the PRI was an important institution in the recruitment of political leaders and, especially, Mexico's presidents. Since then, however, the bureaucracy, specifically the president's cabinet, has produced the country's presidents. Luis Echeverría was the first modern Mexican president never to have won an elected office before assuming the presidency, and Mexico's three subsequent presidents—José López Portillo, Miguel de la Madrid, and Carlos Salinas de Gortari—also came from the bureaucracy. Their technocratic backgrounds are part of a growing tension within the political system between the so-called *técnicos* ("technocrats") and *políticos* ("politicians"). The increasing selection in recent years of young technocrats as political candidates, as well as the recruitment of elected officials into the cabinet, appears to be an effort to resolve the tension and erase the distinction between the two.

Despite the PRI's status as the majority party, it does not include the organized private sector—because of the "unrevolutionary" nature of the private sector, which generally opposed the Mexican Revolution. Instead, business groups are organized into a number of national organizations, including CONCAMIN, the Confederation of National Chambers of Industry, and CONCANACO, the Confederation of National Chambers of Commerce. Both were set up by the government and the groups' leaders work with government officials. Yet because of the groups' access to independent resources, the government has not been able to control them in the way that it has been able to control organizations within the PRI. On the other hand, there has generally existed what one analyst of the Mexican political system has called "an alliance for profits" between the government and the private sector.[2] Put differently, the government has provided business groups with subsidies, protection from foreign competition, lucrative contracts, and the like, in return for their cooperation and support.

For a brief period the PRI (under an earlier name) did include the military sector, but that association was abolished in 1940. The military, nevertheless, has been under the control of civilian political leaders since the 1930s, but that fact does not mean that it is without influence. Military leaders are rewarded for their support by being named state governors, heads of parastate enterprises, and the like. The extent of their involvement in day-to-day policymaking depends on the presence or absence of crises that threaten the stability of the political system. During the 1968 student disturbances the military was actively involved in decision making, and its political involvement has increased as a result of the security threat posed by the Central American conflict and the influx of tens of thousands of refugees into southern Mexico.

Although Mexico is an overwhelmingly Catholic country, the Catholic church has not played a formal or active role in politics until recently. The explanation lies in Mexican history. Like the private sector, the church was "on the wrong side" during the revolution, and its opposition continued until the late 1920s, when a regional rebellion by armed bands of lay Catholics (*cristeros*) was finally crushed by President Calles. Despite the fact that certain policies of postrevolutionary governments, such as the establishment of national textbooks or the prohibiting of church-controlled primary schools, have disturbed the church, for the most part it has developed a good working relationship with the government.

The remaining important organizations or groups that are outside the PRI are the opposition parties. Until recently the most important such party was the Partido de Acción Nacional (PAN), organized in 1939. Its strength has generally been in northern Mexico, particularly in urban areas, and its supporters have included small business people, independent professionals, women, and active middle-class churchgoers. Its opposition to the statist economic policies of the PRI, as well as the nature of its supporters, accounts for its conservative image as a right-of-center party on Mexico's political spectrum. On the other hand, its consistent support of democratic reform and honest elections places it squarely in the tradition of the northern revolutionaries, who originally sparked the revolution of 1910 with their calls for effective suffrage and no reelection. PAN's electoral support has grown steadily over the past several decades. In 1961 it won 7.6 percent of the votes cast nationally; in the presidential election of 1988 it received 18 percent of the total vote.

The main opposition party on the left until recently was the Popular Socialist party (PPS). Founded by Mexico's most famous Marxist, Vicente Lombardo Toledano, this party has worked cooperatively with the PRI. In return, it has received a share of local political positions in areas where it has tended to draw the most votes—in urban areas and, occasionally, among poor Indian peasants in the south. Yet it has rarely been able to win more than 2–3 percent of the total vote cast nationally.

Since the 1988 presidential election, however, the Cardenistas have constituted the principal electoral threat to the PRI from the left.

Cárdenas's Party of the Democratic Revolution (PRD) is far from homogeneous, being a coalition of PRI defectors and communists and Socialists who formerly belonged to the Mexican Socialist party. Whether the PRD can institutionalize itself remains to be seen. In the meantime, the charismatic leadership of Cuauhtémoc Cárdenas and the discontent produced by the government's austerity program and economic liberalization efforts are the glue that keep it together.

Whether the Cardenista Front will ever be able to defeat the PRI depends less on the behavior of Cárdenas than on that of the PRI. Since the early 1960s the PRI's percentage of the vote has steadily declined, from a high of more than 90 percent to a low of 50 percent in the 1988 election according to official figures—or 38–44 percent according to unofficial estimates. Until 1988 the decline in the party's electoral support was paralleled by a steady increase in voter abstention, but in 1988 many voters decided to vote for Cárdenas rather than abstain.

If the PRI continues to lose support, the only way it will be able to maintain control of the political system is through the use of force, fraud, or both. The govenrment is well aware, however, that none of these options represents a long-term solution to the problem. The PRI, therefore, has already made an effort to select more-popular and better-qualified candidates. But better candidates alone will not solve the problem. The PRI must also take steps to rebuild itself as a political institution.

When the official party was founded in 1929, Mexico was basically a rural country with a considerably smaller population. The sectoral organization of the party reflects the social structure of this earlier Mexico. If the PRI wishes to maintain its sectoral organization, it will have to make more of an effort to unionize workers in the rapidly growing service sector, create more groups to incorporate members of the rapidly growing urban middle class into the party, and also incorporate the burgeoning number of urban poor.

If, on the other hand, the government were to decide that the PRI has outgrown its sectoral structure, the party will have to implement policies that are designed to attract the votes of independent-minded individual citizens. In fact, it will have to implement such policies even if the PRI's sectoral organization is maintained, since the PRI has always depended on both corporate and individual support.

The anticorruption campaigns of both President de la Madrid and President Salinas have been efforts to rebuild popular support for the party. Salinas's arrest of La Quina, the notoriously corrupt head of the petroleum workers' union, achieves this goal in two ways. First, it represents an attack against corruption. Second, it helps weaken support for the Cardenista Front while encouraging party discipline within the PRI. Though traditionally strongly supportive of the PRI, La Quina and his followers deserted the PRI's candidate in 1988 because he promised to restructure PEMEX and clean up corruption in the oil industry. The arrest of La Quina, therefore, is a signal to other union bosses that there will be consequences if they fail to support the reform policies of the PRI leadership.

The main source of renewed popular support for the PRI should, of course, ideally come from the efforts of both de la Madrid and Salinas to liberalize Mexico's economic and political systems. So far, such support has not developed. The potential beneficiaries of the opening of the economy begun under de la Madrid and continuing under Salinas are unorganized and, in many cases, have not yet experienced an improvement in either their income or their opportunities to increase it. In contrast, the people who stand to lose as a result of the more open economy are the most organized groups in Mexican society. These include government bureaucrats, workers in government enterprises such as PEMEX, and the owners, managers, and workers in Mexico's most inefficient, unproductive, and uncompetitive companies. These are some of the people whose votes contributed to Cárdenas's surprising show of strength in the 1988 presidential election.

The PRI is therefore engaged in a race against time. It must be able to show that its economic policies can produce economic growth for Mexico and translate that growth into an improvement in the living standards of individuals in all classes. Otherwise, it will continue to lose support. At the same time, the party must continue to liberalize politically for two reasons. First, democratization is necessary to restore the legitimacy of the entire political system, especially because the rest of Latin America has made an important transition from authoritarian to democratic rule. Second, political liberalization is needed to reinforce the economic opening. It is possible, of course, for a more open economy to grow despite the absence of democratic government. But a relatively closed and authoritarian political system will eventually place limits upon the possibilities for such growth.

POLITICAL CULTURE

The changes in Mexico's economic and political systems are reflected in the country's political culture. The conventional wisdom used to be that Mexico's political stability was made possible in part because of the passive and submissive attitudes of the Mexican people toward authority. The same theory was used to explain why Mexicans were able to withstand great suffering, exploitation, and social and economic injustice. Although there is some truth to this characterization, it fails to give enough emphasis to the liberal aspects of Mexican culture. How else is one to understand, for example, the importance that even dictators have given to formal elections or the fact that the much-revered Mexican Revolution originated not so much as a movement for social justice but as an effort to democratize a blatant dictatorship?

With the passage of time and the transformation of Mexico's economy and social structure, the country has become more urban, middle class, and culturally homogeneous. The advent of modern communications has also played a part. To the extent that Mexico has become less isolated and more integrated into the international economy, its culture has also become less authoritarian. No doubt what some Mexican intellectuals refer to as "cultural imperialism," particularly the influence of the United States, has also been important in this transition to more democratic values.

Along with a decrease in authoritarian values has come a decrease in Mexicans' defensiveness, fear of dependence, and sense of inferiority. These traits have until recently been important ingredients of Mexican nationalism. Because of the country's shared 2,000-mile (3,200-kilometer) border with the United States, a history of repeated U.S. invasions or interference in its internal affairs, and the loss of almost half of its territory to its northern neighbor during the nineteenth century, such defensive nationalism is understandable and perhaps was unavoidable. Now, however, it seems to be giving way to a more positive kind of nationalism that is based less on what Mexico is not than on what Mexico is and might be.

To the extent that Mexico is able to succeed in making a peaceful transition from an authoritarian to a democratic regime and from a closed to an open economy, the political culture will continue to evolve in this more positive direction. If, however, Mexico's current economic and political problems prove too great a challenge for its leaders, there is a strong possibility that the country will seek refuge in its past traditions and values. That trend would imply a resurgence of authoritarian values and behavior.

A successful transition to more open political and economic systems does not mean, on the other hand, that Mexico must lose its *mexicanidad*. Western Europe, for example, has managed to industrialize and democratize without the various countries losing their separate cultures and identities, and there is no reason why the Mexican experience should be any different.

PROSPECTS FOR THE FUTURE

There are no guarantees that the attempts to restructure the economy will succeed or that the incipient political reforms will be continued. But even if Mexico does everything right to make a peaceful transition toward more open economic and political systems, external factors could still work against it.

More than two-thirds of Mexico's exports currently go to the United States. Sluggish economic growth in that country would therefore negatively affect Mexico's prospects for reviving its economy and, by extension, for creating a broader base of support for the government's economic restructuring efforts. Increased levels of protectionism in the United States would have a similarly destructive impact. Other external factors that could undermine Mexico's transition to a more open and modern economy include a precipitous drop in oil prices, a substantial increase in interest rates, and a recession in the industrialized countries.

The fate of Mexico's political reform is less linked to external developments, though not entirely divorced from them. To the extent that the rest of Latin America remains committed to democratic government, Mexicans will feel somewhat defensive about their one-party-dominant regime. Yet if Mexico's economic reform efforts fail, the desire on the part of many Mexicans for a more open political system will not necessarily disappear. It may even intensify, reflecting a decision on the part of the Mexican people to have a greater say in the decisions that affect their well-being. There is little doubt, however, that prospects for a more democratic political system would be enhanced by a successful transition to a more open economic system.

What is occurring today in Mexico is a kind of *perestroika a la mexicana*. There are not many precedents for a peaceful and simultaneous transition from a relatively closed economy and political system into relatively open ones. The main cause for cautious optimism is the commitment of Mexico's incumbent political leaders, who correctly believe that traditional political and economic institutions are keeping Mexico from fulfilling its impressive potential as a nation.

NOTES

1. For an earlier version of the discussion of the López Portillo and de la Madrid administrations, see Susan Kaufman Purcell, *Debt and the Restructuring of Mexico*, Critical Issues Series (New York: Council on Foreign Relations, 1988).

2. Clark W. Reynolds, *The Mexican Economy: Twentieth-Century Structure and Growth* (New Haven: Yale University Press, 1970), p. 186.

SUGGESTIONS FOR FURTHER READING

Bailey, John J. *Governing Mexico: The Statecraft of Crisis Management*. New York: St. Martin's Press, 1988.

Bilateral Commission on the Future of United States–Mexican Relations. *The Challenge of Interdependence: Mexico and the United States*. Lanham, Md., and London: University Press of America, 1989.

Camp, Roderic A., ed. *Mexico's Political Stability: The Next Five Years*. Boulder, Colo., and London: Westview Press, 1986.

Grayson, George W., ed. *Prospects for Mexico*. Washington, D.C.: Foreign Service Institute, Department of State, 1988.

Leiken, Robert S. "Earthquake in Mexico." *The National Interest*, no. 14 (Winter 1988/1989):29–42.

Levy, Daniel, and Gabriel Szekely. *Mexico: Paradoxes of Stability and Change*. 2d ed. Boulder, Colo., and London: Westview Press, 1987.

Newell G., Roberto, and Luis Rubio F. *Mexico's Dilemma: The Political Origins of Economic Crisis.* Boulder, Colo., and London: Westview Press, 1984.

Pastor, Robert A., and Jorge G. Castañeda. *Limits to Friendship: The United States and Mexico.* New York: Alfred A. Knopf, 1988.

Purcell, Susan Kaufman. *Debt and the Restructuring of Mexico.* Critical Issues Series. New York: Council on Foreign Relations, 1988.

Purcell, Susan Kaufman, ed. *Mexico in Transition: Implications for U.S. Policy.* New York: Council on Foreign Relations, 1988.

Riding, Alan. *Distant Neighbors: Portrait of the Mexicans.* New York: Alfred A. Knopf, 1985.

Roett, Riordan, ed. *Mexico and the United States: Managing the Relationship.* Boulder, Colo., and London: Westview Press, 1988.

19
Development and Revolution in Cuba

JUAN M. DEL AGUILA

As the only nation in the Western Hemisphere that has adopted revolutionary communism for its model of political development, Cuba stands separate from other Latin American nations. The revolution of 1959 and its subsequent radicalization have attracted the interest of students of politics as well as that of policymakers, journalists, intellectuals, and ordinary people, many of whom have been inspired by "the Cuban example." In addition, the central role played by President Fidel Castro from the beginning of the revolution is a key to understanding developments in Cuba in the years since he and his followers came to power, partly because under his leadership Cuba has become an influential actor in regional politics and has engaged in an unusual degree of revolutionary activism abroad. Like other caudillos (political strongmen) of his generation, President Castro personifies revolutionary Cuba to observers the world over, but as will be made clear in this chapter, his own transformation from an impetuous young revolutionary to an aging dictator parallels the course of the revolution itself.

The politics of revolutionary development have moved Cuba through periods of radical transformation in the economy and the social system, through phases when pragmatism and moderation shaped domestic priorities and affected social attitudes, and finally to the stable totalitarianism of the 1980s characterized by growing difficulties at home and partial retrenchment abroad. In effect, the revolution and its consequences can be understood as an ongoing experiment in the process of achieving mature nationhood, but as with any experiment, Cuba's has been characterized by fits and starts, abrupt policy reversals, intense criticism of the real nature of socialism and revolution, and evident exhaustion.

Cuba's growing participation in the Latin American community, its established role in the Third World, and its membership in the Communist world create opportunities for—but also impose constraints on—its dynamic interaction in international affairs. Hallmarks of the revolution

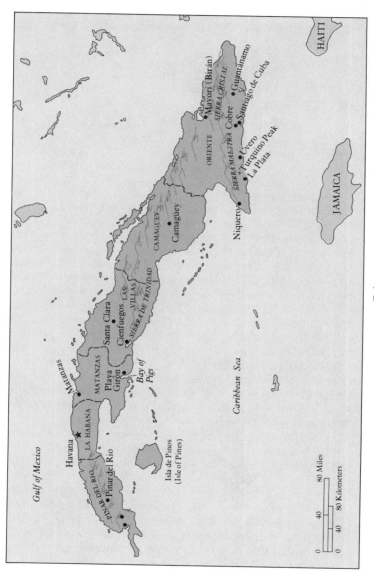

Cuba

have been its external projection and the insistence of Cuba's leaders that the country inspire others to carry out radical revolutions elsewhere. Finally, two basic impulses still shape Cuban behavior, namely, activism abroad and the preservation of national unity, and appreciating the relationship between them is crucial for a comprehensive understanding of the country.

HISTORY, POLITICAL CULTURE, AND EARLY DEVELOPMENT

Cuba, the largest of the Greater Antilles, is located at the entrance of the Gulf of Mexico some 112 nautical miles (208 kilometers) from the United States. Its 44,218 square miles (114,525 square kilometers) of total surface stretch over a varied topography that includes mountain ranges, rolling hills, plains, and hundreds of rivers and streams. The principal mountain ranges lie in the eastern, central, and western provinces, and the highest mountain, Pico Turquino, rises to some 6,500 feet (1,981 meters) in the Sierra Maestra range.

The country's coastline is indented with several deep harbors and ports: Mariel and Havana in the west; Nuevitas, Nipe, and Santiago de Cuba in the east; and along the southern coastline. From the colonial period to the present Cuba has heavily relied on foreign commerce for its prosperity, so that a sound maritime infrastructure is critical for its trade. Since 1959 Cuba has shifted its structure of foreign trade away from the United States and toward the Soviet bloc, so that one can find ships from the Soviet Union and other Eastern European countries anchored in Cuba's harbors. The Cuban merchant marine has also expanded dramatically since 1959.

Unlike many other developing countries, Cuba has not experienced a dramatic rise in population, and its demographic growth rates remain stable. Population growth averages around 1 percent, which alleviates the burden on employment and services that plague many countries in the Third World. Sixty-nine percent of the country's 10 million inhabitants reside in urban areas, and the rest live in small towns and in the less-densely populated rural areas. Most Cubans have lived in large cities and towns since the 1930s, and by the late 1980s over 20 percent of the population lived in the capital city of Havana or its environs. Part of the infrastructure of some of Cuba's larger cities is deteriorating owing to neglect, scarce resources, and the sheer passage of time: Havana was founded by Spanish settlers in 1514, and Santiago de Cuba in 1515.

Caucasians, mulattoes, and blacks are practically the only ethnic groups in the country. Whites make up 66 percent of the population, mulattoes nearly 22 percent, and blacks 12 percent or so. Whites have been the dominant ethnic group during this century, and many are descendants of the creole elite of colonial Cuba. Intraregional and seasonal migration is a fact of life in Caribbean societies, but although migration to Cuba from other Caribbean and Latin American countries has been low, small numbers of migrants from some Caribbean islands settled in Cuba earlier in this century. No Indian subcultures exist, since for all practical purposes the mostly primitive Indian communities that inhabited the island in precolonial times disappeared early in the colonial period.

Although racial differences were evident in prerevolutionary Cuba, no deep racial cleavages existed between whites and nonwhites, and basic social attitudes did not support overt discrimination. Education, occupation, and income levels established social differences among the races, but they also affected status for blacks, whites, and mulattoes as individuals of a particular race. Racial prejudices were found among many whites and between blacks and mulattoes. Subtle forms of segregation were a manifestation of these basic attitudes, but overt racial conflict rarely erupted. Snobbery and elitism often characterized the behavior of the white upper classes, but more than racism shaped such behavior. Changes in the social system and class structure, which have reduced racial and class differences, have further dampened friction among the races but have not eliminated the psycho-social dimensions of racism.

Some scholars like Carlos Moore do maintain that "in social, cultural and psychological terms, race pervades the everyday life of every Cuban, white or black," and that "Cuban society was racist prior to 1959 and is steadfastly so today." Moore and others believe that racism is part of a complex cultural legacy rooted in slavery, subsequently exacerbated by social indifference and political neglect, and that revolutionary intolerance has created new racial barriers. He contends that "revolutionary Cuba is a more intolerant and inhospitable environment for the expression of black distinctiveness than was pre-revolutionary Cuba,"[1] mostly as a consequence of ideological intolerance. On the other hand, the Cuban government considers race and racism to be extremely delicate issues and maintains that the latter is no longer a major social problem. It is thus evident that the issue of race—rooted in Cuba's history and memory— has not disappeared under socialism, partly because racial harmony cannot be achieved by simply declaring that racism has been abolished.

Columbus discovered Cuba during his first trip to the New World in 1492, but because the island lacked substantial mineral wealth and had not developed an advanced indigenous civilization, it remained sparsely populated well into the eighteenth century. The 50,000 or so native Indians at the time of the discovery were gradually subdued by Spanish settlers under the *encomienda* system. They were forced to search for precious minerals, work in agriculture, fish, and also engage in primitive forms of trade. Brutal treatment, disease, poor nutrition, and the harmful effects of servitude itself decimated the Indian population, and little trace of their social system remains. Efforts to Christianize the Indians were not entirely successful, and often the Spanish settlers used violence to instill the "proper" attitudes among the Indians. Catholic missions were established and charged with propagating and maintaining the faith, so that friars and priests played important roles in the early life of the colony. The Catholic church subsequently grew in number, wealth, and influence, and its notions of order, faith, spirituality, and salvation pervaded Cuba's cultural foundation.

The Spanish settlers of Cuba were a heterogeneous lot. Many came from Andalucía and other southern regions of Spain, and as was the case elsewhere in Latin America, the lure of gold, a sense of adventure, and the opportunity to escape the Spanish caste system brought thousands of settlers to Cuba and the New World. But the Cuban colony remained poor, and the prospects of growing fabulously wealthy were greater on the mainland. The colonial regime at this time was weak and ineffective, and Spain itself had little interest in Cuba's development. In his book *The Caribbean*, Franklin Knight writes that "throughout the sixteenth century, the colony [Cuba] virtually stagnated, challenged by pirates, ravaged by hurricanes, plagued by diseases, and depopulated by the magnetic pull of Mexico and Perú."[2] In short, the foundations of Cuba as a colony stemmed from a social system dominated by *peninsulares* and supported by the Catholic church. The native population failed to resist the impact of a stronger culture and quickly disappeared.

Black slaves were brought to Cuba by the thousands from the 1700s to the middle of the nineteenth century, replacing Indians as laborers on sugarcane plantations, as servants in the larger towns and cities, and as manual laborers in service occupations. A census taken in 1791 showed that out of a total population of 273,000, 56 percent of the people were white and that slaves made up the largest proportion of the black population; a century later another census showed that over the entire colonial period, nearly 375,000 black slaves had been brought to Cuba. It is a fact that the slave trade contributed to the wealth of many planters and traders.

Cuba's economy originally revolved around tobacco and, subsequently, coffee cultivation, but it gradually became a plantation economy geared to sugar cultivation, production, and export. The island's geographical location offers the right temperatures as well as the necessary rainfall for sugar production, and the terrain of the lowlands is suitable for harvesting cane. Indeed, economists and historians maintain that the island's comparative advantage in sugar production was soon realized and that earnings from sugar exports financed the imports of foodstuffs, textiles, machinery, and other capital goods.

The combination of sugar, slavery, and the plantation economy shaped the colonial social structure and laid the foundation for an economy geared to foreign commerce, but it did not produce a society of small landowners and rural proprietors. Differences among *peninsulares*, criollos, slaves, and *libertos* (slaves who had obtained their freedom) were evidence of a hierarchical system unmindful of any notion of social equality. As depicted by popular novels, books, and documents of the time, colonial

Cuba remained unaffected by changes taking place elsewhere and there-fore stayed under the tight control of Spain. On the other hand, the benefits of free trade were strongly felt during the English occupation of Havana in 1762–1763, as new markets were found and the economy was further integrated into regional and international commercial net-works. Geopolitical rivalries with Great Britain and the United States in time forced Spain to modify the mercantilist regime, and it gradually gave way to a more open trading system. Spain sought to reestablish political control over its colonial domains, including Cuba, in the early nineteenth century, but the impact of liberal ideas added to the intro-duction of capital and new technology stimulated new thinking.

An influential group of thinkers and wealthy oligarchs like Francisco Arango and Ignacio Montalvo believed in the promise of positivism and individual will, and educators like José de la Luz y Caballero and the priest Félix Varela engendered an early commitment to political inde-pendence and nationhood. Although education was restricted to the creole elite and to the people who could afford it, and was influenced by Catholic beliefs, its benefits were felt by a growing number of progressive criollos. A rift between the people who were committed to the preservation of the colonial regime and those who believed in Cuba's gradual emancipation and eventual independence shaped the politics of the period and forced a reassessment of relations between Cuba and Spain. Racial considerations affected each outlook, and Knight maintains that "the slave society during the nineteenth century was equally one of ferment and strife. Its strengths created its inherent weaknesses. A divided society was also a divisive society. Tensions existed within the white groups as well as between white and nonwhite. In Cuba, the most enduring of the Caribbean slave societies, the white groups split basically between *peninsulares* and *criollos*."[3]

In summary, the colonial system was marked by inequality and hierarchy, and its economic foundation rested on a plantation economy and slavery. Early advocates of Cuba's struggle for independence faced ideological divisions and clashing interests, which allowed Spain to maintain control over the colony. Lacking clear proindependence lead-ership, often fearing the consequences of a social revolution, and without political cohesion or class consciousness, the creole plantocracy accepted its politically subordinate status.

THE STRUGGLES FOR INDEPENDENCE, 1868–1901

The emergence of new political currents in the 1860s stemmed from the need to challenge Spanish domination and to improve Cuba's economic position. On the one hand, a nationalistic and clearly separatist movement advocated confrontation and war against Spain if those were the only means of achieving independence. More moderate elements, represented by the Reformist party founded in 1862, advocated representation for

Cuba in the Spanish Cortes, administrative reforms, and liberal trade policies. The issue of slavery often divided the creoles, as did class and economic differences between the eastern and western planters. The latter feared a social revolution and tended to be more conservative. Still, Spain's refusal to grant meaningful concessions to the Cubans and its failure to satisfy legitimate political demands led to rebellion in 1868 and a decade of bloody and destructive warfare.

The rebels were led by Carlos Manuel de Céspedes, a patriot and moderately wealthy planter from Oriente province. Other political and military leaders like Generals Antonio Maceo and Máximo Gómez fought bravely during the protracted struggle, but latent political divisions among the rebels weakened their effort. Nationalism fed the rebel cause, as did the commitment to emancipate Cuba from colonial domination. Spain poured thousands of troops into Cuba, and sent one of its best generals, Arsenio Martínez Campos, to lead the Spanish forces. Yet the failure to truly carry the war to the western provinces; the deaths of Céspedes, Ignacio Agramonte, and other leaders; the absence of external help; and the lack of support on the part of many Cubans doomed the rebel cause.

Nearly 250,000 people on both sides lost their lives in the struggle, and Cuba's infrastructure was devastated. The war cost Spain approximately $300 million and was both a cause and a consequence of political quarrels among its own elites. Yet Spain and the rebels signed an armistice in 1878 that led to a tenuous peace and a period of self-criticism and questioning on the part of those Cubans who still advocated independence. On the other hand, the Cubans' ability to wage a protracted struggle, endure enormous sacrifices, and exhibit national aspirations demonstrated that a new political consciousness was emerging and that emancipation was achievable. Differences over slavery, regional tensions, and the balance between civilian leaders and military caudillos would have to be resolved before a new war would start, or else Cuba would remain a colony.

Cuba's political economy changed in the last decades of the nineteenth century, partly because the restoration of political stability created economic opportunities for domestic and foreign capital. New technology transformed the sugar industry so that production revolved around foreign-owned industrial complexes, which limited opportunities for local management and participation. A growing worldwide demand for sugar allowed producers to plan with economies of scale in mind, and the industry benefited from new markets, principally in the United States. Spain introduced fees and taxes on Cuba's exports in the early 1890s that adversely affected domestic producers, partly because it feared growing U.S. penetration of Cuba, but these measures did not really isolate Cuba from the United States.

A growing dependence on the U.S. market for trade, investment, technology, and industrial inputs characterized U.S.-Cuban relations in the 1880s and 1890s, even while Spain maintained political control. In 1896 U.S. investments in Cuba were estimated at $50 million, concentrated in mining and sugar holdings. Trade between the two countries was valued at $27 million in 1897, and the composition of that trade showed that the United States exported to Cuba manufactured and industrial goods and imported sugar, molasses, tobacco, and a few nonmanufactured products. U.S. Consul William Elliot Gonzalez publicly recognized that "the Island practically, depends completely on the U.S. market for its sugar exports" and that associated industries like the railroads, warehouses, port facilities, and their financial and labor support structures depended directly on the U.S. market.

There is little doubt that this growing penetration of a weak economy dominated by sugar and its derivative production by a growing capitalist, industrial power meant that the colonial regime was subjected to internal and external pressures. Once again, proindependence forces gathered to challenge Spanish authority and assert claims for independence and sovereignty, and to do so with a new and more compelling sense of unity and national purpose. New leaders, principally José Martí, had forged a more mature vision of political emancipation and nationalism, and the issue of slavery had been laid to rest since its abolition in the 1880s. In short, ideologically and organizationally, the separatists were in a stronger position than in the 1860s, while Spain vacillated between granting meaningful reforms or reimposing absolutist government.

As the founder of the Cuban Revolutionary party (PRC) in exile, and as the intellectual force and principal civilian organizer of the war effort, José Martí represented a younger generation of Cubans committed to the total liberation of the country. Martí believed that war was brutal but necessary, "a political process that would definitively resolve a situation in which fear of war is a paralyzing element," and held that "patriotism is a sacred obligation when one struggles to create conditions in the motherland that would improve the lives of one's countrymen." In the *Manifiesto de Montecristi*, a critical document issued in 1895, the civilian-military leadership spoke for two generations of Cubans and stated that after the war, "the nation would be constituted from its roots, with its own viable institutions, so that a government would be unable to lead it into tyranny." The manifesto asserted that the nation returned to war "with an enlightened and democratic people, cognizant of its own and others' rights," and sure of "its republican education." It is thus quite clear that the people struggling for independence advocated representative government and democratic institutions and were influenced by nationalism, liberalism, and self-determination rather than by absolutism, Marxism, or notions of class struggle.

The war raged back and forth for three years, with the rebels fighting a guerrilla struggle and Spain following a more conventional strategy. Rebel columns moved westward across the countryside, burning and sacking properties and cane fields, attacking small towns, and disrupting the economy. Spain's hated policy of "reconcentration" forced hundreds of thousands of Cubans into fortified towns and military compounds, and hunger, desolation, and brutality decimated the population. Thousands died, including Martí and Maceo, and property losses were valued in the millions of dollars.

A military stalemate between rebel and Spanish forces, and sensationalist accounts of the fighting published in the United States, led to U.S. military intervention in 1898. The Cuban question had become an important issue in U.S. domestic politics, and Spain as well as the rebels had attempted to influence U.S. public opinion. There is solid evidence to show that the McKinley administration preferred a negotiated settlement that would bring independence to Cuba and that it urged Spain to give up its control. Spain rejected diplomatic entreaties and offers of mediation from European powers and obstinately refused to accept either military or political defeat. In April 1898 the U.S. Congress passed a resolution granting President McKinley's request for authority to end hostilities in Cuba, but it also disavowed any interest in exercising sovereignty, jurisdiction, or control over Cuba once Spain had been driven out.

The U.S. occupation of Cuba lasted until 1902, and many students of Cuban politics believe that it created a legacy of resentment and frustration because, in part, U.S. intervention prevented the Cubans from achieving a complete victory over Spain. U.S. military authorities partly rebuilt the nation's infrastructure and brought about significant improvements in public health, education, public administration, and finance, but Cuban nationalists and many intellectuals felt a sense of political impotence and frustration. Subsequently, the inclusion of the Platt Amendment, passed in 1901 by the U.S. Congress, into the Cuban constitution meant that Cuba became a U.S. protectorate rather than a sovereign nation, because the amendment granted territorial concessions to the United States, placed financial restrictions on the Cuban government, and allowed the United States to intervene in Cuba's internal affairs.

Cuba's foreign economic relations were subsequently shaped by a Reciprocity Treaty (1903), which granted preferential treatment to Cuban sugar in the U.S. market and reduced tariffs on U.S. exports to Cuba. U.S. investments in Cuba's sugar industry, cattle industry, public services, utilities, and other properties had reached $200 million by 1909, nearly 50 percent of all foreign investment in Cuba. The Platt Amendment and the Reciprocity Treaty facilitated a growing U.S. influence in Cuba and were often perceived as neocolonialist measures aimed at protecting U.S. interests in the island. Many politicians, businesspeople, owners of sugar estates, and some conservative intellectuals felt that the U.S. "tutelage" was not necessarily detrimental. The U.S. presence thus created a significant political cleavage, separating those people who felt it to be beneficial and necessary for Cuba's early development from nationalists who saw it as a direct infringement of genuine self-determination. The views of Ramón Ruiz illustrate a scholarly consensus on these matters, namely, that the Platt Amendment limited Cuba's first experience in self-government and "offered the Cubans a facile way out of domestic difficulties. Reliance on the United States eventually engendered among Cubans a loss of faith in their Republic and in their own nationality."[4]

THE POLITICAL DEVELOPMENT OF PREREVOLUTIONARY CUBA

Political competition during the early republican period revolved around the Liberal and Conservative parties. These parties—and others—were essentially controlled by the political caudillos José Miguel Gómez and Mario García Menocal, respectively, and did not articulate clear political philosophies or programs. The political system revolved around client arrangements and patronage networks, so that partisan loyalties were often exchanged for political favors. Electoral fraud and administrative corruption were common, and elections were often cynically viewed as attempts by manipulative politicians to preserve or expand personal power. Public office was held in disrepute, politics was used as a means of self-enrichment, and the democratic ideals that had motivated Martí and other revolutionary leaders remained little more than abstractions.

On the other hand, respected intellectuals like Fernando Ortiz and Enrique José Varona formed part of an emerging democratic intelligentsia that rejected politics as a means to private gain and advocated civic-mindedness, cultural emancipation, and above all, honest and democratic government. Varona asserted that "to govern is to watch over compliance with laws, and provide the means for that compliance," and he pointed out that "our public ills are the work of all of us." Ortiz, in turn, criticized the poor conditions found in most of the rural areas, where peasants, seasonal workers, and unskilled laborers toiled under difficult conditions and lived at barely subsistence levels. He attacked the evils of monoculture and the subordination of the economy to foreign capital, and he suggested that the revolutionary generation had betrayed principles articulated earlier. Reformist groups founded the opinion journal known as Revista de Avance, and other people joined the Cuban Council of Civic Renovation. Through writing, public speaking, and political organization, a cultural revival encouraged debate, much of it focused on the need to cleanse the political culture and establish viable institutions. Finally, many critics framed their charges against the postcolonial regime according to anti-imperialistic principles, appealing to students, intellectuals, labor leaders, and others to unite in order to bring about political change.

Gerardo Machado was elected as a popular president in 1924, but he became a virtual dictator following his contrived reelection in 1928 and his violation of constitutional norms. From that point on, politics took on a violent character. Government and opposition alike engaged in terrorism, shootings, and political assassinations, indicating that institutions were unable to resolve political conflicts and that force was seen as a legitimate arbiter of political disputes.

The Great Depression had a devastating effect on the economy. Plummeting sugar prices affected the livelihood of hundreds of thousands of families, and unemployment, social misery, and rural banditry reflected a deeper structural crisis. The government sought to alleviate the problems by acquiring new loans from U.S. bankers, but the country's creditworthiness was shaky and it had previously accumulated substantial debts. Cuba's economic and financial dependence on the United States meant that the impact of the depression was felt in business, finance, public administration, and government itself, so that the options were limited. Breaking the economic bonds with the United States would wreak havoc and plunge the country into instability and chaos. Managing the crisis through technical approaches and financial legerdemain would only postpone the day of reckoning. Robert Smith illustrates the complexity of the situation and its interrelatedness: "During the closing months of 1930 the situation in Cuba degenerated rapidly. The economic picture had been deteriorating for several years and the world-wide depression added problems to an already serious situation. This helped stimulate opposition to Machado, and the threats of disorder mounted."[5]

Student protestors challenged the police in the streets, but resistance to Machado also involved professionals, middle-class elements, labor leaders, and the Communist party. One of the leading anti-Machado organizations was the University Students Directorate, through which a new generation of activists and revolutionaries advocated a complete and definitive change of regime. The Communist party attacked Machado from orthodox Marxist positions, depicting him as the instrument of foreign interests and as the enemy of the working class. The party called for popular mobilization, strikes, and urban confrontations, but its calls failed to spark a popular revolution and often led to internecine struggles with other groups. Finally, the ABC, a secret, cellular organization made up of middle-sector individuals, intellectuals, and students dissatisfied with the politics of the University Students Directorate, played a prominent role in the struggle against the dictator. The ABC stood for liberty and social justice, and its programs called for economic and political reforms. ABC cells engaged in clandestine activities and were often involved in violent incidents—the organization's strategy at one point aimed at Machado's assassination. In short, the opposition was unified in its commitment to driving Machado from power and ending the dictatorship, but it was tactically and ideologically divided. The political agenda of the non-Communist groups called for democratization, socioeconomic change, and a challenge to U.S. interests in Cuba, but their failure to rally mass support against the dictatorship proved to be one of their major weaknesses.

The army proved to be a critical contender, because its support was essential for either keeping Machado in power or shifting the balance to his adversaries. The army was structured on parochial loyalties rather than merit, and its military competence was questionable. It remained the pillar of order and stability, but it also felt the violent political fragmentation that ultimately ousted Machado. Some lower-rank members, many of whom came from humble backgrounds and viewed the army as a vehicle for self-improvement and social mobility, demanded higher pay and an end to the politicization of promotions. Such internal pressure, at a time when a crisis of political authority affected the government's freedom of action and paralyzed decision making, opened the way for an internal revolt led by then-sergeant Fulgencio E. Batista y Zaldívar. Under his leadership, the army sought to contain revolutionary outbursts and directly influence the selection of presidents. It would play a central role during the following decades.

Finally, as had been the case since 1898, the United States played the role of ultimate power broker. In 1933 the new Roosevelt administration, through Sumner Welles as its special ambassador, shaped a resolution to Cuba's political crisis that preserved U.S. interests and restored stability. Welles succeeded in his mediation efforts, partly because the ABC and other groups accepted his presence and partly because the army failed to support Machado at a critical moment. Through his efforts, a weak government under Carlos M. de Céspedes succeeded Machado, but that regime was quickly overthrown. A five-member executive committee headed by Ramón Grau San Martín, a physician and university professor, took power briefly, but it too gave way to a more revolutionary government—still led by Grau. Jaime Suchlicki maintains that these events constitute a "turning point in Cuba's history," marking the "army's entrance as an organized force into the running of government and Batista's emergence as the self-appointed chief of the armed forces and the arbiter of Cuba's destiny for years to come."[6]

The revolutionary government ruled amid great agitation and was opposed by the U.S. embassy, powerful business interests, conservatives fearful of administrative anarchy, and the ABC. Its support came from the University Students Directorate, liberal elements in the press, and, for part of its tenure, Batista and the army. Principally because of the efforts of Antonio Guiteras as minister of government (secretario de gobernación), the government established an eight-hour day for workers, required that at least 50 percent of all employees in industry and commerce be Cuban, proclaimed university autonomy, and granted peasants rights to the land they occupied. In addition, the government dissolved all political parties that had collaborated with Machado, reduced rates on utilities, and granted women the right to vote. Guiteras believed in the need for a radical revolution that would uproot the framework of "economic imperialism" affecting Cuba's economic and political development, but neither he nor Grau could effectively centralize power in order to carry basic reforms forward.

From exile after the revolutionary government's demise and its replacement by a pro-U.S. conservative regime, Guiteras recognized that the "work of a revolutionary government cannot be improvised lightly once in power. It presupposes a preparatory work that [the revolutionary government] could not have had," partly "because it lacked an organized political force able to support it."

One cannot overestimate the impact of the truncated revolution of 1933 on the succeeding generation's psychological makeup, its social agenda, or the political determination of its most able leaders. The incomplete business of 1933 left a sense of frustration among the protagonists of reform and revolution, but in time the goals were rechristened. The failure to democratize politics, achieve economic sovereignty, and cohesively assert a national will shaped the ethos of future reformers and revolutionaries, for whom "the lessons of 1933" laid the foundation for new departures.

SOCIAL DEMOCRACY AND AUTHORITARIANISM: POLITICS IN THE 1940s AND 1950s

After the brief revolutionary interlude in 1933, national politics in Cuba went through a period of realignment and moderate authoritarianism characterized by the conservative domination of weak and undemocratic regimes supported by Batista and the army. Taking advantage of improved economic conditions and secure from military threats or revolutionary outbursts, the regimes governed by partially satisfying political demands and reintroduced client arrangements. On the other hand, electoral irregularities, corruption, episodic repression, and the subordination of civil authority to military pressures retarded the development of viable governing institutions, so the system remained personalist and moderately authoritarian.

In his excellent study *Revolution and Reaction in Cuba*, Samuel Farber suggests that "the contrast between the civilian-democratic and the militarist-authoritarian traditions" formed the key political cleavage and that neither the democratic left in exile nor the Communist party effectively challenged this order. Farber points to relative improvements in civil liberties and a new toleration for moderate domestic opposition groups as evidence of an implicit bargain between the conservative sectors and their opponents, characterized by economic populism and the maintenance of dependent capitalism.[7]

External economic dependence on the United States meant that domestic capital played an increasingly important role, and Cuban interests gradually acquired a growing share of ownership in the sugar industry. Measures like the Reciprocity Treaty and the Jones-Costigan Act in addition to the policies of the Export-Import Bank stabilized Cuba's economy and gave confidence to domestic producers, who always looked to the U.S. market as the preferred outlet for Cuban products. U.S.-

mandated quotas for sugar guaranteed that Cuba's principal export would enter the United States under a preferential tariff and led to the expansion of acreage and production. The United States supplied 54 percent of Cuba's imports in 1933, a figure that increased to nearly 65 percent at the end of the decade and some 81 percent by 1950. What Cuba bought was purchased in the United States, and although having a dynamic market close by proved to be convenient, it also retarded Cuba's industrial development.

A major threshold in the process of political development was reached in 1940 following the enactment of a democratic and progressive constitution, itself the result of political compromises among the democratic left, conservatives, and Communists. This constitution established universal suffrage and freedom of political organization, recognized Western-style civil rights, and abolished the death penalty. Women, children, and workers received social protection, and racial and sexual discrimination were outlawed. Public education was mandated, and the needs of rural children in particular were identified. Private property was legitimated in a broad social context, and the state was charged with "orienting the national economy." Industrial development, agrarian reform, and greater rural-urban integration were set as national priorities, and the state was granted greater powers in national development, public administration, and fiscal and monetary policies.

The constitution reflected a complex bargain between the rising middle sectors and traditional interests, and in explicitly framing a tutelary role for the state in economic and social affairs, it incorporated then-current ideas and political philosophies. If properly observed and enforced, the constitution potentially could have served as the legal and ideological foundation of a lasting democratic order, one that rejected radical approaches but permitted vigorous reformism. Consciously or otherwise, its framers believed that the proper balance between order and liberty had been set and that dependent capitalism could be made to serve broad social interests, not just those of influential elites. Unfortunately, the failure of Cuba's democratic regimes in general and educational institutions in particular to instill the values that a fragile democracy requires if it is to survive a legacy of authoritarianism, corruption, and strongman rule undermined constitutional principles, and violence and gangsterism soon reappeared.

The Auténtico ("Authentic") administrations of Ramón Grau (1944–1948) and his successor Carlos Prío (1948–1952) initiated reforms in agriculture, fiscal management, labor, and education and maintained respect for civil liberties. National elections were competitive and clean, and conservative, liberal, social-democratic and Communist parties received electoral support. Public subsidies, bureaucratic employment, and the creation of new state agencies led to gains among middle-class and professional groups, but agricultural development lagged, and the power of foreign interests was not directly confronted. Worst of all, political violence and urban-based gangsterism threatened the integrity of the democratic regimes, and neither Grau nor Prío was able to stem the violence. Corruption was spawned by a vast system of patronage, payoffs, and bribes, and Grau's minister of education turned his office into a powerful political machine and an illegal financial network. Student activists turned the University of Havana into a haven for gun-toting thugs and criminal factions and often paralyzed the institution through intimidation and brutality. According to Suchlicki,

> An entire system of nepotism, favoritism and gangsterism predominated. Despite numerous accomplishments, the Auténticos failed to provide the country with honest government or to diversify Cuba's one-crop economy. The reformist zeal evident during Grau's first administration had diminished considerably in the intervening decade, and Grau himself seemed softened after years of exile and frustration. When confronted with the reality of Cuban politics, the early idealism and reformism of [student leaders and others] gave way to materialism and opportunism.[8]

The political aspirations and national expectations that had been generated were only partially fulfilled by the two social-democratic administrations: Modernization through reformism did not curb the power of vested interests or foreign capital, and central authority proved weak and incapable of eradicating violence and corruption. To the unfinished agenda of 1933 were added the unrealized promises of the democratic reformers, and scandals and internecine quarrels in Cuba's leadership class eroded public trust in government. The state, supported by neither a dominant class nor a traditional oligarchy, failed to convert diffuse support into legitimately accepted rule, and the nation simply drifted.

Batista's bloodless but effective coup in March 1952 ended the constitutional regime and restored order superficially through political authoritarianism. Cuba's political development was cut short by the coup, and the system proved vulnerable to force. Proclaiming that worry about the lack of guarantees for life and property had led him to accept "the imperious mandate" and usurp power, Batista and his supporters found little resistance to their actions. Prominent national figures, business organizations, labor leaders, a few church officials, and the leadership of the Partido Socialista Popular (PSP—the Communist party) either endorsed the coup or rejoiced at the Auténticos' demise. The Veterans' Association and the Bankers' Association gave their approval, and the Cuban Workers' Confederation pledged to cooperate with the new government. Except for scattered protests by students, denunciations by Catholic lay leaders, and isolated instances of civic resitance, the coup provoked neither massive popular repudiation nor legal-institutional opposition.

During his time in office Batista was unable to legitimate his regime either through elections, good relations with the United States, or negotiations with his opponents. Opposition to Batista included moderate, democratic elements sympathetic to the Auténticos but willing to entertain confrontational approaches; traditional politicians (like those in the Society for Friends of the Republic) who believed that Batista would "come around" if a safe way out of the political stalemate was found; and revolutionaries unwilling to accept halfway solutions or electoral shenanigans. Feeling politically secure, Batista refused calls for new elections and thus spurned a reasonable approach that may have prevented the radicalization of many of his opponents. As a result, insurrection and "armed struggle" became attractive and even justifiable, because there was no viable political center on which a national compromise could be achieved.

Several revolutionary groups, including Fidel Castro's 26th of July Movement, participated in the struggle against the dictatorship. Among these, the Revolutionary Directorate (DR) stood out because of its uncompromising ferocity and violent strategy, aimed at assassinating Batista himself. Led by the charismatic student leader José Antonio Echeverría, the DR was not the vanguard of a social revolution but an organization committed to ending the dictatorship. Ramón Bonachea and Marta San Martín contend that the DR's "immediate task was to overthrow the dictator, establish a democratic form of government, and then carry out a revolutionary program to solve the problems of landless peasants, exploited workers and young people condemned to economic oblivion."[9]

As one of the founders of the 26th of July Movement, and as its undisputed leader, Fidel Castro played a central role in the insurrection against Batista's dictatorship. A group led by Castro attacked a military garrison in the city of Santiago in 1953, but the attack failed and many of Castro's followers were either killed or subsequently arrested and shot. He was captured and tried for subversion, but as a trained lawyer with oratorical skills, Castro used the trial to issue an indictment of the government. Portraying his cause as just and inspired by patriotism and Martí's ideals, Castro called for a return to constitutional government, agrarian reform, profit-sharing arrangements between owners and workers, and social improvements in rural Cuba. He was convicted and sentenced to fifteen years in prison but was subsequently released in 1954 under an amnesty program.

Castro's political beliefs and true intentions before he came to power have been the focus of considerable debate. Some people argue that his commitment to armed struggle reflected the compelling facts that no compromise was possible with Batista and that rebellion itself is justified by lofty principles of Western political theory. Others maintain that Castro harbored Marxist beliefs during his days at the university but that he kept the Communists away from his movement so that it could appeal to the Cuban middle class. Some of his formerly close associates, like Carlos Franqui, say that Castro's caudillo temperament and his egomaniacal pursuit of personal power raised unresolved questions among his followers regarding what path a Castro-led government would take, but that they realized confronting Castro would not be easy. Finally, moderates such as Mario Llerena collaborated with Castro's movement because they sincerely believed in its democratic nature and could not conceive of Castro either as a Communist or as a future dictator.

Fidel Castro himself has given many contradictory accounts of his thinking at the time, describing himself in 1961 as "a Marxist-Leninist until the day that I die," as "a utopian communist captivated by the incontestable truths of Marxist literature," as a "humanist" who believed in "bread and freedom," and as an anti-imperialist revolutionary. Speaking to the Brazilian Frei Betto in 1985, Castro stated that "before I was an utopian communist or a marxist, I was a follower of Martí [*martiano*] and a profound admirer of our people's heroic struggles." In the same interview Castro stated that "I had conceived of a revolutionary strategy that would lead to a profound social revolution, but through phases . . . the masses needed to be taken to the revolution through phases" because their consciousness could not be developed overnight. Finally, Castro reveals that he saw the Communists as "isolated, but as potential allies," and that he had good relations with Communist leaders during his student days.[10] At no time did Castro proclaim his adherence to Western-style democracy or to any other political system that agreed with the aspirations of previous reformers. Only through revolution could Cuba be emancipated, and only through revolution could he become its historical protagonist.

It is thus unequivocally clear that before he came to power, Castro was neither a member of the Communist party nor a doctrinal Marxist. Rather, he was committed to a radical revolution whose final outcome could not have been foreseen but which placed him in the center of power. In addition, one of his top lieutenants, the Argentine revolutionary Ernesto (Che) Guevara was a committed Marxist, as was Fidel's younger brother Raúl Castro. Indeed, the 26th of July Movement itself was divided between moderates who rejected communism as well as traditional Latin American authoritarianism and radicals like Guevara who believed that the solution to the world's problems lay behind the iron curtain. Finally, one of the key documents of the movement, *Nuestra Razón* ("Our Purpose"), defined the revolution's goals as establishing a free and sovereign country, a democratic republic, an independent economy, and a distinct national culture.

A popular view is thus completely discredited, namely, that U.S. policy failures drove Castro and his regime to communism and forced them into the Soviet bloc. For tactical reasons, the rebel leadership did not speak candidly with its own people and uttered deceptive and self-serving statements. At a minimum, *Nuestra Razón* committed the revolutionaries to constitutional government, political pluralism, and respect for civil and property rights. A radical minority led by Castro saw themselves as the self-anointed vanguard of an epic political struggle against capitalism, the Cuban middle class, and U.S. influence in Cuba, and they launched a mass movement that created an unstoppable momentum.

The guerrilla phase of the insurrection ended successfully for the rebels in December 1958. Domestic isolation, rebel victories in eastern Cuba, and loss of support from Washington convinced Batista that his regime could survive only if the guerrillas were defeated. But the army was poorly led, partly because some of its top generals were corrupt and frightened, and a 40,000-man army disintegrated when it faced several popular uprisings, demonstrating a profound loss of morale and an alarming unwillingness to fight a few hundred guerrillas. Cornered and without options, Batista and many of his closest allies fled at dawn on January 1, 1959, paving the way for a total victory by the guerrilla forces.

The breakdown of the authoritarian regime stemmed from its inherent illegitimacy, its refusal to accept an authentic electoral solution during a time of crisis, and its unfounded belief in the use of force and repression. The progressive alienation from the regime by the Cuban middle class reduced the probability that it would become a moderating force and lead a democratic restoration. In a situation in which traditional political forces were discredited and no dependable class base existed, popular support moved toward the revolutionaries. Deeply felt commitments to fundamental change emerged in the midst of an unprecedented vacuum, caused by the collapse of institutions and shifts in the locus of authority over brief spans of time. The guerrillas were able to assume power without direct consent but with massive social approval, and national euphoria was the order of the day.

THE CUBAN REVOLUTION

Neither the insurrection against Batista nor the social revolution that the new regime began to carry out stemmed from deep-seated popular dissatisfaction with the development pattern of Cuba's dependent capitalism. The evidence shows that Cuba had reached a moderate degree of modernization by the late 1950s. Indicators such as literacy rate (75 percent), proportion of the population living in urban areas (around 57 percent), life expectancy (approximately sixty years), and size of the middle class (between 25 and 30 percent of the population) suggest that Cuba's level of development was comparable to that of other more advanced Latin American nations.

On the other hand, urban-rural contrasts were marked, and the quality of life for the average *guajiro* ("peasant") family was well below that of the average urbanite. Health services and educational opportunities were much better in Havana and other larger cities than in the small provincial towns or isolated rural communities, and the best jobs and occupations were not available in rural Cuba. Seasonal unemployment also affected the rural areas disproportionately, and a rural proletariat dependent on the mills for employment saw its economic situation deteriorate once the sugar harvest ended.

In effect, neither the model of Cuba as a chronically underdeveloped society, as depicted by the Cuban government, nor that of an idyllic island characterized by social harmony, a sound economy, and a bustling population fits reality. At the time of the revolution the nation was developing slowly as a dependent capitalist country, in which wealth was not evenly distributed but in which middle sectors and a substantial portion of the working class had made social gains. Although Cuba's political autonomy had remained subject to foreign pressures, the imperatives of capitalist modernization had not obliterated Cuba's cultural integrity, social structure, or economic system.

The success of the revolution can be better explained by political factors than by socioeconomic criteria. The failure of prerevolution governments to develop and nourish viable ruling institutions or to sustain a national ethos of civic-mindedness left those regimes vulnerable to force and strongman rule, and to subversion from within. Legal and constitutional norms were not fully developed, and too many people viewed politics and public office as ways to obtain private, selfish gains. No idea of the public good had taken root, and the political culture revolved around traditional notions of order, loyalty, patrimony, and authority.

The new regime was originally divided among advocates of liberal democracy and a mixed economy and more radical sectors around Castro and Guevara who called for a social revolution. The radicals believed that the basic capitalist system needed to be abolished and the social system uprooted so that the power of vested economic interests, some of them foreign based, could be reduced. In order to eradicate economic evils associated with a dependent capitalist system, statist practices and antimarket doctrines shaped policymaking, and the revolutionary elite was fully aware that to increase state power meant to increase its own. The agrarian reform of 1959 satisfied long-standing claims of peasants and rural workers, and it also made sense politically. The urban reform of 1960, which socialized Cuban-owned businesses and privately owned real estate, adversely affected the private sector's strength. By 1961 banking, wholesale trade, and foreign trade had been fully collectivized, as was 85 percent of all industry and 80 percent of the construction business. This collectivization produced a massive transfer of power and resources from the private economy into the public sector, which was precisely the purpose and intended effect.

Structural changes combined with populist, redistributive measures signaled a willingness to incur domestic costs and foreign anger in order to accelerate the process of radicalizing the revolution. The revolutionary elite believed that to slow down was to court disaster, that momentum itself was proof that the masses supported the regime and enthusiastically joined the assault on capitalism and the private sector. Huge rallies commanded the attention of the populace, and during marathon speeches Castro often mesmerized crowds. The regime realized that social mobilization could serve as a form of explicit consent, and it established mass organizations like the Committees for the Defense of the Revolution, the Federation of Cuban Women, and the Communist Youth Union in order to reach the grass roots.

Once it became evident that a radical social revolution committed to socialism was in the making, led by individuals seeking total power, an opposition emerged that attempted to restrain or defeat the revolutionary elite. As often happens in revolutionary situations, a decisive struggle between radicals and moderates ensued, between people committed to some form of democracy and those who would settle for radical socialism and nothing else. Both sides knew that only one would prevail, that no compromise was possible, and that personal risks were involved. The ranks of the opposition included Catholic organizations, disaffected cadres from Castro's own ranks, respected democratic figures, and other anti-Communist elements.

The Communist party neither carried the Castroites to victory nor became a vehicle on which the revolutionary coalition moved against the private sector and the middle class. Leading Communists like Blas Roca and Aníbal Escalante perceived Castro as an ideological neophyte, unschooled in Marxist verities and unwilling to subordinate his own authority or the power of his movement to orthodox frameworks. The party had criticized the Castroites in the 1950s as "bourgeois adventurers," and its opposition to Batista had been measured, not confrontational. Ideologically, the party still believed in the revolutionary potential of the Cuban working class, and its political work had focused on the labor movement. Needless to say, the party was in no position to assume a leadership role, and its belief that when the revolution came it would become its vanguard, was quickly shattered.

In essence, Castro's relationship with the Communist party stemmed from his desire to limit the damage inflicted on his regime by the defection of non-Communist revolutionaries as well as from the need to enlist Soviet support. The party shrewdly provided organization when Castro's own was being shaken up, and it offered a dialectical explanation for the society's troubles. Andrés Suárez believes that "the Communists played no role, neither in the political leadership of the country nor in the leadership of the students or of the trade unions" but that the party's discipline, support of "national unity," and foreign connections facilitated understandings with Castro.[11]

By the mid-1960s revolutionary changes restructuring class, property, political, and foreign policy relationships had eliminated a dependent capitalist order replete with U.S. influence and moved the country toward radical socialism. The state took over the basic means of production as well as domestic and foreign commerce, industry, transportation, and utilities. Agriculture was reorganized into collective and state farms, but peasants could produce some goods on small, privately owned plots. The mass media was under state control, as was the national system of telecommunications. Party cadres supervised the information network, and Marxism-Leninism shaped the content of public discussion. Dissident intellectuals, nonconformists, and political opponents of the regime were arbitrarily imprisoned, scorned, or forced to leave the country. Nearly 500,000 Cubans had left by the mid-1960s, and this number had grown to over 1 million by the late 1980s.

The regime proscribed dissent and political opposition and forced explicit definitions of loyalty to the system. No opposition parties existed, nor could groups or sectors legally defy the revolutionary state. The legal system came under state control. The court system applied "revolutionary justice" to political offenses, and revolutionary tribunals enforced order and discipline with little evidence of due process. Summary trials of alleged counterrevolutionaries took place, long sentences were imposed on the revolution's opponents, and hundreds were executed. This was a time of social confrontation, characterized by a "we versus they" mentality that divided families and intimidated individuals and groups. Thousands of political prisoners served time during the following decades, and many suffered brutal treatment at the hands of guards and prison officials.

The educational system was radically reorganized and centralized, and education was treated as a key to the process of political socialization. National literacy campaigns pushed literacy rates to the mid-90 percentile, but the quality of instruction left much to be desired. Much of Cuba's history was revised and rewritten, and patriotism and national virtues were highlighted. U.S. influence over Cuba's destiny was made the root of many ills. The number of primary schools went from 7,567 in 1958 to 14,807 in 1968, and enrollment doubled during the same period. Thousands of new teachers were trained, rural education in particular was emphasized and supported, and women enjoyed new educational opportunities. Nelson Valdés has noted that students were "required to devote school time to three types of work: educational, productive and socially useful,"[12] so pupils worked in agriculture and volunteer campaigns while they studied.

Health and social services received considerable attention, and resources were allocated for the construction of clinics, hospitals, day-care centers, and other facilities. Quality of care was very uneven, and the lack of trained personnel affected the delivery of services, but improvements were evident in the rural areas in particular. Life expectancy in Cuba prior to 1959 had been sixty-four years of age, a relatively strong indicator of socioeconomic development. By 1970 Cubans could expect to live to age seventy, and today to about seventy-five. The health-care system is highly regarded, and most of the basic medical services are free.

A great debate over economic policy directly affected the development strategy of the 1960s. On the one hand, socialist ideologues led by Che Guevara argued that a strong moral foundation must be prepared if socialism is to succeed and that egalitarianism, altruism, and collectivism must be its core values. A cultural transformation must accompany structural changes and instill new values and attitudes among the masses. Arguing that the development of revolutionary consciousness was as important as satisfying material expectations, Guevara articulated a utopian view of "the new man" that radical socialism would create. In his famous essay on "Man and Socialism," Guevara's thinking is apparent:

> In these countries [including Cuba] there is no form of education for worthwhile social labor, and wealth remains distant from the masses. Underdevelopment and the habitual flow of capital toward "civilized" countries make it impossible to change rapidly without sacrifice. There remains a long road to be traversed in order to construct a solid economic base; and the temptation to follow the paths of material interest, used as a stimulus for accelerated development, is very great.[13]

On the opposite side stood the more pragmatic policymakers and people schooled in "scientific socialism" rather than in Guevara's utopianism. They knew that Cuba was a poor agricultural country without a large industrial base and with little technological innovation on which to launch grandiose development schemes. Consequently, they held that encouraging production and discipline through material incentives and tangible rewards was probably more effective than abstract appeals to altruism and selflessness.

In the end, the final arbiter of all disputes, Castro himself, settled the issue and approved Guevara's approach, reversing industrialization policies, accepting moral stimuli, and launching the nation on an all-out campaign against underdevelopment that promised to produce 10 million tons (9 million tonnes) of sugar. At its conclusion in 1970 the economy was completely unbalanced, growth rates had plummeted, and scarcity and shortfalls were evident in every sector. Only 8.5 million tons (7.7 million tonnes) of sugar had been produced, and according to Castro, the results constituted a moral defeat. Economists like Carmelo Mesa-Lago, Sergio Roca, and others have demonstrated that long-lasting damage was done to the infrastructure by such a colossally wrongheaded approach to development. Although chastened by the losses in production and national morale, the regime and its leader (who offered to resign but stayed on because the crowds still hailed him) survived their first systemic crisis.

In conclusion, regime consolidation came about through sustained mobilization, direct exhortation, and a top-to-bottom direction of an ongoing revolutionary agenda rather than through elections. Rewards and sanctions were utilized to elicit compliance with revolutionary policies, but care was exercised not to alienate key sectors of the working class, peasantry, and urban proletariat. These sectors formed the class basis for the new regime once the middle class had been destroyed and the upper strata had either left the country or accepted a dramatic loss in privilege and status. Daily life became intensely political.

SOCIETY AND GOVERNMENT IN THE 1970s AND 1980s

Needing to regularize the political process and to establish national ruling institutions through which stability could be preserved, the revolutionary elite succeeded in reorganizing the state and the Communist party and created ruling councils at the local level. Fundamental changes in government became evident, especially in the manner in which central authority is exercised, in President Castro's role as chief decision maker, in the critical role of the Cuban Communist party (PCC), and in the organization of social forces. A new socialist constitution was enacted in 1976, defining the PCC "as the leading force in the state and in society" but also outlining the powers of national, provincial, and local organs. Party congresses in 1975, 1980, and 1986 strengthened the party's hegemonic role, provided forums for discussion of national problems, and set broad strategies for future development.

A new economic model, namely, the Sistema de Planificación y Dirección Económica (SPDE—System of Direction and Economic Planning), framed policies in the late 1970s and early 1980s, taking into consideration criteria such as efficiency, rationality, prices, and other "economic mechanisms." This framework accepted the validity of material incentives and market processes and introduced wage differentials, production norms, monetary controls, and taxes. Mesa-Lago writes that "SPDE takes into account the law of supply and demand and the need of monetary and mercantile relations in the transitional stage"—presumably prior to reaching socialism—but that it does not abolish central planning.[14] It is probable that Soviet pressures, as well as the need to create complementary economic arrangements between Cuba and its socialist trading partners, influenced the decision to introduce the SPDE. Its principal advocate was a Soviet-trained economist, Humberto Pérez, who served as director of the Central Planning Agency.

A central question faced by nondemocratic regimes is the extent to which genuine participation is desirable in order to sustain legitimacy. The balance between spontaneity and control is a crucial issue for the Cuban government, insofar as spontaneity threatens the elite's position, but total control can be maintained only through coercion. Communist regimes in the 1990s face unprecedented internal pressures, either from labor sectors (as in Poland), as a result of unresolved ethnic struggles (as in Soviet Armenia and Azerbaijan), from a desire for independence (as in the Soviet Baltic republics), or from a popular groundswell for reform (as in the German Democratic Republic).

On the other hand, the Cuban regime faces neither ethnic unrest nor expressions of regional supremacy, because of the absence of genuinely oppressed ethnic minorities and because regionalism is simply not a potent political force. In fact, Cuba has achieved a remarkable degree of political stability and continuity, either as a result of genuine national unity or because its ruling elite and the Communist party itself are not completely discredited. Socialism appears to have engendered widespread political passivity, albeit laced with discouragement and sullenness, in the present generation, and nationalism is indeed a galvanizing force. Cubans are constantly told by their government that unity is the supreme value, that social divisions weaken the polity and create opportunities for "the enemy," that vigilance on all fronts is essential, and that "imperialism never sleeps." Although many of these claims are patently fraudulent and little more than shopworn slogans, their impact is considerable. In the absence of contrary information or any real debate on the merits of continuity or change, the status quo is preferred.

The Governmental Framework

Cuba's highest-ranking executive organ is the Council of Ministers (CM), composed of the head of state and government, several vice presidents, the head of the Central Planning Agency, and "others determined by law." Fidel Castro is its president, and he is also head of state and government, first secretary of the Communist party, and commander in chief. In fact, all lines of authority converge on President Castro, so that as Jorge Domínguez and others point out, the "maximum leader's" central role has been formalized. His brother Raúl is the CM's first vice president as well as minister of defense and second secretary of the Communist party. The Castro brothers thus maintain executive control over the central administrative organs, and their personal power is nearly absolute.

The CM has the power to conduct foreign relations and foreign trade, maintain internal security, and draft bills for the National Assembly. It has an executive committee whose members control and coordinate the work of ministries and other central organizations. All of its members belong to the Communist party, and some—like Minister of Culture Armando Hart and Armed Forces Vice Minister Gen. Abelardo Colomé—also belong to the party's Political Bureau.

The Council of State (CS) functions as the executive committee of the National Assembly between legislative sessions, and it is modeled on the Presidium of the Soviet Supreme Soviet. The CS issues decrees, exercises legislative initiative, can order general mobilization, and can replace ministers. It includes some thirty-two members, including eleven out of the fourteen members of the Political Bureau. Influential men like Carlos Rafael Rodríguez, Jorge Risquet, and José R. Machado belong to the CS, as does Cuba's highest-ranking woman, Vilma Espín.

The National Assembly of People's Power (NA) is the national legislature. Deputies are elected for five-year terms, but the Assembly holds only two brief sessions per year. In the 1986–1991 *quinquenio* (five-year term) its 510 deputies each stand for roughly 20,000 inhabitants. Deputies are not directly elected by the people; rather, some are elected by provincial assemblies, and some are appointed.

Among the NA's formal powers, it can decide on constitutional reforms, discuss and approve (but not disapprove) the national budget, plan for economic and social development, and elect judges. In practice, legislative initiative is not exercised, the NA cannot challenge the political leadership, and it is, in fact, a rubber-stamp body. In his study on "The Nature of Cuban Democracy," Archibald Ritter notes that what partly explains the Assembly's impotence is "insufficient time, support staff, and financial resources to permit individual members to scrutinize problem areas, pieces of legislation, and reports independently and carefully."[15] Some of its work takes place in specialized commissions, such as Child Care and Women's Rights, Defense and Internal Order, and Complaints and Suggestions. Nearly 41 percent of its members are workers, technicians, administrative cadres, or professionals, and nearly 20 percent are political or mass organization leaders. Seven percent either belong to the Revolutionary Armed Forces or work for the Ministry of the Interior, an organ charged with internal security. Sixty-five percent are males, and the average age is thirty-eight.

The underrepresentation of workers, peasants, and women suggests that these groups have yet to transform enhanced status into political influence. The typical deputy is a fairly well-educated, probably white, male who is either a full-time party bureaucrat or a white-collar employee. The real center of legislative power and initiative lies in the Council of State, and Ritter's conclusion is that "at the level of the National Assembly, a large proportion of the process of leadership selection and policy formulation is carried out by the party within the shell or framework of the National Assembly."[16]

The Organs of People's Power

Cuba's fourteen provinces are subdivided into 169 municipalities, each governed by an Assembly of Delegates of People's Power. Their members serve terms of two and a half years, and they are directly elected at the grass roots. The nominating process is carefully monitored by the party and by nominating commissions, so that a candidate's political attitudes must be acceptable. Democratic-style campaigning is not permitted, and candidates cannot reach their supporters via independently controlled media. Claims that these assemblies constitute "socialist democracy in action" stretch one's understanding of what democracy really means, and of what constitutes effective political competition in a one-party state in which basic liberties and freedom of speech are severely restricted. Neither claim stands up to scrutiny.

In 1986, 13,256 delegates were elected to these assemblies, 17 percent of them women. A substantial number of these delegates are either Communist party members or leaders in mass organizations like the Federation of Cuban Women or the Committees for Defense of the Revolution. Membership in the party or any of the mass organizations facilitates political mobility and confers higher status. The assemblies provide a local forum for popular grievances and deal with various problems such as repairing dilapidated housing, monitoring conditions in day-care centers, distributing health information, and cleaning up local sites. The assemblies' work may either overlap that of mass organizations or take advantage of proximity at the grass-roots level. The assemblies depend on national organs for resources, which often curtails local initiatives.

The Cuban Communist Party

The Cuban Communist party (PCC) has undergone significant transformations since the 1960s, when Castroites took effective control of its organization and eliminated political adversaries. The party atrophied in the 1960s, and membership was only 55,000 by 1969. Lip service was paid to its leading role, but in fact, the rambunctious politics of the period and the ad hoc manner in which policies were framed forced the party to the sidelines. The "microfaction affair" in 1968, in which orthodox, former PSP cadres led by Aníbal Escalante attempted to sow division in the ranks and provoke Castro's downfall, led to a bitter internal struggle and the subsequent arrest of some thirty-five members of the microfaction. Purges followed, and the guilty party members were sent to jail. This affair severely undermined the party's credibility, but it demonstrated that challenges to Castro could be politically fatal. Scholars often speculate that there are divisions among members of the party's top organs, such as the Central Committee; but if so, these divisions have not erupted into a serious challenge to President Castro.

Scheduled congresses were canceled, and the First Congress did not take place until 1975. Party membership went from 202,807 members and candidates in 1975 to some 481,000 in 1981 and 523,000 or so in the late 1980s. The proportions of workers (43 percent) and women (22 percent) are higher than in the past, and the party is making efforts to recruit quality candidates. Its presence at all levels of government and society and in the armed forces suggests that its vertical and horizontal integration has been effective, as are its penetrative capabilities.

On the other hand, substantive questions emerged in the 1980s regarding the ideological rigor of the cadres, their discipline, and their willingness to lead through example and sacrifice. The regime is aware that it must reinvigorate the party at the grass roots and struggle against atrophy and indolence. President Castro frequently reminds party members of their solemn obligations, of their historical mission on behalf of socialism and the revolution itself, and of the high personal standards expected of leaders and the rank and file. Several cases of corruption among party officials have been uncovered in recent years, and the guilty have lost their membership and are in jail.

The president has revealed that the party's work in Havana is often lax, but that away from the capital the party's performance is adequate. For instance, he explained that in Havana, "everything is more difficult because there are too many chiefs" and that "for several years the role of the party in the provinces is different from the role of the party in the capital." Still, the president concluded that "we have a magnificent party, a healthy and revolutionary party in the capital and throughout the country."[17]

Continuity at the top characterizes the party's ruling elite. Nonetheless, four new members were elected to the Political Bureau in 1986, and stalwart Castroites like former Minister of the Interior Ramiro Valdés, former Minister of Transportation Guillermo García, and former Minister of Health Sergio del Valle were removed. The removal of García and del Valle stemmed from their incompetence in running their respective ministries, but the Valdés dismissal came as a result of a personal quarrel with Raúl Castro. Vilma Espín became the first female full member of the Political Bureau, and two of her associates acquired candidate status. A provincial party secretary, Esteban Lazo (a black), was appointed to the Political Bureau, as was the secretary of the Cuban Workers' Confederation. (The latter was subsequently removed.) Each new member represents an important constituency, and each may have been rewarded for doing good work. Nonetheless, core Castroites like Juan Almeida, Carlos Rafael Rodríguez, Osmany Cienfuegos, and Pedro Miret remained as members. Major decisions in domestic and foreign policy are made by the Political Bureau, so that its members are "the elite of the elite." It can be assumed that decisions are reached by consensus after some discussion, but it is extremely unlikely that individually or as a group, members can effectively oppose President Castro. New members in particular are unlikely to assert themselves in the rarefied air of the group, so bringing in new blood is not necessarily indicative of new policy directions. Within this elite, the lines of accountability run *from* not *toward* President Castro, so personnel changes seldom affect the elite in general, and certainly not the president's absolute power.

In a careful review of changes at the Third Party Congress in 1986, Jorge Domínguez finds that changes in the top organs as well as throughout the PCC's lower ranks suggest that "if the leadership's ossification might have been halted, the party's may have worsened. The Communist Party of Cuba grew little and became more elitist. It is an elite 'vanguard' more than ever."[18] Generational pressures may have been eased somewhat by appointing younger cadres and removing "immovable objects" like Valdés and García, both members of the original revolutionary generation, but the need for bringing skilled individuals who have completed some university training into the party means that Cuba's *nomenklatura* ("privileged class") will dominate internal party affairs for the foreseeable future. The leadership is aware that institutional elitism breeds privileges and inequality, undermines the egalitarian rhetoric of socialism, and leads to the formation of what many people regard as "a new class," but these contradictions are generic to socialism itself.

SOCIAL PROBLEMS AND THE CAMPAIGN OF RECTIFICATION

The 1980s were a most difficult period for Cuba because of unresolved economic difficulties, financial pressures, and ideological erosion. Some of the problems stemmed from Cuba's place in the socialist world and its role as a producer of agricultural products and an importer of technology and capital goods. Under socialism Cuba has not escaped the vagaries of international markets and price fluctuations and has, in fact, been cast as a supplier of agricultural products for metropolitan markets. Growth averaged around 7.0 percent between 1981 and 1985, but then fell sharply. A mere 1.4 percent growth rate was registered in 1986, and the gross social product dropped 3.5 percent in 1987. Annual economic plans are regularly described as "tight" (*tensos*), and early evidence suggests that critical targets set in the 1986–1991 five-year plan will not be met. Economic forecasts were not much better for the rest of the decade, so austerity and hardship rather than improvements were expected.

Cuba is also burdened with a substantial hard-currency debt of more than $6 billion and has had to reschedule some of it. Sugar harvests seldom reach their targets and have stabilized at around 8.3 million tons (7.5 million tonnes) per year. The drop in oil prices has cost Cuba several hundred million dollars since 1985, because through conservation, the country had previously been reexporting some oil. This loss of income has severely restricted imports from capitalist countries, now averaging between 10 and 15 percent of the total. Cuba runs a consistently negative trade balance with the socialist countries, and between 1984 and 1986 accumulated a trade deficit of nearly $6 billion. Lastly, its debt to the Soviet Union alone exceeds $24 billion, and payment has been postponed twice already: in 1972 and again in 1986. Cuba is scheduled to start paying on that debt in 1991, but it could well ask Moscow for further relief.

The regime felt the need to abruptly change course in 1984–1985, when reports showed that the SPDE was failing, that the entire economy was facing crisis in key sectors, and other problems like speculation, profiteering, "subjectivism," and a veritable "anarchy and chaos" plagued the system. President Castro went on the offensive and criticized "a consumer's mentality" that placed consumption over investment, spending over savings, and imports over exports. He urged restraint and sacrifice, but exempted himself or his policies from any criticism. The president commented sarcastically that "no one during these 25 years asked where the money was coming from, where resources were coming from, what mystery or miracle . . . what Aladdin's lamp was that from which we could ask for everything and it never ended."

An "economic war of all the people" was subsequently launched in order to restore economic sanity and a sense of limits, still another massive campaign intended to mobilize the nation and place it on a war footing. A Central Economic Group was established in order to revise targets and bring consumption under control, but the group also took a critical look at the SPDE itself and found it profoundly deficient.

Peasant free markets, which had been permitted so that food shortages could be alleviated through direct sales to the public, were abolished in 1986, because the regime found that producers preferred to sell in these markets at higher prices and thus held back some of the produce sold to the state. Subsequently, street vendors were eliminated as was private manufacturing. Finally, the abysmal performance of state enterprises came under scrutiny, and agriculture, industry, and the sugar industry itself were evaluated. Cuba had failed to meet its export obligations to the socialist community with regard to sugar, citrus, and other goods, and its credibility as a reliable trading partner was in question.

The social impact of a rapidly deteriorating economic condition was perhaps what finally forced the regime to declare a Campaign of Rectification of Errors and Negative Tendencies, because not only was the economic model in crisis but indolence, absenteeism, social disaffection, and "a loss of socialist consciousness" were also rampant. President Castro severely criticized planners, technocrats, administrators, entrepreneurs, and "nameless bureaucrats" for paying too much attention to mechanisms and disregarding political and moral criteria. At the Third Party Congress the president pointed to "the blind belief that the construction of socialism is essentially a question of mechanisms. I think that the construction of socialism and communism is essentially a political task and a revolutionary task, and that it must come from the development of consciousness and from educating men for socialism and communism. . . . I do not have the slightest doubt that the fundamental path is political and revolutionary work."

Most worrisome, the regime found that a new spirit of capitalism had strongly resurfaced, threatening the very belief system on which socialism was presumably founded. The work of an entire generation was in danger, because ideological laxity and sheer laziness (*pancismo*) were widespread. President Castro asserted that "in our search for economic efficiency we have created the conditions where vices and deformations prosper, and what is worse, corruption! That is what hurts." Some enterprising peasants had grown wealthy, and readily boasted of it. The very capitalist ideas of profit and gain, not to mention creature comforts and leisurely habits, were pervasive so that making money was accepted. Hundreds of cases of administrative corruption were found and others of enterprises manipulating production figures and failing to complete projects on time. Upon inspection, the quality of many goods was poor, and parts of the national health system were being mismanaged. A large number of middlemen (*merolicos*) and speculators had made fortunes either through illegal or criminal activities or through rendering services to consumers at inflated prices. President Castro identified speculators who had "100,000, 200,000, 300,000 pesos and came to Havana to buy a house for 60,000, 70,000, or 80,000, houses that the Revolution had given to them," because "there were buyers for everything."

The regime confronted a major dilemma because the political leadership had originally approved the SPDE and several experiments with market forces and some capitalist measures, but the top political leadership is and has always been blameless in its own eyes and cannot be forced to recant. Consequently, President Castro singled out "the leadership cadres, the administrators, that have fallen into demagogic practices. . . . [They] have lacked character, will and responsibility."[19] Not surprisingly, Humberto Pérez was dismissed from the Central Planning Agency, and hundreds of others—including high officials—lost their jobs. The bureaucracy is being shaken up, but cases of corruption, malfeasance, fraud, and thievery are still being found.

The Campaign of Rectification is thus a gigantic moral crusade designed to rid the society of greed and social indolence. Values antithetical to socialism are deeply rooted in the culture, so that socialization efforts and moralistic exhortations did not create Guevara's "new man." This time, "the correct path to socialism" involves not only rectifying past errors, restoring consciousness, and uprooting negative tendencies but also rectifying those errors that are committed while rectifying those errors. The regime is returning to the intense moralism and utopianism of the past, and there is much evidence to suggest that the present generation is unreceptive to the message. Isolated protests have taken place, and many youths in particular seem to be alienated from the system and its aging leader. How long this period of national purification and social cleansing will last is anybody's guess, but since the problems are probably more serious than the regime cares to admit, it is likely that this campaign will last a long time.

THE INTERNATIONAL ARENA

The key factors framing Cuba's role in the world are revolutionary messianism, an anti-U.S. and anti-imperialistic stance, a legacy of defiance, and Marxist-Leninist ideology. President Castro's revolutionary convictions as well as his shrewdness and episodic demagogic outbursts, often in the midst of crisis and bipolar confrontations, make Cuba an influential actor in regional politics and in parts of the Third World. Still, the country's foreign relations, intended to maximize its international standing and degree of influence abroad, are subject to domestic pressures and external constraints.

In the 1960s Cuba's revolutionary messianism led it to support guerrilla movements in several other Latin American and Third World countries, specifically Venezuela, Bolivia, Guatemala, and Nicaragua. Subsequently, Cuba has assisted groups like the M-19 in Colombia, the MIR in Chile, the Tupamaros and Montoneros in Uruguay and Argentina, respectively, and the more recent Farabundo Martí National Liberation Front in El Salvador. Cuban support varies according to political circumstances and the country's own capabilities, but in practically all cases it involves either training guerrillas in Cuba and sending them out or supplying weapons and logistical assistance to such groups. At times, Cuba has provided sanctuary for revolutionaries from various countries, and Sandinista leaders like Tomás Borge and others have spent some time in Cuba. President Castro has repeatedly stated that as a revolutionary country, Cuba is obliged to offer moral as well as material support to revolutionaries fighting their own wars of liberation, and the constitution of 1976 includes this principle.

Through a vigorous assertion of proletarian internationalism, Cuba maintains thousands of cadres abroad on various missions. The regime's view is that through proletarian internationalism, Cubans fulfill their self-imposed revolutionary duties and advance the cause of socialism and Marxism-Leninism, but the policy has explicit geopolitical aims. In the late 1980s, approximately 85,000 Cubans were stationed abroad either as combat troops (in Angola and Ethiopia) or as technical and economic advisers (Nicaragua). Contingents include doctors, nurses, and health-care personnel as well as construction workers, teachers, agronomists, and other professionals. Intelligence people, political operatives, and security personnel serve abroad—often disguised as *internacionalistas* ("internationalist workers")—and supplement the work of intelligence agencies. In some cases Cuba earns hard currency as a result of these missions, because countries like Libya and Angola pay Cuba in dollars for its services while the Cuban government pays its people's salaries in pesos.

On occasion, fulfillment of these international duties leads to war or confrontation with status quo powers (like South Africa) or as was the case in Grenada in 1983, direct clashes with U.S. forces. In Angola, Cuba supports a corrupt Marxist dictatorship, and in Ethiopia it backs a brutal Marxist regime. The Angolan war started in the wake of the Portuguese collapse in southwestern Africa in the mid-1970s, and Cuban forces helped turn the tide for Angola's Popular Movement for the Liberation of Angola (MPLA). Cuban troops have been stationed in Angola since and have fought against South African regulars and guerrillas connected with the Union for the Total Independence of Angola (UNITA). Official Cuban government casualty sources list 2,300 dead, including several hundred from diseases and accidents. (Additional hundreds were wounded.) In all likelihood, this figure underestimates the total number of casualties because not all the bodies were recovered from the battlefields.

In December 1988 agreements signed among Cuba, South Africa, and Angola formalized an end to Cuba's participation in the Angolan War and established a schedule for South African troops to leave Namibia and Cuban troops to leave Angola. All 50,000 Cuban combat troops are to leave by July 1991, and, as of February 1990, several thousand have already returned to Cuba. The peace agreements also called for free elections in Namibia and for its independence. On the other hand, the civil war between UNITA and the Angolan regime continues. There is little doubt that improvements in East-West relations, escalating costs at home, and the failure to achieve a military victory forced Cuba (as well as Angola and South Africa) to negotiate seriously.[20]

In the 1980s Cuba restored diplomatic relations with influential Latin American states like Argentina, Brazil, and Perú. It appears that Havana prefers normalization of state-to-state relations to active support for some guerrilla movements, and key Latin American governments are seeking ways to bring Cuba back into the Latin American community. A process of mutual reciprocity is under way that allows Cuba to expand critical ties in exchange for pragmatic recognition on its part that democratic processes in Latin America are legitimate. Suspicions regarding Cuba's ties to revolutionary networks and its intrusive behavior moderate Latin America's willingness to renew relations, but sectors of the left sympathize with Cuba and often pressure governments to recognize Havana.

Cuba's relations with the Soviet Union are once again undergoing some difficulties owing to Mikhail Gorbachev's reforms and his partial retreat from the international class struggle, which are not appreciated in Havana. President Castro has explicitly rejected *perestroika* and *glasnost* on the grounds that any acceptance of market practices and greater openness could undermine socialism. The president holds that Cuba must remain as the ideological conscience of the Communist world and that "we must have our way of interpreting the revolutionary ideas of Marxism-Leninism." Neither genuine political liberalization nor substantive democratization has taken place, and Cuba is a highly authoritarian one-party state. On the other hand, there is reason to believe that some factions in the regime support the reform movement sweeping parts of the Communist world, and in time they may acquire greater influence in Cuba.

For strategic reasons, Moscow is unlikely to radically cut back on its support to Cuba. The Soviets provide around $5 billion–$6 billion annually in economic assistance, trade subsidies, credits, and other forms of aid. The Soviets pay higher-than-world-market prices for sugar and are Cuba's major supplier of oil and oil products. When prices were high this arrangement proved advantageous to Cuba, but the Soviets have not reduced their prices in recent years despite declines in world oil prices. Cuba receives around 50 percent of all Soviet aid to the Third World, and between 1981 and 1985 the total value of arms transfers from the Soviet Union to Cuba was $3.5 billion. For strategic reasons, Moscow's economic and military support for Cuba will continue, but there is solid evidence that Cuba will not receive major increases in Soviet assistance.

Finally, although U.S.-Cuban relations fluctuate between hostility and tolerance, neither country is prepared to make the crucial political concessions that would lead to a genuine rapprochement. Formal diplomatic relations were broken in 1961, but "interest sections" opened in Washington and Havana in 1977. Issues raised by the United States include Cuba's strategic relationship with the Soviet Union, its revolutionary activism in Africa and Latin America, and problems in the area of human rights. Historical grievances, nationalism, the U.S. economic embargo, and Cuba's insistence on sovereignty and on earning its powerful neighbor's respect shape that country's outlook. Both governments collaborate on matters related to emigration and family reunification, and in 1985 the two signed an agreement allowing thousands of Cubans to emigrate to the United States. Restoring relations with Cuba is not a high priority for the Bush administration, and Cuban officials repeatedly state that they are prepared to wait for a change of official attitude in Washington.

CONCLUSION

Cuba's political development following its independence was characterized by clientelism, strongman rule, and military intervention in politics, and the legitimacy of the early regimes seldom rested on popular consent. In the 1940s and 1950s democratic reformism failed to develop viable ruling institutions, and corrupt governments undermined public support for political democracy. Authoritarian regimes alienated rising middle sectors and relied on coercion rather than on consent, seldom ruling with popular support. Economic dependency made national development difficult and resulted in a social system without cohesion.

Radical structural transformations uprooted capitalism and reordered the political system through mobilization and charismatic rule, because the revolutionary elite believed that development could be achieved only through political and economic centralization. Egalitarianism, unity, and social militancy became the supreme values of the new Marxist order, and pluralism, representative democracy, and a mixed economy were consciously rejected. Private education was abolished, and the state reshaped the entire educational system, expanding health services as well. State control of industry, commerce, telecommunications, agriculture, and even small-scale production created a large bureaucracy, which led to a new technocracy composed of administrators, planners, managers, and "producers of culture and information." A new class with its own vested interests thus appeared.

Finally, a stable regime whose longevity is not entirely dependent on its performance is led by an aging caudillo less and less able to inspire and lead the new generation. Irrefutable signs of ideological erosion, social disaffection, and the Campaign of Rectification itself suggest that socialism's belief system is breaking down in Cuba and that a desperate attempt to restore discipline and zeal is under way. Its prospects, and Cuba's, are not bright.

NOTES

1. All quotes come from Carlos Moore, "Race Relations in Socialist Cuba," in Sergio Roca, ed., *Socialist Cuba: Past Interpretations and Future Challenges* (Boulder, Colo.: Westview Press, 1988), pp. 175–206.

2. Franklin Knight, *The Caribbean* (New York: Oxford University Press, 1978), p. 32.

3. Ibid., p. 119.

4. Ramón Ruiz, *Cuba: The Making of a Revolution* (New York: W.W. Norton and Company, 1968), p. 31.

5. Robert F. Smith, *The United States and Cuba* (New Haven: College and University Press, 1960), p. 127.

6. Jaime Suchlicki, *Cuba: From Columbus to Castro*, 2nd ed., rev. (Washington, D.C.: Pergammon Brassey's, 1986), p. 109.

7. Samuel Farber, *Revolution and Reaction in Cuba, 1933–1960* (Middletown, Conn.: Wesleyan University Press, 1976).

8. Suchlicki, *Cuba: From Columbus to Castro*, p. 125.

9. Ramón L. Bonachea and Marta San Martín, *The Cuban Insurrection, 1952–1959* (New Brunswick, N.J.: Transaction Books, 1974).

10. All of the quotes appear in *Fidel y la Religión* (Santo Domingo, Dominican Republic: Editora Alfa y Omega, 1985).

11. Andrés Suárez, *Cuba: Castroism and Communism 1959–1966* (Cambridge, Mass.: MIT Press, 1967).

12. Nelson P. Valdés, "Radical Transformation of Cuban Education," in Rolando E. Bonachea and Nelson P. Valdés, eds., *Cuba in Revolution* (Garden City, N.Y.: Anchor Books, 1972), p. 433.

13. Quoted from Donald C. Hodges, *The Legacy of Che Guevara: A Documentary Study* (London: Thames and Hudson), p. 96.

14. Carmelo Mesa-Lago, *The Economy of Socialist Cuba* (Albuquerque: University of New Mexico Press, 1981), p. 29.

15. Archibald Ritter, "The Organs of People's Power and the Communist Party: The Patterns of Cuban Democracy," in Sandor Halebsky and John M. Kirk, eds., *Cuba: Twenty-Five Years of Revolution, 1959–1984* (New York: Praeger Publishers, 1985), p. 286.

16. Ibid., p. 289.

17. All of the quotes by President Castro were taken from Fidel Castro, *Por el Camino Correcto* (La Habana: Editora Política, 1987).

18. Jorge I. Domínguez, "Blaming Itself, Not Himself: Cuba's Political Regime After the Third Party Congress," in Roca, ed., *Socialist Cuba*, p. 9.

19. Castro, *Por el Camino Correcto*.
20. For a comprehensive assessment, consult Sergio Díaz-Briquets, ed., *Cuban Internationalism in Sub-Saharan Africa* (Pittsburgh: Duquesne University Press, 1989).

SUGGESTIONS FOR FURTHER READING

Azicri, Max. *Cuba, Politics, Economics, Society*. London: Pinter Publishers, 1988.
Brundenius, Claes. *Revolutionary Cuba: Economic Growth, Income Distribution and Basic Needs*. Boulder, Colo.: Westview Press, 1983.
del Aguila, Juan M. *Cuba: Dilemmas of a Revolution*, rev. ed. Boulder, Colo.: Westview Press, 1988.
Díaz-Briquets, Sergio, ed. *Cuban Internationalism in Sub-Saharan Africa*. Pittsburgh: Duquesne University Press, 1989.
Domínguez, Jorge I. *Cuba: Order and Revolution*. Cambridge: Belknap Press of Harvard University Press, 1978.
Erisman, H. Michael. *Cuba's International Relations*. Boulder, Colo.: Westview Press, 1985.
Horowitz, Irving L., ed. *Cuban Communism*, 7th ed. New Brunswick, N.J.: Transaction Books, 1989.
Kirk, John M. *Between God and the Party: Religion and Politics in Revolutionary Cuba*. Gainesville: University of Florida Press, 1989.
Llovio Menéndez, José L. *Insider: My Hidden Life as a Revolutionary in Cuba*. New York: Bantam Books, 1988.
Mazarr, Michael J. *Semper Fidel: America and Cuba, 1776–1988*. Baltimore: Nautical and Aviation Publishing Company of America, 1988.
Mesa-Lago, Carmelo. *The Economy of Socialist Cuba*. Albuquerque: University of New Mexico Press, 1981.
Pérez, Louis A. *Cuba: Between Reform and Revolution*. New York: Oxford University Press, 1988.
Smith, Wayne S. *The Closest of Enemies: A Personal and Diplomatic Account of U.S.-Cuban Relations Since 1957*. New York: W.W. Norton and Company, 1987.
Stone, Elizabeth, ed. *Women and the Cuban Revolution*. New York: n.p., 1981.
Szulc, Tad. *Fidel: A Critical Portrait*. New York: Morrow and Company, 1986.

20
Costa Rica

MITCHELL A. SELIGSON

Virtually all the studies comparing Central American nations contain the phrase, "with the exception of Costa Rica"; travelogues, and even many academic studies, refer to Costa Rica as the "Switzerland of Central America." The propagation of the notion of Costa Rican exceptionalism has become so widespread that the first-time tourist is likely to be surprised to find a Central American nation, not an alpine one. Yet, as with most stereotypes, there is more than a grain of truth in this one: Costa Rica is different from its neighbors in three very fundamental ways.

First, levels of social and economic development are far higher in Costa Rica than elsewhere in Central America.[1] Life expectancy at birth for Costa Rican males was 71 years in 1987, nearly matching the rate of the United States (72) and dramatically exceeding the male life-expectancy rate in Nicaragua, Costa Rica's neighbor to the north, which was 62. Among females in Costa Rica, life expectancy was even higher, 76 years, compared to 65 in Nicaragua. Infant mortality, a universally used measure for comparing development, stood at 18 per 1,000 live births in 1987, compared to 62 in Nicaragua and 69 in Honduras. In terms of the proportion of college-age students attending an institution of higher education, in 1986 Costa Rica surpassed even Switzerland, with 24 percent enrolled in Costa Rica versus 23 percent in Switzerland. Costa Rica's rate also surpassed the United Kingdom (22 percent) and was nearly twice as high as that for El Salvador (14 percent), its closest competitor in Central America in the area of college enrollments.

Second, Costa Rica has the longest and deepest tradition of democratic governance of any nation in Central America. Indeed, experts in the Latin American field have rated Costa Rica as the most democratic country in all of Latin America for the past decade.[2] Civil liberties, including freedom of press, speech, and assembly, are widely respected and protected. Free and open elections have become the hallmark of Costa Rica's style of politics, with observers throughout the world seeking to copy elements of an electoral system that faithfully guarantees against

Costa Rica

PACIFIC OCEAN

Caribbean Sea

NICARAGUA

PANAMA

0   20   40 Miles
0   20   40 Kilometers

voting fraud and corruption. Human rights, so often brutally abused in other Central American nations, are carefully respected, and one rarely hears of even allegations of their violation.[3]

Third, Costa Rica is a peaceful island in a violent region. It abolished its army some forty years ago and is constitutionally prohibited from forming another one. Although there have been minor incursions and incidents over the years along Costa Rica's northern and southern borders, border guards and paramilitary units have been adequate to cope with these international conflicts. Costa Rica would be incapable of mounting a credible defense against a determined aggressor, but Costa Rica's friends in Latin America have often made it clear that they would use their military forces to deter thoughts of any such move. Indeed, on at least one occasion, Venezuela has gone so far as to land some of its air force planes in Costa Rica as a symbol of its readiness to assist. Strikes and protests are rarely violent, and negotiation is the most common mechanism for resolving disputes. Although Costa Rica has not been immune to terrorist attacks, their number and severity have been quite limited.

Costa Rica, then, stands out from its neighbors as being more advanced socially, economically, and politically and as more democratic and peaceful. There have been many attempts to determine why Costa Rica diverges from the regional pattern. Some studies have focused on historical accidents as an explanation, others on the mixture of resources (especially land and labor), and yet others on questions of ethnic homogeneity. To date, no comprehensive explanation has been established, yet partial explanations incorporating each of the mentioned features seem plausible. In this short introduction to Costa Rica these elements will be articulated as factors that seem to explain Costa Rican distinctiveness.

HISTORY AND POLITICAL CULTURE

Costa Rica, the southernmost country in the group of five colonies that united into a loose federation shortly after gaining independence from Spain in the early 1820s, developed in isolation from its neighbors to the north. This isolation was partially a result of historical factors, since politics pivoted around Guatemala, the colonial seat of power. It was also partially the result of a geographic factor, namely, that the bulk of Costa Rica's population resided in San José, Cartago, and Heredia, towns located on the *meseta central* ("central plateau"), and thus was largely cut off from both the Pacific Ocean and the Caribbean Sea as well as from Nicaragua to the north and from Panama to the south.

Although Costa Rica can boast that it is more than twice the size of El Salvador, its 19,650 square miles (50,900 square kilometers) make it less than half the size of Guatemala and Honduras and only slightly more than one-third the size of Nicaragua. In U.S. terms, it is tiny, about the size of West Virginia. The usable territory is further reduced by the presence of a mountain chain that cuts through the center of the country, running from north to south. The mountain chain is studded with active volcanoes, and the most recent eruption of one, in 1963, caused widespread damage to crops. The net effect of the mountains, volcanoes, and other natural formations is a reduction of arable land to an estimated 53 percent of the total land area.[4]

Costa Rica was further weakened by the absence of large Indian populations widely found elsewhere in Central America. In Guatemala, for example, the conquering Spaniards were able to rely upon a large supply of Indians to undertake heavy labor in the mines and in the fields. Although there is evidence that prior to the conquest there were perhaps as many as 400,000 Indians living in the territory that was to become Costa Rica, by the end of the sixteenth century there were fewer than 20,000—and according to some estimates, as few as 4,500 by 1581.[5]

Isolation, mountains, volcanoes, and the absence of a sizable indigenous work force do not seem to add up to a very promising base for the impressive developments that Costa Rica eventually achieved. Paradoxically, however, what seemed like disadvantages turned out to be significant advantages for Costa Rica. Isolation proved a blessing by removing the country from the civil wars and violence that so rapidly came to characterize postindependence Central America. Later, the dictatorial rule and foreign invasions that plagued the region had little direct impact on Costa Rica. Hence, in contrast to its neighbors to both the north and the south (Nicaragua and Panama), Costa Rica has never experienced an invasion of U.S. Marines. The mountains provided the altitude, and the volcanoes the rich soil, both of which were required for what was to prove to be a highly successful coffee industry. Finally, the absence of a large indigenous population meant that the repressive labor systems (especially the *encomienda* system) that predominated in much of the rest of Latin America could not prosper in Costa Rica.

The colonial period in Costa Rica was one of widespread poverty. Early explorers found little of the gold and silver that so strongly stimulated Spanish migration to the New World. Had they discovered major mines, no doubt they would have found ways of importing a labor force to work them. But the mines were never found, the labor was not imported, and the flood of colonizers who settled elsewhere was only a trickle in Costa Rica. There are reports that as late as 1675 there were only 500–700 Spanish settlers in Costa Rica, and by 1720 the number had barely exceeded 3,000. It was not until the mid-1850s that the total population of the country exceeded 100,000.

The small population, both indigenous and immigrant, together with the absence of major gold and silver mines, meant that agriculture became the principal source of economic activity throughout the colonial period. Although the soil was rich and a wide variety of crops grew well, farming was directed toward subsistence agriculture. As a result, Costa Rica had little to trade in exchange for needed goods that were not available locally. The initial poverty reinforced itself by placing beyond the reach of the settlers the farm tools and other implements and artifacts needed for a more productive economy and a more comfortable life-style.

Throughout the colonial period efforts were made to add vitality to the fragile local economy. Attention was focused on export agriculture, especially cacao and tobacco. Both crops grew well and fetched high prices on the international market, but both eventually failed in Costa Rica. In the case of cacao, which was grown in the tropical lowlands bordering on the Caribbean Sea, marauding Indians from Nicaragua, in league with British pirates, systematically raided the plantations and stole the crop. Tobacco grew in the highlands, and therefore was protected against such raids, but Spain declared a monopoly on tobacco exports and drove down profit margins for producers to the point where the cultivation of tobacco no longer proved worth the effort. By the end of the colonial period Costa Rica had not been able to find a way out of its poverty.

Independence was delivered as a gift to Costa Rica in 1821 when the isthmus, under the leadership of Guatemala, became independent from Spain. Although there was a brief period in which Costa Rica was joined with the other nations of Central America into a federation, shortly afterward independent political rule was established in the nation. Very early on in the postcolonial period the fledgling government took critical steps to help develop a stronger economic base for the country. One of these was the granting of land to all people who were willing to plant coffee on it. As a result, coffee cultivation increased dramatically in the first half of the nineteenth century, and by the 1840s direct exports of Costa Rican coffee to the markets in Europe had begun. The product was well received by the buyers and quickly achieved recognition for its high quality.

Coffee exports soon became the principal engine of economic growth for Costa Rica. The income from these exports made it possible for coffee producers to import new tools and building materials, and the state was also able to invest funds in critical infrastructure projects, especially roads and ports to facilitate the production and export of coffee. One major project that grew out of the effort to facilitate coffee exports was the construction of a railroad to the Caribbean port of Limón. Until the completion of this project, virtually all coffee exports had been shipped to Europe via the Pacific coast port of Puntarenas, around the tip of South America, and then to Europe. The shipping costs of that lengthy voyage were very high and reduced profits for the producers.

The railroad to the Caribbean served to cut those costs. Its construction was financed by a series of foreign loans, which Costa Rica found itself unable to repay even before the railroad was completed. As a result, the U.S.-owned firm that had contracted to build the railroad began to plant bananas to subsidize its construction. From this small start the

United Fruit Company developed, and it became the major economic influence in the Caribbean tropical lowlands of Costa Rica up through the 1930s, after which time the company moved its operations to the Pacific coastal lowlands. Banana cultivation provided employment for the railroad workers who had migrated to Costa Rica from Jamaica and later for job seekers from Costa Rica's highlands. The Jamaican blacks came to be the only demographically significant ethnic minority in the country, although today they account for less than 2 percent of the population.

Coffee and bananas proved to be the mainstays of the economy through the middle of the twentieth century. Over the years coffee fields were expanded to cover a wide area along the chain of mountains that runs through the country, an expansion caused by farmers in search of new land on which to grow coffee. As the territory suitable for coffee growing shrank, settlers moved to other areas where they planted basic grains; in the higher mountain regions, they grew vegetables or raised dairy cattle. In the province of Guanacaste, the broad flatlands proved suitable for cattle raising, and a major export industry of fresh beef developed between Costa Rica and the United States. When the United Fruit Company left the Caribbean lowlands because of the onset of debilitating banana diseases there, those banana fields lay abandoned until the 1950s when the discovery of new, resistant varieties allowed other companies to reinitiate the banana industry in that area. The economy of the 1980s, then, rested upon the export of coffee, bananas, and beef. The recent introduction of so-called nontraditional crops, such as flowers, melons, tropical fruits, and vegetables, has also begun to produce significant export earnings.

Although agriculture has been the traditional base of the economy, Costa Rica's joining the Central American Common Market in the early 1960s led to significant industrialization. By the mid-1980s agriculture was producing only one-fifth of the gross domestic product, and industry nearly one-third. The growth of industry has paralleled the growth of urbanization, and in the mid-1980s nearly half of the population was urban.

POLITICS AND PARTIES[6]

Poverty and the absence of a wealthy ruling class that derived its power from a slave or Indian population proved to be factors that favored the development of democracy in Costa Rica. Local government had its origins in colonial Costa Rica when local *cabildos* (city councils) were established in 1812. When independence was announced, a procedure was established that involved the popular election of delegates to a constitutional convention, and indirect, representative democracy was established in the first constitutional arrangements. A weak presidency was created, with the term of office limited to only three months, within a rotating directorate.

But all was not favorable for democratic rule. The system was weakened by regional rivalries between the two major population centers, San José and Cartago, and civil wars punctuated the first twenty years of independence, as did coups, assassinations, and invasions. In 1844 a new constitution was drafted and approved, and it divided the government into three separate branches: legislative, executive, and judicial. Voting rights were established, but restrictions were many: To be eligible to vote, one had to be married, male, a property owner, and at least twenty-five years of age. Less than 3 percent of the population voted in the first elections under this new constitution. But even this limited form of democracy was extinguished by a coup within two years.

Additional efforts at constitution making, more coups, and counter-coups occurred until 1890. In that year a period of political stability and democratic rule was initiated that lasted, virtually unbroken, until 1948. Direct elections were instituted in 1913, and a new constitution drafted in 1917 granted numerous social guarantees to the working population. Although this document was to be replaced in 1919, in the years that followed Costa Ricans made continual improvements in the election laws and procedures. In 1925 the secret ballot was instituted, and in 1927 the Civil Registry, which made a verifiable voter-registration system possible, was established.

Political parties were first organized in the nineteenth century, but they were little more than loose, personalist coalitions built around the leading economic interests until 1940. In that year the coffee oligarchy elected Rafael Angel Calderón Guardia to power and was surprised when he quickly moved in a populist direction. Calderón, a physician who had developed a large following among the urban poor, embarked upon a major program to introduce social legislation. In 1942 he began a social security program and approved a minimum wage law. He also established an eight-hour workday and legalized unions. In 1943, after the Nazi invasion of the Soviet Union, he formed an electoral alliance with the Costa Rican Communist party, known as the Partido Vanguardia Popular. This party, organized in 1929, had attempted to run candidates for local office in the 1932 elections, but after it was barred from doing so, it became increasingly involved in labor protests that took place during the Great Depression, especially among banana workers.

The alliance between Calderón and the Communists caused great concern and division within Costa Rica, but in the 1944 elections the alliance forces won, supporting a candidate of Calderón's choosing. With World War II over and the cold war beginning, the wartime alliance of convenience with the Communists became the target of increasingly strong protests within Costa Rica, and in 1948 a coalition of the traditional coffee oligarchy in league with young reformist social democrats defeated Calderón, who was once again running for the presidency. The legislature, however, had the responsibility of declaring the results of the election, and with Calderón's supporters in the majority, it annulled the election.

The reaction to the maneuver was swift and violent. An armed group led by José (Pepe) Figueres Ferrer organized in the mountains to the south of the capital and began a series of skirmishes with the government forces, aided by unionized banana workers. After a brief but bloody civil war, Figueres triumphed. He took over the government and ran it for a year and a half, during which time a new constitution was drafted and approved. Although it was a modern constitution, guaranteeing a wide range of rights, it outlawed parties that were perceived as threatening to democratic rule, such as the Communist party.

Four major consequences of the civil war of 1948 have served to shape Costa Rican politics ever since. First, the new constitution abolished the army and replaced it with a paramilitary force of civil guards. Without an army, it is far more difficult for dissenting forces to engineer a coup, and indeed, there have been no successful attempts to dislodge civilian rule since 1948. Second, Figueres did what no other successful leader of a coup in Latin America has ever done: He voluntarily turned the control of the government over to the victor of the annulled election. By doing so, he firmly established a respect for elections that had been growing in Costa Rica since the turn of the century. Third, the civil war largely delegitimized the Communist party, and since that time, even after the elimination of the constitutional prohibition on Communist candidates running for office, the voting strength of the Communist party has not exceeded 3 percent of the total presidential vote. Fourth, Figueres ushered in with him a group of social reformers who, while in many ways merely expanded upon programs begun by Calderón, sought to spur economic development and social progress without resorting to outright socialist schemes.

Once Figueres relinquished power he began to build a new party, called the National Liberation Party (PLN), to compete in the 1953 elections, which he won handily. From the moment of that election through 1990, the presidency has oscillated between control by the PLN and control by a coalition of opposition forces.

GOVERNMENTAL STRUCTURE

Since 1949 Costa Rica has operated under the constitution that grew out of the 1948 civil war. Power is shared among the president, a unicameral legislature, and the courts. Members of the legislature and the president are elected every four years. Candidates for the legislature, representing each of the seven provinces of the country, are selected by party conventions. The ability of a sitting president to implement programs has always depended upon the strength of congressional support.

In order to implement the wide range of social and economic development programs envisioned by the leaders of the PLN, numerous autonomous and semiautonomous agencies have been created. Hence, one agency handles electric and telephone services, another water supply, and yet another automobile and home insurance. These agencies have been a positive force for development and have spawned many creative ideas. For example, the automobile and home insurance agency also runs the fire department, which guarantees that it is in the insurance agency's interest to have an efficient fire-fighting service. The autonomy of these agencies has helped to isolate them from partisan political pressure. Yet, along with their autonomy has come the problem of an excessive decentralization of control. As a result, central planning and budgetary control have become extremely difficult as agencies and their functions have proliferated over the years.

POLICYMAKING

The modern state that Costa Rica has evolved into can be largely credited with the achievements that were noted at the beginning of this chapter. The high standard of living that has been attained, however, has been built on an economy that remains largely agrarian based. Most industrialization is of the assembly type, and as much as 90 cents of each dollar of output is made up of imported materials. The continuously growing government and para-statal bureaucracies have further increased costs without adding to production.

By the mid-1970s it was beginning to become clear that the growth model of the post-civil-war period was running out of steam and that the economy could no longer support the expense of a widespread social welfare net and a bloated public sector. Yet little was done to correct the system under successive PLN presidents. Then, beginning in 1980, under the leadership of an opposition president, the system began to come apart. In order to shore up local production and consumption, and taking advantage of cheap loans being offered by foreign banks that were awash in petrodollars as a result of the dramatic rise in world petroleum prices, Costa Rica began to borrow wildly. Over a very short span of time the country's foreign debt grew to the point at which it exceeded the equivalent of the total annual national production, and by 1982 Costa Rica had one of the highest per capita foreign debts in the world. The local currency was devalued again and again, inflation and unemployment rose, and the system seemed headed for a crash.

By late 1981 the future seemed grim indeed. Yet, while similar circumstances have led to coups in other Latin American countries, Costa Ricans waited patiently for the elections of 1982, and once again voted in the PLN. A dramatic plan for recovery was put in place by the victorious president, and the plan proved successful in stabilizing the economic picture. Inflation dropped, employment rose, the currency was revalued, and an effort was made to rationalize the foreign debt. These actions restored confidence in the system, but they did not return to the citizens the benefits of the growth that had been lost during the 1980–1982 period. Belts had to be tightened, taxes were increased, and prices rose. Economic growth picked up a bit, but there was no dramatic recovery.

THE INTERNATIONAL ARENA

In 1986 the PLN broke the pattern of electoral victory that had normally oscillated between the opposition party and itself by winning the election. It did so under the leadership of Oscar Arias Sánchez, and Arias took power in an increasingly threatening international environment brought on by the crisis in Nicaragua.

When the Sandinista revolutionaries were fighting to overthrow the Somoza dictatorship in the late 1970s, they found extensive support in their neighbor to the south. Although Costa Rica remained officially neutral in that conflict, there was a long-standing antipathy for Somoza and the harsh dictatorial regime that he represented. Public support for a Sandinista victory was overwhelming, and there is much evidence that the government of Costa Rica did what it could to help.[7]

Once the Sandinistas took power, however, relations between Costa Rica and the new regime rapidly deteriorated. Costa Ricans rapidly perceived the revolution as having a Marxist-Leninist orientation, and as such, it presented two threats to Costa Rica. First, it was a threat because of the fear that Communist "expansionism" would mean Nicaragua would eventually attempt to take over Costa Rica. Second, it presented a threat to internal stability because it was feared that disgruntled Costa Ricans, especially among the university youth, would turn to revolutionary activity. In fact, in a small way the second expectation was realized. Terrorism, which had been almost unknown in Costa Rica, erupted with a number of ugly incidents in which lives were lost, and several clandestine "people's prisons" were discovered that were apparently designed to be used to hide victims of political kidnappings. With the Reagan administration in the White House, yet a third fear gripped Costa Ricans. This was the fear that the United States would invade Nicaragua, possibly using Costa Rican territory as a base of operations. Such an event would thrust Costa Rica into an international military conflict for which it was not prepared and which it did not want. Indeed, as the Iran-Contra hearings were to later demonstrate, a clandestine airstrip was built in Costa Rica to help ferry arms to the contra rebels, and a plan was evolved for a so-called Southern strategy involving Costa Rican territory.

On top of all of these concerns was the growing problem of Nicaraguan refugees. As the contra war grew in ferocity and the Nicaraguan economy deteriorated, waves of refugees joined those already in Costa Rica who had fled the initial takeover of the Sandinistas. If the contras or a direct U.S. invasion were able to overthrow the Sandinistas, it was feared there would be yet another, far larger wave of immigrants made up of the defeated Sandinistas who, it was not doubted, would begin planning for a new invasion. In short, Costa Ricans mortally feared being caught up in an impossible international conflict that could only result in deep harm being done to their country's national economy, society, and moral fiber.

Upon assuming office Oscar Arias dedicated himself to bringing peace to the region. Doing so was not only appropriate for a country that had long been noted for its internal peace and lack of an army but also urgently needed if Costa Rica hoped to avoid the problems noted above. Arias managed to draw together the leaders of all of the Central American countries and develop a peace plan that was not only to involve Nicaragua but would also serve to end the civil war in El Salvador and the guerrilla war in Guatemala. For his efforts Arias was awarded the Nobel Peace Prize, but the far more important prize of peace has eluded him, at least as of this writing.

CONCLUSIONS

In the 1990 elections the PLN lost the presidency to an opposition coalition led by the son of Calderón Guardia. Within a few months of this loss, the Sandinistas in Nicaragua were defeated in an upset election. These two elections saw the new decade emerging with new leadership in these two Central American neighbors. The dominant parties of the decade of the 1980s, the PLN in Costa Rica and the FSLN in Nicaragua, were being asked by the voters to take a back seat and allow fresh faces to try their hand at economic development, democratization, and peace. The dramatic changes in the Soviet Union and Eastern Europe did not go unnoticed in Central America, as capitalism and democracy rapidly began to replace socialism and dictatorship. In this context, peaceful, democratic Costa Rica faces new opportunities for regional leadership as the one country in Central America with a long tradition of democracy. On the domestic scene, however, the growing international debt and the inability of Costa Rica to pay even the interest on that debt cast a dark cloud over the country's economic and political future. The ability of coffee, banana, and beef exports to cover the costs of financing growth is clearly limited. Nontraditional exports might someday help, but the debt simply seems too large and the market for these new exports too small for one to be optimistic. And yet, Costa Rica's open, democratic style of governance seems to enable the country to withstand crises that would cause others to wilt. If the past is any guide to the future, Costa Rica will rise to the test and overcome its problems.

NOTES

1. The data in this paragraph are drawn from the World Bank, *World Development Report, 1989* (New York: Oxford University Press, 1989), pp. 220–221, 226–227.

2. See Kenneth F. Johnson, "The 1980 Image-Index Survey of Latin American Political Democracy," *Latin American Research Review* 38:3 (1982):193–201.

3. The Latin American Studies Association reports that the National Reconciliation Commission established as part of the Central American peace accord of 1987 found that "no one in Costa Rica claimed that there were systematic violations of human rights or denial of freedom of expression in the country" (Latin American Studies Association, "Final Report of the LASA Commission on Compliance with the Central America Peace Accord" [Pittsburgh: LASA, March 15, 1988], p. 8).

4. There are several estimates. See Carolyn Hall, *Costa Rica: Una interpretación geográfica con perspectiva histórica* (San José, Costa Rica: Editorial Costa Rica, 1984), especially pp. 261–267.

5. Hall reports 17,166 in 1569 (ibid., p. 72), whereas another source reports the lower figure (Mitchell A. Seligson, *Peasants of Costa Rica and the Development of Agrarian Capitalism* [Madison: University of Wisconsin Press, 1980], p. 4).

6. This section draws on Mitchell A. Seligson, "Costa Rica and Jamaica," in Myron Weiner and Ergun Ozbudun, eds., *Competitive Elections in Developing Countries* (Durham, N.C.: Duke University Press, 1987).

7. See Mitchell A. Seligson and William Carroll, "The Costa Rican Role in the Sandinista Victory," in Thomas W. Walker, ed., *Nicaragua in Revolution*, pp. 331–344 (New York: Praeger, 1982).

SUGGESTIONS FOR FURTHER READING

Bell, John Patrick. *Crisis in Costa Rica.* Austin: University of Texas Press, 1971.

Biesanz, Richard, Karen Zubris Biesanz, and Mavis Hiltunen Biesanz. *The Costa Ricans.* Englewood Cliffs, N.J.: Prentice-Hall, 1982.

Booth, John A. "Representative Constitutional Democracy in Costa Rica: Adaptation to Crisis in the Turbulent 1980s." In Steve C. Ropp and James A. Morris, eds., *Central America: Crisis and Adaptation*, pp. 153–188. Albuquerque: University of New Mexico Press, 1984.

Edelman, Marc, and Joanne Kenan, eds. *The Costa Rica Reader.* New York: Grove Weidenfeld, 1989.

Gudmundson, Lowell. *Costa Rica Before Coffee: Society and Economy on the Eve of the Export Boom.* Baton Rouge: Louisiana State University Press, 1986.

Hall, Carolyn. *Costa Rica: A Geographical Interpretation in Historical Perspective.* Boulder, Colo.: Westview Press, 1985.

Seligson, Mitchell A. *Peasants of Costa Rica and the Development of Agrarian Capitalism.* Madison: University of Wisconsin Press, 1980.

————. "Ordinary Elections in Extraordinary Times: The Political Economy of Voting in Costa Rica." In John A. Booth and Mitchell A. Seligson, eds., *Elections and Democracy in Central America*, pp. 158–184. Chapel Hill: University of North Carolina Press, 1989.

Seligson, Mitchell A., and Edward N. Muller. "Democratic Stability and Economic Crisis: Costa Rica, 1978–1983." *International Studies Quarterly* 31 (September 1987):301–326.

21
Nicaragua:
Revolution Under Siege

JOHN A. BOOTH

Nicaragua, though relatively blessed with rich soil, ample land, gold, timber, and energy potential, has been cursed by its geography and politics. Because the Lago de Nicaragua and the Río San Juan provide an excellent waterway across the meso-American isthmus, they have attracted extensive foreign interference in Nicaraguan politics. Nicaragua has had several spurts of modernization and development, but civil wars and foreign intervention have reversed them. Fifteen years of economic growth in the 1960s and 1970s have been wiped away as Nicaragua has again fallen into war and has become an object of U.S.-Soviet conflict. In July 1979 a revolutionary coalition led by the Sandinista National Liberation Front (FSLN) toppled the four-decade-old Somoza regime. Despite the Sandinistas' subsequent struggle to build a new Nicaragua, their revolution became mired in many of Nicaragua's traditional problems. In February 1990 Nicaraguan voters, tired of war and economic difficulties, voted the FSLN out of power and began a new era in the nation's history.

POLITICAL HISTORY AND CULTURE

Located astride the Central American isthmus, Nicaragua (1988 population estimated at 3.6 million) has three main regions: a Pacific lowland of rich soils, the mountainous Central Cordillera, and the swampy, forested Atlantic lowland. Just before the Spanish colonized Nicaragua, Nicaragua's indigenous population was roughly 1 million, mostly sedentary agriculturalists who lived west of the Central Cordillera. Despite Indian resistance, a 1524 expedition firmly established Spanish control. Slavery, imported diseases, and the killing of those natives who resisted conquest reduced the Indian population to fewer than 100,000 by 1600. The surviving Indians were mostly absorbed through intermarriage into

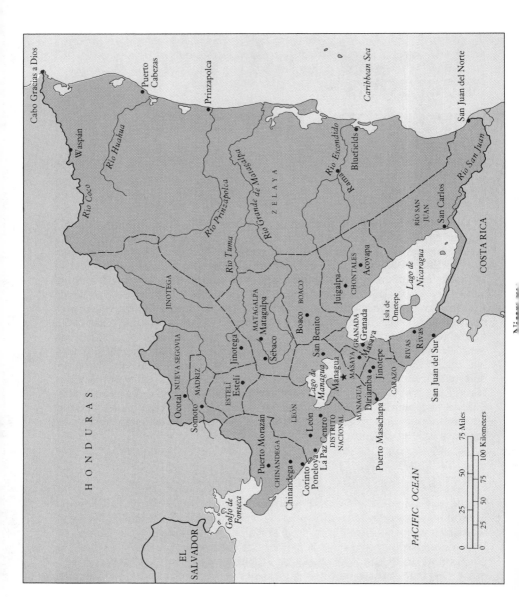

an emergent Spanish-speaking mestizo population and culture.[1] Near the bottom of the social pyramid, poor mestizos cultivated small subsistence farms. At the top, heirs of the conquerors and land grantees evolved into a wealthy upper class of large hacienda owners who dominated Nicaraguan society and institutions.

Nicaragua is today divided geographically and culturally. Atlantic Nicaragua, with only a tenth of the population (mostly blacks and Indians) spread across half the national territory, remains culturally, racially, linguistically, and geographically isolated. The Pacific and Central Cordillera zones together contain 90 percent of the country's populace, preponderantly Hispanic mestizos. Western Nicaragua's cultural homogeneity and integration have been advanced by relatively easy communications, especially through the capital city of Managua (1988 pop. est. 1 million).

Political History

Conflict over economic policy and politics developed in the late colonial period between the landed elites of north-central León and southern Granada. This rivalry gave rise to chronic, often violent nineteenth- and twentieth-century conflict between two clan-based, regional political parties, the Granada-centered Conservatives and the Liberals of León, typically led by personalistic caudillos. Civil war was frequent and ingrained, and the Liberal-Conservative schism deeply divided society across class lines. By the early twentieth century, however, the parties' ideological differences had largely vanished.

In 1856 Liberals invited a filibusterer from the United States, William Walker, and a mercenary army to help them oust the Conservative government. Walker himself seized power, however, and declared his intention to annex Nicaragua to the United States as a slave state. Conservatives elsewhere in Central America sent troops to oust Walker. The ensuing war toppled the filibusterer in 1857 and ushered in thirty-seven years of Conservative rule.

Liberals returned to power in 1893 under modernizing strongman José Santos Zelaya, who soon ran afoul of U.S. intentions to build a transisthmian canal in either Nicaragua or Panama. Panama was ultimately chosen, and Zelaya began to negotiate with possible competitors, prompting the United States to intervene in a 1909 Conservative rebellion against him. The United States secured its canal monopoly by sending troops to help topple Zelaya and to back weak Conservative regimes until the mid-1920s.

In 1927 the United States again sent marines to Nicaragua to stop another civil war but decided to let the Liberals take power in 1932. This decision failed to bring peace, however, because the maverick Liberal leader Augusto C. Sandino revolted against the U.S. occupation. To fight Sandino and to maintain order, the United States organized, trained, and commanded a new national guard. After the U.S. pullout in 1933 (leaving Sandino undefeated and uncowed), the new guard commander, Liberal Anastasio Somoza García, used the force to murder Sandino and seize power. Somoza García (1936–1956), followed by his sons Luís (1956–1967) and Anastasio Somoza Debayle (1967–1979), employed the guard to rule Nicaragua. They used the Liberal party (rechristened Liberal Nationalist [PLN]) to mobilize phony election-year demonstrations, pass legislation, staff government posts, and distribute the patronage and corrupt access to public funds that bought cooperation. Rule by the Somozas became increasingly repressive and violent in the 1970s.

Political Culture

Several historical factors have shaped modern Nicaraguan political culture. One, the Liberal-Conservative conflict for control of national institutions never became peacefully competitive, and most rulers assumed power by force or electoral fraud. Two, dictators of one party or the other held power for lengthy periods, repressing the opposition and ruling corruptly. Three, armed foreign (especially U.S.) intervention on behalf of both parties and foreign manipulation of domestic politics produced a curious combination of antiforeign nationalism and dependency upon foreign patronage and allies. Four, the bureaucracy, military, and judiciary were partisan rather than politically neutral or technically expert. Five, rarely in Nicaraguan history prior to 1979 did citizens really take part in making public decisions or choosing leaders. Six, violence was common in politics and in the service of elite economic interests; rebellions were frequent. Seven, institutional leadership has historically come from wealthy Liberal and Conservative landed families. Since 1920 both parties have felt middle-class challenges to their leadership, including Sandino (the illegitimate son of a small landowner), Anastasio Somoza García (from a second tier of downwardly mobile Liberal landowners), and several middle-class reform parties and movements, including the FSLN.

These factors have left Nicaraguans alienated from and cynical about their leaders, and prone to blame the government for many of their problems. Nicaraguans also have a strong sense of personal independence, spontaneity in their relationships, and a deep loyalty to Catholicism.[2] Such traits have at times contributed to rebellion against authoritarian rule, especially when it was unjust, capricious, or too repressive.

Economy

Since colonial days Nicaragua has exported agricultural products. The Spanish and their heirs engaged in export-oriented cattle and cacao production, whereas many mestizo smallholders grew staples for the internal market. Coffee growing spread after 1850 as the landed elite appropriated coffee land from the mestizos and a few remaining Indian communities. Coffee quickly became Nicaragua's principal export and has remained one of the two top crops ever since. Concentration of land ownership rose rapidly, and the production, milling, and exporting of coffee became the major source of wealth of the national elite. Road and rail construction and government modernization were pursued in the late nineteenth and early twentieth centuries to facilitate the exportation of coffee and promote economic growth. But this era of "progress" also reduced Nicaragua's domestic food production and increased dependency upon imported food and vulnerability to external commodity-price cycles. The material condition of much of the population worsened.

After World War II the Nicaraguan economy diversified. Land ownership further concentrated as speculators rushed to grow cotton in the Pacific zone and squeezed out still more small farmers. The cotton boom increased the number of rural wage workers, reduced living standards for many peasants, and increased the concentration of wealth. In 1960 Nicaragua joined the Central American Common Market (CACM) to promote industrialization and further develop export agriculture. On the surface the CACM succeeded, as overall growth statistics were impressive in the 1960s and early 1970s. However, the great social and economic changes caused by this growth were among the major causes of the anti-Somoza rebellion and Sandinista revolution. Repression of labor actually reduced real working-class wages in the 1960s and 1970s and hurt the general standard of living. Income and wealth inequality increased. Nicaragua industrialized by depending on cheap imported raw materials and expanding Central American consumer markets, but both were lost in the mid-1970s. Unemployment then shot up, and inflation rose; a terrible earthquake in Managua in 1972 further damaged the economy.

As working-class living standards fell, unions and professional groups demanded increased wages and related reforms. When such demands were met with repression, wage demands changed to calls for political reform. Repression eventually drove labor to ally with the growing anti-Somoza opposition, and businesspeople grew unhappy with the government's economic mismanagement in the early 1970s. When Anastasio Somoza Debayle greedily exploited his power to enrich himself after the Managua quake, he alienated many of his former economic allies, and business groups began to agitate for political reform and for the end of Somoza rule.

The Insurrection and Sandinista Revolution

Political and economic opposition to the Somozas grew in the 1960s and early 1970s along with the Nicaraguan economy's rapid but distorted growth. Of the rash of rebel groups that appeared in the early 1960s, only the Marxist-Leninist FSLN survived, but the national guard easily controlled the Sandinistas until the mid-1970s, when Anastasio Somoza Debayle sharply escalated repression. This new repression and economic recession in the mid- and late 1970s turned more and more of Somoza's once-reformist opponents into rebels and allies of the now rapidly growing FSLN. When spontaneous popular revolts against the dictatorship boiled up all over Nicaragua in late 1978, the opposition united behind the FSLN, whose military ranks rapidly swelled. A Sandinista military offensive in June and July of 1979 beat down the guard's resistance. Somoza eventually fled, the guard collapsed, and the Sandinista-led coalition took power on July 19, 1979.

POLITICS AND GOVERNMENT IN REVOLUTIONARY NICARAGUA

Political Parties

The FSLN was founded in 1961 as a political-military movement by a handful of Marxist-Leninists, including Carlos Fonseca and Tomás Borge. The Sandinistas emulated the guerrilla strategies of Castro and Sandino in their struggle to topple the Somozas and implement a socialist revolution. The national guard's counterinsurgency contained the FSLN for fifteen years but never eliminated it. Meanwhile, the Sandinistas built a base among university students and both Catholic and Protestant groups. As unrest grew and repression against all opposition escalated in the mid- and late 1970s, the FSLN won peasant and worker support, and the adoption of a broad coalitional strategy in 1977 by the FSLN's main faction[3] attracted many people from other movements and groups. Eventually, several thousand men and women fought the national guard under the FSLN banner, giving the Sandinistas dominance in the victorious rebel coalition. The FSLN quickly organized itself into a modern Marxist party that penetrated all levels of government, controlled the armed forces and key ministries, and massively organized popular support.

The years of Somoza manipulation and corruption left both the traditional Liberal and Conservative parties discredited. Conservatives had actively collaborated with the Somozas at times, but some factions survived into the revolutionary era. One, the Democratic Conservative party (PCD), had a representative on the revolutionary Junta (1980–1984) and held several seats in the National Assembly after 1984. Several other opposition parties first helped overthrow Somoza and then became opponents of the FSLN; they included the Independent Liberal party (PLI), which split from the PLN in the 1940s, and the Nicaraguan Social Christian (PSCN) and Popular Social Christian (PPSC) parties. Three tiny parties criticized the FSLN from the left—the Socialist Party (PSN), the Communist Party (PCN), and the Marxist-Leninist Popular Action Movement (MAP-ML). In the late 1980s several new small parties and splinters formed, and prospects for opposition party realignment grew.

After a decade of revolution, political parties still played many traditional roles. The dominant FSLN tolerated opponents and was willing to share modest amounts of authority with and to be influenced by its collaborators in the anti-Somoza struggle. The FSLN's tolerance of its opponents varied according to the behavior of the opposition and the political necessities imposed and opportunities offered by external pressures. The FSLN politicized the armed forces and bureaucracy, much like their Liberal and Conservative predecessors did. The FSLN's control of key power centers and its manipulation of other political forces often neutralized both its opponents and its allies. Opposition parties were ineffective, and their popular support was quite limited until the 1989–1990 election campaign.[4] In that campaign, over a dozen parties united to form the United Nicaraguan Opposition (UNO). Even then, however, the opposition proved divisive, personalistic, and mutually distrustful—traits that have long made Nicaraguan political coalitions unstable. Even with its victory in 1990, UNO seemed unlikely to remain unified once in power.

The Armed Opposition and the Contra War

Following a Nicaraguan tradition, some opponents, encouraged and financed by the United States, took up arms against the Sandinistas. These rebels, known as "contras" (from the Spanish word for counter-revolutionary), waged a growing guerrilla war from 1981 to 1988 and forced the government to mobilize a massive army for counterinsurgency. By 1986, with $100 million in U.S. funding and other aid, the rebels put several thousand troops into Nicaragua. The government reacted by building a massive, Soviet-armed, counterinsurgency-oriented army of 90,000 regulars and reserves. The regime's military countermeasures were very successful, but financing the war devastated the Nicaraguan economy, and revolutionary programs and the draft antagonized many citizens.

Despite vigorous U.S. efforts, the contra leadership suffered from repeated divisions and corruption. In 1988, with renewal of U.S. funding uncertain and no prospects of a military victory or of U.S. military intervention on their side, the contras signed a temporary cease-fire. They then withdrew most of their forces to Honduras and began to disband. The United States managed to hold the contra forces together until after the 1990 election but then began to work for their demobilization.

Interest and Pressure Groups

Business Groups

In the 1950s there were few formally organized interest and pressure groups, but during the Central American Common Market boom, such organizations multiplied rapidly. Business groups became active campaigners for social and political reforms, attempted to negotiate Somoza out of power in 1978, and took part in strikes to weaken the regime. Business groups led by the Superior Council of Private Enterprise (COSEP) played a major role in opposition to the revolution. Business interests disliked FSLN rule and the increased government control of the economy. They took a major role in promoting the UNO coalition in the 1990 election.

Labor

Under the Somozas, labor was both manipulated and repressed by the regime. It was also divided among competing confederations. Ultimately, most peasant unions, industrial unions, and professional associations joined the anti-Somoza coalition in the late 1970s. Under the revolutionary government, labor organization was at first encouraged and spread rapidly, and the new Sandinista Workers Confederation (CST) attempted to attract unions to the Sandinista banner. However, when the CST supported government austerity programs, worker resentment grew and fueled resistance to the CST. The government then curtailed strikes for several years, and some independent confederations joined the anti-Sandinista opposition.

Religious Groups

For decades the Catholic church supported the Somoza regime, but following the Second Vatican Council (1962), liberation theology and a new church commitment to the poor led to growing social Christian activism. With the 1968 appointment of Miguel Obando y Bravo as archbishop of Managua,[5] church collaboration with the regime ended. When the national guard attacked Catholic social activists, many of them began to support the FSLN and its fighters. After 1979 the Catholic church hierarchy became increasingly critical of the revolution and helped lead the Sandinistas' opposition. Protestants had gained a substantial foothold in the poorer Nicaraguan communities by the 1960s and similarly radicalized after suffering repression. Many Protestants also fought with the Sandinistas, and after 1979 many evangelical churches supported the revolution.

GOVERNMENT AND POLICY

Governmental Structure

The Somoza dynasty corruptly ruled Nicaragua by using the national guard for security and repression and the PLN to manipulate policy and elections. Except for the Central Bank, the national bureaucracy and the judiciary were inept, partisan, and vehicles for patronage and corruption. After 1979 the National Directorate (DN) of the FSLN sought to revamp radically the Nicaraguan political system. The DN's nine members, all top Sandinista commanders, acted as a board of directors for the revolution, the FSLN, and the government. Several DN members held key ministerial positions.

Although it kept most of the old bureaucracy while reforms were being made, the revolutionary junta in 1979 abolished the old constitution and created a Council of State that represented elements of the rebel coalition. The junta and the council extensively restructured the government and nationalized major economic sectors and the property of the Somozas and their cohorts. A new police force and army were created from the ranks of Sandinista soldiers, and the police and army were fused with the FSLN to ensure the security of the revolution. Public policies and services (education, health, agrarian reform) were restructured to benefit the poor majority. Controversial special courts were set up to punish national guard members and Somoza collaborators. The FSLN mobilized tens of thousands of people to support its programs through women's, youth, labor, and neighborhood organizations. Beginning in 1981 the junta invoked a state of emergency that sharply constrained civil liberties.

The regime consolidated after 1984, when Nicaraguans elected FSLN candidate and DN member Daniel Ortega Saavedra president and chose Sandinistas for almost two-thirds of the new National Assembly's seats. The Assembly wrote a constitution, adopted in early 1987, that formally established a presidential government with divided powers and checks and balances. The overwhelming political advantage of the FSLN, however, effectively circumscribed most formal restraints on its power. The constitution provided for a mixed economy, political pluralism, and international nonalignment and guaranteed a wide array of civil liberties and rights. Many such rights were constrained by the state of emergency, however, which remained in effect until 1988.

During its first term from 1985 through 1990, the Assembly's strong FSLN majority ensured legislative cooperation with the Sandinista leadership's policies. The Assembly did serve as a sounding board for policy, and opposition concerns did have influence despite the FSLN's huge majority. The presidency evolved toward a powerful Mexican-style institution, increasingly taking on planning functions. The regulatory apparatus that grew and changed so much after 1979 became too costly, corrupt, and inefficient after 1985, leading to huge layoffs of public employees and further administrative reorganizations in 1988 and 1989.

Highly criticized special courts for counterrevolutionary crimes persisted until early 1988. The regular judiciary developed only moderate independence from the executive branch, which in turn only partly complied with judicial rulings against it. The suspension of constitutional protections for much of the time from 1981 until early 1988 made citizens' recourse to the judiciary difficult.

Policymaking

Goals

The consensual goals of the revolutionary coalition in 1979 were to destroy the political and economic foundations of the Somoza regime and to eliminate human rights abuses. The revolution succeeded in destroying the old regime, but success in the area of human rights was more elusive. At first political freedom was extensive, but by 1981 economic problems, internal resistance, and the challenge from the United States and the contras had led to sharp constraints on civil liberties. As economic problems and the contra war intensified and as mobilization for defense grew, restrictions on strikes, liberty of expression and association, intimidation and repression of opponents, and abuses of authority and due process became more common. Nevertheless, Nicaragua never suffered from the murderous practices of neighboring Guatemala and El Salvador. However, the fact that the Sandinistas proved capable of sharply relaxing repression at times (1984, 1988) made its imposition all the more glaring, particularly in light of the early revolutionary goals.

Other goals, some influenced by the Marxist-Leninist ideology of the Sandinista leadership, quickly drew criticism and contributed to the breakdown of the revolutionary coalition in the early 1980s. First, the FSLN wanted economic recovery; but it also wanted to socialize key profit-generating economic sectors in order to promote its redistributive policies of wage increases, agrarian reform, increased business regulation, and expanded services. The revolutionary government established a mixed economy that reserved about half of the economy for the private sector, but that also quickly generated major contradictions. The private sector's reluctance to invest slowed production, increased unemployment, and reduced the tax revenues needed for social programs. In order to save the revolution, the government ultimately had to adopt many policies that most favored its least-preferred group—large private commercial agriculture—at the expense of peasants and workers.

The FSLN also wanted to establish a "participatory democracy" that would emphasize distributive justice over constitutional formalism and be guided by a dominant FSLN, rather than being electorally competitive. Uniquely among Marxist-Leninist revolutionaries, the Sandinistas eschewed a one-party monopoly and allowed other forces to participate in politics. This stance ensured and at once legitimized a soon-antagonistic domestic opposition, which most revolutions have crushed but the FSLN did not.

The sincerity of the Sandinistas' commitment to political pluralism and a mixed economy was hotly debated. FSLN leaders argued that the commitment was strategic and fundamental, since to have adhered to a traditional Marxist model would have doomed the revolution because of Nicaragua's proximity to and dependence upon the United States. Their critics, citing key speeches and documents of the FSLN, said that both pluralism and the mixed economy were only tactics to entrench the Sandinistas so that they might ultimately and fully socialize the economy and crush political opposition. Although only time will reveal the winner of this debate, during their first decade in power the Sandinistas proved quite pragmatic and flexible. Political flexibility was shown especially in the holding of the national elections of 1984 and 1990 under laws shaped by the opposition parties, the reversal of a long-standing pledge not to negotiate with the contras, and the 1988 cease-fire. Proof of the FSLN's commitment to pluralism and electoral democracy came definitively with the party's decision to accept defeat in the 1990 election and pass power to the UNO coalition's victorious candidate, Violeta Barrios de Chamorro.

Performance

Until 1983 revolutionary economic policy permitted economic recovery from the 1978-1979 war, but after that the combined impact of declining terms of trade, revolutionary economic reforms, economic mismanagement, and the contra war were profoundly negative for the economy and many individuals. Many rural Nicaraguans received agricultural land as a result of the extensive agrarian reform, but most urban dwellers saw their services, quality of life, income, and standard of living steadily deteriorate. Much of the private sector was angry; it disinvested and mobilized politically against the government. Many peasants in areas afflicted by the war came to resent the government because of the turmoil or because they were relocated for military reasons. In 1987 and 1988 economic performance plunged, and in 1988 and 1989 the government made major economic and monetary reforms intended to restore private-sector and foreign-government confidence by reducing economic controls. Before the reforms could be assessed, Hurricane Joan—the worst natural disaster ever to befall Nicaragua—hit in September 1988. Destruction of crops, roads, bridges, agricultural machinery, homes, and vital natural resources was calamitous, perhaps doing more economic damage than the previous decade's two wars.[6]

THE INTERNATIONAL ARENA

The fundamental goals of the Sandinista revolutionary government were to defend the revolution from external threat (especially from the United States), to sharply reduce extensive U.S. influence over Nicaraguan affairs, and to diversify Nicaraguan diplomatic, commercial, and financial dependence. Among the policies adopted in pursuit of these goals were a nonaligned status (formally enshrined in the 1987 constitution) and membership in the Non-Aligned Movement; diplomatic relations with many new countries; new commercial, political, and aid links to Eastern and Western Europe; and the building of a new police and army with weapons and advice from Soviet-bloc countries. For over ten years of great struggle, the revolutionary government defended itself from the United States, but many key policy goals had to be sacrificed. Some diversification of external relations was achieved, but dependence had been more shifted and spread around than reduced.

Debt and Trade

The Sandinistas quickly renounced their desire to repudiate Somoza's foreign debts when they realized how important credit would be to the economy. Since 1979 Nicaragua's export earnings have covered only about a quarter to a third of the country's import needs. This trade deficit has been financed by external borrowing, which has resulted in a huge foreign debt ($1,955 per capita in 1987, compared to total per capita production of $879).[7] Continued renegotiation of the debt has kept interest payments below foreign earnings. Most of the credit came from Western national and multilateral sources until the mid-1980s; declining Western credit has since been replaced mainly by the Eastern bloc. Nicaragua's trade, once divided rather evenly between the United States, the CACM, and elsewhere, has shifted. The CACM's collapse in the late 1970s greatly cut trade with Central America, and the United States embargoed trade with Nicaragua, so both exports and imports have shifted toward Europe, Asia, and the Eastern bloc. Petroleum, once acquired from Mexico and Venezuela, is now obtained from the Soviet Union. The United States trade embargo was lifted in March 1990.

Relations with the United States

During the Carter administration, U.S. dissatisfaction with the Sandinistas was temporarily muted, and more than $100 million in aid was released or appropriated. However, relations cooled quickly as the Carter and Reagan administrations accused Nicaragua of supporting El Salvador's guerrilla insurgents. U.S. aid to Nicaragua was suspended, and the U.S. Central Intelligence Agency (CIA) began to organize and finance exiled former national guard elements into the first contra forces in 1981. Angered by Nicaragua's growing Soviet and Cuban links, U.S. policy became increasingly hostile and included diplomatic pressure to isolate and discredit Nicaragua as well as credit and trade embargoes. Nicaragua pressed for bilateral talks, but such efforts proved fruitless except briefly in 1983. The war and the U.S. refusal to negotiate with Nicaragua were major reasons for Nicaragua's acceptance of the Central American peace accord in August 1987. The victory of Violeta Chamorro in the 1990 election held forth the prospect of rapidly improving U.S.-Nicaraguan relations. Both the Bush administration and Chamorro called for demobilization of the contras.

Relations with Western Europe

Nicaragua partly succeeded in balancing U.S. hostility by seeking good relations with Western Europe. Spain and the Scandinavian countries were particularly helpful, and the European Community provided moderate amounts of credit and assistance until the mid-1980s. Even conservative Britain disagreed with U.S. policy toward Nicaragua. Although clearly a Marxist-Leninist party itself, the FSLN especially cultivated the

European social-democratic movement. However, by the mid-1980s general disenchantment with Nicaragua's eroding human rights record had grown, and European Community assistance had thus fallen off sharply. Scandinavian and Spanish aid programs continued, however.

Relations with the Soviet Bloc

From the outset, the Sandinistas sought and received advice and arms from the Soviet bloc, although no military accords were established with the USSR. Cuba was very generous with both reconstruction assistance and military aid. Soviet-bloc economic assistance, trade, and credit remained modest until U.S. pressures began to isolate Nicaragua. The Soviets and the Eastern-bloc countries began to supply Nicaragua with petroleum and credit when other sources dried up in the mid-1980s, eventually leaving Managua heavily dependent on the Eastern bloc. Trade with the Soviet bloc also jumped after the U.S. commercial embargo began. Military assistance increased rapidly in the mid-1980s as the contra war heated up, and Soviet military aid was instrumental in the Nicaraguan response to the contras. The USSR and Cuba both pressed Nicaragua to avoid isolation from the West, and the Soviets cut aid after 1987 to encourage Nicaragua to move toward a negotiated settlement of its war and conflicts with neighbors.

Relations with Latin America

Neighboring Central American nations began to regard the Sandinista government with increasing apprehension after 1979, fearing Nicaragua's growing military power and its early support for Marxist rebels in El Salvador. As U.S. pressure won Honduran, Costa Rican, and Salvadoran cooperation in the contra war, Nicaragua's relations with those countries became extremely tense and armed clashes on the Honduran and Costa Rican borders became common.

Other Latin American nations generally supported Nicaragua, especially in multilateral settings like the OAS, and criticized U.S. policy in the isthmus. When tensions in Central America aroused fears of regional war or direct U.S. military intervention, Mexico, Venezuela, Colombia, and Panama formed the Contadora Group to promote peace in Central America, and other nations supported them. Contadora's peacemaking efforts were frustrated largely by U.S. opposition. As U.S. support for the anti-Sandinista rebels flagged as a result of the Iran-Contra scandal, however, Central American nations led by Costa Rica and Guatemala themselves acted to seek peace. In August 1987 they signed a Central American peace accord in which they effectively recognized the legitimacy of each others' regimes and agreed to stop supporting each others' rebels. Nicaragua accepted the accord, implemented some democratic reforms, and entered into negotiations with the contras that led to the March 1988 cease-fire. Tensions in the region then eased somewhat, but critical international security issues remained to be negotiated under the auspices of Contadora. Nicaragua's 1990 election was set ahead several months under terms of later agreements among the Central American presidents.

CONCLUSION

The historic victory of UNO's Violeta Barrios de Chamorro over the FSLN's Daniel Ortega by a 55 to 41 percent margin may well have marked the end of the Sandinista revolution. Nicaraguan voters did in one day what the U.S.-backed contras were unable to do in nine years of war—remove the FSLN from ruling power. The United States, however, was deeply responsible for the UNO victory because its economic embargo and the contra war had generated the two major issues of the campaign— Nicaragua's dismal economy and the highly unpopular military draft.

The new government faced formidable economic and political difficulties. Even with UNO's 51 seats in the 92-place National Assembly, Chamorro would begin her term facing several great difficulties. The economy was in terrible shape, much of the nation's infrastructure had been destroyed by war, and the society had become badly polarized. Despite UNO's campaign pledge to continue agrarian reform, many UNO backers expected the return of confiscated property and the rollback of certain revolutionary economic programs. Because the ideological differences among UNO's constituent parties were extreme, ranging from communists and socialists to archconservatives, the coalition's prospects to hold together throughout its six-year term seemed very poor. With only 55 percent of the Assembly votes, UNO lacked sufficient voting strength to make changes in the 1987 constitution.

The FSLN's historic decision to accept its loss and assume the role of an opposition party by no means spelled the end of the Sandinistas. They captured 39 of 92 National Assembly seats, including one for President Ortega, and would clearly constitute the strongest, best organized, and most disciplined party in the legislature. The FSLN also retained considerable influence over the officer corps of the armed forces and enjoyed extensive influence in its affiliated mass organizations, including the labor movement. As an opposition party, the FSLN hoped to defend the key constitutional, institutional, and policy changes it had won while in power; rebuild its popular appeal; and return to office via the 1996 elections.

The 1990 election and the FSLN's decision to step down constituted a historic watershed in Nicaragua's turbulent history. Nevertheless, realistic prospects for Nicaragua to break out of its traditional cycles of war and repression would depend on the ability of the new government, the Sandinistas, and other elites to accommodate each other. In early 1990 there existed both internal and external pressures for Nicaraguans to work toward such accommodation. President Ortega and the FSLN took a major step in that direction with the decision to step down, and Violeta Chamorro reciprocated with a call for reconciliation.

However, promoting reconciliation and building greater democracy in such a situation would certainly not prove easy. The absence of a democratic tradition and an elite commitment to democratic political rules, and the extreme divisiveness and lack of trust among opposition political elites, were obstacles to the continued democratization of Nicaragua. The traditional proneness of political forces in Nicaragua to seek foreign help could also easily complicate domestic conflict resolution efforts. When one adds to these cultural tendencies and traditional divisions the bitterness and anger spawned by the years of civil war, it appeared that internal conflict could well persist without a definitive accord between the Sandinistas and the opposition.

NOTES

1. Today only about 3 percent of Nicaraguans are Indians, and they are concentrated mainly in the Atlantic zone. There are roughly 85,000 Miskitos, 8,000 Sumus, 1,500 Ramas, and 800 Garifonas. See Martin Diskin et al., *Peace and Autonomy on the Atlantic Coast of Nicaragua* (Pittsburgh: Latin American Studies Association, September 1986), p. 9.

2. Jose Luis Velazquez P., *Sociedad civil y dictadura* (San Jose: Libro Libre, 1986), pp. 66–69; Thomas W. Walker, *Nicaragua: Land of Sandino* (Boulder, Colo.: Westview Press, 1981), pp. 70–75.

3. Known as the Terceristas, this faction was led by the Ortega Saavedra brothers, Daniel and Humberto. The divisions in the FSLN in the late 1970s, while serious, were largely over tactics rather than over serious ideological differences. When the Nicaraguan people rebelled against the regime in late 1978, the FSLN leadership quickly healed its breach and has been quite unified ever since.

4. The Interamerican Research Center's survey of Managua residents (*Nicaraguan Public Opinion,* poll taken on June 4–5, 1988 [Los Angeles: June 30, 1988], p. 29) reported 9 percent total identification with opposition parties, versus 28 percent with the FSLN.

5. Mons. Obando is now a cardinal.

6. Miami *Herald,* October 30, 1988, p. 1; *Barricada Internacional,* October 27, 1988, pp. 1–9; November 24, 1988, pp. 5–8.

7. Based on Inter-American Development Bank, *Economic and Social Progress in Latin America: 1988 Report* (Washington, D.C.: IDB, 1988), pp. 464–468, Table B-1.

SUGGESTIONS FOR FURTHER READING

Americas Watch. *Human Rights in Nicaragua: August 1987 to August 1988.* New York: August 1988.

Booth, John A. *The End and the Beginning: The Nicaraguan Revolution,* 2d ed. Boulder, Colo.: Westview Press, 1985.

Colburn, Forrest D. *Post-Revolutionary Nicaragua: State, Class, and the Dilemmas of Agrarian Policy.* Berkeley: University of California Press, 1986.

Hodges, Donald C. *The Intellectual Foundations of the Nicaraguan Revolution.* Austin: University of Texas Press, 1986.

Millett, Richard. *Guardians of the Dynasty: A History of the U.S. Created Guardia Nacional de Nicaragua and the Somoza Family.* Maryknoll, N.Y.: Orbis Books, 1977.

Nolan, David. *The Ideology of the Sandinistas and the Nicaraguan Revolution.* Coral Gables, Fla.: Institute of Interamerican Studies, University of Miami, 1984.

O'Shaughnessy, Laura Nuzzi, and Luis H. Serra. *The Church and Revolution in Nicaragua.* Monographs in International Studies, Latin America Series no. 11. Athens: Ohio University, 1986.

Spalding, Rose J., ed. *The Political Economy of the Revolutionary Nicaragua.* Boston: Allen and Unwin, 1987.

Vilas, Carlos M. *The Sandinista Revolution: National Liberation and Social Transformation in Central America.* New York: Monthly Review Press, 1986.

Walker, Thomas W., ed. *Nicaragua: The First Five Years.* New York: Praeger, 1986.

———. *Nicaragua: The Land of Sandino,* 2d rev. ed. Boulder, Colo.: Westview Press, 1986.

———. *Reagan Versus the Sandinistas: The Undeclared War on Nicaragua.* Boulder, Colo.: Westview Press, 1987.

22
El Salvador

ENRIQUE BALOYRA

Where did the current Salvadoran nightmare come from? How could it have been avoided? How is it going to end?

SOCIETY

Comparisons to Cuba and Vietnam notwithstanding, Salvadoran politics of the 1980s are rooted in a unique combination of factors affecting that society's ability and willingness to cope with economic modernization and political democratization.

El Salvador's uniqueness is manifold. For the most part and unlike other Latin American countries, it has not been divided by ethnic conflict nor has it been ruled by caudillos. Miscegenation and transculturation were so thorough that the word *ladino* (assimilated Indian) became obsolete to the Hispanicized mestizos, the overwhelming majority of the population. Salvadoran economic dependence has been less a question of neglect and disinterest by foreigners managing local assets from a global perspective than one of assimilating the costs of unpredictable cycles of export commodities. There are no foreign plantations in El Salvador, and, in the main, the economy has remained under national control. In addition, there have been no landings by U.S. Marines, and anti-U.S. sentiment is a contemporary phenomenon.

During colonial times, with land relatively available and labor scarce, the key issue of production was maintaining a reliable supply of labor. By the mid-sixteenth century the *encomienda* (permanent assignments of Indian villages to individuals who supposedly protected and Christianized Indians in return for their labor) were being replaced by *repartimientos* (weekly allocations of Indian laborers), and the *encomienda* was limited to tribute paid by villages. Large farms (haciendas) eventually absorbed most of the noncommunal lands but left large tracts underutilized. Excluded from the *repartimientos*, hacendados relied on debt peonage and retail stores (*tiendas de roya*) to keep laborers permanently attached

484

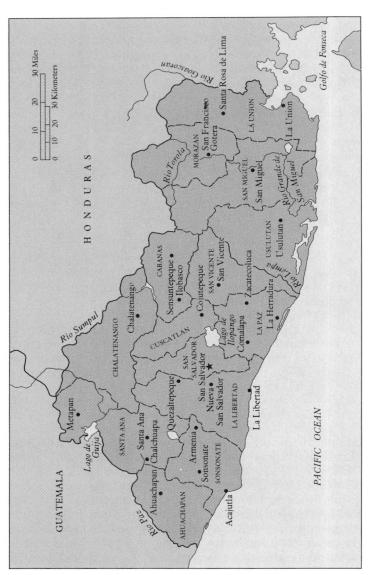

El Salvador

to their farms. Labor permanence in the farms created patron-client bonds that endured until recently.

The absence of precious metals and the marginal location of the country outside the main routes of trade kept Salvadoran society relatively stagnant during the next two centuries. Cocoa and indigo were the main export products, but competition and European protectionism limited the gains of export agriculture. Political and economic subordination to Guatemala depressed these gains even further. By the end of the colonial period, no more than one-half of the cultivable land was in commercial agriculture, and the remaining areas survived by growing maize and beans. There was little unemployment, but illiteracy was epidemic. There were no newspapers and no public debate to speak of.

Independence from Spain in 1821, and then from Mexico in 1823, did not settle the larger political questions and, if anything, may have worsened the material conditions of life of the poorest cultivators. As the population grew, access to and control of land became more important than the availability of labor. As was the case in the rest of the isthmus, liberals lined up behind free trade and anticlericalism, and conservatives insisted on tariffs and greater identification of church with state. Personal rivalries complicated these cleavages. El Salvador's enthusiasm for a Central American union exposed the country to the machinations of foreign caudillos, particularly Guatemala's Rafael Carrera. Local armies were recruited to fight for or against the federation or confederation of the time. Between 1825 and 1871 there were about twenty-five major armed conflicts that brought much devastation. The only major conflict deviating from this pattern was the rebellion of Nonualco Indians perpetrated by Anastasio Aquino in 1833. But this was a protest about worsening social conditions, military conscriptions, and new taxes enacted in 1832—not an ethnic conflict.

With the defeat of the conservatives in 1871, Salvadoran politics entered a period of "bourgeois revolution" as liberals finally managed to impose their version of political economy. Laissez-faire became the order of the day, but only after communal lands were abolished and government policy was reoriented to promote the cultivation and export of coffee. Coffee replaced indigo as the predominant export product, became the growth engine of the economy, and effected a profound transformation of property and production relations in the countryside.[1]

Where did this scheme go awry so that today's economic problems developed?

People moderately acquainted with El Salvador's politics of disaster know that rapid population growth (3 percent per year in 1971–1983) compounded the problems of a mini-state (8,295 square miles [21,484 square kilometers] in size) with a high density of population (690 persons per square mile [265 per square kilometer] and 5.7 million total population in 1987) and few natural resources. Other people believe that the country's backwardness is the basic reason for which El Salvador has remained a predominantly rural society sustained by agriculture.[2] But the problem lies elsewhere.

To be sure, El Salvador still has a predominantly agricultural economy. From 1980 to 1987 agriculture accounted for about one-fourth of the gross domestic product, and in 1985 about 685,000 people, or 43 percent of a labor force of 1,586,000, were employed in agriculture. These figures represent a relative decrease from the 65.4 percent engaged in agriculture in 1950, but an absolute increase over the total of 447,000 at that time. Meanwhile, the number of people in industry and services (308,000) increased at a faster rate but remained below the number in agriculture (594,000). Given the very high average annual growth rates of the labor force during those years, absorption of labor into *any* occupational category appears to have been more crucial to the economy than any absolute or relative decline in agriculture.[3] In addition, with a bloated service sector disguising unemployment and underemployment, and with an industrial sector unable to absorb more than 19 percent of the labor force during that time, it is hard to see how labor concentration in agricultural occupations could be considered the most problematic aspect of the economy.[4]

The metaphor of a race is frequently utilized in describing situations of economic inequality. In the case of coffee cultivation in El Salvador, the "race" started between 1880 and 1912. Many would-be planters could not afford to wait five years until the plants had yielded their first crop, and many who entered the race came to rely on credit advances, utilizing anticipated profits as collateral. To obtain credit, planters frequently had to agree to sales contracts in which purchase prices were calculated at below-market rates. In many cases, the creditors were larger planters who also were *beneficiadores* (coffee processors) and export brokers. When market prices softened, profits dwindled or disappeared; repayment became difficult or impossible. Absent any official relief, repossession followed.

In short, the race was more favorable to those people who had resources sufficient to carry them through long periods of bad luck. With time, the number of small family farms multiplied and their size decreased, while the size of a more or less constant number of large multifamily farms continued to increase. In the early 1960s these large farms, representing less than one-half of 1 percent of the 226,800 farms in the country and averaging about 502 acres (203 hectares) in size, accounted for 38 percent of the land under cultivation. By contrast, the more than 207,000 smallest farms, averaging 4.10 acres (1.6 hectares) and representing 91 percent of all farms, accounted for only 22 percent. In 1978, according to some estimates, 1,139 large proprietors representing 0.08 percent of the economically active population (estimated at 1,420,000) controlled about 68 percent of the net surplus of production. At about the same time, during the late 1970s, households in the top 5 percent income bracket controlled 21.4 percent of the national income, whereas a majority of wage earners, concentrated in the five lowest brackets, controlled only 22.5 percent. These discrepancies may appear sufficient for producing civil war in El Salvador, but comparable data for Mexico and for the rest of Central America would indicate that El Salvador's was hardly the worst case of socioeconomic inequality. So why El Salvador?

In terms of the labor market, the logic was simple. So long as there was an oversupply of workers, labor would remain exceedingly cheap in El Salvador—a condition deemed vital by export producers seeking to remain competitive. Natural population growth guaranteed that this would continue to be the case unless workers were able to unionize. It is here that the power of the state was brought to bear: first, in the late nineteenth century, in enforcing vagrancy laws that made laborers available to cultivators on a permanent basis, and, later on, since the late 1920s, in preventing the organization of rural unions.[5] These became possible only in the 1980s after much violence and bloodshed.[6] In the meantime, as long as emigration to Honduras was possible, and marginal land and seasonal work were available as safety valves, authoritarian capitalism could survive in El Salvador with a minimal level of repression.

It was the more subtle aspects of the interaction between demography and economy that began to unravel things. First was the extraordinary pressure for access to land. Beginning in 1960 the land to human ratio shrank in El Salvador to a point where, in 1980, there were only 1,234 acres (.5 hectares) per economically active person in agriculture—a 50 percent drop. With export agriculture dedicating more and more land to nontraditional crops—particularly cotton and sugarcane—the land available for domestic-use agriculture diminished markedly. Between 1950 and 1980 the area dedicated to cotton and sugarcane in El Salvador increased 289 and 154 percent, respectively, and vast tracts were turned over to grazing, thereby further depriving peasants of access to even the marginal lands that they exploited for subsistence agriculture. In other words, peasants were driven to the wall because of the success, not the failure, of export agriculture.

Why did Salvadoran industry fail to grow rapidly enough to absorb the increasing number of workers released from agricultural occupations? First, no rival group of entrepreneurs emerged to dispute the economic supremacy of the oligarchy. A relatively small number of planters controlled the economy through their tenure of the largest farms as well as through their controlling shares in production and exports, foreign exchange, and domestic credit. This supremacy has been called "the magic square of oligarchic domination." Capital was reproduced by and new wealth came to essentially the same group of people, and there was little capital available for diversification outside this circle. Second, although most oligarchic families diversified their holdings, they failed to adopt a wage and employment policy that would have enlarged the market. Third, as a result, economies of scale were available only if

Salvadoran-made goods had access to a larger Central American market, a condition that did not last long. Fourth, there was little foreign investment, and much of that was scared off during the preliminary stages of civil war in the mid-1970s.

It must be noted that not only indifference and callousness but also attempts to improve the lot of the less fortunate may have worsened the situation in El Salvador. For example, in 1965 the government of Col. Julio Adalberto Rivera established minimum agricultural wages. Growers reacted by discontinuing the two free daily meals to their farm hands, by releasing young people and women from their traditional marginal tasks, and by relying less on permanent *colonos* and more on temporary workers paid at lower, unregulated wages.[7] Wage labor was brought about by the modernization of agriculture and proved to be profoundly traumatic and destabilizing, undermining the traditional client-patron arrangements found in the countryside and replacing them with a more impersonal, but no more equitable, labor market.

In summary, a very robust impetus for agricultural modernization combined with fast demographic growth, an unequal distribution of property, and a small territory combined to deteriorate the material conditions of life for thousands of agricultural workers in El Salvador. The "proletarization" of peasants into agricultural workers made them available for political mobilization, and eventually there emerged organizers willing and able to lead them into the politics of protest and insurrection.

THE STATE: FROM LIBERAL OLIGARCHY
TO REACTIONARY DESPOTISM

In El Salvador, the maldistribution of the gains of the export trade cannot be blamed on the unhindered operation of market forces. Ever since colonial times, political power has been utilized in El Salvador to create and perpetuate economic advantage and social privilege. Following independence, the woes of the politics of Central American unification distracted but did not deter the local economic elite from a project of export diversification. The liberal sentiment predominating in the country embraced this project, which came to fruition in the 1870s. There was prosperity and growth, but the majority of citizens were not benefited.

The oligarchic regime that emerged from this transformation was more stable, as improved communications and a permanent army facilitated the maintenance of internal order; and there was a more orderly presidential succession, with the domestic political process coming under civilian control. But the Salvadoran state remained private, as the oligarchy continued to manage the key political transactions and policy questions, and to keep them from public scrutiny. "Official business," in short, was the business of a few family clans. For two generations (1871–1927) these families managed the regime quite well.[8]

Basically the same group of individuals controlled politics and the economy, but in 1927–1931 they became divided over how to cope with the world economic crisis and increasing social protest. The overthrow of President Arturo Romero in December 1931 underscored the fact that, in the absence of effective national party organizations, the obstructionism of the oligarchy and the high level of mobilization of the lower classes would overwhelm any attempt to consolidate a democratic regime through reformism and elections. Reaction to the peasant insurrection of 1932, organized by the tiny Communist party of El Salvador (PCS) and brutally suppressed, indefinitely postponed any prospect of relief.

The collapse of the oligarchic regime brought the military to power, first through personalist dictators (1932–1945) and then in a more institutional fashion. The oligarchy lost control of the government but not of the sources of economic power. The country remained backward, particularly under the rule of Gen. Maximiliano Hernández Martínez (1932–1944), who increased the power of the government through monetary and fiscal controls—including the creation of the Central Bank and the Mortgage Bank in 1934 and the imposition of exchange controls in 1935—that ended reckless monetary speculation and offered a measure of protection to the smaller capitalists.

Beginning in 1948 military reformers sought to find ways to trickle some benefits down to the lower classes, but the military appeared incapable of finding enough consensus and sufficient resolve to overcome the resistance of the oligarchy. In the late 1960s and throughout the 1970s the Salvadoran armed forces found it more difficult to maintain equilibrium between prosperity and order. In the late 1960s the emergence of parties that could defeat the military-backed party at the polls, particularly the Christian Democratic party (PDC) and the National Revolutionary Movement (MNR), complicated government-opposition relations. A 1969 war with Honduras, which brought thousands of Salvadoran emigrants back into the country, temporarily reversed this trend; but in 1972 and 1977 military presidents had to perpetrate massive electoral frauds to install their handpicked successors in office. In 1976 the military had to withdraw a project of "agrarian transformation," their most serious blueprint for reform to date, but this defeat strained the tacit division of power between the oligarchy and the military. Hitherto, neither side had challenged the other so openly; indeed, they remained deadlocked in the precarious balance acknowledged by their tacit pact. But the regime had degenerated into a sort of reactionary despotism, and the resulting political illegitimacy and social irresponsibility were increasingly difficult to defray without augmenting the level of official repression.

World economic recession hit El Salvador twice in the 1970s, changing the delicate mixture of repression and reform toward the former. Urban guerrillas began to appear, kidnapping the wealthy and collecting fabulous ransoms for their war chests.[9] As order began to unravel, the people who could afford it spent massive amounts of money on their own protection. Others went further, taking matters into their own hands and organizing death squads. Apparently, they acted in concert with military intelligence (ANSESAL), the treasury police, the national guard, and the Nationalist Democratic Organization (ORDEN), a paramilitary organization of peasants created by Colonel Rivera in 1966. Priests and labor organizers were murdered in rural areas. The teacher's union (ANDES) became the backbone of the growing insurgency, and it was joined by university students and radicalized middle-class elements. The Catholic church, led by Archbishop Oscar Arnulfo Romero, found itself opposing the established order. In 1977 the Carter administration, unable to persuade President Carlos Humberto Romero to curb official violence, suspended all military aid to El Salvador.

In 1979 the Sandinista revolution and the destruction of the national guard in Nicaragua solidified a tenuous consensus within the military of El Salvador about the need for change. On October 15 a group of colonels and majors deposed General Romero and thus ended the tacit alliance between officers and the oligarchy. Apparently, the military felt that it could not continue to shelter the oligarchy from the social and political consequences of its economic selfishness without destroying its own institution in the process. But the military could agree on little else. The Carter administration tried to help fill the political vacuum and prevent another revolutionary victory in the Isthmus. U.S. efforts hinged on constructing a centrist coalition that could implement social reforms, defeat the left politically, and co-opt the more recalcitrant elements of the right.

In December 1979 the social democrats in the provisional government delivered an ultimatum to the armed forces, demanding clarification of past abuses of human rights and a prompt enactment of social reforms. When the military refused to cooperate, the social democrats resigned en masse, and the government fell apart. On New Year's Eve, José Napoleón Duarte reversed a long-standing party policy and led the PDC into an alliance with the military in a new junta. Early 1980 was decisive. Mario Zamora, the PDC's most popular young politician, and Archbishop Romero were assassinated in February and March, respectively. In addition, the PDC split over the military's inability to curb death-squad activity and guarantee basic citizens' rights in the wake of the civil war that erupted over the reform measures that were decreed on March 7.[10] Rubén Zamora and others left the PDC and created the Popular Social Christian Movement (MPSC). In August the MPSC and Guillermo Ungo's MNR joined in the creation of the Democratic Revolutionary Front (FDR), which later became allied with the guerrilla front (FMLN).[11] Thus solidified were two alliances: the military and the PDC, on the one hand, against the FDR and the FMLN, on the other. The contradictory nature of these alliances reinforced the growing polarization and undermined attempts at creating the broad coalition of moderates required to promote a peaceful solution to the crisis.

Following early attempts to change the basic Carter blueprint that almost ended in disaster, the Reagan administration adopted that blueprint in the hopes that it would automatically lead to victory. But the Reagan administration remained focused on Nicaragua, and the Salvadoran situation failed to sort itself out. The PDC played a pivotal role in this effort, remaining in power through most of the 1980s and exhausting itself in the process.[12]

THE POLITICAL SPECTRUM

Ultimately, the increasing differentiation of a society into more diverse groups with conflicting interests must be reflected in the increasing modes and levels of participation within the political community.[13] In the nineteenth century the principal distinction between parties in El Salvador had to do with whether they were officialist or oppositionist. These became somewhat permanent categories in themselves. By 1918 the officialists were sufficiently concerned with the outcome of a presidential election that they launched the most organized "official" party of the period, the Red League. But it was not until the 1930s that larger groups resembling modern political parties appeared. Of these, only the Communist party of El Salvador (PCS), founded in 1930, remains today. All others, including President Arturo Araujo's Salvadoran Labor party, have disappeared.[14]

During the period of military presidents (1932–1979), the survival of reactionary despotism in El Salvador depended on the government's ability to control the social consequences of agrarian modernization and to exclude from effective participation any actor who could undermine the status quo. Incumbents relied on the more sophisticated official parties. The first of these was the Revolutionary party of Democratic Unification (PRUD), founded by Col. Oscar Osorio in 1950; another was the National Conciliation party (PCN), created in 1961, which supported the candidacy of Colonel Rivera. Neither the PRUD nor the PCN delivered for the Salvadoran military the performance of the official party of Mexico (PRI), which they consciously tried to imitate. PRUD and PCN served as patronage machines and to legitimize electoral manipulation. They did not participate in crucial policy decisions, which were transacted between the government and the primary organizations of the private sector—particularly the Association of Coffee Processors and Exporters (ABECAFE), the National Association of Private Enterprise (ANEP), the Industrialists' Association (ASI), and the Salvadoran Chamber of Commerce. Except for the Popular Salvadoran party (PPS), which represented very specific interests, the Salvadoran oligarchy did not feel compelled to organize its own political party during this time. Thanks to the adoption of a system of proportional representation for the unicameral national legislature (*Asamblea Legislativa*) and the creation of a Central Council of Elections, which made vote counting more aboveboard, the

PDC and the MNR made some inroads into the system. But the prospects for change remained unaltered: Unionization and elections would eventually lead the armed forces to support a truly reformist government or to prepare to fight a civil war. Ironically, once the military opted for the former in 1980, it found itself engaged in the latter.

How wide and how viable is the political spectrum of contemporary Salvadoran politics? Despite some controversy about their nature and relevance to those politics, the Salvadoran elections of 1982–1988 had a positive impact in the process of transition. First, they represented a peaceful alternative to the ongoing conflict. With negotiations thwarted by the oligarchy and the military, the Duarte administration successfully reincorporated the FDR to the political process. This move closed a cycle of incorporation initiated in September 1981, when the Salvadoran right realized that it had to organize a political party, the Nationalist Republican Alliance (ARENA), and compete in elections if it did not want to abandon the field to the PDC. With the MPSC and the MNR offering their own presidential candidate in 1989, all the major political alternatives were represented.

Second, with allies of the extreme left and right legally represented and engaged in campaigns and elections, the issue of violence was joined. Much as ARENA needed to manage internal tension between its more moderate and more violent elements around former army major and presidential candidate Roberto D'Aubuisson, the MPSC and the MNR had to declare their stance on the question of FMLN violence and distance themselves somewhat from guerrilla leaders such as the ERP commander, Joaquín Villalobos. Inevitably, such actions led to a delegitimation of violence.

Third, even apparent setbacks—such as the PDC defeats in 1982 and 1988, the split of the PDC in 1988, and the ARENA victory in 1989—open possibilities for a realignment away from the alliances that froze the political process throughout the five years from 1983 to 1988. In essence, by enabling the downloading of contestation and conflict resolution from the civil war to the political process, elections have been efficient instruments of political transition in El Salvador.

The results of those elections also illuminate the actual correlation of forces and anticipate the possible changes resulting from the reincorporation of the democratic left (see Table 22.1). First, assuming the number of eligible voters to be around 2,750,000, there is little question that a fairly sizable contingent of people is yet to be incorporated fully. Many such people may lack the documents necessary for registration, others may be unable to vote owing to transportation stoppages and/or intimidation by the guerrillas, and still others may be growing weary with frequent elections and lackluster governments, as evidenced by declining turnouts. All of these factors suggest that there is room for new coalitions and different outcomes.

Table 22.1 Results of Recent Elections in El Salvador

	Voting Turnout	Vote PDC	Vote ARENA	Vote PCN	Others Right	Total Valid	Null and Blank
(National totals, in thousands)							
1982[1]	1,485.2	526.9	383.6	249.0	149.0[2]	1,308.5	176.7
1984[3]	1,412.6	549.7	376.9	244.6	95.1[4]	1,266.3	146.3
1984[5]	1,524.1	752.6	651.7			1,404.4	119.7
1985[6]	1,107.5	505.3	286.7	80.7	90.5[4]	965.2	142.2
1988[7]	1,150.9	326.7	447.7	78.8	77.5[8]	930.7	220.2
(National totals, in percentages)							
1982[1]		40.3	29.3	19.0	11.4	88.1	
1984[3]		43.4	29.8	19.3	7.5	89.6	
1984[5]		53.6	46.4			92.1	
1985[6]		52.4	29.7	8.4	9.5	87.2	
1988[7]		35.1	48.1	8.5	8.3	80.9	

[1]Constituent Assembly elections of March 28, 1982.
[2]Including Democratic Action (AD), Popular Salvadoran party (PPS), and Popular Orientation party (POP).
[3]Presidential primary election of March 25, 1984.
[4]Including AD, PPS, POP, the Authentic Institutional party of El Salvador (PAISA), and the Stable Republican Movement of the Center (MERECEN).
[5]Runoff presidential election of May 6, 1984.
[6]Legislative and municipal elections of March 31, 1985.
[7]Legislative and municipal elections of March 20, 1988.
[8]Includes all the parties in note 4 plus the Renovating Action party (PAR) and the Liberation party (PL).

Sources: Computed from Foreign Broadcast Information Service, Central America (April 2, 1982), I; CIDES Centroamerica, El Salvador, Resumen, Vol. 3, No. 108 (March 28–April 3, 1984), p. 1; "Computos oficiales, 25 de marzo de 1984," and "Computos oficiales, 6 de mayo de 1984," Estudios Centroamericanos, Vol. 39, Nos. 426, 427 (April–May 1984), pp. 365–366; "Resultados oficiales, 20 Marzo 1988," Estudios Centroamericanos, Vol. 43, Nos. 473, 474 (March–April 1988), pp. 285–295.

Second, the right remains a formidable force that must be reckoned with. In five elections, the average proportion of the vote going to ARENA was 36.6 percent; minor and generally rightist parties managed an additional 9.2 percent in four elections. At the very least, these figures imply a continuation of a relatively polarized National Assembly, even after the left offers candidates in 1991. The constitution of 1983 reflects this polarization, and it will be a while before a reformist

Assembly can amend it and eliminate articles restricting social reforms. Finally, in 1988, even at its worst moment of disarray, the PDC—which had averaged nearly 45 percent of the vote—remained the choice of more than one-third of the electorate.

In a nutshell, there are three viable political forces in El Salvador that could have similar shares of a future enlarged electorate. These trends hardly conjure up a specter of inevitable disaster. If anything, they hint at the possibility of institutionalizing pluralism in El Salvador.

PROSPECTS

Can effective solutions to the crisis be forthcoming from the rough and tumble of electoral campaigns and alliances? Are there inexorable forces at work?

In 1988, after numerous manmade and natural disasters—with civil war displacing 15 percent of all families, inflicting some 60 thousand deaths, and driving half a million people out of the country; with real salaries below three-fourths of their 1980 level, official unemployment hovering around 30 percent, 75 percent of the population living in poverty, and average annual growth rates of GDP below 1 percent; and with two consecutive years of drought and a major earthquake in 1986— the Salvadoran transition appeared stalled.

Despite the efforts of many people, no new formula of domination had been found to replace reactionary despotism, as centrists and moderates appeared incapable of agreeing on a common project that could attenuate violence, neutralize armed extremists of all stripes, and produce a national reconciliation. President Duarte fell gravely ill with cancer, and the PDC split again following a serious setback at the hands of ARENA in the legislative and municipal elections of March 20. Meanwhile, growing impatience with the inability of $3.2 billion of U.S. economic aid and military assistance to make a difference in the conflict, and alarm at the prospect of an ARENA victory in the presidential elections of 1989, threatened to undermine a bipartisan consensus in the U.S. Congress to stay the course in El Salvador.

In March 1989, the ARENA candidate, Alfredo Cristiani, won the presidential election. While liberals in the U.S. Congress suggested that further aid must be conditioned to human rights, little changed over the next year. Guerrilla activities continued, including an urban offensive in November 1989. There was no apparent resurgence of death-squad activities.

Whatever the merits of U.S. policy, Salvadorans must bear primary responsibility for a national tragedy that they very much brought on themselves. But nothing is foreordained in El Salvador. Just as in the Ivory Coast, coffee cultivation could have produced a more equitable distribution of property. Much as in Brazil, a reformist faction could have emerged from the coffee oligarchy to diversify the economy and gradually democratize politics and society. As was the case in Venezuela, military professionals may prevail and, for the sake of their institution, redefine their role. And, unlikely as it seems, at least some Salvadoran guerrillas may accept an honorable settlement and continue their struggle through peaceful means.

Nothing will happen automatically, and making democratic values a part of Salvadoran culture will take at least a generation. But if total disaster is to be averted, democratic politics remains a viable alternative in El Salvador, particularly when the country is confronted by over-whelming problems for which there are no immediate solutions. Even without a civil war going on, any government trying to consolidate a democratic regime in El Salvador would generate much discontent while servicing the foreign debt and reactivating the economy; creating con-ditions for investment and living wages; respecting opposition rights while coping with the efforts of antidemocratic elements to destroy the regime; reasserting civilian supremacy over a self-styled hegemonic military; and depending on continued U.S. assistance while preventing U.S. foreign policy from unleashing itself in the country. A government may hardly be expected to deliver a sterling performance in the face of such issues, but central to the entire effort is the ability to guarantee the physical security and basic rights of citizens. Such a guarantee is a tall order, and the solutions are very difficult to bring about. But all the more reason to imagine that Salvadorans may finally understand the futility of violence and take democratic politics seriously.

NOTES

1. Between 1870 and 1891, the value of indigo exports dropped from US $2.6 million to less than one million, while the value of coffee exports increased from US $80,000 to US $4.8 million.

2. If by "urban" we mean places with more than 100,000 inhabitants, only the San Salvador metropolitan area would qualify as a city. In 1975, only 14 percent of the population lived there, and the majority of the urban population was concentrated in cities with less than 50,000 inhabitants.

3. The average annual rates of growth of the labor force were 3.47 in the 1960s, 2.98 in the 1970s, and 3.12 in the 1980s.

4. In 1985, only 53 percent of the economically active population resided in urban areas. In addition, 41 percent of these were in the "informal" sector instead of in the money economy.

5. This "interference" was required when the system of satellite agriculture which kept renters, sharecroppers, and colonos more or less tied to the fincas and large farms would not deliver enough manpower—a rarity in the twentieth century—or when those available took advantage of favorable circumstances to demand higher wages.

6. There were attempts at organizing unions before this. The most militant were the initially reformist Christian Federation of Salvadoran Peasants (FECCAS), founded in 1964; and the Union of Rural Workers (UTC), established in 1974. In 1976, the two merged into the Federation of Rural Workers (FTC). In 1968,

the Salvadoran Communal Union (UCS) was created with the support of the American Institute of Free Labor Development (AIFLD). By the late 1970s all of these organizations had incurred the wrath of the oligarchy and counted several, in some cases hundreds, of their members among the victims of repression in El Salvador.

7. Since the late 1960s, as demand for land for cotton cultivation went up, many *hacendados* began to ask *colonos* for payment in cash, rather than in kind, for share-cropping and squatting rights. In addition, conversion to stock raising led to massive expulsions of peasants from the land. These brought about land invasions, strikes, and bloody confrontations. The trend was reinforced in recent years, particularly in farms that could be affected by the agrarian reform statute of 1980.

8. I use oligarchic regime to mean "the rule of a few governing for themselves," reserving the term oligarchy for "a reduced group of individuals who control a socioeconomic system and enjoy most of its benefits."

9. The five dominant guerrilla groups of El Salvador emerged as follows. In 1970, a splinter group of the Communist Party of El Salvador formed the Popular Liberation Forces (FPL), under the leadership of Salvador Cayetano Carpio (Marcial). The FPL adhered to the theory of prolonged popular war but, in 1971, adherents of the *foco* theory recognized by the late Ernesto (Che) Guevara, left to the FPL to establish the People's Revolutionary Army (ERP). In 1975, following the assassination of ERP leader Roque Dalton, a group created the Armed Forces of National Resistance (FARN). The smaller and lesser known Revolutionary Party of Central American Workers (PRTC) and Armed Forces of Liberation (FAL) were created in the mid-1970s and in 1980, respectively. Beginning in 1983, following the suicide of Marcial in Managua, the Farabundo Martí National Liberation Front (FMLN) became a more unified body representing these five organizations. The ERP's Joaquín Villalobos emerged as the ablest military commander of the guerrillas whereas the FAL's Shaifk Handal utilized his status as PCS secretary general to increase his leverage in the rebel alliance.

10. These included the nationalization of banking (Decree No. 158), and agrarian reform (Decree No. 153).

11. Ungo had been Duarte's running mate in 1972.

12. Except for the period of June 1982 through May 1984, during which Dr. Alvaro Magaña served as provisional president.

13. By "political community" I mean that institutional arena or space where groups and individuals adopt public identities, in the realm of official business and the media, to organize and express themselves while seeking to influence policy.

14. During his twelve-year reign, General Martínez banned all political organizations, except for his Pro-Fatherland "party."

SUGGESTIONS FOR FURTHER READING

Books

Anderson, Thomas P. *Matanza: El Salvador's Communist Revolt of 1932*. Lincoln: University of Nebraska Press, 1971.
Baloyra, Enrique A. *El Salvador in Transition*. Chapel Hill, N.C.: University of North Carolina Press, 1982.

Browning, David. *El Salvador: Landscape and Society.* Oxford: Clarendon Press, 1971.

Bulmer-Thomas, Victor. *The Political Economy of Central America Since 1920.* London: Cambridge University Press, 1987.

Castro Morán, Mariano. *Función política del ejército salvadoreño en el presente siglo.* San Salvador: UCA Editores, 1984.

Colindres, Eduardo. *Fundamentos económicos de la burguesía salvadoreña.* San Salvador: UCA Editores, 1977.

Krehm, William. *Democracies and Tyrannies of the Caribbean.* Westport, Conn.: Lawrence Hill and Company, 1984.

Montgomery, Tommie Sue. *Revolution in El Salvador, Origins and Evolution.* Boulder, Colo.: Westview Press, 1982.

Webre, Stephen. *José Napoleón Duarte and the Christian Democratic Party in Salvadoran Politics, 1960–1972.* Baton Rouge: Louisiana State University Press, 1979.

White, Alastair. *El Salvador.* New York and Washington: Praeger Publishers, 1973.

Williams, Robert G. *Export Agriculture and the Crisis in Central America.* Chapel Hill: University of North Carolina Press, 1986.

Articles

Baloyra-Herp, Enrique A. "Reactionary Despotism in Central America," and Browning, David. "Agrarian Reform in El Salvador." *Journal of Latin American Studies,* XV, 2 (November 1983), pp. 295–319 and 399–426, respectively.

Cáceres, Luis René. "Será El Salvador otra Corea del Sur? Comentarios al modelo de promoción de exportaciones." *Occasional Paper Series, Latin American and Caribbean Center, Florida International University,* #19 (October 1986).

Centro de Investigación y Acción Social (CINAS). *El Salvador: Crisis Económica,* #9 (January 1987).

Diskin, Martin, and Kenneth Sharpe. "Facing Facts in El Salvador." *World Policy Journal,* I, 2 (Spring 1984), pp. 517–548.

Fundación Salvadoreña para el Desarrollo Económico y Social (FUSADES). *Cómo está nuestra economía?* (April 1988).

Fundación Salvadoreña para el Desarrollo Económico y Social (FUSADES). *Encuesta Sobre Clima de Negocios y Coyuntura Industrial* (May 1988).

Karl, Terry. "After La Palma: The Prospects for Democratization in El Salvador." *World Policy Journal,* II, 2 (Spring 1986), pp. 305–330.

Keogh, Dermot. "The Myth of the Liberal Coup: The United States and the 15 October 1979 Coup in El Salvador." *Journal of International Studies,* XIII, 2 (Summer 1984), pp. 153–183.

López, Roberto. "The Nationalization of Foreign Trade in El Salvador: The Myths and Realities of Coffee." *Occasional Paper Series, Latin American and Caribbean Center, Florida International University,* #16 (March 1986).

Villalobos, Joaquín. "El estado actual de la guerra y sus perspectivas." *Estudios Centroamericanos.* XLI, 449 (March 1986), pp. 169–202.

Zaid, Gabriel. "Enemy Colleagues." *Dissent* (Winter 1982), pp. 13–38.

23
Guatemala: The Politics of Unstable Stability

ROLAND EBEL

"Guatemala Begins New Civilian Era" screamed the ten-inch banner headline in *El Grafico* on January 15, 1986. The previous evening thousands of Guatemalan citizens had massed in front of the Palacio Nacional to hear the first freely elected president in twenty years give his inaugural address. The fact that the *fiesta popular,* as the occasion was billed, degenerated into a riot when President Vinicio Cerezo Arevalo arrived two hours late did not dampen the country's enthusiasm for the young Christian Democrat who had survived three attempts on his life before ending two decades of military dominance of the political system. Today Guatemalans can be happy, he told his audience, "because we are returning to our own house" even if the house "is in the worst condition ever encountered by any chief executive."

The *fiesta popular* riot was not the only indicator of the nation's unease. Massed outside the National Theater, where the new president had earlier been sworn in, was a group of women known as the Mutual Aid Group (GAM) demanding to know the whereabouts of the thousands of *desaparecidos* who literally had "disappeared" during the last fifteen years of military rule.[1] Elsewhere in the city, some 2,000 homeless people had invaded privately owned land in the Monte Maria section chanting, "A government of the people, for the people, and by the people" as they marked out their illegally obtained homesites.

Vinicio, as he is popularly called, was well aware of the difficulties facing his administration in January 1986. The five-year decline in the Guatemalan economy had reached crisis proportions. Exports were down, the GNP showed a negative growth rate, monetary reserves had been exhausted, and unemployment was skyrocketing. The new president faced a cruel dilemma. To bring the Guatemalan economy back into a growth phase he had to motivate the business community to invest and produce more. At the same time there were pent-up demands for a

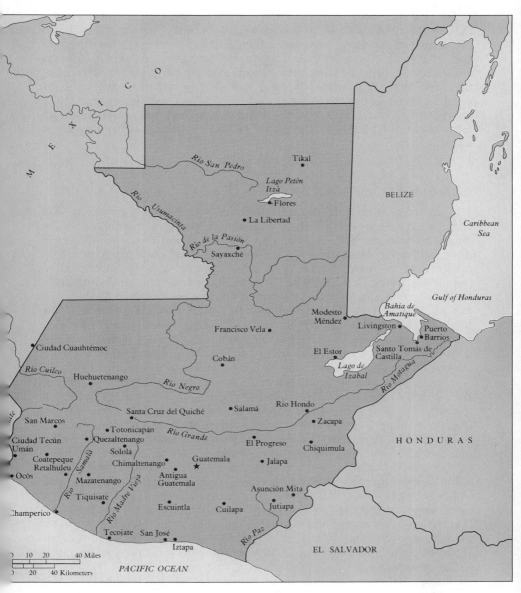

Guatemala

fairer distribution of land and national income by the "popular sectors" that had supported his candidacy.

He also had intractable problems on the political front. Cerezo knew that he was being allowed to take power by the sufferance of the military. The army commanders, wearied by their inability to manage the economy and unable, because of their human rights record, to obtain foreign assistance, were willing to turn power over to the civilians. However, they also made it abundantly clear that they would not give up their control of the countryside, where they had successfully suppressed a guerrilla uprising, or accept an investigation into what the Kissinger Commission had termed "the brutal behavior of the security forces" in doing so.[2]

THE SOCIAL STRUCTURE

Guatemala is roughly the size of Tennessee, but its topography and climate vary enormously—from the cool, wheat-growing mountainous areas, through the coffee-growing piedmont, to the banana and cotton areas of the Caribbean and Pacific coasts. The national population of 8 million can be divided into three broad groups: a fairly sophisticated population living in Guatemala City and its environs, a rural and small-town ladino (Latin or mestizo) population concentrated in the eastern part of the country, and the indigenous population (55 percent of the total) located in the western uplands. Guatemala's Indians are divided into some twenty-one different language groups, and although their culture has been enormously disrupted by the counterinsurgency war, many villages still retain much of their traditional character.

The largest, and in many ways the most economically dynamic of the Central American countries, Guatemala achieved an average economic growth rate of 5.7 percent per year between 1961 and 1975—driven largely by export agriculture and by sales of light manufactured goods to the Central American Common Market. As a result, Guatemala City and the urban middle class both grew substantially. Glitzy new shopping malls and condominiums popped up in the urban center, and affluent suburbs mushroomed on the hills overlooking the city. The middle and upper-middle classes also enjoyed an expansion in both educational and employment opportunities during this period. By the 1980s, however, the national economy had turned sour, registering negative growth, balance-of-payments deficits, and greatly increased inflation. Unemployment, officially listed at 14.5 percent in 1986, is believed to be closer to 50 percent.

Guatemala's macroeconomic success during the 1960s and 1970s did not automatically translate into "microeconomic" benefits for the masses. According to a U.S. AID study in 1982, the nation had the most unequal land distribution pattern in Latin America as well as the most regressive tax structure.[3] Its literacy level of 56.6 percent and a life expectancy of only sixty-two years place it among the sociologically least developed countries in the Western Hemisphere.

GUATEMALAN POLITICAL DEVELOPMENT: 1524–1985

Colonial Guatemala

In 1527, three years after Pedro de Alvarado defeated Tecun Uman, the Quiche king, the Capitanía del Reino de Guatemala was established to govern the new Spanish territory ranging from Chiapas in southern Mexico to Costa Rica—an enormous distance for that day of 1,350 miles (2,170 kilometers).

Since Guatemala also contained one of the densest concentrations of sedentary Indians in the empire, which were the source of both tribute and labor, the territory quickly evolved a highly stratified and exploitive economic and social system. At the same time, the province was also part of a vast empire that was politically and socially very fragmented. Clashing interests between landowners and merchants, rural ladinos and Indians, provincial towns and the capital city ultimately created a situation in which independence was seen as "an alternative to possible civil war."[4] As things turned out, independence did not prevent civil war; it just postponed it.

The Liberal Synthesis

Although independence came peacefully to Guatemala on September 15, 1821, the struggle between Liberal and Conservative political factions launched the country into 167 years of oscillation between despotism and anarchy—with periodic and short-lived democratic interludes. Between 1829 and 1838 Guatemala was a part of the United Provinces of Central America and was governed by the Liberal caudillo, Mariano Gálvez, who sought to modernize and Europeanize the country. In 1838 the Liberals were overthrown by a Conservative caudillo, Rafael Carrera, who sought to reimpose "a disciplined state with restored Hispanic institutions."[5] However, by 1871 the Liberals, under Gen. Justo Rufino Barrios, had managed to fight their way back into power.

In many respects the Liberals were the *desarrollistas* ("developmentalists") of their day. They believed that economic progress could best be achieved by tying an economy to the world economic system. The trading of primary products for manufactured goods was seen as the natural outworking of the international economic law of "comparative advantage." To achieve this, a domestic social system had to be built that would encourage and support the "productive" sectors of the society, namely, the producers of agricultural products (mostly coffee) for export. Thus, the improvement of the economic infrastructure with the aid of foreign capital was stressed; empty lands were opened up to settlement and cultivation—often to foreigners; Indian *ejidos* (village lands) were put on the open market with the expectation that they would become more productive under private ownership; public education and laws designed to modify the Indian culture were put forward as a means of achieving social modernization; and legislation designed to ensure a cheap and dependable labor supply for commercial agriculture and public works was enacted.

The Liberal program, which entailed European immigration, foreign loans, agro-export agriculture, private enterprise, and the Westernization of the Indian, worked quite well to enhance the economy of the nation as a whole and to produce great wealth for the coffee elite. However, its effects upon the masses were disastrous. Large numbers of Indians were dispossessed of their ancestral lands, either because they did not hold title to them or because they were bought out; whole villages lost title to their *ejidos*; foreign capital produced foreign debt; and the country's dependency on the exportation of coffee turned Guatemala into a monocultural economy.

The Revolutionary Decade

The revolution that overthrew the Liberal "dictator," Gen. Jorge Ubico, on July 1, 1944, was largely brought about by frustrated and idealistic urban middle-class groups who had been inspired by the democratic and progressive rhetoric of the Atlantic Charter issued by Roosevelt and Churchill during the dark days of 1941. The political program of the idealists who elected Dr. Juan José Arévalo president in 1945 on a platform of "spiritual socialism" was directed toward five utopian and, for an underdeveloped country, largely incompatible goals. The first goal had as its objective the destruction of all vestiges of Ubico's centralized control structure and the diffusion of decision-making power among well-institutionalized legislative, judicial, and local government bodies. The second goal was to open up the political system to competitive elections at all levels. To this end, political parties and interest groups were encouraged to organize. Third, economic development was to take place through import substitution, land reform, and the full utilization of unused agricultural land. Fourth, better distribution of economic output was to be achieved by legalizing collective bargaining, enacting minimum wage and severance pay laws, and by the establishment of an Institute of Social Security (IGSS) to administer a range of social services. Fifth, social modernization was to be attained through broadened educational opportunities and the creation of trade unions and other agencies of mass mobilization.

The major difficulty with Arévalo's "populist" program was that it tried to do too much too fast. Both the new leader and his political objectives initially enjoyed high legitimacy throughout the country. However, these objectives, when translated into concrete programs, were often incompatible (apportioning scarce resources to both industrial development and social welfare, for example), and the new president was not an accomplished administrator. Thus, the legitimacy of the new government gradually melted away, and Arévalo had to put down over twenty attempted coups against his government during the five years of his presidency.

His successor, Col. Jacobo Arbenz Guzmán, was elected overwhelmingly in 1950 after his major competitor had been assassinated. However, the Revolutionary party of National Unity (PRUN) that supported him was seriously divided between the *arevalistas*, who wanted to see moderate change, and the *arbencistas*, who found the pace of change too slow. In addition, a number of parties on the right were determined to combat the growing power of left-wing elements in the Arbenz coalition.

Rather than attempting to broaden the base of his support or conciliate the disaffected groups, Arbenz increasingly implemented the programs and policies of the left. The agrarian-reform committees, dominated by urban ladinos, alienated the Indians; the growing influence of Communist leaders in Guatemala's trade unions and government agencies alarmed the middle classes; the confiscation of 26,000 acres (10,530 hectares) of United Fruit Company land under the famous Agrarian Reform Law of 1952 antagonized the United States; and the threat to arm the industrial workers to preserve the revolution provoked the army. Arbenz's ordering of a shipment of arms from Czechoslovakia in May 1954 was the "trigger" that provoked the United States into assisting an exile army, led by dissident Col. Carlos Castillo Armas, to overthrow him.

What had begun as an attempt to achieve planned social, economic, and political reforms ended with the unleashing of all of the "Machiavellian" tendencies in the society. The violence, hostility, and political chaos of the next thirty years must be considered, at least in part, as the legacy of the idealism of Arévalo and Arbenz.

The Military-Civilian Coalition (1970–1985)

Between 1954 and 1970 the civilian and military leaders of Guatemala were groping to find a way to manage an increasingly conflictual society. Between 1944 and 1954 the nation had experienced a significant economic boom, which had benefited the elites and the middle classes and had also produced a literal explosion of middle- and upper-sector interest groups, each of which reserved the right to petition, strike, or demonstrate on behalf of its constituents. However, the workers and campesinos, who were not enjoying the same rising living standards, were now demanding the right to regain the organizational rights they had enjoyed during the revolutionary decade and to participate in the economic and political life of the nation. These demands were supported by progressive, largely foreign, Roman Catholic and Protestant missionaries imbued with the concepts of liberation theology and by a guerrilla movement, the Revolutionary Armed Forces (FAR), which continually caused trouble for the government after 1963.

Beginning with the elections of 1970 the Guatemalan military and segments of the economic and political elites succeeded in creating a military-civilian coalition that, while faction-ridden and often violent, succeeded in managing Guatemala's conflict-ridden society for a decade and a half. The coalition was built around a number of tacit assumptions. First, a limited number of traditional political parties acceptable to the military-civilian elite were to be allowed to compete for office, namely, the center-left Christian Democratic party (DCG), the old *arevalista* "populist" tradition in the form of the Partido Revolucionario (PR), a moderate military-developmentalist party from the 1960s (Institutional Democratic party [PID]), and the National Liberation Movement (MLN)— a civilian party representing the anti-Communist tradition of Castillo Armas.

Second, the military would control the executive while civilians would be allowed to dominate Congress and manage the political parties. This arrangement would be accomplished by drawing up party slates with a military officer at the head of the ticket while civilians ran for congressional and municipal posts. These slates linked competing sectors of the economic elite and the middle class with the various factions of the military. Third, within limits, the military would permit its various internal factions to compete for power through the electoral process— although a totally unacceptable result could be altered by falsifying the returns. Fourth, public policy would be oriented toward defending private property, stimulating the growth of a capitalist economy, expanding employment opportunities for the middle classes, and providing a minimal level of social welfare for select segments of the urban masses without seriously changing the social structure.

As a result of the operation of these intraelite understandings, Guatemala during this period evolved a moderately stable political system at the top although it was plagued with increasing unrest and dissatisfaction at the bottom. The military remained in charge of overall policy but governed with at least the minimal consent of Congress. The entrepreneurial elites, along with their multinational partners, operated the economy in conjunction with the middle-class technocrats, who ran the Central Bank, the autonomous government agencies, and the economic and planning ministries.

National decision making was largely built around direct interaction and bargaining between the upper-sector interest groups (e.g., the Guatemalan Association of Agriculturalists, the Chamber of Commerce, and the Chamber of Industry) and the "state" as represented by the presidency, the ministries, and the autonomous agencies. The state mediated policy disputes between these powerful economic sectors and their interest-group representatives and coordinated national policy. Although the Guatemalan political parties were important in recruiting political leaders, once these leaders were in place they gave way to the economic and technical power of the upper-sector groups and the military.

Officially excluded from this system, the popular sectors were beginning once again to bestir themselves. After the initial eradication of campesino and most trade-union organizations by Castillo Armas in 1954, a number of select trade unions were allowed to reorganize during successive administrations—particularly those with links to the Christian Democrats and the AFL-CIO. At the same time, the U.S. AID mission encouraged the establishment of rural cooperatives, again largely under Christian Democratic auspices. By the early 1970s a number of labor confederations felt strong enough to support their members in a number of strikes against both national and multinational companies. However, it was the formation of the National Committee of Trade Union Unity (CNUS) in March 1976 and a threatened general strike (over the repression of the Coca-Cola Company trade union) just one month after a Guatemala City earthquake that led to a major breakthrough in lower-sector militancy. President Kjell Laugerud García (1974–1978), recognizing the need for national unity and social peace if the country were to recover from the earthquake, began to listen to union demands, permitted the formation of the Campesino Unity Central (CUC), and also opened up the electoral register to a number of new political parties.

THE BREAKDOWN OF THE MILITARY-CIVILIAN COALITION

The Laugerud reforms, George Black has written, "were too lukewarm to neutralize the Left, but were enough to allow it some space to reorganize."[6] However, the reforms also opened up a political Pandora's box. To add to the trade-union militancy, ecclesiastical base communities (i.e., local Roman Catholic religious study groups) and the CUC succeeded in organizing areas of the countryside that had been quiescent for decades.

When Gen. Romeo Lucas García was elected in 1978 on a coalition ticket made up of PID, PR, and a smaller right-wing party (Authentic Nationalist Center [CAN]), both the military and the dominant economic groups, led by the Coordinating Committee of Agricultural, Commercial, Industrial, and Financial Associations (CACIF), were prepared to repress any further mass agitation. This determination led to a cycle of political violence that included a recrudescence of guerrilla activity in the countryside and intense counterviolence against moderate party and trade-union leaders from "hit squads" organized by the MLN and the army. By the end of 1980 the military-civilian coalition was facing a full-scale guerrilla war, and other pressures were mounting against the Lucas regime. Junior officers were becoming increasingly concerned about the corruption and politicking among the senior officers, many of whom had enriched themselves by buying up cheap public land and by diverting funds from the public agencies they ran; the business class was becoming panic-stricken over the five-year slide in the Guatemalan economy; the civilian politicians wanted a fair chance at power and the economic opportunities it afforded; and the United States wanted a "clean" government as an ally against the Sandinistas in Nicaragua.

The coalition unraveled completely in the elections of 1982 when both the right-wing MLN and CAN (as well as the centrist Christian Democrats) ran candidates against Lucas's handpicked successor. When electoral fraud became obvious, these parties, as well as sectors of the army, combined to overthrow the Lucas regime.

The seventeen-month presidency of Gen. Efraín Ríos Montt (March 23, 1982–August 8, 1983) has yet to be fully understood. An active Pentecostal layman (whose brother was a Roman Catholic bishop) who had been fraudulently denied the presidency by Laugerud in 1974 when he ran on a ticket supported by the Christian Democrats and two smaller parties, Ríos was brought to power by victorious junior officers to implement an essentially incompatible agenda: conduct free elections, root out military corruption, end state terrorism, stimulate a flagging economy, and defeat the leftist insurgency.

In an attempt to implement this agenda, the Ríos Montt regime became a strange mixture of authoritarianism, counterinsurgency terrorism, and reformism. Although initially promising to hold free elections quickly, Ríos (after offering the guerrillas an amnesty) imposed a state of siege and quietly postponed elections. He also forcefully and successfully prosecuted the war against the guerrillas. The counterinsurgency strategy, nicknamed *frijoles y fusiles* ("beans and guns"), called for the creation of strategic hamlets in guerrilla areas that would be supplied by the government with *frijoles* and other necessities. The peasants living in them were required to join "civil patrols" to protect the hamlets against "internal subversion" and guerrilla attacks. Indian villages deemed sympathetic to the insurgents were to be destroyed.

However, there was also a reformist side to Guatemala's Pentecostal president. He succeeded in ending most of the urban violence, greatly lowered corruption in both the army and the bureaucracy, introduced Indian representation in the Council of State (a corporatively organized government advisory body that had been substituted for the National Congress, which had been shut down), and sought to restructure the tax system. Every Sunday evening President Ríos, an accomplished lay preacher, would deliver a televised homily to the nation to push his famous "three-finger" campaign: *No robo, no miento, y no abuso* ("I will not rob, I will not lie, and I will not abuse authority").

Although successful in containing the guerrilla movement, the Ríos Montt regime had begun to unravel by the end of 1982. Roman Catholics disliked his evangelicalism and were furious when he maintained a correct, but cool, stance toward a papal visit; civilian politicians resented his postponement of elections; the business community opposed a 10 percent ad valorem tax he was proposing to shore up government revenues; the agrarian sector was fearful of persistent talk about an agrarian-reform program; the officer corps resented the power of the junior officers in the administration; and the United States sought something more than "active neutrality" from Guatemala in its campaign against the Sandinista regime in Nicaragua. A threat by Mario Sandoval Alarcón, leader of the MLN, to overthrow the Ríos Montt regime with his own private army persuaded the warring factions in the military to unite against the president. He was deposed by the army on August 8, one day after his successor, Gen. Oscar Humberto Mejía Víctores, had returned from paying a "courtesy call" to U.S. officials on the aircraft carrier *Ranger*.

At first it appeared that the Mejía Víctores regime represented a step backward in Guatemala's political development. Urban violence increased, the Council of State was dissolved, and the economy continued to deteriorate. However, because of the need for U.S. military aid, the new regime began to move toward a democratic opening. Elections for a constitutional convention were announced for 1984, and presidential and congressional elections were set for 1985. General levels of violence and human rights abuses also began to drop in 1984.

When the antimilitary, center-left Christian Democratic party won a surprising plurality of the votes in the 1984 election for the Constituent Assembly, the central question for the military regime became which parties should be allowed to compete for power in 1985. Initially, the army hoped to reconstitute the military-civilian coalition that had managed the political process throughout the 1970s. However, the growing antagonism between the civilian politicians of the MLN and the army negated this option. Thus, when the deteriorating economic conditions in Guatemala made it all the more desirable for the military to turn matters over to the civilians, General Mejía decided to open up the contest to all the legally inscribed parties.

A total of twelve parties grouped in eight slates competed for the presidency on November 3, 1985 (see Table 23.1). It is generally believed that the military had hoped that the center-right Union of the National Center (UCN), led by newspaper publisher Jorge Carpio Nicolle, would win. However, the UCN's reputation as the "army party" plus the division of the vote among at least three other center-right groups enabled the DCG once again to win. It also won 51 of the 100 seats in Guatemala's unicameral Congress.

Cerezo came to power stating that he currently held 30 percent of the "power" but that by the end of his term he hoped to have 70 percent. His strategy to achieve this aim was fourfold: not to disturb the army, to engage in *concertación* ("negotiation") with CACIF, to allow a limited amount of political agitation by lower-sector groups, and to secure international loans.

In a certain respect, he has had more success with the army than with the business community. He has resisted prosecuting human rights abuses and has developed ties with a group of younger, development-

Table 23.1   The Guatemalan Elections of 1985

	First Round	Second Round	Congress
DCG	38.6%	68.4%	51 seats
UCN	20.2	31.6	22
PCN-PR	13.8		11
MLN-PID	12.6		12 (6/6)
CAN	6.3		1
PSD	3.4		2
PNR	3.1		1
PUA-FUN-MEC	1.9		0

Sources: George E. Delury, ed., *World Encyclopedia of Political Systems and Parties,* 2nd ed. (New York: Facts on File Publications, 1987), Vol. 1, p. 443; Arthur S. Banks, ed., *Political Handbook of the World* (Binghampton, N.Y.: CSA Publications, State University of New York, 1987), p. 231.

oriented officers. However, his call for the economic elites to pay their "social debt" through increased taxation led to massive demonstrations and shutdowns by the business community and organized labor in the fall of 1987.

THE GUATEMALAN POLITICAL CULTURE

As the administrative center of the Spanish Empire in Central America, Guatemala has probably most fully perpetuated the traditional traits of Hispanic culture in the region: personalism, patrimonialism, hierarchy, and militarism. And given the existence of a large, settled Indian population, the political culture took on an exploitive and authoritarian character as well.

To better understand the nature of the Guatemalan political culture, one can identify three political subcultures, each with a somewhat distinct set of political orientations. The business elite is characterized by what might be called "cosmopolitanism"—an orientation toward the world culture rather than toward one's own national culture. Cosmopolitans bank in Panama, shop in Miami, and send their children to university in the United States. Upper-class cosmopolitans do not participate actively in party politics, but they do use their upper-sector interest groups, like CACIF, to pressure and/or bargain with the government. Cosmopolitans also often look to the army to protect their interests.

The political orientations of the politically active urban middle and lower sectors can be typified by what Glen C. Dealy has called "the spirit of *caudillaje*," namely, a value system in which the pursuit of power becomes the "referent for life's activities." In a *caudillaje* culture, he states, "everyman endeavors to be the public man. That is, he strives to practice in everyday life those virtues historically associated with public leadership": dignity, generosity, manliness (*machismo*), grandeur, and leisure.[7] Because these classes have traditionally not had the income to travel widely, they are much more nationalistic in their political feelings. This *caudillaje* culture produces the manipulative, exploitive, and opportunistic political personality one so often associates with the country's officer corps and party, trade-union, and student political leaders.

Finally, the political culture of the Indian population can be termed "parochial," namely, historically resistant to national influences. Traditionally, Indian attitudes have centered around the protection of the village against national and ladino political penetration. Traditional Indian institutions were designed to produce consensus, and leadership rested upon those individuals who conformed to the village religious and social norms. The counterinsurgency war and the emergence of a cadre of university-trained Indian leaders has, however, politicized many younger Indians, destroyed their parochial orientations, and "resocialized" many of them into *caudillaje* patterns of behavior.

One final feature of Guatemala's culture merits mention because of the importance of its long-term impact, namely, the growing Protestantism of the country. Although traditionally a strong Roman Catholic country, recent years have seen an amazing growth in both mainline and Pentecostal denominations. In fact, it has been estimated that half of all of Guatemala's active churchgoers are now Protestant. Since Protestantism stresses such virtues as hard work, frugality, and honesty (e.g., Ríos Montt's famous three-finger campaign), the potential cultural impact of this movement on the country could be enormous.

THE POLITICAL STRUCTURE

Three generalizations can be made about the pattern of political parties and interest groups that contend for power and articulate interests in Guatemala. First, interest groups have traditionally been more powerful than political parties because they are usually older, wealthier, and better organized. Second, both sets of political organizations, with the exception of the guerrilla groups, carry on the bulk of their activities within the capital city. In this context, national politics is often city politics. Third, political parties and interest groups function as "power contenders." That is, each political organization brings a particular resource or weapon into the political arena with which it seeks to threaten or coerce the government or the other power contenders in the system. The army can threaten a coup, the students a demonstration, the unions a strike, the business community a lockout, the church a pastoral letter, a political party a "no" vote in Congress, etc. As a result, government policy is often subject to a "veto" by some form of direct action on the part of one or more of the system's power contenders.

From 1963 to 1983 the military permitted a "licensed" four-party system to give legitimacy to the military-civilian coalition that ran the country. Each party represented one of the major political traditions of the nation that had emerged out of the revolutionary decade. The Partido Revolucionario (PR), founded in 1957, represented the populist tradition of *arevalismo*. Based on an urban middle-class constituency, the PR achieved a surprising victory in 1966 when it elected a civilian law professor, Julio César Méndez Montenegro, to the presidency. However, shocked by an overwhelming defeat by Gen. Carlos Arand Osorio (known as "the butcher of Zacapa") in 1970, the party's *caudillaje* leadership allied it with the military-dominated PID in the elections of 1974, 1978, and 1982. As a result, a number of the PR's leaders reaped financial rewards from the corruption of those years.

The National Liberation Movement (Movimiento de Liberación Nacional—MLN), which represents the "antipopulist," anti-*arbencista* tradition, was founded by President Carlos Castillo Armas in 1956.[8] The most right-wing of the major parties, it has championed the interests of the agro-export sector. The dominant civilian party in the military-civilian coalition during the late 1960s and early 1970s, the MLN went into opposition after 1976 when President Kjell Laugerud, whom it had backed in 1974, moved his regime in a more centrist direction. The party's longtime leader, Mario Sandoval Alarcón, has called the MLN "the party of organized violence" dedicated to the eradication of communism and those people who would greatly modify the land-tenure system. Sandoval is generally believed to have organized many of the assassination squads that terrorized centrist and democratic-left politicians during the 1970s, and his threat to put the party's paramilitary cadres in the streets to overthrow Ríos Montt was one of the factors that motivated the army to remove him.

The Institutional Democratic party (PID) was formed in 1965 as the electoral vehicle of the army with support from bureaucrats and elements of the technocratic middle class. Embracing a vague military-developmentalist philosophy, the party, after losing to the PR's Méndez Montenegro in 1966, concluded various electoral alliances with the PR and the MLN to control the presidency from 1970 to 1982.

The Guatemalan Christian Democratic party (DCG) emerged in 1955 out of a Roman Catholic political movement organized by Archbishop Mariano Rossell y Arellano to combat the alleged Communist leanings of Arbenz. Over the years it has gradually assumed the position of being the strongest of the parties of the "democratic left," and as such, more than 250 of its leaders have been assassinated by the death squads. The party's successful campaigns in 1984 and 1985 were based on support from the trade unions, the cooperative movement, and the urban middle class.

Between 1976 and 1978 President Kjell Laugerud permitted the official registration of a number of "party committees"—political organizations that could not run their own candidates but could form coalitions with registered parties. As a result, Guatemala's licensed four-party system has become a multiparty one (see Table 23.1). The most important of the new parties is the Union of the National Center (Unión del Centro Nacional—UCN), founded in 1984 by Jorge Carpio Nicolle, publisher of *El Gráfico*. Something of a personalistic party, the UCN follows an essentially developmentalist line and finished second in the elections of 1985. A diagram of the evolution of Guatemala's party system is presented in Figure 23.1.

As the parties gear up for the presidential elections of November 1990, the Christian Democrats seem to be losing ground. The corruption issue is hurting Cerezo, and the party is split between the old "social Catholic" wing that supports the "grand old man" of the party, René deLeon Schlotter, and the neoliberal Cerezo wing that supports Alfonso Cabrera. Their strongest challenger would appear to be the former presidential candidate of the UCN, newspaper publisher Jorge Carpio Nicolle. Another candidate with growing strength is the Protestant former head of state, Gen. Efraín Ríos Montt, who has a reputation for moral rectitude and law and order. A number of lesser candidates, including the popular mayor of Guatemala City, round out the list.

Guatemala's political structure is not limited to political parties, and four other elements have to be noted: associational interest groups, institutional interest groups, guerrilla groups and other types of combat organizations, and mass organizations. The most important of the upper-sector associational interest groups is the Coordinating Committee of Agricultural, Commercial, Industrial, and Financial Associations (CACIF), which serves as the umbrella organization for most of the modern sectors of the economy: the Chamber of Commerce, the National Union of Agriculturalists, etc. A number of agricultural chambers have split with CACIF over differences concerning Cerezo's currency exchange and export tax policies.

CACIF has been one of the most vocal opponents of Cerezo's tax policies and, under the leadership of the losing presidential candidate, Jorge Serrano Elias, joined with labor in a series of demonstrations and business strikes against the government in 1987.

Under Cerezo, the Guatemalan trade-union movement is beginning to emerge as a counterweight to CACIF. There are three major trade-union confederations, which together claim (erroneously) to have a million members: the Guatemalan Confederation of Syndical Unity (CUSG), a trade-union confederation with links to the AFL-CIO but which considers itself to be a "constructive critic" of the government;[9] the Union of Guatemalan Workers Syndicates (UNSITRAGUA), generally considered to be at odds with the regime; and the Coordinating Committee of Guatemalan Workers (CGTG), a trade-union confederation with Christian Democratic links. Massive strikes in January 1988 saw these organizations subsumed, along with CUC and the University Students

512

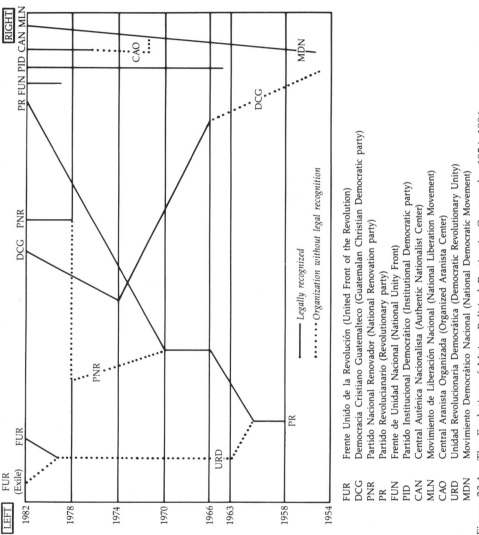

FUR   Frente Unido de la Revolución (United Front of the Revolution)
DCG   Democracia Cristiano Guatemalteco (Guatemalan Christian Democratic party)
PNR   Partido Nacional Renovador (National Renovation party)
PR   Partido Revolucianario (Revolutionary party)
FUN   Frente de Unidad Nacional (National Unity Front)
PID   Partido Institucional Democrático (Institutional Democratic party)
CAN   Central Auténica Nacionalista (Authentic Nationalist Center)
MLN   Movimiento de Liberación Nacional (National Liberation Movement)
CAO   Central Aranista Organizada (Organized Aranista Center)
URD   Unidad Revolucionaria Democrática (Democratic Revolutionary Unity)
MDN   Movimiento Democrático Nacional (National Democratic Movement)

Figure 23.1.   The Evolution of Major Political Parties in Guatemala, 1954–1986

Association (AEU), under a new leftist umbrella group, the Popular Labor Action Unity (UASP).

Institutional interest groups such as the church, the army, the bureaucracy, the universities, and the press are important power contenders, but in almost every case, these groups are highly fragmented. The army, for example, is not only internally divided by rank (i.e., junior versus senior officers), it is also broken up into various cliques or support networks (called *promociones*) based on graduating class. These *promociones* often have links with private-sector groups through which access to government is exchanged for personal business opportunities. The Roman Catholic church also is split between the more conservative, pro-Vatican clergy and the more radical priests, like Padre Andrés Girón, who follow the tenets of liberation theology.

What George Black calls "the Guatemalan left" is composed of an alliance of guerrilla organizations, left-wing political parties (such as the Communist Guatemalan Labor party [PGT], the United Front of the Revolution [FUR], and the Democratic Socialist party [PSD]), lower-sector interest groups such as the Campesino Unity Central (CUC) and the National Committee of Trade Union Unity (CNUS), and radical middle-class organizations such as the Guatemalan Committee of Patriotic Unity (CGUP) and the Robin Garcia Revolutionary Student Front. It also includes the Guatemalan National Revolutionary Union (URNG), a coalition of the four major guerrilla groups fighting the government.[10] The right also has a "guerrilla force" made up of the Secret Anticommunist Army (ESA), generally believed to be associated with the extremist wing of the MLN, and the Esquadrón de la Muerte. These organizations have been responsible for hundreds of political killings since 1978.

In summary, the current elected government of Guatemala confronts a series of power contenders—political parties, interest groups, guerrilla organizations of both the left and the right, and mass organizations—each with its own agenda and each with sufficient power to seriously disrupt the political process. Through the first half of Vinicio Cerezo's term, it was the willingness of the military high command to support the Christian Democratic majority that enabled him to survive.

THE CONSTITUTION OF 1985

On May 31, 1985, Guatemala ratified its twentieth constitutional document.[11] Although the new constitution perpetuates Guatemala's traditional presidential system, a number of significant changes were made. Presidential and congressional terms were increased from four to five years, thus extending the mandate (and the power) of an elected government. The size of Guatemala's unicameral Congress was increased from 66 to 100 seats, of which 25 are elected by proportional representation.

The method of electing the president has also been changed. Under the 1965 constitution, if no candidate had received an absolute majority, the Congress was charged with picking the winner. Under the new constitution, if there is no winner with a majority, the top two candidates submit to a runoff.

The judiciary is headed by a nine-member Corte Suprema de Justicia, four of whom are directly chosen by Congress. The remaining five members are appointed by Congress from a list submitted by the bar association and the deans of Guatemala's four law schools.

Two days before turning power over to Cerezo, the Mejía government established a National Security Council to monitor the policies of the new government, and the creation of this institution has had a double effect. On the one hand, it places serious constraints on what Cerezo can do, but on the other, it also guarantees him a measure of military support.

Thus far, the actual (as opposed to the constitutional) decision-making system remains the time-honored process of "vertical bargaining" between the major power contenders and the president—with one difference: Cerezo's legislative majority has strengthened his hand with respect to economic and social matters. Ultimately, however, his staying power rests with the military.

DOMESTIC AND FOREIGN POLICY

At his inauguration, Vinicio Cerezo declared, "In 126 days I will change the country," and to do so, he developed a strategy involving both foreign and domestic policy. In foreign policy, Cerezo has continued the policy of "active neutrality" in the conflicts in Central America as the best way of enhancing Guatemala's international image and obtaining foreign loans and credits.

President Cerezo's policy toward Central America created problems for him in his relations with the U.S. government. He found himself pressured by the Reagan administration to take a harder line against the Sandinistas, while many liberal congressmen criticized Guatemala for failing to investigate past human rights abuses. In spite of this, U.S. aid to Guatemala has increased substantially.[12]

Active neutrality also led to Guatemala's playing host to the Central American states in 1986 and 1987 in Esquipulas, a picturesque town near the Honduran border, where the so-called Arias (or Guatemala) peace plan was adopted.

With respect to domestic policy, Cerezo announced early in his term a National Social and Economic Reordering Plan designed to create a "new set of owners" who would diversify the productive structure and widen national and international markets. However, this program came under almost immediate attack. Business was opposed to the higher export taxes and controlled exchange rates needed to increase government revenues in order to create new jobs, and organized labor objected to the increase in inflation that resulted from the lifting of price controls needed to induce business to increase investment. Peasants, who took Cerezo's desire to create "a new set of owners" seriously, demanded that state land, some of which had fraudulently been taken over by the generals, be apportioned to the landless. Cerezo, while permitting some *campesino* agitation to be orchestrated by his wife, Raquel Blandón de Cerezo, and by Padre Andrés Girón, was not prepared to personally step foot in the swamp of agrarian reform.

Although the president was able to push his economic proposals through the DCG-dominated Congress, a drop in coffee prices in 1986, a cut in the U.S. sugar import quota, and a decrease in cotton production produced a shortfall in revenue. To counteract this problem, the government in 1987 enacted a new property tax law that required all owners to prepare self-assessments (*autoavalúo*) of their properties under "pain of perjury." These taxes, along with a projected utility rate hike of 40 percent, stimulated massive protests in the fall of 1987 that united CACIF, the trade unions, and even some *milperos* (small Indian proprietors) against the government. When the protests were renewed in January 1988 with an outpouring of 70,000 trade-union demonstrators and a call by ex-presidential candidate, Jorge Serrano Elías, for a "revolution that will give us the satisfaction two years of democracy hasn't produced," Cerezo made a U-turn and agreed to much of labor's social agenda, particularly price controls on 14 consumer items, generalized wage hikes, and recognition of 173 new trade-union organizations.

Cerezo also changed direction on the human rights demands of the Mutual Aid Group. Not wanting to offend the army, he had adamantly refused to push ahead strongly on investigating the whereabouts of the so-called *desaparecidos,* and he had also refused to tamper with the army's control of the countryside through the strategic hamlet programs or the village civil-defense patrols. However, as part of his agreement with the trade unions on March 9, 1988, he agreed to set up a commission to investigate human rights abuses.

By May Day (Guatemala's Labor Day) none of UASP's affiliated organizations were satisfied with the government's progress on the March accords. Congress had refused to pass the wage increases, and the government appeared to be dragging its feet in recognizing the new unions. In addition, the Campesino Unity Central (CUC) denounced continuing human rights abuses by the civil-defense patrols in the countryside and demanded their termination. Thus, UASP used the May Day celebration to protest the government's foot-dragging.

The urban middle and lower sectors were not the only groups antagonistic to the Cerezo government. A group of military field commanders, calling themselves the "Officers of the Mountains," launched a military uprising 11 days later, complaining that the government was negotiating with leftists while they were "bleeding in the mountains" fighting terrorists. The coup attempt, while not successful, forced Cerezo to back away from his agreement with the popular sectors. Under pressure from business, the government lifted price controls on many items, devalued the quetzal (thereby making this currency cheaper for the agro-export elite to buy with U.S. dollars), and unveiled a long-term economic plan, called Guatemala 2000, that promised more freedom for private enterprise. With that, the UASP called for progressive work stoppages, which continued off and on throughout the rest of 1988.

On May Day, one year later, 40,000 workers used the occasion to protest once again the president's failure to live up to the March accords. Throughout the summer of 1989, teachers, postal employees, road workers, nurses, and other public employees were perpetually on strike. On May 9 the Cerezo administration again weathered an abortive coup with the backing of the army high command.

It is ironic, in light of the history of the violent antagonism between the Christian Democrats and the army, that the military has become the regime's major support. Having relinquished power in order to gain international legitimacy and the economic benefits that go with that legitimacy, the generals do not want to see the civilian government fail. So long as Cerezo does not attempt to disturb the countryside by terminating the strategic hamlets and the civil-defense patrols, and so long as he does not cave in on agrarian reform, he will probably retain that support. However, continued agitation by the nation's many "power contenders," major new successes by the URNG guerrilla coalition, or a disputed election in November 1990 could end Guatemala's democratic experiment.

The government's "neoliberal" economic policies, embodied in its Guatemala 2000 plan, have resulted in improved economic growth rates and substantial increases in business investment. A negative result, however, has been the upturn in inflation and unemployment. The nation has benefited from these policies; the masses have not. In the meantime, bombs were set off in the wealthy hotel district, the URNG guerrillas inch closer to the capital city, strike threats continue, and the Cerezo administration becomes more isolated.

On September 27, 1989, as troops surrounded the National Palace and helicopters flew overhead, rumors of a new coup attempt abounded. The government denied it. . . .

NOTES

1. The president of the Guatemalan Supreme Court reported that over 100,000 Indian children had been orphaned by the death of at least one parent between 1980 and 1984.

2. "In the cities they have murdered those even suspected of dissent. In the countryside, they have at times killed indiscriminately to repress any sign of support for the guerillas" (*Report of the National Bipartisan Commission on Central America* [Washington, D.C., January 1984], p. 100).

3. Piero Gleijese, "Guatemala," in Abraham F. Lowenthal, ed., *Latin America and Caribbean Contemporary Record*, Vol. 5, 1985–1986 (New York: Holmes and Meier, 1988), p. B301.

4. Ralph Lee Woodward, *Central America: A Nation Divided* (New York: Oxford University Press, 1976), p. 50.

5. Ibid., p. 113.

6. George Black, *Garrison Guatemala* (New York: Monthly Review Press, 1984), p. 39.

7. Glen C. Dealy, *The Public Man: An Interpretation of Latin American and Other Catholic Countries* (Amherst: University of Massachusetts Press, 1977), pp. 34–35.

8. In 1954 Castillo Armas founded the National Democratic Movement (MDN), which split into the MDN and MLN in 1960. The MDN ceased to function following the military coup of 1963.

9. *Central America Report* 13:21 (June 13, 1986):172.

10. "Guatemala—The War Is Not Over," *NACLA Report on the Americas*, Vol. 17, No. 2 (March-April 1983), p. 10.

11. This figure includes provisional constitutions, enacted constitutions, constitutive acts, etc.

12. Richard Millett, "Guatemala," in Abraham F. Lowenthal, ed., *Latin America and Caribbean Contemporary Record*, Vol. 6, 1986–1987 (New York: Holmes and Meier, 1988), pp. B310–B311.

SUGGESTIONS FOR FURTHER READING

Adams, Richard N. *Crucifixion by Power: Essays on Guatemalan National Social Structure, 1944–1966.* Austin: University of Texas Press, 1970.

Adams, Richard N., Roland H. Ebel, et al. *Community Culture and National Change.* New Orleans: Middle American Research Institute, Tulane University, 1972.

Black, George. *Garrison Guatemala.* New York: Monthly Review Press, 1984.

Calvert, Peter. *Guatemala: A Nation in Turmoil.* Boulder, Colo.: Westview Press, 1985.

Carmack, Robert M., ed. *Harvest of Violence: The Maya Indians and the Guatemala Crisis.* Norman: University of Oklahoma Press, 1988.

Castellanos Cambranes, Julio. "Origins of the Crisis of the Established Order in Guatemala." In Steve C. Ropp and James A. Morris, eds., *Central America: Crisis and Adaptation,* pp. 119–152. Albuquerque: University of New Mexico Press, 1984.

Dealy, Glen Caudill. *An Honorable Peace in Central America.* Pacific Grove, Calif.: Brooks/Cole Publishing Company, 1988.

Ebel, Ronald H. "The Development and Decline of the Central American City State." In Howard J. Wiarda, ed., *Rift and Revolution: The Central American Imbroglio,* pp. 70–104. Washington, D.C.: American Enterprise Institute for Public Policy Research, 1984.

Handy, Jim. *Gift of the Devil: A History of Guatemala.* Boston: South End Press, 1984.

Immerman, Richard H. *The CIA in Guatemala: The Foreign Policy of Intervention.* Austin: University of Texas Press, 1982.

Jonas, Susanne. "Guatemala: Land of Eternal Struggle." In Ronald H. Chilcote and Joel C. Edelstein, eds., *Latin America: The Struggle with Dependency and Beyond.* Cambridge, Mass.: Schenkman Publishing Company, 1974.

———. *Guatemala: The Coming Explosion.* Boulder, Colo.: Westview Press, 1990.

Jonas, Susanne, and David Tobis, eds. *Guatemala.* New York: North American Congress on Latin America, 1974.

McClintock, Michael. *The American Connection,* Vol. 2, *State Terror and Popular Resistance in Guatemala.* London: Zed Books, 1985.

Melville, Thomas, and Marjorie Melville. *Guatemala: The Politics of Land Ownership.* New York: Free Press, 1971.

Painter, James. *Guatemala: False Hope, False Freedom.* London: Latin American Bureau, 1987.

Plant, Roger. *Guatemala: Unnatural Disaster.* London: Latin American Bureau, 1978.

Schlesinger, Stephen, and Stephen Kinzer. *Bitter Fruit: The Untold Story of the American Coup in Guatemala.* Garden City, N.Y.: Anchor Press/Doubleday, 1983.

Schneider, Ronald M. *Communism in Guatemala, 1944–1954.* New York: Frederick A. Praeger Publishers, 1958.

Trudeau, Robert H. "The Guatemalan Election of 1985: Prospects for Democracy." In John A. Booth and Mitchell A. Seligson, eds., *Elections and Democracy in Central America,* pp. 93–126. Chapel Hill: University of North Carolina Press, 1989.

Weaver, Jerry L. "Political Style of the Guatemalan Military Elite." In Kenneth Fidel, ed., *Militarism in Developing Countries.* New Brunswick, N.J.: Transaction Books, 1975.

Williams, Robert G. *Export Agriculture and the Crisis in Central America.* Chapel Hill: University of North Carolina Press, 1986.

24
Honduras

MARK B. ROSENBERG

Honduras has managed to avoid the political extremes that characterize the politics of the three countries with which it shares borders: Nicaragua, El Salvador, and Guatemala. Since 1982 the country has had two elected civilian presidents, and it has become a critical ally of the United States and the recipient of an unprecedented amount of foreign assistance. Because of its unique geographic location at the epicenter of the region's conflict, it now plays a major role in the efforts to bring peace to the troubled isthmus.

HISTORY AND POLITICAL CULTURE

The size of Tennessee, Honduras is the most mountainous country in Central America. A recent census placed the population at about 4.4 million people; most of them are mestizo, but small concentrations of African Americans can be found in the north coast areas as well as on the bay islands. Although Roman Catholicism is the dominant religion, Protestantism has made important inroads in the population in recent years. The population tends to be concentrated in the interior of the country, which is almost uniformly higher than 1,000 feet (305 meters) in elevation. The country's capital is Tegucigalpa (3,200 feet [975 meters]), and it has a population of about 600,000. San Pedro Sula, located in the fertile Sula Valley, has a population that has ballooned to about 300,000 in recent years. This latter city is the economic heart of the country—producing almost 40 percent of the gross national product.

One of the poorest countries in Latin America, Honduras has rarely been able to compete successfully with its Central American neighbors. The Honduran economy is heavily dependent on the production of agricultural exports, and bananas and coffee account for about one-half of all export income. Industrial production lags far behind that of the other Central American countries, and since the outbreak of regional hostilities, capital investment has been negligible. The national currency has been under severe pressure because of massive capital flight, gov-

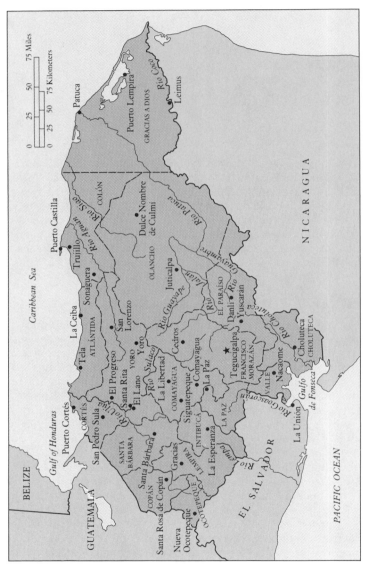

ernment deficit financing, and a high value relative to the U.S. dollar. Although the official exchange rate is two lempiras to one dollar, a parallel market places the value of the dollar at closer to three lempiras. Just under 50 percent of the population still lives in the countryside, where there is serious pressure for land reform. Migrants from conflicts in Nicaragua, El Salvador, and Guatemala have taken temporary refuge in the country, placing a great strain on its limited resource base.

Even though Honduras has one of the oldest political party systems in Latin America, civilian caudillos and military strongmen have dominated Honduras's recent history.[1] In the early 1930s a National party caudillo was elected to the presidency, and through a series of constitutional manipulations by a rubber-stamp national Congress, Tiburcio Carías Andino stayed in power until 1949. His rule was partisan in nature, and members of the opposition Liberal party still remember the "Cariato" with some bitterness because of the repression that its party leaders suffered. Carías's minister of defense was named by a Constitutional Assembly to succeed the dictator in 1949. Juan Manuel Gálvez was then followed by Julio Lozano Díaz, who was named chief of state following indecisive presidential elections in 1954.

Lozano's two-year rule was marked by repression and arbitrariness. He was booted from office in a military coup, the country's first in the twentieth century. Following eighteen months of military control, Ramón Villeda Morales was named by the national Congress as president of the country. When he took office in 1958, Villeda was the first Liberal to assume the presidency in over three decades. He initiated a number of important programs—social security, a labor code, and agrarian reform[2]—and is the only civilian president in recent Honduran history to have had a "populist" approach to governance. During this period urban and rural labor deepened their organizational efforts, which placed increasing pressure on the military government to respond to labor's growing list of demands for reform.

Fearful of the divisive leadership style of his apparent successor, the military aborted the 1963 presidential elections and once again took over the governing of the country in October of that year. Unlike after the previous coup, the military now made an alliance with the National party, whose leading operative was a close adviser to the military officer who ruled the country. For the next eight years the country's political direction was determined by Gen. Oswaldo López Arellano, who had been a member of the first military junta, and by National party leader Ricardo Zuñiga Agustinus. The latter was a shrewd political insider with an intense appetite for manipulation and intrigue.

The military–National party alliance lasted for almost eight more years and was punctuated by two important events. First, in the context of growing popular dissatisfaction with the government's lackluster performance, municipal elections were held in 1968. Violence, ballot-box stuffing, and confusion marked this effort and resulted in a Liberal party boycott of the unicameral national Congress. Second, a 100-hour war with El Salvador one year later left much destruction in Honduras, particularly in the border areas. This conflict provided the military government with a unique opportunity to unite the country's divisive forces around the banner of nationalism.[3]

Following this nationalistic exercise, López Arellano promised to return the country to democratic rule. A national pact was subscribed to by both parties, elections were held, and the National party candidate was narrowly elected to assume the presidency. But when Ramón Ernesto Cruz took office in mid-1971 he confronted three major obstacles. First, a still-ambitious López Arellano had remained in his post as chief of the armed forces. Second, Zuñiga had also remained in the government as a cabinet minister, and third, organized labor had high expectations about the new president's ability to effect the needed reforms. From the outset it was clear that López wanted to return to the presidency, and Zuñiga himself could not be denied an important role in decision making inasmuch as he controlled the party apparatus. Labor's commitment to reform was much greater than its support for democracy.

Cruz's inability to consolidate power around himself, his utter administrative incapacity, and a growing popular mobilization forced Cruz from power via a telephone coup in late 1972. Leaving Zuñiga and the National party out of the power equation, López Arellano returned to office with a broad, populist base of support, including urban and rural labor, businesspeople, the Catholic church, and López's own armed forces.

From 1972 to 1975 López Arellano pursued agrarian reform, state enterprises were established to promote development, and public investment increased significantly. But by mid-1975 the government had come under increasing opposition from conservative, landed interests and a united private sector, which realized that military rule ultimately was not in their best interests. López was booted from power in 1975 by his own military when it was revealed that he and members of his government had taken a payoff from a U.S. multinational to lower the government's high banana-export taxes.

López's ouster provided an opportunity for both the Liberal and the National parties to push for a transition to civilian democratic rule. During this period (1975–1982), senior military officers held power. First, Gen. Juan Alberto Melgar Castro ruled from 1975 to 1978. More conservative and cautious than López, Melgar was less reformist than his predecessor. He did convene a quasi-parliamentary body that formally included almost all of the country's political forces except the two dominant political parties, which refused to participate. This council set forth a new electoral law and worked directly with the president in addressing other issues of national concern.[4]

When Melgar appeared to become too ambitious politically, he was deposed by his senior military commander, Gen. Policarpo Paz García, in 1978. In reality, Paz was acting on behalf of other senior military commanders, who had earlier formed a Superior Council of the Armed Forces, a deliberative body that met periodically to coordinate civil and military policy. Paz's primary mission was to return the country to civilian rule. With Somoza's ouster in 1979 and growing U.S. pressure for democratization, Paz called for constitutional elections in 1980 and presidential elections in 1981. It was during the later years of his rule that military corruption became particularly acute.

Liberal party leader Roberto Suazo Córdova was elected president in 1981, and he came to power with a convincing electoral mandate, having soundly defeated the omnipresent Ricardo Zuñiga. Despite the clear public expectation that he would open the democratic political space, Suazo pulled an old National party trick by seeking an alliance with a hard-line anti-Communist military officer, Gustavo Alvárez Martínez.

Using a national security approach to governance, Alvárez quickly assumed a leading role in the civilian democratic government. His goals coincided with the emerging U.S. approach to Central America, which gave Honduras a key role in the effort to strengthen the nascent anti-Sandinista (contra) forces into a credible fighting force.[5] Despite the new democratic context, Suazo's four-year rule was pockmarked by human rights violations and numerous denunciations of Alvárez and his national security model.[6] Alvárez himself was kicked out of the country in 1984, but his legacy was an environment in which democracy was superseded by national security.

Presidential elections in late 1985 brought another Liberal into power, as José Azcona Hoyo, an engineer, was elected despite President Suazo's efforts to keep him out of office. Preferring another Liberal candidate, Suazo had engineered a political crisis shortly before the elections that had nearly prompted a military coup. His machinations did have the effect of keeping a youthful and charismatic National party candidate from winning the election, even though Rafael Leonardo Callejas did have the greatest popularity in the country. Thus, when he entered office in January 1986 Azcona and his political forces were debilitated by a divisive intraparty electoral campaign. His own aloof political style and his commitment to political cronies who had no large vision of national affairs effectively handicapped any possibility for the aggressive leadership that was needed to resolve festering national problems. Like Suazo, Azcona disappointed reform-oriented democratic forces who believe in civilian governance.

POLITICAL STYLE

The country's difficulty in establishing and consolidating a democratic order can be understood within the context of its political style, which has several important characteristics. First, Honduran politics is not yet governed by regulations that prevent the arbitrary exercise of power, and the formal rules of political life do not effectively govern the conduct of officeholders. Institutionalized public politics have not yet taken precedence over "palace" and "barracks" politics. Noninstitutionalized government is the norm; people take precedence over rules; personalism is a way of life. Because no single set of rules has been accepted, key authority roles are subject to continual redefinition in accordance with the particular needs of the moment. Thus, the political system in Honduras is more akin to a game in which power for power's sake becomes the all-consuming objective.

Second, Honduran politics of the last three decades can be understood as a personal struggle to control or influence the national government through a search for stable, but often short-lived, political coalitions. Networks based upon party affiliation give organizational coherence to a candidate's political aspirations, and coalitions also help to define an aspirant's power relations, both horizontally with other elites (and their respective coalitions) and vertically to the bases of society.

Politicians tend to emphasize competition and power, not rule making and not national problem solving. They spend as much time and effort looking backward to protect themselves as looking forward to anticipate programs. Accordingly, political rewards are related back to groups jockeying for power, not forward to their consequences for society. Active development efforts are reduced to minimal efforts at incrementalism. There is no tradition of public interest that can be defined beyond the narrow interests of the personal ruler and the coalition in power.

Third, rule in Honduras is a dynamic world of political will and action that is determined by personal authority and power instead of by institutions. It is a system of relations based upon shifting coalitions that link rulers and would-be rulers with patrons, associates, clients, supporters, and rivals. The necessity of meeting specific client needs, and the intensity of those clients' expectations and demands, mitigate against general pressure for responsive government. Shortages of human and material resources impose certain imperatives on public office holders that work against obeying any notion of the public good. *Chamba* (the provision of employment) becomes one of the principal modus operandi of government. Indeed, government jobs are viewed as entitlements and rewards for personal loyalty rather than as public trusts and responsibilities. There are few incentives to perform official duties with probity because the imperative of meeting clients' needs has precedence.

The Honduran public sector is a primary object of power, not so much because of its role in the country's development, but because it is the mechanism through which private need can be addressed. Offering an arena in which individuals and factions struggle for power and position, the public sector is not an arena in which groups or parties compete for policies and constitutional norms. The public sector in Honduras has historically been the major arena of privilege, far exceeding in importance the economic, social, and religious arenas where elites normally interact. Power is ultimately defined in terms of one's ability to turn public authority into private benefit in both a material and a symbolic sense.

MAJOR INTEREST GROUPS

Since the early 1950s, the Honduran political arena has gradually opened to an expanding list of urban and rural organizations, but this opening has been fitful. For instance, the return to democracy in the early 1980s was accompanied by new state-directed repression and human rights violations, and one Honduran commentator has likened this period to the repressive years of the Carías dictatorship.[7] However, Honduran interest groups generally have a great deal of access to both civilian and military decision makers. Indeed, one of the distinguishing characteristics of Honduran political life is the fact that it has been the military, not the civilians, who have consistently been responsive to popular needs.

In general, two interests tend to have the most power in Honduras: the country's armed forces and the U.S. embassy. First, the Honduran military functions as the country's most important interest group, and since 1956 it has been the critical element in coalition formation. Like other interest groups, the Honduran military is not a monolith—it is subject to factionalism and divisiveness, both of which can be impediments to the formation of stable coalitions. Nonetheless, the military plays a key role in society because power is typically checked by countervailing power, not by institutional rules.

Constitutionally, the military enjoys a great deal of autonomy. Article 227 of the constitution of 1982 stipulates that the military is under the control of the chief of the armed forces—only through him can the president of the country mobilize troops. The military also controls the police force, organized as the Public Security Forces (FUSEP). Composed of the army, air force, navy, and FUSEP, the Honduran military has oscillated in ruling style from authoritarianism (1963–1971) to populist reformism (1972–1975) and back to authoritarianism (1975–1981). Decisions are made through the Superior Council of the Armed Forces, currently composed of the country's top sixty active-duty officers. Although the chief of the armed forces is the key military officer in the country, he tends to rely on loyal battalion commanders who directly control troops.

Despite the fact that military rule during the late 1970s degenerated into rampant corruption and mismanagement, the military has been able to maintain a high profile in the democratic political arena. The continuing military presence can be explained by "push" and "pull" factors. As a result of the former, senior military officers have been able to impose their definition of national security policy on civilians. Because of the latter, civilian mismanagement and disputes have kept the military engaged in political questions as mediators and brokers for rival civilian leaders. For instance, in April 1985 the military played a key role in breaking a civilian deadlock over succession in the Liberal party.

In Honduras, like most other Central American countries, the U.S. embassy is the most important external influence on domestic politics, and this influence is registered in both direct and indirect fashion. First, the U.S. embassy is a critical source of political legitimacy for domestic political participants, because without recognition and approval by the U.S. embassy, a would-be politician will encounter difficulty in seeking a top leadership position. Second, the U.S. government is the most important source of material resources in the country, particularly through its development assistance programs administered by the U.S. Agency for International Development. Although U.S. assistance was meager in the 1970s, it expanded during the 1980s to become a central pillar of the country's economy.

Third, the U.S. embassy has come to play a pivotal role in the formulation of Honduran security policy, particularly regarding the Sandinista government of Nicaragua. Two central features of this policy have been Honduras's willingness to allow the anti-Sandinista forces to use Honduran territory and the periodic deployment of U.S. forces throughout the Honduran countryside in joint military maneuvers with the Honduran armed forces. In the process, Honduran security interests have become an adjunct of U.S. regional security concerns. A primary beneficiary of U.S. policy has been the Honduran military, which has taken advantage of U.S. security interests as a means by which to enhance its own institutional position in Honduran society.

With regard to Honduras's domestic political agenda, however, the United States has not completely dominated. On security issues, there have been differences between the embassy and the Honduran government over the extent to which the latter should be overtly hostile to Nicaragua and on the manner in which U.S. material support for the anti-Sandinista forces should be managed. In the economic arena, the United States has been unable to convince either democratic government of the need to devalue the country's currency. When a major narcotics dealer was forcefully removed from Honduras by the United States, a public demonstration at the U.S. embassy degenerated into violence, and the embassy annex was burned and pillaged. To the dismay of U.S. officials, Honduran security forces were not called into action until most of the damage had occurred.

Two political parties continue to dominate Honduran political life. The Liberal and National parties have periodically alternated in power since the early 1900s, and both parties have been dominated by leading personalities over the years—the former by caudillo Modesto Rodas Alvarado and the latter by Ricardo Zuñiga Agustinus. Neither leader attempted to modernize his respective party, and neither could ever transcend the tendency toward patronage that characterizes both. Since their deaths, both parties have struggled to become more program and reform oriented. Only the National party, under the leadership of the youthful Rafael Leonardo Callejas, has been able to restructure and modernize itself. However, like its counterpart, this party is still driven by a top-down mentality that concentrates power at the top of the party structure.

Only two minor parties have been able to challenge the traditional parties. The Innovation and Unity party (PINU) was formed in the late 1960s by progressives from the Liberal party. Following a social-democratic philosophy, PINU has consistently outlined a reform-oriented approach to government. It was the first party to consciously incorporate leaders from organized labor into its ranks and propose them as candidates for the unicameral national Congress. Another party, the Christian Democrats (PDCH), emerged from the rural land struggles during the 1960s in southern Honduras. Initially the party was closely identified with the Catholic church, but it has gradually become more progressive than the church and maintains strong ties with rural peasant organizations. Despite the clear alternatives that both of these minor parties offer, they have had only limited success in attracting voters. In the most recent presidential elections their total combined support was less than 100,000 votes.

In addition to the political parties, Honduras has a range of important labor and private-sector organizations that have periodically enjoyed deep access into the public sector. The formal organization of the Honduran labor movement dates from 1954 and the successful strike of workers on the north coast banana plantations. The Honduran Workers' Confederation (CTH) is the country's most important and powerful labor organization. Bringing together the Labor Federation of Northern Workers (FESITRANH), the Central Federation of Free Workers' Unions of Honduras (FECESITLIH), and the peasant-based National Association of Honduran Peasants (ANACH), the CTH works closely with the U.S.-sponsored Inter-American Institute of Free Labor Development and the Inter-American Regional Organization of Workers. The CTH has periodically been a major force for social change in the country, particularly in the late 1960s and early 1970s. More recently it played a key role in supporting the military's mediation in the civilian succession crisis of 1985. Stridently anti-Communist, the CTH is governed by an old-guard leadership that is well connected both nationally and internationally.

Six years after the CTH was founded in 1964 the General Confederation of Workers (CGT) was established as a social-Christian alternative to the CTH. The major source of power within the CGT has been the National Union of Peasants (UNC), a militant rural peasant organization established as an alternative to the ANACH. However, while the latter has tended to work fairly closely with the country's agrarian-reform institute, the UNC has constantly been at odds with that agency. The UNC has about 30,000 families associated with it.

The country's most militant labor organization has been the United Federation of Honduran Workers (FUTH), which is Marxist oriented.

Having attracted unions from both of the other federations, FUTH's most important base of support comes from workers in the public utilities union (STENEE) and the beverage workers' union (STIBYS).

Like most labor movements throughout Latin America and the Caribbean, the Honduran one has both sectarian and ideological as well as generational differences that divide it. The more militant labor groups have been the targets of repression and divide-and-rule tactics by the government. There has been very little concerted effort made for the purpose of enhancing labor's share of the economic or political pie. Indeed, the recent tendency by political parties to name high-profile labor leaders to senior party positions has further divided labor as to the strategy it should pursue.

Honduras's private sector has traditionally been one of the weakest in Central America. Early dependency on foreign-owned banana companies and a limited resource base stunted the formation of a national capitalist class that could be a driving source of local entrepreneurship. Indeed, until the early 1960s the Honduran private sector was dominated by importers and agro-exporters (bananas, beef, lumber). When regional economic integration efforts through the Central American Common Market accelerated during that decade, a more nationalistic entrepreneurial group emerged in Honduras. It tended to look to the state for subsidies, guaranteed loans, and protectionism and was an important force pushing for expansion and modernization of the country's infrastructure.

Like most groups in Honduras, the private sector is not a monolith. There are many splits and divisions within the group: industrialists versus businesspeople; exporters versus importers; Tegucigalpa versus San Pedro Sula; and Arabs (Turcos) versus native-born Hondurans (Indios). The most powerful economic forces tend to be clustered in competitive investor groups whose assets are diversified across a range of different economic activities both in the country and elsewhere in Central America and the United States. The recent economic crisis is promoting a diversification of investment into activities that generate foreign exchange, particularly through agro-exporting.

Three private-sector organizations have historically represented the private sector in the country's political arena. The oldest and most distinguished organization is the Cortes Chamber of Commerce (CCIC), which represents a broad range of business interests in San Pedro Sula. Reorganized in 1951, the CCIC actually serves as the most significant development agency in the north coast area. The CCIC provides almost constant input to the government on a range of policy issues and is one of the country's most effective pressure groups on issues of both regional and national importance.

A Honduran Council of Private Enterprise (COHEP) was created in 1968 to represent the private sector before the government on policy issues. Uniting over thirty private-sector associations, COHEP has not had the ongoing policy impact that its founders intended. Nonetheless, it has frequently served as a sounding board for new policy initiatives and functions as a high-level forum for the development of consensus on issues affecting the private sector.

The Honduran Federation of Ranchers and Farmers (FENAGH) was established in the late 1960s as a national-level interest group to counteract the rising pressure in the countryside for agrarian reform. FENAGH has been a continual opponent of the agrarian-reform agency, which it believes is partial to the interests of the landless peasants. Although FENAGH's initial efforts to arrest the reform movement were not successful, continual pressure through the mid-1970s gradually reduced the momentum for reform and then paralyzed it under the democratically elected governments of the 1980s.

In recent years the Honduran Association of Coffee Producers has emerged to oppose U.S. and Honduran support for the anti-Sandinista efforts in southern Honduras. APROCAFE has been especially vocal about the damage that anti-Sandinista forces have caused in the fertile coffee-producing areas near the Nicaraguan border, where hundreds of Honduran families have been displaced because of hostilities. The association has actively pressured the Honduran and U.S. governments for reparations and has even sent emissaries to the U.S. Congress to discuss the situation. It is one of the few private-sector-only organizations to directly involve itself in the broader issues of Honduras's role in the anti-Sandinista effort.

Even with this array of interests in Honduran society, the presence of the military and the U.S. embassy distort the political interplay that might develop if these two institutions were less powerful. The current democratization efforts might help to restore a more effective balance among civilian interests if the U.S. penchant for regional security anchored by the anti-Sandinista efforts is modified. If it is not modified, the Honduran military and the U.S. embassy will continue their predominant political roles in the country.

GOVERNMENT AND POLICYMAKING

Centralization, personalism, and the vertical nature of politics in Honduras give any sitting president an important role in policymaking. Normally the president, if he is a civilian, will be the leader of one of the two major parties. He will have arrived in power by virtue of the following conditions: He does not, for philosophical or practical reasons, constitute a threat to either the Honduran armed forces or the U.S. government; he is so involved in coalition building and patronage politics that he will have little time to focus on more-enduring political issues and their policy implications.

Once he is in office, the president of the country is under enormous pressure from followers to provide jobs, recommendations, and other forms of reward for the loyalty and support that his followers provided.

Interparty enmity is so deep and partisanship is such a prevailing way of life that it is difficult for the chief executive to provide consistent leadership that transcends parochial needs. Thus, the public sector is an important mechanism through which the president can reward and pacify loyal followers.

It is difficult for public policy initiatives to fare well in this context. Because the entire government apparatus is dependent on the chief executive, by tradition, the executive defines or structures non-security-related policy initiatives either through legislation or policy decrees. The nonprogrammatic orientation of the traditional parties and the limited interinstitutional policy coordination at the cabinet level reduce the prospects for policy that can address on-going problems. Thus, while the chief executive can play a dominant role in new policy initiatives, he rarely does because of the incentives to focus on other, more pressing problems.

In its most recent incarnation, the unicameral Congress of Honduras has had several important functions, many of which have had little to do with the legislative process or the representation of constituency interests. Under President Roberto Suazo Córdova (1982–1986), Congress tended to be only a rubber stamp. There was little interest or capacity to promote independent policy initiatives, and Congress only became a source of opposition to the president when he tried to extend his stay in power beyond the constitutionally mandated four-year period.

The next Congress became more interested in independent policy initiatives and was not as servile to the president as its predecessor. Its committees and subcommittees more vigorously pursued legislation and gave more careful oversight to the executive branch. However, it still served as a source of political patronage for party leaders, who directly select the 134 deputies from lists of loyal supporters. In turn, sitting deputies provide important patronage possibilities for loyal party activists under their leadership.

By tradition, the Congress has also served as an important platform for ambitious political leaders, and the body's president tends to be a candidate in the next presidential election. Therefore, legislative behavior often is molded to that individual's personal political agenda rather than to a wider set of public policy issues. This situation becomes especially likely as the four-year term closes.

Like the Congress, the Honduran judiciary has tended to be more important for patronage and political-support functions than for the administration of justice. Traditionally, the judiciary has been used as an instrument by the executive to promote the party in power. Political penetration starts at the top with the Supreme Court, which is nominally appointed by Congress every four years to coincide with the new presidential term. In practice, the president or his top party leadership designates Supreme Court magistrates. In turn, the president of the court names lower-court judges, numbering about 400. A career-judiciary law has not yet been implemented, therefore judges tend to be named as a result of their political loyalty and reliability rather than for their legal skills.

The National Electoral Tribunal (TNE) has primary responsibility for voter registration and coordinates and supervises national presidential elections. The tribunal's leadership is composed of representatives of the country's four political parties and a delegate from the Supreme Court. Because of the country's tradition of fraudulent elections, inter- and intraparty competition, and the personal ambitions of senior party officials, the tribunal is a major arena of political conflict in the country. The party representatives are selected on the basis of their loyalty to party superiors rather than because of their national stature and credibility. Thus, rather than being a neutral and apolitical mediator of electorally generated tensions in the country, the TNE reflects and reinforces these tensions, frictions, and hostilities, especially within and through the parties. Because each of the eighteen administrative departments of the country has its own tribunal, these problems are spread throughout the system. In a real sense, while the tribunal system is supposed to provide important arbitration in cases of political conflict, it usually reinforces and maintains tension.

One of the major issues of contention of the TNE focuses on the administration of the National Registry of Persons (RNP), which has primary responsibility for updating and maintaining the national electoral census. The work of the RNP is nominally technical in nature: Without a smooth and efficient tracking mechanism of Honduran citizens, an accurate voting list would be impossible. However, there is very little confidence among the country's rival political factions that the RNP can be run apolitically.

Like the leadership of the TNE, the RNP's presidency changes every year to give equal participation in its administration. Thus, like other aspects of the public sector, the RNP has continually been assaulted by rival party officials eager to ensure short-term enrollment advantages for their organizations. Although the possibilities for overall list manipulation appear to be small, administrative and personnel discontinuities promoted by the RNP's politicization have weakened the political system's overall capability to promote greater confidence in the democratic process.

THE INTERNATIONAL ARENA

Honduras occupies a critical geographic position in the Central American isthmus. It is the only country with Central American neighbors on three different borders, and such a location gives it special responsibilities, opportunities, and burdens in international relations and foreign policy. However, there has been little serious thought in the country about regional geopolitics and how the country might take advantage of its location.

Prior to the Sandinista revolution of 1979, Honduras had followed a policy of isolation from its neighbors. Beyond the intraregional rivalries engendered by the unequal development of the Central American Common Market, the occasional border dispute, and the deadly 100-hour war with El Salvador in 1969, its foreign policy tended to be a low-key exercise aimed at maintaining cordial relations with the United States. With the emergence of the revolutionary government in Nicaragua in 1979 and the possibility for revolution in neighboring El Salvador, however, the region—and Honduras—assumed a new and higher profile in U.S. national security concerns.

The Honduran role in the U.S. security policy for Central America was first articulated by Carter administration officials in 1979 when they pointed to the country's potentially key role in the maintenance of regional security. In mid-1980 one official stated that "Honduras' location between Nicaragua and El Salvador gives it a key geopolitical position in the 'bridge-building' process we hope will emerge in Central America."[8] During that year the United States initiated a new and unprecedented military assistance program, including the provision of significant levels of military arms, training, and joint military maneuvers.

U.S. security assistance to Honduras had the primary impacts of modernizing the Honduran military and enhancing its logistical and organizational capacities. Two regional U.S. security objectives were continually put forth: to reduce the flow of arms from Nicaragua through Honduras intended for guerrillas in El Salvador and to enhance the defensive capacity of the Honduran armed forces in the event of a Sandinista incursion. The latter objective was intimately linked to Honduras's willingness to let anti-Sandinista guerrillas use Honduran territory for training and sanctuary.

The country's willingness to assume a role as a U.S. security surrogate can be linked to several factors. First, the commitment was largely made by the Honduran military and only later ratified by democratically elected civilian leaders. Second, this role was the subject of constant pressure from the United States, even to the point where other objectives in the relationship between the two countries were given much lower priority. Third, agreement was tied to a significant increase in badly needed U.S. economic assistance, which has come to play a leading role in the Honduran budget.

The national security model embraced in Honduras had two major implications for domestic politics. First, it gave the military a strong advantage at all levels of national decision making, even within the context of the mandate given to civilian decision makers through democratic elections. Second, it had the effect of closing the political arena and reducing the political space available for dissident groups and individuals. Human rights violations became more persistent, and politically related disappearances burgeoned.[9]

WHAT NEXT?: THE UNFINISHED AGENDA

As Honduras enters the last decade of the twentieth century, important domestic and international issues need to be addressed. At the level of domestic politics, a major question is the durability of the country's democracy. The presidential elections of 1989 have introduced a new generation of younger and more programmatically oriented civilian leaders. The most direct impact of this leadership change will be registered through the traditional parties, which are both under pressure to modernize and promote a public policy that addresses the country's critical rural and urban problems. Agrarian reform is still a major concern, and pressure is growing for improved urban services and the expansion of employment opportunities. Indeed, the Honduran economy was moribund throughout the 1980s, and the civilian leaders will need to aggressively promote economic development if conditions in both rural and urban areas are not to deteriorate further.

Civilian leaders must still worry about the armed forces, whose appetite for power was enhanced during two Liberal party presidencies. If the military is to be kept out of the presidential palace, civilians will need to become much more competent at national problem solving. A critical new problem that must be resolved between both groups concerns the flow of narcotics through the country. Throughout 1988 charges and countercharges between the military and civilians were exchanged about each other's complicity in international drug trafficking.

In the international arena, Honduras confronts a U.S. policy of support and encouragement for the anti-Sandinista forces who are located on the border with Nicaragua. Numbering over 12,000 combatants, this force is now a major security problem for Honduras. Difficult negotiations with the United States are in the offing concerning the U.S. military presence in Honduras, and tensions linger with El Salvador over the border areas in dispute since the 1969 war.

A more difficult issue revolves around Honduras's role in the region's future. Given the country's critical geopolitical position in Central America, Honduras will be in an important position to determine the success or failure of regional peace initiatives such as the Arias peace plan. Further, Honduras could also be pivotal to the region's hopes for a newly initiated Central American Common Market. These issues will place enormous burdens on the country's democratic leadership, which has much work to do if it is to protect itself and the country from anxious military officers.

NOTES

1. James A. Morris, *Honduras: Caudillo Politics and Military Rulers* (Boulder, Colo.: Westview Press, 1984), chap. 6.

2. Mario Posas and Rafael del Cid, *La construcción del sector público y del estado nacional de Honduras, 1876–1979* (San José, Costa Rica: EDUCA, 1979), pp. 113–124.

3. Thomas P. Anderson, *The War of the Dispossessed: Honduras and El Salvador, 1969* (Lincoln: University of Nebraska Press, 1981).

4. Longino Becerra, *Evolución histórica de Honduras* (Tegucigalpa: Editorial Baktun, 1983), pp. 207–212.

5. Roy Gutman, *Banana Diplomacy: The Making of American Policy in Nicaragua, 1981–1987* (New York: Simon and Schuster, 1988), pp. 45–49.

6. Leticia Salomón, "La doctrina de la seguridad nacional en Honduras," *CEDCH Especial No. 33* (Tegucigalpa) (February 1988), pp. 5–7.

7. Juan Ramón Martínez, "Carías, Suazo Córdova y Alvárez Martínez: ¿la misma lógica?" *Cambio Empresarial* 3:12 (1988):42–43.

8. Mark B. Rosenberg, "Honduran Scorecard: Military and Democrats in Central America," *Caribbean Review* 12:1 (1983):12–13.

9. Americas Watch Committee, *Human Rights in Honduras: Central America's "Sideshow"* (New York: 1987), pp. 64–71.

SUGGESTIONS FOR FURTHER READING

Human Rights in Honduras: Central America's "Sideshow." New York: Americas Watch, 1987.

Oseguera de Ochoa, Margarita. *Honduras hoy: sociedad y crisis politica.* Tegucigalpa: Centro de Documentacion, 1987.

Posas, Mario, and Rafael del Cid. *La construcción del sector público y del estado nacional de Honduras, 1876–1979.* San José: EDUCA, 1979.

Rosenberg, Mark B., and Philip L. Shepherd, eds. *Honduras Confronts Its Future: Contending Perspectives on Critical Issues.* Boulder, Colo.: Lynne Rienner Publishers, 1986.

Rudolph, James D., ed. *Honduras: A Country Study.* Washington, D.C.: Government Printing Office, 1983.

Salomon, Leticia, ed. *Honduras: panorama y perspectivas.* Tegucigalpa: Centro de Documentacion de Honduras, 1989.

25
The Dominican Republic: The Challenge of Preserving a Fragile Democracy

MICHAEL J. KRYZANEK

The Dominican people often tell visitors that although Christopher Columbus first landed in what is now the Bahamas, the New World that the Spanish explorers developed actually began in Santo Domingo, the capital city of the Dominican Republic. As a result of the early Spanish colonization, the Dominican Republic today is a country rich in history and tradition. A walk through the old section of Santo Domingo with its restored churches and colonial-era offices serves to remind visitors that the Dominican Republic is a place that is deeply Spanish, not just in terms of history and language, but in cultural patterns, religion, social norms, and governing practices.

And yet traveling outside of Santo Domingo to the sugar-producing regions to the east, or north to the agricultural heartland called the Cibão, one is struck by the fact that the Dominican Republic is a country that has obviously been influenced by neighboring Haiti. Sugarcane cutters, poor farmers, and other people at the bottom of the socioeconomic ladder are often recent émigrés from Haiti. Forced to leave their homeland because of economic decay, political oppression, and in some cases slavelike business arrangements between governments, Haitians have come across the border in large numbers. Today the Dominican Republic is a country in which well over a third of the population is black, and a majority of the people are mulattoes (a mixture of black and white).

Although the Spanish heritage and socioracial composition help to define the unique identity of the Dominican Republic, it is the nature of the economy and the quality of life that are critical in understanding this country and what it means to be a Dominican. From a statistical point of view, the Dominican Republic is a classic Third World nation. With a per capita income level of $1,400, an unemployment rate that

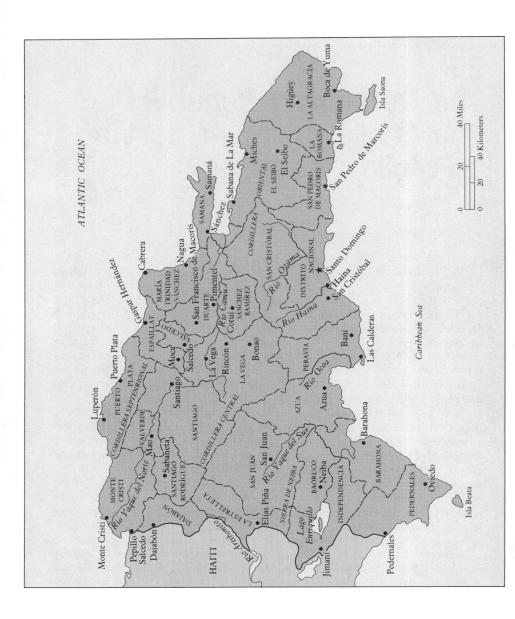

normally hovers around 25 percent, a foreign debt of nearly $4 billion, and serious deficiencies in literacy, infant mortality, life expectancy, and nutrition, most Dominicans must face hardship and frequent shortages.

The Dominican Republic, however, is not a country trapped in a perpetual state of underdevelopment and dependency. Since the conclusion of the civil war in 1965, government leaders have attempted to shake the country loose from its reliance on agriculture by taking steps to diversify its economic base. Increasingly, the Dominican Republic is being viewed as a country that has more to offer than its chief staple crop, sugar. Tourism, mining, manufacturing, and the apparel industry are all growing areas of commerce as foreign, and in particular U.S., firms continue to be impressed with the Dominican Republic as a site for investment.

Despite this mixture of modernization and underdevelopment, the Dominican Republic remains a country of deep social disparity. Although the middle and upper classes (which make up about 20 percent of the population) have benefited somewhat from the transition to a more diversified economy, the remainder of the people have experienced little change in their lives and are the ones who have been hurt most by external economic conditions and government-imposed austerity policies. Sugar workers and tenant farmers in the rural areas and the vast army of the urban unemployed and underemployed continue to feel the effects of an economy that is often forced to respond to fluctuations in the U.S. sugar quota, unreliable foreign investment, restrictive loan guarantees imposed by the International Monetary Fund, and roller-coaster prices for OPEC oil.

The fact that the Dominican Republic has traditionally been greatly affected by decisions and conditions in other countries has created a dynamic tension between foreign influence and domestic priorities. Whether the dominant factor was the Spanish, the Haitians, the United States, the International Monetary Fund, or OPEC, the Dominican Republic has had two responses—one internal and uniquely Dominican and one external and the result of numerous dependent relations. The tension between the two has frequently shaped events in the Dominican Republic in the past and will undoubtedly have the same impact in the future.

HISTORY AND POLITICAL CULTURE

The development of the Dominican Republic from a colonial outpost of Spain to a respected but still-struggling democracy in Latin America was not achieved without considerable political conflict and personal struggle. The pattern of Dominican government, starting with the administration of the New World by Diego Columbus (Christopher Columbus's son) to the current succession of democratically elected leaders, has been, to say the least, highly changeable. The Dominican Republic is a country that has endured invasions and occupations, conspiracies and revolutions, dictators and demagogues, and yet it has been able to reach a point in its history where democratic governance is increasingly being accepted as the proper foundation upon which to build a modern state. But despite the current era of democracy enjoyed by the Dominican people, the historical legacy is sad.

The era in which the Dominican Republic was the center of the New World was a short one. After about fifty years as the capital of the Spanish colonial operation, the Dominican Republic slipped into centuries of neglect. When the Spanish left for larger, more profitable conquests of Cuba and Mexico, the Dominican Republic became a pawn that was fought over by a succession of foreign powers and an occupation army from Haiti.

It was not until 1844, when the Haitian occupiers left, that Dominicans could claim independence. Dominican patriots led by Juan Pablo Duarte were instrumental in driving the Haitians out and in exciting their countrymen about the prospects for developing a new democratic state. But Duarte's vision of an independent and democratic Dominican Republic was dashed as a long series of military dictators stripped the treasury and drove the Dominican Republic into debt.

The assassination of the dictator Ulises Heureaux in 1899 offered Dominicans the opportunity to fulfill a lifelong dream of democracy. Almost immediately, however, the country slipped into a factional war among various personalistic groups anxious to control the new democracy. The instability created by the warring factions nearly devastated the economy and triggered a predictable response from the foreign sector.

In 1904 President Theodore Roosevelt announced the creation of a receivership arrangement for the Dominican Republic in which U.S. customs officials would collect duties on Dominican exports, pay off outstanding debts owed to European and U.S. creditors, and provide local government officials with a percentage of the returns for domestic use. Although the Dominicans ratified this agreement and benefited from the accounting expertise of the U.S. customs officials, the receivership was but another example of internal instability and administrative inefficiency spurring foreign intervention.

Despite a period of political calm during the receivership, the conflict among the rival groups became so serious and devastating to the economy that in 1916 the Wilson administration ordered U.S. troops into the country as a stabilizing force. For eight years U.S. administrators and marine contingents controlled Dominican affairs and created a modernization program that brought a great deal of change to the country. Yet despite the reforms and public-works projects, the U.S. occupiers began facing a loose but dedicated band of guerrillas and an increasingly nationalistic population. With the onset of the Harding administration the United States was anxious to leave the Dominican Republic, and in 1924 the occupation ended with some visible successes but also a recognition on the part of Washington that such interventions create more problems than they solve.

One of the long-term problems that the U.S. occupation created was the formation of a local constabulary that was designed to maintain order once the marines left. This so-called *guardia* would, in but a few short years, become the base of social control for Rafael Leonidas Molina Trujillo, who quickly rose up through the ranks to become the Dominican Republic's most powerful leader.

The thirty-one-year rule of Rafael Trujillo has been described as Latin America's most complete dictatorship. The Dominican Republic was controlled by one man and his extended family from 1930 to 1961, and that control was often achieved through brutal repression. The Dominican Republic during the Trujillo years became a country in which opposition politics and dissent were crushed and democracy was transformed into a kind of cult of personality with *el presidente* as the center of the political system.

As the world became more aware of the repressive nature of Trujilloism, the system of control that he had built gradually came tumbling down. Opposition leaders and intellectuals became more forceful in their attacks on Trujillo, the United States tired of supporting an ally who had become an embarrassment, and most important, the middle class in the country came to realize that the leader's corruption and control were harming the economy and limiting their ability to advance.

On May 30, 1961, as he traveled home, Rafael Trujillo was brutally murdered by a gang of assassins, and his death completed one of the saddest chapters in Dominican history. Although Trujillo brought stability and a degree of modernization to the Dominican Republic, the march toward democracy had been delayed, and the Dominicans were forced to endure another period of authoritarian rule and self-serving leadership.

Trujillo's death left a void in the body politic of the Dominican Republic. Trujillo's son Ramfis and his last puppet president, Joaquín Balaguer, at first attempted to maintain control, but internal political opposition increased, and support from the United States all but disappeared. After some six months Ramfis was forced into exile, leaving Balaguer behind to deal with a rapidly deteriorating situation. Balaguer, however, was no longer solely in command of Dominican politics, as the elites had established a Council of State and prepared the country for democracy.

By 1962 the Dominican Republic was fully immersed in democratic politics. Political exiles returned, parties and independent unions began to form, demonstrations became commonplace, and the free interchange of ideas had replaced Trujillo's cult of personality. After but a year of transition the Dominican Republic was moving toward its first open election in over thirty years. The clear favorite to win the presidency was the charismatic leader of the Partido Revolucionario Dominicano (PRD), Juan Bosch. The leading exile politician during the Trujillo era,

Bosch represented what Dominicans yearned for—a liberal, democratic politician pledged to create social reform.

Juan Bosch won an overwhelming victory in the presidential election of 1962 and proceeded to begin making good on his promises to the Dominican people. Unfortunately, Bosch's style of governing and his political skills were not as strong as his charismatic manner. Bosch alienated key elites by appointing leftists to his inner circle and failed to effectively present his reform program. The internal tensions created by Bosch led to his removal from office by the military after only nine months.

With Bosch gone, the conservative elites sought to regain control over Dominican politics, but the stability that returned to the Dominican Republic during the post-Bosch era masked the anger and frustration of those Dominicans who felt that democracy had been betrayed. The Dominican Republic became a nest of conspirators plotting ways in which to reestablish constitutional rule and return Juan Bosch to the presidency.

On April 24, 1965, the plotting came to an end as supporters of Juan Bosch moved to seize power. Rebels took to the streets, occupied the National Palace, and went on the radio to urge the people to support the revolution. The early successes of the rebels, or "constitutionalists," were short-lived as counterrevolutionary groups led by conservative military units moved to crush the rebellion. Heavy fighting ensued in the capital city of Santo Domingo as both sides sought to achieve a quick victory.

As has been the case often in the Dominican Republic, internal instability triggered U.S. involvement. Convinced by U.S. Ambassador Tapley Bennett of Communist infiltration of the "constitutionalist" camp and the possibility of a "second Cuba" in the U.S. traditional sphere of influence, President Lyndon Johnson ordered U.S. military forces to be sent to the Dominican Republic to protect and evacuate U.S. citizens. Once in the Dominican Republic, however, the 23,000 troops allied with the conservative military units as they forced the constitutionalists into a small section of the city and made it impossible for the rebels to capture key positions. Within six months of their arrival in the Dominican Republic the U.S. troops had departed, as the two warring parties had signed a cease-fire agreement and pledged to hold new elections in June 1966.

The people of the Dominican Republic were left numb by the failed revolution. The June elections held no real meaning since in the minds of many Dominicans the battle for democracy had already been lost. Juan Bosch returned from exile and participated in the election, but he and his PRD were defeated by Joaquín Balaguer, who also had returned from exile and had pledged to bring the country back to normalcy. Although Bosch remained popular, Dominicans came to realize that electing Bosch and the PRD might rekindle the revolutionary climate in the country and create another round of fighting and U.S. intervention.

Joaquín Balaguer ruled the Dominican Republic from 1966 to 1978, a period of time marked by significant economic advances and effective subversion and repression of the political opposition. Despite his quiet and shy demeanor, Balaguer proved to be a master politician, as he mixed traditional paternalistic qualities of leadership with small doses of controlled democracy and an occasional acceptance of repression. Helped by high prices for sugar, public and private investment from the United States, and a demoralized and factionalized opposition, Balaguer was able to bring the Dominican Republic to a kind of normalcy.

Unlike Trujillo, Balaguer sought to remain in power through the ballot box. In 1970 and 1974 Balaguer was reelected to the presidency, although the opposition PRD boycotted the elections and the turnout on both occasions was low. Balaguer's attempt to remain in office by running again in 1978, however, was challenged by a rejuvenated PRD. This time the PRD was led, not by a romantic social democrat, but by a millionaire rancher, Antonio Guzmán. After years of remaining on the sidelines, moderates in the PRD were able to control the party hierarchy and fashion a candidacy that would attract a wide range of voters and provide a responsible alternative to Balaguer.

Although Balaguer tried to distance himself from the outward signs of authoritarian rule, when it came to accepting the results of the 1978 presidential election he reverted to an old Trujillo tactic. Very early on in the 1978 presidential vote counting it became clear that Guzmán and the PRD were headed for victory. As the vote totals continued to mount against Balaguer, military units moved into the central electoral headquarters and confiscated the ballot boxes. Fortunately for Antonio Guzmán, the democratic opposition in the Dominican Republic had a strong supporter in President Jimmy Carter, who forcefully alerted Balaguer to the aid implications of the vote shutdown. The economic pressure from the White House on Balaguer was so intense that the voting process was resumed, and Guzmán eventually was declared the winner.

The election of Antonio Guzmán was in many respects a turning point in Dominican history. For the first time in the country a sitting president had agreed to hand over power to an opposition leader. Moreover, the United States publicly gave its approval to the Guzmán administration and sent a message to conservative elements in the country that Washington wanted Guzmán to be given more of a chance for survival than Juan Bosch had had. Most important, the Dominican people seemed better prepared for this new round of democracy, and there was a fragile consensus among key elites in the country that Balaguer's style of authoritarianism was no longer appropriate for the Dominican Republic.

Once in office Antonio Guzmán set out to reform the political character of Dominican life. The PRD president immediately began to depoliticize the military by firing, retiring, or reassigning potentially dangerous staff members. Political exiles were encouraged to return home, and dissident parties such as the Dominican Communist party were allowed to function openly again. The climate of politics also changed as the incessant repression and undercurrent of fear left Dominican life.

But although Guzmán made significant advances in the political arena, he had less success in addressing the pressing social and economic challenges faced by his country. Almost immediately upon taking office Guzmán faced a host of problems, from a devastating hurricane to falling prices for staple crops like sugar. Tensions in the country rose as wage increases were denied, and social groups from campesinos to teachers charged the government with bad faith and insensitivity to their claims.

In the midst of the turmoil surrounding the Guzmán presidency were mounting charges that the president, his family, his advisers, and many PRD legislators were using their offices for personal gain. The allegations of corruption took a tragic turn in July 1982 when Antonio Guzmán committed suicide. Feeling personally responsible for the corruption that had reached the inner circle of his family, Guzmán shot himself just one month before he was to leave the presidency.

The death of Antonio Guzmán overshadowed another important milestone in Dominican democratic development. Because Guzmán had promised when he took office the he would not seek another term, the PRD had nominated Salvatore Jorge Blanco to be its candidate for the presidency in 1982. Jorge won handily, and thus there was a second peaceful transfer of power, only this time the transfer was within an established social-democratic party.

The Jorge administration will be remembered as the one that turned the Dominican Republic's attention away from political reform and toward economic and financial restructuring. As reserves dwindled and debt mounted, Jorge turned to the International Monetary Fund for assistance. In return for a $500-million loan arrangement, the IMF required a number of internal reforms, including a major change in the currency exchange rate.

After much internal debate and controversy over the IMF recommendations, the Jorge administration made a series of policy decisions that brought long-needed reforms in the areas of currency exchange, taxation, budget formation, and bank management. When Dominicans became aware that life under the new reforms would mean a round of austerity, they took to the streets. In the worst incident of urban violence since the civil war, over sixty Dominicans were killed in rioting in April 1984. The Jorge administration, which prided itself as a champion of human rights, was now being castigated as an authoritarian repressor.

As the 1986 election approached, it was clear that the PRD was no longer viewed as the only party capable of running the country. Despite the fact that the IMF reforms eventually did help to stabilize the economy and allow the government to regain its standing with eager creditors, Dominicans were anxious for a change and for a more calming influence in the National Palace.

Since Joaquín Balaguer had run and won on the platform of returning the country to normalcy in 1966, it was no surprise when the wily politician returned to politics and pledged to extricate the Dominican Republic from its economic and financial morass. Despite his age (over eighty), health problems (nearly blind), and a questionable background (ties to Trujillo and a twelve-year authoritarian regime), Balaguer was able to narrowly defeat the PRD candidate, Jacobo Majluta, and again step into the National Palace. At his inauguration Balaguer pledged to bring honesty back to government, to address the nagging unemployment problem in the country, and to look closely at the previous arrangements made with international lending organizations, and once in office he moved quickly to put his mark on the Dominican economy. He pushed hard to increase public-works expenditures in order to reduce unemployment, foreign investment and tourism were encouraged, and more-liberal monetary policies loosened credit and helped revive the building industry.

Despite these positive developments, Balaguer still had to face up to the fact that he was the president of a poor, dependent nation. Low world prices for sugar coupled with a severe cutback in the U.S. quota forced Balaguer to seek markets in Eastern Europe and the Soviet Union and to begin the dismantling of certain unprofitable state enterprises. Balaguer's approach of attacking unemployment through public-works projects and loose credit ushered in a period of substantial growth in the Dominican Republic, but at the same time it heightened inflation and unleashed a new round of strikes and demonstrations. The man famed for his ability to bring back normalcy was by 1988 being viewed as the source of social and economic decay.

As the Dominican Republic headed toward the presidential election of 1990, confidence in the Balaguer administration and in the vitality of Dominican democracy was called into question. The election became a contest between two aging caudillos as Balaguer and the ever-resilient Juan Bosch tried to convince the Dominican electorate that they could lead the country out of its current economic and social malaise. The campaign for president accented personalities rather than policies as both Balaguer and Bosch played to the fears and emotions of their fellow Dominicans. Balaguer stressed his competence as an administrator while subtly reminding voters of Bosch's Marxist past. Bosch, on the other hand, sought out the support of the urban masses and criticized Balaguer for the high inflation rate, food shortages, and the breakdown of essential public services. At the conclusion of 1989, Bosch was running slightly ahead of Balaguer, with Peña Gómez and Majluta far behind. Most observers of Dominican politics felt that the race for the presidency would continue to remain close, with both Balaguer and Bosch seeking to form electoral alliances with Peña Gómez and Majluta in order to secure victory.

POLITICAL GROUPS AND POLITICAL PARTIES

Like most countries in Latin America, the Dominican Republic is made up of numerous social, economic, and political groups. Although the Dominican military remains the key "power contender" in politics and is often supported by the traditional landed elite and the church, national leaders cannot ignore an ever-growing number of newer power-seeking groups that have the ability to affect the decision-making process. One of the most significant changes in the composition of group activity in the Dominican Republic is the influence that the business, financial, and professional sector has on national life. Trade associations, commercial organizations, and various informal networks of lawyers, doctors, bankers, and businesspeople now can be viewed as critical participants in the process of formulating and implementing national policy.

Although most of the power wielded by the old and new elites in the Dominican Republic is exercised behind the scenes and is often the result of personal and family relationships, Dominicans who do not have a prominent position in society nevertheless participate in a political system that has become increasingly open. Some of the most vigorous protest in recent years has come from union and student groups upset about minimum wage restrictions and budget cuts. The rural campesinos, on the other hand, have consistently avoided pressure politics and have only started to form cooperatives and interest associations.

One of the most interesting facets of group dynamics in the Dominican Republic is the influence of the foreign community. Diplomats; corporate investors; international banking, loan, and aid officials; multinational enterprises; and the steady stream of consultants and advisers who visit the country have become an important part of the Dominican policy process. Because the Dominican Republic relies so heavily on trade, aid, and capital from abroad, those individuals or groups that provide the essential ingredients for Dominican modernization have steadily gained access to government officials and key leaders in the private sector.

Although the democratic vitality of the Dominican Republic is seen in the influence of a broad range of groups and interests, one of the keys to the apparent success of Dominican democracy is the political party system. Even during the darkest days of the Trujillo dictatorship, exiles in Puerto Rico and the United States maintained an active opposition and dreamed of the time when they would be able to return to their country and replace authoritarian rule with party democracy. Today political parties in the Dominican Republic are active, although there are some disturbing signs that the unity and ideological purity that they showed while out of power may be in jeopardy now that democracy has become the accepted system of governance.

The premier democratic political party in the Dominican Republic has been the Partido Revolucionario Dominicano (PRD). The PRD under the guidance of Juan Bosch was the voice of opposition during the Trujillo dictatorship and eventually became the governing party in 1962. After twelve years of Balaguer's quasi-democracy, the PRD finally got another chance to build Dominican democracy, but unfortunately, democratic dreams and political power do not necessarily make a good combination. Since taking power in 1978 the PRD has been engulfed in an intraparty dispute over ideology, leadership, corruption, and policy, and moderates like Jacobo Majluta have squared off against leftists like José Francisco Peña Gómez for control of the party.

While the PRD regroups and attempts to iron out the deep personal fissures within its party, Joaquín Balaguer heads a party he founded prior to the 1986 election. In a masterful political stroke, Balaguer joined his personalistic Partido Reformista with the Social Christian party, one of many third parties in the Dominican party system. The resulting merger created a new party, the Social Christian Reform party (PRSC), and gave Balaguer a stronger and more legitimate political base from which to seek the presidency.

In the 1990 election campaign, the PRD fell completely apart as the embarrassment of the public trial of former Dominican president Jorge Blanco on corruption charges and factionalism rendered the organization powerless. Although the PRD continued to function as a political party, its leaders, such as Peña Gómez and Jacobo Majluta, formed their own organizations and attempted to separate themselves from the negative image linked with the PRD label. What was once a party that held out the promise of popular rule and social reform was transformed into a minor player in Dominican politics.

Prior to 1986, party politics in the Dominican Republic was dominated by the PRD and the Reformistas, but the resurgence of Juan Bosch contributed to the development of a new political party. After being pushed out of power in 1963 Bosch broke with the PRD and formed the Partido Liberación Dominicano (PLD). The PLD is a leftist party that is strongly nationalistic and critical of both the PRD and the PRSC for abandoning the urban and rural poor. In the 1986 election Bosch and the PLD received 18 percent of the vote, and the party has an excellent chance of winning the presidency in 1990.

THE GOVERNMENT

Although the Dominican constitution mandates a tripartite governing structure much like that in the United States, in reality political power is not distributed evenly in the country, nor are there adequate checks and balances in the governing system. Since Dominican democracy is still in its infancy, the country's governing institutions have not been able to mature or develop a sense of independence.

Describing the Dominican executive branch, especially during the administrations of Joaquín Balaguer, is quite simple. The Dominican president prefers to centralize most, if not all, government decisions in his hands. Balaguer's leadership style is akin to paternalism in that the Dominican president receives a steady stream of visitors in his office and his home and personally responds to the problems or concerns that are presented to him. Balaguer, of course, cannot be everywhere or manage every aspect of public policy, but his approach is definitely personalistic and designed to show his people that he is running the country.

In recent years the Dominican president has been forced to work very closely and in some instances to share power with the president of the Central Bank, the secretary of finance, and a number of other officials in areas critical to the management of the Dominican economy. Because the Dominican government is deeply involved in food subsidy programs, infrastructure construction, tourism, trade relations, investment enhancement, and sugar refining, the president is also required to deal with a wide range of public agencies and enterprises.

Although the checks-and balances system is more form than substance, Dominican presidents like Balaguer have had to learn how to handle the military so as to maintain the country's fragile democratic structure. Some, like Guzmán, boldly challenge the officer corps with forced retirements and reassignments; others, like Jorge, shower the military with pay increases and arms purchases. Balaguer's approach to the military is to periodically reshuffle military personnel and overlook much of the corruption and repression that emanates from within the armed forces. No matter what the approach, Dominican presidents are keenly aware that democratic governance and their jobs are dependent on developing a working relationship with the military.

Although government power in the Dominican Republic is securely positioned within the executive branch, the legislative and judicial branches have begun to play more of a role in national life since 1978. The two-house Dominican legislature traditionally was a quiet institution that either was an empty showcase of democracy or a rubber stamp of executive power. The PRD's return to power in 1978 revived the legislative branch and helped to make it more of a partner in developing national policy. During the Guzmán and Jorge administrations and the Balaguer regime, issues of national concern were debated vigorously in the legislature, and executive initiatives were no longer automatically approved.

The Dominican judiciary has also begun to exert greater independence since the return of democracy in 1978. Long the bastion of patronage and corruption, the judiciary engaged in a long battle with the Jorge government over pay increases and judicial appointments. Dominican justices, however, continue to shy away from challenges to executive power and have yet to earn the trust of the people, especially at the local level where money paid by lawyers to judges and court clerks is the standard means of moving a trial forward. Perhaps the most serious indictment of the Dominican judicial system is the undercurrent of violence and repression that remains a part of Dominican national life. Abuses of criminal rights, violations of due process, inhumane prison conditions, and torture surface periodically with little sign that the judicial system has the will or the power to correct the situation.

In analyzing the decision-making process in the Dominican Republic, one cannot ignore the role of the bureaucracy, especially the importance of the state enterprises. Since the time of Rafael Trujillo the Dominican government has been a major employer in the country and has been responsible for controlling key sectors of the economy such as the sugar industry, electricity, and construction. These state enterprises have become massive bureaucracies employing thousands of Dominicans and have developed a reputation for mismanagement, corruption, and waste. One of the key challenges for President Balaguer and future leaders of the Dominican Republic is to make the state enterprises efficient and profitable. Many foreign observers have recommended that the Dominicans move toward privatization of the enterprises, or at least a gradual dismantling of state involvement.

GOVERNMENT POLICY

Public policymaking in the Dominican Republic can best be described as government officials reacting to a series of economic and social crises that have the potential to create political unrest. Falling prices for sugar, burgeoning debt payments, dependency on foreign oil, consistently high unemployment rates, and an ever-growing population demanding food, housing, and education combine to make the Dominican policy process confused and often contentious. As a result of the multitude of challenges facing the Dominican Republic, political leaders must be deft balancers as they attempt to address the country's dependency and debt without antagonizing the urban and rural poor by implementing harsh austerity measures.

Despite the fact that the Dominican Republic is a poor country that has traditionally relied on the sugar trade to generate revenue, government leaders have sought to transform the country into a major assembly and manufacturing center. Although the Dominican Republic is a long way from this goal, the government is actively seeking foreign investors to its industrial free zones (IFZs). The IFZs offer foreign companies an attractive location for their assembly and manufacturing enterprises along with low wages, weak or nonexistent unions, lengthy grace periods for taxation, and a work force that is anxious to learn and perform assigned tasks. At present there are eleven IFZs in operation employing over 100,000 Dominicans, and more zones are planned as the Dominicans gradually attempt to diversify their economy.

Even while the Dominicans work to restructure their economy and seek ways to lessen their reliance on agricultural commodities like sugar, new forms of dependency arise. The most serious is the country's foreign debt. Dominican government officials are concerned about the debt problem, not only because the yearly service payments ($740 million in 1987) place a drain on the economy, but because the efforts to lessen the debt obligations often require stringent controls on public-employee salaries, higher prices for basic goods, and import restrictions. Furthermore, the dependency on foreign loans and the demands that the creditors make upon the Dominican government prompted President Balaguer to state that the Dominican Republic will not jeopardize its development in order to meet debt payments or to abide by loan requirements.

INTERNATIONAL RELATIONS

The Dominican Republic, despite its small size (roughly equivalent to New Hampshire and Vermont combined), is actively involved in international and regional affairs and has developed a reputation as a model for other countries that are experiencing challenges similar to those faced by the Dominicans. The relative success of Dominican democracy and the moderation of its politics, for example, prompted President Reagan to single out the Dominican Republic as the "beacon of hope for Latin America."

The status of the Dominican Republic as an influential small state in the Western Hemisphere, however, is not merely the function of a democratic government and moderate politics. The Dominican Republic is situated in a strategic location in the Caribbean between Puerto Rico and Cuba and abuts the Mona Passage, a key transportation route in the region. The United States has long recognized the strategic importance of the Dominican Republic and continues to view the importance of good relations between the two countries in geopolitical terms. Furthermore, with an uncertain governing climate in neighboring Haiti and Castro's Cuba retaining its close ties to the Soviet Union, the United States values the democratic stability of the Dominican Republic.

The history of the U.S. interest and involvement in the Dominican Republic has helped foster growing feelings of nationalism and independence among the country's people. Dominicans still accept the North Americans readily when they arrive in the country, but the many instances of intervention and economic control have convinced the country's leaders to diversify its ties. As a result, the Dominican Republic has sought greater involvement in Caribbean affairs, particularly in economic and trade matters. Also, the Dominican Republic has developed oil-for-sugar arrangements with Mexico and Venezuela and has negotiated loan agreements with these two Latin American giants. Last, the Dominican government has formed closer ties to European, Pacific Basin, and now Eastern-bloc nations, and trade with Common Market countries, Japan, and Taiwan has increased significantly.

Despite the efforts of the Dominicans to diversify their ties and lessen their dependence on the United States, trade relations, investment interest, and migration patterns require that the Dominicans maintain what has certainly been a "special relationship." Currently the U.S. share of Dominican exports is 70 percent, and the U.S. investment share in the Dominican Republic is 63 percent. Dominicans continue to arrive in the United States looking for work and have made New York the city with the second-largest population of Dominicans (Santo Domingo being the first). These circumstances are not likely to change in the near future, and as a result, the Dominican Republic will continue to be a nation that relies on decisions made in government offices in Washington or corporate boardrooms in New York.

CONCLUSION

Over the years the Dominican Republic has been described and analyzed from a number of different perspectives. Most observers of this country have accented the long struggle of the Dominicans to develop a democratic governing system despite the harsh realities of authoritarian rule. Others have stressed the constant battle of the Dominicans to establish a more independent economic base and to free their country from its reliance on sugar revenue and international lending. Although each of these perspectives remains relevant today, it is important that they be examined as part of a new theme that seems appropriate for understanding the country as it heads into the 1990s.

At the heart of this new theme of Dominican national life is the fact that democratic governance, at least for the time being, has been established. The question now becomes how the Dominican leaders and the Dominican people can maintain a form of government that they and their predecessors worked and died for in the face of mounting economic and financial crises, growing social polarization, and increased political factionalism. After achieving their historic goal the Dominicans now are faced with the challenge of preserving democracy at a time when both internal and external conditions threaten the shaky foundation upon which the governing system has been built. As Dominicans are finding out every day, maintaining and advancing a democracy is a complex balancing act that requires patience, diligence, and the art of compromise—character traits that are often at a premium in a developing country.

SUGGESTIONS FOR FURTHER READING

Atkins, G. Pope. *Arms and Politics in the Dominican Republic.* Boulder, Colo.: Westview Press, 1981.

Atkins, G. Pope, and Larman Willson. *The United States and the Trujillo Regime.* New Brunswick, N.J.: Rutgers University Press, 1972.

Bell, Ian. *The Dominican Republic.* Boulder, Colo.: Westview Press, 1981.

Black, Jan Knippers. *The Dominican Republic: Politics and Development in an Unsovereign State.* Boston: George Allen and Unwin, 1986.

Bosch, Juan. *The Unfinished Experiment: Democracy in the Dominican Republic.* New York: Praeger, 1963.

Calder, Bruce. *The Impact of Intervention: The Dominican Republic During the U.S. Occupation of 1916–1924.* Austin: University of Texas Press, 1984.

Crassweller, Robert. *Trujillo: The Life and Times of a Caribbean Dictator.* New York: Macmillan, 1966.

Gleijeses, Piero. *The Dominican Crisis.* Baltimore, Md.: Johns Hopkins University Press, 1978.

Kryzanek, Michael J., and Howard J. Wiarda. *The Politics of External Influence in the Dominican Republic.* Stanford, Calif.: Hoover Institution Press, 1988.

Logan, Rayford W. *Haiti and the Dominican Republic.* New York: Oxford University Press, 1968.

Lowenthal, Abraham F. *The Dominican Intervention.* Cambridge, Mass.: Harvard University Press, 1972.

Martin, John Bartlow. *Overtaken by Events: The Dominican Crisis from the Fall of Trujillo to the Civil War.* New York: Doubleday, 1966.

Rodman, Selden. *Quisqueya: A History of the Dominican Republic.* Seattle: University of Washington Press, 1964.

Slater, Jerome. *Intervention and Negotiation: The United States and the Dominican Republic.* New York: Harper and Row, 1970.

Welles, Sumner. *Naboth's Vineyard: The Dominican Republic, 1844–1924.* New York: Payson and Clarke, 1928.

Wiarda, Howard J. *The Dominican Republic: Nation in Transition.* New York: Praeger, 1988.

———. *Dictatorship and Development: The Methods of Control in Trujillo's Dominican Republic.* Gainesville: University of Florida Press, 1970.

Wiarda, Howard J., and Michael J. Kryzanek. *The Dominican Republic: A Caribbean Crucible.* Boulder, Colo.: Westview Press, 1982.

26
Panama's Struggle for Democracy

STEVE C. ROPP

Panama is in the midst of a political transition of historic proportions. Traditionally a country governed by civilians, it has been ruled for more than two decades by the military. This period of military rule came to an abrupt end in December 1989 when the Bush administration sent in U.S. troops to destroy the Panamanian Defense Forces (PDF) and to capture Gen. Manuel Antonio Noriega. The new civilian government established following the invasion has attempted to consolidate its political control and to institutionalize democratic forms of participation.

When the military came to power in 1968, under the leadership of Gen. Omar Torrijos Herrera, it did so as an agent of social change. However, the military's social-reform agenda gradually fell by the wayside as top officers became increasingly concerned with their own personal well-being.

The trend toward self-serving corruption within the PDF was epitomized by the emergence of General Noriega as commander in chief following Torrijos's death in 1981. As head of the intelligence branch within the PDF, Noriega was in a position not only to spy on his fellow officers but to control lucrative illicit activities. The rapidly growing Medellín drug cartel allegedly found his services useful for the laundering of their cocaine profits, and by the mid-1980s the PDF had become a "drug trafficking–military" mafia masquerading as a formal military institution.

Although Panama had been undergoing a crisis of military rule since the mid-1970s, this crisis began to draw increasing international attention in 1987, when a high-ranking member of the PDF openly denounced General Noriega, setting off a wave of civilian unrest. The Reagan administration supported the civilian opposition and made it clear that it viewed Panama as one of the region's few remaining military dictatorships. However, it soon became apparent that the United States had badly misjudged the difficulty of removing Noriega. Economic sanctions

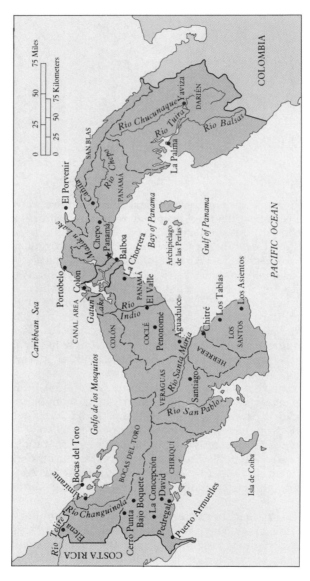

Panama

applied in 1988 and 1989 hurt the Panamanian economy but did not lead to significant political change.

Panama's crisis of military rule became so intense that it eventually prompted a U.S. invasion. In broad terms, this crisis can be viewed as the result of one permanent historical reality combining with a more recent institutional trend. The permanent reality is the country's role as a "strategic bridge" for the transportation of goods from around the world. From this perspective, cocaine is simply the last of a long list of illicit goods that have crossed the isthmus since colonial times. The recent institutional trend is the growing political and economic power of the military. Historically a weak institution, it was only in the late 1960s that military leaders consolidated the institutional base that allows them to dominate politics.

The U.S. invasion temporarily removed the military from politics and reduced the involvement of the Panamanian government in illicit activities such as drug trafficking. However, there is a sense of nervous anticipation in U.S. policymaking circles as the year 2000 approaches. Can Panama's fledgling democracy survive the political and economic vicissitudes of the 1990s, or will there be an eventual return to military rule? And, even assuming continued civilian rule, would there be sufficient political stability to ensure a smooth transfer of the canal? A closer look at Panama's history and current political process may allow one to make a few preliminary judgments.

HISTORY AND POLITICAL CULTURE

The Republic of Panama is a small, narrow country that joins Central America to South America. Shaped like a giant "S" some 420 miles (675 kilometers) long, it winds from the border of Costa Rica in the west to Colombia in the east. In total area, Panama encompasses some 29,209 square miles (75,651 square kilometers), making it slightly larger than the state of West Virginia. The population of about 2 million is largely composed of mestizos and mulattoes together with black West Indians brought to Panama in the late nineteenth century to help construct the canal. Small numbers of native Indians occupy some of the interior provinces as well as the San Blas islands along the northern coast.

Panama is as much a location as it is a country. Its lack of significant size and its position between the Atlantic and Pacific oceans make Panama a vital strategic bridge. Although geography is not always destiny, the enduring legacy of the country's location has been to constantly reinforce a particular kind of laissez-faire economic thought and open economic practices.

Faith in the benefits of an open economy developed during colonial times when the isthmus served as a major transit point linking Spain to its most important colonial possessions along the west coast of South America. Legal trade with the Spanish colonies was supplemented by contraband trade in slaves and other commodities. These illicit activities, particularly critical to the isthmian economy in hard economic times, served as a precursor to the more recent illicit traffic under military rule in commodities such as drugs and high-technology items.

The result of Panama's early function as a strategic bridge was to concentrate economic resources and political power in the hands of a small, Hispanic urban commercial class. The politicians who assumed leadership positions in Panama following independence in 1903 did not have ties to a traditional agrarian sector. Panama had never developed an *encomienda* system because of its lack of a large Indian population, and unlike its Central American neighbors, Panama never experienced a nineteenth-century coffee boom.

Since 1903 Panamanian politics has been dominated by a struggle for power between the largely white urban commercial class and nonwhite groups that have been excluded from the full benefits of nationhood. During the periods of French and U.S. canal construction (1878–1914), large numbers of black workers were imported from Caribbean countries such as Jamaica and Barbados. These workers spoke English and were physically incorporated as an underclass into the U.S.-controlled Canal Zone. Although their wages were low compared to those for white workers from the United States, these workers constituted an urban labor elite when compared with Panama's mestizo and black Spanish-speaking populations.

During the 1920s and 1930s the Panamanian economy deteriorated owing to the termination of canal construction activities and, later, the Great Depression. Resentment began to grow, particularly among mestizos from the interior provinces, against the West Indian blacks and against members of the urban commercial elite, who were viewed as natural allies of the United States. This resentment crystallized in 1923 with the formation of Community Action, a movement whose intent was to gain entrance for mestizo professionals and urban day laborers to the more lucrative jobs associated with the canal.

In the 1930s Arnulfo Arias emerged as the leader of this highly nationalistic movement. Elected president in 1940, he quickly promulgated a new constitution that contained discriminatory provisions against West Indians. The political crisis precipitated by this constitutional change was resolved when the United States, upset with Arias's anti-U.S. actions, helped remove him from office. Although the political crisis associated with the rise of Community Action became more attenuated with the passage of time, Arnulfo Arias remained a major fixture in Panamanian politics until his death in 1988.

The struggle for power since independence between upper- and lower-class groups has been influenced during more recent times by the reemergence of the Panamanian military as a political force. The army was disbanded shortly after independence because it was viewed as a threat to both the political hegemony of the urban commercial elite and the United States. However, through a slow evolutionary process, the army was reassembled out of the small police force that had taken its place. By the early 1950s the national police had been turned into a national guard and a colonel had been elected president with military backing.

After a turbulent period of civilian democracy during the late 1950s and 1960s, the military coup against Arnulfo Arias brought Gen. Omar Torrijos to power. Torrijos quickly built a political base among marginal groups in both Panama City and the countryside. Farm collectives were formed, labor unions organized, and the government expanded dramatically to accommodate popular needs.

Panamanian politics thus reveals a consistent dynamic beneath its surface complexities. This dynamic pits the urban commercial class against groups traditionally excluded from the full benefits of Panama's location. During the 1930s and 1940s Arias led a movement for the inclusion of rural mestizos and urban day laborers in these benefits; in the 1970s the military spearheaded attempts to include additional marginalized rural and urban groups. The effort to restore civilian rule in Panama, which resulted in the U.S. military invasion of 1989, is reflective of this same dynamic and of the continuing need to reach an accommodation between upper and lower class interests.

POLITICAL PARTIES AND INTEREST GROUPS

After the coup of 1968 the Panamanian military became the central actor in domestic politics. For the first ten years the military governed directly, and political party activity was banned. However, deteriorating economic conditions in the mid-1970s led General Torrijos to reassess the costs and benefits of direct military rule, and in 1978 he formed the Democratic Revolutionary party (PRD) to incorporate the various groups that supported his military regime as the country moved toward a democratic opening.

Formation of the PRD suggested that the military wished to give permanent institutional form to its reformist ideals through the establishment of a new political party that would regularly win elections with military backing. The idea was not a new one as attested to by the existence of other similar Latin American parties such as Mexico's PRI. However, compared to the PRI, the PRD was not nearly as successful in consolidating its electoral grip. When presidential elections were held in 1984 the military had to resort to fraud to ensure a victory for the party's candidate, because even with full government backing, the PRD received fewer votes than the party of Arnulfo Arias.

Twenty years of military governance led to the establishment of a political system artificially dominated by one political party. And yet the country's natural tendency is to engage in multiparty politics. During the 1964 presidential elections nineteen political parties fielded seven presidential candidates, although many of these parties were really nothing more than highly personalistic factions formed to align with larger electoral coalitions.

Even though Panama's political parties changed little during twenty years of military rule, there have been significant changes in the relative importance and strength of the various interest groups. General Torrijos encouraged the formation of new labor unions to strengthen his popular base, and labor was legally empowered by the formal recognition of these new unions and by the passage of a new labor code in 1972, which significantly improved the bargaining position of workers.

Other groups that have experienced significant change since 1968 are business organizations and the Catholic church. The business sector has diversified and expanded to the point that there is no direct correspondence between its interests and those of most traditional political parties. This fact was apparent in 1987 when businesspeople organized against General Noriega under the banner of the National Civic Crusade. Similarly, the Catholic church, a historically docile institution, has become increasingly involved in politics. Responding to the general call during Vatican II for more vigorous reformist policies, the church has increasingly demonstrated its willingness to enter the political arena.

Although Panamanian politics has retained many of the features it exhibited prior to twenty years of military rule, there have been a number of significant changes. Certain groups such as labor have grown stronger as a result of their privileged status during this period. Others, such as the urban commercial elite, have grown relatively weaker after two decades of sitting on the political sidelines.

One of the most significant changes has been the growing gap between the traditional political parties and the newly emerging sectors and interest groups. The party leadership is aging and increasingly out of touch with the realities of a new generation of Panamanians, whose aspirations the party leaders have not been able to fully ascertain. A massive movement of rural dwellers to Panama City has created a new electorate that is largely detached from the patterns of self-interest and coercion that assured its vote for particular parties in the past. This detachment of leaders from followers enhances the unpredictability and volatility of electoral politics in the 1990s.

FORMAL GOVERNMENT STRUCTURES

As in many other Latin American countries, there is an important distinction to be made in Panama between formal government structures and those informal structures that frequently determine policy outcomes. During the 1970s, the Panamanian military became a new "branch" of government that determined how the civilian components of the government would perform. Yet it would be an unfair characterization of the relationship between the military and the civilians to suggest that the latter played no role in the affairs of state. For this reason, it is important to discuss not only the informal structures that gave the military influence but also those formal civilian institutions that enhanced or constrained military actions.

Panama's formal government structures largely derive from the country's long association with Colombia. Following independence in 1903 a constitution was drafted that created a centralized unitary government with executive, legislative, and judicial branches. The new government structure was very much in the Iberian political tradition, with the executive branch intended to dominate the other two. The president appointed provincial governors so his power extended directly down to the regional level; although local municipalities theoretically possessed some autonomy, this idea was not honored in practice.

When the Panamanian military seized power in 1968 it considerably altered the traditional civilian structure. The National Assembly, which had come to be viewed by the military as an elite-dominated institution, was replaced with a much larger legislature whose members were elected from the country's 505 municipal subdistricts. The traditional political parties were banned from electoral participation, and short legislative sessions ensured that there would be no time to mount meaningful challenges to military executive authority.

The 1972 constitution, which created this new "popular legislature," also recognized the central role within the executive branch of General Torrijos and the defense forces. Although there was still a civilian president, real power was given to Torrijos as "maximum leader" of the Panamanian Revolution. The impotency of the president within this new constitutional structure was best expressed by the fact that he could neither appoint nor remove military personnel. The PDF legally became a fourth branch of government since the other three branches were constitutionally required to act in "harmonic collaboration" with the military.

During the early 1970s the military governed directly. However, by the mid-1970s it had become obvious that the country's growing economic problems were undermining the regime's base of popular support and that the costs of direct rule would soon begin to escalate. As a result, General Torrijos began to move Panama back toward its more traditional government structures. Most important, this change meant the holding of direct presidential elections and the reestablishment of the National Assembly.

Torrijos's attempt to reduce the PDF's direct role in politics led him to modify the 1972 constitution, and as a result, political parties could once again organize in order to participate in the 1984 presidential and legislative elections. Although something like a "democratic opening" thus took place, it is important to note its limits. The PDF ensured its future political role through, one, manipulation of the 1984 elections to guarantee victory for its presidential candidate and, two, control of the

National Assembly through the military-backed Democratic Revolutionary party.

The death of General Torrijos in 1981 did not fundamentally alter this relationship between the PDF, which controlled the levers of power, and those civilian institutions formally charged with governing. Power continued to flow from the commander in chief of the defense forces and his general staff to the legislative branch through military control of the official party. And it continued to flow to the executive branch through military selection of presidential candidates, electoral fraud, and early "retirement" for presidents who challenged the PDF. During late 1989, General Noriega attempted to strengthen his grip over the civilian government by restoring the larger legislature that had supported military rule during the 1970s. But following the U.S. military invasion, the new civilian government abolished this larger legislature, replacing it with the traditional National Assembly.

GOVERNMENT POLICIES

Observers of Panamanian politics under military rule noted a curious blend of populist development policies mixed with more conventional ones. Populist policies, aimed at the redistribution of goods to the popular sectors, were the natural result of the military's disdain for the urban commercial elite, which dominated policy formation prior to 1968. The simultaneous pursuit of more conventional development policies, emphasizing continued growth of the more dynamic areas of the private sector, reflected the permanent historical reality of Panama's open trading economy.

Major components of the military's populist policies have included the implementation of land reform, enactment of a progressive labor code, and efforts to regain national control of the Panama Canal. The land reform program was aimed not only at including the traditionally marginalized rural groups in national development but at creating a popular following for the military in areas where the urban commercial elite did not have a strong base of support. Collective farms were organized, and considerable amounts of readily available public lands were distributed to small farmers.

Like the rural poor, Panama's urban work force had not received many benefits prior to the military coup of 1968. The urban commercial elite had historically implemented policies that prevented the formation of large and effective unions and had opposed changes in the labor code that would have improved the workers' economic lot. New labor legislation was introduced by General Torrijos in 1972 that significantly improved the bargaining position and job security of workers, and union membership grew rapidly between 1972 and 1976.

Perhaps the military's broadest popular constituency consisted of those Panamanians who wished to see the canal brought under national control. General Torrijos worked hard during the early 1970s to create an international support group that would help speed negotiations with the United States for a new treaty. Highly nationalistic Third World countries, such as Cuba, were encouraged to support Panama's cause as well as countries such as Venezuela and Costa Rica that have more-moderate democratic governments. Through such international coalition building as well as support for changes in the treaty arrangements on the part of several U.S. presidential administrations, Torrijos was able to achieve his goal. In 1978 a treaty was ratified that returned the Canal Zone to Panama and stipulated that Panama would gain full control of the canal in the year 2000.

The military's more conventional approach to development emphasized further growth in the highly dynamic service sector. Because of its geographic location, Panama has attracted a host of activities associated with the growth of global multinational corporations. The military government revised the banking laws so that Panama quickly became a regional center for the accumulation and transfer of "Latindollars." The number of offshore banks grew from 30 in 1970 to 100 in 1980, and assets rose accordingly.

In the mid-1970s the military began to move away from its populist policies because of a variety of internal and external constraints. Domestically, the urban commercial elite was showing less and less willingness to invest in an economy over which it had no control. The public sector had grown dramatically, as is generally the case under populist rule, and this fact had increased the burden on public finances. And although the world's bankers had initially been willing to subsidize populist policies in exchange for favorable banking laws, the growth of Panama's international debt had made this policy less feasible by the late 1970s.

Populist policies were very much absent in the early 1980s, but populist rhetoric continued to flourish, and after 1987 there was a resurgence of nationalism encouraged by U.S. attacks on Gen. Manuel Noriega and his corrupt military officers. The canal issue was once again revived, with Noriega claiming that the United States wished to retain its military bases in Panama after the year 2000. However, populist policies differed considerably from those of earlier years in that their sole objective was to retain support for the existing military leadership. Following the U.S. invasion and restoration of civilian rule, populist rhetoric was toned down and there was little discussion of the canal issue. The new government headed by President Guillermo Endara concentrated on issues of more immediate concern such as rebuilding the police force and restoring the health of the shattered national economy. Under such circumstances, it was not possible to assess the nature of the policies that the civilians would pursue over the longer term.

PANAMA IN THE WORLD

Panama's recent involvement in world affairs has been conditioned both by its central geographic location and by the existence of a corrupt military government with populist roots. The uses to which Panama has been put by various international groups in recent times are reflective of both of these facts. For example, the Medellín cartel discovered in the early 1980s that the existence of an international banking system in Panama that relied on the U.S. dollar and was under the control of unscrupulous military officers provided the perfect vehicle for its money-laundering activities.

The country's geographic location and the fact that General Noriega was a military intelligence officer meant that Panama also attracted the attention of various foreign intelligence services. The United States took the lead in this regard, finding Noriega a useful source of information on the activities of leaders such as Fidel Castro and Daniel Ortega. In exchange for intelligence information and help in defending U.S. regional interests, various administrations were willing to overlook drug-related activities within the PDF.

The United States was not alone in its attraction to this part of Central America. For more than a decade Israel maintained close ties to Panama's military regime, finding Panama useful not only as a source of information concerning activities of the Palestine Liberation Organization in Central America but for purchases of proscribed high-technology items. Cuba is another country that maintained close ties to the Panamanian military. Fidel Castro's motivations for maintaining such ties were similar to those of Israel—intelligence information and purchases of prohibited goods through the Colón Free Zone.

During the 1970s General Torrijos sought to increase Panama's bargaining leverage in the treaty negotiations with the United States by expanding ties with Third World governments. Later General Noriega sought to offset U.S. pressure to resign by further expanding relations with the Soviet Union, Cuba, and Nicaragua. In doing so, he hoped to obtain not only rhetorical support but also military help. Cuban-manufactured arms were shipped to Panama, and Cubans advised Noriega concerning the training of his paramilitary forces.

Panama's international contacts multiplied rapidly during the 1970s and 1980s as a consequence of these and other factors. Prior to the 1968 military coup the nation's foreign policy was largely the product of its bilateral relations with the United States. Although the U.S. military invasion has led to a reemphasis on U.S.-Panamanian relations, the country's international contacts remain quite substantial. In the economic realm, the United States no longer exerts a hegemonic influence in Panamanian affairs. Countries such as Japan and Taiwan look to Panama as a logical location for banking, production, and transshipment activities, and their economic roles have expanded accordingly.

CONCLUSION

Panama is undergoing a political transition of historic proportions that has been vastly complicated by the 1989 U.S. military invasion. Since the founding days of the Republic, the commercial elite has struggled with populist forces for control of the state, creating an unending cycle of unstable elitist and populist governments. Relying on the growing institutional power of the military, the populists finally managed to consolidate their rule during the 1970s. The U.S. invasion destroyed this populist government by attacking its "central nervous system" (the military), but enduring civilian governing institutions have not yet been produced to replace the military.

Forecasting Panama's political future is a risky business at best, but that future does not look particularly bright. The U.S. invasion has temporarily masked the historical antagonisms between the commercial elite and populist forces. However, as the economy rebounds and the direct U.S. military presence is reduced, these traditional antagonisms will once again surface. Unless the civilian government can bring about a historical reconciliation between Panama's feuding power blocs, Panama's political path to the millennium will be rocky indeed.

SUGGESTIONS FOR FURTHER READING

Dinges, John. *Our Man in Panama*. New York: Random House, 1990.

Farnsworth, David N., and James W. McKenney. *U.S.-Panama Relations, 1903–1978: A Study in Linkage Politics*. Boulder, Colo.: Westview Press, 1983.

Furlong, William L., and Margaret E. Scranton. *The Dynamics of Foreign Policy Making: The President, the Congress, and the Panama Canal Treaties*. Boulder, Colo.: Westview Press, 1984.

Jorden, William J., *Panama Odyssey*. Austin: University of Texas Press, 1984.

LaFeber, Walter. *The Panama Canal: The Crisis in Historical Perspective*. New York: Oxford University Press, 1978.

McCullough, David. *The Path Between the Seas: The Creation of the Panama Canal, 1870–1914*. New York: Simon and Schuster, 1977.

Pippin, Larry LaRae. *The Remon Era*. Stanford, Calif.: Institute of Hispanic American and Luso-Brazilian Studies, 1964.

Ropp, Steve C. *Panamanian Politics: From Guarded Nation to National Guard*. Stanford, Calif.: Hoover Institution, 1982.

United States, Library of Congress, Federal Research Division. *Panama: A Country Study*. Washington, D.C.: 1989.

27
Haiti:
The Failures of Governance

GEORGES A. FAURIOL

Haiti, the second-oldest independent nation in the Western Hemisphere, is about a decade away from its bicentennial and has little to show for it. Discovered by Columbus in 1492 during his first voyage to the Americas, the nation's experience since then has encompassed all shades of development experience—except perhaps that of effective modern political and economic management. In spite of this unhappy and at times tragic record, Haiti has from time to time entered the consciousness of the international community, most recently as a result of the fall of the Duvalier dynasty in 1986 and its convoluted aftermath.

These facts would not be all that dramatic were it not for the dysfunctional character of Haiti's political dynamics, economic features, and social institutions. Born out of the economic excesses of slavery and the political violence of the French Revolution, Haiti emerged in 1804 as an independent nation. Its economy in ruins and its population exhausted, Haiti's career as a modern nation began without any foreign friends. In fact, its early status as an outcast among the community of nations further increased its vulnerability to both internal and external threats. At the beginning of the twentieth century this overlap of threats ultimately generated direct U.S. political and military administration (1915–1934). In a more recent period the difficulties experienced by Haiti's development process have also introduced into the life of the nation a broad array of foreign government and multinational economic assistance organizations as well as nongovernmental groups.

Despite these misfortunes, Haiti has not lost the basic features of its national character. Its roots lie in a hybrid of French eighteenth-century colonialism, African culture, a marginal brand of Catholicism, and the aftereffects of the United States' strategic sweep in the Caribbean region. Indeed, the African cultural and spiritual features have remained almost unaltered for a majority of the population since they were first imported in the seventeenth century. The vitality of this primarily rural environment

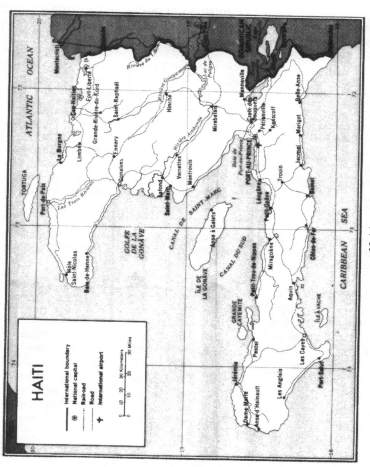

Haiti

has survived in the face of economic adversity and the unusual disinterest of the political leadership in the process of national development.

Roughly the size of the state of Maryland, Haiti occupies the western third of the island of Hispaniola, which it shares with the Dominican Republic. It lies at a crossroads of trading passages and strategic interests—Cuba lies to the immediate west across the Windward Passage, the open waters of the Atlantic Ocean bound Haiti on the north, and the Caribbean Sea lies to the south. Haiti remains ethnically and culturally distinct, being 95 percent black and the only independent French-speaking nation in the Western Hemisphere.

With an estimated average per capita GNP income of a little over $300, Haiti is also the poorest country in the region. In fact, a 23 percent literacy rate and a life expectancy of fifty-five years ranks Haiti near the bottom on a global basis. A mountainous topography coupled with a failing agricultural program and land-management neglect have not only concentrated the country's 5.5 million people into the nominally fertile 30 percent of the country but have also in recent years accentuated the flows of out-migration. Revenues from coffee, a few odd agricultural and mineral exports, and offshore manufacturing have had limited economic impact, leaving much of the work force on the margins of national life. Haiti's best talent has left for other shores, including the United States where the current population of Haitian origin may be as high as 1 million.

Study of the Haitian experience is frustrating because of an absence of identifiable political and economic development strategies. In practice, the most charitable characterization of Haiti's public administration since the nineteenth century is that the government has been at its relative best when pursuing a policy of benign neglect—leaving most of Haiti's peasants to their own autonomous devices. A very small and generally urbanized political and economic elite has for the most part directed priorities at maintaining its own fragile status quo and in sustaining a limited enclave of export-oriented commercial activity. Some writers speak of a "kleptocracy," or "predatory state," and of the "politics of squalor." Some allude to the "colonial" or "self-colonized" character of the Haitian society. Others borrow from development literature and assess Haiti in the context of a "transitional society."[1] What, in fact, is a viable characterization of Haiti's politics and development process?

THE FORMATION OF THE HAITIAN STATE

The Caribbean entered the historical record of the European world in 1492, the year Columbus discovered Haiti. Some 300 years later, Haiti fought its way to independence from France in 1804. In between there flourished a plantation colony characterized by extraordinary wealth and deep social and racial divisions. Few factors have had a more dramatic impact on today's Caribbean polities than their transformation some 300 years ago from small colonies of settlement into economic dependencies of European powers.

The environment of sugar and slaves came crashing down in Haiti in the late eighteenth century. Saint-Domingue, as Haiti was then known, was the crown jewel of France's overseas empire. But the importation of over 800,000 African slaves created an untenable socioeconomic milieu. Open racial and color conflict was set in motion with the violent explosions of the French Revolution after 1789, and what followed was the Haitian Revolution of 1789–1804, which ravaged the country to the core. In the bloody confusion, blacks, lighter-skinned mulattoes, and whites built complex alliances and were helped along by the intervention of British, Spanish, and naturally, French forces.

After independence in 1804 the early Haitian leaders faced the traditional patterns of nineteenth-century power politics. As a smaller state, Haiti was treated as an object of policy, if dealt with at all. A spiritual heir to the French Revolution, it also provided a serious challenge as the first non-European postcolonial state in the modern world. According to diplomatic historian Rayford Logan's characterization, Haiti started out as a "power and enigma," turned into an "anomaly," became a "threat," and ultimately was an "outcast" among the nations of the earth.[2]

Lacking any viable institutions, Haiti initially evolved a remarkable collection of powerful personalities who shaped the nation's style of governance—authoritarian, personalist, anchored in coercive power: Jean-Jacques Dessalines (1804–1806), Haiti's first emperor and efficient exterminator of the whites in Haiti; Henri Christophe (1807–1820), Haiti's first crowned king; Alexandre Pétion (1807–1818), Haiti's first president for life; and Jean-Pierre Boyer (1818–1843), who ruled over an increasingly crippled nation. At mid-century another extraordinary figure appeared—Faustin Soulouque (1847–1859), later Emperor Faustin I. He ordered a general massacre of the mulattoes, led the country in several abortive campaigns into neighboring Dominican Republic, and further precipitated Haiti's deterioration.

By the dawn of the twentieth century Haiti was in debt to French, German, and U.S. financial interests. France had underwritten all external loans between 1825 and 1896 and owned the National Bank. The Germans held the trading sector. Most imports came from the United States, and after 1900 U.S. influence expanded into banking.

The 1915 U.S. intervention in Haiti was the result of severe disarray in that country's politics—suffice it to say that the degeneration of Haitian politics had indeed attained a new plateau. Of the twenty-two presidents who served between 1843 and 1915, one finished his term in office, three died a natural death while in office, one was blown up with the presidential palace, another one was probably poisoned, one was hacked to pieces, and one resigned. The fourteen others were overthrown. The sorry state of Haitian finances was also perceived by Washington as a

Trojan horse for European intervention in the Caribbean. The object of the U.S. action was, not to expose Haiti to U.S. exploitation, but to promote Haitian political stability, financial rehabilitation, and economic development.

Yet Haiti was one of the United States' least successful interventions. True, a minimum of financial order was established, debt was reduced, and the administrative infrastructure was improved, but the U.S. presence did not lead to democratic virtues or greater management capabilities among the Haitian elite. Violent anti-U.S. feelings triggered a review of U.S. policy in 1930. Faced with similar problems in Nicaragua, President Hoover and his successor, Franklin D. Roosevelt, became determined that the United States would exit from Haiti's tropical imbroglio as quickly as possible. Following the 1915–1934 U.S. period were twenty years during which Haitian governance slowly decayed under the weight of presidential excesses. This period came to an uninspired end with the 1957 elections that brought François Duvalier to power. What ensued was a harsh family rule that was to last until his son's downfall in 1986.

THE CHARACTER OF SOCIETY

More than any other country in the Western Hemisphere, the structure of Haitian politics underscores the isolated and traditional character of the country's society. Formal ideology is not a particularly useful component in explaining the course of Haitian developments. The character of the polity is therefore best assessed by a review of the following factors: religion, the nation's rural-urban bifurcation, cultural values, and the Haitian society's world view.

Religious institutions are numerically and culturally important in the Caribbean, but in Haiti established churches have been to a degree displaced or absorbed by indigenous cults and practices derived from tradition and folklore. Although marginal in much of the region (the Rastafarians in Jamaica, for example), Voodoo in Haiti has been enriched by both Christianity and ancestral African rites for over three centuries to provide Haitians with a great emotional outlet.

Basic to Voodoo is the ancestral past and its impact on the present. There is a fatalism in its cosmos that does not leave much room for shaping the present or the future. Nature and humans contend with each other in a process forwarded by appeals to the many spirits who control all forces. An individual struggles to survive within an essentially static hierarchy.

This defensive character of Haitian religious culture has intermixed with the country's unique historical experience. The product of slavery and of harsh colonial conditions, the very origins of modern Haiti were fixed in a rejection of the white race, if not entirely of the culture that it represented. That viewpoint took its toll on the Haitian psyche. Although French and modernizing sociopolitical influences engaged the minute portion of the nation represented by the elite, the vast majority of the population remained tied to the slave experience and its eradication with the revolution of 1804. More African and Creole than French, more illiterate than not, and historically more isolated than any other country in the Caribbean, Haitian culture has to a degree generated an enduring demoralized attitude regarding the nation's potential.

This fact has been made more acute by the exploitative preferences of the two sectors of Haitian society that might have taken the country out of its long dead-end run: the mulatto (lighter-skinned) minority and the black governing elite. Neither group has viewed its place in life as involving a contribution to the national good, hard work, or an expansion of the political and social framework of traditional society. Elites have viewed themselves as the caretakers of the Haitian estate, an opportunity to enrich themselves without interference from or interfering in the life of the rest of the nation. Under this precept, neither economic growth, social enlightenment, nor political modernization have taken deep root.

In this context, the geographical separation of the elite from the masses, and of the urban population from the rural one, has been a politically salient feature of the country. Accounting for perhaps 80 percent of the population, the rural peasantry has been excluded from national decision making, and the fact that serious national debates take place partly in French, a language the vast majority of the population does not speak, underlines the curious nature of Haitian political relationships. But what has made life bearable for the average Haitian is the fact that the government has historically not intruded into their lives. Until this century "government" was, in fact, locally visible through the most tenuous of administrative systems. After 1957 the Duvalier regimes modernized this process considerably through a local security presence.

The heart of Haiti is its inner country—rural, poor, and dedicated to basic agricultural production. Long periods of isolation have made this part of Haiti a conservator of African traditions, and the traditional milieu is still the dominant environment of Haiti today. Roughly 80 percent of the population is made up of peasants who speak Creole and no French, are essentially illiterate, and live in social conditions reminiscent of past centuries; Voodoo is the religion despite the strong presence of Catholic and Protestant churches.

The other world of Haiti is built primarily around the capital and a few secondary towns. It is not only urban but also coastal in character, and this portion of Haiti is more literate and French-speaking. If the nation has developed any capital wealth since independence, this is where it is to be found. An urbanized and somewhat cosmopolitan elite has dedicated itself to trading as opposed to developing the interior of the country. This community includes the mulatto economic elite in uneasy association with the black political classes, to which in recent decades has been added a very small, semipermanent expatriate population from the four corners of the world.

INSTITUTIONAL PATTERNS

The absence of a viable political development process has stunted the growth of socioeconomic and political interest groups normally found in a modernizing society. Likewise, the weakness of Haitian institutions has for the most part made it very difficult for the process of change to be channeled toward productive ends.

Government administration has constituted a center of influence, if for no other reason than it has represented the source of jobs, money, gifts, and public favors—if not outright access to the national treasury. The urbanized sector for the most part consists of a docile, lower-middle class of Haitian society. Unionization, paralyzed under the Duvaliers, has not been a factor despite the limited rebirth of a trade-union movement in recent years. At its most senior echelon, the public sector has included the lucky few who have had access to corrupt government patronage emanating from the presidential palace.

The Catholic church is the one institution whose presence and local relevance have often rivaled those of the government. If nothing else, since the 1860s the church has fulfilled an important educational mission and has provided isolated communities with the rudiments of continuity and linkage to the outside world. Not surprisingly, the spiritual and political worlds have occasionally overlapped. As recently as the 1960s François Duvalier pushed through a "Haitianization" of the clergy, also reviving age-old frictions regarding appointments of the church hierarchy in Haiti. As elsewhere in the region, the clergy is split between conservative and liberal contingents, with the latter's influence gaining ground; the Catholic church even played a decisive role in the 1986 ouster of Jean-Claude Duvalier. In recent years the Catholic church and other religious denominations have become the conduit through which human rights and other sociopolitical concerns are exposed to the world community.

Consolidation of political power in the hands of strongmen has made the armed forces the institutional pillar of society. Born out of revolutionary violence and later suffering socioeconomic destruction, Haiti never succeeded in constructing the structures of a civilian society capable of minimizing the rule of force. Part of Haiti's history is the story of competing mercenary bands (cacos) and peasant groups (piquets) fighting a ragtag military. The deinstitutionalization that has marked portions of the nation's experience was reversed during the U.S. occupation after 1915. Ironically, the most visible product of this period turned out to be the Garde d'Haiti—later transformed into today's army. The armed forces remain by default the only organization with a national political reach and a semblance of institutional cohesion.

Not surprisingly, Haiti's low level of political participation has generated few alternative institutions. Perhaps the weakest link lies in the absence of a diverse civilian political elite. Not only has the economic poverty of the nation centralized national authority into a minute urban constituency, but the political ravages of recent Haitian dictatorships have also decimated civilian political leadership. As a consequence, there is no competitive political party structure, a weakness that is not likely to be overcome quickly in a society used to authoritarian rule. Likewise, modern social or political pressure groups (for example, labor unions or the media) have found little opportunity for growth. The small modern business community, because of the nation's co-optive political dynamics, has remained generally uninterested in or incapable of acting as an autonomous interest group. In the 1980s Haiti's large exile community did come forth as an outside pluralistic (and so far, fractionalized) source of influence (and money).

This lack of political parties and interest groups does not mean that Haiti's large rural peasantry and marginal population are politically inert. In fact, it is the occasional outbursts of what constitutes the majority of the population that have given Haiti its complex character. With no institutional channels, these outbursts (such as the one that led to Duvalier's ouster in 1986) have represented very real but unstructured political frustrations. Disconnected from elite political agendas, however, these violent expressions have not resulted in any institutional changes. Rural society still remains tied to traditional forms of belief and localized family and community structures.

THE DUVALIER ERA

The Duvalier era began in 1957 (Papa Doc became president for life in 1964) during a period of political confusion that included the collapse of the previous government (Paul Magloire), violence, and fraudulent elections. François Duvalier was the product of a movement toward a return to black culture and of a political resurgence that took hold during the U.S. occupation (1915–1934). In the 1920s a Haitian intellectual class had begun to evolve a potent political racialism derived from a reevaluation of the country's African tradition. This racialism initially evolved into a conception associated with the French-African negritude movement, which entailed a belief in the distinctive character of an African environmental heritage and a rejection of the superiority of European culture. As a form of "cultural decolonization," it was later elaborated by Haitians, including François Duvalier, into a powerful rationale of black political power, which through the early 1970s constituted the framework of government control.

Who was François Duvalier? The person who held such a spell over Haitian affairs after 1957 was a soft-spoken physician and part-time ethnologist. A black, or *noir*, by Haitian standards, Duvalier had four children, including one son, Jean-Claude (later to be known as Baby Doc). Unlike many of his colleagues in Haitian history, François Duvalier was never a military man, and as a result of his writings, he was perceived as something of an intellectual. These characteristics confounded most observers and political opponents and initially misled the United States into assuming that Haiti was distancing itself from the norm of Haitian history.

Duvalier was committed to bringing to the surface the nation's black heritage, even at the cost of isolating the country from external ties and sources of assistance (as ultimately was the case in the 1960s). But his policies ultimately created a monster. "Duvalierism" was made up of a curious combination of negritude, quasi-radical nationalism, and fascist tendencies. The search for a "new equilibrium" signaled a shift in political and economic power—from the predominant mulatto elite to a new black middle class acting in the interest of the peasant masses. But in practice, the Duvalierist ideology was little more than gestures. Corruption, income inequalities, illiteracy, and environmental degradation were compounded by a continuing brain drain.

But Duvalier was a shrewd autocrat, ruthlessly suppressing any groups that might have challenged his authority. The power of the mulatto elite was eroded, the political power of the Roman Catholic church was reduced by allowing the government to have a say in the nomination of the Haitian church's leadership (which until then had been essentially French), and the army was purged and brought into line. A powerful paramilitary organization (Volontaires de la Securité Nationale [VSN])—the famed Tonton Macoutes (TTMs)—was established to protect the regime and enforce its directives.

Confounding most predictions, Jean-Claude Duvalier (Baby Doc) did initially show considerable durability after taking over in April 1971 following his father's death. Jean-Claude was then nineteen years old and had come to power through the political dictates of his father. An unknown quantity, whose contact with the outside was very limited, and surrounded all his life by presidential advisers, family members, and security guards, he was ultimately greatly influenced by two important women: his politically powerful mother (Simone) and his dynamic and controversial wife, Michèle. His marriage to Michèle Bennett, daughter of a mulatto business family, created much attention not only because of the cost of the wedding but also because the marriage provided a link between the mulatto business community and the black government leadership.

François Duvalier's political and foreign policy isolation was initially replaced by his son's "economic revolution." The latter was a rather vague design to modernize the economic structure of Haiti, based on a broader popular participation and the political changes pursued by François Duvalier. Naturally, the reality was quite different. Operationally this policy implied greater solicitation of economic assistance from major donor countries (United States, France, Canada) and a consortium of international and private lending agencies. Yet the authoritarian and often aimless nature of Haitian governance continued to cloud all external relationships, including ties with the United States, and ultimately led to Duvalier's downfall in 1986.

THE IMPACT OF THE INTERNATIONAL ARENA

Overall, Haitian diplomacy has followed an isolationist policy. This has been characterized by a strong disinclination to be visibly associated with mainstream Third World politics, including the Non-Aligned Movement and most North-South disputes. These factors alone greatly differentiate Haitian policy from the policies of the country's Caribbean and Latin American neighbors.

Haiti's main concern has remained the management of its ties with the preponderant center of power, Washington, D.C. François Duvalier faced an informal political boycott of his regime throughout most of the 1960s, a situation made manageable because of the Haitian government's inward-looking tendency. After 1971 a mild renaissance of Haitian economic perspectives under Jean-Claude Duvalier led to a revival of foreign investments and tourism, and a conglomeration of national and multinational aid agencies was lured by the Haitian government's expressions of commitment to socioeconomic development.

The Reagan administration came to power disposed to reassess ties with the Duvalier regime, and the latter was inclined to cooperate, shaken as it was by the refugee crisis, economic downturn, and troubles with foreign aid. The U.S. administration showed a willingness to accept slow progress toward political reform if gains could be achieved in three other areas: the immigration problem, Haitian economic and social development, and U.S. foreign aid. In tandem, Duvalier announced a framework for gradual "democratization." The details were vague, but the timing was important, for it preceded Haiti's incorporation into the Caribbean Basin Initiative, a major framework of U.S. policy in the region.

However, Duvalier's weak leadership caved in to pressures from a corrupt and conservative political elite that had the most to lose from even mild liberalization policies, and there was soon a retreat in Duvalier's on-and-off efforts to open Haiti to modernization. In 1982–1983 an ouster of technocrats was followed by arrests and intimidation as allies of Duvalier's powerful mother and the old Papa Doc guard returned to replace the departed modernizing factions.

Already facing mounting criticism abroad, Duvalier soon had to address Catholic church militancy, which helped mobilize Haitians. This mobilization was sanctioned during a visit by Pope John Paul II in March 1983 when his airport sermon referred to "injustices" and the need for a more equitable society in Haiti. These remarks were seen as an indication of the church's intent to champion change by taking on an active political role. The church even encouraged Haitians to protest in the streets, a process that led to a war of nerves with the government in late 1985 and January 1986, and the church acted in cooperation with international and U.S. human rights groups to focus on the regime's corruption and human rights abuses.

A majority of U.S. congressional members became skeptical of the U.S. government's vague optimism about Haiti's political progress, and the racial element of U.S.-Haitian relations also played a crucial role in changing U.S. perceptions of Duvalier, for U.S. blacks took a special interest in change in Haiti. Racial, religious, and humanitarian concerns had, in fact, captured the attention of the U.S. black community as a whole early on. Ultimately, the Duvalier regime's overall ineptitude isolated it from much of its traditional key sources of economic support (the United States, West Germany, France, and Canada). When merged with racial and humanitarian considerations, this isolation left the Duvalier regime undefended.

The actual collapse of the regime began in November 1985 with a series of spontaneous riots in Gonaïves that turned into a major anti-government protest. The government's security forces responded harshly, and more protests swept the country. Arrests of opposition figures further infuriated the public, which was being given a blow-by-blow account of events through domestic radio reports. In December 1985 the government shut down Radio Soleil, the Catholic church's radio station, which had become the most popular source of information. When the government hoped to defuse tension by freeing some opposition leaders and lifting the ban on Radio Soleil in January 1986, it was too late. Indeed, this eleventh-hour flexibility only persuaded critics of Duvalier's imminent departure. Finally, on February 6, 1986, at 2:00 P.M., Duvalier left Haiti on a U.S. military transport plane destined for exile in France.

When it came to developing a transition regime in February 1986, the list of possible leaders was frighteningly small. No one had really been in charge of the movement that brought down Duvalier, even though the Catholic church had provided some institutional cohesion. The U.S. embassy mid-wifed a transition regime whose leadership (headed by Gen. Henri Namphy) appeared agreeable to Duvalier, but the broader picture turned out to be much more uncertain. Secretary of State George Shultz's call for democracy in Haiti a week before Duvalier's collapse had covered up the fact that this objective could not be accomplished in the near term. Policy designs were catapulted into the future without defining the near-term process, and Haiti paid the price for this lack of definition when elections in late 1987 did not come up to expectations. The short-lived 1988 government of civilian Leslie Manigat subsequently gave way to General Namphy (himself thrown out of office by another military commander, Gen. Prosper Avril, in September 1988). In March 1990 General Avril resigned and was replaced by Ertha Pascal-Trouillot, the only woman on Haiti's Supreme Court. The provisional president stated that her only goal was to lead the country to early elections. The U.S. ambassador called it "a great day for this country, a great day for democracy."[3]

THE HAITIAN CHALLENGE

Haiti's tragic history does not suggest an obvious source of hope regarding the course ahead. The years after 1957 only demonstrated that the supposed economic reforms of Jean-Claude Duvalier and his father's brutal political tendencies were but continuations of Haiti's lack of national viability, and alternatives have not clearly surfaced in the wake of Duvalier's collapse. Although mass opposition forced the regime's ouster, the interim government that followed it (1986–1988) was a direct product of the Duvalier era. Like their predecessors, the new regimes have not been able to tackle Haiti's major social and ecological crises. Given the country's malnutrition rate and deforestation, any future Haitian government faces a daunting task.

A nation whose track record of purposeful government is practically nonexistent, in tandem with a desperate socioeconomic environment, faces limited choices. Haiti has a reservoir of individual skills and political acumen, but the major challenge lies in the pooling of these human resources and the development of relevant economic and political organizations. Although there are egalitarian and cooperative features in the nation's peasant environment, Haiti's traditional political culture and linguistic bifurcation are profound obstacles to the development of a modern democratic government. In addition, the dubious interest of portions of the elite for collaborating in the economic, political, and cultural integration of the nation renders near-term national development problematic at best.

Haiti is likely to stagnate and fail to find clear-cut political and economic solutions. Humanitarian concerns will continue to dominate, and fears of political catastrophe will attract external interest. Foreign government and aid agencies will attempt to set priorities in the hope of generating true technocratic developments. These efforts will interact with a Haitian political leadership that, given the difficult circumstances, is likely to be tempted by the viability of a generally authoritarian, if hopefully a socially conscious, government.

NOTES

1. See the "Suggestions for Further Reading," particularly Fass (1988), Nicholls (1979), Morse (1988), and Rotberg (1971).
2. Rayford W. Logan, *The Diplomatic Relations of the United States with Haiti, 1776–1891.* Chapel Hill: University of North Carolina Press, 1971.
3. *New York Times,* March 14, 1990.

SUGGESTIONS FOR FURTHER READING

Abbott, Elizabeth. *Haiti: The Duvaliers and Their Legacy.* New York: McGraw-Hill, 1988.

Bellegarde-Smith, Patrick. *Haiti: The Breached Citadel.* Boulder, Colo.: Westview Press, 1990.

Diederick, Bernard, and Al Burt. *Papa Doc: The Truth About Haiti Today.* New York: McGraw-Hill, 1969.

Dupuy, Alex. *Haiti in the World Economy: Class, Race, and Underdevelopment Since 1700.* Boulder, Colo.: Westview Press, 1989.

Fass, Simon M. *Political Economy in Haiti: The Drama of Survival.* New Brunswick, N.J.: Transaction Books, 1988.

Fauriol, Georges A. *Foreign Policy Behavior of Caribbean States: Guyana, Haiti, and Jamaica.* Lanham, Md.: University Press of America, 1984.

Green, Graham. *The Comedians.* New York: Penguin Books, 1965.

Healy, David. *Gunboat Diplomacy in the Wilson Era: The U.S. Navy in Haiti, 1915–1917.* Madison: University of Wisconsin Press, 1976.

Heinl, Gordon Debs, and Nancy Gordon Heinl. *Written in Blood: The Story of the Haitian People.* Boston: Houghton Mifflin, 1978.

Herskovitz, Melville J. *Life in a Haitian Valley.* Garden City, N.Y.: Doubleday, 1971.

Laguerre, Michel. *The Complete Haitiana: A Bibliographic Guide to the Scholarly Literature, 1900–1980.* 2 vols. New York: Kraus International, 1982.

Leyburn, James G. *The Haitian People.* 2d edition. New Haven, Conn.: Yale University Press, 1966.

Logan, Rayford W. *The Diplomatic Relations of the United States with Haiti, 1776–1891.* Chapel Hill: University of North Carolina Press, 1941.

Lundhal, Mats. *Peasants and Poverty: A Study of Haiti.* New York: St. Martin's Press, 1979.

Miller, Jake C. *The Flight of Haitian Refugees.* New York: Praeger, 1984.

Morse, Richard M., ed. *Haiti's Future: Views of Twelve Haitian Leaders.* Washington, D.C.: Wilson Center Press, 1988.

Nicholls, David. *From Dessalines to Duvalier: Race, Colour, and National Independence in Haiti.* Cambridge: Cambridge University Press, 1979.

Ott, Thomas O. *The Haitian Revolution, 1789–1804.* Knoxville: University of Tennessee Press, 1973.

Preeg, Ernest H., and Anthony P. Manigat. *The Haitian Crisis: Two Perspectives.* Miami: Institute of Interamerican Studies, University of Miami, 1988.

Rotberg, Robert I. *Haiti: The Politics of Squalor.* Boston: Houghton Mifflin, 1971.

Schmidt, Hans. *The United States Occupation of Haiti, 1915–1934.* New Brunswick, N.J.: Rutgers University Press, 1971.

Weinstein, Brian, and Aaron Segal. *Haiti: Political Failures, Cultural Successes.* New York: Praeger, 1984.

Part 4

Conclusion: Latin America and its alternative futures

HOWARD J. WIARDA
HARVEY F. KLINE

A LIVING LABORATORY

Latin America is one of the world's most exciting living laboratories of social and political change. Capitalist, socialist, feudal, and mercantilist economies exist in a variety of forms, along with numerous hybrids of these major types. The political structures vary from repressive authoritarian regimes, which ignore democratic processes and ride roughshod over human rights, to liberal and democratic polities, whose citizens are as free as any in the world. In between are a variety of halfway houses, with combined civilian and military features, and transitional regimes of various kinds, some tending toward democracy, others seemingly going back toward authoritarianism. The social systems also range from feudal and two class to multiclass pluralistic to socialist—again with many combinations from nation to nation and within single nations. The most primitive and backward conditions prevail in some areas, the most sophisticated and modern in others.

What helps make Latin America such a fascinating laboratory for comparative sociological and political science study is not only these differences but the common background of the countries that make up the area. Few parts of the world offer such fruitful conditions for research on the processes of comparative change and modernization. Iberian institutions were set down in an unknown and almost virgin New World territory. Of course, for a full understanding of the area, one must take account of the different patterns of the Spanish and Portuguese settlements—the distinct conditions encountered, the differing geographic and climatic conditions, the varying numbers and levels of native Indian civilizations, the distinct socioeconomic patterns that evolved, and the differential importance the colonizing countries assigned the far-flung territories—but still the point holds. Here was a new and largely unsettled territory that suddenly and dramatically experienced the indelible imprint of Iberian-style Westernization. The Spanish and the Portuguese gave the region a common language, religion, and legal system, common forms of social organization and methods of economic enterprise, common intellectual and educational traditions, a common structure of political authority and political culture, and common ways of behaving and of understanding. In studying Latin America, such shared conditions enable one to hold some factors constant, almost as though the area were a scientific laboratory, in examining both the parallels and the divergences of national developmental experiences.

Although Latin America's common colonial and historical backgrounds should be emphasized in connection with certain parallels in the developmental patterns, the diversity of the area is equally striking. Comparative analysis, after all, requires that both similar and differential aspects be studied. This book seeks to stress both aspects: the general and continental patterns are described in Part 1, and the diverse national experiences are stressed in the chapters on specific countries.

Although both countries share a Spanish colonial background, Argentina and Paraguay are quite different; though Peru, Bolivia, Ecuador, Mexico, and Guatemala all had large pre-Columbian Indian civilizations, their patterns of development have been far from identical. The developmental experiences of the plantation systems of the Caribbean nations and Brazil have similarly been distinctive. Comparative Central American development, the comparative developmental experiences of the Andean nations, or those of the Southern Cone (Argentina, Chile, Uruguay) provide fascinating areas for study. Some countries, such as Mexico and Peru, were closely structured on the Spanish colonial system while other areas were characterized by colonial neglect. Those areas receiving the strongest Spanish influence were those with the greatest quantities of gold and silver and with large Indian civilizations to provide an abundance of cheap labor. These differing patterns of conquest and colonization in turn shaped the distinct developmental patterns—authoritarian or democratic—of the future Latin American nations.

The chapters on specific countries in this book point up the immense richness and diversity of the Latin American nations. Only with extreme care is it possible to generalize about all the nations of the area or to fashion a Latin America policy that applies to the region as a whole. The book describes traditional, liberal, socialist, and corporatist polities and influences as well as various combinations of them. It examines civilian governments and military regimes and other situations in which the distinction between civilian and military is blurred. Within the military category, there exist rightist and repressive regimes and leftist and nationalistic ones. There are countries that fit the general pattern of Latin American development as outlined in Part 1, other countries that fit the general pattern only partially, and still others that hardly fit it at all. Hence, it is important to stress both the common currents in Latin America and the differences from country to country, both the main themes and the variations. The Latin American nations are incredibly complex and exceedingly diverse (and becoming more so), although the cultural and sociopolitical traditions in which they exist and behave politically are often common ones. In this book's discussion and study, it is both the common patterns and the nuances that command attention, both the main roots and trunk and the several branches, both the constants and the variables in this intriguing living laboratory.

CONTINUITY AND CHANGE

Although the main structures of Latin American society and polity remained quite stable for a long period of time, extending from the colonial period into the nineteenth century, in recent decades the change process has been greatly accelerated. This book identifies six major areas of change: political culture and values, the economic structure, social and class structure, political groups and organizations, the range of public policy, and the international environment.

The country chapters make clear the degree to which Latin American political culture is undergoing transformation. New values and ideologies—socialism, corporatism, populism, Marxism, liberalism—have challenged the old belief systems, and new communications and transportation grids are increasingly breaking down traditional isolation. Although there is enormous variation from country to country, it is plain that the older Catholic, authoritarian, and hierarchical assumptions are being questioned everywhere, the older bases of legitimacy are being challenged, and a great variety of new ideologies are competing for people's minds.

The economic system has also altered dramatically. Although one may still find a few countries that conform to the stereotype, these are no longer just sleepy, rural, agricultural entities. Argentina, Brazil, Mexico, and Venezuela (and to a lesser degree Chile, Colombia, and Peru) have taken their place among the more industrialized and productive nations of the world. In these and other countries, subsistence agriculture coexists with modern industries and agribusinesses. Manufacturing, mining, and services in many countries generate as much GNP as agriculture. The older feudalistic concepts and structures have gradually given way to modern capitalist or socialist ones, and Latin America has become much more integrated than in the past with the international economic order. This integration has quickened economic life and provided new prosperity, but it has also helped lead to today's severe economic problems of debt and stagflation.

These economic changes have served to accelerate social change. A new labor class has risen up, and in many countries a strong middle sector has also evolved, wresting power from the old elites but often so internally divided as to offer few possibilities for stable rule. The elite groups themselves are now increasingly differentiated between old landed wealth and new industrial, banking, commercial, and manufacturing elements. The social composition of the church and the military officer corps has changed from upper to middle class. An urban subproletariat has emerged in all the countries of Latin America, and in the countryside the lethargic and tradition-bound peasant of the past has become restless and, in some cases, organized and mobilized.

The political system has changed concomitantly. New political parties have been formed, often replacing elite factions; they are organized around new ideological principles and often are mass based. Large-scale organizations of workers, peasants, university students, and professionals have emerged. These are no longer nations in which a handful of oligarchs, clerics, and military officers dominate national life; increasingly competitive and pluralistic societies have evolved, and there is a great variety of competing interests. The United States is a major influence on the Latin American political systems, bringing both benefits and a situation of dependency.

Not only have the major participants and the group structure changed but the extent of government policy has greatly expanded. In addition to agrarian reform, economic development, urban policy, and family planning, major issue areas now encompass housing, water supplies, education, health care, electric power, literacy programs, irrigation, highways, drugs, debt, and reforestation. New norms of honesty and efficiency coexist with older systems of patronage and favoritism, and governments are increasingly judged on the basis of their ability to deliver the services and programs the people have come to expect. Human rights have recently become a major issue.

The international environment in which the Latin American countries operate has also changed. The traditional isolation is breaking down at a rapid rate, and Latin America no longer produces chiefly for itself but for the international market. At the same time, it is increasingly dependent on that market for goods it does not have or produce, such as oil (with some notable exceptions like Venezuela) and heavy machinery. The breakdown of the traditional isolation covers not just the economic marketplace but the marketplace of ideas as well. Latin America is caught up in all the social, cultural, and political transformations shaking the rest of the world. "Civilization" no longer stops at the Rio Grande; Latin America is as much a part of modern civilization as the United States is, and in some areas—international law and diplomacy, music, sociology and political science, the social and political experiments its regimes are undertaking, to say nothing of soccer—it may well be leading the way. The cold war has also come to Latin America, and the countries of Central America and the Caribbean particularly have been sucked up into the East-West conflict.

And yet, with all these changes, one should not lose sight of the continuities. Elitist and authoritarian structures persist in various countries. The pervasiveness of family structure, kinship, and patron-client relations is apparent, and corporatist and personalist politics often predominate. The older belief systems and ways of behaving are powerful, and modern organizations and associational groups are often weak or nonexistent. Revolutionary breakthroughs have occurred in some countries, but in others the pace of change has been more gradual and evolutionary. Nor should one underestimate the ability of the traditional elites and ruling groups to accommodate and co-opt the new social forces as they have others in the past. In this way, although some limited change goes forward, the basic structure of power and society may be perpetuated. Indeed, it is largely the clashes and conflicts between these rival conceptions, the change-oriented forces on the one hand and the defenders of the status quo (albeit modified) on the other, that lie at the heart of contemporary Latin American politics. The struggle is certain to continue, as are the varied efforts of individual countries to reach some kind of compromise and reconciliation between them.

SOME NEW COMMON CURRENTS

Although Latin America is exceedingly diverse and the weight of the past hangs heavily over the area, there are some new common currents, highlighted in the country chapters, that command serious attention. These changes have taken place relatively recently—over the last two decades—and they imply some profound present and future transformations for Latin American political society. Although the reader is encouraged to look for other common currents and nuances derived from a systematic comparison of the country chapters, let us here offer, in the form of a set of hypotheses for further study, what to us as editors seem to be among the most important nuances and departures from the past stemming from these varied treatments.

1. *Accelerated change and the supplanting of the traditional order.* Since 1930 (somewhat earlier in the cases of Mexico, Argentina, and Chile), the feudal, two-class, oligarchic, and elite-dominated systems have been set aside and in some cases eclipsed; now these changes are proceeding more rapidly and reaching deeper into society. The Latin American countries are no longer a group of simple, traditional banana republics; they have become increasingly complex, mobilized, dynamic, multifaceted, even revolutionary nations.

2. *A growing differentiation among social and political groups.* Throughout the area, competitive labor and peasant movements, populist and middle-sector groups, political parties and other newer power contenders have challenged the wealth and position of the older elites. There is a growing pluralism in society and polity marked by increased competitiveness, challenge, division, and societal fragmentation.

3. *The emergence of a conflict society.* Although the older order is declining and a new one emerging, neither seems sufficiently well established or legitimate enough in most countries to rule effectively by itself or in coalition. The result in most countries of Latin America has been not a peaceful, stable transition to bourgeois, stable, moderate, middle-of-the-road, happy, and democratic politics but a continuing situation of conflict and discord over the nature and future of national politics.

4. *The radicalization of the younger generation.* One has to be impressed by the degree to which the younger generation of opinion leaders in Latin America, especially the university students, has been radicalized. Since roughly the mid-1960s, this new element (in many countries, the majority of the population) has largely abandoned its older allegiance to liberalism and republicanism in favor of more-radical solutions. In some countries, the politically aware and involved younger generation is almost totally socialist and Marxist. In some countries, socialism is coming to represent the midpoint of the political spectrum, not the fringe. In these countries, the question is no longer whether or not socialism is coming to Latin America but when and in what form.

5. The decline of U.S. influence. Along with radicalization has come a downward slide in the position of the United States. Although many Latin American nations remain dependent on the United States, they have begun to take an increasingly independent stance. The U.S. model, culture, and society are no longer so widely admired; Latin America is expanding its trade and contacts with other parts of the world, including the socialist one; U.S. foreign-assistance programs are much smaller than they used to be; Cuba has definitively broken out of the U.S. sphere of influence; businesspeople from other countries (Japan, West Germany, Italy, France) are beating out U.S. competitors for the major contracts. The era of U.S. dominance and hegemony is ending as Latin America takes charge of its own future. Some people attribute the trend to the declining international status of the United States; others to the declining position in the world—relatively—of the U.S. economy. Whatever one decides on these questions (too complex to be resolved here), it seems that, along with the deterioration of the traditional order and the new thrust toward greater radicalism on the part of some elements of the younger generation, the role and influence of the United States throughout the area have significantly diminished.

The strong U.S. presence in Central America probably represents a temporary blip on this downward curve and not a reversal of it. Overall, what impresses one is the pragmatism, despite frequent rhetorical flourishes to the contrary, on the part of both parties: a growing sense of limits in the United States about what it realistically can and cannot do in Latin America and a corresponding realism on the part of the Latin American nations in dealing with the United States. For even with the decline of U.S. influence throughout the area, the United States remains a major presence and power with which the Latin Americans must deal pragmatically, and most Latin American leaders recognize that fact. At the same time, they have also, prudently, begun to diversify their international relations.

6. The decline of Latin America's historical developmentalist model. With the ebbing of U.S. influence in Latin America, the classic Latin American developmentalist formula has also been challenged. That formula, as outlined in Chapter 7, involved the gradual accommodation and co-optation of new and rising power contenders into the political system without the interests of the traditional elites being discarded in the process. The model is now not only being challenged by other, more radical alternatives but in several countries it is collapsing from within. Rather than a peaceful and accommodative process of change, Latin American political society is now often characterized by a deep fragmentation of social and political groups, escalating conflict, increasing violence and class strife, and perhaps periodic long-term breakdowns. It seems that the consensual society of the past is being replaced by a society of discord, deterioration, and irreconcilable divisions. The old norms and institutions are in decline, and there are no adequate new

ones to serve as replacements. A political and institutional vacuum is developing in some countries in which strife and violence are everyday occurrences, political disputes have polarized, and the middle way is being ground down between left and right extremes.

7. Economic crisis. One key cause of the current decline and malaise is economic crisis. Most of the Latin American nations are in desperate financial trouble. Relative to the industrialized countries of the North, they have been in a steadily worsening terms-of-trade situation ever since the 1920s. Expenses and outflow far exceed income, inflation is rampant, expectations have outstripped production, growth has slowed and barely keeps pace with population. For many people, standards of living are falling. There is little new investment and few new loans are available. Spiraling oil prices have wreaked general disaster, foreign debts have piled up, and some nations may be forced to default on their loans. The economic pie has stopped expanding in some countries and in some others may even be contracting. First, such a shrinking economic pie means that some groups and individuals receive less and thus have increasing grounds for discontent. Second, it threatens the entire historical model of accommodative, co-optive politics since it means there are no new pieces to hand out to an increasingly impatient population.

8. Military authoritarianism. The immediate response to these series of crises in the 1960s and 1970s was a rash of military coups and the coming to power of a host of generally right-wing authoritarian regimes. At the end of 1977 fourteen of the twenty Latin American countries were under military rule. The causes of this resurgence of military rule included the factors noted earlier: economic crisis, the failure of civilian politics and politicians and of the historical Latin American co-optive model, the challenge of rising revolutionary movements, and the like. The military regimes frequently suspended or curbed human rights, sought to snuff out potential leftist challenges, and ruled brutally and oppressively. But military rule was a response to an existing vacuum and an effort to stem chaos and disintegration. Along with a new web of political controls, the military initiated forms of state capitalist development, centralizing both public and private power in its own hands and desperately seeking to hold a nation together while it tried to fashion a new developmental formula. But in the early 1980s the pendulum began to swing back the other way. Several military regimes had been thoroughly discredited by their mismanagement of their nation's economic accounts and their indiscriminate use of repression, and a number of new democratically elected governments were inaugurated. But the military remains in the wings, and as the economic and political crises intensify, it seems in several countries to be prepared to return to center stage.

9. State socialism. It is often only a short step in Latin America from state capitalism to state socialism, and given the socialist ideology of

many members of the Latin American younger generation—sometimes both civilian and military—that prospect has become a major alternative for the future. In countries where a large share of the national product is already in state hands, all that is required for that transition to occur is a shift in the political leadership. That happened under General Velasco in Peru and partially under General Torrijos in Panama. Socialism may thus come to some Latin American countries, not through mass revolution from below, but through decree law from above. Venezuela and Costa Rica have opted for a gradual and parliamentary route to social democracy, but in other countries it could—and has—come quite abruptly. Meanwhile, others are arguing for privatization and a freeing up of the Latin American economies.

10. Democratization. Since 1979, a number of transitions to democracy have occurred in Latin America. On the South American continent— in Argentina, Bolivia, Brazil, Ecuador, Peru, Uruguay, and Chile—military regimes have been replaced or have given way to democratic ones. In quite a number of countries of the Caribbean and Central America, democratization has also gone forward—although there the new civilian, elected governments frequently have to share power with the armed forces. But even in some of these Central American mixed systems, political conditions are better now than they were at the beginning of the 1980s.

Latin America is now more urban, literate, and middle class than it was in the 1960s; the social basis for democracy is therefore also more solid than it used to be. The U.S. government has supported the transitions to democracy for both moral and political reasons and because it is widely recognized that it is in the interests of the United States to do so. But militarism remains a problem in Latin America, socioeconomic conditions remain abysmal in many countries, and the new democratic regimes have not really delivered on their promises. It remains an open question whether these new openings to democracy can be effectively consolidated or whether the new democracies are just a temporary phenomenon—fated once again, as part of a long and often dreary cycle, to give way to military authoritarianism.

These democratic openings have served, at least for now, to diminish the appeals of the more radical ideologies, both left and right. Although the Cuban Revolution has not been successful economically, it has settled down and become more bureaucratic. That helps explain the increased willingness of the Latin American nations to accept the Cuban Revolution as a fact that may or may not have relevance for them. Our prognosis is that although the Cuban Revolution is unlikely to be repeated in very many other countries in Latin America in its Cuban form, other socialist formulas may be tried. These would probably be eclectic and nationalistic efforts, however, growing out of local needs and circumstances rather than being copies of what is a unique and in many ways distinctly Cuban experience.

Another fascinating area of study is provided by the internal dynamics of the military, in or out of power, and its relationship with civilian groups. In quite a number of countries, the military is divided among left, center, and right factions. These factions are then entwined with corresponding factions among civilian elements. Many current crises in Latin America involve not just competition between the civilian and military authorities but complex patterns of one overlapping civilian-military group competing with another civilian-military group (or several such groups).

There is similarly a vigorous debate about the future of the Latin American economies. Will they be capitalist, socialist, or that hybrid called state capitalism? Many analysts have concluded that the Latin American economies are woefully outdated as well as graft ridden, inefficient, and patronage dominated. They are badly in need of reform as well as of new capital investment. But the sorely needed investment will not come as long as the overall systems are so inefficient; on the other hand, governments that make reforms toward a more efficient economy often have to sacrifice their basis of patronage support in the process. How Latin America resolves these complex issues of political economy will be one of the crucial questions of the 1990s.

THE FUTURE

Latin America remains as diverse as ever, and the range of developmental options will no doubt remain wide. We would anticipate that in quite a number of countries (probably the majority), democracy will remain the preferred form of government. But democracy will continue to struggle in such countries as Brazil and Peru, and there may well be some backsliding toward renewed military authoritarianism in these and others. There is a good chance that the appeal of a single-party integrating mechanism like Mexico's PRI will continue, but the pressures from the left for a more thoroughgoing and radical restructuring, as in Cuba or Nicaragua, will also remain strong.

Nor should one underestimate either the capacity of some of the authoritarian military regimes to hang on to power (although these regimes will probably evolve in new directions) or the capacity of the military to come back into power. One should not be surprised to see state capitalist systems become populist and state socialist systems (the current prevailing form), almost overnight in some cases.

One should also not be surprised by the adaptability of traditional elitist elements. Latin American elites tend to be very practical and flexible, and although it may sound ideologically inconsistent, they are capable of leading their nations in new directions. The elites, after all, frequently have strong anti-U.S. sentiments and are often strongly nationalist in their own way. We would not be surprised if even those regimes that are dominated by elites, who can be quite accommodative,

decide that their best interests lie in leading the process of social change—
even including the nationalization of some U.S. holdings—rather than
being overcome by it. Meanwhile, the left will continue to push in more
radical directions while other elements will try to see if the center can
hold.

All of these factors lend a dynamic flexibility and fascination to Latin
American politics that we find exciting. It is healthy and exhilarating
that there are not one or two routes to modernization but many varied
ones. Democracy seems to be the preferred route for growing numbers
of people in Latin America, but even democracy takes many different
forms and still may not be all that stable. We think it would be boring,
as well as historically and factually inaccurate, to say that there is only
one road for all nations to follow. That idea is too easy and too simple.
It is far more interesting and invigorating to wrestle with the realities
that Latin America has several alternative futures and that the balance
of forces is changing. Development may take a number of forms and
need not correspond to any preconceived notions.

Whatever direction development takes in Latin America, one should
bear in mind the following caveats.

1. Development is a long, difficult, arduous, wrenching process. It
will not come about through the use of antiseptic phrases and slogans.
For some countries poor in resources, it may not come at all.

2. The capacity of the United States to influence future outcomes is
likely to be limited. Latin America is highly nationalistic and has recently
begun to expand its trade and relations outside the North American
orbit. Latin America neither wishes to, nor because of history and
tradition can, follow exactly the development model of the United States.
Hence, there are likely to be increasing problems and tensions in North-
South, U.S.–Latin American relations centering on major political and
economic issues.

3. Latin American development will be carried out largely by the
Latin American nations themselves and on their own terms. They will
learn to devise development strategies and formulas that are attuned to
their own desires and traditions rather than to imitate entirely those of
the already developed nations. Further, such development is likely to
be in accord with the special nature of Latin American society and its
institutions (as outlined in Part 1) and may not conform to the U.S.
and West European experiences. There will probably be various overlaps
of imported U.S. and European institutions coupled with traditional
Latin American ways of doing things.

4. It is thus our obligation to seek to understand Latin America and
its distinctive development processes, not from a U.S. perspective, but
on Latin America's own terms, through its perspectives, and not by
means of our own rose-colored lenses. We should keep our eyes and
minds open to the distinct characteristics of another culture area rather
than seek to interpret it wholly from a North American viewpoint. Only

then can we begin to understand what Latin America is all about, develop an empathy for and a comprehension of a foreign area whose assumptions and operating procedures are often imitative of as well as different from our own, and appreciate Latin America's development aspirations, not from some haughty or "superior" North American perspective, but through the givens and dynamics of Latin American political society itself.

About the Editors
and Contributors

CONTRIBUTING EDITORS

Howard J. Wiarda is Professor of Political Science and Comparative Labor Relations at the University of Massachusetts/Amherst; Research Associate of the Center for International Affairs, Harvard University; Adjunct Scholar of the American Enterprise Institute for Public Policy Analysis in Washington, D.C.; and Associate of the Foreign Policy Research Institute in Philadelphia. He served as Lead Consultant to the National Bipartisan Commission on Central America and, by appointment of the President of the United States, on the White House Task Force on Project Economic Justice. His most recent books are *The Democratic Revolution in Latin America, Foreign Policy Without Illusion,* and the second edition of *New Directions in Comparative Politics* (Westview Press, 1990).

Harvey F. Kline is Professor of Political Science and Chair at The University of Alabama. His most recent books are *Colombia: Portrait of Unity and Diversity* and *The Coal of El Cerrejón: Dependent Bargaining and Colombian Policy Making.*

CONTRIBUTORS

Enrique Baloyra is Associate Dean of the Graduate School of International Studies at the University of Miami at Coral Gables and author of *El Salvador in Transition* and of numerous articles and essays about that country.

John A. Booth is Professor and Chair of Political Science at the University of North Texas. A specialist on Central American politics, he is the author of *The End and the Beginning: The Nicaraguan Revolution* (Westview Press, 1985) and of many scholarly articles on Central America and Mexico and is the coeditor of *Elections and Democracy in Central America.*

Juan M. del Aguila is Associate Professor of Political Science and Director of the Center for International Studies at Emory University. He is the author of *Cuba: Dilemmas of a Revolution* (Westview Press, 1988) as well as numerous journal articles and book chapters about Cuban politics and Soviet-Cuban foreign policy in Latin America.

Roland Ebel, who teaches political science at Tulane University, is author of *Political Modernization in Three Guatemalan Indian Communities.* He has also written widely on national and local politics in Central America. His paper on

589

the character of the Central American city-state was published by the Kissinger Commission. He is currently working on a study of the Cerezo regime in Guatemala.

Georges A. Fauriol is Director and Senior Fellow of the Latin American Program at the Center for Strategic and International Studies. In addition to numerous journal articles, he has authored four books, most recently *The Third Century: U.S. Latin American Policy Choices for the 1990s* and *Guatemala's Political Puzzle*, both published in 1988.

Eduardo A. Gamarra is Assistant Professor of Political Science at Florida International University. He is coauthor of *Revolution and Reaction: Bolivia 1964–1985* and is coeditor of the *Latin America and Caribbean Contemporary Record*.

Michael J. Kryzanek is Professor of Political Science at Bridgewater State College in Massachusetts. He has published widely on the Dominican Republic, the Caribbean, and U.S.–Latin American relations. Professor Kryzanek has written two books on the Dominican Republic, both as coauthor with Howard J. Wiarda: *The Dominican Republic: A Caribbean Crucible* (Westview Press, 1982) and *The Politics of External Influence in the Dominican Republic*. Professor Kryzanek is currently working on a book about leaders, leadership, and U.S. policy in Latin America.

Ronald H. McDonald is Professor of Political Science at the Maxwell School, Syracuse University, and former chair of the department. He is the author of *Party Systems and Elections in Latin America* and coauthor of *Party Politics and Elections in Latin America* (Westview Press, 1989).

James M. Malloy is Professor of Political Science at the University of Pittsburgh. He is coeditor of *Latin America and Caribbean Contemporary Record*. His most recent books are *Authoritarians and Democrats: Regime Transition in Latin America* (with Mitchell A. Seligson) and *Revolution and Reaction: Bolivia 1964–1985*.

John D. Martz is Professor of Political Science at the Pennsylvania State University. He is editor of *Studies of Comparative International Development*. His most recent book is *United States Policy in Latin America*.

David J. Myers is Associate Professor of Political Science at the Pennsylvania State University. He is coeditor of *Venezuela: The Democratic Experience* as well as author of various articles about Venezuelan and Brazilian politics. He is currently completing a book on urban politics and regime consolidation in Venezuela.

David Scott Palmer is Professor of Political Science and International Relations at Boston University. From 1976 to 1988 he served at the Foreign Service Institute as Chairman for Latin American and Caribbean Studies. His published work includes studies of Peruvian politics, Latin American insurgencies, military regimes in Latin America, and redemocratization in the region.

Susan Kaufman Purcell is Vice President for Latin American Affairs at the Americas Society in New York City. Her publications on Mexico include *Mexico* *in Transition: Implications for U.S. Policy, Debt and the Restructuring of Mexico-United States Relations,* and *The Mexican Profit-Sharing Decision: Politics in an Authoritarian Regime.*

Riordan Roett is the Sarita and Don Johnston Professor and Director of the Latin American Studies Program at The Johns Hopkins University School of Advanced International Studies (SAIS) in Washington, D.C. Dr. Roett also directs the school's Center of Brazilian Studies and is past president of the Latin American Studies Association. A fourth edition of his *Brazil: Politics in a Patrimonial Society* will appear in 1990.

Steve C. Ropp is Professor of Political Science at the University of Wyoming. He is the author of *Panamanian Politics: From Guarded Nation to National Guard* and coeditor, with James A. Morris, of *Central America: Crisis and Adaptation.*

Mark B. Rosenberg is Professor of Political Science and Director of the Latin American and Caribbean Center at Florida International University. An associate editor of *Hemisphere,* Dr. Rosenberg has authored and coedited numerous works on Honduras and Central America.

Richard S. Sacks is a free-lance writer who has published extensively on Paraguay. He has worked as a newspaper and wire-service reporter and has traveled in Europe, the Near East, Africa, and South America. He holds a masters degree in international relations from SAIS.

Mitchell A. Seligson is Professor of Political Science and Director of the Center for Latin American Studies of the University of Pittsburgh. His most recent book is *Elections and Democracy in Central America,* coedited with John A. Booth.

Paul E. Sigmund is Professor of Politics at Princeton University. He is the author of fourteen books, including *The Overthrow of Allende and the Politics of Chile, 1964–1976* and *Multinationals in Latin America,* and coauthor of *The Military Institution in Latin America.* He has recently completed *Liberation Theology at the Crossroads: Democracy or Revolution?*

Peter G. Snow, Professor of Political Science at the University of Iowa, is the author of *Argentine Radicalism and Political Forces in Argentina* and of many articles on Argentine politics published in Argentine, Mexican, Spanish, British, German, and U.S. scholarly journals.

Iêda Siqueira Wiarda taught in the Department of Political Science, University of Massachusetts/Amherst; she is now Specialist in Iberian-Brazilian Culture, Hispanic Division, Library of Congress. She has been course chairperson, Foreign Service Institute, Department of State, and has worked as a consultant to various governmental and private agencies, especially in the areas of inter-American relations, population, and public policy. She is the author or coauthor of *Family Planning Activities in a Democratic Context: The Case of Venezuela; Women, Population,* *and International Development in Latin America;* and *The Transition to Democracy in Spain and Portugal.*

Gary W. Wynia is William Kenan Professor of Political Science at Carleton College. He is the author of various articles and of *The Politics of Latin American Development, Argentina in the Postwar Era,* and *Argentina: Illusions and Realities.*

Index